Introduction to
Econometrics
Principles and Applications
Eighth Edition

GMK Madnani

Oxford & IBH Publishing Co. Pvt. Ltd.
New Delhi
(A Unit of CBS Publishers & Distributors Pvt Ltd **)**

CBSPD

CBS Publishers & Distributors Pvt Ltd

New Delhi • Bengaluru • Chennai • Kochi • Kolkata • Lucknow • Mumbai
Hyderabad • Jharkhand • Nagpur • Patna • Pune • Uttarakhand

Introduction to
Econometrics
Principles and Applications
Eighth Edition

ISBN-13: 978-81-204-1719-9
ISBN-10: 81-204-1719-4

OXFORD & IBH
New Delhi
(*A Unit of* CBS Publishers & Distributors Pvt Ltd)

Published by **Satish Kumar Jain** and produced by **Varun Jain** for

CBS Publishers & Distributors Pvt Ltd
4819/XI Prahlad Street, 24 Ansari Road, Daryaganj, New Delhi 110 002, India.
Ph: 011-23289259, 23266861   Website: www.cbspd.com
                                e-mail: delhi@cbspd.com

Corporate Office: 204 FIE, Industrial Area, Patparganj, Delhi 110 092
Ph: 011-4934 4934   Fax: 011-4934 4935

                e-mail: publishing@cbspd.com; publicity@cbspd.com

Branches

- **Bengaluru:** Seema House 2975, 17th Cross, KR Road, Banasankari 2nd Stage, Bengaluru 560 070, Karnataka, India
  Ph: +91-80-26771678/79   Fax: +91-80-26771680   e-mail: bangalore@cbspd.com
- **Chennai:** 7, Subbaraya Street, Shenoy Nagar, Chennai 600 030, Tamil Nadu, India
  Ph: +91-44-26680620, 26681266   Fax: +91-44-42032115   e-mail: chennai@cbspd.com
- **Kochi:** 42/1325, 1326, Power House Road, Opp KSEB, Power House, Ernakulum Kochi 682 018, Kerala, India
  Ph: +91-484-4059061-65,67   Fax: +91-484-4059065   e-mail: kochi@cbspd.com
- **Kolkata:** 147, Hind Ceramics Compound, 1st Floor, Nilgunj Road, Belghoria, Kolkata-700056, West Bengal, India
  Ph: +033-25633055, 033-25633056   e-mail: kolkata@cbspd.com
- **Lucknow:** Basement, Khushnuma Complex, 7 Meerabai Marg (Behind Jawahar Bhawan), Lucknow-226001, UP, India
  Ph: +0522-4000032   e-mail: tiwari.lucknow@cbspd.com
- **Mumbai:** PWD Shed, Gala no 25/26, Ramchandra Bhatt Marg, Next to JJ Hospital Gate no. 2, Opp. Union Bank of India, Noorbaug, Mumbai-400009, Maharashtra, India
  Ph: 022-66661880/89   e-mail: mumbai@cbspd.com

Representatives

• Hyderabad	0-9885175004	• Jharkhand	0-9811541605	• Nagpur	0-8692091830
• Patna	0-9334159340	• Pune	0-9664372571	• Uttarakhand	0-9716462459

Printed at Chaman Enterprises, Daryaganj, New Delhi, India

Preface to the Eighth Edition

It is generally argued that econometrics is suitable for those select students who possess substantial level of knowledge of statistics and mathematics. Established texts also use sophisticated mathematical tools which are beyond the comprehension of students with different backgrounds.

The primary intent of writing this text, as one may refer from the accompanying preface of the first edition, was to design a text on Econometrics which makes only modest mathematical demands on the students.

Recurring and consistent demand of the text clearly demonstrates the fact that our esteemed teachers approve the approach to the subject as it also accommodates the students with different background of statistics and mathematics. On the other, drastically changed business scenario has also prompted use of econometric techniques by the management 'Gurus', consequently therefore, researchers prefer more empirical material in the texts of Econometrics for drawing useful inferences from abstract econometric models. To fill this need within given constrains and perspective of new material, every edition required omitting nonessential details, improving the exposition of previous matter and, finally integrating all the matters to make every chapter econometrically sound and easily accessible to those who are less acquainted with the intricacies of the subject.

Two empirically based appendixes; one on estimation of non-linear relations and growth models; and the other on estimation of qualitative models are added in the present edition.

The model validation also presents larger problems for the students. This incited us to club all the "test-statistics" under one new chapter- *"How to investigate the goodness of econometric model"*.

— GMK. Madnani

Preface to the First Edition

Perhaps the most significant development in economics since the Second World War has been the increased application of quantitative methods to the problems of economics; and econometrics is one of such methods which is widely used in nearly every branch of economic research.

So far econometric studies possessed restricted appeal and were considered a highly specialised tool of research. But with the growing interest in quantitative aspect of economics, econometrics has acquired great significance. Yet, unfortunately, this field of knowledge has not become so popular with our students of economics at the postgraduate level, probably for two reasons: (i) that students are often discouraged due to the esoteric and highly specialised nature of this body of knowledge, and (ii) the presentation of this subject has mostly remained too complex for the interested students even with an advanced background knowledge of mathematics and statistics. This lamentable tendency has always posed a challenge to me as a teacher of quantitative methods in economics; and the result of this challenge is this book.

During the development of the manuscript, therefore, my prime goal was to design a textbook on econometrics which makes only modest mathematical demands on the students; yet, it gives enough 'feel' of the subject and stimulate them to be unafraid of further study in applied mathematics and statistics. With this as my objective, I have persistently stressed simplicity, clarity and the significance of the basic concepts involved in econometric techniques rather than the rigour and extent of their availability. Nevertheless, in a quest for the attainment of this goal every care has been taken that such an objective is achieved without losing flavour of modern econometrics and without leaving out too many things. The present text, therefore, does not cover all but merely intends to serve as a worthwhile introduction for the beginners to whet their appetites for learning as much about econometrics as is dictated by their University Syllabus.

This book, hence needs to be judged by the accomplishments rather than by its omissions.

The book is divided into two main parts. Part one, consisting of Chapters 1 to 3, deals with basic ideas of theory of Statistics which are important for understanding the principles of econometrics. Part two, consisting of chapter 4 through 13, contains an exposition of all basic econometric methods. While all the topics explored here represent standard topics dealt in all econometrics texts, but as mentioned above, their approach and simplicity in treatment should appear unique. The use of every technique has been supported with a numerical example to make the students know both; how things are done and why.

My debts are great and too many; specially like the debt of my former teachers, which I cannot even dare to acknowledge. I am greatly indebted to the authors of more advanced texts; it is only inadequately recognised in the bibliography given at the end of the text. I am grateful to my colleagues for advice and criticism; of course I remain responsible for the final adaptations, inclusions and exclusions of the material in the text.

Udaipur, 1980   *G.M.K. Madnani*

Contents

PART ONE
BASIC STATISTICAL THEORY

Elementary Statistics: A Review

To help the beginner to understand and benefit from this book, the first part deals with a few basic but important topics on Statistics essential for the understanding of the theory of Econometrics.

A brief review of some of the basic concepts of statistics that are used repeatedly in this book, are presented in first three chapters.

1.1 POPULATIONS AND SAMPLES

The *population* is an abstract term that refers to the totality of all conceptually possible observations, measurements or outcomes of some specified kind. The number of conceptually possible observations is called the size of the population. The size varies according to the population being investigated. For example, a study of monthly incomes may be conducted at a district, State and country level. In the first instance, the population will consist of the incomes of one district; in the second case, all the residents of the State; in the third case, the incomes of all the citizens of the country.

A population may be *finite*, when it consists of a given number of observations or values; or it may be *infinite*, when it includes an infinite number of observations. Most of the populations with which we deal in econometrics are infinite.

Related to the concept of a population is the concept of a sample. A *sample* is a set of observations selected from the population. The number of observations included in the sample is called the *size* of the sample.

In econometrics our attention is confined to samples drawn in accordance with some specified chance mechanism. Such samples are called *probability samples*; an important type of probability sample is the *random sample*. In finite populations, a random sample is obtained by giving every individual in the population an equal chance of being chosen; in case of infinite populations, sample is random if each observation is independent of every other observation.

Populations and samples are studied through their characteristics. The most important of these characteristics are the *Mean*, the *Variance* and the *Standard deviation*. Characteristics of a population are called *parameters*;

the characteristics of sample are called *statistics*. The basic numerical measures of population and samples along with their usual symbols are:

Parameters (Population)	Statistics (Sample)
1. Population mean: μ	Sample mean: $\overline{X}$
2. Population variance: σ_x^2	Sample variance: S_x^2
3. Population standard deviation: σ_x	Sample standard deviation: S_x

Statistics deals with phenomena that can be either measured or counted. With respect to a phenomenon that can be measured, we speak of a *variable*— meaning a homogeneous quantity whose magnitude can change at different points of time. If a phenomenon can only be counted but not measured, we speak of an *attribute*. An attribute refers to the presence or absence of a given characteristic in a sample or population. The antithesis of a variable is a *constant*. A constant is a magnitude that does not change at different points of time. When a constant is joined to a variable, it is often referred to as the *coefficient* of that variable. However, a coefficient may be symbolic rather than numerical; for example, symbol *a* stands for a given constant in the expression *ax*, and is called the coefficient of *x*. This symbol is supposed to represent a given constant, and yet, since no specific value has been assigned to it, it can take virtually any value. In short, therefore, it is a constant that is variable. To identify its peculiar status, it is also termed as *parametric constant* or *parameter*.

If the quantity in question is a variable and not a constant, one may be interested in the source of variation so that it could be controlled. In case of a variation that cannot be fully controlled, its existence is due to chance. The variables whose values cannot be fully controlled or determined prior to observations are called *random variables* or *stochastic variables*. In contrast, a *non random* or *non stochastic* variable is one that is fully controllable or at least fully predictable.

A variable may be continuous or non-continuous in nature. A *continuous variable* is a variable that can assume any value on the numerical axis or a part of it. Time, temperature, income, price, expenditure and such similar variables can be classified as continuous. In contrast, a *discrete variable* is one that can assume only some specific values on the numerical axis. These values may not be separated by intervals of equal length.

Those variables which the model is intended to explain are called *endogenous variables* (originating from within), those variables which are assumed to be determined by the forces external to the model, and whose magnitudes are only accepted as given data are called *exogenous variables* (originating from without). Endogenous variables are regarded as stochastic, whereas the exogenous variables are truly nonstochastic or can be so regarded.

At times exogenous variables are classified as *instruments* and *noninstruments*. An instrument is an exogenous variable that is *specifically* manipulated so as to achieve some targets. Government expenditure, taxes and subsidies are examples of instrument exogenous variables.

1.2 DISTRIBUTIONS

The concept which is related to the organisation of data is that of *distribution*. In case of data relating to samples, we have frequency distributions, while probability distributions are associated with populations. The *frequency distribution* is an organised presentation of the observed values of a variable in a sample; it shows the number of observations for each value of the variable in the sample (in case of discrete variable) or the number of the observations in each interval of values of the variable in the sample (in case of continuous variable). The number of observations in each class is called *absolute frequency*. In contrast, *relative frequency* gives the proportion of observations rather than their number for each class.

Distributions may be presented in a tabular form on a graph or with a mathematical formula. Graphically frequency distributions of discrete variables are presented by a *frequency polygon* or a *histogram*. An important feature of the histogram is that its area represents the sum of the relative frequencies and hence it is equal to 1. Table 1.1 and Figs. 1.1, 1.2 and 1.3 illustrate these definitions.

Table 1.1: Frequency Distribution of X (Family Income)

Values of income (Rs.) X_1	Absolute frequency f_i	Relative frequency f_i/n
1	20	$\dfrac{20}{1000} = 0.02$
2	200	$\dfrac{200}{1000} = 0.20$
3	540	$\dfrac{540}{1000} = 0.54$
4	220	$\dfrac{220}{1000} = 0.22$
5	20	$\dfrac{20}{1000} = 0.02$

Assume that we take a sample of the daily incomes of 1000 persons from a village. It is observed that 20 individuals have an income of Re. 1; 200 individuals have an income of Rs. 2; 540 individuals have an income of Rs. 3; 220 individuals have an income of Rs. 4; and 20 individuals have an income of Rs. 5.

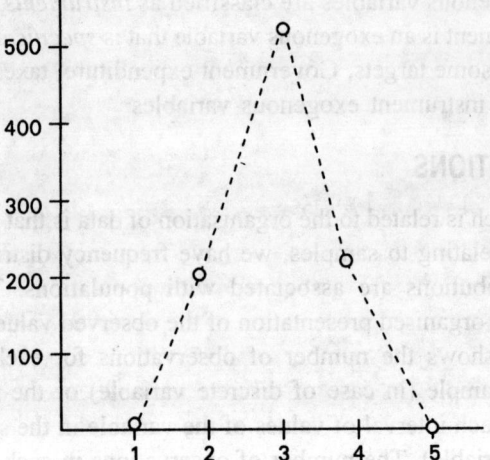

Fig. 1.1: Frequency Polygon (absolute frequency)

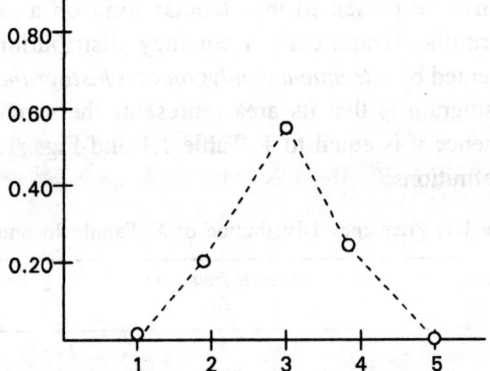

Fig. 1.2: Frequency Polygon (relative frequency)

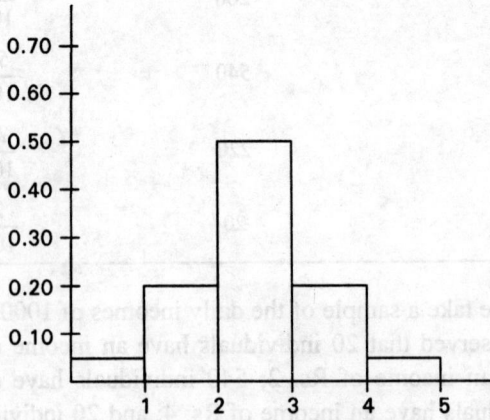

Fig. 1.3: The Histogram

The above information constitutes the frequency distribution of the variable—*income*.

In a population the concept corresponding to frequency distribution is known as probability distribution. In a population, each and every value of a variable has some probability of occurring; in other words, each value of a random variable has some probability associated with itself. The sum of the probabilities of all values is equal to one. *The probability distribution* describes every value of the random variable along with the probability of its occurrence. Probability distributions can be of discrete and continuous variables. Just as frequency distributions can be examined by studying their mean and variances, a probability distribution can be summarised in terms of a few of its characteristics known as the *moments* of the distribution. Two of most widely used moments are the *expected value* and the *variance*.

The four basic theoretical probability distributions are: the Normal Distribution, the Chi-square Distribution, the *t*-Distribution and the *F*-Distribution. These are distributions of corresponding statistics: the Z, χ^2, t and F statistics. These statistical formulae transform the units of original population parameters into units of sampling distribution of these statistics. The probabilities of these distributions have been computed by various statisticians and have been tabulated. Thus by using the appropriate transformation procedure one can find the probabilities of the original distribution indirectly instead of estimating these probabilities directly from the original distributions which involve highly complex expressions.

1.3 STATISTICAL INFERENCE

Statistical inference is concerned with generalisations (or making inferences) about the populations on the basis of information contained in the sample. On this account, statistical inference may be viewed as *inductive reasoning*. Extension from particular to the general is called *inductive inference*.

New knowledge is found through two kinds of inferences; of which one is inductive while the other is *deductive inference*. Inductive inference involves element of uncertainty in the conclusions. One simply cannot make perfectly certain generalisations on the basis of experimentation. However, the degree of uncertainty can be measured in inductive inference, if the experiment has been performed in accordance with certain principles. In statistics, uncertainty is measured in terms of probability, and the central problem of analytical statistics is that of inductive inference.

Deductive inference, which can be described as a method of deriving information from the accepted facts, involves no uncertainty in the conclusions. The conclusions reached by deductive inference are conclusive.

While deductive inference is extremely important, much of the new knowledge in the real world comes about by the process of inductive inference. In mathematics, for instance, deductive inferences are used while in the empirical science inductive inferences are mostly used to find new knowledge.

The purpose of statistical inference is to make a judgement about the particular parameters on the basis of sample statistics. These judgements are mere guesses endowed with a certain degree of reliability which can be increased with different sampling techniques. The judgement relating to population parameters are of two types; one is concerned with *estimation* of a parameter, the other with *testing* (some) *hypothesis* about the parameter.

The estimation is done with the help of an *estimator*. Estimator, therefore, is a formula which describes a procedure of guessing (or obtaining) the value of given population parameter. A specific value of an estimator is called *estimate* (of parameter). On the other hand, hypothesis testing involves an *a priori* assumption about the value of a parameter. The hypothesis is tested against the information provided by sample in the form of a *test-statistic*.

In statistical inference we are, therefore, concerned with the value of an estimate or of a test statistic which in turn represents a guess concerning the relevant population parameter. Different samples would lead to different guesses, i.e., some values will be close to the value of the parameter than the others. But, in reality we deal with only one sample and therefore we obtain only one value (guess). Nonetheless, it is also important to know what the guesses might have been had we had different samples from the population. There could be three possibilities: (a) that all the possible samples lead to guesses which are always near the true value of the parameter, (b) that all possible samples lead to widely different guesses and only few are near the true value, and (c) that all the possible samples give rise to the same values but these are far from the true value of the parameter. In the first case any sample value is obviously quite reliable, in the second only some of the guesses can be near the true value, but in the third case no guess can be found to be true for the population parameter. As such reliability of a guess can be known only by knowing the behaviour of all the guesses that could be made on the basis of all the possible samples and in fact, we can draw infinite number of samples from a given population. It is on this logic that the concept of *sampling distribution* has been evolved.

Various methods are used for making statistical inference. These methods are based on following four situations that are encountered in the process of inference:

    (i)   the population as it actually is,

   (ii)   the relationship between the characteristics of this population and the characteristics of many samples drawn from this population,

 (iii)   the relationship between characteristics of the many samples and the characteristics of one sample, and

 (iv)   the one sample that one actually observes in practice.

Now suppose our problem is to infer from the observed sample (i.e., situation (iv)), the characteristics of the true (but unobservable) population (i.e., situation (i)). To do this, we make use of the laws provided by the situations (ii) and (iii).

1.4 SAMPLING DISTRIBUTION

Distribution relating to an estimate of a specific population parameter is called a *sampling distribution* of that estimate. Suppose, for example, that we wish to estimate the mean family income of a particular district in a given year on the basis of a sample of say, 100 families. Assume that we use mean of the samples to estimate the population (family incomes of the district) mean. We can draw an infinite number of samples from the district and calculate the value of the sample mean from each sample. These values can now be arranged in the form of a (frequency) distribution which would be called a sampling distribution of sample mean. Note that although the population of all families in the district is a finite one, the number of samples that we can draw from this population is infinite as long as we allow each family to be included in any sample. Such sampling is called sampling with replacement. We would know all about the possible behaviour of our guesses by studying the resulting sampling distribution. Had we used some other estimator, e.g., mode or median in place of mean, the resulting distribution would have been called sampling distribution of mode or median. As such we can obtain sampling distribution of any estimator or test statistic.

We did not refer to size of the sample while understanding the concept of sampling distribution. It is quite obvious that samples of different sizes give different types of information about the population from which they are drawn. To avoid the effects that are due to the change in size of the samples, a sampling distribution always refers to samples of the same size. The effects of changing the sample size are then studied by comparing the different sampling distributions built with different size of samples.

Furthermore, it can also be seen that sampling distribution of sample mean, in fact, is a probability distribution; because the income of the family as well as the mean income of the sample (drawn from the district), both are random variables.

But how does sampling distribution help to obtain a good or reliable guess?

Suppose we have obtained the sampling distribution of sample mean for the above example of family incomes. In case the mean of the sampling distribution turns out to be the value which is equal to the true value of the parameter, then the mean is said to be a good guess (or a good estimate) for the population parameter. To generalise, we say that an estimator is said to be a *good estimator* if the mean of the sampling distribution of that estimator is found to be equal to the true value of the parameter. An estimator would be a *perfect estimator* if its sampling distribution is concentrated entirely in one point and the point is also the true value of the parameter. Needless to say, perfect estimators are very rare and can be obtained only if there is no variation in the population so that every sample drawn from the population gives rise to same mean value which also happens to be the true value of the parameter. Naturally, therefore, we have to be satisfied by less than a 'perfect guess'; but again one can ask—to what limit? Statisticians provide this limit by stating some properties of an estimator that are commonly considered desirable for an estimator to be called a good estimator. The desirable statistical properties fall into two categories: small sample (or finite-sample) properties and large sample (or asymptotic) properties. Underlying both these sets of properties is the notion that an estimator has a sampling distribution.

1.5 CLASSICAL AND BAYESIAN INFERENCES

In Statistical terminology, an unbiased estimator is considered desirable because, as more and more samples are taken, the average value of the sample estimates will then tend toward the true value of the parameter. Again, in the class of unbiased estimators a minimum variance unbiased estimator is preferred because on average it yields values that are closer (in terms of squared differences) to real parameter than are those obtained from any other unbiased estimator. On the other, the methods of interval estimation and hypothesis testing are also evaluated in terms of their performance in a large number of repeated samples.

The underlying logic for using repeated samples is to acquire high probability of giving correct results, that is; to justify the concepts such as 95% levels of significance. This technique is called *classical* approach of statistical inference. To be precise, *classical type of statistical inference* has the following two characteristics:

1. Test procedures and estimators are evaluated in terms of their properties in repeated samples. In other words inferences (made in the form of point estimation, interval estimation and testing of hypothesis) are based on sampling distribution.
2. The probability of an event is defined in terms of the limit of the relative frequency of that event.

In contrast, the basis of *Baye's statistical inference* is Baye's theorem.

In Bayesian framework, probability is defined in terms of a degree of belief and, therefore, the properties of estimators and test procedures in repeated samples are of no interest. The degree of belief which differs from individual to individual, may be in the form of quantitative and/or qualitative information but in no case it depends on the relative frequency of the event in a large number of hypothetical experiments.

In Bayesian approach, therefore, unknown parameter can be expressed in terms of a subjective distribution which is called a *prior distribution* or prior density function. Prior distribution when combined with the sample information becomes a *posterior distribution* which forms the main feature of Bayesian analysis.

Classical statistics prescribes inferential techniques based on sample information alone. In Bayesian methods we have an additional ingredient: the prior distribution. This is combined with likelihood function which comes from the sample information. As such many statisticians strongly support the use of Bayesian inferential techniques. They argue that the classical approach either ignores past information or at the most incorporates the prior information in an adhoc manner. The Bayesian approach on the other modifies subjective prior information through the currently available sample information and avoids the necessity of assuming repeated samples and of using arbitrary levels of significance.

There are others who reject the Bayesian approach mainly because it is based on the notion of subjective prior information. For instance, information like the fact that the demand function has a negative slope, that the marginal propensity to consume is less than one, etc., which according to Bayesian should be incorporated in these models as prior information which classical econometricians ignore. There is a point in this argument; but one should not push it too far.

Assume that one estimates the demand function and obtains its positive slope. This suggests that the researcher should examine his data more closely or that there are some specification errors which he should check. On the other, a procedure that is contained to yield only negative slopes might not reveal such deficiencies in the data or model specifications. However, if the researcher has full confidence in the quality of data and specifications of model, prior information of above nature will surely enhance his results for better. But such is a very rare case in most of econometric work (that researcher has full confidence in data and specifications) and hence the Bayesian methods, though theoretically sound, cannot be applied without due considerations. Nor can Bayesian approach be regarded as a complete substitute for the sampling theory approach.

Throughout this text, classical approach has been followed while discussing the various econometric techniques of estimation. It is not because one is siding with 'Classical Approach'; rather because most econometric practice is in that tradition.

1.6 CENTRAL LIMIT THEOREM

Two important theorems, which relate the true population parameters to the parameters of the sampling distribution, are used most often in econometric theory.

Theorem I: If population of a certain variable X has a *normal distribution* with known mean $= \mu$ and variance $= \sigma_x^2$, and if repeated random samples of size n are taken from this population and for each sample the sample mean is computed $(\overline{X}_i)$, then the theoretical distribution of the sample means (i.e., sampling distribution of sample mean) will be *normal* with the *same mean* of the population $= \mu$ and *variance* $= \sigma_x^2/n$.

That is to say; if $\quad X_i \sim N(\mu, \sigma_x^2)$

$$\text{then, } \overline{X}_i \sim N(\mu, \sigma_x^2/n)$$

Theorem II: Suppose that the random variable X in the above case does not possess a normal distribution. What can one say about the distribution of $\overline{X}_i$ under such a situation?

According to another mathematical theorem, it may be said that if X possesses a distribution (whatsoever) with mean $= \mu$ and variance $= \sigma_x^2$, then the sampling distribution of $\overline{X}_i$ approaches a normal distribution with mean $= \mu$ and variance $= \sigma_x^2/n$ as the sample size n increases. This is known as *Central Limit Theorem.*

That is to say; if $\quad X_i \sim (\mu, \sigma_x^2)$

$$\text{then, } \overline{X}_i \to N(\mu, \sigma_x^2/n) \text{ for } n \to \infty$$

Probability and Related Distributions

2.1 CONCEPT OF PROBABILITY

Statistical analysis is an integral part of econometrics, while statistical theory rests upon the laws of probability. As such it is essential to learn about the probability theory to understand and interpret the general implications of econometric research.

Since our interest is mainly to understand the practical applicability of statistics in econometrics, this chapter and the next are in the nature of a summary.

There are certain notions which are impossible to define adequately, and probability is one such notion. But still the concept of probability is frequently used in many branches of science as well as in every day life. Various definitions of probability have been given. The statistical definition begins with the idea of a relative frequency. *Probability* is the limiting value of the relative frequency as the number of trials approaches infinity; symbolically

$$p = \underset{n \to \infty}{\text{Lt.}} \frac{m}{n} \qquad \qquad ...(i)$$

where p stands for probability of the event whose relative frequency is $\frac{m}{n}$. This definition assumes that limit is finite.

[If in n trials an event happens m times, then the relative frequency of the event is $\frac{m}{n}$.]

There is a condition which must get fulfilled if the above definition is to be accepted; i.e., the sequence of experiment or trials which becomes infinite must be a random sequence. By a random sequence we mean that any arbitrary selection from n trials gives the same value for p as the original n trials. For example, we take n_1 trials out of total n trials according to any arbitrary principle. Assume further that we observe that the event whose probability we want to compute occurs m_1 times among n_1 trials. Then we must have $p = \underset{n_1 \to \infty}{\text{Lt.}} \frac{m_1}{n_1}$, to be same value as obtained by (i).

Probability is an abstract concept; but since it involves the notion of a relative frequency that is observable, we can estimate probabilities from the empirical data.

The probability of any event can assume any value between zero and one. Symbolically

$$0 \leq p(X_i) \leq 1$$

If the probability of variable X assuming a particular value, say X_i, is equal to zero, this means that the variable cannot assume the value X_i. In other words, a probability of zero corresponds to the impossibility of occurrence. If the probability of a particular value, say X^* is equal to unity, this means that this value always occurs; i.e., the value X^* is the only value that the variable can assume. Thus the probability of one corresponds to certainty. Any probability between zero and one corresponds to uncertainty.

There are several rules for the calculation of probabilities of occurrence of one or more events simultaneously. These rules are known as the Laws of Probability.

2.2   BASIC LAWS OF PROBABILITY

There are four basic laws of probability:

1. *Addition Rule: Mutually exclusive events.* If two events A and B are mutually exclusive, the probability of either A or B occurring is the sum of their separate probabilities. Symbolically we may write this law as

$$p(A \text{ or } B) = p(A) + p(B)$$

For example, assume that we throw a die and we want to find the probability of either two (event A) or six (event B) appearing on the die. These events are mutually exclusive.

Probability of throwing two is $\dfrac{1}{6}$; probability of throwing six is $\dfrac{1}{6}$. The probability of throwing either two or six with an unbiased die, therefore, is

$$p = \frac{1}{6} + \frac{1}{6} = \frac{1}{3}$$

The same rule can be extended to the occurrence of three or more mutually exclusive events.

2. *Multiplication Rule: Independent events.* If two events are independent the probability of both events A and B occurring simultaneously is the product of their individual probabilities. Symbolically:

$$p(A \text{ and } B) = p(A) \cdot p(B)$$

Suppose event A refers to the winning of a cricket match by the Indian team playing against the Australian team, and event B refers to winning by a red horse in a race. These two events are obviously independent. How to determine the probability of both these events occurring simultaneously?

Since we assume that the Indian and Australian teams are equally good, the probability of our winning is $\frac{1}{2}$. Furthermore, assuming that in the horse race there are five horses running, all in equally good shape so that the probability of the red horse winning is $\frac{1}{5}$. Therefore,

$$p(A) = \frac{1}{2} \text{ and } p(B) = \frac{1}{5}$$

$$\therefore \qquad p(A \text{ and } B) = \frac{1}{2} \times \frac{1}{5} = \frac{1}{10}$$

The same rule can be extended to the occurrence of three or more independent events.

3. *Multiplication Rule: Dependent events.* If two events are dependent on each other, the probability of both occurring simultaneously is given by the probability of one event multiplied by the probability of the other, given that the first event has occurred. Symbolically:

$$p(A \text{ and } B) = p(A) \cdot p(B/A)$$

or, $\qquad p(A \text{ and } B) = p(B) \cdot p(A/B)$

The notation $p(B/A)$ refers to the conditional probability of B, that is, the probability of B occurring when event A has already occurred.

Consider an urn in which there are two red balls and three black balls. The probability of drawing a red ball at random, $p(A) = \frac{2}{5}$, since there are two red balls among the five balls in the urn.

Consider now the probability of drawing a black ball $p(B)$, after a red ball has been drawn. This is called conditional probability, $p(B/A) = \frac{3}{4}$. When one red ball has been drawn, four balls are left in the urn; three of these four balls are black. Hence conditional probability of the event B after A is known to have happened is $\frac{3}{4}$.

Hence the probability of drawing a red ball and then a black ball will be

$$\left(\frac{2}{5}\right)\left(\frac{3}{4}\right) = \frac{3}{10}$$

What will be the probability of drawing a black ball and then a red ball?

4. *Addition Rule: Events not mutually exclusive.* If two events are not mutually exclusive, the occurrence of either event A or event B means the occurrence of either A and B or both A and B. The probability of either A or B is given by

$$p(A \text{ or } B) = p(A) + p(B) - p(A \text{ and } B)$$

For instance in playing cards, let A designate the occurrence of a 'Heart' and let B designate the occurrence of a 'King'. What is the probability that a card chosen at random will be either a Heart or a King?

The events are not mutually exclusive, since a king can be a king of hearts. Hence we use the rule 4.

$$p(A) = \frac{13}{52}; \quad p(B) = \frac{4}{52}$$

$$p(A \text{ and } B) = p(A)\, p(B) \qquad\qquad \text{(by rule 2)}$$

$$\therefore \quad p(A \text{ and } B) = \left(\frac{13}{52}\right)\left(\frac{4}{52}\right) = \frac{1}{52}$$

Hence, $\quad p(A \text{ or } B) = \dfrac{13}{52} + \dfrac{4}{52} - \dfrac{1}{52} = \dfrac{4}{13}$

For three events, say A, B and C, which are not mutually exclusive, the probability of either A or B or C is determined from the following formula:

$$p(A \text{ or } B \text{ or } C) = p(A) + p(B) + p(C) - p(A \text{ and } B)$$
$$- p(A \text{ and } C) - p(B \text{ and } C)$$
$$+ p(A \text{ and } B \text{ and } C)$$

2.3 PROBABILITY DENSITY FUNCTION

Random variable can be discrete or continuous; we shall, therefore, examine the probability distribution of discrete and continuous variables separately.

2.3.1 Probability Density Function of a Discrete Random Variable

Consider a throw with two unbiased coins. The coins are thrown independently. The number of heads (or tails) in each throw can now be regarded as a random variable X. The following outcomes are possible:

Outcomes	Number of heads (X)	Probability of (X): f(X)
TT	0	1/4
TH	1	1/4
HT	1	1/4
HH	2	1/4

An alternative way of presenting the above information is

X	f(X)
0	1/4
1	1/2
2	1/4

The above distribution is known as probability distribution which can be described through probability density function.

Let us now give the definition of probability density function.

If X is a discrete random variable assuming values: $x_1, x_2, x_3, ..., x_n$ with associated probabilities; $f(x_1), f(x_2), ..., f(x_n)$, then the set of pairs:

$$
\begin{array}{cc}
x_1 & f(x_1) \\
x_2 & f(x_2) \\
x_3 & f(x_3) \\
\vdots & \vdots \\
\vdots & \vdots \\
x_n & f(x_n)
\end{array}
$$

is called the discrete probability density of X.

The graphical representation of probability distribution may be uniform or non-uniform. If all the permissible values of X have equal probability of being observed, the probability distribution is called the *uniform* or *rectangular* distribution. This type of distribution is shown in Fig. 2.1 and Table 2.1.

Table 2.1

Outcomes on throwing a die (x)	Probability of $x = f(x_i)$
1	1/6
2	1/6
3	1/6
4	1/6
5	1/6
6	1/6
	$\Sigma f(x_i) = 1$

In econometric applications mostly non-uniform probability distributions are observed. In such cases each value of the random variable has different probability of being observed.

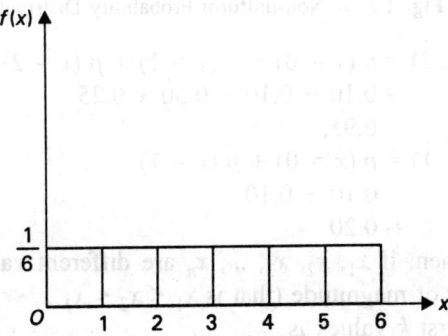

Fig. 2.1: A Uniform Probability Distribution

For example, suppose that random variable X denotes the number of children per family and that X can take values from 0 to 4. The graph of such non-uniform probability distribution is shown in Fig. 2.2 and Table 2.2.

Table 2.2

No. of children per family (x)	No. of families (f)	Proportion of families $p = f(x_i)$
0	2	2/20 = 0.10
1	2	2/20 = 0.10
2	10	10/20 = 0.50
3	5	5/20 = 0.25
4	1	1/20 = 0.05
	20	$\Sigma f(x_i) = 1$

For some problems, we need to find probability that X will assume a value less than or equal to a given number. Such probabilities are called *cumulative probabilities* and are usually denoted by $F(X)$. The cumulative probability is the sum of individual probabilities. For example the probability of having three or less children (from the above non-uniform distribution) is

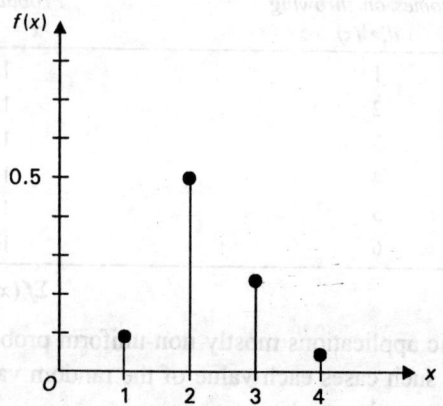

Fig. 2.2: A Non-uniform Probability Distribution

$$p(0 \le x \le 3) = p(x = 0) + p(x = 1) + p(x = 2) + p(x = 3)$$
$$= 0.10 + 0.10 + 0.50 + 0.25$$
$$= 0.95;$$

and, $P(0 \le x \le 1) = p(x = 0) + p(x = 1)$
$$= 0.10 + 0.10$$
$$= 0.20$$

In general, then, if $x_1, x_2, x_3, ..., x_n$ are different values of X given in increasing order of magnitude (that is $x_1 < x_2 < x_3 ... < x_n$), the cumulative probability of first k values is

$$F(x_k) = f(x_1) + f(x_2) + ... + f(x_k) = \sum_{i=1}^{k} f(x_i)$$

Since the values outside the range of X (i.e., values smaller than x_1 or larger than x_n) occur only with probability equal to zero;

$$\therefore \qquad F(x_k) = \sum_{x=-\infty}^{k} f(x_i)$$

The important points related to cumulative probability are:

(i) If x_n is the largest value of X, then $F(x_n) = 1$
(ii) $F(-\infty) = 0$, $F(\infty) = 1$; where F is the cumulative distribution of a non-decreasing random variable x.

2.3.2 Probability Density Function of a Continuous Random Variable

If a random variable is continuous, it can assume an infinite number of values in an interval with specific probability. We regard a probability distribution as a continuous function of the random variable in this case and call it *Probability density function.*

Assume that a random variable X can vary continuously from $X = x_1$ to $X = x_n$; we then, define the probability density function by the following integral:

$$\int_{x_1}^{x_n} f(x)\, dx$$

The integration from x_1 to x_n in case of the continuous variable is analogous to the summation of probabilities in the discrete case.

In general, if X is a continuous random variable, then the probability that it assumes a value in the interval from a to b is determined by the following

$$p(a < x < b) = \int_{a}^{b} f(x)\, dx$$

where $f(x)$ is the relevant probability density function. Since the probability that X will assume any value is 1 (i.e., it is a certainty);

$$p(-\infty < x < +\infty) = \int_{-\infty}^{+\infty} f(x)\, dx = 1$$

Furthermore, the probability that X will assume any value less than or equal to some specific value x_0 is,

$$F(x) = \int_{-\infty}^{x_0} f(x)\, dx$$

where F (as in discrete case) represents the cumulative probability of x.

Let us take a hypothetical example to understand the above terms.

Consider a continuous random variable X that can assume all values between 2 and 6 with equal probability. The probability density function is:

$$f(x) = \frac{1}{4}$$

What is the probability that X will be smaller than or equal to 5?

The reason why the probability density $= \frac{1}{4}$, can easily be seen if we compute the cumulative function over the entire range of X (i.e., between 2 and 6):

$$\int_2^6 f(x)\, dx = \int_2^6 \left(\tfrac{1}{4}\right) dx = \left[\frac{1}{4}x\right]_2^6 = 1$$

Now to obtain the probability the X will be smaller than or equal to 5, we have to find,

$$p\,(2 \le x \le 5) = \int_2^5 \left(\tfrac{1}{4}\right) dx = \frac{3}{4}.$$

The probability that X will be between 3 and 4 is given by

$$p\,(3 \le x \le 4) = \int_3^4 \left(\tfrac{1}{4}\right) dx = \frac{1}{4}$$

The cumulative probability distribution for a random variable X, normally distributed with mean μ and standard deviation σ is

$$F(x) = \frac{1}{\sigma\sqrt{2\pi}} \int_{-\infty}^{x_i} \exp.\left[-\frac{1}{2\sigma^2}(x_i - \mu)^2\right] dx_i$$

where $\pi = 3.1416$ and 'exp' is the *exponential base* $= 2.71828....$ The probability density function obtained by differentiating the above cumulative function with respect to x_i is given by

$$f(x) = \frac{1}{\sigma\sqrt{2\pi}} \exp.\left[-\frac{1}{2\sigma^2}(x_i - \mu)^2\right]$$

The probability of observing any given value, say x_i, may now be evaluated, assuming μ and σ to be given.

2.3.3 Joint Probability Distributions

So far we have concerned ourselves with only one random variable (continuous or discrete) and its probability distribution. Such distributions are termed as *univariate distributions*.

We may now consider a sample which involves more than one random variable at a time. The corresponding probability distribution is then called

Multivariate distribution. As an example, let us consider a case involving only two variables, i.e., a case of *bivariate* distribution.

Assume that we observe two characteristics of a person in a very large sample. By denoting X for the sex of the person and Y for smoking characteristic, we obtain the following probabilities:

Probability of male smoker	= 0.6
Probability of female smoker	= 0.1
Probability of male non smoker	= 0.1
Probability of female non smoker	= 0.2

The above collected information can be presented in the form of Table 2.3.

Table 2.3

Values of Y	Values of X		Marginal probability of Y : f(y)
	Male: x_1	Female: x_2	
Smoker: y_1	$f(x_1, y_1) = 0.6$	$f(x_2, y_1) = 0.1$	$f(y_1) = 0.7$
Non smoker: y_2	$f(x_1, y_2) = 0.1$	$f(x_2, y_2) = 0.2$	$f(y_2) = 0.3$
Marginal probability of X : f(x)	$f(x_1) = 0.7$	$f(x_2) = 0.3$	1

The probability that X assumes a given value x and Y assumes a given value y is called the *Joint probability* of x and y and is denoted as $f(x, y)$. For instance in the above table (joint) probability of female being non smoker is $f(x_2, y_2) = 0.2$.

The probability that X will assume a given value x whatever the value of Y, is called the *Marginal probability* of x; while the distribution of these probabilities is called the *Marginal distribution* of X. This is given in the bottom row of the above table. Similarly, the marginal distribution of Y consists of probabilities of different values of Y regardless of the values assumed by X. Such distribution is given in the last right hand column of Table 2.3. For example, the probability of male (whether smoker or non smoker) is 0.7 and the probability of non smoker (whatever sex) is 0.3.

Marginal probability distributions are, in fact, univariate distributions and thus are denoted in the same way: $f(x)$ and $f(y)$. Also, as we can observe from Table 2.3, the probabilities of the marginal distribution of any variable (say X) are determined by adding up the corresponding probabilities over all values of the other variable (i.e. Y); so that in general,

$$f(x_i) = \sum_{j=1}^{\infty} f(x_i, y_j) = f(x_i, y_1) + f(x_i, y_2) + \cdots\cdots$$

$$f(y_i) = \sum_{j=1}^{\infty} f(x_j, y_i) = f(x_1, y_i) + f(x_2, y_i) + \cdots\cdots$$

Finally, there is a concept of *Conditional probability*. We referred to this under rule 3 of the Probability Laws.

The probability that X is equal to x given that Y is equal to y_1 is known as the conditional probability of X, given Y. It is denoted by $f(x/y)$ Thus $f(y/x)$ depicts the conditional probability of Y, given X. Also;

$$f(x/y) = \frac{f(x, y)}{f(y)}: \text{conditional probability of } X.$$

$$f(y/x) = \frac{f(x, y)}{f(x)}: \text{conditional probability of } Y.$$

Applying the above rule, the probability that a person be a female, given that she be a smoker, is

$$f(x_2/y_1) = \frac{f(x_2, y_1)}{f(y_1)} = \frac{0.1}{0.7} = 0.143$$

The probability that the person is a smoker, given that person be a female, is

$$f(y_1/x_2) = \frac{f(y_1, x_2)}{f(x_2)} = \frac{0.1}{0.3} = 0.333$$

2.4 CHARACTERISTICS OF PROBABILITY DISTRIBUTIONS

2.4.1 Mathematical Expectation or Expected Value

Probability distributions like ordinary frequency distributions contain various characteristics with which these distributions are identified. The most common characteristics, as we know, are the mean and variance which are defined in terms of mathematical expectation or expected values in case of probability distributions.

The mathematical expectation is computed by multiplying all possible values of random variable by their respective probabilities and then summing the products.

Mathematical expectation, thus, characterises the central tendency of the probability distribution; hence arithmetic mean of a frequency distribution is in fact the mathematical expectation of a probability distribution. This may be understood by considering a simple example. Suppose we observe a sample of 20 families classified by the number of children and tabulated as shown in Table 2.2 given in the case of non-uniform probability distribution under section 2.3.1.

The number of children per family denoted by x can be regarded as the different values which random variable X can assume. Let us obtain the average number of children per family. This is given by:

$$\bar{x} = \frac{\sum\limits_{i=0}^{4} f_i x_i}{\sum\limits_{i=0}^{4} f_i}$$

$$= \frac{1}{20} (2 \times 0 + 2 \times 1 + 10 \times 2 + 5 \times 3 + 1 \times 4)$$

i.e., $\quad \bar{x} = 2.05$

The same result would be obtained if we calculate mathematical expectation of x as per above definition. Mathematical expectation of x, denoted by $E(x)$ is then given by:

$$E(x) = (0 \times 0.10 + 1 \times 0.10 + 2 \times 0.50$$
$$+ 3 \times 0.25 + 4 \times 0.05)$$

$$E(x) = 2.05$$

i.e., $\quad E(x) = \bar{x} = 2.05$

The analogy between the mean of an ordinary frequency distribution and the expected value of a discrete random variable should, therefore, be clear. This is the reason why $E(x)$ is identified with population mean μ.

Generalising now, if a discrete random variable X possesses the following probability function:

X	$f(x)$
x_1	$f(x_1)$
x_2	$f(x_2)$
x_3	$f(x_3)$
$\vdots$	$\vdots$
x_n	$f(x_n)$

then expected value or mathematical expectation of X is

$$E(X) = x_1 \cdot f(x_1) + x_2 \cdot f(x_2) + x_n \cdot f(x_n)$$

or, $\quad E(X) = \sum_{i=1}^{n} x_i \cdot f(x_i)$

If X is continuous random variable with probability density function $f(x)$, then we merely replace the summation by integration:

$$E(X) = \int_{-\infty}^{+\infty} x \cdot f(x)\, dx.$$

The integration is carried out from $-\infty$ to $+\infty$ so that all possible values of X in the population are covered.

There are certain probability distributions for which expected value of the variable may not exist. A classical example in this respect is the problem called *St. Petersburg paradox*. The problem is why people are unwilling to make bets at better than 50–50 odds when their (mathematical) expectations of winning money, in a particular kind of gamble, are greater the more money they bet. The expected gain in *St. Petersburg** problem is infinity.

The concept of mathematical expectation is important in the derivation of various theorems in mathematical statistics.

We will indicate briefly seven rules for employing the notations of mathematical expectation in various computations in econometrics.

1. If X is a random variable (continuous or discrete) and a and b are constants, then

$$E(aX + b) = a\, E(X) + b$$

X-discrete variable:

$$E(aX + b) = \sum (ax_i + b)\, f(x_i)$$

$$= \sum ax_i\, f(x_i) + \sum bf(x_i)$$

$$= a \sum x_i\, f(x_i) + b \sum f(x_i)$$

$$= a\, E(X) + b$$

X-continuous variable: $\displaystyle E(aX + b) = \int_{-\infty}^{+\infty} (ax + b)\, f(x)\, dx$

$$= \int axf(x)\, dx + \int bf(x)\, dx$$

$$= a\, E(X) + b$$

2. The mathematical expectation of a sum (or a difference) of random *independent* variables is the sum (or difference) of their individual expected values; i.e.,

$$E(X + Y + Z \,......) = E(X) + E(Y) + \cdots\cdots$$

Let us consider a simple case involving two variables only:

$$E(X + Y) = \sum_i \sum_j (x_i + y_j)\, f(x_i, y_j)$$

$$= \sum_i \sum_j x_i\, f(x_i, y_j) + \sum_i \sum_j y_j\, f(x_i, y_j)$$

$$= \sum_i x_i \sum_j f(x_i, y_j) + \sum_j y_j \sum_i f(x_i, y_j)$$

But $\displaystyle \sum_j f(x_i, y_j) = f(x_i)$ = marginal probability of X

and $\displaystyle \sum_i f(x_i, y_j) = f(y_j)$ = marginal probability of Y

Therefore, $\displaystyle E(X + Y) = \sum_i x_i \cdot f(x_i) + \sum_j y_j \cdot f(y_j)$

$$= E(X) + E(Y)$$

---

*For St. Petersburg problem See problem No. 3 under Assignment 2.3

3. The expected value of a linear combination of random variables is equal to the linear combination of their expected values, i.e.,

$E(aX + bY + cZ + ...) = aE(X) + bE(Y) + ...$
where $a, b, c, ...$ are constants.
Let us take a simple case

$$E(aX + bY) = \sum_i \sum_j (ax_i + by_j) f(x_i, y_j)$$

$$= \sum_i \sum_j ax_i f(x_i, y_j) + \sum_i \sum_j by_j f(x_i, x_j)$$

$$= a \sum_i x_i \sum_j f(x_i, y_j) + b \sum_j y_j \sum_i f(x_i, y_j)$$

$$= aE(X) + bE(Y)$$

4. The expected value of a constant is equal to that constant, i.e., $E(k) = k$, where k is some constant

$$E(k) = \sum_i k \cdot f(k) = k \sum f(k) = k$$

5. The expected value of the product of two *independent* variables is equal to the product of the expected values of the two variables, i.e.,

$$E(XY) = E(X) E(Y)$$

$$E(XY) = \sum_i \sum_j x_i y_j f(x_i, y_j)$$

Since X and Y are independent, their joint probability is given by:

$$f(x_i, y_j) = f(x_i) f(y_j)$$

$\therefore$
$$E(XY) = \sum_i \sum_j x_i y_j f(x_i) f(y_j)$$

$$= \sum_i x_i f(x_i) \cdot \sum_j y_j f(y_j)$$

$$= E(X) E(Y)$$

We should note here the difference in the expected value of a sum and the expected value of a product. The expected value of a sum is always equal to the sum of expected values; whereas the expected value of a product is equal to the product of expected values only if the variables are uncorrelated (independent).

6. If X and Y are two *independent* variables, then their covariance is equal to zero, i.e.,

$$\text{Cov } (X, Y) = 0$$

Let us first understand the concept of *covariance*. Consider any two series of n-sample observations on X and Y variables:

$$X : x_1 \; x_2 \; ... \; x_n$$
$$Y : y_1 \; y_2 \; ... \; y_n$$

At times we are interested in knowing the way in which the variables change together. In the language of statistics, how do they covary? The covariance between X and Y is defined as;

$$\text{Cov } (X, \; Y) = \frac{\sum\limits_{i=1}^{n}(X_i - \overline{X})(Y_i - \overline{Y})}{n}$$

If the variables X and Y are not changing together (i.e., if they are independent), their covariance is equal to zero, because the numerator in that case will turn out to be zero.

The covariance may also be described in terms of mathematical expectation,

$$\text{Cov } (X, \; Y) = \frac{1}{n} \sum (X_i - \overline{X})(Y_i - \overline{Y})$$

i.e., $\text{Cov } (X, \; Y) = E \left\{ [X - E(X)][Y - E(Y)] \right\}$

Let us now examine the rule 6

$$\begin{aligned}
\text{Cov } (X, \; Y) &= E \left\{ [X - E(X)][Y - E(Y)] \right\} \\
&= E \left\{ XY - Y \cdot E(X) - X \cdot E(Y) + E(X) \cdot E(Y) \right\} \\
&= E(XY) - E(Y) \cdot E(X) - E(X) \cdot E(Y) + E(X) \cdot E(Y) \\
&= E(XY) - E(X) \cdot E(Y)
\end{aligned}$$

Since X and Y are independent,

$$E(XY) = E(X) \; E(Y)$$

Therefore, $\text{Cov } (X, \; Y) = E(X) \cdot E(Y) - E(X) \cdot E(Y) = 0$

That is to say, if the two variables are independent their covariance is zero. But the converse may not be true. In other words, though the covariance between the variables be zero, they may not be independent. As an example consider the following hypothetical table.

Values of X	Values of Y		$f(x)$
	0	1	
1	0	$\frac{1}{3}$	$\frac{1}{3}$
2	$\frac{1}{3}$	0	$\frac{1}{3}$
3	0	$\frac{1}{3}$	$\frac{1}{3}$
$f(y)$	$\frac{1}{3}$	$\frac{2}{3}$	1

Let us now determine Cov (X, Y) from this table.

$$\text{Cov } (X, Y) = E \{[X - E (X)] [Y - E (Y)]\}$$

i.e. $$\text{Cov } (X, Y) = E (XY) - E (X) \cdot E (Y)$$

$$E (X) = 1 \times \frac{1}{3} + 2 \times \frac{1}{3} + 3 \times \frac{1}{3} = 2$$

$$E (Y) = 0 \times \frac{1}{3} + 1 \times \frac{2}{3} = \frac{2}{3}$$

$$E (XY) = \sum_i \sum_j x_i y_j \, f(x_i, y_j)$$

$$= \left(1 \times 1 \times \frac{1}{3}\right) + \left(2 \times 0 \times \frac{1}{3}\right) + \left(3 \times 1 \times \frac{1}{3}\right) = \frac{4}{3}$$

Therefore, Cov $(X, Y) = \dfrac{4}{3} - (2)\left(\dfrac{2}{3}\right) = 0$

Thus, we obtain zero covariance between the two variables. But are the variables, X and Y, independent? No, because the marginal and conditional distributions are not the same. [X and Y are said to be independent if

$$p (X = x_i, Y = y_i) = p (X = x_i) \cdot p (Y = y_i),$$

otherwise they are said to be dependent.]

The preceding analysis shows that independence between the two random variables is a *sufficient* condition but not a *necessary* condition for zero covariance.

7. If X is a random variable and a and b are constants, then

$$\text{Var } (aX + b) = a^2 \, \text{Var } (X)$$

Proof: $\text{Var } (aX + b) = E (aX + b) - E (aX + b)]^2$

(By definition of second moment)

$$= E [(aX + b) - (a\mu + b)]^2$$
$$= E [aX - a\mu]^2$$
$$= E [a^2 (X - \mu)^2] = a^2 E [(X - \mu)^2]$$
$$= a^2 \, \text{Var } (X)$$

2.4.2 Moments and the Mathematical Expectation

The application of the above rules enables us to determine special characteristics of a probability distribution called *Moments*. The moments represent a family of parameters which characterise a probability distribution.

Two kinds of moments can be distinguished; moments about the origin and moments about the mean (or mathematical expectation).

Given a random variable X and its probability distribution, we define the *n*th moment about the origin (i.e., about zero) as:

Discrete variable: $\quad E(X^n) = \sum x_i^n \cdot f(x_i)$

Continuous variable: $\quad E(X^n) = \int\limits_{-\infty}^{+\infty} x^n \cdot f(x)\,dx$

Suppose now that $n = 0$, i.e., the 0th moment about origin is

$$E(X^0) = E(1) = 1$$

Suppose; $\qquad\qquad n = 1$, i.e., the first moment about origin is

$$E(X^1) = E(x) = \mu \text{ (population mean)}$$

In other words, the first moment about the origin of a random variable is the mathematical expectation of the random variable. This allows us to establish relation between any moment about the origin and the mathematical expectation:

nth moment:	$E(X^n) = E(x_i - 0)^n$
First moment:	$F(X^1) = E(x_i - 0)^1$
Second moment:	$E(X^2) = E(x_i - 0)^2$
Third moment:	$E(X^3) = E(x_i - 0)^3$ and so on.

A very important class of moments are the moments about the mathematical expectation. These can be obtained by merely replacing the zero by the mathematical expectation, thus

nth moment about mathematical expectation of X is given;

$$E[x_i - E(x)]^n \text{ or, } E(x_i - \mu)^n$$

These moments help us to describe the various characteristics of the probability distributions.

(i) Zero-th moment denoted as μ_0 about the mathematical expectation is equal to one.

$$\mu_0 = E(x_i - \mu)^0 = E(1) = 1$$

(ii) The first moment (μ_1) about the mathematical expectation is zero.

$$\mu_1 = E(x_i - \mu)^1 = E(x_i) - E(\mu) = \mu - \mu = 0$$

(But the first moment about the origin is population mean.)

(iii) The second moment (μ_2) about the mathematical expectation is variance.

$$\mu_2 = \sum(x_i - \mu)^2 = \text{Variance.}(X)$$

$$\left[\text{Since,} \qquad \sigma^2 = \sum \frac{(x_i - \mu)^2}{n} = \frac{1}{n}\sum(x_i - \mu)^2 \right.$$

$$\left. = \frac{1}{\Sigma f_i}\sum(x_i - \mu)^2 = E(X_i - \mu)^2 \right]$$

The second moment therefore measures the dispersion of probability distribution about the mean of the distribution.

(iv) The third moment (μ_3) about the mathematical expectation is a measure of the skewness of the distribution.

$$\mu_3 = E\,(x_i - \mu)^3$$

It measures the degree to which probability distribution is symmetrical about mathematical expectation. If $\mu_3 = 0$, the distribution is symmetrical.

(v) The fourth moment (μ_4) about the mathematical expectation is a measure of kurtosis of the distribution. It measures the degree of flatness of peakedness at the highest point on the curve.

$$\mu_4 = E\,(x_i - \mu)^4$$

2.5 IMPORTANT THEORETICAL PROBABILITY DISTRIBUTIONS

An extensive use of following four probability distributions is made in the Econometric Theory.

The Normal Distribution

The best known of all the theoretical probability distributions is the normal distribution. It is a bell-shaped curve which extends indefinitely in both directions and is symmetrical round the mean of the variable, whose values are measured on the horizontal axis. The vertical axis depicts the value of the probability density function.

A continuous random variable X is said to be normally distributed if its probability density function has the following form:

$$f(x) = \frac{1}{\sigma\sqrt{2\pi}}\ \exp.\left[-\frac{1}{2}\cdot\frac{(X-\mu)^2}{\sigma^2}\right],$$

$$-\infty < X < \infty$$

where μ and σ^2, known as the *parameters of the distribution*, are the mean and the variance of the distribution respectively.

The Properties of the Distribution

(i) It is symmetrical around its mean value.
(ii) Approximately 68 per cent of the area under the normal curve lies between the values of $\mu \pm \sigma$, about 95 per cent of the area lies between $\mu \pm 2\sigma$, and about 99.7 per cent of the area lies between $\mu \pm 3\sigma$.
(iii) It should be obvious that the probability of X_i will be different according to probability density function which mainly depends on the two parameters, μ and σ^2. Though the different normal distributions would lead to different probabilities but the difference will only be due to differences in their means and variances. Due to this fact, every normal distribution is transformed to specific normal distribution for which the areas have been calculated and tabulated. This specific distribution is called **Standard Normal Distribution** or **Gauss Distribution**.

The standard normal distribution is the probability distribution of a variable Z which has a normal distribution with zero mean and unit variance, i.e.,

$$Z \sim N(0, 1).$$

The probabilities of various values of Z have been tabulated by Gauss and are shown in the Appendix. To use this table, one has to convert the given normally distributed variable X with mean μ and variance σ^2 into a standardised normal variable Z by the following transformation:

$$Z_i = \frac{X_i - \mu}{\sigma} \sim N(0, 1)$$

Substituting Z into normal probability density function given above, following expression is obtained:

$$f(Z) = \frac{1}{\sqrt{2\pi}} \exp.\left(-\frac{1}{2}Z^2\right)$$

This describes the probability density function of the standarised normal variable.

The Chi-Square (χ^2) Distribution

Let $X_1, X_2, ..., X_v$ are the normal and independent set of variables, suppose these are normalised by taking their respective standard normal values:

$$Z_1 = \left(\frac{X_1 - \mu_1}{\sigma_1}\right) \sim N(0, 1);$$

$$Z_2 = \left(\frac{X_2 - \mu_2}{\sigma_2}\right) \sim N(0, 1),...,$$

$$Z_v = \left(\frac{X_v - \mu_v}{\sigma_v}\right) \sim N(0, 1).$$

The sum of the squares of the normalised variables has a Chi-square distribution;

$$\chi^2 = \sum Z_i^2 = \sum \left(\frac{X_i - \mu_i}{\sigma_i}\right)^2$$

with v degrees of freedom. The number of degrees of freedom is equal to the number of independent variables.

Properties of the χ^2 Distribution

(i) The χ^2 distribution is skewed to the right, the degree of skewness depends on the degrees of freedom. As the degrees of freedom increase, the distribution becomes increasingly symmetrical. As a matter of fact, for degrees of freedom more than 100, the variable:

$$\sqrt{2\chi^2} - \sqrt{2v-1}$$

can be treated as a standard normal variable: v is the degrees of freedom.

(ii) The mean of χ^2 distribution is v and its variance is $2v$.

(iii) If Z_1 and Z_2 are two independent Chi-square variables with v_1 and v_2 degrees of freedom, then, the sum $Z_1 + Z_2$ is also a Chi-square variable with $df = v_1 + v_2$.

The Student's t-Distribution

If Z_1 is a standardised normal variable; $Z_1 \sim N(0, 1)$, and another variable Z_2 is an independent variable that follows the Chi-square distribution with v degrees of freedom, then the quantity t defined as $t = Z_1/\sqrt{Z_2/v} = Z_1\sqrt{v}/\sqrt{Z_2}$ follows student's t-distribution with v degrees of freedom.

Properties of the t-distribution

(i) The t-distribution, like the normal distribution, is symmetrical about zero but flatter than the normal distribution. This means that the area at the tails is larger for the t-distribution than for the standard normal distribution. However, as the sample size becomes larger (i.e., degrees of freedom increase), the t-distribution approximates the normal distribution. If $n > 30$, one makes a very small error if one decides to use Z instead of t.

(ii) The mean of t-distribution is zero and variance $v/(v - 2)$, hence always greater than 1.

(iii) The range of t-values is $-\infty < t < +\infty$.

The values of t-distribution are tabulated in the Appendix.

The F-Distribution

If two variables Z_1 and Z_2 are independently distributed χ^2-variables with v_1 and v_2 degrees of freedom respectively, the statistic

$$F = \frac{Z_1/v_1}{Z_2/v_2}$$

follows F-distribution (after the name of Fisher) with v_1 and v_2 degrees of freedom.

The above ratio of F-statistic can also be viewed in terms of the ratio of two independent estimates of variances, and the F-distribution is then used to test the equality of these estimates. For this reason the F-statistic is called the variance ratio and is described as:

$$F = \frac{\hat{\sigma}_1^2}{\hat{\sigma}_2^2} = \text{variances ratio, with } v_1 \text{ and } v_2 \text{ degrees of freedom.}$$

Properties of F-distribution

(i) The value of F-statistic is always positive and the range of values of F is $0 \leq F \leq +\infty$.

(ii) Like the Chi-square distribution, the F-distribution is also skewed to the right. It can, however, be shown that as v_1 and v_2 increase, the F-distribution approaches normal distribution.

(iii) The mean value of F-distribution is $(v_1/v_2) - 2$ which is defined for $v_2 > 2$, and its variance is:

$$\frac{2v_2^2 (v_1 + v_2 - 2)}{v_1 (v_2 - 2)^2 (v_2 - 4)} \text{ which is defined for } v > 4.$$

(iv) There is a formal relationship between t and F-statistic as applied in regression analysis. The square of a t-statistic with v degrees of freedom has F-distribution with 1 and v degrees of freedom; that is:

$$t_{(v)}^2 = F_{(1, v)}$$

2.6 THE LOGNORMAL DISTRIBUTION

A random variable (x), the logarithm of which $(\log_e x)$ is normally distributed, is said to have the lognormal distribution.

That is, if: $y = \log_e x \sim N(\mu, \sigma^2)$ then, $x = e^y$ has lognormal distribution. The mean and variance are defined as:

Mean: $\qquad E(x) = E(e^y) = \exp. \left(\mu + \frac{1}{2}\sigma^2 \right)$

Variance: $\quad$ Var. $(x) = $ Var. $(e^y) = \exp. (2\mu + \sigma^2 (e^{\sigma^2} - 1))$

The frequency density curve of the lognormal distribution, unlike that of normal distribution, is asymmetric exhibiting a long tail in the positive direction as depicted in Fig. 2.3.

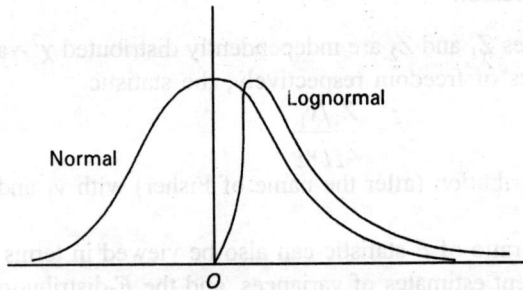

Fig. 2.3: Lognormal Distribution

It is, therefore, defined only for positive values of x. Since many variables in economics can not assume negative values and also do not have symmetric distribution as the normal, the lognormal distribution may be more appropriate in such economic applications than normal.

2.7 SUBJECTIVE PROBABILITY AND BAYE'S THEOREM

The concept of probability given under 2.1 is based on an idea of limiting relative frequency. Such a concept was developed to describe games of chance where trials are repeated a large number of times under identical conditions. There are, in fact, situations where it may not be possible to repeat the trials (or experiments) under identical conditions. For instance, in social sciences, where controlled experimentation is not possible, this concept of *long run frequency* is rather difficult to accept. Almost all decisions made in the sphere of economics do not depend on outcomes of repetitive experiments. A firm deciding on raising prices has to make the decision on the basis of some probability about what the competitive firms will do, but these probabilities are necessary subjective and have no relative long frequency distributions. Such concept is explained under section 1.5 of first Chapter.

A different interpretation of probability which has been used in social sciences and even in Econometrics, is that of subjective degree of belief. For example, we often say, "The chances of his securing I class in the examination are 50%" *or*, "There are 99% chances that it will rain today". These are probability statements but they do not describe any long run or limiting relative frequency. The probabilities are in the form of subjective degree of belief and therefore based on subjective judgement of the likelihood of the events in above statements.

Subjective probabilities vary from person to person. Nevertheless, it is possible to give objective interpretation to these subjective probabilities through a statistical procedure widely known as Baye's theorem.

Baye's theorem: This theorem is based on the concept of subjective probability via conditional probabilities discussed earlier.

We know that $P(X/Y)$ is the conditional probability of X, given Y; and $P(Y/X)$ is the conditional probability of Y, given X.

Also, $\quad P(X/Y) = \dfrac{P(XY)}{P(Y)}$ and, $P(Y/X) = \dfrac{P(XY)}{P(X)}$

Hence, $\quad P(X/Y) = \dfrac{P(Y/X) \cdot P(X)}{P(Y)}$ $\qquad$ ...(i)

Let us now substitute H (denoting Hypothesis) for X, and D (denoting Data) for Y so that (i) can now be written as:

$$P(H/D) = \frac{P(D/H) \cdot P(H)}{P(D)} \qquad \text{...(ii)}$$

Equality (ii) involves yet another interpretation of probabilities. Taking right hand side of (ii):

(a) $P(D/H)$ is the probability of observing the data (D) given that Hypothesis (H) made is true. This is called *likelihood function*.
(b) $P(H)$ is the probability that Hypothesis (H) is true before observing the data. This is called *prior probability*.

(c) $P(D)$ is the unconditional probability of observing the data (D) whether or not H is true.

On the left hand side of (ii), we have:

(d) $P(H/D)$ which indicates the probability that H is true after observing the data (D). This is called the *posterior probability*.

Equality (ii) can also be expressed as:

$$P(H/D) \propto P(D/H) \times P(H) \qquad \text{...(iii)}$$

That is, *posterior probability* is proportional to the product of *likelihood function* and *prior probability*.

This is a simple version of Baye's theorem. This theorem thus helps to generate posterior probabilities from prior probabilities and likelihoods. If the prior probability is interpreted as a subjective degree of belief, the posterior probability is obtained by combining subjective belief with objective information on an observed event.

The Baye's theorem describes the procedure that combines a prior distribution with observed information to form a posterior distribution.

For continuous distributions (iii) may be written as:

$$f(\theta/D) = \frac{L(D/\theta) \cdot f(\theta)}{\left[L(D/\theta) \cdot f(\theta)\right] d\theta} \propto f(D/\theta) \times f(\theta)$$

Here 'f' stands for probability density and $f(\theta/D)$ is the posterior probability density function of θ (or probability of parameter θ) after the sample data (D) has been observed.

$L(D/\theta)$ is the likelihood function, which denotes the **likelihood of** observing sample data (D) given the parameter (θ).

$f(\theta)$ is the prior probability density function representing the **prior belief** regarding the value(s) of the parameter(s) before observing data (D).

ASSIGNMENTS

1. Assume three independent random variables X, Y and Z.
   Given that: $E(X) = 1$, $E(Y) = -5$, and $E(Z) = 6$
   Determine: $E(2X)$, $E(4Y)$, $E(5Z)$, $E(X + Y + Z)$, $E(XY)$,
   $E(XZ)$, $E(YZ)$, and $E(3XY - 6YZ + 4XZ)$.

2. Assume two independent variables. The probability density function of X is $f(X) = \dfrac{1}{4}$,
   $(1 \leq X \leq 5)$. The probability density function of Y is $f(Y) = \dfrac{1}{3}$, $(3 \leq Y \leq 6)$.
   Determine: $E(X)$, $E(Y)$, $E(X + Y)$, and $E(XY)$.

3. Suppose you are asked to toss a coin and you are paid Rs. 2 if you get heads in the first toss, but not in the second; Rs. 4 if you get heads in the first and the second tosses but not in the third; Rs. 8 if you get heads in the first, second and third toss but not in the fourth; and so on. How much would you expect to win from such a game?

Derivation and Properties
of Estimators

3.1 ESTIMATOR—ESTIMATION

Whenever we take a sample, we do so with an idea of learning something about the population from which the sample is drawn. In statistical terminology, this learning is termed as *statistical inference* which is of two kinds; *estimation* and *hypothesis testing*. Both types of statistical inference utilise the information provided by the sample for drawing some conclusions about the parameters of the population; yet each type of inference uses this information in different ways. The information by the sample is given by sample observations: X_1, X_2, ..., X_n. In estimation we use some formula or rule (called estimator) in which we substitute the sample observations to obtain numerical result (called estimation) of the population parameter(s). In hypothesis testing we combine the prior information that we may have with the information provided by the sample. Such prior information may concern the assumption about the form of distribution of the population of interest, the value of some parameter other than which is required to be obtained or some specification concerning parameter of interest. Estimation, as we shall observe in the course of this book, has been given more importance in the econometric theory than hypothesis testing.

The theory of estimation is divided into two parts: *point* estimation and *interval* estimation. The aim of point estimation is to obtain a single value which is the best guess of the parameter of interest. In interval estimation the object is to obtain interval within which the true value of the parameter may be said to lie with some given level of probability which expresses the confidence we have that the value lies within the stipulated range. Hence the interval itself is called *confidence interval*.

There are various methods with which we may obtain point estimation or point estimates of the parameters of economic relationships. There is naturally a problem of choosing the one which gives us the best estimate. Also, how are we to decide whether any estimate is the best or whether it is good or better than another obtained by a different method?

That is; we need to devise a criterion to call an estimator a best one. We, therefore, have to do two things: (a) to specify various properties of an estimator that go to make it a best estimator and, (b) to devise different methods that could give rise to estimators that possess at least some of these desirable properties.

3.2 PROPERTIES OF ESTIMATORS

As stated above, in econometric terminology the term estimator is used to denote the method or function by which we calculate the value of a (unknown) parameter; while the term estimate is used to refer the result from applying that method. For example, in order to know about the population mean we use sample observations: X_1, X_2, ..., X_n and insert it in the function $\dfrac{\Sigma X_i}{n}$ which is called estimator of the population mean. The numerical result which is obtained by using the sample observations in the estimator is called estimate.

Assume some random variable X whose distribution is characterised by a specific parameter θ, which we want to estimate. Thus the parent population consists of all possible values of X and θ is one of the parametric characteristics of this population. An estimator of θ is denoted by $\hat{\theta}$ and since it is obtained by substituting the sample observations of X into a formula, we write

$$\hat{\theta} = \hat{\theta}\,(X_1, X_2, ..., X_n)$$

which is read as "$\hat{\theta}$ is a function of X_1, X_2, ..., X_n."

Since the accuracy of an estimator, in general, increases with the number of observations in the sample data, the desirable properties of the estimators are divided into two groups depending upon the size of sample.

Finite sample or small sample properties refer to properties of the sampling distribution of an estimator based on any fixed sample size. On the other hand asymptotic or large sample properties are the properties of the sampling distribution of the estimator which is obtained from a sample whose size approaches infinity.

3.2.1 Small Sample Properties of Estimators

The desirable properties or the main criteria for a good estimator obtained from small samples are:

(1) Unbiasedness, (2) Least Variance, (3) Minimum Mean Square Error, (4) Efficiency, (5) Best Linear Unbiasedness, and (6) Sufficiency.

(1) *Unbiasedness:* The bias of an estimator is defined as the difference between its expected value and the true value of the parameter. Mathematically,

$$\text{Bias} = E\,(\hat{\theta}) - \theta$$

An estimator is unbiased if bias = 0, i.e., $E\,(\hat{\theta}) - \theta = 0$. Therefore, we say, $\hat{\theta}$ is an unbiased estimator of θ if $E\,(\hat{\theta}) = \theta$.

When the bias is positive, that is, when the mean value of the distribution is larger than its parameter, then the estimator is said to be *upward biased*, Conversely, when the bias is negative, the estimator is *biased downwards*.

A concept related to bias is *sampling error*.

Sampling error = $\hat{\theta} - \theta$; Bias = E (Sampling error)

That is, sampling error is simply the difference between the value of estimator and the true value of the parameter to be estimated. The extent of this error shall vary from sample to sample.

Biased and unbiased estimators have been illustrated in Figs 3.1 and 3.2.

Since the distribution is assumed to be a symmetric one, the mean is shown at the centre of the distribution, and it is equal to the true value of the parameter in Fig. 3.1; it is not equal to the true value of the parameter in Fig. 3.2.

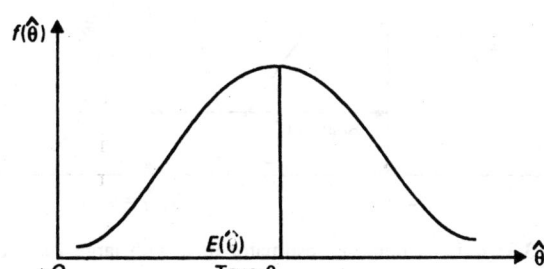

Fig. 3.1: $\hat{\theta}$ is an unbiased estimator of θ

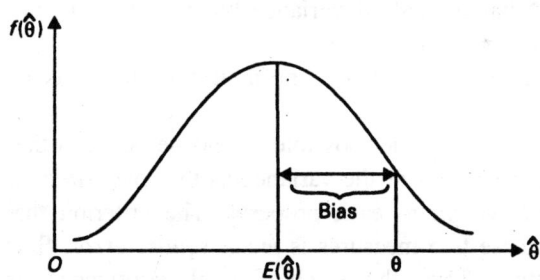

Fig. 3.2: $\hat{\theta}$ is a biased estimator of θ

Unbiasedness is a desirable property but not particularly important by itself. It is because this property tells us nothing about the dispersion of the distribution of the estimator. An estimator which is unbiased, but one which has a large variance, will frequently lead to estimates that are quite different from true value of the parameter. On the other hand an estimator which has a very small variance but is biased, is equally (and even more) less useful. In the light of this argument it seems desirable to examine the variance of the distribution of the estimator also.

(2) *Least Variance (or Best Estimator)*: An estimator is best when it possesses the smallest variance as compared to any other estimator which is obtained by a different method.

In the terminology of mathematical statistics, $\hat{\theta}$ is the best estimator of θ if Var $(\hat{\theta})$ < Var (θ^*); where θ^* is any other estimator (not necessarily unbiased), i.e.,

$$E\,[\hat{\theta} - E\,(\hat{\theta})]^2 < E\,[\theta^* - E\,(\theta^*)]^2$$

Here also, the minimum variance property by itself is rather meaningless; because low variance is desirable along with small bias. A diagrammatic representation of this idea is given in Fig. 3.3.

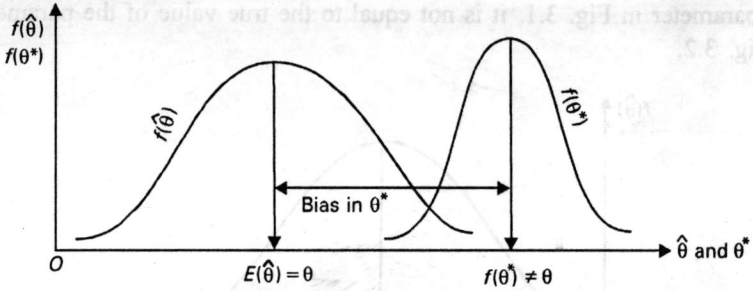

Fig. 3.3: $\hat{\theta}$ is an unbiased estimator of θ with large variance
θ^* is biased estimator of θ with small variance

Figure 3.3 shows the distribution of two estimators of θ, namely θ^* and $\hat{\theta}$. Of these θ^* has a smallest variance but is not unbiased, $\hat{\theta}$ has larger variance than θ^* but is unbiased.

The question now arises; which one should be chosen as an 'appropriate' estimator?

Unfortunately it is just not possible to choose between the two; because we cannot use either bias or the variance as the sole criterion. We must, in fact, give some weight to each property. The criterion that gives equal importance to these two measures is *mean square error*. Since variance is in the square units of bias, the giving of equal importance to bias and to the variance implies that equal importance is attached to variance and to the square of bias.

(3) *Minimum Mean-square-error (MSE)*: MSE is defined as the expected value of the squared difference of the estimator around the true population parameter.

$$\text{MSE}\,(\hat{\theta}) = E\,(\hat{\theta} - \theta)^2$$
$$= E\,[\hat{\theta} - E\,(\hat{\theta}) + E\,(\hat{\theta}) - \theta]^2$$
$$= E\,[\hat{\theta} - E(\hat{\theta})]^2 + E\,[E\,(\hat{\theta}) - \theta]^2 + 2E\,\{[\hat{\theta} - E\,(\hat{\theta})]\,[E\,(\hat{\theta}) - \theta]\}$$

But $\quad E\,[\hat{\theta} - E\,(\hat{\theta})]^2 = \text{Var}\,(\hat{\theta})$; and

$$[E(\hat{\theta}) - \theta]^2 = [\text{bias }(\hat{\theta})]^2.$$

Also; $E\{[\hat{\theta} - E(\hat{\theta})][E(\hat{\theta}) - \theta]\}$

$$= E\{\hat{\theta} \cdot E(\hat{\theta}) - [E(\hat{\theta})]^2 - \hat{\theta}\theta + \theta \cdot E(\hat{\theta})\}$$
$$= [E(\hat{\theta})]^2 - [E(\hat{\theta})]^2 - \theta \cdot E(\hat{\theta}) + \theta \cdot E(\hat{\theta})$$
$$= 0$$

Therefore, MSE $(\hat{\theta})$ = Var $(\hat{\theta})$ + [bias $(\hat{\theta})]^2$

In other words MSE is the sum of two quantities; the squares of bias and variance. If one of these two components gets smaller at the expense of the other, the net benefit is reflected by the MSE. Hence we would want an estimator to possess the smallest MSE rather than the smallest of any one of its two components.

(4) *Efficiency:* There is a lack of general agreement as to the most appropriate definition of this property of the estimator. Some econometricians equate efficiency with minimum MSE of the estimator, others define efficiency only in the context of asymptotic properties rather than finite sample properties, and others consider an estimator to be efficient if it is unbiased and at the same time has a minimum variance. The last view has become quite common among the present day econometricians.

Statistically $\hat{\theta}$ is an efficient or best estimator if the following two conditions are fulfilled:

(i) $E(\hat{\theta}) = \theta$

and (ii) $E[\hat{\theta} - E(\hat{\theta})]^2 < E[\theta^* - E(\hat{\theta}^*)]$, where θ^* is another unbiased estimator of θ. Thus, in comparing two unbiased estimators, the one which possesses the smaller variance shall be more efficient than the other estimator. For example, comparing between sample mean and sample median as estimator of population mean, sample mean is a more efficient estimator of the population mean relative to sample median. It is so because though both are unbiased estimators, the variance of sample mean is smaller than the variance of sample median.

However, it would be a tedious job to choose (efficient one) amongst the large number of unbiased estimators. But this difficulty is surmounted by *Cramer-Rao Inequality*. This inequality enables us to construct a lower limit (but greater than zero) for the variance of any unbiased estimator, provided we can specify the functional form of the parent population. We shall be referring to this inequality under the maximum likelihood method of estimation.

(5) *Best, Linear, Unbiasedness (BLU):* An estimator is BLU if it is linear, unbiased and has the smallest variance as compared with all other linear unbiased estimators of the true θ. The best and unbiasedness properties of

the estimator have been discussed above. Linearity of the estimator is described by the functional form that it possesses with the sample observations. For example, the sample mean $\overline{X}$ is a linear estimator; because

$$\overline{X} = \frac{\Sigma X_i}{n} = \frac{1}{n}\left[X_1 + X_2 + ... + X_n\right]$$

$$= \frac{1}{n}X_1 + \frac{1}{n}X_2 + ... + \frac{1}{n}X_n,$$

that is, each observation is related in linear form in the estimator $\dfrac{\Sigma X_i}{n}$.

(6) *Sufficiency:* Another finite sample property of an estimator which is sometimes mentioned is sufficiency. An estimator is said to be sufficient if it utilises all the information about the true parameter that is provided by the sample. This means that no other estimator can add any further information about the parameter of interest. Thus between the two unbiased estimators, say mean and median, sample median is not a sufficient estimator because it uses only the ranking and not the values of sample observations. The relevance of sufficiency lies in the fact that this property is a necessary condition for efficiency. An estimator cannot be efficient unless it makes use of all the sample information.

Before closing the discussion on the desirable properties of the estimators, let us ask ourselves which one is the most important desirable property?

Unfortunately not all econometricians agree on any single property in this regard. It is because, since the choice of estimator depends crucially on the prospective use of that estimator. In some cases unbiasedness may be most desirable, in others it may be the maximum precision though the estimator may be biased. Again at times we desire estimator with minimum MSE. In applied econometrics, we cannot rely on only one desirable property. It would be worthwhile to quote here Econometrician R.J. Ball. According to him, *"Desirable properties for estimates are a matter of choice to some extent by the statistician. There is no law that says that bias, sufficiency or efficiency should be ranked in some unique order. The most desirable characteristic in each particular study depends to a large extent on the purpose of the study."*

3.2.2 Large Sample Properties of Estimators

Asymptotic properties relate to the estimators which are obtained from the large samples; i.e., when sample size $n \to \infty$. The term asymptotic here refers to asymptotic distribution of an estimator. If the distribution of an estimator tends to become more and more similar in the form of some distribution as $n \to \infty$, then such a specific distribution is called asymptotic distribution of that estimator. Generally distribution of an estimator as $n \to \infty$ collapses on one point ultimately. For instance, in case of distribution of sample mean, its mean is equal to the population mean and its variance is equal to $\dfrac{\sigma^2}{n}$; where σ^2 is the population variance and n is the sample size.

Obviously as $n \to \infty$, $\dfrac{\sigma^2}{n}$ approaches zero and the distribution will collapse on the population mean. A graphical representation of such distribution (in the ultimate form) would show a straight vertical line of height equal to 1 and not as a normal (asymptotic) distribution. Asymptotic distribution (which may degenerate), but the form that it tends to put on in the last part of its journey to the final collapse.

Having discussed the meaning of asymptotic distribution let us now turn to the properties of such distributions of the estimators. They are:

(1) Asymptotic unbiasedness, (2) Consistency, and (3) Asymptotic efficiency.

(1) *Asymptotic Unbiasedness:* An estimator is an asymptotically unbiased estimator of true parameter, if $\lim\limits_{n \to \infty} . E(\hat\theta_n) = \theta$; subscript in $\hat\theta$ denotes the sample size.

∴ Asymptotic bias of $\hat\theta = \lim\limits_{n \to \infty} . [E(\hat\theta_n) - \theta]$

This definition merely states that an estimator is asymptotically unbiased if its bias vanishes as $n \to \infty$. It is important to note here that if the estimator is unbiased (in small samples) it is also asymptotically unbiased; but the converse is not necessarily true.

An example of a biased but asymptotically unbiased estimator is the sample variance.

$$\hat\sigma^2 = \frac{1}{n}\Sigma\left(X_i - \overline{X}\right)^2$$

$$\lim\limits_{n \to \infty} . E(\hat\sigma^2) = \lim\limits_{n \to \infty} . \left(\frac{n-1}{n}\right)\sigma^2 = \sigma^2 \qquad \text{(see page 48)}$$

(2) *Consistency:* An estimator $\hat\theta$ is a consistent estimator of θ if it satisfies the following two conditions;

(i) $\hat\theta$ is asymptotically unbiased,

$$\lim\limits_{n \to \infty} E(\hat\theta) = \theta$$

(ii) the variance of $\hat\theta$ approaches zero as n tends to infinity,

$$\lim\limits_{n \to \infty} [\text{Var}(\hat\theta)] = 0$$

To see whether an estimator is consistent, we should therefore examine its bias and variance as sample size is increased. If both bias and variance decrease as n becomes larger, and at the limit (as $n \to \infty$) both become zero, then estimator is assumed to possess the property of consistency. This is illustrated in Fig. 3.4, which shows that as the sample size increases from 20 to 100 observations both bias of $\hat{\theta}$ and its variance decrease.

Again, sum of squared bias and variance is equal to the MSE, the disappearance of the bias and variance as $n \to \infty$ is equivalent to the disappearance of the MSE, so that we can also say;

θ is a consistent estimator of $\hat{\theta}$, if $\lim_{n \to \infty}$. MSE $(\hat{\theta}) = 0$

More formally, an estimator $\hat{\theta}$ is said to be a consistent estimator of θ if the probability of the absolute value of the difference between $\hat{\theta}$ and θ being less than k (an arbitrarily small positive quantity) approaches unity:

$$\lim_{n \to \infty}. P\{|\hat{\theta} - \theta| < k\} = 1, \, k > 0$$

where P stands for probability. It can also be expressed as:

$$\text{plim. } \hat{\theta} = \theta,$$
$$\scriptstyle n \to \infty$$

where term *plim.* means probability limit.

It is to be noted that the properties of unbiasedness and consistency are conceptually very much different. The property of unbiasedness and consistency are conceptually very much different. The property of unbiasedness can hold for any sample size, whereas consistency is strictly a large-sample property.

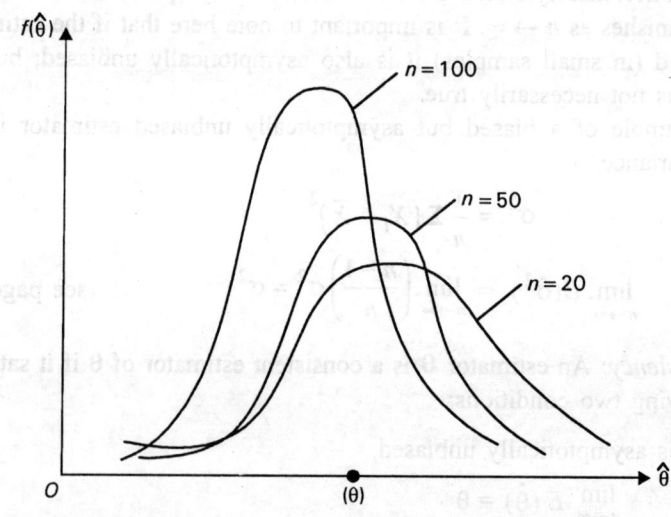

Fig. 3.4

(3) *Asymptotic efficiency:* $\hat{\theta}$ is an asymptotically efficient estimator of θ, if

   (i) $\hat{\theta}$ is consistent, and
   (ii) $\hat{\theta}$ has a smaller asymptotic variance as compared to any other consistent estimator.

The establishment of the first condition does not pose any difficulty. To establish whether consistent estimator satisfies the second condition is more difficult. It is because the variance of any consistent estimator goes to zero as $n \to \infty$. So in the present situation when we are comparing consistent estimators, we choose the one whose variance goes faster to zero (as $n \to \infty$) and call it asymptotically more efficient.

For example consider two estimators, $\hat{\theta}$ and θ^*, whose distributions have the following means and variance;

Mean   : $E(\hat{\theta}) = \left(\dfrac{n-1}{n}\right)\theta;$ $E(\theta^*) = \left(\dfrac{n+1}{n}\right)\theta$

Variance : $\text{Var}(\hat{\theta}) = \dfrac{\sigma^2}{n^2};$ $\text{Var}(\theta^*) = \dfrac{\sigma^2}{n}$

Both estimators are asymptotically unbiased and consistent; since their bias and variance become zero as $n \to \infty$;

$$\lim_{n \to \infty} E(\hat{\theta}) = \theta; \quad \lim_{n \to \infty} E(\theta^*) = \theta$$

$$\lim_{n \to \infty} \text{Var}(\hat{\theta}) = 0; \quad \lim_{n \to \infty} \text{Var}(\theta^*) = 0$$

However, the variance of $\hat{\theta}$ goes faster to zero as $n \to \infty$. Thus $\hat{\theta}$ is asymptotically more efficient than the alternative consistent estimator θ^*.

3.2.3 Application

To bring forth the basic ideas underlying the foregoing discussion, let us take an example.

Example: Examine the desirable properties in case of following three estimators which have been proposed to estimate true mean (μ) from a random sample of observations on $X_1, X_2, X_3, ..., X_n$.

(It is assumed that parent population is normally distributed.)

(i) $\overline{X} = \dfrac{\Sigma X_i}{n}$ (ii) $\hat{\mu} = \dfrac{\Sigma X_i}{n+1}$

(iii) $\mu^* = \dfrac{X_1}{2} + \dfrac{\displaystyle\sum_{i=2} X_i}{2n}$

I. Small Sample Properties:

(a) *Unbiasedness*

(i) $E(\overline{X}) = E\left[\dfrac{\Sigma X_i}{n}\right] = \dfrac{1}{n}\sum_{i}^{n} E(X_i) = \mu$

Hence $\overline{X}$ is unbiased.

(ii) $\quad E\,(\hat{\mu}) = E\left[\dfrac{\Sigma X_i}{n+1}\right] = \left(\dfrac{n}{n+1}\right)\sum_i^n E(X_i)$

$$= \left(\dfrac{n}{n+1}\right)\mu \neq \mu$$

Hence $\hat{\mu}$ is *biased*.

(iii) $\quad E\,(\mu^*) = E\left[\dfrac{X_1}{2} + \dfrac{\displaystyle\sum_{i=2} X_i}{2n}\right]$

$$= \dfrac{1}{2}\,E\,(X_1) + \dfrac{1}{2n}\sum_{i=2} E(X_i)$$

$$= \dfrac{1}{2}\mu + \left(\dfrac{n-1}{2n}\right)\mu = \left(\dfrac{2n-1}{2n}\right)\mu \neq \mu$$

Hence μ^* is *biased*.

(b) *Efficiency:* Only $\overline{X}$ is to be examined for this property ($\because$ other two estimators are biased)

$\text{Var}\,(\overline{X}) = \dfrac{\sigma^2}{n}$. With the help of Cramer-Rao inequality it can be shown that $\dfrac{\sigma^2}{n}$ is the minimum variance amongst the unbiased estimators of μ. This $\overline{X}$ is an efficient estimator of $\hat{\mu}$.

(c) *BLU:* $\overline{X}$ satisfies the condition of linearity. It is also best (because it has minimum variance) and unbiased.

II. *Asymptotic properties:*

(a) *Asymptotic unbiasedness*

(i) $\lim\limits_{n\to\infty}.\,(\overline{X}) = \lim\limits_{n\to\infty}\,(\mu) = \mu$

Hence $(\overline{X})$ is asymptotically unbiased.

(ii) $\lim\limits_{n\to\infty} E\,(\hat{\mu}) = \lim\limits_{n\to\infty}\left(\dfrac{n}{n+1}\right)\mu = \mu.$

Hence $(\hat{\mu})$ is asymptotically unbiased.

(iii) $\lim\limits_{n\to\infty} E(\mu^*) = \lim\limits_{n\to\infty}\left(\dfrac{2n-1}{2n}\right)\mu = \mu$

Hence μ^* is asymptotically unbiased.

(b) *Consistency*

(i) $\text{Var}\,(\overline{X}) = \dfrac{\sigma^2}{n}. \quad \therefore \lim\limits_{n \to \infty}\left(\dfrac{\sigma^2}{n}\right) = 0$

$\overline{X}$ is therefore, a consistent estimator.

(ii) $\text{Var}\,(\hat{\mu}) = \text{Var}\left[\dfrac{1}{n+1}\Sigma X_i\right]$

$$= \left(\dfrac{1}{n+1}\right)^2 \Sigma\,\text{Var}\,(X_i) = \left(\dfrac{1}{n+1}\right)^2 n\cdot\sigma^2$$

$\therefore \lim\limits_{n \to \infty}\dfrac{n}{(n+1)^2}\,\sigma^2 = 0$; hence $\hat{\mu}$ is consistent estimator.

(iii) $\text{Var}\,(\mu^*) = \text{Var}\left[\dfrac{X_1}{2} + \dfrac{\sum\limits_{i=2} X_i}{2n}\right]$

$$= \dfrac{1}{4}\,\text{Var}\,(X_1) + \left(\dfrac{1}{2n}\right)^2 \sum_{i=2}\text{Var}\,(X_i)$$

$$= \left(\dfrac{n^2 + n}{4n^2}\right)\sigma^2$$

$\therefore \lim\limits_{n \to \infty}\left(\dfrac{n^2 + n}{4n^2}\right)\sigma^2 = \dfrac{\sigma^2}{4} \neq 0.$

Hence μ^* is *not* consistent estimator.

(c) *Asymptotic efficiency*

Only $\overline{X}$ and $\hat{\mu}$ satisfy the condition of consistency and thus needs to be examined for this property. $\overline{X}$ is efficient even in case of small samples, hence it is asymptotically efficient as well.

$$\text{Var}\,(\hat{\mu}) = \dfrac{n\sigma^2}{(n+1)^2} = \left(\dfrac{n}{n+1}\right)^2\left(\dfrac{\sigma^2}{n}\right)$$

In large samples $\left(\dfrac{n}{n+1}\right)$ will be close to infinity; as such asymptotic

variance of $\hat{\mu} = \dfrac{\sigma^2}{n}$; which is same as that of $\overline{X}$. It follows, therefore, that $\hat{\mu}$ is also asymptotically efficient.

3.3 ALTERNATIVE METHODS OF ESTIMATION

There are various methods of estimation which lead us to estimators that possess different properties. These estimators are known by the names that indicate the nature of the technique used in deriving the formula.

The method of moments, least squares method and the maximum likelihood method; all three methods lead to estimators which are known by the names of these techniques.

I. Method of Moments: This is the oldest estimation method in statistics. The underlying principle in this method is that the sample moments reflect the population characteristics in the sense that the *expected values of the sample moments are equal to the population moments.*

First, however, let us define sample moments.

Sample moments: Let $X_1, X_2, ..., X_n$ be a random sample from the density function: $f(X)$. Then the rth sample moment about *zero* is given by:

$$m'_r = \frac{1}{n} \sum_{i=1}^{n} X_i^r \qquad \qquad ...(1i)$$

In particular, if $r = 1$ (i.e., first moment),

$$m'_1 = \frac{1}{n} \sum_{i=1}^{n} X_i^1 = \overline{X};$$

that, is first sample moment is sample mean. [Under section 2.4.2, other moments about origin and expected value have been discussed.]

Let us now examine how expected value of rth sample moment is equal to the rth population moment.

From (i);
$$m'_r = \frac{1}{n} \sum_{i=1}^{n} X_i^r$$

$$\therefore \quad E(m'_r) = E\left[\frac{1}{n} \sum_{i=1}^{n} X_i^r\right]$$

$$= \frac{1}{n} E\left[\Sigma X_i^r\right] = \frac{1}{n} \Sigma E(X_i^r)$$

$$= \mu'_r \text{ (By definition of population moment)}$$

In a specific case when $r = 1$;

$$E(m'_1) = E(\overline{X}) = \mu$$

That is to say that first sample moment which depicts the sample mean, its expected value is the population mean. Next, let us examine the variance of $\overline{X}$.

By definition:
$$S_{\overline{x}}^2 = E(\overline{X} - E(\overline{X}))^2 = E[\overline{X} - \mu]^2$$

$$S_{\bar{x}}^2 = E \left[\frac{1}{n} \Sigma (X_i - \mu) \right]^2$$

$$S_{\bar{x}}^2 = \frac{1}{n^2} E \left[\Sigma (X_i - \mu) \right]^2$$

It can be proved that:

$$S_{\bar{x}}^2 = \frac{1}{n^2} \Sigma E (X_i - \mu)^2$$

$$S_{\bar{x}}^2 = \frac{1}{n^2} \Sigma \sigma^2$$

$$S_{\bar{x}}^2 = \frac{\sigma^2}{n}$$

Thus the variance of the sample mean is equal to the population-variance divided by the sample size.

This fact is to extreme importance in applied statistics. It implies that, whatever the population (provided it has a finite variance), the distribution of the sample mean (i.e., sampling distribution of mean) becomes more and more concentrated near the population mean as the sample size increases. This proof forms the basis of the *Central Limit Theorem*.

Do the estimators obtained from this procedure possess the desirable properties?

Let us examine the properties of two basic estimators; i.e., sample mean ($\bar{X}$) and sample variance (S_x^2).

(i) *Sample mean is an unbiased estimator of the population mean.*

Sample mean: $\bar{X} = \dfrac{\Sigma X_i}{n} = \dfrac{1}{n} \sum_i^n X_i$

Taking expected values: $E(\bar{X}) = \dfrac{1}{n} \Sigma E(X_i)$

$$= \frac{1}{n} \sum_i \mu = \frac{1}{n} (n \cdot \mu) = \mu$$

(ii) *Sample variance is a biased estimator of the population variance.*

Sample variance is $S_x^2 = \dfrac{\Sigma (X_i - \bar{X})^2}{n}$. Taking expected values;

$$E(S_x^2) = E \left\{ \frac{1}{n} \Sigma \left(X_i - \bar{X} \right)^2 \right\}$$

$$= E \left\{ \frac{1}{n} \Sigma (X_i - \mu - \bar{X} + \mu)^2 \right\}$$

$$= E\left\{\frac{1}{n}\Sigma(X_i-\mu)^2 + \frac{1}{n}\Sigma(\overline{X}-\mu)^2\right.$$

$$\left. -2(\overline{X}-\mu)\cdot\frac{1}{n}\Sigma(X_i-\mu)\right\}$$

$$= E\left\{\frac{1}{n}\Sigma(X_i-\mu)^2 + (\overline{X}-\mu)^2 - 2(\overline{X}-\mu)^2\right\}$$

$$= \frac{1}{n}\Sigma E(X_i-\mu)^2 - E(\overline{X}-\mu)^2$$

$$= \frac{1}{n}\cdot\Sigma\sigma^2 - \frac{\sigma^2}{n}$$

$[\because$ population variance $\sigma^2 = E(X_i-\mu)^2]$

$$\therefore \quad E\left(S_x^2\right) = \left(\frac{n-1}{n}\right)\sigma^2$$

That is to say, $E(S_x^2) \neq \sigma^2$ and hence sample variance is not the unbiased estimator of the population variance.

Nevertheless we can, by a little manipulation, obtain unbiased estimator as follows:

$$E\left(S_x^2\right) = \left(\frac{n-1}{n}\right)\sigma^2$$

i.e. $$\left(\frac{n}{n-1}\right)E\left(S_x^2\right) = \sigma^2$$

or, $$\left(\frac{n}{n-1}\right)E\left\{\frac{\Sigma(X-\overline{X})^2}{n}\right\} = \sigma^2$$

or, $$\left(\frac{n}{n-1}\right)\cdot\frac{1}{n}\Sigma E(X-\overline{X})^2 = \sigma^2$$

or, $$\left(\frac{1}{n-1}\right)\Sigma E(X-\overline{X}) = \sigma^2$$

or, $$E\left\{\frac{\Sigma(X-\overline{X})^2}{n-1}\right\} = \sigma^2$$

i.e., an unbiased estimator of population variance $(\hat{\sigma}^2)$ from the sample observations may be obtained by the formula: $\dfrac{\Sigma(X_i-\overline{X})^2}{n-1}$.

Hence it can be shown:

(i) For random sample from any population, the sample mean is an unbiased, best linear unbiased, best linear unbiased, asymptotically unbiased, and consistent estimator of the population mean.

(ii) For random sample from any population, the sample variance is a biased but asymptotically unbiased and consistent estimator of the population variance.

Therefore, under very general conditions, the estimators derived by the methods of moments are:

(a) consistent estimators and squared error consistent estimators. An estimator is said to be squared error consistent if $\lim_{n \to \infty} E[(\hat{\theta} - \theta)^2] = 0$ holds good, and

(b) asymptotically normal but not BAN estimators. (BAN stands for Best, Asymptotically and Normal.)

II. Least Squares Method: The method of least squares, which has long been used, consists in the choice of an estimator so that sum of squares of the deviations of the sample observation from the estimate (obtained through the estimator) is a minimum. To obtain such estimator, we make use of simple calculus. The results of maximum likelihood estimation and estimation by the method of least squares are frequently (but not always) identical.

This method has been discussed in detail in Chapter 5.

III. Maximum Likelihood Method: The most important procedure of estimation in econometrics is R.A. Fisher's method of maximum likelihood. The basic principle underlying this technique of estimation is that different populations generate different samples, and that any given sample is more likely to have come from some population than from others. Assume that we obtain a sample of n observations of whose parent population is normal. In fact our sample might have been generated by many different normal populations. But suppose the mean of our observed sample is 10. Now, we ask ourselves; to which population does our sample most likely belong? In general, as we have said, any normal population could be its parent population and the one which has mean equal to 10 (or near about 10) is likely to generate samples with mean equal to 10. The point in argument is illustrated in Fig. 3.5. X_1, X_2, ...X_{11} depict 11 specific sample observations. These observations could have come from any of the normal populations A, B or

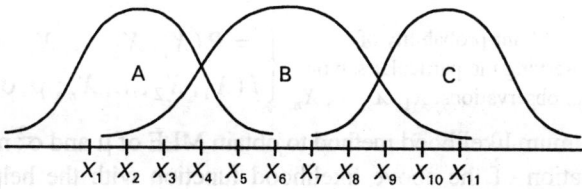

Fig. 3.5

C. The probability of obtaining our sample from *A* or *C* appears to be very small, but the probability of getting the same sample from population B is very high. As such we say that the particular sample is more likely to have come from population B than from populations *A* or *C*.

In Fig. 3.5 we did not refer to the variance of the different populations, and as we know, every population is characterised by its mean and variance. A sample with large variance is more likely to be obtained from a population with large variance than from a population with a small variance. In other words we ought to consider combinations of specific mean and variance of the population in relation to combinations of specific mean and variance of (observed) sample.

With this background let us now define the maximum likelihood estimator in a formal way.

Assume that X is a random variable with a known parent population. This population is characterised by different parameters; say, $\theta_1, \theta_2, ..., \theta_K$. Suppose that a sample of n observations, $X_1, X_2, ..., X_n$, is obtained; then the maximum likelihood estimators of $\theta_1, \theta_2, ..., \theta_K$, are those values of these parameters that would generate our observed sample most often. In 'probability' terms, the maximum likelihood estimators of $\theta_1, \theta_2, ... \theta_K$ are those values for which the probability of given set of sample observations is the maximum. That is to say, to obtain a maximum likelihood estimators of $\theta_1, \theta_2,... \theta_K$, we have to find those values which maximise the function:

$$f(X_1, X_2, ..., X_n).$$

Obtaining the maximum likelihood estimator (MLE) involves specifying the likelihood function and then finding those values of parameters which give this function its maximum value.

A likelihood function, usually denoted by l, refers to the formula of joint probability distribution of the sample. A random sample $X_1, X_2, ... X_n$ in fact represents a set of n independent random variables with exactly the same probability distributions. The likelihood function l is, therefore, defined by the formula of the joint probability distribution of the sample as:

Likelihood function: $l = f(X_1, X_2, ..., X_n)$,

or, $\qquad l = f(X_1) \cdot f(X_2) \cdot f(X_3)...$

(Since observations are independent).

Hence if we draw a random sample of n observations from the population of a variable $X \sim N(\mu, \sigma^2)$, the general expression of the likelihood function is:

$$\begin{array}{l} \text{Joint probability of} \\ \text{observing the particular sample} \\ \text{with observations: } X_1, X_2, ..., X_n \end{array} \left\{ \begin{array}{l} = P(X_1, X_2, ..., X_n) = \\ l(X_1, X_2, ..., X_n; \mu, \sigma^2) \end{array} \right.$$

The maximum likelihood method to obtain MLE of μ and σ^2 now consists of maximisation of the above likelihood function with the help of simple calculus.

To grasp the basic idea underlying this method, let us derive MLE of a normally distributed random variables X; i.e., $X \sim N(\mu, \sigma^2)$.

Thus our problem now is to obtain MLE of the parameters μ and σ^2 from a sample of n independent observations of X.

The likelihood function would be:

$$l(X_1, X_2, ..., X_n; \mu, \sigma^2)$$

Since we know the normal density function is represented by;

$$\frac{1}{\sqrt{2\pi\sigma^2}} \, \exp. \left[-\frac{1}{2} \left(\frac{X - \mu}{\sigma} \right)^2 \right],$$

the probability of each observation in the sample will be given as under:

$$p(X_1) = \frac{1}{\sqrt{2\pi\sigma^2}} \, \exp. \left[-\frac{1}{2} \left(\frac{X_1 - \mu}{\sigma} \right)^2 \right]$$

$$p(X_2) = \frac{1}{\sqrt{2\pi\sigma^2}} \, \exp. \left[-\frac{1}{2} \left(\frac{X_2 - \mu}{\sigma} \right)^2 \right]$$

$$\vdots$$

$$p(X_n) = \frac{1}{\sqrt{2\pi\sigma^2}} \, \exp \left[-\frac{1}{2} \left(\frac{X_n - \mu}{\sigma} \right)^2 \right]$$

The joint probability of the n-sample values is given by the likelihood function:

$$l = \frac{1}{\sqrt{2\pi\sigma^2}} \, \exp. \left[-\frac{1}{2} \left(\frac{X_1 - \mu}{\sigma} \right)^2 \right] \cdot \frac{1}{\sqrt{2\pi\sigma^2}} \, \exp. \left[-\frac{1}{2} \left(\frac{X_2 - \mu}{\sigma} \right) \right]$$

$$...... \frac{1}{\sqrt{2\pi\sigma^2}} \, \exp. \left[-\frac{1}{2} \left(\frac{X_n - \mu}{\sigma} \right)^2 \right]$$

$$l = \left\{ \frac{1}{\sqrt{2\pi\sigma^2}} \right\}^n \exp. \left[-\frac{1}{2} \sum_{i}^{n} \left(\frac{X_i - \mu}{\sigma} \right)^2 \right]$$

$$l = \left(\sigma\sqrt{2\pi} \right)^{-n} \exp. \left[-\frac{1}{2} \sum_{i}^{n} \left(\frac{X_i - \mu}{\sigma} \right)^2 \right]$$

Our next problem is to see for what values of μ and σ^2 is this function maximum.

We, therefore, equate partial derivatives of this function to zero; but to simplify the derivations, we first express the exponential function in logarithmic form as under:

$$L = -\frac{n}{2} \log_e \sigma^2 - n \log_e \sqrt{2\pi} + \left\{ -\frac{1}{2} \Sigma \left(\frac{X_i - \mu}{\sigma} \right)^2 \log_e e \right\}$$

(where $L = \log_e l$)

$$L = -\frac{n}{2} \log_e \sigma^2 - n \log_e \sqrt{2\pi} - \frac{1}{2\sigma^2} \Sigma (X_i - \mu)^2$$

We apply *order conditions* to function L; which is logarithmic transformation of likelihood function l.

Will the results be affected?

No, since the logarithm of l is a *monotonic function* of L. This means that whenever l is increasing, its logarithm (i.e. L) is also increasing, and whenever l is falling, L is also falling. Therefore, the point corresponding to the maximum of l is also the point which corresponds to the maximum of L.

Hence we maximise L;

$$\frac{\partial L}{\partial \mu} = -\frac{1}{2} \sigma^{-2} \sum 2 (X_1 - \mu)(-1) = 0 \qquad \text{...(i)}$$

$$\frac{\partial L}{\partial \sigma^2} = -\frac{n}{2} \sigma^{-2} + \sigma^{-4} \sum (X_i - \mu)^2 = 0 \qquad \text{...(ii)}$$

Solving the above two equations for σ^2 and μ;

$$\Sigma X_i - n\mu = 0 \qquad \text{(from first equation)}$$

i.e.,
$$\hat{\mu} = \frac{\Sigma X_i}{n} = \overline{X} \qquad \text{(sample mean)}$$

$$-\frac{n}{\hat{\sigma}^2} + \frac{\Sigma (X_i - \mu)^2}{\hat{\sigma}^4} = 0 \qquad \text{(from second equation)}$$

i.e.,
$$\frac{1}{\hat{\sigma}^2} \left[-n + \frac{\Sigma (X_i - \mu)^2}{\hat{\sigma}^2} \right] = 0$$

or;
$$\frac{\Sigma (X_i - \mu)^2}{\hat{\sigma}^2} = n$$

i.e.,
$$\frac{\Sigma (X_i - \mu)^2}{n} = \hat{\sigma}^2 \qquad \text{(sample variance)}$$

Thus it has been established that for a random sampling from a $N(\mu, \sigma^2)$ population, the sample mean and sample variance are the maximum likelihood estimators of the population mean and population variance respectively.

One of the important feature of the maximum likelihood method is that it generates estimators with *desirable asymptotic properties*, and under very general conditions a maximum likelihood estimator is consistent, asymptotically unbiased and asymptotically efficient. The likelihood function also helps us to determine the Cramer-Rao Lower Bounds for the variances of the distribution of estimators obtained above.

$$L = f(X_1, X_2, ..., X_n; \mu, \sigma^2)$$

The above function is differentiated twice and crosswise with respect to μ and σ^2. The results so obtained are placed in the form of a matrix, called *Information matrix*, as follows:

$$\begin{bmatrix} -E\left(\dfrac{\partial^2 L}{\partial \mu^2}\right) & -E\left(\dfrac{\partial^2 L}{\partial \mu \partial \sigma^2}\right) \\ -E\left(\dfrac{\partial^2 L}{\partial \mu \partial \sigma^2}\right) & -E\left(\dfrac{\partial^2 L}{\partial \left(\sigma^2\right)^2}\right) \end{bmatrix}$$

Substituting the corresponding values and then *inverting the matrix*, we obtain;

$$\begin{bmatrix} \left(\dfrac{n}{\sigma^2}\right) & 0 \\ 0 & \dfrac{n}{2\left(\sigma^2\right)^2} \end{bmatrix}^{-1} = \begin{bmatrix} \dfrac{\sigma^2}{n} & 0 \\ 0 & \dfrac{2\left(\sigma^2\right)^2}{n} \end{bmatrix}$$

The Cramer-Rao lower bound for the variance of the normal distribution of the estimator (mean) is, therefore, given by the element in the upper left corner, i.e., $\dfrac{\sigma^2}{n}$.

The method of maximum likelihood as applied to a Simple Linear Regression Model has been once again discussed in Chapter 5.

3.4 MEANING OF HYPOTHESIS TESTING

At the beginning of this chapter we observed that there are essentially two kinds of statistical inferences: estimation and hypothesis testing. Both are concerned with learning something about an unknown aspect of a population on the basis of sample information. We have so far discussed the problems relating to estimation; presently our concern shall be the problem of testing hypotheses.

A *hypothesis* is a theoretical proposition that is capable of empirical verification or disproof. It may be viewed as an explanation of some event or events, and which may be true or false explanation.

Three forms of hypotheses are generally described is statistics; *maintained, simple* and *composite*. Those assumptions that are not exposed to any test are called the maintained hypotheses; while the remaining are called testable hypotheses. The testable hypothesis is called the *null* hypothesis. The term null refers to an idea that there is "no difference between the true value and the value that we hypothesise." Since null hypothesis is a testable hypothesis, there must also exist a counter proposition to it in order to test our hypothesised proposition. The counter proposition is called *alternative* hypothesis. Usually we depict the null hypothesis by symbol H_0 and the alternative hypothesis by H_A. Suppose null hypothesis is that the population mean $\mu = 15$; and an alternative hypothesis may be framed as: $\mu \neq 15$ or, say, $\mu = 20$. The two situations are different and therefore can be described in symbolic form as follows:

Situation A	*Situation B*
(Composite Hypothesis)	(Simple Hypothesis)
$H_0 : \mu = 15$	$H_0 : \mu = 15$
$H_A : \mu \neq 15$	$H_A : \mu = 20$

In situation *B*, the implication is that μ can either be 15 or 20. In other words we are sure that there is no other value which μ can assume. Situation *A* states that value of μ may be greater or lesser than the value hypothesised in the null hypothesis. Such type of hypotheses are called composite hypothesis: whereas the type of hypotheses shown under situation *B* are called simple hypothesis.

The first step in hypothesis testing is that of formulation of the null hypothesis and its alternative. The next step consists of devising a *criterion of test* that would enable us to decide whether the null hypothesis is to be rejected or not. For this purpose the whole set of values of the population is divided into two regions: the *acceptance region* and *rejection region*. The acceptance region includes the values of the population which have a high probability of being observed, and the rejection region or *critical region* includes those values which are highly unlikely to be observed. The test is then performed with reference to *test-statistic*. The empirical tests that are used for testing the hypothesis are called *tests of significance*. If the value of the test-statistic falls in the critical region, the null hypothesis is rejected; while if the value of test-statistic falls in the acceptance region, the null hypothesis is not rejected.

3.5 TYPES OF ERRORS AND LEVEL OF SIGNIFICANCE

The procedure by which we are able to reject our null hypothesis, is called *criterion of test*. In other words criterion of test refers to setting up of the boundary between critical and acceptance regions. The setting up of the boundary between these two regions is determined by many considerations; such as, the prior information concerning the distribution of the test-statistic, by the specification of the alternative hypothesis and by the cost involved in arriving at an incorrect conclusion.

The test criterion, however, may not always give us correct conclusions. In making any decision we are liable to commit one of the two types of error explained in the following table.

Decisions $\downarrow$	Facts	
	H_0 *true*	H_A *true*
H_0 accepted	Correct decision	*Type II* error committed
H_A accepted	*Type I* error committed	Correct decision

In other words, whenever we happen to incorrectly reject the null hypothesis, we make error of type I and whenever we happen to incorrectly accept the null hypothesis, we make error of type II. As a simile, type I error is '*convicting an innocent*', while that of type II is '*letting go a guilty*'.

The probability of making type I error is denoted by α and the probability of making type II error is denoted by β; obviously we always want to minimise both α and β; but more so in case of α (so that the chances of convicting an innocent are minimised to the lowest level.) It is, therefore, that level of significance is set by keeping in view the probability of committing type I error . *Choosing a certain level of probability with which we would be willing to risk error of type I, is called level of significance.* Generally in practice a level of significance of 0.05 or 0.01 is customary. If, for example, a 0.05 or 5 per cent level of significance is chosen in designing a test of hypothesis then there are only five chances in 100 that we would reject the (null) hypothesis when it should be accepted. Alternatively, this means that we are 95 per cent confident that we have made the right decision; and only with five per cent of probability that we might have gone wrong.

The general idea behind the two types of errors can also be illustrated by an example of testing null hypothesis against simple alternative hypothesis. Assume that we obtain a sample of n-observations. We are to examine whether this sample belongs to a normal population A with mean = μ_A or population B with mean = μ_B. (We are not considering the variances of the populations sample for the time being.)

So we have: $H_0 : \mu = \mu_A$

$\qquad\qquad H_A : \mu = \mu_B$

To carry out the test we have to establish the boundary between the critical and acceptance regions. This will depend, as we have explained, on the chosen level of significance and the alternative hypothesis. The level of significance may be chosen *a priori* as, say, five per cent. Since the alternative hypothesis is that $\mu = \mu_B$ and assuming that $\mu_B > \mu_A$, only high values of observed sample mean $\overline{X}$ (which is test-statistic in the present case) relative to μ_A would constitute evidence against H_0.

The two distributions *A* and *B* are compared diagrammatically in Fig. 3.6 wherein we show the probabilities of two types of error involved in hypothesis testing.

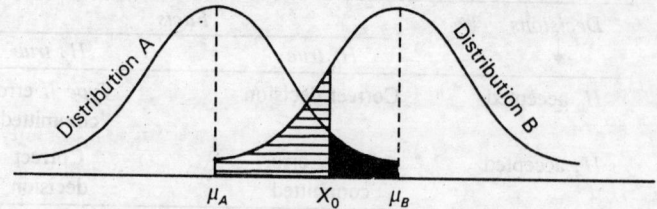

Fig. 3.6

Error type I is committed whenever $\overline{X}$ falls to the right of the boundary point X_0 (assuming that H_0 is true) and its probability is given by the chosen level of significance (i.e., five per cent) and corresponds to the blackened area. The error type II occurs whenever we do not reject H_0 when it is in fact false. This happens whenever $\overline{X}$ falls to the left of X_0 (assuming that H_0 is not true). The probability of making this error is given by the striped area in Fig. 3.6. As could be visualised, the decrease in the probability of one type of error can be brought about only at the cost of increase in the probability of another type of error. We can decrease the probability of error type I by shifting the boundary point X_0 further to the right. But by doing so we would obviously increase the striped area which represents the probabilities of error type II. Then, the question arises, how to decrease the probabilities of both types of error simultaneously? The only way in which we can reduce the probabilities of both kinds of error at the same time is by increasing the size of sample.

3.6 POWER OF A TEST

In the above discussion we considered the case of testing a simple hypothesis to understand the types of errors. Let us now consider a case of null hypothesis against a composite hypothesis:

$$H_0 : \mu = \mu_A$$
$$H_A : \mu \neq \mu_A$$

So far the probability of error type I is concerned it shall be given by the level of significance but the probability of error type II (i.e., area of not rejecting H_0 when it is false) will now depend on the value of μ itself. If the value of μ_A is closer to μ, the probability of error type II will be high as compared to probability of this error if the value of μ_A had been away from value of μ.

For instance, the null hypothesis states that $\mu = 20$, then probability of not rejecting H_0 is obviously greater if the true mean is 25 than if it is 30. This is because the striped area, as shown in Fig. 3.7 (a) and (b), will then increase.

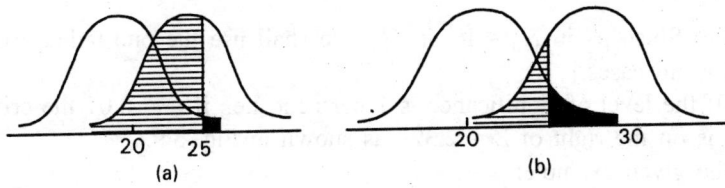

Fig. 3.7

Thus the probability of error type II can be determined for any value of μ. The smaller this probability, the better is the test in discriminating between true and false hypothesis. In Figs. 3.7 (a) and (b), the test will discriminate more clearly between null and alternative hypothesis if the alternative mean is 30 than if it is 25.

In terminology of statistics, the lower the probability of incorrectly accepting H_0 (i.e., letting go a guilty), the more powerful is our test. That is to say, the power of a test is measured by the probability of rejecting H_0 when it is false. Since the probability of error type II is the probability of incorrectly accepting H_0, *the power of test is given* by: {(1 – probability of type II error)}. Again, since the probability of error type II depends on the value of μ, the power of test will also depend on value of μ (in relation to its value in alternative hypothesis).

If we plot the probabilities of incorrectly accepting H_0 on the vertical axis against the corresponding values of μ on the horizontal axis, we obtain a graph as illustrated in Fig. 3.8. This is called *power function of a test*.

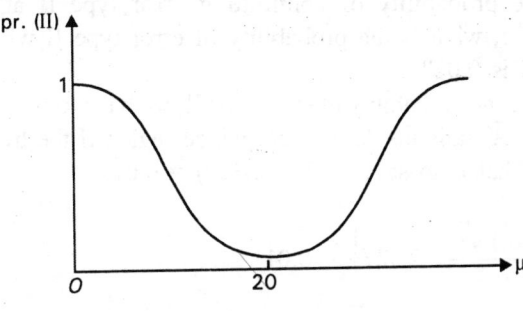

Fig. 3.8

The general idea behind the two types of error can be explained by the following example.

Suppose we consider the following hypothesis concerning the mean of a variable; $X \sim N(102, 25)$

$$H_0 : \mu_0 = 100$$
$$H_A : \mu_A = 105$$

We assume that test-statistic is based on sample size 100. Our problem is to determine the probabilities of error type II corresponding to 1, 5 and 10 per cent levels of significance.

[*Note:* Since μ_0 in $H_0 < \mu_A$ in H_A, we shall use the one tailed critical region in all cases.]

(a) If the level of significance is 1 per cent; i.e., if $\alpha = 0.01$ the critical region is on the right of $Z = 2.327$ as shown in Fig. 3.9.

In the given example:

$$Z = \frac{102 - 100}{\sqrt{25/100}} = 4$$

Since this value is in the critical region: the decision would be rejection of null hypothesis which states that $\mu = 100$.

This analysis indicates that if we want to avoid making error type I with 99 per cent confidence, then null hypothesis should be rejected. As such we are aware of the probability of making error of type I only.

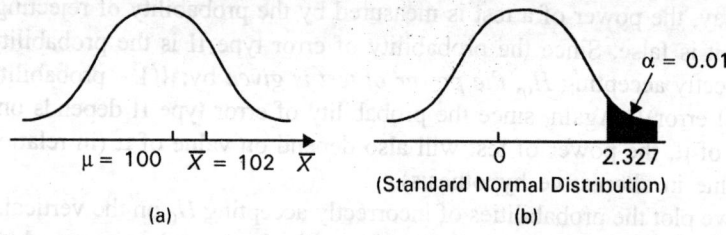

(a)   (b)

Fig. 3.9

What is the probability of committing error type II at this level of significance? Or, what is the probability of error type II when probability of error type I is 0.01?

To determine the probability of error type II, we have to find the probability that a value of $\overline{X}$ falls inside the acceptance region if the true mean is not 100 but 105. That is to say, $P(Z > 2.327) = 0.01$.

or, $P\left\{\dfrac{(\overline{X} - \mu_0)\sqrt{n}}{\sigma} > 2.327\right\} = 0.01$

or, $P\left\{\overline{X} > \mu_0 + 2.327\left(\dfrac{\sigma}{\sqrt{n}}\right)\right\} = 0.01$

But $\left[\mu_0 + 2.327\left(\dfrac{\sigma}{\sqrt{n}}\right)\right] = \left\{100 + 2.327\left(\dfrac{5}{10}\right)\right\} = 101.1635$

We have to determine the probability $\overline{X} < 101.1635$ given that the mean of $\overline{X}$, $E(\overline{X})$, is 105. To do this we make the appropriate transformation to standard normal variable. We can write

$$P\{\overline{X} < 101.1635 \mid E(\overline{X}) = 105\} = P\left[Z < (101.1635 - 105)\frac{\sqrt{n}}{\sigma}\right]$$

$$= P[Z < (101.1635 - 105)\, 0.5]$$

$$= P[Z < -1.9183]$$

From the normal probability Table we find

$$P[Z < -1.9183] = 0.0274$$

That is, the probability of making type error II is 0.0274 at 1 per cent level of significance.

(b) If the level of significance is five per cent, i.e., if $\alpha = 0.05$, the critical region is on the right of $Z = 1.645$ as shown in Fig. 3.10 (b).

To determine the probability of error type II, we now have to find,

$$P\,(Z > 1.645) = 0.05$$

In the present case

$$\overline{X} = \mu_0 + 1.645\left(\frac{\sigma}{\sqrt{n}}\right)$$

$$\overline{X} = 100 + 1.645\,(0.5) = 100.8225$$

The probability that $\overline{X} < 100.8225$, given that the mean of $\overline{X} = 105$ is,

$$P\left[\overline{X} < 100.8225 \mid E(\overline{X}) = 105\right]$$

$$= P\left[Z < (100.8225 - 105)\frac{\sqrt{n}}{\sigma}\right]$$

$$= P[Z < -2.0887]$$

$$= 0.0185$$

That is, the probability of making error type II is 0.0185.

(c) If the level of significance is 10 per cent, i.e., if $\alpha = 0.10$, the critical region is on the right of $Z = 1.280$ as shown in Fig. 3.10 (a).

To determine the probability of error type II, we now have to obtain, $P\,(Z > 1.280) = 0.10$. In the present case

$$\overline{X} = \mu_0 + 1.280\left(\frac{\sigma}{\sqrt{n}}\right)$$

$$\overline{X} = 100 + 0.6400 = 100.6400$$

The probability that $\overline{X} < 100.6400$, given that mean of $\overline{X} = 105$ is:

$$P\left[\overline{X} < 100.64 \mid E(\overline{X}) = 105\right] = P\left[Z < (100.64 - 105)\frac{\sqrt{n}}{\sigma}\right]$$

$$= P[Z < 2.18] = 0.0146$$

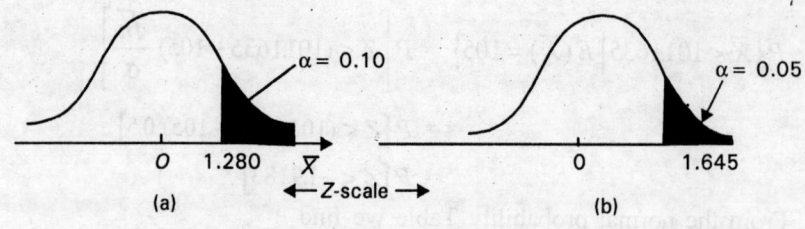

Fig. 3.10

That is, probability of making error type II is 0.0146.

The results may now be summarised as follows:

Probability of Error I (α)	Probability of Error II (β)
0.01	0.0274
0.05	0.0185
0.10	0.0146

These results show that the two probabilities are inversely related.

3.7 MAJOR STEPS IN HYPOTHESIS TESTING

Following are the six steps that are to be strictly followed in the procedure for testing a hypothesis:

1. Formulation of the null and alternative hypotheses.
2. Decision about the level of significance of the test.
3. Decision about the location of the critical region.
4. Decision about the appropriate test (of significance).
5. Computation of the chosen test-statistic from the sample observations.
6. Comparison of the sample value of the chosen statistic with the theoretical (tabulated) value that define the critical region so as to reject or accept the null hypothesis.

Let us examine each step separately.

Step 1: The object of statistical inference is to derive conclusions about the population parameter from the sample statistics. Such an inductive inference is known to be a hazardous process. In fact, it is a theorem of logic that in inductive inferences uncertainty is present. Certain rules are to be followed to measure the level of uncertainty and decide whether to accept or reject our conclusions. To do this, the best way is to compare the sample estimate with the true value of the population parameter. How can such comparison be possible when true value of population parameter is unknown. To meet out this difficulty, some assumption about the value of the true population parameter is made. This is then formulation of null hypothesis. Of course it may be difficult to hypothesise any special value for the true population parameter. There could be a very large number of hypothetical values which may be compatible with our sample estimate. To avoid such problem, it has become customary in econometrics to make the hypothesis that the true population parameter is equal to zero.

Step 2: In making any decision, one is liable to commit one of the following types of errors:

Error type I: Rejects the null hypothesis, when it is actually *true*.

Error type II: Accepts the null hypothesis, when it is actually *wrong*.

Obviously, one would want to minimise the probability of being wrong in all cases. In other words, one would like to minimise type I and type II errors. But unfortunately, for any given sample size, it is not possible to minimise both the errors simultaneously.

The classical approach to this problem is to assume that a type I error is likely to be more serious in practice than a type II error. Therefore, one should try to keep the probability of committing a type I error at a fairly low level, such as 0.01 or 0.05, and then try to minimise the type II error as much as possible.

The probability of type I error is called the *level of significance*. Choosing a certain level of significance would mean specifying the probability of committing a type I error.

Step 3: The critical region includes the values of the variable which have low probability (of 5 per cent or 1 per cent) of being observed. That is to say, the critical region includes only those values that correspond to the level of significance. But the critical region may be chosen at

   (i) the right end
   (ii) the left end
   (iii) half at each end of the distribution of the variable.

In the first and second cases, it involves one-tail test and in the third case it involves a two-tail test. The decision on 'which of the two to choose' would depend on the form in which the alternative hypothesis is expressed.

Alternative hypothesis can be in three forms:

Form 1. $H_1 : \mu \neq \mu_0$

Form 2. $H_1 : \mu > \mu_0$

Form 3. $H_1 : \mu < \mu_0$

The location of the critical region would depend on the direction to which the inequality sign points.

One has to choose the right tail as the critical region if the inequality sign is *greater than*; the left hand tail as the critical region if the inequality sign is *less than*, and a two-tail critical region when the inequality sign is—*not equal to*.

In econometrics, we usually choose two-tail critical region.

Step 4: The choice among the various tests of significance depends on two things:

  (a) Size of sample, and (b) information on population variance.

  (i) If the variance of parent population is known, Z-test is appropriate (irrespective of the normality of the population and the sample size).
  (ii) If the variance of the parent population is not known but the size of sample is large (it is greater than 30 observations), Z-test is still appropriate because the estimate of the population variance from a large sample is a satisfactory estimate of the true population variance.
  (iii) If the variance is not known and also the size of sample is small (less than 30 observations), t-test is appropriate provided that the parent population is normal.
  (iv) It has been established that: $t^2 = F$.
       (See page 74)

  F-statistic is used for conducting various tests of significance in econometric applications; specially in analysis of variance.

Step 5: Once the decision has been taken about the particular test of significance, the test-statistic has to be computed from the observed sample observations to conduct the required test.

Step 6: The final step of the hypothesis testing is to compare the computed value of the test-statistic with that of tabulated theoretical value of this statistic.

If the computed value falls in the critical region, the null hypothesis is rejected (i.e., alternative hypothesis is accepted).

If the computed value falls outside the critical region, the null hypothesis is accepted (i.e., alternative hypothesis is rejected).

ASSIGNMENTS

  1. Explain the following:
     (i) Is the choice of an estimator $\hat{\alpha}$ (of a parameter α) to minimise $E|\hat{\alpha} - \alpha|$ the same thing as minimising $|E(\hat{\alpha}) - \alpha|$?
     (ii) Does the consistency of an estimator imply that its variance approaches zero as the sample size increases without limit?
     (iii) Why is asymptotic efficiency defined only for consistent estimators?
  2. Examine whether following statements are true or false.
     (i) Consistent estimators are asymptotically unbiased.
     (ii) Bias and error are the two statistical terms which refer to the same characteristic of an estimator.
     (iii) Mean Square Error is the difference of two quantities; variance and square of bias.
     (iv) Sample variance is unbiased estimator of the population variance.
     (v) Level of significance depends on the test of significance.

(vi) Non-correlation between the two variables does not mean independency between them.

(vii) Power of a test is defined as $(1-\alpha)$; α is probability of type I error.

(viii) The level of probability with which we would be willing to risk type II error is called *level of significance*.

3. Discuss which of the two properties; unbiasedness and efficiency, is more desirable property of an estimator to be used to estimate the annual exports of each product in a developing country, when:

   (a) you wish to establish a long run average annual growth rate for total exports;
   (b) you wish to establish import controls for a given year based on amount of foreign exchange available from exports.

4. A random sample; $X_1, X_2, ..., X_n$; is drawn from a normal population with mean 3 and standard deviation σ. Find the MLE of σ.

5. A random sample of size N is taken from a normal population for random variable X with mean μ and $\sigma = 1$. Obtain the MLE of μ.

6. Suppose a random variable X has probability function: $f(X) = 2k\,X^k$. A sample of size n is taken; show that the maximum likelihood estimator for k is given by

$$\left\{ \frac{-n}{\Sigma \log X} \right\}.$$

7. x is distributed as $f(x) = ae^{-bx}$, $x \geq 0$.
   y is distributed as $f(y) = ce^{-dy}$, $y \geq 0$. Obtain the MLE of parameters a, b, c and d. Are these unbiased and consistent?

8. Given sample size $n = 100$, sample mean $X = 102$ and the sample standard deviation $= 15$. Test the following hypothesis of the population mean, H_0: $\mu = 100$, H_A: $\mu = 105$. Which hypotheses should be accepted with the probability of making type I error controlled at $\alpha = 0.05$?

   Also find the probability of making type II error, β, if the above decision rule is used.

9. Consider the following statement of hypothesis concerning a variable $X \sim N$ $(\mu; 90,000,00)$

$$H_0: \mu = 25,000$$
$$H_A: \mu = 30,000$$

   Assume that test-statistic is based on sample size 4 and the chosen levels of significance are 1 per cent, 5 per cent, and 10 per cent. Determine the corresponding probabilities of error type II.

10. "The method recommended by most statisticians in testing hypothesis, is to keep the probability of committing an error of the first kind on a given level and then to construct the test in such a way as to minimise the chance of not rejecting the false hypothesis (i.e., committing an error of the second kind)." Explain fully the types of errors referred in the above statement. How could these be minimised?

11. Explain clearly the concepts of consistency and asymptotic unbiasedness of an estimator.

   Suppose the σ^2 is the parameter to be estimated in a normal parent population: $N(X; \mu, \sigma^2)$, μ being known. Show that $\left(\dfrac{n}{n-1} \right) S^2$, where n is the sample size and S^2 is the sample variance, is an unbiased estimate of σ^2.

12. Define the term 'Best critical region'.

    Given a random sample of size n from a normal population with unknown mean, μ and known variance, σ^2, how would you devise a test of the hypothesis $\mu = 1$ against the alternative $\mu \geq 1$? What is the test?

    Show that the power of the test of any value of $\mu > 1$ increases with the sample size.

    How would you test the above hypothesis if the variance is not known?

13. Explain clearly the concepts of consistency, unbiasedness, efficiency and sufficiency of an estimate. What is the use of these concepts in estimation problem?

    The radius of a circle is measured with an error of observation which follows a normal distribution with mean zero and unknown variance. Given n independent measurements of radius, find an unbiased estimate of the area of the circle.

14. Let $x \sim N(\mu, 16)$. The null and alternative hypothesis are $H_0: \mu = 10$, $H_A: \mu \geq 10$. A random sample of size 16 is available. Two tests are proposed:

    (a) Reject H_0 if and only if $\bar{x} > 11.64$

    (b) Reject H_0 if and only if $\bar{x} < 8.04$ or, $\bar{x} > 11.96$.

    Tabulate the power function of each of the proposed tests. Which of the two tests would you recommend? Why?

ANOVA and Regression Analysis

One of the most elegant, powerful and useful techniques in modern statistical method is of *analysis of variance and covariance* developed by R.A. Fisher.

4.1 CONCEPT OF ANALYSIS OF VARIANCE (ANOVA)

With the method of analysis of variance, total variation in a variable can be reduced into different components associated with possible sources of variability whose relative importance we wish to assess. For example, assume that we have five plots of land. We are using different fertilisers, different system of irrigation and different seeds on these plots to cultivate wheat. Our problem is to examine variation in yields of wheat per acre of land due to the above three factors. With the method of analysis of variance it is possible to break the total variation in yield into three components. A component due to type of fertiliser, another due to type of seed and third due to type of irrigation. This method, therefore, is conceptually the same as regression analysis where our object is to determine the factors (explanatory variables) which cause the variation in the dependent variable. In regression analysis the total variation in the dependent variable is split into two components: the variation explained by the regression line (i.e., by the explanatory variables), and the unexplained variation. Coefficient of determination is also obtained to know the percentage of explained part of variation in the total variation. As such the objective in both the methods is that of determination of various factors which cause variations in the dependent variable.

However, there are significant differences between the two methods. The most important being: regression analysis provides numerical values of the influence of the various explanatory factors on the dependent variable in addition to the information concerning the different components responsible for bringing variation in dependent variable. It is only the latter type of information which is provided by the method of analysis of variance. Nevertheless, considering from the statistical point of view, this method stands in its own right. This method is of great importance and used in regression analysis for conducting various tests of significance.

In this chapter we, therefore, aim to study regression analysis from the view of analysis of variance which provides an illuminating and complementary way of looking at the problem of statistical inference.

4.2   METHOD OF ANALYSIS OF VARIANCE AS STATISTICAL METHOD

As already stated, the aim of this method is to split the total variation of a dependent variable around its mean into the components which may be attributed to specific causes. For the sake of simplicity we assume that there is only one factor (X) which influences the variable (Y) under study. Let us suppose also that we have four sub-samples of Y and our problem is to establish whether the difference between the means of four sub-samples is significant or whether it may be attributed to chance. If X is an important cause of variation in Y, the difference between the means of the sub-samples will be large and this will be shown by a large dispersion of the means of sub-samples around common mean $\overline{Y}$. If X is not an important source of variation in Y, the difference between the means of sub-samples will be small and this fact will be reflected by a small variance of the distribution of sampling means of sub-samples around common mean $\overline{Y}$.

The comparison between the two variances is done through the F-statistic (F stands for the name of Fisher who invented this statistic) which in fact is the ratio of two variances under study. If the two variance estimates are close to each other, their ratio will approach unity. The greater the difference between the two variances the greater is the value of F-ratio which in turn suggests that the difference between two variances is significant.

We illustrate the method of analysis of variance with the following hypothetical example.

Four random samples of size $n_1 = n_2 = n_3 = n_4 = 5$ with means $\overline{Y}_1 = 2$, $\overline{Y}_2 = 3$, $\overline{Y}_3 = 4$ and $\overline{Y}_4 = 7$ are given.

Our problem is to test the difference between these means of sub-samples.

We assume that the samples are drawn from four different populations which have a normal distribution with means μ_1, μ_2, μ_3, and μ_4 respectively and with equal standard deviation σ. We want to test hypothesis $H_0 : \mu_1 = \mu_2 = \mu_3 = \mu_4$ against alternative hypothesis; H_1: μ_i's are not equal. If H_0 is true, then all the four populations may be considered as one population with mean μ $(= \mu_1 = \mu_2 = \mu_3 = \mu_4)$ and standard deviation σ, i.e., $Y \sim N(\mu, \sigma^2)$. This will also mean that all the four samples are drawn from this one population.

On the basis of *Central limit theorem*, the sampling distribution of sample means $\overline{Y}_1, \overline{Y}_2, \overline{Y}_3$ and $\overline{Y}_4$ can be depicted as:

$$\overline{Y}_1 \sim N(\mu, \sigma_{\overline{Y}_1}^2) \sim N\left(\mu, \frac{\sigma^2}{n_1}\right)$$

$$\overline{Y_2} \sim N(\mu, \sigma_{\overline{Y_2}}^2) \sim N\left(\mu, \frac{\sigma^2}{n_2}\right)$$

$$\overline{Y_3} \sim N(\mu, \sigma_{\overline{Y_3}}^2) \sim N\left(\mu, \frac{\sigma^2}{n_3}\right)$$

$$\overline{Y_4} \sim N(\mu, \sigma_{\overline{Y_4}}^2) \sim N\left(\mu, \frac{\sigma^2}{n_4}\right)$$

And if null hypothesis were true ($\mu_1 = \mu_2 = \mu_3 = \mu_4$) then all the four formulations shall form a single large population; $Y \sim N(\mu, \sigma^2)$.

Thus to test null hypothesis, we need common mean μ and common variance σ^2.

(i) Common mean μ can be computed by taking into consideration all the four samples together (see Table 4.1),

$$\hat{\mu} = \frac{\Sigma Y_i}{N} = \frac{\sum\limits_{j}^{n}\sum\limits_{i}^{k} Y_{ji}}{N} = 4$$

where, $N = n_1 + n_2 + n_3 + n_4$ and

$k = $ number of samples

(ii) Common population variance can be obtained in two ways. Firstly, an unbiased estimator of common variance from the given four samples may be obtained by the following formula:

$$\hat{\sigma}^2 = \frac{\sum\limits_{j=1}^{k} n_j(\overline{Y}_j - \overline{Y})^2}{k-1} \; ; \; k = \text{number of samples.}$$

This formula is based on the differences between the sample means $(\overline{Y}_j)$ and the common population mean $(\overline{Y})$. If H_0 is true, then the sample means should not differ significantly from each other and also from the overall mean $\overline{Y}$. This, in turn, implies that the estimate $\hat{\sigma}^2$ will also be smaller if the null hypothesis is true. Therefore the estimate of $\hat{\sigma}^2$ is an important factor of the test of difference between means of various samples; and also as we observe from the formula; it actually reflects the variation between sample means. Hence it is called *Variation between.*

Secondly, an unbiased estimator of common variance σ^{2*} may be obtained by pooling together the variances of the sub-samples through the following formula:

$$\sigma^{*2} = \frac{n_1 s_1^2 + n_2 s_2^2 + n_3 s_3^2 + n_4 s_4^2}{(n_1 + n_2 + n_3 + n_4) - k}$$

Table 4.1: The Data

Samples				Total observation
I	II	III	IV	
2	3	5	6	2
3	4	5	8	3
1	3	5	7	1
3	5	3	4	3
1	0	2	10	1
				3
				4
				3
				5
				0
				5
				5
				5
				3
				2
				6
				8
				7
				4
				10
$\Sigma Y_{1i} = 10$	$\Sigma Y_{2i} = 15$	$\Sigma Y_{3i} = 20$	$\Sigma Y_{4i} = 35$	$\sum_{j}\sum_{i} = 80$
$\overline{Y}_1 = 2$	$\overline{Y}_2 = 3$	$\overline{Y}_3 = 4$	$\overline{Y}_4 = 7$	$\overline{Y} = 4$
$S_1^2 = 0.80$	$S_2^2 = 2.80$	$S_3^2 = 1.60$	$S_4^2 = 3.40$	

But $\quad n_1 s_1^2 = n_1 \left\{ \dfrac{\sum\limits_{i}^{n_1}(Y_{1i} - \overline{Y}_1)^2}{n_1} \right\} = \sum\limits_{i}^{n_1} \left(Y_{1i} - \overline{Y}_1 \right)^2$

....

....

$n_4 s_4^2 = n_4 \left\{ \dfrac{\sum\limits_{i}^{n_4}(Y_{4i} - \overline{Y}_4)^2}{n_4} \right\} = \sum\limits_{i}^{n_4} \left(Y_{4i} - \overline{Y}_4 \right)^2$

$$\sigma^{*2} = \frac{\sum\limits_{i}^{n_1} \left(Y_{1i} - \overline{Y}_1 \right)^2 + ... + \sum\limits_{i}^{nk} \left(Y_{ki} - \overline{Y}_k \right)^2}{N - k}$$

or,

$$\sigma^{*2} = \frac{\sum\limits_{j=1}^{k} \sum\limits_{i}^{nk} \left(Y_{ji} - \overline{Y}_j\right)^2}{N-k}$$

As could be observed, this formula examines the variations within each sample and hence is called *Variation within*.

We have now two unbiased estimates of population variance. Estimate $\hat{\sigma}^2$ reflects the variation between the sample means and therefore depends on the validity of the null hypothesis. Estimate σ^{*2} reflects the variation *within* the samples and is, therefore, independent of the null hypothesis.

Since the two estimates of variance are independent, it can be shown that their ratio follows and F-distribution with $\{(k-1)$ and $(N-K)\}$ degrees of freedom.

$$F^* = \frac{\left[\sum\limits_{j=1}^{k} n_j \left(\overline{Y}_4 - \overline{Y}\right)^2\right] \div (k-1)}{\left[\sum\limits_{j=1}^{k} \sum\limits_{i=1}^{nk} (Y_{ji} - \overline{Y}_i)^2\right] \div (N-k)}$$

The calculated F^* variance ratio is compared with the tabulated value of F. If $F^* > F$, H_0 is rejected; i.e., we accept that the difference between the sample means is significant. If $F^* < F$, H_0 is accepted; i.e., we accept that the sample means are not significantly different.

Applying the procedure described above to the example given in Table 4.1, we obtain following estimates of overall variance.

1. The estimate of *Variation between* is

$$\hat{\sigma}^2 = \frac{\sum\limits_{j=1}^{k} n_j \left(\overline{Y}_j - \overline{Y}\right)^2}{k-1}$$

$$= \frac{n_1\left(\overline{Y}_1 - \overline{Y}\right)^2 + n_2\left(\overline{Y}_2 - \overline{Y}\right)^2 + n_3\left(\overline{Y}_3 - \overline{Y}\right)^2 + n_4\left(\overline{Y}_4 - \overline{Y}\right)^2}{4-1}$$

$$= \frac{5(2-4)^2 + 5(3-4)^2 + 5(4-4)^2 + 5(7-4)^2}{3}$$

i.e., $\hat{\sigma}^2 = \dfrac{20 + 5 + 0 + 45}{3} = 23.333$

2. The estimate of *Variation within* is

$$\sigma^{*2} = \frac{\sum\limits_{j}^{} \sum\limits_{i}^{nj} (Y_{ji} - \overline{Y}_j)^2}{N-k}$$

$$\sigma^{*2} = \frac{\sum_{1}^{5}(Y_{1j} - \overline{Y}_1)^2 + \sum_{1}^{5}(Y_{2j} - \overline{Y}_2)^2 + \sum_{1}^{5}(Y_{3j} - \overline{Y}_3^5)^2 \sum(Y_{4j} - \overline{Y}_4)^2}{20 - 4}$$

i.e., $\sigma^{*2} = \dfrac{4 + 14 + 8 + 20}{16} = 2.875$

3. Observed variance ratio $F^* = \dfrac{23.333}{2.875} = 8.115$

4. The tabulated value of F at 5% level of significance with (3, 16) degrees of freedom is found to be $F_{0.05} = 3.24$.

5. Since $F^* > F$, we reject the null hypothesis and accept that there is a significant difference in the means obtained from the four samples.

The above test can also be performed in another way which is based on the following important relationship.

$$\sum_{j=1}^{k}\sum_{i=1}^{nj}(Y_{ji} - \overline{Y})^2 \quad = \quad \sum_{j=1}^{k} n_j(\overline{Y}_j - \overline{Y})^2 \quad + \sum_{j=1}^{k}\sum_{i=1}^{nj}(Y_{ji} - \overline{Y}_j)^2$$

$$\left\{\begin{array}{c}\text{Total sum of squared}\\ \text{deviations}\end{array}\right\} = \left\{\begin{array}{c}\text{Sum of squares}\\ \text{between samples}\end{array}\right\} + \left\{\begin{array}{c}\text{Sum of squares}\\ \text{within samples}\end{array}\right\}$$

i.e. Total Variation in Y = between variation + within variation. This relation can be easily proved as under:

$$\left(Y_{ji} - \overline{Y}\right) = \left(Y_{ji} - \overline{Y}\right) + \overline{Y}_j - \overline{Y}_j = \left(Y_{ji} - \overline{Y}_j\right) + \left(\overline{Y}_j - \overline{Y}\right)$$

Therefore;

$$\left(Y_{ji} - \overline{Y}\right)^2 = \left(\overline{Y}_{ji} - \overline{Y}_j\right)^2 + 2\left(Y_{ji} - \overline{Y}_j\right)\left(\overline{Y}_j - \overline{Y}\right) + \left(\overline{Y}_j - \overline{Y}\right)^2$$

Summing over all values, we obtain:

$$\sum_{j=1}^{k}\sum_{i=1}^{ni}\left(Y_{ji} - \overline{Y}\right)^2 = \sum_{j}\sum_{i}\left(Y_{ji} - \overline{Y}_j\right)^2 + 2\sum_{j}\sum_{i}\left(Y_{ji} - \overline{Y}_j\right)\left(\overline{Y}_j - \overline{Y}\right)$$

$$+ \sum_{j}\sum_{i}\left(\overline{Y}_j - \overline{Y}\right)^2$$

But, $2\Sigma\Sigma\left(Y_{ji} - \overline{Y}_j\right)\left(\overline{Y}_j - \overline{Y}\right) = 2\sum_{j}\left[\left(\overline{Y}_j - \overline{Y}\right)\sum_{i}\left(Y_{ji} - \overline{Y}_j\right)\right] = 0$

$$\left\{\because \sum_{i}\left(Y_{ji} - \overline{Y}_j\right) = 0\right\}$$

Therefore,

$$\sum_{j=1}^{k}\sum_{i=1}^{nj}\left(Y_{ji} - \overline{Y}\right)^2 = \sum_{j}^{k}\sum_{i}^{nj}\left(Y_{ji} - \overline{Y}_j\right)^2 + \sum_{j}^{k} n_j\left(\overline{Y}_j - \overline{Y}\right)^2$$

Substituting the values in the above relation from our example;

$$\left.\begin{array}{l} \displaystyle\sum_{j}^{4}\sum_{i}^{5}\left(\overline{Y}_{ji} - \overline{Y}\right)^2 = 116 \\[3mm] \displaystyle\sum_{j}n_j\left(\overline{Y}_{ji} - \overline{Y}\right)^2 = 70 \\[3mm] \text{and, } \displaystyle\sum_{j}^{4}\sum_{i}^{5}\left(Y_{ji} - \overline{Y}_j\right)^2 = 46 \end{array}\right\} \text{ So that, } 116 = 70 + 46$$

The results obtained above are put in a table of the Analysis of Variance which merely describes the proposition:

$$\sum_{j}\sum_{i}\left(Y_{ji} - \overline{Y}\right)^2 = \sum_{j}n_j\left(\overline{Y}_{ji} - \overline{Y}\right)^2 + \sum_{j}\sum_{i}\left(Y_{ji} - \overline{Y}_j\right)^2$$

in a particular procedure.

Table 4.2: Table of Analysis of Variance

Source of variation	Sum of squares (SS)	Degrees of freedom (Df)	Mean sum of squares (MSS)	F^*
Between samples	70	$(4-1) = 3$	$\dfrac{70}{3} = 23.3$	$F^* = \dfrac{23.3}{2.8}$
Within samples	46	$(20-4) = 16$	$\dfrac{46}{16} = 2.8$	$= 8.321$
Total	116	$(20-1) = 19$		$F_{0.05} = 3.24$

It may be observed that the above procedure has neatly divided the total sum of squares and total degrees of freedom into two components; between samples and within samples variation.

The technique of partitioning a sum of squared deviations from a mean into two components which, under a null hypothesis, follow the F-distribution is known as the Analysis of Variance.

4.3 REGRESSION ANALYSIS AND ANALYSIS OF VARIANCE

In regression analysis, the squared deviations from mean has been minimised and it has been proved in 5.8 that

$$\sum_{i}^{n}\left(Y_i - \overline{Y}\right)^2 = \sum_{i}^{n}\left(\hat{Y}_i - \overline{Y}\right)^2 + \sum_{i}^{n}\left(Y_i - \hat{Y}\right)^2$$

$$\left\{\begin{array}{c}\text{Total sum of}\\\text{squared}\\\text{deviations}\end{array}\right\} = \left\{\begin{array}{c}\text{Sum of squared}\\\text{deviations from}\\\text{regression line}\end{array}\right\} + \left\{\begin{array}{c}\text{Square Sum}\\\text{of residual}\\\text{terms}\end{array}\right\}$$

That is, $\qquad \sum y_i^2 \qquad = \qquad \sum \hat{y}_i^2 \qquad + \qquad \sum e_i^2$

$$\text{(Total Variation)} = \left(\begin{array}{c}\text{Explained}\\\text{variation}\end{array}\right) + \left(\begin{array}{c}\text{Unexplained}\\\text{variation}\end{array}\right)$$

In other words, in the regression analysis the total variations are split into explained (by explanatory variables) and unexplained (error terms) variations against *between* and *within variations* in case of analysis of variance procedure. This suggests that one can compile an *Analysis of Variance type of Table* for the regression analysis also in order to judge the overall significance of the (regression) results.

Table 4.3

Source of variation	Sum of squares (SS)	Degrees of freedom (df)	Mean sum of squares
Explained (ESS)	$\Sigma \hat{y}_i^2$	$k-1$	$\dfrac{\Sigma \hat{y}_i^2}{(k-1)}$
Residual (RSS)	Σe_i^2	$n-k$	$\dfrac{\Sigma e_i^2}{(n-k)}$
Total (TSS)	Σy_i^2	$n-1$	$\dfrac{\Sigma y_i^2}{n-1}$

Arrange the various sum of squares and their associated *df* in Table 4.3, which is the standard form of the AOV table. From the results of Table 4.3, obtain *F*-statistic:

$$F = \frac{\text{MSS of ESS}}{\text{MSS of RSS}} = \frac{\Sigma \hat{y}_i^2 / k - 1}{\Sigma e_i^2 / n - k}$$

Assuming that the regression model consists of only one explanatory variable, then:

$$F = \frac{\Sigma \hat{y}_i^2 / 2 - 1}{\Sigma e_i^2 / n - 2} = \frac{\hat{\beta}^2 \Sigma x_i^2}{\Sigma e_i^2 / n - 2} \qquad \text{...(4.1)}$$

It can be proved that:

$$E\left(\hat{\beta}^2 \Sigma x_i^2\right) = \sigma^2 + \beta^2 \Sigma x_i^2 \qquad \text{...(4.2)}$$

$$E\left(\frac{\Sigma e_i^2}{n-2}\right) = E(\hat{\sigma}^2) = \sigma^2 \qquad \text{...(4.3)}$$

Therefore, if β is, in fact, zero, equations (4.2) and (4.3) both provide identical estimates of true σ^2. In this situation explanatory variable has no linear influence on dependent variable Y whatsoever and the entire variations in Y are explained by the random disturbances U_i. If on the other hand, β is not zero, (4.2) and (4.3) will be different and part of the variations in Y can be ascribed to X. Therefore, the F ratio defined by (4.1) provides a test of the null hypothesis: $\beta = 0$.

To illustrate, consider the following data to construct the analysis of variance table for a simple regression model:

$$Y_i = \alpha + \beta X_i + U_i.$$

Given

$$\overline{Y} = 321.75 \qquad \Sigma xy = 43147.33$$
$$\overline{X} = 350.00 \qquad \Sigma x^2 = 46510.00$$
$$n = 12 \qquad \Sigma y^2 = 40068.25$$

On calculation we find that, $\hat{\beta} = 0.9277$, $\hat{\alpha} = -2.945$.

Since $\Sigma e_i^2 = \Sigma y_i^2 - \hat{\beta} \Sigma x_i y_i$

$$\therefore \ \Sigma e_i^2 = 40.47, \ \sqrt{Var\ \hat{\beta}} = \sqrt{\frac{4.047}{\Sigma x_i^2}} = 0.009328 \text{ and } R^2 = 0.998$$

The regression results are: $\hat{Y}_i = -2.945 + 0.9277 X_i$, $R^2 = 0.998$

$$(0.0093)$$

Table 4.4: Table of Analysis of Variance

Source of variation	Sum of squares	Degrees of freedom	Mean sum of squares	F*
Explained	$\Sigma \hat{y}_i^2 = 40027.28$	$k - 1 = 1$	40027.78	$\begin{cases} \dfrac{40027.78}{4.047} \\ = 9890.72 \end{cases}$
Residual	$\Sigma e_i^2 = 40.47$	$n - k = 10$	4.047	
Total	$\Sigma y_i^2 = 40068.25$	$n - 1 = 11$		

The observed F^* is much higher than the tabulated $F = 4.96$ with $(1, 10)$ degree of freedom. Hence we reject the null hypothesis and accept that the regression is significant, that is, X is a significant explanatory factor of the variation in Y.

There is an interesting relationship between the F-test of significance and t-test discussed earlier. It can be shown that:

Square of the t-value with $n - k$ degrees of freedom is an F-value with 1 and $n - k$ degrees of freedom.

$$t = \frac{\hat{\beta}}{SE\left(\hat{\beta}\right)} = \frac{\hat{\beta}}{\sqrt{Var\left(\hat{\beta}\right)}}$$

But $\quad Var\left(\hat{\beta}\right) = \dfrac{\hat{\sigma}^2}{\Sigma x_i^2} = \dfrac{\Sigma e_i^2 / n - 2}{\Sigma x_i^2}$

Therefore, $\quad t^2 = \dfrac{\hat{\beta}}{Var\left(\hat{\beta}\right)} = \dfrac{\hat{\beta}^2}{\left[\dfrac{\Sigma e_i^2}{n-2}\right]\left[\dfrac{1}{\Sigma x_i^2}\right]}$

That is, $\qquad t^2 = \dfrac{\hat{\beta}^2 \Sigma x_i^2}{\Sigma e_i^2 / n - 2} = F \qquad$ as per eq. (4.1)

Note here that the numerator degrees of freedom of the F ratio must be 1 (one) for proving that: $t^2 = F$.

If we assume $H_0 : \beta = 0$ then, for the above illustration, t value is found to be 99.4532. This t has 10 df. Under the same hypothesis the F value was 9890.72 with 1 and 10 df.

Hence, $(99.4532)^2 = F$ value.

4.4 REGRESSION ANALYSIS AND ANALYSIS OF VARIANCE COMPARED

Following are the main differences and similarities between the two procedures:

1. In both the methods, the total variation in Y is split into two components, in regression analysis the components are: explained and residual while in analysis of variance; the components are: between and within.
2. The null hypothesis tested in the method of analysis of variance is; $H_0 : \mu_1 = \mu_2 = \mu_3 \ldots = \mu$ against alternative $H_1 : \mu_j$'s are not equal. In contrast, the test performed in regression analysis in a test concerning the overall explanatory power of the regression as measured by R^2. We have shown above that the F-test, in fact is equivalent to testing of overall significance of regression.
3. It is also proved above that t and F tests are equivalent and the relationship between them is found to be as $t^2 = F$.

Summarising therefore, it may be said that though both the methods aim at the same object; the regression analysis is a more powerful method than the analysis of variance method; specially when we are concerned with the study of economic relationships involving market data which are not experimental. It is because, regression analysis provides a numerical estimate for the influence of each explanatory variable over and above the information provided by the analysis of variance method. But in certain cases, such as when we study the influence of qualitative factors on a certain variable, the analysis of variance method is more appropriate. It is because we cannot quantify the qualitative variables hence their influence cannot be assessed by regression analysis. On the other hand, since in the analysis of variance method we do not need the values of explanatory variable(s), this procedure can very well examine the effect of qualitative explanatory factors on the dependent variable. Remember that the regression technique requires the knowledge of the values of explanatory variable(s) along with the values of dependent variable, but Analysis of Variance method is based solely on the values of dependent variable. (See example solved under 4.2)

Analysis of Variance, therefore, commands its hold in at least two fields of study:

(i) For the analysis of qualitative variables which cannot be approximated by dummy variables in regression analysis, and

(ii) For the analysis of experimental data where it is required to examine to logical evaluation of the effects of each additional variable on the value of independent variable.

The technique of Analysis of Variance is of great help in the regression analysis for empirically testing the various hypothesis in Econometrics. Three such tests are described under.

4.5 STATISTICAL TESTS BASED ON ANALYSIS OF VARIANCE

4.5.1 Testing the Equality between Coefficients Obtained from Different Regressions or Different Samples

Many a time a researcher estimates a regression equation separately for several sets of data and his problem is to test whether some or all the parameters are the same for all different sets of data. Such instances are numerous in econometric research.

Assume that we have two samples on the variables:

Y and X containing n_1 variables:

and, Y and X containing n_2 observations

We obtain two estimates of the same relationship for these two samples;

$$\hat{Y} = \hat{b}_0 + \hat{b}_1 X \text{ for } n_1 \text{ observations}$$

and, $Y^* = \beta_0 + \beta_1 X$ for n_2 observations.

Our problem is to examine whether these two estimated relations differ significantly. If yes, then we can conclude that the relationship changes from one sample to the other.

For instance, suppose that we have the data on consumption and disposable income for the two periods 1950–1959 and 1960–1969. We estimate the consumption functions separately for these periods. We could then ask:

Are the two estimated functions different statistically?

Does the marginal propensity to consume differ statistically in the functions?

Prof. G.C. Chow suggested F-test to answer these questions. This test is also known as *Chow test* for testing equality of two regressions. We explain this test in the following steps.

Step 1: Fit the pooled regression with number of observations $(n_1 + n_2)$ and estimate unexplained variation Σe_i^2

i.e., obtain $\hat{Y}_p = \hat{a}_0 + \hat{a}_1 X$ and,

$\Sigma e_p^2 = \Sigma y_p^2 - \Sigma \hat{y}_p^2$ with $(n_1 + n_2 - k)$ degrees of freedom, p stands for pooled data.

Step 2: Fit the regression for each sample separately.

For sample one: $\hat{y}_1 = \hat{b}_0 + \hat{b}_1 X$ and $\Sigma e_1^2 = \Sigma y_1^2 - \Sigma \hat{y}_1^2$

For sample two: $\hat{y}_2 = \hat{\beta}_0 + \beta_1 X$ and $\Sigma e_2^2 = \Sigma y_2^2 - \Sigma \hat{y}_2^2$

Step 3: Compute F^* ratio as under;

$$F^* = \frac{\left\{ \Sigma e_p^2 - \left(\Sigma e_1^2 + \Sigma e_2^2 \right) \right\} \div k}{\left(\Sigma e_1^2 + \Sigma e_2^2 \right) \div (n_1 + n_2 - 2k)}$$

We test the null hypothesis;

$$H_0 : \hat{a}_1 = \hat{b}_1 = \hat{\beta}_1$$

against alternative $H_1 : H_0$ is not correct.

If $F^* > F_{0.05}$, we reject the null hypothesis, that is, we accept that the two functions are different.

An Example: A sample of 20 observations on X and Y is to be used for estimating linear function $Y = \beta_0 + \beta_1 X + U$.

The first ten observations yield the following results:

$$\bar{X} = 15.30 \qquad \Sigma x_t^2 = 78$$
$$\Sigma x_i y_i = -1568.0$$
$$\bar{Y} = 160 \qquad \Sigma y_t^2 = 45600$$

The ten subsequent observations yield:

$$\bar{X} = 14.08 \qquad \Sigma x_i^2 = 98.16$$
$$\Sigma x_i y_i = -2308.80$$
$$\bar{Y} = 160 \qquad \Sigma y_i^2 = 62440$$

Our problem is to see whether the function changed over the two periods or two samples.

Since in the present example we are not given the pooled results, we may compute F^* in the following way.

$$F^* = \frac{\Sigma e_1^2 / (n_1 - 2)}{\Sigma e_2^2 / (n_2 - 2)} \quad \text{with } \{(n_1 - 2), (n_2 - 2)\} \text{ degrees of freedom.}$$

On calculation, we obtain the following results:

	$\hat{\alpha}$	$\hat{\beta}$	R^2	Σe^2	df
For 1st ten observations:	467.58	−20.103	0.69	14078.49	8
For 2nd ten observations:	437.18	−23.521	0.87	8134.72	8

$$\therefore \quad F^* = \frac{14078.49 \div 8}{8134.72 \div 8} = \frac{1759.80}{1016.84} = 1.731$$

Tabulated $F_{0.05}$ with (8, 8) degrees of freedom = 3.44. Since $F^* < F$, we accept the null hypothesis, i.e., the two functions do not differ statistically.

4.5.2 Testing the Sensitiveness or Regression Coefficient with the Size of the Sample

Many times the researcher may want to know how his estimated regression behaves outside the sample data which he has used for the estimation. In other words he wants to find out whether estimates will be different in enlarged sample (than the size of sample used by him) or will they remain stable over time (i.e., large in cross-section samples).

Here again *Chow-test* (in a bit different form) is used to test the sensitiveness of the regressions.

Suppose the original sample size is n_1 and we have obtained the regression;
$\hat{y} = \hat{\alpha} + \hat{\beta}X$ and

$$\Sigma e^2 = \Sigma y^2 - \Sigma \hat{y}^2 \text{ with } (n_1 - 2) \text{ degrees of freedom.}$$

Again suppose with an augmented sample of $(n_1 + n_2)$ observations (n_2 are new observations), we obtain regression:

$$\hat{Y} = \hat{b}_0 + \hat{b}X$$

and $\qquad \Sigma e_a^2 = \Sigma y_a^2 - \Sigma \hat{y}_a^2$ (a stands for augmented sample)
with $(n_1 + n_2 - k)$ degrees of freedom.

Compute F^* ratio in the following way:

$$F^* = \frac{\left(\Sigma e_a^2 - \Sigma e^2\right) \div n_2}{\Sigma e^2 \div (n_1 - 2)}$$

We test the null hypothesis

$$H_0 : \hat{\beta} = \hat{b} \text{ against } H_1 : \hat{\beta} \neq \hat{b}$$

If $F^* > F$, we reject the null hypothesis, i.e., we accept that the structural coefficients are unstable and that their values change with the increase in the size of the sample.

4.5.3 Testing the Restrictions Imposed on the Relationship between Two or More Parameters of a Function

This test was suggested by G. Tintner.

Suppose from a cross-section data on 30 firms of an industry, Cobb-Douglas form of production function $Q = A_0 L^\alpha K^\beta$ is estimated. Assume that the regression results obtained are.

$$\hat{Q} = \hat{A}_0 L^{0.82} K^{0.23} \qquad R^2 = 0.77$$

Since it is observed that the sum of coefficients is nearly unity $(0.82 + 0.23 = 1.05)$, it appears that the industry in question might have experienced constant returns to scale. We, therefore, want to test the statistical reliability of this presumption. In other words, we want to test the hypothesis: $H_0 : \alpha + \beta = 1$

against alternative: $H_1 : \alpha + \beta \neq 1$

For this, we estimate the production function in two different ways: (i) by imposing a restriction of $\alpha + \beta = 1$, and (ii) without imposing any restriction. We obtain sum of squared errors in both the cases and compute F-statistic in the following way:

Suppose the results in these two cases are:

With restriction: $\hat{Q} = \hat{A}_0 L^{0.74} K^{0.26}$ and $\Sigma e_1^2 = 6.45$; $R^2 = 0.65$

Without restriction: $\hat{Q} = \hat{A}_0 L^{0.82} K^{0.23}$ and $\Sigma e_2^2 = 4.64$; $R^2 = 0.77$

We compute F^* in the following way:

$$F^* = \left\{ \frac{\Sigma e_1^2 - \Sigma e_2^2}{\Sigma e_2^2} \right\} (n - k); \text{ which follows}$$

F-distribution with $\{1, (n - k)\}$ degrees of freedom.

In our example;

$$F^* = \left\{ \frac{6.45 - 4.64}{4.64} \right\} (30 - 3) = 10.5323$$

But $F_{0.05} = 4.20$ with $(1, 28)$ degrees of freedom.

Since $F^* > F$, we reject null hypothesis and conclude that the industry in question had not experienced constant returns during the sample period.

[**Note:** Testing of returns to scale through t-test has also been discussed in Section 7.5.4. of Chapter 7]

ASSIGNMENTS

1. Explain the underlying idea in the technique of *Analysis of Variance*. In what way does this technique differ from *regression analysis*? Explain the importance of each technique in Econometric studies.

2. Show the statistic $F^* = \left(\dfrac{n - k}{k - 1} \right) \left(\dfrac{R^2}{1 - R^2} \right)$ and $t^2 = F^*$

Hint: $F = \dfrac{ESS/k - 1}{RSS/n - k}$

$$= \left(\frac{n - k}{k - 1} \right) \left(\frac{ESS}{TSS - ESS} \right)$$

$$= \left(\frac{n - k}{k - 1} \right) \left[\frac{ESS/TSS}{1 - (ESS/TSS)} \right]$$

$$= \left(\frac{n - k}{k - 1} \right) \left(\frac{R^2}{1 - R^2} \right)$$

where k is total number of parameters to be estimated of which one is intercept term.

3. The *Phillips curve* implies that there is a negative relationship between the percentage change in wages and unemployment rate. Phillips curve relation was fitted to a certain data and following ANOVA table was obtained:

Source of Variation	SS	df	MSS
Due to regression	2.153	1	2.153
Due to residual	1.144	11	0.104
Total	3.297	12	

Do the data support the existence of the Phillips curve relationship?

4. Two saving functions: $S = f(Y)$ are fitted to two periods separately for the following data:

Period I	Savings (S) Rs. lakhs	Income (Y) Rs. lakhs	Period II	Savings (S) Rs. lakhs	Income (Y) Rs. lakhs
1960	3.6	88	1969	5.9	155
1961	2.1	94	1970	9.0	167
1962	0.8	100	1971	9.5	177
1963	2.0	106	1972	8.2	186
1964	1.0	110	1973	10.4	197
1965	1.2	119	1974	15.3	211
1966	4.1	127	1975	19.4	228
1967	5.0	135	1976	17.5	239
1968	4.3	143	1977	19.9	252

Examine whether MPS differ in the two periods.

5. In order to examine whether or not there is difference in the MPC of two samples, following consumption functions were estimated from the data:

$\hat{C}_1 = 120 + 0.90Y \quad n_1 = 35, \ R_1^2 = 0.92, \ \Sigma e_1^2 = 3251$
$\qquad \quad (5.6)$

$\hat{C}_2 = 160 + 0.82Y \quad n_2 = 30, \ R_2^2 = 0.95, \ \Sigma e_2^2 = 4532$
$\qquad \quad (8.5)$

$\hat{C} = 250 + 0.70Y \quad n = 65, \ R^2 = 0.92, \ \Sigma e^2 = 16320$
$\qquad \quad (6.2)$

Would you accept the hypothesis that there is no difference between MPC of the two samples?

(The brackets are the *t*-values of the coefficients.)

PART TWO

ECONOMETRIC PRINCIPLES

Definition and Scope
of Econometrics

The economic theories we learn in classrooms attempt to define the relationships among different economic variables. These relationships are, at times, described in mathematical forms. Their purpose is to help us understand better the economic world we live in.

However, theories have to be checked against data obtained from the real world. If empirical data verify the relationship proposed by the theory, we may accept it: otherwise we must reject the relationship. To provide a better guidance for economic policy-making, we also need to know the quantitative relationships between the different economic variables. For example: if investment is proposed to be increased by 15 per cent, we must know by how much the national income will be expected to increase. We obtain these quantitative measurements from the data taken from the real world. If the theory is compatible with the actual data, we accept the theory as valid. If the theory is incompatible with the observed behaviour, we either reject the theory or, in the light of the empirical evidence of the data, modify it.

5.1 WHAT IS ECONOMETRICS?

The field of knowledge which helps us to carry out evaluation of economic theories in numerical terms, is Econometrics.

The name 'Econometrics' was introduced in 1926 by a Norwegian economist and statistician, Ragnar Frisch. The term was actually modelled on the expression 'Biometric' which appeared late in the 19th century to denote the field of biological studies employing statistical methods.

Econometrics is the science which combines economic theory with economic statistics and tries by mathematical and statistical methods to investigate the empirical support of the general schematic law established by economic theory. Econometrics, therefore, makes concrete certain theoretical economic laws by utilising economics, mathematics and statistics.

Although measurement is an important role of econometrics, the scope of econometrics is much broader as described by leading econometricians while defining this field of knowledge.

(i) Econometrics may be defined as the social science in which the tools of economic theory, mathematics, and statistical inference are applied to the analysis of economic phenomena. (Arthur S. Goldberger, *Econometric Theory,* 1964, page 1.)

(ii) Econometrics, the result of a certain outlook on the role of economics, consists of the application of mathematical statistics to economic data to lend empirical support to the models constructed by mathematical economics and to obtain numerical results. (Gerhard Tintner, *Methodology of Mathematical Economics and Econometrics,* 1968, page 74.)

(iii) ...... econometrics may be defined as the quantitative analysis of actual economic phenomena based on the concurrent development of theory and observation, related by appropriate methods of inference. (Samuelson, Koopmans, and Stone, *Econometrica,* Vol. 22, April 1954, pages 141-146.)

(iv) ...... econometrics is the branch of economics concerned with the empirical estimation of economic relationships. The 'metric' part of the world signifies measurement; and econometrics is basically concerned with measuring economic relationships. (Michael D. Intriligator, *Econometric Models, Techniques and Applications,* 1980, page 2.)

(v) Econometrics may be defined as statistical observation of theoretically founded concepts; or alternatively as mathematical economics working with measured data. (Jan Tinbergen, *Econometrics,* 1951.)

(vi) A main task of econometric theory is to provide a bridge between the exact relationships of economic theory and the disturbed relationships of economic reality (A.S. Goldberger, *Econometric Theory,* 1964, page 2.)

Econometrics may be considered as the integration of economics, mathematics and statistics for the purpose of providing numerical values for the parameters of economic relationships and verifying economic theories. In a way, it is a special type of economic analysis and research in which the general economic theory, formulated in mathematical terms (i.e., mathematical economics), is combined with empirical measurement (i.e., statistics) of economic phenomena. Economic statistics provides numerical data for econometrics and therefore, the success of econometrics depends upon the availability of good data.

In words of Jan Tinbergen,

(vii) "Econometrics is the name for a field of science in which mathematical-economics and mathematical-statistics are applied in combination. Econometrics, therefore, forms a borderland between two branches of science, with the advantages and disadvantages thereof, advantages; because new combinations are introduced which often open up new perspectives; disadvantages, because the work in this field requires skill in two domains which either takes up too much time or leads to insufficient training of its students in one of the two respects." [*Econometrics,* 1953 (Second impression, page 3)]

5.1.1 Indian Scholars of Econometrics*

The first major application of Econometrics was made in draft Second Five Year Plan prepared by Prof. P.C. Mahalanobis. This was the first Indian contribution to econometrics.

Other Indian econometricians who have contributed significantly to economic science, to Indian economic development, to International trade, and to Indian reforms are many. They have been honoured with Fellowship of Econometric Society (formed in 1932): P.C. Mahalanobis (1951), Amartya Sen (1968), Sukhamoy Chakarvarty (1969), A.L. Nagar (1970), T.N. Srinivasan (1970), C.R. Rao (1972), B.S. Minhas (1973), Jagdish Bhagwati (1973), Partha Dasgupta (1975), Mukul Mazumdar (1976), Avinash Dixit (1977), Prasantha Pattanaik (1978), G.S. Maddla (1981), Pradeep Dubey (1990), Kaushik Basu (1991), Debraj Ray (1993), Abhijit Banerjee (1995), Bhaskar Dutta (1996), Tanan Mitra (1997), V.V. Chari (1998), Vijay Krishna (2002), Kalyan Chatterjee (2003) and Arunava Sen (2003).

5.2 METHODOLOGY OF ECONOMETRICS

Starting from the relationships of economic theory, econometric inquiry generally proceeds along the following lines:

Step 1: Specify mathematical equation(s) to describe the relationships between economic variables as proposed by economic theory (*Specification*).

Step 2: Design methods and procedures based on statistical theory to obtain representative sample(s) from the real world.

Step 3: Development of methods of estimating the parameters of the specified relationship(s) described in step 3 (*Estimation*).

Step 4: Development of (statistical) methods of testing the validity of theory by using estimated parameters obtained by step 4 (*Verification*).

Step 5: Development of methods of making economic forecasts or policy implications based on the estimated parameters in case the theory stands out the test evolved under step 5 (*Application*).

The requirements and the possible errors in the above steps may be described through the chart on the next page.

---

* Economic and Political Weekly, February 7, 2004. Page 543.

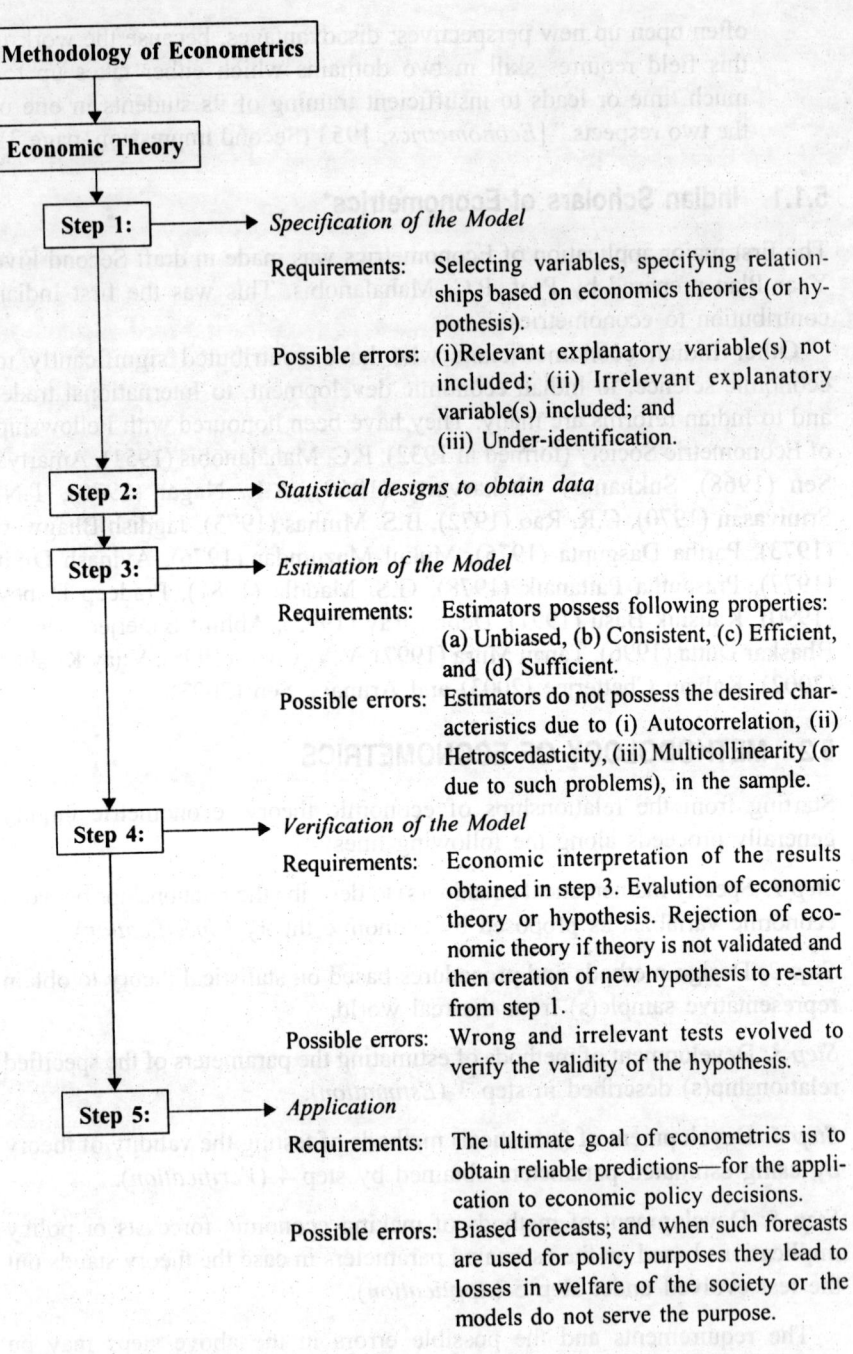

At times it is argued that why should one make a start from abstract economic theories which were never tested against the economic reality. After all economic theories were formulated only on the basic principles of the functioning of economic system and by applying deductive procedure. Such an argument of *measurement with no theory* is not without pitfalls.

For instance, how is one to know which of the mass data available are of interest in any particular situation? Furthermore, measurement alone is not sufficient. It may yield results which may not be meaningful, e.g., it may be found that the number of calves and the number of babies born in Delhi show a strong statistical correlation, which clearly does not make any sense.

Ideally, it is the theory which provides us an unambiguous ground for choosing the relevant variables. It is only when the complete searching of the theory does not give us any direction should we proceed to adopt the *measurement with no theory* approach.

When the term 'econometrics' was first used in the 1930s, it conveyed both the development of pure theory from a mathematical viewpoint and the empirical estimation of economic relationships. Now it signifies primarily the latter; the mathematical development of economic theory is now called mathematical economics. Very often, students wrongly assume econometrics as synonymous with the application of mathematics to economics. Econometrics is by no means the same as mathematical economics, nor is it identical with economic statistics. The relationship amongst these three branches of science is as described under:

5.2.1 Econometrics and Mathematical Economics

Mathematical economics puts the literary form of economics in terms of mathematical symbols. Such economics is merely an approach to economic analysis but does not differ from the non-mathematical approach to economics in any fundamental way. The major difference between the mathematical economics and the so-called *literary economics* lies principally in the fact that in the former the assumptions and conclusions are stated in mathematical symbols and equations rather than in words and sentences in the process of reasoning. Both describe the same economic relationships but in an exact form. Neither economic theory nor mathematical economics allows for random elements which might affect the (exact) relationship and render it *stochastic* in character. Relations in economic theory or in mathematical economics are of *non-stochastic* form. It is in this regard that econometrics differs from mathematical economics.

As explained in the chart above, although econometrics presupposes the economic theory in the mathematical form (step 1 in the chart), it does not assume that economic relations are nonstochastic (or exact).

Econometrics assumes every economic relation as a stochastic one, i.e., it assumes the presence of disturbances in the exact behavioural patterns as suggested by economic theory or mathematical economics. There are many reasons for assuming the presence of disturbance term in the exact relations to render it stochastic. Furthermore, econometric methods provide numerical values for the coefficients of the relationships under investigation. These values, as explained in the chart, are of great importance in making policy decisions. Mathematical economics does not provide such numerical values. But by combining mathematical formulations of theory with empirical data, econometrics enables us to pass from the abstract theoretical scheme to numerical results in concrete cases. In this way econometrics provides a bridge between the exact relations of economic theory and disturbed relations of economic reality.

5.2.2 Econometrics and Statistics

Statistics, as we all know, deals with collection of data, its tabulation in a desired form and then perhaps also the detection of relation between economic variables under investigation. Thus economic statistics is mainly a descriptive aspect of economic theory. Statistics also, as in the case of mathematical economics, does not provide the numerical values of the parameters involved in the economic relationships. Statistics provides numerical data for econometrics but does not itself make concrete the relationships between the economic magnitudes.

Economic statistics also differs from mathematical (or modern or inferential) statistics. The latter which is based upon the theory of probability, deals with the methods of measurement which are developed on the basis of controlled or carefully planned experiments. These statistical methods can be applied in economic relationships because such experiments cannot be designed (except in a very few cases, e.g., agricultural experiments or industrial experimentation) for economic phenomena. Yet fundamental ideas of mathematical statistics are applicable in econometrics; but they are not applied blindly or by analogy. They are used only after adapting them to random or stochastic behaviour occurring in economic problems. These adapted statistical methods are then called econometric methods.

5.3 GOALS OF ECONOMETRICS

Mathematical economics and economic statistics, as explained above, are the important aspects of econometrics. Mathematical formulations of theory provide rigour and precision while statistics provides the life-blood or the raw materials to this new field of knowledge, that is, econometrics.

But what is the prime goal(s) of econometrics?

Econometrics helps us to achieve the following three goals:

1. Judge the validity of the economic theories;
2. Supply the numerical estimates of the coefficients of the economic relationships which may be then used for sound economic policies; and
3. Forecast the future values of the economic magnitudes with certain degree of probability.

5.3.1 Verification of Economic Theories

Regardless of its elegance and logical consistency, no theory can stand on its own merits without some empirical testing; and econometrics enables us to make such empirical testing.

In the earlier stages of the development of economic theory, a so-called armchair economist might have speculated, through deductive procedure, about the forces that determine prices, production, investment, employment, etc., without concern for the ability of his theories to stand up under rigorous empirical tests. In other words, the economic theories thus developed in an abstract level were not tested against economic reality.

Econometrics aims primarily at the verification of economic theories and thereby helps us to know and decide how well economic theories expounded so far explain the actual behaviour of the economic units.

5.3.2 Estimation of Coefficients of Economic Relations

Econometrics is concerned with the analysis of measures of economic activity. It is constantly extending into areas of applications wider than statistics and economics themselves. Various econometric techniques are applied in order to obtain reliable estimates of the individual coefficients of the economic relationships from which different parameters of economic theory may be evaluated. For instance, econometrics can supply estimates of elasticities, multiplier coefficients, technical coefficients of production, marginal costs, marginal revenues, etc. The knowledge of all such coefficients is extremely valuable for the formulation of the sound economic policies.

For example, a producer suspects that the demand for his product is relatively inelastic. This is extremely valuable for the producer to know that, within a specified probability limit, this elasticity of demand is between say, –0.3 and –0.5. It does not then pay the manufacturer to decrease the price of the product because his receipts would be reduced. Econometrics can provide such estimates of elasticities. Knowledge of demand and supply elasticities permits an estimate of the incidence of sales taxes to the government. Will the consumer or the producer bear most of the tax? How much more? The answers to all such questions are provided by econometrics.

Estimation of production functions enable us to compare marginal productivities of labour and capital in various firms and industries; and also provide an insight of *returns to scale* the industry is experiencing.

Above examples show how useful econometrics can be for sound economic policies.

5.3.3 Forecast the Future Values of Economic Magnitudes

Apart from the evaluation of theory and estimation of numerical values of the coefficients of economic relations, econometric models can also be used for forecasting. Presently forecasting is becoming increasingly important both for the regulation of developed economies as well as for the planning of the economic development of undeveloped countries.

For example, from the estimate of the marginal propensity to consume, the investment multiplier can be computed by a simple formula: $k = \dfrac{1}{1 - MPC}$. Then, for a given increase in investment, the net eventual increase in national income, other things being equal, can be predicted within specified probability limits. If this forecast value of increase in national income turns out to be lower than what is desired, the government must take different measures in order to achieve that target. In this way the 'forecasts' enable the policy maker to judge whether it is necessary to take any measures in order to influence the relevant economic variable.

5.4   THE NATURE OF THE ECONOMETRICS APPROACH

The various steps described in the chart (section 5.2) form important stages in the methodology of any econometric research.

Let us restate them in the form of different stages which every researcher must take into account if nonsense or ambiguous results are to be avoided.

Stage 1: The first and the foremost step of every econometric research is the specification of the model. This will involve determination of:

(a)   the dependent and explanatory variables to be included in the model,
(b)   the *a priori* assumptions about the size and the sign of the parameters (on the basis of theoretical criteria) of the model, and
(c)   the mathematical form of the model.

As already discussed, the specification of the econometric model will have to be based on economic theory.

Stage 2: Estimation of the model by means of appropriate econometric method will include the following steps:

(a)   Collection of data on the variables included in the model. (Cross-section or Time-series).
(b)   Examination of multicollinearity problem.
(c)   Examination of the identification conditions if the model involves more than single equation.
(d)   Choice of appropriate econometric technique for estimation of the model.

Stage 3: The estimated model is to be evaluated on the basis of certain criteria to see whether the estimates are reliable.

The evaluation consists of deciding whether the estimates of the parameters are theoretically meaningful and statistically significant. The following three criteria are used for such evaluation:

(a) *Economic 'a priori' criteria:* These are determined by the principles of economic theory. If estimates of the parameters turn up with sign and size not conforming to *a priori* criteria, they should be rejected unless there is a good reason to believe that in the particular instance the principles of economic theory do not hold. In such cases the reasons for accepting the estimates with the *different* (from economic theory) sign and size must be stated clearly.

(b) *Statistical criteria (First-order tests):* These tests are determined by statistical theory and include correlation coefficient and the standard deviation (or standard error) of the estimates. The square of the correlation coefficient (called Coefficient of Determination) computed from the sample data explains the percentage of the total variations in the dependent variable due to changes in explanatory variables. The standard error of the estimates describes the dispersion of the estimates around the true parameter. Hence the larger the standard error, the less reliable it is and vice versa.

(c) *Econometric criteria (Second-order tests):* These tests are given by the theory of econometrics. Such tests help us to establish whether the estimates have the desirable properties of unbiasedness, consistency, sufficiency, etc. If the assumptions of the econometric technique applied (for the estimation of the parameters) are not satisfied the estimates cease to possess some of the desirable properties. The assumptions of the various econometric techniques differ and hence there are various econometric criteria for each method. For instance, Durbin-Waston *d-Statistic* is one of the econometric criteria used in evaluation of the estimates (to test the validity of the assumption of non-autocorrelated disturbance terms). Another example is the 'test' to establish the identification conditions of a relationship.

The researcher must use all the above criteria; economic, statistical and econometric before he accepts or rejects the estimates.

Stage 4: The final stage is to examine the forecasting power of the model.

One of the major objectives of econometrics is forecasting. By forecasting* we mean the prediction of values of certain variables outside the available sample of data. Forecasting is closely related to policy choice and policy evaluation. In fact, most methods of policy evaluation rely upon a specific type of forecast. Therefore the forecaster and decision maker are often combined in the same person or agency responsible for both forecasting and policy evaluation.

---

*Forecasting is a special kind of prediction. By prediction we do not necessarily mean explanations of events that will occur in the future. One may attempt to predict events that have occurred but which have not been observed.

It is essential to examine the forecasting power of the model. Many a times, the model may be 'economically' meaningful and, statistically and econometrically correct for the sample period for which the model has been estimated, yet it may possess very poor forecasting power. This may be due to sensitiveness of the structural parameters involved in the model; or due to the following reasons:

(a) The values of the explanatory variables used in the forecast may not be accurate;
(b) The estimates of the coefficients may not be correct due to deficiencies in the data used.

One procedure to establish the forecasting power of the model is to use the estimates of the model for a period not included in the sample. The estimated value (i.e., forecast value) is then compared with the actual (i.e., realised value) magnitude of the relevant dependent variable. The difference between these two values is tested statistically. If after conducting the desired test of significance we observe that this difference is significant, we conclude that the forecasting power of the model is poor.

There are various tests for establishing the forecasting power of the model.

5.5 THEORETICAL AND APPLIED ECONOMETRICS

Econometrics, as in the case of all sciences, can also be distinguished into two branches: *Theoretical and Applied.* Theoretical econometrics deals with the development of the appropriate methods for measuring economic relationships described by econometric models. These methods may be classified into two groups:

(a) Single-equation techniques which are applied to one relationship at a time; and
(b) Simultaneous-equation techniques which are applied to all the relationships of the model simultaneously.

Also it is the concern of theoretical econometrics to spell out the assumptions of these methods, their properties, and what happens to these properties when one or more of the assumptions of the method are not fulfilled.

Applied econometrics describes the practical value of econometric research. It deals with the applications of econometric techniques developed in theoretical econometrics to different fields of economic theory for its verification and forecasting. Presently more and more empirical studies in the fields of market demand and supply, production functions, cost functions, consumption and investment functions, are being carried out with the help of econometrics. The applied econometrics has made it possible to obtain numerical results from these studies which are of great importance to our planners.

ASSIGNMENTS

1. 'Econometrics is a branch of Economics in which measurement of the relationships discussed in *a-priori* economic analysis are studied. In this sense, econometrics plays a service function for economic analysis, but in a more positive role it may also lead to the discovery of new relationships or theories hitherto unsuspected from *a-priori* consideration alone.'
   Discuss the above statement given by an econometrician Prof. Klein.

2. How would you define Econometrics? How does it differ from Mathematical economics and Statistics?
   Describe the main steps involved in any econometric research by taking an example from economic theory.

3. Considering the following relations, how would you explain that economic theory postulates exact relationships between the economic variables. How can these be transformed into econometric relations?

   (a) Demand function: $D_x = \alpha + \beta_1 p_x + \beta_2 y$
        D_x = quantity demanded, p_x = price, and y = income.

   (b) Supply function: $S_x = \alpha + \beta_1 p_x + \beta_2 p_f$
        S_x = quantity supplied, p_x = price, and p_f = price of factor input.

   (c) Cost function: $C = \alpha + \beta x$
                   C = total cost, and x = total output.

   (d) Consumption function; $C = \alpha + \beta Y$
                   C = Consumption expenditure, and
                   Y = disposable income.

   (i) What is the economic meaning of the coefficients involved in all the above relationships?

   (ii) What would you expect the sign and size of the coefficients to be in each of the above relationships?

4. What is Econometrics and what are its components? Describe the function of each component. Give examples in support of your answer.

5. Name and describe three relationships studied in Economic theory which can be estimated as subject matter of Econometrics. What are the parameters of these relationships?

6. Write an essay on the need for and the inherent difficulties of the use of the *probability approach* to Economics.

7. Do you agree with the view that in econometrics, as distinct from mathematical economics, one cannot neglect the stochastic variables in the relationships being considered? Give reasons for your answer.

8. Write an essay discussing the inter-relationship among Mathematical Economics, Economic Statistics and Econometrics.

9. Differentiate between Economic and Econometric Model. Describe the methodology involved in an econometric model.

10. Discuss the role of measurement in Economics.

6

Simple Regression Estimation and Testing Procedures

Most of economics is concerned with relations among variables. These relations when phrased in mathematical terms can predict the effect of one variable on another. For example, assuming that income, prices and all other determinants of demand are constant, we can express the quantity demanded (q) as a function of the price (p) of that commodity only. This may be put in the form: $q = f(p)$. Similarly we are familiar with other functions (with different assumptions), such as, Supply functions: $S = f(p)$; Cost functions: $C = f(Q)$; Utility functions: $U = f(q = $ quantity consumed); Production functions: $Q = f(x_1, x_2...$: amounts of different inputs); and many others. These functional relationships define the dependence of dependent variable upon the independent variable (s) in the specific form. The functional form may be linear, quadratic, logarithmic, exponential or hyperbolic.

In this chapter we shall consider a simple linear regression model, that is; a relationship between two variables related in a form of linear function.

We shall first discuss two important forms of relation; stochastic and non-stochastic which are important relations in econometric methods.

6.1 STOCHASTIC* AND NON-STOCHASTIC RELATIONS

A relation between X and Y characterised as $Y = f(X)$ is said to be deterministic or nonstochastic if for each value of independent variable (X) there is one and only one corresponding value of dependent variable (Y). On the other hand, a relation between X and Y is said to be stochastic if for a particular value of X there is whole probability distribution of values of Y. In such case for any given value of X, the dependent variable Y assumes some specific value only with some probability. Let us illustrate the distinction between stochastic and nonstochastic relations with the help of demand function.

---

* The word 'Stochastic' comes from a Greek word 'Stokhos' meaning 'a bull's eye'. The outcome of throwing darts on a board is a Stochastic process; a process fraught with misses.

Assuming that demand for a certain commodity depends on its price (other determinants taken to be constant) and functional form being linear, the relationship can then be put as:
$$q = f(p) = \alpha + \beta p.$$
Suppose for a particular data on p and q we obtain; $\alpha = 25$ and $\beta = -2$ so that demand equation becomes:
$$q = 25 - 2p.$$
The above relation between p and q is such for a particular value of p, say two units; there is only one corresponding value of q, which is 21 units. If the price is five units, the quantity demanded turns out to be 15 units and so on. This is, therefore, a deterministic (nonstochastic) relation since for each price there is always only one corresponding quantity demanded or sold. But such an exact and deterministic relation between p and q is never true in the real world. The deterministic behaviour of the above relationship breaks down when *Ceteris Paribus* condition is relaxed. We, therefore, rewrite the demand equation as:
$$q = 25 - 2p + U;$$
where U is commonly known as *random disturbance*, since it disturbs an otherwise deterministic relation. On assumption of certain probability distribution of this random error term, there will be more than one quantity demanded for each price as shown in the table given on next page.

A diagrammatic representation of the stochastic and non-stochastic relations is shown in Figs. 6.1 and 6.2.

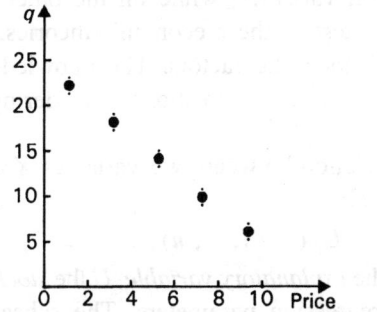
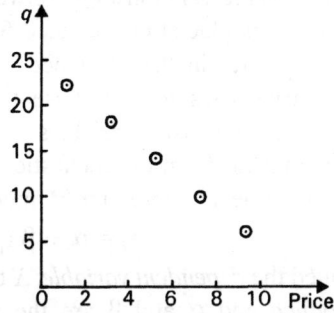

Fig. 6.1: Stochastic Relation   **Fig. 6.2:** Nonstochastic Relation

The relation $q = 25 - 2p + U$ is a stochastic one because with presence of the disturbance term, there are three quantities demanded for each price with different probabilities.

We also observe that in stochastic relations different values of independent variable (p) give rise to different probability distributions of dependent variable (q). In the given example; when $p = 1$ we obtain probability distribution I of values of q with mean = 24 and variance = 0.5; if $p = 2$ we obtain another probability distribution II of values of q with mean = 21

	Stochastic Relation			Probability Distribution of U	
p	$q\ (= 25 - 2p + U)$		Mean value (q)	U	$f(U)$
				−1	0.25
				0	0.50
				+1	0.25
1	I	23 with probability 0.25 24 " " 0.50 25 " " 0.25	24		
2	II	20 with probability 0.25 21 " " 0.50 22 " " 0.25	21		
⋮		⋮			
10	III	4 with probability 0.25 5 " " 0.50 6 " " 0.25	5		

and variance = 0.5. Thus, the probability distributions of dependent variable differ in respect of mean but not in variance. In economic theory all relations are stated in a non-stochastic form but in reality such relations never exist.

6.2   THE SIMPLE LINEAR REGRESSION MODEL

Relationships suggested by economic theory are usually specified as exact or deterministic relationships between variables; while on the other hand much stress is placed on the need for testing these economic theories. This implies a belief in the existence of stochastic factors. The knowledge of econometrics tries to test these theoretical propositions considering the existence of stochastic variables.

The simplest form of stochastic relation between two variables X and Y is called a linear* regression** model:

$$Y_i = \alpha + \beta X_i + U_i \ (i = 1, ..., n)$$

Y is called the *dependent variable*, X the *explanatory variable*, U the *stochastic disturbance* and α and β are the regression parameters. The subscript i

---

* The term 'linear' can be interpreted in two different ways.

A function is said to be linear in X if X appears with a power or index of 1 only and is not multiplied or divided by any other variable.

A function is said to be linear in the parameter β, if β appears with a power 1 only and is not multiplied or divided by any other parameter.

Of the above two interpretations of linearity, linearity in parameters is relevant for our Regression Model.

** The term 'regression' is also used in two different ways:

'Classical' (or Least Squares) regression   or 'Bivariate' regression. If Y_i is a random variable and X is not (or vice versa), we have least square regression. If both y_i and x_i are random variables, we have a bivariate regressions.

refers to the ith observation. α and β are to be estimated on the basis of the given data on the variables X and Y.

The stochastic nature of the regression model implies that for every value of X there is a whole probability distribution of values of Y. In other words the value of Y can never be predicted exactly. This uncertainty concerning the value of Y arises because of the presence of the stochastic term U which imparts randomness to Y. How are we to justify the insertion of the U-term in the model?

Ignoring for the moment the probability that the theory may be incorrect, we can give the following reasons for the insertion of the disturbances term in our model:

(a) *Due to errors in equation:* Suppose, in the model $Y = \alpha + \beta X + U$; Y denotes the consumption expenditure and X denotes disposable income; as such our model states that consumption expenditures of households depend entirely on their disposable incomes. In fact there are many other factors, such as, size—composition of family, age variations, habits, tastes, etc., on which the consumption expenditure depends, yet we have ignored them. Definitely, therefore, to the extent that we ignore these factors which influence that consumption we are trying to explain. We would not expect our relationship to be exact unless these factors are assumed to remain constant. If all these factors remained constant while our data on Y and X were being collected, our simple model ought to give an exact relationship between consumption expenditure and disposable income. Unfortunately, this is never the case and insertion of U in the model represents agglomerate effect of all these omitted variables.

(b) *Due to errors in measurement* (Errors in variables): Another justification for the insertion of a disturbance term is that it represents the measurement errors in the recording or processing of the sample data on Y. Thus, the disturbance term also reflects the errors in the regress and (or dependent variable).*

(c) *Due to imperfect specification of the mathematical form of the model*: We may have linearised a possibly nonlinear relationship between X and Y. Or we may have left out of the model some equations. It is because the economic phenomena are much more complex than a single equation may reveal. For example, price determines and is determined by the quantity supplied (or quantity demanded) in the market. Under such circumstances if we attempt to study the phenomena with a single equation model, we are bound to commit an error. Thus the disturbance term represents such an

---

* The observations on regressors (or explanatory variables) are assumed to be error free. This is the basic requirement for keeping error terms not related with explanatory variables. Consequences of such errors are dealt in Chapter 11.

error which may be due to the imperfect specification of the form of the model, that is, of the number of its equations.

(d) *Due to aggregation:* We often use aggregate data, such as aggregate consumption or aggregate income; in which we add magnitudes referring to individuals whose behaviour is dissimilar. Thus aggregation of data introduce error in the relationship. Such aggregations may be in the form of: aggregation overtime, spatial aggregation, cross-section aggregation and so on.

Thus we measure as many factors as possible and include them in our equation of the model as separate variables, while we dispose of all the remaining under the heading "random disturbances" relying on laws of probability to tell us what to expect from the neglected factors. Putting it straight, insertion of U in our model, in a way depicts *confession of our ignorance.*

It follows, therefore, that the consumption expenditure Y (dependent variable) will depend not only on the disposable income X (explanatory variable) but also on a large number of random causes which we summarise in the form of stochastic disturbances. The probability distribution of Y and its characteristics are then determined by the values of X and the probability distribution of U.

For the full specification of the model we must notify the following three things:

1. The mathematical form of the relation between the variables considered in the model.
2. The probability distribution of disturbance term.
3. The nature of the values of the explanatory variables.

For a simple linear regression model, these specifications are grouped in the form of five basic assumptions; usually known as Assumptions of Linear Regression Model.

Assumption 1. U_i is a random real variable and has normal distribution.
Assumption 2.   The mean value of U_i is *zero.* $E(U_i) = 0$ $(i = 1, ..., n)$
Assumption 3.   The variance of U_i is constant.

$$E(U_i^2) = \sigma^2 \ (\sigma^2 \text{ is a constant})$$

The assumption is known as the assumption of *Homoscedasticity.*

Assumption 4.   The disturbance terms of different observations (U_i, U_j) are independent. $E(U_iU_j) = 0$ $(i \neq j)$
The assumption is known as the assumption of *Nonautocorrelation.*

Assumption 5.   The explanatory variable(s) is nonstochastic variable and is measured without error; U_i is independent of the explanatory variable(s).
$E(X_i\ U_j) = X_i\ E(U_j) = 0$, for all $i, j = 1, ..., n$.

The regression equation: $Y = \alpha + \beta X + U$ along with the given five assumptions represents the *Classical Linear Regression Model*. The five assumptions have important roles to play in the sampling distributions of parameters: α and β. They, therefore, need to be understood very clearly.

The first four assumptions relate to distribution of U while the last one concerns the explanatory variable. The assumptions 1 and 2 state that for each value of X, U is normally distributed with zero mean, that is U is continuous variable symmetrically distributed around zero. The third assumption of homoscedasticity means that every distribution of U has the same variance σ^2 (which is assumed to be some constant value) whose value is not known. In other words this assumption states that for all values of X_i, whether lower or higher, the variance of the distribution of U remains same. Thus first three assumptions fully specify the distribution of U. The interpretation of the fourth assumption is that our observations are independent of each other so that the disturbances of different observations turn out to be non-autoregressive. The final assumption which refers to the explanatory variable states that values of X_i are controllable and predictable and that the covariance between U and X is zero; that is explanatory variable is independent of the disturbance term.

6.2.1 IMPORTANCE OF ASSUMPTIONS OF RESIDUALS

(i) *Independency and Constant Variance:* After we compute the regression equation, we should examine the residuals $(Y - \hat{Y})$ where $\hat{Y}$ is the estimate of Y from the fitted equation $\hat{Y} = \hat{\alpha} + \hat{\beta} X$. One may notice a peculiar characteristic in the values of residuals; that is, the magnitude of residuals systematically may increase or decrease with the values of the independent variable X. This dependency of residuals is termed as problem of *heteroscedasticity*. Sometimes the absolute values of the residuals exhibit a systematic pattern, such as, at first the values appear to increase, then decrease and then again increase. This indicates the violation of another assumption of 'independency of residual terms' and is known as *autocorrelation*. These two problems of autocorrelation and heteroscedasticity have been examined in detail in chapter 9 on violation of assumptions.

(ii) *Left out Variables:* In many empirical works, the residuals cluster form definite patterns. Such patterns are possibly caused by some omitted variables. As such, when the values of residuals are arranged in a systematic way with respect to a variable which is left out from the regression, the residual form into clusters.

The variables are, at times, ignored by the investigator because they are difficult to be quantified, e.g., managerial input, quality of labour and technology in the production function. A part of influence of such omitted variables is captured by the included variables while a portion (depending on the nature of included variable) is retained by the residuals. In such situations, we may be able either to say something about the direction of the bias in the estimated coefficients or to insert some substitute variables that capture the effects. These substitute variables are called *Proxy variables*. A detailed discussion on various types of mis-specifications of such nature is given in Chapters 10 and 11.

(iii) *Nonlinearity:* Sometimes systematic pattern in residuals are produced because of wrong functional form assumed by us. While explaining the estimation procedure, only linear form was assumed. But such an assumption may be unduly limiting in some cases and one may wish to utilize less restrictive functional form, say, log-normal or semi-log. There can be other functional form as well. The estimation of functional form other than linear can be done after making suitable transformation of the variables so long as the residual is additive to the transformed equation. A detailed analysis on estimation of various functional forms is given in the seventh chapter.

(iv) *Data Deficiencies:* The procedure of least-squares for estimation of regression equation is based on minimisation of sum of squares of vertical (or horizontal) distances of the data points from the estimated line. Nevertheless, it is important to realize that other estimation techniques are feasible and occasionally desirable.*

However, the loss associated with each deviation from the line of best fit is different in different procedures of estimation. Loss associated in case of least-squares procedure is more than what it is in case of procedure that minimises absolute deviations in case of each deviation from the line of best fit.

In case of least-squares procedure, since we minimize the sum of squared deviations, the loss associated with each individual deviation is that deviation squared. (For example, if $d = 8$, loss = 64, if $d = -2$, loss = 4.)

In case of least-absolute-value procedure of estimation, the loss is absolute value of deviation (that is, if $d = 8$, loss = 8; if $d = -2$, loss = 2).

The loss function of both the procedures are symmetric with respect to sign of deviation, but the least-squares loss function penalizes large deviations more than the least-absolute-value loss function. In other words, we say that the least-squares procedure of estimation gives more weightage to the large deviation and hence it is very sensitive to data points which lie far from the rest of the observation points. We call such data points *outliers*.

---

* (a) We can think of passing a line in such a way that the sum of squares of the perpendicular distances are minimized rather than vertical or horizontal. Such an estimated regression line is called *orthogonal regression*.

 (b) Secondly, we may in certain situations minimize the sum of absolute distances rather than the sum of squares of the distances. The estimators developed by such a procedure are called LAR (Least Absolute Residual) or MAD (Minimum Absolute Deviations) estimators.

'Outliers' are caused by abnormalities in the data. The estimated line shifts very significantly when 'outliers' are retained or removed from the rest of observations. Hence there is a dilemma; whether to retain or reject the outliers from the data. If we estimate a regression equation, look at the residuals, then decide which observations are outliers. We re-estimate the equation omitting these observations, the standard errors and confidence intervals we report now are no longer valid (since some observations have been dropped). On the other, if we do not discard these outliers, even in views of some information we have on them, the results we get are not meaningful. Hence leaving the outliers in, produces meaningless results while discarding them produces uncertain standard errors. The best course is to estimate the regressions with and without outliers to get a good 'feel' for the sensitivity of the results to the precision of the outliers and then decide accordingly. But in case there are many extreme observations and that we have a strong a-priori reason to discard them, an alternative procedure is to apply method of minimizing the sum of absolute errors: $\Sigma |Y_i - \hat{\alpha} - \hat{\beta}X_i|$ rather than the procedure of OLS. The method of LAR (Least Absoulte Residual) is computationally complicated to be discussed in the present text.

6.2.2 Impact of Assumptions of Residuals on Dependent Variables

The effect of first three assumptions on the probability distribution of dependent variable Y can now be rationalised.

(a) In the equation $Y_i = \alpha + \beta X_i + U_i$; Y_i is a linear function of U_i. Since it is assumed that U is normally distributed, it follows that Y_i is also normally distributed.

(b) $Y_i = \alpha + \beta X_i + U_i$; $\therefore E(Y_i) = E(\alpha + \beta X_i + U_i)$

$$= \alpha + \beta X_i \; [\because E(U_i) = 0]$$

Therefore, we say that mean of Y_i is given by $(\alpha + \beta X_i)$

(c) Var $(Y_i) = E(Y_i - \bar{Y})^2 = E[Y_i - E(Y_i)]^2$

$$= E[\alpha + \beta X_i + U_i - (\alpha + \beta X_i)]^2$$

$$= E(U_i)^2$$

$$= \sigma^2 \left[\because E\left(U_i^2\right) = \sigma^2\right]$$

Therefore, we say that variance of Y_i is equal to σ^2.

Thus with the first three assumptions of U, we are assuming indirectly that Y_i is normally distributed variable with mean $(\alpha + \beta X_i)$ and variance σ^2; symbolically;

$$Y_i \sim N\left(\alpha + \beta X_i, \sigma^2\right)$$

We illustrate this in Fig. 6.3.

$Y = \alpha + \beta X$ represents the population regression line. This regression line is unknown since we do not know the exact values of α and β. We try to estimate their values on the basis of sample data. On substituting these estimated values in the population regression line we obtain sample regression line which in turn serves as an estimate of the population regression line. If the estimated values of α and β are given by $\hat{\alpha}$ and $\hat{\beta}$ respectively then sample regression line is given by: $\hat{Y}_i = \hat{\alpha} + \hat{\beta}X_i$; $\hat{Y}_i$ represents the fitted values of actually observed values Y_i. We cannot expect the observed values (Y_i) to lie exactly on the sample regression line $(\hat{\alpha} + \hat{\beta}X_i)$. Values of Y_i and $\hat{Y}_i$ will differ and this difference is called a residual and symbolised as e_i.

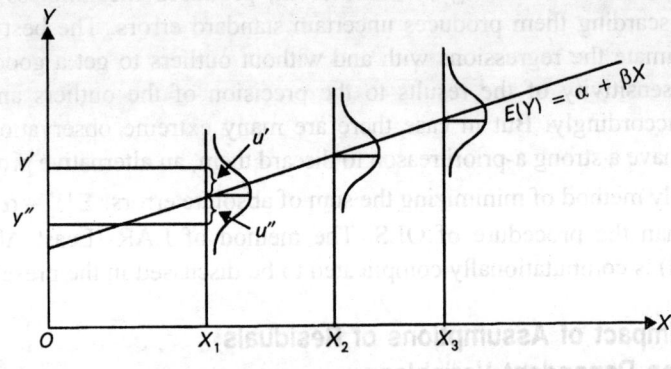

Fig. 6.3
(See fig. 9.8 also for exact representation of distribution of *U*)

∴ The true relationship is given by:

$$Y_i = \alpha + \beta X_i + U_i$$

and, the estimated relationship is represented by:

$$Y_i = \hat{\alpha} + \hat{\beta}X_i + e_i$$

The difference between these two relations along with the difference between residual and disturbance has been illustrated in Fig. 6.4.

AA' is the true regression line and *B'B* is the estimated regression line. *P* represents one of the observations in the sample data. e_i differs from U_i because the true values of the parameters are different from their estimated values. In fact we can view the residual e_i as the estimate of the disturbance U_i.

6.3 ESTIMATION OF REGRESSION PARAMETERS

Estimation of α and β by least squares method (OLS) or classical least squares (CLS) involves finding values for the estimates $\hat{\alpha}$ and $\hat{\beta}$ which will minimise the sum of the squared residuals: Σe_i^2.

From fitted regression line:

$$Y_i = \hat{\alpha} + \hat{\beta}X + e_i; \text{ we obtain:}$$

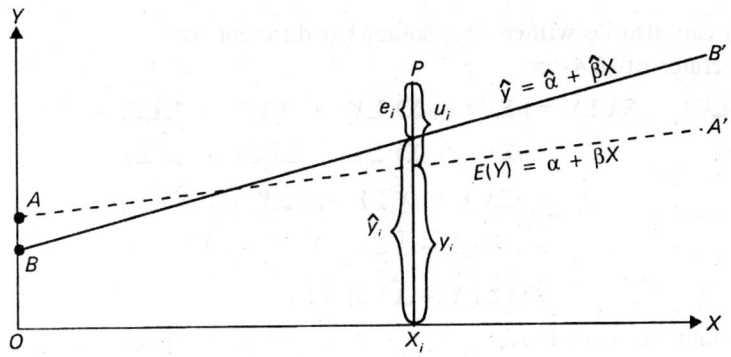

Fig. 6.4

$$e_i = Y_i - (\hat{\alpha} + \hat{\beta}_i)$$

$$\therefore \quad \sum_{i=1}^{n} e_i^2 = \sum_{i=1}^{n} (Y_i - \hat{\alpha} - \hat{\beta}X_i)^2$$

To find the values of α and β that minimise this sum, we have to differentiate with respect to $\hat{\alpha}$ and $\hat{\beta}$ and set the partial derivatives equal to zero.

$$\partial/\partial\hat{\alpha}\left[\Sigma e_i^2\right] = -2\Sigma\,(Y_i - \hat{\alpha} - \hat{\beta}X_i) = 0$$

$$\partial/\partial\hat{\beta}\left[\Sigma e_i^2\right] = -2\Sigma X_i\,(Y_i - \hat{\alpha} - \hat{\beta}X_i) = 0$$

or, equivalently, $\Sigma Y_i = n\hat{\alpha} + \hat{\beta}\Sigma X_i$ ...(6.1)

$$\Sigma X_i Y_i = \hat{\alpha}\Sigma X_i + \hat{\beta}\Sigma X_i^2 \qquad \text{...(6.2)}$$

From (6.1) we have,

$$n\hat{\alpha} = \Sigma Y_i - \hat{\beta}\Sigma X_i$$

$$\hat{\alpha} = \overline{Y} - \hat{\beta}\overline{X} \qquad \text{...(6.3)}$$

Substituting value of $\hat{\alpha}$ in (6.2) we get

$$\Sigma X_i Y_i = (\overline{Y} - \hat{\beta}\overline{X})\,\Sigma X_i + \hat{\beta}\Sigma X_i^2$$

$$\Sigma X_i Y_i = \overline{Y}\Sigma X_i - \hat{\beta}\overline{X}\,\Sigma X_i + \hat{\beta}\Sigma X_i^2$$

$$\Sigma X_i Y_i - \overline{Y}\Sigma X_i = \hat{\beta}(\Sigma X_i^2 - \overline{X}\Sigma X_i)$$

$$\therefore \qquad \hat{\beta} = \frac{\Sigma X_i\,Y_i - \overline{Y}\Sigma X_i}{\Sigma X_i^2 - \overline{X}\Sigma X_i}$$

$$= \frac{n\Sigma X_i\,Y_i - \Sigma Y_i\Sigma X_i}{n\Sigma X_i^2 - (\Sigma X_i)^2} \qquad \text{...(6.4)}$$

(6.4) can also be written in a somewhat different way.
Numerator of (6.4) is:

$$
\begin{aligned}
n\Sigma X_i Y_i - \Sigma X_i \Sigma Y_i &= n\Sigma X_i Y_i - \Sigma Y_i \Sigma X_i + (\Sigma X_i \Sigma Y_i - \Sigma X_i \Sigma Y_i) \\
&= n\Sigma X_i Y_i - \Sigma Y_i \Sigma X_i - \Sigma X_i \Sigma Y_i + \Sigma X_i \Sigma Y_i \\
&= n\Sigma X_i Y_i - n\overline{X}\,\Sigma Y_i - n\overline{Y}\Sigma X_i + n^2 \overline{X}\,\overline{Y} \\
&= n(\Sigma X_i Y_i - \overline{X}\Sigma Y_i - \overline{Y}\Sigma X_i + n\,\overline{X}\,\overline{Y}) \\
&= n\{\Sigma (X_i - \overline{X})(Y_i - \overline{Y})\}
\end{aligned}
$$

Denominator of (6.4) is:

$$
\begin{aligned}
n\Sigma X_i^2 - (\Sigma X_i)^2 &= n\Sigma X_i^2 - 2(\Sigma X_i)^2 + (\Sigma X_i)^2 \\
&= n\Sigma X_i^2 - 2\Sigma X_i \Sigma X_i + (\Sigma X_i)^2 \\
&= n\Sigma X_i^2 - 2n\overline{X}\,\Sigma X_i + n^2 \overline{X}^2 \\
&= n(\Sigma X_i^2 - 2\overline{X}\Sigma X_i + n\overline{X}^2) \\
&= n\Sigma (X_i - \overline{X})^2
\end{aligned}
$$

$$
\therefore \quad \hat{\beta} = \frac{n\Sigma (X_i - \overline{X})(Y_i - \overline{Y})}{n\Sigma (X_i - \overline{X})^2}
$$

Now denoting $(X_i - \overline{X})$ as x_i and $(Y_i - \overline{Y})$ as y_i we get;

$$
\hat{\beta} = \frac{\Sigma x_i y_i}{\Sigma x_i^2} \qquad\qquad ...(6.5)
$$

6.3.1 Estimation of a Function with Intercept Zero

Suppose it is desired to fit the line: $Y = \alpha + \beta X + U$, subject to the restriction $\alpha = 0$.

To estimate β, the problem is put in a form of restricted minimisation problem and then *Lagrange method* is applied.

We minimise:
$$
\sum_{i=1}^{n} e_i^2 = \sum_{i=1}^{n}(Y_i - \hat{\alpha} - \hat{\beta}X_i)^2
$$

Subject to:
$$
\hat{\alpha} = 0
$$

The composite function then becomes: $Z = \Sigma(Y_i - \hat{\alpha} - \hat{\beta}X_i)^2 - \lambda\hat{\alpha}$, where λ is Lagrange multiplier, and we minimise the function with respect to $\hat{\alpha}$, $\hat{\beta}$ and λ:

$$
\partial Z/\partial\hat{\alpha} = -2\Sigma(Y_i - \hat{\alpha} - \hat{\beta}X_i) - \lambda = 0 \qquad\qquad ...(i)
$$

$$
\partial Z/\partial\hat{\beta} = -2\Sigma(Y_i - \hat{\alpha} - \hat{\beta}X_i)\,X_i = 0 \qquad\qquad ...(ii)
$$

$$
\partial Z/\partial\lambda = -\hat{\alpha} = 0 \qquad\qquad ...(iii)
$$

Substituting (iii) in (ii) and rearranging we obtain

$$-2\Sigma X_i(Y_i - \hat{\beta}X_i) = 0$$

$$\Sigma Y_i X_i - \hat{\beta}\Sigma X_i^2 = 0$$

$$\hat{\beta} = \frac{\Sigma X_i Y_i}{\Sigma X_i^2}$$

This formula involves the actual values of the variables, and not their deviations, as in the case of unrestricted value of β.

6.4 STATISTICAL PROPERTIES OF LEAST SQUARES ESTIMATOR

(i) *Linearity*

$$\hat{\beta} = \frac{\Sigma(X_i - \bar{X})(Y_i - \bar{Y})}{\Sigma(X_i - \bar{X})^2} \qquad \text{(from 6.5)}$$

$$\hat{\beta} = \frac{\Sigma Y_i(X_i - \bar{X}) - \bar{Y}\Sigma(X_i - \bar{X})}{\Sigma(X_i - \bar{X})^2}$$

$$\hat{\beta} = \frac{\Sigma Y_i(X_i - \bar{X})}{\Sigma(X_i - \bar{X})^2} \qquad [\because \bar{Y}\Sigma(X_i - \bar{X}) = 0]$$

$$\hat{\beta} = \frac{\Sigma Y_i x_i}{\Sigma x_i^2}$$

Let us suppose that,

$$\frac{x_i}{\Sigma x_i^2} = k_i \ (i = 1, ..., n)$$

$$\therefore \quad \hat{\beta} = \sum_{i=1}^{n} k_i Y_i \qquad \qquad ...(6.6)$$

Similarly (6.3) gives $\hat{a} = \bar{Y} - \hat{\beta}\bar{X} = \frac{1}{n}\Sigma Y_i - \bar{X}\Sigma k_i Y_i$

$$\therefore \quad \hat{\alpha} = \Sigma\left[\frac{1}{n} - \bar{X}k_i\right]Y_i \qquad \qquad ...(6.7)$$

Thus both $\hat{\alpha}$ and $\hat{\beta}$ are expressed as linear functions of the Y's.

(ii) *Unbiasedness:*

$$\hat{\beta} = \Sigma k_i Y_i \qquad \qquad \text{(from 6.6)}$$

$$= \Sigma k_i(\alpha + \beta X_i + U_i)$$

$$= \alpha\Sigma k_i + \beta\Sigma k_i X_i + \Sigma k_i U_i \qquad \qquad ...(6.8)$$

$$\therefore \quad k_i = \frac{x_i}{\Sigma x_i^2} \qquad \therefore \Sigma k_i = \frac{\Sigma x_i}{\Sigma x_i^2} = 0;$$

and, $\quad \Sigma k_i X_i = \Sigma k_i \ (x_i + \overline{X}) = \dfrac{\Sigma x_i^2}{\Sigma x_i^2} = 1 \hspace{3cm} ...(6.9)$

Substituting these values in (6.8) we obtain,

$$\hat{\beta} = \beta + \Sigma k_i U_i \hspace{4cm} ...(6.10)$$

$$E (\hat{\beta}) = E (\beta) + \Sigma k_i E (U_i) = \beta$$

Equation (6.7) gives,

$$\hat{\alpha} = \Sigma \left(\frac{1}{n} - \overline{X} k_i \right) Y_i$$

$$= \Sigma \left(\frac{1}{n} - \overline{X} k_i \right) (\alpha + \beta X_i + U_i)$$

$$= \alpha + \beta \frac{1}{n} \Sigma X_i + \frac{1}{n} \Sigma U_i - \alpha \overline{X} \Sigma k_i - \beta \overline{X} \Sigma k_i X_i - \overline{X} \Sigma k_i U_i$$

$$= \alpha + \beta \overline{X} + \frac{1}{n} \Sigma U_i - \beta \overline{X} - \overline{X} \Sigma k_i U_i$$

$$= \alpha + \frac{1}{n} \Sigma U_i - \overline{X} \Sigma k_i U_i \hspace{3cm} ...(6.11)$$

$$\therefore \ E(\hat{\alpha}) = \alpha + \frac{1}{n} \Sigma E(U_i) - \overline{X} \Sigma k_i E(U_i)$$

$$E(\hat{\alpha}) = \alpha$$

Thus, we prove that $\hat{\alpha}$ and $\hat{\beta}$ are unbiased estimators of α and β.

(iii) *Minimum variance of $\hat{\alpha}$ and $\hat{\beta}$*: Now we have to establish that out of the class of linear unbiased estimators of α and β; $\hat{\alpha}$ and $\hat{\beta}$ possess the smallest sampling variances. For this we shall first obtain the variance of $\hat{\beta}$ and then establish that it is the minimum variance.

$$\text{Var} (\hat{\beta}) = E[(\hat{\beta} - \beta)^2]$$

$$= E[\Sigma k_i U_i)^2] \hspace{3cm} ...\text{from equation (6.10)}$$

$$= E \left[k_1^2 U_1^2 + k_2^2 U_2^2 ... + k_n^2 U_n^2 + 2 k_1 k_2 U_1 U_2 + ... \right.$$

$$\left. + 2 k_{n-1} k_n U_{n-1} U_n \right]$$

$$= E \left[k_1^2 U_1^2 + k_2^2 U_2^2 ... + k_n^2 U_n^2 \right] +$$

$$E \left[2 k_1 k_2 U_1 U_2 + ... + 2 k_{n-1} k_n U_{n-1} U_n \right]$$

$$= E\left[\Sigma\left(k_i^2 U_i^2\right)\right] + 2E\left[\sum_{i \neq j} k_i k_j U_i U_j\right]$$

$$= \Sigma k_i^2 E(U_i^2) + 2\Sigma k_i k_j E(U_i U_j) = \sigma^2 \Sigma k_i^2 \quad [\because E(U_i U_j) = 0]$$

$$\Sigma k_i = \frac{\Sigma x_i}{\Sigma x_i^2}$$

$$\therefore \quad \Sigma k_i^2 = \frac{\Sigma x_i^2}{(\Sigma x_i^2)^2} = \frac{1}{\Sigma x_i^2}$$

$$\therefore \quad \text{Var}(\hat{\beta}) = \sigma^2 \Sigma k_i^2 = \frac{\sigma^2}{\Sigma x_i^2} \qquad \qquad ...(6.12)$$

$$\text{Var}(\hat{\alpha}) = E\left[(\hat{\alpha} - \alpha)^2\right]$$

$$= E\left[\Sigma\left(\frac{1}{n} - \bar{X} k_i\right)^2 U_i^2\right] \qquad \text{(from equation 6.11)}$$

$$= \sigma^2 \Sigma\left(\frac{1}{n} - \bar{X} k_i\right)^2$$

$$= \sigma^2 \Sigma\left(\frac{1}{n^2} - \frac{2}{n}\bar{X} k_i + \bar{X}^2 k_i^2\right)$$

$$= \sigma^2\left(\frac{1}{n} - \frac{2\bar{X}}{n}\Sigma k_i + \bar{X}^2 \Sigma k_i^2\right)$$

$$= \sigma^2\left(\frac{1}{n} + \frac{\bar{X}^2}{\Sigma x_i^2}\right) \qquad \left(\because \Sigma k_i = 0 \text{ and } \Sigma k_i^2 = \frac{1}{\Sigma x_i^2}\right)$$

Again; $\quad \dfrac{1}{n} + \dfrac{\bar{X}^2}{\Sigma x_i^2} = \dfrac{\Sigma x_i^2 + n\bar{X}^2}{n\Sigma x_i^2} = \dfrac{\Sigma X_i^2}{n\Sigma x_i^2}$

$$\therefore \qquad \text{Var}(\hat{\alpha}) = \sigma^2\left(\frac{1}{n} + \frac{\bar{X}^2}{\Sigma x_i^2}\right) = \sigma^2\left(\frac{\Sigma X_i^2}{n\Sigma x_i^2}\right) \qquad ...(6.13)$$

$\hat{\alpha}$ and $\hat{\beta}$ are also 'Best' estimators: In order to establish that $\hat{\beta}$ possesses the minimum variance property (Best), we compare its variance with that of some alternative, unbiased estimator of β, say β^*.

Suppose $\beta^* = \Sigma w_i Y_i$ where constant $w_i \neq k_i$, but $w_i = k_i + c_i$

$$\therefore \qquad \beta^* = \Sigma w_i (\alpha + \beta X_i + U_i)$$

$$= \alpha \Sigma w_i + \beta \Sigma w_i X_i + \Sigma w_i U_i \qquad ...(6.14)$$

$$\therefore \qquad E(\beta^*) = \alpha\Sigma w_i + \beta\Sigma w_i X_i \qquad \left[\because E(U_i) = 0\right].$$

Since β^* is assumed to be an unbiased estimator which implies that $\Sigma w_i = 0$ and $\Sigma w_i X_i = 1$ in the above equation.

But, $\qquad \Sigma w_i = \Sigma(k_i + c_i) = \Sigma k_i + \Sigma c_i$

$$\therefore \qquad\quad \Sigma c_i = 0 \quad \because \Sigma k_i = \Sigma w_i = 0$$

Again, $\Sigma w_i X_i = \Sigma (k_i + c_i)X_i = \Sigma k_i X_i + \Sigma c_i X_i$

$$\therefore \qquad\quad \Sigma c_i X_i = 0 \quad \because \Sigma w_i X_i = 1 \text{ and } \Sigma k_i X_i = \Sigma k_i x_i = 1.$$

Also $\therefore \Sigma c_i x_i = \Sigma c_i X_i + \overline{X}\Sigma c_i = 0$

Thus we have shown that if β^* is to be unbiased estimator then following results must hold true.

$$\Sigma w_i = 0, \ \Sigma w_i X_i = 1, \ \Sigma c_i = 0, \ \Sigma c_i X_i = \Sigma c_i x_i = 0 \qquad \qquad ...(6.15)$$

The variance of this assumed estimator β^* is then

$$\text{Var } (\beta^*) = E \ (\beta^* - \beta)^2]$$

$$= E\left[\left(\Sigma w_i U_i\right)^2\right] \qquad\qquad \text{(from 6.14)}$$

$$= \sigma^2 \Sigma w_i^2$$

[By following exactly the same arguments that we used in obtaining Var $(\hat{\beta})$.]

$$\therefore \quad \text{Var } (\beta^*) = \sigma^2 \Sigma w_i^2$$

But $\qquad \Sigma w_i^2 = \Sigma(k_i + c_i)^2 = \Sigma k_i^2 + 2\Sigma k_i c_i + \Sigma c_i^2$

$$\Sigma k_i c_i = \Sigma c_i \cdot \frac{x_i}{\Sigma x_i^2} = \frac{\Sigma c_i x_i}{\Sigma x_i^2} = 0 \qquad\qquad \text{(By 6.15)}$$

$$\therefore \qquad \Sigma w_i^2 = \Sigma k_i^2 + \Sigma c_i^2; \text{ so that}$$

$$\text{Var } (\beta^*) = \sigma^2\left(\Sigma k_i^2 + \Sigma c_i^2\right) = \sigma^2\Sigma k_i^2 + \sigma^2\Sigma c_i^2$$

$$\text{Var } (\beta^*) = \text{Var } (\hat{\beta}) + \sigma^2\Sigma c_i^2$$

Σc_i^2 must be positive; so that Var (β^*) > Var $(\hat{\beta})$

In case $\Sigma c_i^2 = 0$, then Var (β^*) = Var $(\hat{\beta})$.

This proves that $\hat{\beta}$ possesses minimum variance property.

In the similar way we can prove that the least squares constant intercept $\hat{\alpha}$ possesses minimum variance, in other words it is also a 'Best' estimator.

We take a new estimator α^*, which we assume to be a linear function of the Y_i's, with weights $w_i = k_i + c_i$, as earlier.

Least squares $\hat{\alpha}$ was;

$$\hat{\alpha} = \Sigma\left(\frac{1}{n} - \bar{X}k_i\right)Y_i \qquad \text{(from 6.7)}$$

By analogy, $\quad \alpha^* = \Sigma\left(\frac{1}{n} - \bar{X}w_i\right)Y_i = f(Y)$

Since we want α^* to be an unbiased estimator of the true α, that is, $E(\alpha^*) = \alpha$, we substitute for $Y_i = \alpha + \beta X_i + U_i$ in α^* and find the expected value of α^*

$$\alpha^* = \alpha\left(1 - \bar{X}\Sigma w_i\right) + \beta\left(\bar{X} - \bar{X}\Sigma w_i X_i\right) + \Sigma\left(\frac{1}{n} - \bar{X}w_i\right)U_i$$

$$E(\alpha^*) = \alpha\left[1 - \bar{X}\Sigma E(w_i)\right] + \beta[\bar{X} - \bar{X}\Sigma E(w_i X_i)] + \Sigma E\left(\frac{1}{n} - \bar{X}w_i\right)U_i$$

$E(\alpha^*) = \alpha$, if and only if,

$$E(w_i) = 0, \; E(w_i X_i) = \frac{1}{n}, \text{ and } E(w_i U_i) = 0$$

that is, if $\Sigma w_i = 0$, $\Sigma w_i X_i = 1$ and $\Sigma w_i U_i = 0$.

These conditions imply that $\Sigma c_i = 0$ and $\Sigma c_i X_i = 0$.

Variance of this assumed estimator α^* is then

$$\text{Var}(\alpha^*) = E(\alpha^* - \alpha)^2 = \sigma^2\Sigma\left[\frac{1}{n} - \bar{X}w_i\right]^2$$

$$= \sigma^2\Sigma\left[\frac{1}{n^2} + \bar{X}^2w_i^2 - 2\frac{1}{n}\bar{X}w_i\right]$$

$$= \sigma^2\left[\frac{n}{n^2} + \bar{X}^2\Sigma w_i^2 - 2\bar{X}\frac{1}{n}\Sigma w_i\right]$$

$$= \sigma^2\left[\frac{1}{n} + \bar{X}^2\Sigma w_i^2 - \frac{2}{n}\bar{X}\Sigma w_i\right]$$

Since $\Sigma w_i = 0$ and $\Sigma w_i^2 = \Sigma k_i^2 + \Sigma c_i^2$, we have

$$\text{Var}(\alpha^*) = \sigma^2\left[\frac{1}{n} + \bar{X}^2\left(\Sigma k_i^2 + \Sigma c_i^2\right)\right]$$

$$\text{Var}(\alpha^*) = \sigma^2\left[\frac{1}{n} + \frac{\bar{X}^2}{\Sigma x_i^2}\right] + \left[\sigma^2\bar{X}^2\Sigma c_i^2\right]$$

The first term is the variance of $\hat{\alpha}$, hence

$$\text{Var}(\alpha^*) = \text{Var}(\hat{\alpha}) + \sigma^2\bar{X}^2\Sigma c_i^2.$$

But, $\Sigma c_i^2 > 0$; because not all c_i's are zero.

Therefore, $\text{Var}(\alpha^*) > \text{Var}(\hat{\alpha})$.

Thus we have proved that the least squares estimators of linear regression model are Best, Linear and Unbiased (BLU) estimators.

One may ask why so much importance is attached to the BLU properties of the ordinary least squares estimates? (See 6.5.1 below)

6.5 THE GAUSS-MARKOV THEOREM

According to the *Gauss-Markov theorem*, under the five basic assumptions of the classical linear regression model, the least-squares estimators are linear and unbiased estimators. These are also the best of all linear unbiased estimators; i.e., the estimators have minimum variance within the class of linear unbiased estimators. Sometimes this theorem is referred to as the BLUE theorem, where BLUE is an acronym for *Best Linear Unbiased Estimator*, and the least-squares estimators are, therefore, also referred to as BLU estimators. This theorem has been proved under section 6.4 above.

6.5.1 Importance of the BLU Properties

(a) *Linearity:* This property is desirable because it facilitates the computations of the estimates.

(b) *Unbiasedness:* By itself, this property is not useful. The only assurance it gives is that if we have a very large number of samples, the estimators of the parameters obtained from these samples will on the average give the true value of β's.

(c) *Best:* Also in this case, least variance property by itself is not particularly desirable, because an estimate may have zero variance and yet have an enormous bias.

However, the minimum variance property becomes desirable when combined with unbiasedness. The importance of this property is apparent when we want to apply the standard tests of significance for $\hat{\alpha}$ and $\hat{\beta}$ and to construct confidence intervals for these estimates.

6.6 MAXIMUM LIKELIHOOD ESTIMATORS

We observe following two important features in the derivation of the results in sections 6.3 and 6.4.

(a) We do not make use of all the assumptions relating to disturbance terms while proving the BLU properties of the least squares estimators.*

---

* The OLS method does not depend on the assumption of normality for the residuals U_i. But we make this assumption to facilitate the construction of confidence intervals and application of tests of significance.

For example, for establishing the property of linearity we made use of the assumption regarding covariance between disturbance and explanatory variable $E(X_iU_i) = 0$. Again unbiasedness required this assumption along with that of the mean of disturbance terms $[E(X_iU_i) = 0$ and $E(U_i) = 0]$. For the derivation of variance of the parameters and their minimum variance property depended on the assumptions relating to homoscedasticity and non-autoregressive nature of the disturbance terms

$$\left[E\left(U_i^2\right) = \sigma^2 \text{ and } E(U_i \, U_j) = 0\right].$$

(b) While establishing these properties we do not make any assumption about the specific form of the distribution of the disturbance terms. Actually we do not make use of assumption relating to normality of U while proving $\hat{\alpha}$ and $\hat{\beta}$ as BLUE.

Let us now suppose that we make use of assumption of normal distribution of disturbance terms along with other assumptions for obtaining different estimators of β and α.

Will these estimators of α and β (say α^* and β^*) be different from least squares estimators $\hat{\alpha}$ and $\hat{\beta}$?

Will such estimators possess the desirable properties?

Maximum likelihood estimators of the parameters are obtained by using the assumption of normality of U.

The maximum likelihood estimators of the parameter of a given population are considered to be those values of the parameters which should generate the observed sample most often. To find these estimators we have to determine the likelihood function for the observations in the sample and then maximise it with respect to the unknown parameters.

In our model: $Y_i = \alpha + \beta X_i + U_i$, sample consists of n observations on Y and X. Since U_i is assumed to be normally distributed, Y_i is also normally distributed. In other words variables $(\alpha + \beta X_1)$, $(\alpha + \beta X_2)$, ..., $(\alpha + \beta X_n)$ are distributed normally with mean $(\alpha + \beta X_i)$ and a common variance equal to σ^2.

Therefore, the likelihood function: $l\,[Y_1, Y_2...Y_n: (\alpha + \beta X_i), \sigma^2]$ will be written as

$$l = \frac{1}{\sqrt{2\pi\sigma^2}}\, \exp. \left[-\frac{1}{2}\left(\frac{Y_1 - \alpha - \beta X_1}{\sigma}\right)^2\right]$$

$$\times \frac{1}{\sqrt{2\pi\sigma^2}}\, \exp. \left[-\frac{1}{2}\left(\frac{Y_2 - \alpha - \beta X_2}{\sigma}\right)^2\right]...$$

$$\times \frac{1}{\sqrt{2\pi\sigma^2}}\, \exp. \left[-\frac{1}{2}\left(\frac{Y_n - \alpha - \beta X_n}{\sigma}\right)^2\right]$$

$$\therefore \qquad l = \left(\frac{1}{\sqrt{2\pi\sigma^2}}\right)^n \exp.\left[-\frac{1}{2}\sum_{i=1}^{n}\left(\frac{Y_i - \alpha - \beta X_i}{\sigma}\right)^2\right]$$

Taking logarithms on both sides;

$$\log_e l = L = -\frac{n}{2}\log_e 2\pi - \frac{n}{2}\log_e \sigma^2 - \frac{1}{2\sigma^2}\sum_{i=1}^{n}(Y_i - \alpha - \beta X_i)^2$$

α, β and σ^2 are the three parameters.

Differentiating with respect to each of them we obtain,

$$\frac{\partial L}{\partial \alpha} = -\frac{1}{2\sigma^2}\sum_i 2(Y_i - \alpha - \beta X_i)(-1)$$

$$\frac{\partial L}{\partial \beta} = -\frac{1}{2\sigma^2}\sum_i 2(Y_i - \alpha - \beta X_i)(-X_i)$$

$$\frac{\partial L}{\partial \sigma^2} = -\frac{n}{2\sigma^2} + \frac{1}{2\sigma^4}\sum_i (Y_i - \alpha - \beta X_i)^2$$

Equating each of these three equations to zero and putting 'star' mark on the parameters to distinguish them from least squares estimators, we get:

$$\frac{1}{2\sigma^{*2}}\Sigma(Y_i - \alpha^* - \beta^* X_i) = 0 \qquad \qquad ...(6.16)$$

$$\frac{1}{2\sigma^{*2}}\Sigma X_i(Y_i - \alpha^* - \beta^* X_i) = 0 \qquad \qquad ...(6.17)$$

and, $$\frac{-n}{2\sigma^{*2}} + \frac{1}{2\sigma^{*4}}\Sigma(Y_i - \alpha^* - \beta^* X_i)^2 = 0 \qquad ...(6.18)$$

The first two equations reduce to the Least Squares Normal Equation:

$$\Sigma Y_i = n\alpha^* + \beta^*\Sigma X_i$$

$$\Sigma X_i Y_i = \alpha^*\Sigma X_i + \beta^*\Sigma X_i^2;$$

which proves that the Maximum Likelihood Estimators (MLE) of α and β are the same as the least squares estimators. Hence they would also possess all the desirable properties.

The third equation gives us the most important result, i.e., the maximum likelihood estimator of variance of disturbance terms; σ^2. We could not get such estimator under least squares methods.

From (6.18),

$$\sigma^{*2} = \frac{1}{n}\Sigma(Y_i - \alpha^* - \beta^* X_i)^2 \qquad \qquad ...(6.19)$$

Since $\quad\alpha^* = \hat{\alpha}$ and $\beta^* = \hat{\beta}$, $\quad\therefore Y_i - \alpha^* - \beta^* X_i = e_i$

$$\therefore \qquad \sigma^{*2} = \frac{1}{n}\sum_{i=1}^{n} e_i^2 \qquad\qquad\qquad ...(6.20)$$

Equation (6.20) states that the MLE of the variance of the disturbances equal to the sample variance of the least squares residual.

Let us now examine whether this estimator also possesses the required properties.

Since this is a maximum likelihood estimator of σ^2, it has all the desirable asymptotic properties, but its 'small sample properties' need to be established. In other words we want to examine whether or not σ^{*2} is an unbiased estimator of σ^2.

$$y_i = Y_i - \bar{Y} = \left[(\alpha + \beta X_i + U_i) - (\alpha + \beta \bar{X} + \bar{U})\right]$$

$$y_i = \beta(X_i - \bar{X}) + (U_i - \bar{U})$$

$$y_i = \beta x_i + (U_i - \bar{U})$$

Therefore, $\quad e_i = \beta x_i + (U_i - \bar{U}) - \hat{\beta} x_i \quad$ (by substituting in $e_i = y_i - \hat{\beta} x_i$)

$$e_i = (U_i - \bar{U}) - (\hat{\beta} - \beta) x_i$$

$$\therefore \qquad \Sigma e_i^2 = \Sigma \left[(U_i - \bar{U}) - (\hat{\beta} - \beta) x_i\right]^2$$

$$\Sigma e_i^2 = \Sigma(U_i - \bar{U})^2 - 2(\hat{\beta} - \beta)\Sigma x_i (U_i - \bar{U}) + (\hat{\beta} - \beta)^2 \Sigma x_i^2$$

$$\therefore \quad E\left[\Sigma e^2\right] = E\left[\Sigma(U_i - \bar{U})^2 - 2(\hat{\beta} - \beta)\Sigma x_i (U_i - \bar{U}) + (\hat{\beta} - \beta)^2 \Sigma x_i^2\right]$$

Taking each term of R.H.S separately:

(i) $$\Sigma E(U_i - \bar{U})^2 = E\left[\Sigma U_i^2 - \frac{1}{n}(\Sigma U_i)^2\right] = (n-1)\sigma^2$$

(ii) $$E\left[(\hat{\beta} - \beta)\Sigma x_i (U_i - \bar{U})\right] = E\left[\frac{\Sigma U_i x_i}{\Sigma x_i^2}(\Sigma U_i x_i - \bar{U}\Sigma x_i)\right]$$

$$\left(\text{Since by (6.10)}, (\hat{\beta} - \beta) = \Sigma k_i U_i = \frac{\Sigma x_i U_i}{\Sigma x_i^2}\right)$$

$$= E\left[\frac{(\Sigma U_i x_i)^2}{\Sigma x_i^2}\right]$$

$$= \sigma^2 \qquad\qquad \text{(see derivation of 6.12)}$$

(iii) $$E\left[(\hat{\beta} - \beta)^2 \Sigma x_i^2\right] = \frac{\sigma^2}{\Sigma x_i^2} \cdot \Sigma x_i^2 = \sigma^2 \quad \text{(By 6.12)}$$

$$\therefore \qquad E\left[\Sigma e_i^2\right] = (n-1)\sigma^2 - 2\sigma^2 + \sigma^2 = (n-2)\ \sigma^2$$

or, $\qquad E\left(\sigma^{*2}\right) = \dfrac{1}{n}\ E\left(\Sigma e_i^2\right) = \left(\dfrac{n-2}{n}\right)\sigma^2$

So we have;

$$E(\sigma^{*2}) = \left(\dfrac{n-2}{n}\right)\sigma^2 \qquad \qquad ...(6.21)$$

This shows that σ^{*2} is a biased estimator σ^2. We make use of result this to obtain an unbiased estimator of σ^2.

From (6.21) we obtain

$$\left(\dfrac{n}{n-2}\right)E(\sigma^{*2}) = \sigma^2$$

$$\therefore \quad \left(\dfrac{n}{n-2}\right)E\left[\dfrac{1}{n}\Sigma(Y_i - \hat{\alpha} - \hat{\beta}X_i)^2\right] = \sigma^2$$

[on substituting for σ^{*2} from (6.19)]

$$\left(\dfrac{n}{n-2}\right)E\left(\dfrac{\Sigma e_i^2}{n}\right) = E\left(\dfrac{\Sigma e_i^2}{n-2}\right) = \sigma^2 \qquad ...(6.22)$$

That is; $\left(\dfrac{\Sigma e_i^2}{n-2}\right)$ is the unbiased estimator of true variance of U.

Note: An unbiased estimator of σ^2 in case of two explanatory variables is given by equation 8.27 of chapter 8.

6.7   THE SAMPLING DISTRIBUTION OF THE LEAST SQUARES ESTIMATORS

Since least squares estimators are linear combinations of independent normal variables $Y_1, Y_2, Y_3, ...Y_n$; $\hat{\alpha}$ and $\hat{\beta}$ must also be normally distributed with following characteristics:

(i) $\hat{\alpha}$ and $\hat{\beta}$ are unbaised estimators, their means being equal to their true values α and β.

(ii) Variance of each estimator is known.

Both these results may be stated in summary form:

$$\hat{\alpha} \sim N\left[\alpha, \sigma^2\left(\dfrac{1}{n}+\dfrac{\overline{X}^2}{\Sigma x_i^2}\right)\right]$$

$$\hat{\beta} \sim N\left(\beta, \frac{\sigma^2}{\Sigma x_i^2}\right)$$

Variances of the parameters are directly related to the variances of the disturbances, thus following points should be noted carefully:

(i) Larger the value of σ^2, the larger the variances of $\hat{\sigma}$ and $\hat{\beta}$. In other words the greater the dispersion of the disturbance terms around the population regression line, the greater the dispersion in the values of estimated regression parameters.

(ii) Σx_i^2 is in the denominator of the variance formula of both estimators. This means the more dispersed the values of the explanatory variables (i.e. larger Σx_i^2), the smaller the variances of $\hat{\alpha}$ and $\hat{\beta}$. If $\Sigma x_i^2 = 0$ or nearer to zero; i.e. when $X_1 = X_2 = X_3 = \dots X_n$ both variances would be infinitely large.

(iii) The variance of $\hat{\alpha}$ is smallest when $\overline{X} = 0$ or near to zero.

$$\left(\text{Note that when } \overline{X} = 0, \text{Var} (\hat{\alpha}) = \frac{\sigma^2}{n}\right)$$

6.8 CONFIDENCE INTERVALS AND HYPOTHESIS TESTING

Construction of confidence intervals is important in order to achieve precision of $\hat{\alpha}$ and $\hat{\beta}$. We have all the information concerning the distribution of $\hat{\alpha}$ and $\hat{\beta}$ in order to standardise them.

In our case, $Z = \dfrac{\hat{\beta} - \beta}{\sigma\sqrt{\dfrac{1}{\Sigma x_i^2}}}$ and, $Z = \dfrac{\hat{\alpha} - \alpha}{\sigma\sqrt{\dfrac{\Sigma X_i^2}{n\Sigma x_i^2}}}$

or, $Z = \left(\hat{\beta} - \beta\right)\dfrac{\sqrt{\Sigma x_i^2}}{\sigma}$ and, $Z^* = \dfrac{\left(\hat{\alpha} - \alpha\right)\sqrt{n}\sqrt{\Sigma x_i^2}}{\sigma\sqrt{\Sigma X_i^2}}$

where Z is $N(0, 1)$.

σ represents the variance of the unobservable disturbances which is unknown. If we substitute unbiased estimator of σ^2 in the standard normal variable Z, the resulting variable $\left(\dfrac{Z\sqrt{n-2}}{V}\right)$ follows the *t-distribution* with $(n - 2)$ degrees of freedom.

In case of $\hat{\alpha}$, $Z = \dfrac{\left(\hat{\alpha} - \alpha\right)\sqrt{n\Sigma x_i^2}}{\sigma\sqrt{\Sigma X_i^2}}$, $V^2 = \dfrac{\Sigma e_i^2}{\sigma^2} = \dfrac{(n-2)\sigma^{*2}}{\sigma^2} = \dfrac{(n-2)\sigma^{*2}}{\sigma^2}$

$$\therefore \qquad t = \frac{(\hat{\alpha} - \alpha)\sqrt{n\Sigma x^2}}{\sigma\sqrt{\Sigma X_i^2}} \cdot \sqrt{(n-2)} \frac{\sigma}{\sqrt{n-2} \cdot \sigma^*}$$

$$t = \frac{(\hat{\alpha} - \alpha)\sqrt{n\Sigma x_i^2}}{\sigma^*\sqrt{\Sigma X_i^2}} \qquad \qquad ...(6.23)$$

Thus by transforming the *Z-variable to t-variable* the unknown true disturbance variance σ^2 has disappeared and we have a test function which depends solely on the sample observations and the hypothetical value of α.

By rearranging in terms in *t*-expression:

$$\hat{\alpha} - \alpha = t \cdot \sigma^* \sqrt{\frac{\Sigma X_i^2}{n\Sigma x_i^2}}$$

or,
$$\alpha = \hat{\alpha} \pm t \cdot \sigma^* \sqrt{\frac{\Sigma X_i^2}{n\Sigma x_i^2}}$$

Therefore 95% confidence limits for α are:

$$\hat{\alpha} \pm t_{0.025} \cdot \sigma^* \sqrt{\frac{\Sigma X_i^2}{n\Sigma x_i^2}}$$

In the similar fashion, to carry out tests on β, we have

$$Z = \frac{(\hat{\beta} - \beta)\sqrt{\Sigma x_i^2}}{\sigma}, \text{ and } V = \frac{\sqrt{n-2} \cdot \sigma^*}{\sigma}$$

$$\therefore \qquad t = \frac{(\hat{\beta} - \beta)\sqrt{\Sigma x_i^2}}{\sigma} \cdot \sqrt{n-2} \cdot \frac{\sigma}{\sqrt{n-2}\sigma^*}$$

$$= \frac{(\hat{\beta} - \beta)\sqrt{\Sigma x_i^2}}{\sigma^*} \qquad \qquad ...(6.24)$$

$$\therefore \qquad \hat{\beta} - \beta = t \cdot \frac{\sigma^*}{\sqrt{\Sigma x_i^2}}$$

or,
$$\beta = \hat{\beta} \pm t_{0.025} \cdot \frac{\sigma^*}{\sqrt{\Sigma x_i^2}}$$

gives the 95% confidence limits for β.

t-statistic derived under (6.23) and (6.24) are also important if we want to test hypothesis concerning regression parameters.

One hypothesis of usual interest is that we hypothesise that there is no relationship between the explanatory variable X and the dependent variable

Y in the regression model: $Y = \alpha + \beta X$. This in other words means that the population regression line is horizontal. As such the null hypothesis of no relationship between X and Y is

H_0: $\beta = 0$ and, alternative hypothesis H_A: $\beta \neq 0$

To test H_0 against H_A we utilise *t-statistic* given in (6.23) and (6.24) and determine the acceptance and critical regions.

If we assume H_0: $\beta = 0$ is true, then the test ratio of (6.24) becomes

$$t = \frac{\hat{\beta}\sqrt{\Sigma x_i^2}}{\sigma^*} = \frac{\hat{\beta}}{\text{SE}(\hat{\beta})} \left(\because \sigma_\beta^2 = \frac{\sigma^{*2}}{\sigma x_i^2} \right),$$

which has *t-distribution* with $(n - 2)$ degrees of freedom. The boundary between the acceptance and critical region can be determined from the table of *t-distribution* for and given level of significance and for any number of degrees of freedom.

To perform a two-tailed test with five per cent level of significance and $(n - 2)$ degrees of freedom, the acceptance region is defined by:

$$-t_{0.025} \cdot \text{SE}(\hat{\beta}) \leq \hat{\beta} \leq + t_{0.025} \cdot \text{SE}(\hat{\beta})$$

6.9 GOODNESS OF FIT (R^2)

So far we were concerned with the estimation and precision of regression parameters. Let us now consider the regression line as a whole and examine its goodness of fit. Suppose a sample regression line has been obtained by the method of least squares. Fig. 6.5 shows the breakdown of the variation of Y_i into two components; explained and unexplained.

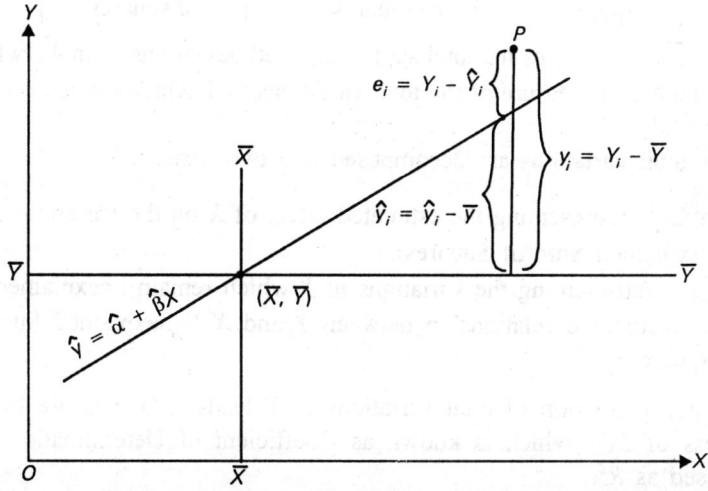

Fig. 6.5

Recall that, $Y_i = \hat{Y}_i + e_i$

or, $Y_i - \overline{Y} = (\hat{Y}_i - \overline{Y}) + e_i$

For all the observations this will turn to:

$$\Sigma(Y_i - \overline{Y}) = \Sigma(\hat{Y}_i - \overline{Y}) + \Sigma e_i$$

$$\Sigma(Y_i - \overline{Y})^2 = \Sigma\left[(\hat{Y}_i - \overline{Y}) + e_i\right]^2$$

$$= \Sigma(\hat{Y}_i - \overline{Y})^2 + 2\Sigma(\hat{Y}_i - \overline{Y})e_i + \Sigma e_i^2$$

But $\Sigma(\hat{Y}_i - \overline{Y})e_i = \Sigma(\hat{\alpha} + \hat{\beta}X_i - \overline{Y})e_i$

$$= \hat{\alpha}\Sigma e_i + \hat{\beta}\Sigma X_i e_i - \overline{Y}\Sigma e_i$$

$$= 0 \quad (\because \Sigma e_i = 0 \text{ and } \Sigma X_i e_i = 0)$$

Again; $\Sigma(\hat{Y}_i - \overline{Y})^2 = \Sigma(\hat{\alpha} + \hat{\beta}X_i - \overline{Y})^2$

$$= \Sigma\left[(\overline{Y} - \hat{\beta}\overline{X}) + \hat{\beta}X_i - \overline{Y}\right]^2$$

$$= \Sigma\left[\hat{\beta}(X_i - \overline{X})\right]^2$$

$$= \hat{\beta}^2\Sigma(X_i - \overline{X})^2.$$

$\therefore$ $\qquad \Sigma(Y_i - \overline{Y})^2 = \hat{\beta}^2\Sigma(X_i - \overline{X})^2 \quad + \quad \Sigma e_i^2$

or, $\qquad\qquad \Sigma y_i^2 \quad\quad = \hat{\beta}^2\Sigma x_i^2 \qquad\quad + \quad \Sigma e_i^2$

$$\qquad\qquad\quad \downarrow \qquad\qquad\quad \downarrow \qquad\qquad\quad\quad \downarrow$$

$$\left\{\begin{array}{c}\text{Total sum of} \\ \text{squares}\end{array}\right\} = \left\{\begin{array}{c}\text{Explained sum} \\ \text{of squares}\end{array}\right\} + \left\{\begin{array}{c}\text{Unexplained sum} \\ \text{of squares}\end{array}\right\}$$

$\Sigma(Y_i - \overline{Y})^2$ represents the total sum of squared deviations from $\overline{Y}$, which we may take as a measure of the total variations in Y which are required to be explained.

These total variations are decomposed into two parts:

(i) $\hat{\beta}^2\Sigma x_i^2$: representing the estimated effect of X on the variations in Y (Explained Sum of Squares).

(ii) Σe_i^2: representing the variations in Y which remain unexplained by the estimated relationship between Y and X (Unexplained Sum of Squares).

This decomposition of total variations in Y leads to a measure of the 'goodness of fit'—which is known as Coefficient of Determination and symbolised as R^2.

$$R^2 = \frac{\text{Variations explained}}{\text{Variations required to be explained}}$$

$$R^2 = \frac{\hat{\beta}^2 \, \Sigma x_i^2}{\Sigma y_i^2} = \frac{\Sigma y_i^2 - \Sigma e_i^2}{\Sigma y_i^2} = 1 - \frac{\Sigma e_i^2}{\Sigma y_i^2} \qquad \qquad ...(6.25)$$

It is easy to see in (6.25) that limits of R^2 are zero and unity. If our fit is perfect, $\Sigma e_i^2 = 0$ and $R^2 = 1$; indicating the best fit. At the other extreme if our estimated sample regression line is horizontal ($\beta = 0$), then

$$\Sigma e_i^2 = \Sigma y_i^2, \text{ and } R^2 = 0. \text{ Thus, } 0 \le R^2 \le 1$$

R^2, in fact, is equal to the square of the simple correlation coefficient between X and Y.

We know, $\qquad r = \dfrac{\Sigma x_i y_i}{n \sigma_x \sigma_y} = \dfrac{\Sigma x_i y_i}{\sqrt{\Sigma x_i^2 \, \Sigma y_i^2}}$

By eq. (6.5), $\quad \hat{\beta} = \dfrac{\Sigma x_i y_i}{\Sigma x_i^2}$ and by (6.25), $R^2 = \dfrac{\hat{\beta}^2 \, \Sigma x_i^2}{\Sigma y_i^2}$

$$\therefore \qquad R^2 = \left(\frac{\Sigma x_i y_i}{\Sigma x_i^2} \right)^2 \frac{\Sigma x_i^2}{\Sigma y_i^2} = \frac{(\Sigma x_i y_i)^2}{\Sigma x_i^2 \, \Sigma y_i^2}$$

$$= \left(\frac{\Sigma x_i y_i}{\sqrt{\Sigma x_i^2 \, \Sigma y_i^2}} \right)^2 = r^2$$

$\therefore \qquad R^2 = r^2$

Since, $\qquad 0 \le R^2 \le 1$

$\therefore \qquad 0 \le r^2 \le 1$ or $-1 \le r \le +1$

We compute R^2 for *example 1*, given under section 6.12 as follows,

$$\Sigma y_i^2 = 19837; \ \Sigma x_i^2 = 604.8; \text{ and, } \hat{\beta} = 5.54$$

$\therefore \qquad \hat{\beta}^2 \, \Sigma x_i^2 = (5.54)^2 \, (604.8) = 18562.28$

$$\therefore \qquad R^2 = \frac{18562.28}{19837} = 0.936.$$

This suggests that 93.6 per cent of the total variations in Y can be attributed to the variations of the fitted value of Y, i.e., $\hat{Y}$; or we say that our regression line fits the given data well.

In this way R^2 measures the proportion of variations in the dependent variable that is explained by the independent variables. This particular definition has a valid interpretation only when our regression model contains the constant term. Secondly, value of R^2 depends on sum of squares of the residuals. Whenever we include an additional variable in the regression equation, Σe_i^2 is sure to decrease and hence R^2 is sure to rise. But such an increase in R^2 with the inclusion of additional variable in the model is just a mathematical property and therefore it may or may not describe the importance of inclusion of the additional variable in the regression equation. Thus we must remember that even though R^2 does measure the proportion of variations in the dependent variable that is explained by the fitted regression equation, it should not always be taken as a determinant of 'goodness of fit'.

6.10 FORECASTING ABILITY AND R^2

One of the major objectives of econometrics is forecasting. A forecast is a quantitative estimate about the likelihood of future events based on past or current information. The past and current information is in the form of a regression model that we estimate. We then make the prediction of values of certain variable by using information contained in the estimated model.

We must not forget that forecasting ability of any econometric model (through confidence intervals) is quite different from the examination of model through classical tests; F, R^2 and t.

A regression model can have significant t-statistic and a high R^2 and still forecast very badly period after period. This may be due to structural change during the forecast period which is not explained by the estimated model. On the other, a model with low R^2 and insignificant regression coefficients may provide good forecasts. This may happen because there is little variation in the dependent variable, so that although it is not explained well by the model it is easy to forecast.

The prediction can be attempted in two alternative ways; either our forecast is single value or we can estimate an interval within which the value of the variable will most probably lie. The first method yields a *point forecasts* (predicting a single number in each forecast period), while the second yields an *interval forecasts* (indicating an interval in which we hope the actual value will lie).

Forecasting is closely related to policy evaluation. Infact, most methods of policy formulation and evaluation reply upon a specific type of forecast. It is, therefore, useful to distinguish between various types of forecasts:

(a) Conditional *vis-a-vis* Unconditional forecasts
(b) Ex-post *vis-a-vis* Ex-ante forecasts.

Conditional-Unconditional Forecasts: In a conditional forecasts, the values for one or more explanatory variables are not known with certainty. Certain values are, therefore, assumed for them to produce forecast of the dependent variable. Such predictions are termed conditional because they depend solely on the values that explanatory variables shall assume in the forecast period. In an unconditional forecasts, values for all the explanatory variables are known with certainty in the forecast period.

Ex-post and Ex-ante Forecasts: In an ex-post forecasts, the forecast period is such that the sample observations on both dependent and independent variables are known with certainty. As such ex-post forecasts can be checked against the existing data. Such forecasts, therefore, also provide a means of evaluating the predictive power of the estimated model. An ex-ante forecast predicts values of dependent variable beyond the estimation period given the information of explanatory variable with or without certainty depending on the nature of the data. Both types of forecasts are explained in a line-diagram above.

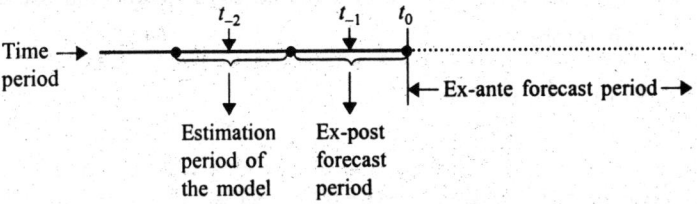

An ex-post forecast is an unconditional forecast while ex-ante forecast may also be unconditional.

Main goal of applied econometric work is not only to make forecast but rather a *good forecast*. A good forecast is the one which yields a forecast error with minimum variance.

How does forecast error creep in?

There are at least *four* distinct sources of such an error:

(i) The very (random) nature of disturbance term in the model itself signifies the fact that the forecasts will deviate from true values even if the model is specified correctly and its parameter values are exactly known.

(ii) The procedure of estimating the regression parameters is based on sampling distribution; that is, the estimated parameters will not only differ from sample to sample but also from true parameter values (of course on the average they will be equal to the true values). As such the parameters themselves introduce errors in the forecasts.

(iii) In case of conditional forecasts, errors are introduced when certain values on explanatory variable(s) are assumed in the period in which the forecast is to be made.

(iv) Errors may creep in due to mis-specification of the model. This introduces specification bias in the values of parameters and hence in the forecasts.

Forecasting through an econometric model is, therefore, a complicated process. We shall discuss here the problems of obtaining *good forecasts* using only a single-equation regression model in two different cases; conditional forecasting and unconditional forecasting.

Unconditional Forecasting: In all applied econometric work, it is generally preferred to generate unconditional forecasts, because the value of explanatory variable is either known with certainty or can be forecasted easily and precisely in the forecasting period. The magnitude of forecasting error thus gets minimised. Recall simple regression model considered in earlier chapters.

$$Y_t = \alpha + \beta X_t + U_t \qquad\qquad t = 1, 2, .., T$$
$$U_i \sim N\,(0,\, \sigma^2)$$

Our problem is: Given a value X_{T+1} what is the best forecast of Y in the period $(T + 1)$. Let this forecast of Y be denoted by $\hat{Y}_{T+1}$ and the forecast error by $\hat{e}_{T+1}$. Therefore,

$$e_{T+1} = \hat{Y}_{T+1} - Y_{T+1}$$
$$E\,(\hat{e}_{T+1}) = E\,[\hat{Y}_{T+1} - Y_{T+1}]$$
$$E\,(\hat{e}_{T+1}) = E\,[\hat{\alpha} + \hat{\beta} X_{T+1} - \alpha - \beta X_{T+1} - U_{T+1}]$$
$$E\,(\hat{e}_{T+1}) = E\,[-U_{T+1}],$$

[on the assumption that the parameters α and β are known exactly; i.e., $\hat{\alpha} = \alpha;\ \beta = \hat{\beta}$]

$$E\,(\hat{e}_{T+1}) = 0$$

Let the variance of forecast error be denoted by e_f^2, therefore;

$$e_f^2 = E\,(\hat{e}_{T+1}^2) = E\,[(-U_{T+1})^2] = \sigma^2$$

Hence we write: $\hat{e}_{T+1} \sim N\,(0,\, \sigma^2)$.

The existence of forecast error is brought about because the forecast value Y_{T+1} can not be guaranteed to lie on the true regression line due to the presence of the disturbance term U. Since this error is normally distributed with zero mean and constant variance of σ^2, we can normalize the forecast error to examine statistical significance of the forecasted value Y_{T+1}.

We have, $\hat{e}_{T+1} \sim N(0, \sigma^2)$

Therefore; $$\lambda = \frac{\hat{e}_{T+1} - 0}{\sigma} = \frac{\hat{Y}_{T+1} - Y_{T+1}}{\sigma},$$

where λ shall be normally distributed with zero mean and unit standard deviation.

Hence; Prob. $\left[-\lambda_{.05} \le \dfrac{\hat{Y}_{T+1} - Y_{T+1}}{\sigma} \le \lambda_{.05} \right] = 0.95$

The value of $\lambda_{.05}$ can be had from a table of Normal Distribution variable.

95% confidence interval of the forecast can now be written as:

$$\underbrace{\hat{Y}_{T+1} - \lambda_{.05}\sigma}_{\hat{Y}_{T+1}^{(*)}} \le Y_{T+1} \le \underbrace{\hat{Y}_{T+1} + \lambda_{.05}\sigma}_{\hat{Y}_{T+1}^{(**)}}$$

The intervals are depicted in the figures (6.6a) and (6.6b).

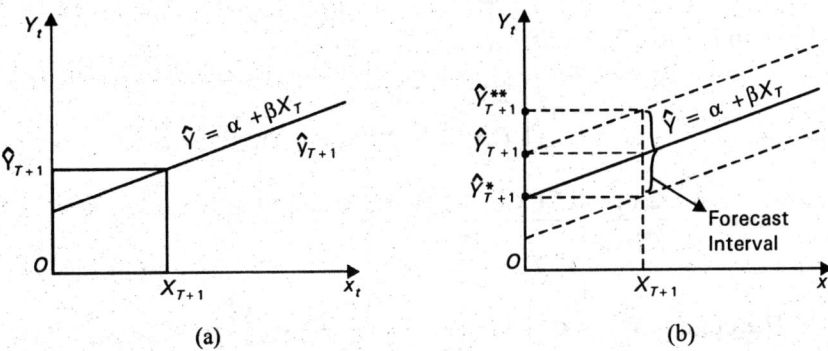

Fig. 6.6: (a) & (b) Forecast intervals when α and β are exactly known.

In the above discussion, it is assumed that the parameters α and β are known exactly. This, of course, is never true; rather α and β are also random variables which are estimated from the given sample. How shall the forecast be affected considering such a situation.

The forecast error shall then be defined as:

$$\hat{e}_{T+1} = \hat{Y}_{T+1} - Y_{T+1}$$

$$= \hat{\alpha} - \hat{\beta}X_{T+1} - \alpha - \beta X_{T+1} - U_{T+1}$$

$$= (\hat{\alpha} - \alpha) + (\hat{\beta} - \beta) X_{T+1} - U_{T+1}$$

Mean: $\quad E(\hat{e}_{T+1}) = E(\hat{\alpha} - \alpha) + E(\hat{\beta} - \beta) X_{T+1} + E(-U_{T+1}) = 0$

(Since $\hat{\alpha}$ and $\hat{\beta}$ are unbiased estimators)

Variance: $\quad E\left[(\hat{e}_{T+1})\right] = \sigma_f^2$

$$= E[(\hat{\alpha} - \alpha)^2] + E[(\hat{\beta} - \beta)^2] X_{T+1}^2 + E[(-U_{T+1})^2]$$

$$+ 2E[(\hat{\alpha} - \alpha)(\hat{\beta} - \beta)] X_{T+1}$$

$$= \text{Var.}(\hat{\alpha}) + 2X_{T+1} \text{Cov.}(\hat{\alpha}, \hat{\beta})$$

$$+ X_{T+1}^2 \cdot \text{Var}(\hat{\beta}) + \sigma^2 \qquad ...(6.26)$$

From OLS procedure, we obtained:

$$\text{Var}(\hat{\alpha}) = \sigma^2 \left(\frac{\Sigma X_T^2}{T\Sigma x_t^2}\right), \quad \Sigma x_t^2 = \Sigma(X_T - \bar{X})^2 \qquad ...(6.27)$$

$$\text{Var}(\hat{\beta}) = \left(\frac{\sigma^2}{\Sigma x_t^2}\right) \qquad \qquad \text{...(6.28)}$$

$$\text{Cov}(\hat{\alpha}, \hat{\beta}) = \sigma^2 \left(\frac{(-)\overline{X}}{\Sigma x_t^2}\right) \qquad \qquad \text{...(6.29)}$$

Substituting (6.27), (6.28) and (6.29) in (6.26);

$$\sigma_f^2 = \sigma^2 \left[\frac{\Sigma X_T^2}{T\Sigma x_t^2} - \frac{2\overline{X} X_{T+1}}{\Sigma x_t^2} + \frac{X_{T+1}^2}{\Sigma x_t^2} + 1\right]$$

Since $\quad \dfrac{\Sigma X_T^2}{T\Sigma x_t^2} = \dfrac{\Sigma(X_T - \overline{X})^2 + T\overline{X}^2}{T\Sigma x_t^2} = \dfrac{1}{T} + \dfrac{\overline{X}^2}{\Sigma x_t^2}$

Therefore; $\quad \sigma_f^2 = \sigma^2 \left[\dfrac{1}{T} + \dfrac{\overline{X}^2}{\Sigma x_t^2} - \dfrac{2\overline{X} X_{T+1}}{\Sigma x_t^2} + \dfrac{X_{T+1}^2}{\Sigma x_t^2} + 1\right]$

$$= \sigma^2 \left[1 + \frac{1}{T} + \frac{\overline{X}^2 - 2\overline{X} X_{T+1} + X_{T+1}^2}{\Sigma x_t^2}\right]$$

$$= \sigma^2 \left[1 + \frac{1}{T} + \frac{(X_{T+1} - \overline{X})^2}{\Sigma x_t^2}\right]$$

$$= \sigma^2 \left[1 + \frac{1}{T} + \frac{x_{T+1}^2}{\Sigma x_t^2}\right] \qquad \qquad \text{...(6.30)}$$

(6.30) describes that the forecast error is sensitive to the size of sample (T), to the variance of X and to the distance of X_{T+1} from the mean of X. The large the sample size (T) and greater the variance of X (i.e. Σx_i^2), the smaller the error of forecast will be. Also, error forecast will be smaller if X_{T+1} happens to be equal or nearer the sample mean of X. This then suggests that best forecasts about Y are for the values that are around its mean value. Therefore, it is not correct to show the confidence bands as parallel lines depicted in figures (6.6a) and (6.6b). The size of the error grows as one moves away from the mean value. A more accurate representation of the error region is a curved one as shown in figure (6.7).

To obtain 95% forecast interval; we write

$$\lambda = \frac{\hat{Y}_{T+1} - Y_{T+1}}{\sigma_f} \sim N(0, 1)$$

since we use unbiased and consistent estimator $\hat{\sigma}^2 \left(= \dfrac{\Sigma e_t^2}{T-2}\right)$ in place of true σ^2, λ shall follow t-distribution with $(T-2)$ degrees of freedom. The 95% confidence interval for $\hat{Y}_{T+1}$ is then given by:

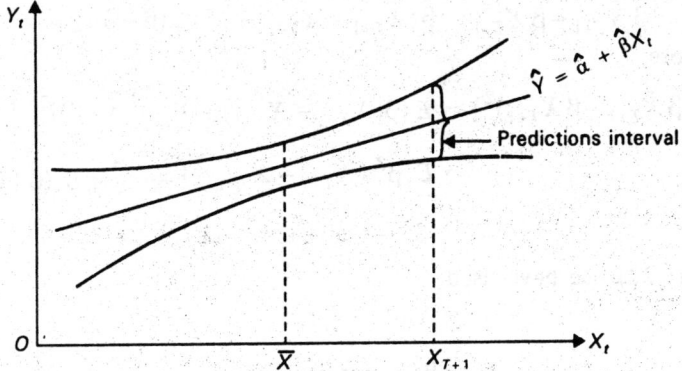

Fig. 6.7: When α and β are not known exactly.

$$\hat{Y}_{T+1} - t_{.05}(\sigma_f) \le Y_{T+1} \le \hat{Y}_{T+1} + t_{.05}(\sigma_f)$$

where

$$\sigma_f = \hat{\sigma}^2 \left[1 + \frac{1}{T} + \frac{x_{T+1}^2}{\Sigma x_t^2} \right]$$

Conditional Forecasting: When the explanatory variable needs also to be predicted or assumed in the forecast period in order to predict the dependent variable (Y), it is a conditional type of forecasting. One may intuitively expect that such forecasts of Y are less reliable than in the unconditional case of forecasting. As we observe below, the 95% confidence intervals for the forecast error get increased in magnitude in this type of forecast.

To begin: we consider the model:

$$Y_t = \alpha + \beta X_t + U_t \qquad\qquad t = 1, 2, .., T.$$

$$\text{and, } \hat{X}_{T+1} = X_{T+1} + V_{T+2}$$

$$U_t \sim N(0, \sigma^2), \text{ and}$$

$$V_t \sim N(0, \sigma_v^2)$$

U_t and V_t are not correlated, $\hat{X}_{T+1}$ and $\hat{\beta}$; $\hat{X}_{T+1}$ and $\hat{\alpha}$ are also not related.

The forecast error is then defined as:

$$\hat{e}_{T+1} = \hat{Y}_{T+1} - Y_{T+1} = (\hat{\alpha} - \alpha) + (\hat{\beta}\hat{X}_{T+1} - \beta X_{T+1}) - U_{T+1}$$

Mean:

$$E(\hat{e}_{T+1}) = E(\hat{\alpha} - \alpha) + E(\hat{\beta}\hat{X}_{T+1} - \beta X_{T+1}) - E(U_{T+1})$$

$$= E[\hat{\beta}(X_{T+1} + U_{T+1})] - \beta X_{T+1}$$

$$= \beta X_{T+1} - \beta X_{T+1} = 0$$

Variance: $E[(\hat{e}_{T+1})^2] = \sigma_f^2$

$$= E[(\hat{\alpha} - \alpha)^2] + E[(\hat{\beta}\hat{X}_{T+1} - \beta X_{T+1})^2]$$

$$+ E[(U_{T+1})^2] + 2E[(\hat{\alpha} - \alpha)(\hat{\beta}\hat{X}_{T+1} - \beta X_{T+1})] \qquad ...(6.31)$$

Since $\hat{\beta}\hat{X}_{T+1} - \beta X_{T+1} = \hat{\beta}(\hat{X}_{T+1} - X_{T+1}) + X_{T+1}(\hat{\beta} - \beta)$,
therefore;

$$E[(\hat{\beta}\hat{X}_{T+1} - \beta X_{T+1})^2] = E[\hat{\beta}(\hat{X}_{T+1} - X_{T+1}) + X_{T+1}(\hat{\beta} - \beta)]^2$$

$$= E[\hat{\beta}^2(\hat{X}_{T+1} - X_{T+1})^2] + X_{T+1}^2 E[(\hat{\beta} - \beta)^2]$$

$$= [\beta^2 + \text{Var}(\hat{\beta})]\sigma_v^2 + X_{T+1}^2 \cdot \text{Var}(\hat{\beta}) \quad ...(6.32)$$

In (6.32), we have used

$$V_{T+1} = \hat{X}_{T+1} - X_{T+1}$$

$$\hat{\beta}^2 = \beta^2 + \text{Var}(\hat{\beta}), \text{ and}$$

$$\text{Cov}(\hat{\beta}, U_{T+1}) = 0$$

Simplifying last term of (6.31); we obtain:

$$E[(\hat{\alpha} - \alpha)(\hat{\beta}\hat{X}_{T+1} - \beta X_{T+1})] = E[(\hat{\alpha} - \alpha)\hat{\beta}(\hat{X}_{T+1} - \hat{X}_{T+1})]$$

$$+ X_{T+1} \cdot E[(\hat{\alpha} - \alpha)(\hat{\beta} - \beta)]$$

$$= X_{T+1} \text{Cov}(\hat{\alpha}, \hat{\beta}) \quad ...(6.33)$$

Substituting (6.32), and (6.33) in (6.31)

$$\sigma_f^2 = \text{Var}(\hat{\alpha}) + [\beta^2 + \text{Var}(\hat{\beta})]\sigma_v^2 + X_{T+1}^2 \text{Var}(\hat{\beta})$$

$$+ 2X_{T+1}\text{Cov}(\hat{\alpha}, \hat{\beta}) + \sigma^2$$

$$\sigma_f^2 = \text{Var}(\hat{\alpha}) + \text{Var}(\hat{\beta})(X_{T+1}^2 + \sigma_v^2) + 2X_{T+1}\text{Cov}(\hat{\alpha}, \hat{\beta})$$

$$+ \sigma^2 + \beta^2\sigma_v^2 \quad ...(6.34)$$

When we put (6.34) in terms of least squares estimators, it becomes:

$$\sigma_f^2 = \sigma^2\left[1 + \frac{1}{T} + \frac{x_{t+1}^2 + \sigma_v^2}{\Sigma x_t^2}\right] + \beta^2\sigma_v^2 \quad ...(6.35)$$

where $\quad x_{t+1}^2 = (X_{T+1} - \overline{X})^2$.

On comparing (6.30) with (6.35), we observe that the stochastic nature of the forecast value of explanatory variable (X) increases the error by $\beta^2\sigma_v^2$ and σ_v^2 in the numerator of the last term of the bracket. Both these are non-negative quantities and tend to zero only when the forecast on X_{T+1} is made with zero error variance. The 95% interval associated with the forecast value of Y_{T+1} will naturally be larger than the intervals described under unconditional type of forecasting.

In the present case, it is not possible to describe the confidence intervals. It is because forecast variable $\hat{Y}_{T+1}$ is not normally distributed (it involves sum of the products of normally distributed variables).

6.11 REPORTING THE RESULTS OF REGRESSION ANALYSIS

The results of regression analysis derived above are reported in conventional format. It is not sufficient merely to report the estimates of α and β. In practice we report regression coefficients together with their standard errors and the value of R^2. It has become customary to present the estimated equation with standard errors placed in parentheses below the estimated parameter values. These results are supplemented by R^2, the value of which is written on right hand side of the estimated regression equation.

In case of *example 1* in 6.12 below;

$$Y_i = 92.89 + 5.54 \, X_i \qquad R^2 = 0.935$$
$$(4.39) \quad (0.347)$$

Some econometricians report the *t-ratios* of the estimated coefficients in place of standard errors. This way of presentation makes the testing of hypothesis easier and direct. Thus the other form of presentation of results for the same example will be:

$$Y_i = 92.89 + 5.54 \, X_i \qquad R^2 = 0.935$$
$$(21.17) \quad (15.97)$$

6.12 APPLICATIONS

Example 1: Obtain the usual regression results from the following data of 20 pairs of observations on X and Y:

$$\Sigma X_i = 228, \ \Sigma Y_i = 3121, \ \Sigma X_i Y_i = 38927, \ \Sigma X_i^2 = 3204,$$
$$\Sigma x_i y_i = 3347.60, \ \Sigma x_i^2 = 604.80 \text{ and } \Sigma y_i^2 = 19837.$$

We are supposed to fit a linear relation between Y (dependent variable) and X (explanatory variable).

(*i*) Estimation of $\hat{\alpha}$ and $\hat{\beta}$

$$\Sigma X_i = 228; \ n = 20; \ \therefore \ \overline{X} = 11.4$$
$$\Sigma Y_i = 3121; \ n = 20; \ \therefore \ \overline{Y} = 156.05.$$

By (6.5), $\qquad \hat{\beta} = \dfrac{3347.6}{604.8} = 5.54.$

By (6.3), $\qquad \hat{\alpha} = 156.05 - (5.54)(11.40) = 92.89.$

Then our estimated sample regression line is:

$$\hat{Y}_i = 92.89 + 5.54 \, X_i.$$

(ii) *Estimation of Variances*

By (6.12) and (6.13), $\text{Var} (\hat{\alpha}) = \sigma^2 \left(\dfrac{\Sigma X_i^2}{n \, \Sigma x_i^2} \right)$ and $\text{Var} (\hat{\beta}) = \dfrac{\sigma^2}{\Sigma x_i^2}.$

Since σ^2 is unknown we substitute σ^{*2} (an unbiased estimator of variance of disturbance) in place of it to obtain:

$$\text{Var} \, (\hat{\alpha}) = \frac{\sigma^{*2} \, \Sigma X_i^2}{n \, \Sigma x_i^2} \text{ and Var } (\hat{\beta}) = \frac{\sigma^{*2}}{\Sigma x_i^2}$$

where, $\qquad \sigma^{*2} = \dfrac{\Sigma e_i^2}{n-2}$ $\hspace{5cm}$ (by 6.22)

$$\therefore \qquad \sigma^{*2} = \frac{\Sigma e_i^2}{n-2} = \frac{\Sigma y_i^2 - \hat{\beta}^2 \Sigma x_i^2}{n-2}$$

$$= \frac{19837 - (5.54)^2 (604.8)}{20 - 2} = 70.82.$$

$$\therefore \qquad \text{Var} \, (\hat{\alpha}) = 70.82 \left[\frac{3204}{(20)(604.8)} \right] = 18.75 \quad \therefore \text{ S.E of } \hat{\alpha} = 4.33$$

and, $\qquad \text{Var} \, (\hat{\beta}) = \dfrac{70.82}{604.8} = 0.117 \quad \therefore \text{ S.E of } \hat{\beta} = 0.34$

(iii) *Construction of Confidence Intervals.* Suppose we wish to set up a confidence interval for α and β at probability level $p = 0.95$. In other words we want to find the value of t that cuts-off 0.025 of the area at the tail end of the distribution on both sides. Thus with 18 degrees of freedom, we look up the row labelled '18' and column labelled '0.025' in the t-table. This value is 2.101.

Therefore, the 95 per cent confidence intervals for α and β are:

$$92.89 - (2.101) \, (4.34) \leq \alpha \leq 92.89 + (2.101) \, (4.33)$$
$$83.79 \leq \alpha \leq 101.99$$

and, $\qquad 5.54 - (2.101) \, (0.34) \leq \beta \leq 5.54 + (2.101) \, (0.34)$
$$4.83 \leq \beta \leq 6.25.$$

(iv) *Hypothesis Testing*

Supposing that $\quad H_0 \colon \beta = 0$, and
$$H_A \colon \beta \neq 0$$

We have defined the acceptance region at 5 per cent level of significance:

$$-t_{.025} \, (\text{SE of } \hat{\beta}) \leq \hat{\beta} \leq + t_{.025} \, (\text{SE of } \hat{\beta})$$

i.e., $\quad -t_{.025} \leq \dfrac{\hat{\beta}}{(\text{SE of } \hat{\beta})} \leq + t_{.025}$

$$\frac{\hat{\beta}}{\text{SE} \, (\hat{\beta})} = \frac{5.54}{0.34} = 16.29; \; t_{.025} \, (n = 18) = 2.101$$

Since the value 16.29 lies outside the acceptance region, the hypothesis of no relationship between X and Y is to be rejected.

Example 2: Following table gives the gross national product (X) and demand for food (Y) measured in arbitrary units, in an undeveloped country over a ten-year period. Estimate the food function: $Y = \alpha + \beta X + U$.

Year	1960	1961	1962	1963	1964	1965	1966	1967	1968	1969
Y	6	7	8	10	8	9	10	9	11	10
X	50	52	55	59	57	58	62	65	68	70

We are required to estimate the food function: $Y = \alpha + \beta X + U$ and compute:

   (i) Coefficient of Determination,
   (ii) Standard Errors of the regression estimates, and
   (iii) Conduct test of significance at 5 per cent level of significance.

From the worksheet of Table 6.1 on page 130, we obtain following data:

$$\Sigma X_i = 596, \ \Sigma Y_i = 88, \ \Sigma X_i Y_i = 5325, \ \Sigma X_i^2 = 35916$$

$$\Sigma x_i y_i = 80.20, \ \Sigma x_i^2 = 394.4, \quad \begin{cases} \Sigma y_i^2 = 21.60 \text{ and } n = 10. \\ \Sigma y_i^2 = \Sigma Y_i^2 - n\,\bar{Y}^2 \end{cases}$$

Therefore,
$$\hat{\beta} = \frac{\Sigma x_i y_i}{\Sigma x_i^2} = \frac{80.22}{394.4} = 0.2033$$

$$\hat{\alpha} = \bar{Y} - \hat{\beta}\bar{X} = 8.8 - 0.2033 \ (59.6) = -3.32$$

$$\hat{\sigma}_u^2 = \frac{\Sigma e_i^2}{n-2} = \frac{5.27}{10-2} = 0.6587$$

$$\text{Var} \ (\hat{\alpha}) = \hat{\sigma}_u \frac{\Sigma X_i^2}{n\,\Sigma x_i^2} = 5.999; \ \text{SE} \ (\hat{\alpha}) = 2.45$$

$$\text{Var} \ (\hat{\beta}) = \frac{\hat{\sigma}_u^2}{\Sigma x_i^2} = 0.00167; \ \text{SE} \ (\hat{\beta}) = 0.041$$

$$R^2 = \frac{\hat{\beta}^2 \ (\Sigma x_i^2)}{\Sigma y_i^2} = 0.756$$

The summary results are:

$$\hat{Y}_i = -3.32 + 0.2033 \ X_i \qquad R^2 = 0.76$$
$$\text{SE} \ (\hat{\beta}_i) \qquad (2.45) \qquad (0.041)$$
$$t^* \qquad -1.35 \qquad 4.96$$

The variable X explains 76 per cent of the total variations in Y. Only $\hat{\beta}$ is statistically significant at 5 per cent level of significance; $\hat{\alpha}$ is not significant.

Example 3: The least squares estimate of α in $Y = \alpha + \beta X + U$ is

$$\hat{\alpha} = \Sigma \left(\frac{1}{n} - \bar{X} w_i \right) Y_i \ \text{where} \ w_i = \frac{x_i}{\Sigma x_i^2} \ \text{with Var} \ (\hat{\alpha}) = \sigma_u^2 \left(\frac{1}{n} + \frac{\bar{X}^2}{\Sigma x_i^2} \right)$$

Table 6.1: Worksheet for estimation of the food function: $Y = \alpha + \beta X + U$

n	Y_i	X_i	X_i^2	X_iY_i	$y_i = (Y_i - \bar{Y})$	$x_i = (X_i - \bar{X})$	x_iy_i	$x_i^2 = (X_i - \bar{X})^2$	$\hat{Y}_i = (\hat{\alpha} + \hat{\beta}X_i)$	$e_i = (Y_i - \hat{Y}_i)$	e_i^2
1	6	50	2500	300	-2.8	-9.6	26.88	92.16	6.84	-0.85	0.72
2	7	52	2704	364	-1.8	-7.6	13.68	57.76	7.25	-0.25	0.06
3	8	55	3025	440	-0.8	-4.6	3.68	21.16	7.86	0.13	0.02
4	10	59	3481	590	1.2	-0.6	-0.72	0.36	8.67	1.32	1.74
5	8	57	3249	456	-0.8	-2.6	2.08	6.76	8.27	-0.27	0.07
6	9	58	3364	522	0.2	-1.6	-0.32	2.56	8.47	0.53	0.28
7	10	62	3844	620	1.2	2.4	2.88	5.76	9.28	0.71	0.50
8	9	65	4225	585	0.2	5.4	1.08	29.16	9.87	-0.90	0.81
9	11	68	4624	748	2.2	8.4	18.48	70.56	10.51	0.49	0.24
10	10	70	4900	700	1.2	10.4	12.48	108.16	10.91	-0.91	0.83
$n = 10$	$\Sigma Y_i = 88$ $\bar{Y} = 8.8$	$\Sigma X_i = 596$ $\bar{X} = 59.6$	$\Sigma X_i^2 =$ 35916	$\Sigma X_iY_i =$ 5325	$\Sigma y_i = 0$	$\Sigma x_i = 0$	$\Sigma xy_i =$ 80.22	$\Sigma x_i^2 =$ 394.4	$\Sigma \hat{Y}_i = 88$	$\Sigma e_i = 0$	$\Sigma e_i^2 =$ 5.27

Show that no other linear unbiased estimate of α can be constructed with smaller variance.

Let us take the expression:

$$\text{Var}\ (\hat{\alpha}) = \sigma_u^2 \left(\frac{1}{n} + \frac{\overline{X}^2}{\Sigma x_i^2} \right) = \sigma_u^2 \left(\frac{\Sigma x_i^2 + n\overline{X}^2}{n\Sigma x_i^2} \right)$$

$$= \sigma_u^2 \left(\frac{\Sigma X^2 - n\overline{X}^2 + n\overline{X}^2}{n\Sigma x_i^2} \right) \qquad \because \Sigma x_i^2 = \Sigma X^2 - n\overline{X}^2$$

$$= \sigma_u^2 \left(\frac{\Sigma X_i^2}{n\Sigma x_i^2} \right)$$

To show that no other linear unbiased estimator of α can be constructed with smaller variance, refer to 6.4 where we have proved that $\hat{\beta}$ and $\hat{\alpha}$ are the best estimators in the model: $\hat{Y} = \hat{\alpha} + \hat{\beta}X$.

Example 4: Let $\hat{\alpha} = \sum_{i=1}^{n} c_i Y_i$ where $Y_i = \alpha + \beta X_i + U_i$. Using Lagrangian multipliers, find the weights c_i $(i = 1, ..., n)$ which will make $\hat{\alpha}$ a best linear and unbiased estimate of α and show that:

$$c_i = \left(\frac{1}{n} - \frac{\overline{X} x_i}{\Sigma x_i^2} \right)$$

We are given that;

$$\hat{\alpha} = \Sigma c_i Y_i$$
$$\hat{\alpha} = \Sigma c_i (\alpha + \beta X_i + U_i)$$
$$\hat{\alpha} = \alpha \Sigma c_i + \beta \Sigma c_i X_i + \Sigma c_i U_i$$
$$E\ (\hat{\alpha}) = \alpha \Sigma c_i + \beta \Sigma c_i X_i$$

$\hat{\alpha}$ would be an unbiased estimator of α if $\Sigma c_i = 1$ and $\Sigma c_i X_i = 0$.

Using these two conditions, we proceed to minimise the var $(\hat{\alpha}) = \sigma_u^2 \Sigma c_i^2$ with the help of Lagrange's method.

Let the new function be Z; so that

$$Z = \Sigma c_i^2 - \lambda \left(\Sigma c_i - 1 \right) - \mu \Sigma c_i X_i$$

μ and λ are two Lagrangian multipliers. To minimise Z, differentiate it partially w.r.t. c_i $(i = 1, ..., n)$, λ and μ and equate to zero.

$$\frac{\partial Z}{\partial c_i} = 2\Sigma c_i - \lambda - \mu \Sigma X_i = 0 \qquad \qquad ...\text{(i)}$$

$$\frac{\partial Z}{\partial \lambda} = \Sigma c_i - 1 = 0 \qquad \qquad ...\text{(ii)}$$

$$\frac{\partial Z}{\partial \mu} = \Sigma c_i X_i = 0 \qquad \qquad \dots\text{(iii)}$$

From (i), $\qquad \Sigma c_i = \lambda + \mu \Sigma X_i$ ($\because$ λ and μ are unknown multipliers and division by 2 will not make any change)

but from (ii), $\quad \Sigma c_i = 1;$

$\therefore \qquad \qquad \qquad \lambda = \dfrac{1}{n} - \mu \overline{X}$

$\therefore \qquad \qquad \Sigma c_i = \left(\dfrac{1}{n} - \mu \overline{X}\right) + \mu \Sigma X_i = \left(\dfrac{1}{n} - \mu x_i\right) \qquad \dots\text{(iv)}$

From (iii), $\qquad \Sigma c_i X_i = 0$

$$\Sigma \left(\frac{1}{n} - \mu x_i\right) X_i = 0, \quad \therefore \mu = \left(\frac{\overline{X}}{\Sigma x_i^2}\right)$$

Substituting μ in (iv), the desired result is obtained,

i.e., $\qquad \qquad \Sigma c_i = \left\{\dfrac{1}{n} - \left(\dfrac{\overline{X}}{\Sigma x_i^2}\right) x_i\right\}$

ASSIGNMENTS

1. Determine whether the following models are linear in the parameters, or the variables, or both. Which of these models are linear regression models?

   (a) $\quad Y_i = \alpha_0 + \dfrac{\beta}{X_i} + U_i$

   (b) $\quad I_n Y_i = \alpha_0 + \beta X_i + U_i$

   (c) $\quad Y_i = \alpha_0 + \beta I_n X_i + U_i$

   (d) $\quad I_n Y_i = I_n \alpha_0 + \beta I_n X_i + U_i$

   (e) $\quad Y_i = \alpha_0 X_i^{\beta} + U_i$

   (f) $\quad Y_i = \alpha_0 + \beta^3 X_i + U_i$

   Note: I_n = natural log (i.e., log to the base e); U_t is the stochastic disturbance term.

2. The following sums were obtained from 16 pairs of observations on X and Y.
   $\Sigma Y_i^2 = 526$, $\Sigma X_i^2 = 657$, $\Sigma Y_i X_i = 492$, $\Sigma Y_i = 63$, $\Sigma X_i = 96$. Estimate the parameters in the model: $Y_i = \alpha + \beta X_i + U_i$ and R^2. Test the hypothesis that $\beta = 2.0$.

3. A sample of 20 observations corresponding to the regression model:
   $Y_i = \alpha + \beta X_i + U_i$ gave the following data:
   $\Sigma Y = 21.9$, $\Sigma (Y - \overline{Y})^2 = 86.9$, $\Sigma (X - \overline{X})(Y - \overline{Y}) = 106.4$
   $\Sigma X = 186.2$, $\Sigma (X - \overline{X})^2 = 215.4$

   Estimate α and β and calculate estimates of variance of your estimates. Estimate the conditional mean value of Y corresponding to a value of X fixed at $X = 10$.

4. The following table shows the investment expenditure and the long-run interest rate over the ten-year period:

Year	:	1958	1959	1960	1961	1962	1963	1964	1965	1966	1967
Investment	:	656	804	836	765	777	711	755	747	696	787
Interest	:	0.05	0.045	0.045	0.055	0.06	0.06	0.06	0.05	0.07	0.065

Test the hypothesis that investment is interest elastic by fitting a regression line to the above data and conducting the relevant tests of significance.

5. Given the following data:
$\Sigma x_i y_i = 200$, $\Sigma x_i^2 = 100$, $\Sigma Y_i^2 = 500$, $\overline{X} = 100$, $\overline{Y} = 150$. $n = 27$, estimate the parameters in the model: $Y = \alpha + \beta X_i + U_i$ and test the hypothesis $H_0 : \beta = 1.5$ against the alternative hypothesis $H_1 : \beta > 1.5$.

6. The true relationship between X and Y in the population is given by:
$Y_i = 2 + 3X_i + U_i$. Suppose the values of X in the sample of 10 observations are 1, 2, 3, ..., 10. The values of the disturbances are drawn at random from a normal population with zero mean and constant variance:
$U_1 = 0.464$, $U_2 = 0.06$, $U_3 = 1.48$, $U_4 = 1.02$, $U_5 = 1.39$, $U_6 = 0.91$, $U_7 = -1.50$, $U_8 = -0.69$, $U_9 = 0.18$ and $U_{10} = -1.37$.
   (a) Present the 10 observed values of X and Y.
   (b) Estimate the least squares estimates of the regression coefficients and their standard errors.
   (c) Obtain the predicted value of Y for $X = 12$.

7. Suppose that our regression model does not contain a constant term that is, $Y_i = \beta X_i + U_i$. Show that the least squares estimate of β is $\hat{\beta} = \dfrac{\Sigma X_i Y_i}{\Sigma X_i^2}$. Under what conditions, if any, will β be equal to the least squares estimator of b in $Y_i = a + bX_i + U_i$? How would you define R^2 in the estimation of $Y_i = \beta X_i + U_i$?

8 Prove that the estimated regression coefficients for a linear regression equation with an intercept term are identical to those obtained for the same linear regression equation without an intercept term, but for which all variables are replaced by deviations from their mean values.

9 Suppose the explanatory variable X in $Y_i = \alpha + \beta X_i + U_i$ can only assume the values of 0 and 1. The sample consists of n_1 observations for which $X = 0$, and n_2 observations for which $X = 1$. Let $\overline{Y_1}$ be the mean value of Y for n_1 observations for which $X = 0$, and $\overline{Y_2}$ be the mean value of Y for the n_2 observations for which $X = 1$.
Find $\hat{\alpha}$, $\hat{\beta}$, Var $(\hat{\alpha})$ and Var $(\hat{\beta})$.

10 Assume it is given from theoretical consideration that the total amount of inventories of a commodity X held in stock is an increasing linear function of the rate of change of price of X.
In symbolic notation: $Y_t = \alpha + \beta (P_t - P_{t-1})$, where Y_t denotes inventories in month t and p_t is the price in month t. The following sample of observation is given:

(t)	0	1	2	3	4	5	6	7	8	9	10
(Y_t)	15	20	15	25	30	40	50	45	55	50	60
(P_t)	10	9	6	4	4	5	7	9	13	16	19

   (a) Estimate the parameters of inventory function by least squares.
   (b) What percentage of the total variation in inventories is explained by the price spread?
   (c) Test the significance of regression coefficients.

11. The following data gives the production of coal and the number of wage-earners in the coal industry:

Output
(million tonnes) } 210.8 210.1 211.5 208.9 207.4 205.3 198.8
192.1 183.2 176.8

Number of
workers (000's) } 706.2 703.1 701.8 699.1 697.4 795.3 692.7
630.2 602.1 531.0

(a) Estimate the (linear) production function of coal.
(b) Find average and marginal productivity of labour.
(c) Estimate *t-ratios* and test their significance.

12. Suppose that Mr. A estimates a consumption function and obtains the results:
$$\hat{C} = 15 + 0.81\, Y_d \qquad R^2 = 0.99$$
$$(3.1) \quad (18.7) \qquad n = 19$$
$\hat{C}$ is consumption; Y_d is disposable income, the numbers in parentheses are *t-ratios*.
(a) Test the significance of Y_d statistically using *t-ratios*.
(b) Determine the estimated standard derivations of the parameter estimators.
(c) Construct a 95 per cent confidence interval for the coefficient Y_d.

13. Prove that the estimated regression line $\hat{Y} = \hat{\alpha} + \hat{\beta} X$ passes through the point of the means $(\overline{X}, \overline{Y})$.

14. Show that the OLS estimator $(\hat{\beta}_0)$ of the model: $Y_t = \hat{\beta}_0 + U_t$ $(t = 1, 2, \dots n)$ is given by the mean value of Y, that is; $\hat{\beta}_0 = \overline{Y}$. Also prove that, if U satisfies the standard assumptions,

(i) $E(\hat{\beta}_0) = \beta_0$ and,

(ii) $\mathrm{var}\,(\hat{\beta}_0) = \left(\dfrac{1}{n}\right)\sigma_u^2$.

15. The true relations between Y and X is given by:
$$Y_i = \alpha_0 + \beta_1 X_i + U_i, \qquad (i = 1, 2, \dots, n)$$
An investigator attempts to estimate β_1 without considering an intercept term α_0.
(i) Show that the estimates of β_1 will be biased.
(ii) Derive an expression of this bias.
(iii) Under what conditions would bias be zero?

Functional Forms of Regression
Models and Methods of Estimation

One of the strict assumptions of the classical linear regression model is that the regressand Y is a linear function of the regressors $X_1, X_2, \dots X_k$.

It may be noted here that the word regressor(s) has been used in place of explanatory variable(s). Distinction is to be made between an explanatory variable and the regressor that represents it in any regression model. For example, if we consider consumption (Y) to be a function of disposable income (X) and write $Y = f(X) = \alpha + \beta_1 X + \beta_2 X^2$ then, income is an explanatory variable while regressors are two; income and income squared. What classical model requires is that Y be a linear function of the regressors.

Linear assumption may be unduly limiting in some cases. Also, the economic theory that proposes that Y is a function of X rarely specifies the exact functional form. Unless theory indicates unambiguously that the linear form is an adequate representation of the true relation, it is well to adopt other than linear functional form.

In the present chapter we examine some of the commonly used functional forms and their special features.

7.1 FUNCTIONAL FORMS

1. *Double-log, Log-linear, or Constant-elasticity Models*
   Consider the following model:

$$Y_i = \alpha_0 X_i^{-\beta} e^{U_i}$$

which may be expressed alternatively as

$$I_n Y_i = I_n \alpha_0 - \beta I_n X_i + U_i$$

where I_n = natural log (i.e., log to the base e, where e = 2.718). The logarithms of the variables Y and X are linearly related in the model, hence the name double-log or log-linear model. If all the assumptions of classical linear regression model hold true, the parameters of the above model can be estimated by method of OLS by letting: $Y^* = \alpha - \beta X_i^* + U_i$
where $Y_i^* = I_n Y_i$, $X_i^* = I_n X_i$ and $\alpha = I_n \alpha_0$.

The OLS estimators $\hat{\alpha}_0$ and $\hat{\beta}$ thus obtained will be BLUE of α and β respectively.

The important feature of this model is that the slope coefficient β measures the elasticity of Y with respect to X. Thus, if Y depicts the quantity of a commodity demanded and X its unit price, β measures the price elasticity of demand. The diagrammatic representation of the model can be shown in the form of Fig. 7.1 (a) and (b).

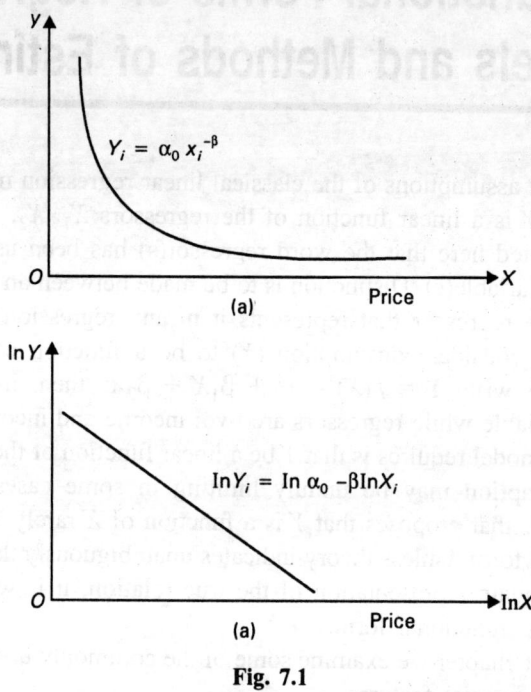

Fig. 7.1

The log-linear model possesses two special characteristics:

(i) The model assumes that the elasticity coefficient between Y and X (which is β) remains constant throughout; hence the alternative name constant-elasticity model.
(ii) Although $\hat{\alpha}_0$ and $\hat{\beta}$ are unbiased estimators of α_0 and β, $\hat{\alpha}_0$ [= antilog $(\hat{\alpha}_0)$] is a biased estimator. Nevertheless it is a consistent estimator of α_0. But since the intercept term is of secondary importance in most practical problems, one need not worry about obtaining its biased estimate.

2. *Semilog Models*
The models of the following two forms are called semilog models:

$$I_n Y_i = \alpha_0 + \alpha_1 X_i + U_i,$$
$$\text{and,} \quad Y_i = \beta_0 + \beta_1 I_n X_i + U_i$$

In the first model, it can be shown that the slope coefficient α_1 measures the proportional change in Y for a given absolute change in X, that is:

$$\alpha_1 = \frac{d}{dX_i}(I_n Y_i) = \left(\frac{1}{Y_i}\right)\left(\frac{dY_i}{dX_i}\right) = \left(\frac{dY_i}{Y_i}\right)\left(\frac{1}{dX_i}\right) = \frac{\Delta Y/Y}{\Delta X}$$

Therefore, $\quad \alpha_1 = \dfrac{\text{Proportional change in } Y}{\text{Absolute change in } X}$

The above model (see Fig. 7.2) is, therefore, most appropriate in the situations where it is observed that for a given change in X, Y changes by a constant percentage amount. Hence, this model is also called a constant growth model.

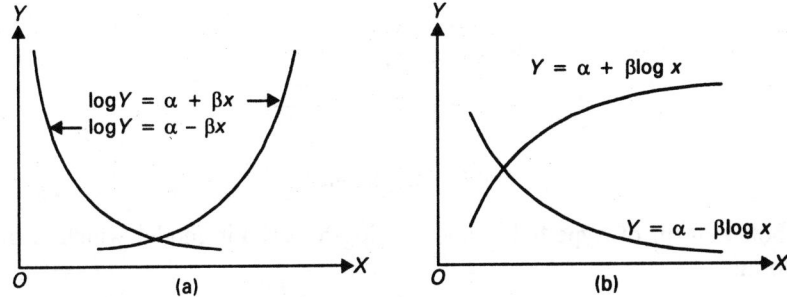

Fig. 7.2: Semilogarithmic Models

In the second model, it can be shown that slope coefficient β measures absolute change in mean value of Y for a given proportional change in X;

$$\frac{dY_i}{dX_i} = \beta_1\left(\frac{1}{X_i}\right)$$

$$\beta_1 = \frac{\Delta Y}{\Delta X/X}$$

$$\beta_1 = \frac{\text{Absolute change in } Y}{\text{Proportional change in } X}$$

Therefore, in situations where it is observed that for a given proportional change in X, Y changes by a constant absolute amount, the second model is most appropriate.

3. *Reciprocal Transformation or Hyperbolic Models*

The model of the form: $Y_i = \alpha + \beta\left(\dfrac{1}{X_i}\right) + U_i$ is called reciprocal transformation model. If α and β are positive, this model shows that Y

decreases nonlinearly as X increases. The special feature of this model, as shown in Fig. 7.3, is that the Y declines continuously as X increases and eventually becomes asymptotic constant value equal to the intercept term of the model. Such models have, therefore, built in them an asymptotic value or limit value which the dependent variable will take when the value of X variable increases indefinitely. An estimate of the asymptotic value is provided by $\hat{\alpha}$.

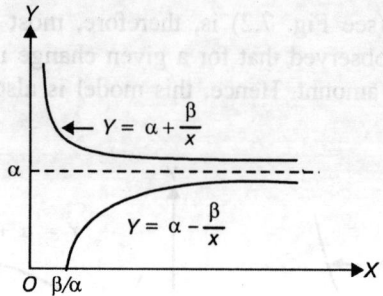

Fig. 7.3: Hyperbolic

Another form of hyperbolic model is log-hyperbolic model which is of the form:

$$I_n Y_i = \alpha - \beta \left(\frac{1}{X_i} \right) + U_i$$

Or, $Y_i = e^{\alpha - \beta/X_i} U_i$

Its shape is described in Fig. 7.4.

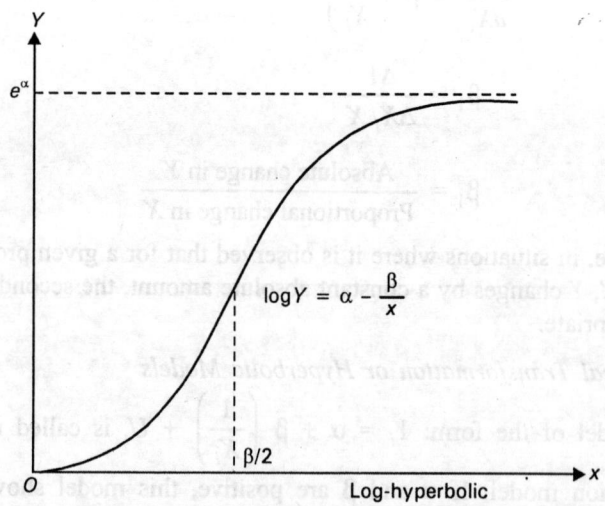

Fig. 7.4: Log-hyperbolic

Differentiating; we obtain,

$$\frac{dY}{dX} = e^{\alpha - \beta/X}\left(\frac{\beta}{X^2}\right),$$

hence slope is positive for positive X.

Second derivative; $\dfrac{d^2Y}{dX^2} = e^{\alpha - \beta/X}\left(\dfrac{\beta^2}{X^4} - \dfrac{2\beta}{X^3}\right),$

hence there is *point of inflexion* where X is $\beta/2$.

To the left of this point, the slope increases with X; to the right of it, the slope diminishes. An asymptotic value is e^{α}, hence as X tends to infinity $Y \rightarrow e^{\alpha}$.

All possible forms of models that are used in empirical research have been described in Table 7.1; wherein slope and elasticity coefficients have also been derived for each functional form.

7.2 CHOICE OF FUNCTIONAL FORM

The choice among alternative functional forms described above involves a compromise among several criteria including economic theory, goodness of fit, and simplicity. No definite role cites which form is an appropriate one for a given problem. The researcher has to decide this for himself depending on the peculiar problem under study. However one can observe the following general criteria for a specific functional form.

The *first* and the *foremost* criterion is that one should rely on economic theory as much as possible in choosing functional forms. Indeed, the objective of econometrics is to give empirical content to economic theory.

Fitting by various functional forms and choosing a 'nice-looking' one without any theoretical justification is merely a *measurement without theory*. Such an approach, as already emphasised, will be absurd. It would simply be a statistical exercise, not an econometric analysis.

Second, the simple form is to be preferred to the more complicated one if the two can explain the problem equally well. Though it is not always obvious; which of the two forms is the simpler, yet it is reasonable to assert that the smaller the number of parameters, the simpler the function.

The *third* criterion is that the functional form should fit the data well otherwise the chosen model will not have good prediction power. The common agreement on the criterion of goodness of fit is to rely on $\overline{R}^2$. The higher the value of $\overline{R}^2$, the larger the proportion of the dependent variable explained by a set of independent variables.

One should be cautions while applying this criterion. The determination coefficient; R^2 may be misleading as a measure of goodness of fit when the regressand has been transformed. For instance, if a double-log form has been the functional form, the R^2 measures the proportion of the variation of

Table 7.1: Alternative Functional Forms

Name of Function	Algebraic Relation	Slope	Elasticity Coefficient
1. Linear	(i) $Y = \alpha + \beta X$	$(+)\ \beta$	$(+)\ \beta\left(\dfrac{X}{Y}\right)$
	(ii) $Y = \alpha - \beta X$	$(-)\ \beta$	$(-)\ \beta\left(\dfrac{X}{Y}\right)$
2. Quadratic	(i) $Y = \alpha + \beta_1 X - \beta_2 X^2$	$(+)\ (\beta_1 - 2\beta_2 X)$	$(+)\ \dfrac{(\beta_1 - 2\beta_2 X)}{Y}$
	(ii) $Y = \alpha - \beta_1 X - \beta_2 X^2$	$(-)\ (\beta_1 - 2\beta_2 X)$	$(-)\ \dfrac{(\beta_1 - 2\beta_2 X)}{Y}$
3. Hyperbolic	(i) $Y = \alpha + \dfrac{\beta}{X}$	$(-)\ \dfrac{\beta}{X^2}$	$(-)\ \beta\left(\dfrac{1}{XY}\right)$
	(ii) $Y = \alpha - \dfrac{\beta}{X}$	$(+)\ \dfrac{\beta}{X^2}$	$(+)\ \beta\left(\dfrac{1}{XY}\right)$
4. Semilogarithmic	(i) $\log_e Y = \alpha + \beta X$ or, $Y = e^{\alpha + \beta X}$	$(+)\ \beta Y$	$(+)\ \beta(X)$
	(ii) $\log_e Y = \alpha - \beta X$ or, $Y = e^{\alpha - \beta X}$	$(-)\ \beta Y$	$(-)\ \beta(X)$
	(iii) $Y = \alpha + \beta \log_e X$ or, $e^Y = a + X^{\beta}$	$(+)\ \dfrac{\beta}{X}$	$(+)\ \beta\left(\dfrac{1}{Y}\right)$
	(iv) $Y = \alpha - \beta \log_e X$ or, $e^Y = a + X^{-\beta}$	$(-)\ \dfrac{\beta}{X}$	$(-)\ \beta\left(\dfrac{1}{Y}\right)$

(Contd.)

(Table 7.1 Contd.)

Name of Function	Algebraic Relation	Slope	Elasticity Coefficient
5. Log-quadratic	(i) $\log_e Y = \alpha + \beta_1 X - \beta_2 X^2$ (ii) $\log_e Y = \alpha - \beta_1 X - \beta_2 X^2$	(+) $Y(\beta_1 - 2\beta_2 X)$ (−) $Y(\beta_1 - 2\beta_2 X)$	(+) $(\beta_1 - 2\beta_2 X)\, X$ (−) $(\beta_1 - 2\beta_2 X)\, X$
6. Log-Hyperbolic (Log-inverse)	(i) $\log_e Y = \alpha + \dfrac{\beta}{X}$ or, $Y = e^{\alpha + (\beta/X)}$	(−) $\dfrac{\beta Y}{X^2}$	(−) $\beta \left(\dfrac{1}{X}\right)$
	(ii) $\log_e Y = \alpha - \dfrac{\beta}{X}$ or, $Y = e^{\alpha - (\beta/X)}$	(+) $\dfrac{\beta Y}{X^2}$	(+) $\beta \left(\dfrac{1}{X}\right)$
7. Double logarithmic	(i) $\log_e Y = \alpha + \beta \log_e X$ or, $Y = aX^\beta$	(+) $\dfrac{\beta Y}{X}$	(+) β
	(ii) $\log_e Y = \alpha - \beta \log_e X$ or, $Y = aX^{-\beta}$	(−) $\dfrac{\beta Y}{X}$	(−) β

the logarithm of Y that has been accounted for, which is not the same thing as the proportion of the variation of Y. To put such a model on a comparable footing with one that simply has Y as the regressand, we should take antilogs of the calculated values of (Log Y) and find their coefficient of determination with the observed values of Y. A detailed account on such other related problems is presented under Section 8.6 in Chapter 8.

7.3 TESTS FOR LINEARITY

So far our main problem had been that of estimating the parameters of a model, the functional form of which is assumed to be known. In other words, we do not make use of any statistical test before we commit ourselves to a specific functional form. But we may want to consider the specification of the functional form as a testable rather than a *maintained hypothesis*. The hypothesis to be tested in this context would be that of linearity. That is, we may like to test the hypothesis that the population regression equation is linear with respect to variables against some alternative hypothesis.

The following three different tests of linearity have been suggested:

1. The simplest test is to test the hypothesis of linearity against the alternative hypothesis which assumes a power function of a specific degree as an alternative to the linearity.

Suppose we propose two alternative functional forms for a data under study:

Linear: $Y_i = \alpha + \beta_1 X_i + U_i$

Cubic: $Y_i = \alpha + \beta_1 X_i + \beta_2 X_i^2 + \beta_3 X_i^3 + U_i$

We may not wish to test the hypothesis that the population regression equation is linear against the alternative hypothesis that regression equation is represented by a polynomial of degree three. The formulation would be,

$$H_0: \beta_2 = \beta_3 = 0$$
$$H_A: H_0 \text{ is false.}$$

If H_0 comes out to be true, it would mean that the variation of Y from observation to observation is not affected by X_i^2 and X_i^3; in other words the addition of X_i^2 and X_i^3 contribute nothing to the explanation of variations in Y. That is, our regression equation ought to be linear one.

The basic idea underlying the test is that a linear function is a special case of a power function, namely, a power function of degree one. If the coefficients attached to the higher powers of the explanatory variables are all zero, the given power function reduces to a simple linear regression.

To test the null hypothesis of $\beta_2 = \beta_3 = 0$, F-statistic will have to be computed:

$$F = \frac{\left(ESS_Q - ESS_L\right)/Q - L}{RSS_Q/N - Q}; \text{ where}$$

ESS_Q = Explained Sum of Squares (i.e., $\Sigma \hat{y}i^2$) when cubic form of equation is fitted to data

ESS_L = Explained Sum of Squares (i.e., $\Sigma \hat{y}i^2$) when linear form of equation is fitted to data

RSS_Q = Residual Sum of Squares in case of cubic form of equation

N = Total number of observations

$L = 2$ ($\because$ there are two parameters, including constant term, in linear form)

$Q = 4$

F-statistics can also be defined in terms of R^2.

$$F = \left(\frac{ESS_Q - ESS_L}{RSS_Q}\right)\left(\frac{N-Q}{Q-L}\right)$$

$$F = \frac{(ESS_Q/TSS) - (ESS_L/TSS)}{1 - (RSS_Q/TSS)}\left(\frac{N-Q}{Q-L}\right)$$

$$F = \left(\frac{R_Q^2 - R_L^2}{1 - R_Q^2}\right)\left(\frac{N-Q}{Q-L}\right)$$

Example: Suppose for a data; $N = 31$, a researcher obtained the following results:

$$Y_t = \alpha + \beta_1 X_t + U_t \qquad\qquad \bar{R}^2 = 0.944$$
$$Y_t = \alpha + \beta_1 X_t + \beta_2 X_t^2 + \beta_3 X_t^3 + U_t \qquad \bar{R}^2 = 0.984$$

Which form should he accept for the data under study?

In the above example, $N = 31$, $L = 2$, $Q = 4$, $\bar{R}_Q = 0.984$ and $\bar{R}_L^2 = 0.944$. We are to test the hypothesis; $H_0: \beta_2 = \beta_3 = 0$ against the alternative that H_0 is not true at 1 per cent level of significance.

First, we must obtain the values of uncorrected R^2's. We know

$$\bar{R}^2 = R^2 - \left(\frac{K-1}{N-K}\right)(1 - R^2)$$

Substituting the relevant values, we obtain; $R_L^2 = 0.946$ and $R_Q^2 = 0.986$. The value of F-statistics is then;

$$F = \left(\frac{R_Q^2 - R_L^2}{1 - R_Q^2}\right)\left(\frac{N-Q}{Q-L}\right) = 38.57$$

The tabulated value of $F(2, 27)$ at 1 per cent level of significance is 5.49; the null hypothesis has, therefore, to be rejected.

The drawback in the above test is that we have to commit ourselves to the functional form of a specific degree as an alternative to the linear model. In the following tests the hypothesis that the population regression equation is linear with respect to the variables is tested without specifying the alternatives functional form(s).

2. The obvious implication of linearity is that the slope and the intercept of the regression equation must remain constant over all values of the explanatory variable. To examine this, we divide the sample observations into subsamples; estimate the slope and intercept for each subsample and then test whether these are statistically different from one subsample to another. If they turn out to be different, it would mean that the population regression equation does not conform with the linearity.

Given sample of N observations is, first, arranged so that

$$X_1 \leq X_2 \leq X_3 \leq ... \leq X_N.$$

The sample is then divided, say, into two subsamples:

Subsample 1: $X_1, X_2, ... X_m$

Subsample 2: $X_{m+1}, X_{m+2}, ... X_N$

We make use of *dummy* variables to set up the regression model as follows (Refer Chapter 11 for such estimation technique)

$$Y_i = \alpha + \beta_1 X_i + \beta_2 D_{i1} + \beta_3 (X_i D_{i1}) + \beta_4 D_{i2} + \beta_5 (X_i D_{i2}) + Ui$$

$D_1 = 1$ if i belongs to subsample 1.

$\quad = 0$, otherwise.

$D_2 = 1$ if i belongs to subsample 2.

$\quad = 0$, otherwise.

The hypothesis of linearity can then be tested as follows

$$H_0: \beta_2 = \beta_3 = \beta_4 = \beta_5 = 0$$

$$H_A: H_0 \text{ is false.}$$

The regression equation with respect to first subsample shall be:

$$Y_i = (\alpha + \beta_2) + (\beta_1 + \beta_3) X_i + U_i$$

The regression equation with respect to second subsample shall be:

$$Y_i = (\alpha + \beta_4) + (\beta_1 + \beta_5) X_i + U_i$$

If H_0 is true, then both depict the same intercept ($= \alpha$) and slope ($= \beta_1$)

To test the null hypothesis, F-statistic, as described in Test 1 is to be computed.

3. The third test of linearity which does not rely on the specification of the alternative functional form is based on the examination of the residual patterns. The usual assumption about the disturbance terms is that they are randomly scattered around the population regression line; i.e., they should tend to have no special pattern about the population line. If the population regression is not linear, the scatter of the disturbance terms around the straight line will no longer be random.

The most common way of examining the pattern of disturbance terms, therefore, is to plot the residuals (e_i's) against the observed dependent variable. If the pattern of residuals show a $\cap$ or $\cup$ shapes, then it may be said that a linear equation does not fit the data properly.

The difficulty in this test is that the disturbance terms (i.e., deviations from the population regression line) are not observable. We just approximate them with residuals (i.e., deviations from the sample regression line). The problem is that the independency amongst the disturbances does not go with the independency amongst the residuals. In other words the residuals may not be independent even if the disturbances themselves are.

7.4 TIME AS A TREND VARIABLE

At times the OLS estimation of a regression model leads to a spurious relation between the dependent and explanatory variables even though there may not be any causal relation among them. This happens when the variables happen to be moving in the same direction over a period of time. The significant association which is obtained under such situation is spurious and does not reflect the influence of one variable on the movement of the other. This problem is met out by introducing the time or trend variable in addition to several other explanatory variables.

The time variable is introduced for the following two reasons:

(i) The trend variable acts as a substitute for a basic variable which is not directly observable (or its data is not available) but is known to affect the dependent variable. For instance, in production theory, technology is one such variable, the impact of which is definitely felt yet it cannot be observed directly. It may, therefore, be convenient to assume that technology is some function of time measured chronologically. Again, in some situations, it may be that a basic variable affecting dependent variable is so closely related to time that it is advisable cost-wise to introduce the time variable itself rather the basic variable.

(ii) Our interest may be to examine how dependent variable behaves over a period of time. In this case, the objective is not to look for the causes behind the upward or downward trend but simply to describe the data over time. Also, at times it may be necessary to eliminate the trend component from the time-series data (so as to obtain trend-corrected variables) before making the data usable for the study under investigation. The present section is concerned with this specific problem. That is, in what different ways the growth of the variable over the period can be measured. The growth path may be of linear form or quadratic, or cubic, and so forth, or logarithmic or exponential, or trigonometric, or any one of a large number of other forms.

Alternative Functional Forms Used for the Trend Equation

(i) *Linear Trend-Equation:* $Y_t = \alpha + \beta t + U_t$.

In this form, β is the nature of a constant absolute increment in Y per unit of time and, in the normal case of positive β, implies *decelerating compound growth rate* in the dependent variable Y.

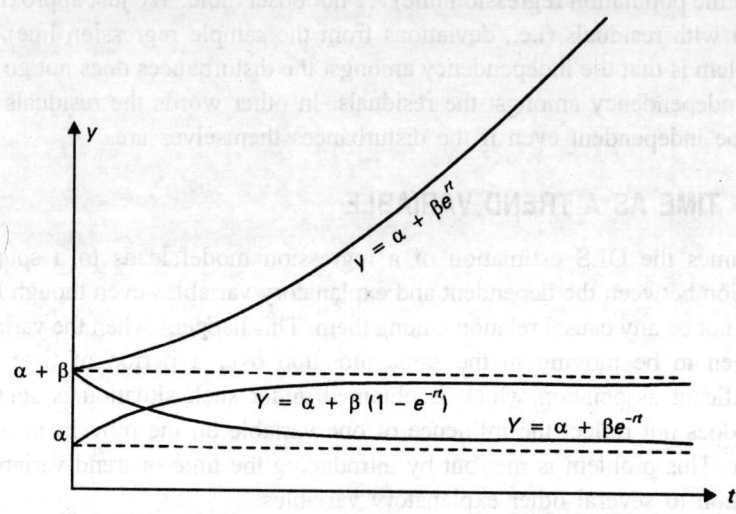

$$y = \alpha + \beta e^{\gamma t}$$

$$Y = \alpha + \beta (1 - e^{-\gamma t})$$

$$Y = \alpha + \beta e^{-\gamma t}$$

Fig. 7.5

(ii) *Exponential Trend-Equations:*

$$Y_t = \alpha + \beta e^{\gamma t}$$
$$Y_t = \alpha + \beta e^{-\gamma t}$$
$$Y_t = \alpha + \beta (1 - e^{-\gamma t})$$

α, β and γ are positive constants in these trend-equations. The Fig. 7.5 shows their graphs.

(iii) *Logistic Trend-Equation:* $Y_t = \dfrac{\alpha}{1 + \beta e^{-\gamma t}}$

This is an *S*-shaped curve as shown in Fig. 7.6.

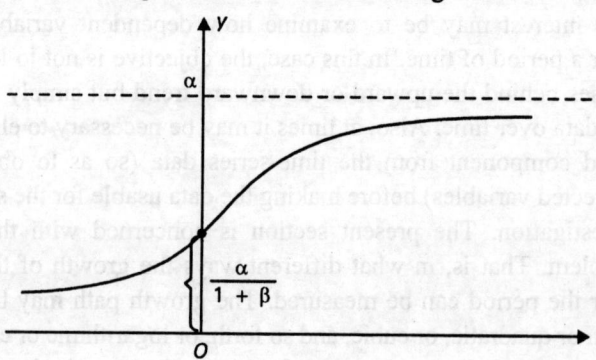

Fig. 7.6

It is used in studying the growth of population. Its salient feature is that the rate of growth begins at a low level, reaches maximum, and then declines so that the growing quantity approaches a definite maximum value or asymptotic value = α.

7.5 ESTIMATION OF NONLINEAR REGRESSION MODELS

7.5.1 Intrinsically Linear Model

As explained earlier, these models are nonlinear with respect to the variables but linear with respect to the parameters to be estimated. The basic common characteristic of such models is that they can be converted into ordinary linear models by a suitable transformation of the variables. Transformation involved is nothing more than relabeling the variables which appear in nonlinear form.

We discuss the following forms of intrinsically linear models.

(i) *Transformation of Polynomials:* If the function is a polynomial in the explanatory variables, the regression model is

$$Y_i = \beta_0 + \beta_1 X_i + \beta_2 X_i^2 + \cdots + \beta_n X_i^n + U_i$$

where, X_i is nonstochastic and U_i satisfies all the assumptions of the classical linear regression model.

For OLS computation of the parameter estimates, we relabel the nonlinear variables as under:

$X^2 = Z_1$, $X^3 = Z_2$, ... and proceed with the application of OLS to the linear relation:

$$Y_i = \beta_0 + \beta_1 X_i + \beta_2 Z_{1i} + \beta_2 Z_{2i} + \dots + U_i$$

Similarly, all the nonlinear models we have discussed under Section 7.1 can be converted to linear models by a suitable transformation.

(ii) *Transformation of Constant Elasticity Model:* The double log form, which incorporates a constant elasticity is very common in econometric estimation.

The nonlinear relations:

$$Y = \alpha X_1^{\beta_1} X_2^{\beta_2}$$

may be written as,

$$\log Y = \log \alpha + \beta_1 \log X_1 + \beta_2 \log X_2$$

which is again a linear relationship:

$$Y^* = \alpha^* + \beta_1 X_1^* + \beta_2 X_2^*$$

Now in case the classical linear regression model is to be appropriate for the above log-linear equation, a special assumption about the disturbance term for the original model is required. The disturbance term may be introduced in original form in two ways:

(a) as an multiplicative term; then the original model is described as:

$$Y_i = \alpha X_1^{\beta_1} X_2^{\beta_2} U_i$$

This is, then, called a multiplicative model*.

(b) as an additive term; then the original model is described as:

$$Y_i = \alpha X_1^{\beta_1} X_2^{\beta_2} + U_i$$

In above case, no transformation of the variables could lead to a regression equation that would be linear in the β's, so the equation would have to be classified as intrinsically non-linear.

Our concern under this section is with intrinsically linear models; that is multiplicative form of model:

$$Y_i = \alpha\, X_1^{\beta_1} X_2^{\beta_2} U_i$$

We can not set $E(U) = 0$ in this multiplicative form, because then the function (on the average) would vanish. Instead either of the following convenient forms has to be considered:

$$Y_i = \alpha\, X_1^{\beta_1} X_2^{\beta_2}\, 10^{U_i} \qquad\qquad ...(7.1)$$

$$Y_i = \alpha\, X_1^{\beta_1} X_2^{\beta_2}\, e^{U_i} \qquad\qquad ...(7.2)$$

In the form (7.1), the log to the base 10 will have to be used, while in form (7.2) the log to the base e (natural logarithms) will have to be used for transformation purposes so that;

$$Y_i^* = \alpha^* + \beta_1 X_1^* + \beta_2 X_2^* + U_i \qquad\qquad ...(7.3)$$

where the star marked variables are either *log* to the base 10 or *log* to the base e of the original values of the variables. We can retain the usual assumptions:

$$E(U_i) = 0;\; E(U_i^2) = \sigma_u^2,\; E(U_i U_j) = 0 \text{ for } i \neq j, \text{ and, } E\,(UX) = 0.$$

But one point is to be noted here regarding the statistical properties of the constant term (α).

Equation (7.3) is linear with respect to α^* ($= \log \alpha$) and the β's but not with respect to α. Hence, if the assumption of the classical normal linear regression model are satisfied, the OLS estimators of α^*, β_1 and β_2 will possess the desirable statistical properties.

Will the desirable properties be carried over to $\hat{\alpha}$? Unfortunately answer is No.

This can be understood as follows:

$\alpha^* = \log \alpha$, taking antilog;

$\alpha = e^{\alpha^*}$ (in case log to the base e has been used)

---

* When explanatory variables enter multiplicatively rather than additively into the model, it is called Multiplicative Model.

Thus, the obtained estimate of α would be

$$\hat{\alpha} = e^{\hat{\alpha}*}$$

But $\hat{\alpha}$ is not an unbiased estimator of α despite the fact that $E(\hat{\alpha}*) = \alpha*$.
In other words what is required to be noted here is that

$$e^{E(\hat{\alpha}*)} = e^{\alpha*},$$

hence, $$E(\hat{\alpha}) = e^{\alpha*}$$

which is not equal to α to make $\hat{\alpha}$ an unbiased estimator.

However the bias and variance tends to zero as $n \to \infty$; that is $\hat{\alpha}$ inherits all the desirable asymptotic properties from $\alpha*$ but not the small sample properties.**

Again, in this model:

$$E(Y) \neq \alpha X_1^{\beta_1} X_2^{\beta_2}$$

because $$E(e^U) \neq e^{E(U)} = e^0 = 1$$

That is, $E(e^U) \neq 1$ but is equal to some constant value other than unity.

Hence $$E(Y) = \alpha E(e^U) X_1^{\beta_1} X_2^{\beta_2} = (\alpha C) X_1^{\beta_1} X_2^{\beta_2}$$

(where C depicts some constant value).

7.5.2   Intrinsically Nonlinear Model

Such models, as defined above, are non-linear with respect to variables as well as with respect to the parameters.

(i) Additive Constant Elasticity Model comes under this category:

$$Y_i = \alpha X_1^{\beta_1} X_2^{\beta_2} + U_i \qquad \qquad ...(7.4)$$

There exists no transformation that would convert (7.4) into a linear relationship with respect to parameters. However if X_1 and X_2 are nonstochastic and U_i satisfies all the assumptions of classical linear regression model, the technique of maximum likelihood method of estimation is used to estimate such a model.

The likelihood function for sample of size N is given by:

$$L = \frac{N}{2} \log 2\pi - \frac{N}{2} \log \sigma^2 - \frac{1}{2\sigma^2}\left[\Sigma \left(Y_i - \alpha X_i^{\beta_1} X_2^{\beta_2} \right)^2 \right]$$

** If we assume that U_i in the traditional form of (7.3) is normally distributed with zero mean and constant variance σ^2, the model before transformation may be put as $Y_i = \alpha X_1^{\beta_1} X_2^{\beta_2} \eta_i$ with the assumption that the logarithm (to the base 10 or e) of η_i is normally distributed with zero mean and variance σ^2. Alternatively, η_i would be called log-normal.

A variable is said to be log-normally distributed if and only if its logarithm is normally distributed. (Refer section 2.6)

To maximise this function, obtain partial derivatives with respect to α_1, β_1, β_2 and σ^2, and equate it to zero. This leads to a system of *four* equations which are again nonlinear with respect to the four unknowns. The solution of such system of equation is obtained through computer. The value of the parameters that maximise the value of L are the desired maximum likelihood estimates of α, β_1, β_2 and σ^2. They possess the desirable asymptotic properties.

(ii) CES (Constant Elasticity of Substitution) production function is also an example of intrinsically nonlinear model

$$Q_i = A\left[\alpha K_i^{-\rho} + (1-\alpha) L_i^{-\rho}\right]^{-v/\rho} e^{U_i} \qquad ...(7.5)$$

where, Q_i = output, K_i = capital input, L_i = labour input, e = 2.71828..., parameters A, α, v and ρ are called 'efficiency', 'distribution', 'returns to scale' and 'substitution' parameters respectively.

By taking logarithms (to the base e) of both sides of (7.5), we obtain:

$$\log Q_i = \log A - \frac{v}{\rho}\log\left[\alpha K_i^{-\rho} + (1-\alpha) L_i^{-\rho}\right] + U_i$$

If K_i and L_i are nonstochastic and independent of U_i, also the likelihood function is maximised with the help of computer to obtain maximum likelihood estimates of A, α, v and ρ.

7.5.3 Estimation of Constant-Elasticity Models

Example 1: Table 7.2 presents the total net investment (I) and interest rate (i). It is required to estimate the total net investment function for the economy as a whole, assumed to be of the form:

$$I = f(i) = \alpha\,(i)^\beta$$

The relevant calculations are shown in the Worksheet 7.2.

(i) $\qquad \hat{\beta} = \dfrac{\Sigma x_i y_i}{\Sigma x_i^2} = \dfrac{(-)3.4866}{2.6891} = (-)\,1.2966$

$$\log_e \alpha = \left\{\bar{Y} - (-1.2966)(1.5157)\right\} = 3.0812$$

(ii) $\qquad R^2 = \dfrac{\hat{\beta}\,\Sigma x_i y_i}{\Sigma y_i^2} = \dfrac{4.5149}{4.8566} = 0.93$

(iii) $\qquad \hat{\sigma}_u^2 = \dfrac{\Sigma e_i^2}{n-2} = \dfrac{0.3416}{9} = 0.0379$

(iv) $\quad$ Var $(\hat{\beta}) = \dfrac{\hat{\sigma}_u^2}{\Sigma x_i^2} = \dfrac{0.0379}{2.6891} = 0.0141$

$\therefore$ SE $(\hat{\beta}) = \sqrt{0.0141} = 0.1188$

Table 7.2: Worksheet for Model: $I = \alpha (i)^\beta_U$

n	I (million Rs.)	i (percent)	Y = $\log_e(I)$	X = $\log_e(i)$	X_i^2	X_iY_i	x_i $(X - \bar{X})$	y_i $(Y - \bar{Y})$	x_iy_i	x_i^2	y_i^2
1	9.0	2.0	2.1972	0.6931	0.4804	1.5229	-0.8226	1.0811	-0.8893	0.6766	1.1688
2	5.5	3.0	1.047	1.0986	1.2069	1.8728	-0.4171	0.5886	-0.2455	0.1740	0.3464
3	8.5	2.0	2.1401	0.6931	0.4804	1.4833	-0.8226	1.0240	-0.8423	0.6767	1.0486
4	4.0	4.0	1.3863	1.3863	1.9218	1.9218	-0.1294	0.2702	-0.0350	0.0167	0.0730
5	3.5	5.0	1.2528	1.6094	2.5901	2.0162	0.0937	0.1367	+0.0128	0.0188	0.0187
6	2.5	6.0	0.9163	1.7918	3.2104	1.6418	0.2761	-0.1998	-0.0552	0.0762	0.0399
7	3.0	4.0	1.0986	1.3863	1.9218	1.5230	-0.1294	-0.0175	+0.0023	0.0167	0.0003
8	1.5	6.0	0.4055	1.7918	3.2104	0.7266	0.2761	-0.7106	-0.1962	0.0762	0.5049
9	1.2	8.0	0.1823	2.0794	4.3239	0.3791	0.5637	-0.9338	-0.5264	0.3177	0.8720
10	1.8	7.0	0.5878	1.9459	3.7865	1.1438	0.4302	-0.5283	-0.2273	0.1851	0.2791
11	1.5	9.0	0.4055	2.1972	4.8277	0.8909	0.6815	-0.7106	-0.4843	0.4644	0.5049
$n = 11$	=	=	$\Sigma Y =$ 12.2771	$\Sigma X =$ 16.6729	$\Sigma X_i^2 =$ 27.9603	$\Sigma X_iY_i =$ 15.1222	$\Sigma x_i = 0$	$\Sigma y_i = 0$	$\Sigma x_iy_i =$ (-)3.4866	$\Sigma x_i^2 =$ 2.6891	$\Sigma y_i^2 =$ 4.8566

$\bar{Y} = 1.1161; \ \bar{X} = 1.5157$

(v) The regression results can now be presented in the following form:
$$\log_e I = 3.0801 - 1.2957 \log_e(i) \qquad R^2 = 0.93$$
$$(0.1188)$$

or, $\quad \hat{I} = \alpha * (i)^{-1.2965}$ where, $\alpha* = \log_e 3.0801$

The results show that the constant interest-elasticity is $(-)\ 1.2965$, that is, the demand for investment is interest-elastic.

The elasticity-coefficient is statistically significant.

Example 2: Estimate production function of a Cobb-Douglas form, for an industry on the basis of the cross sectional data concerning a random sample of eight firms given in Table 7.3.

The various calculations involved in the estimation are given in Worksheet 7.3.

The function to be fitted is: $Q = AL^{\alpha}K^{\beta}$

i.e., $\qquad\qquad \log_e Q = \log_e A + \alpha \log_e L + \beta \log_e K + \log_e U$

(i) Substituting from Worksheet 7.3 the relevant quantities, we obtain:
$$\hat{\alpha} = \frac{(0.8646)(0.2658) - (0.6189)(0.3594)}{(1.5049)(0.2658) - (0.6189)^2} = 0.4349$$

$$\hat{\beta} = \frac{(0.3594)(1.5049) - (0.6189)(0.8646)}{(1.5049)(0.2658) - (0.6189)^2} = 0.3395$$

and, $\log_e A = \bar{Y} - \hat{\alpha}\bar{X}_2 - \hat{\beta}\bar{X}_3$
$$= 5.0486 - (0.4349)\ 0.7554 - (0.3395)\ 0.9721$$
$$= 4.3900$$

(ii) $\quad R^2 = \dfrac{\hat{\alpha}\Sigma x_2 y_i + \hat{\beta}\Sigma x_3 y_i}{\Sigma y_i^2}$

$$= \frac{(0.4349)(0.8646) + (0.3395)(0.3594)}{0.5021}$$

$$= 0.9918$$

(iii) $\quad \Sigma e_i^2 = 0.0041$

$$\therefore \hat{\sigma}_u^2 = \frac{\Sigma e_i^2}{8-3} = 0.0008$$

(iv) $\quad \text{Var}(\hat{\alpha}) = \dfrac{(0.0008)(0.2656)}{0.01696} = 0.0128$

$$\therefore \text{SE}(\hat{\alpha}) = \sqrt{0.0128} = 0.1133$$

$$\text{Var}(\hat{\beta}) = \frac{(0.0008)(1.5049)}{0.01696} = 0.0727$$

$$\therefore \text{SE}(\hat{\beta}) = \sqrt{0.0727} = 0.2697$$

Table 7.3: Worksheet for Model: $Q = A L^{\alpha} K^{\beta} U$

n	Output Q	Labour L	Capital K	Y $\log_e Q$	X_2 $\log_e L$	X_3 $\log_e K$	y_i $(Y_i - \bar{Y})$	x_2 $(X_2 - \bar{X}_2)$	x_3 $(X_3 - \bar{X}_3)$	y_i^2	x_2^2	x_3^2	yx_2	yx_3	$x_2 x_3$
1	100	1.0	2.0	4.6052	0.0000	0.6931	−0.4434	−0.7554	−0.2790	0.1966	0.5706	0.0778	0.3349	0.1237	0.2107
2	120	1.3	2.2	4.7875	0.2624	0.7885	−0.2611	−0.4928	−0.0836	0.0682	0.2428	0.0337	0.1286	0.0479	0.0905
3	140	1.8	2.3	4.9417	0.5878	0.8329	−0.1069	−0.1676	−0.1392	0.0004	0.0281	0.0194	0.0179	0.0149	0.0233
4	150	2.0	1.5	5.0107	0.6931	0.9163	−0.0379	−0.0623	−0.0558	0.0004	0.0039	0.0031	0.0023	0.0021	0.0035
5	165	2.5	2.8	5.1052	0.9163	1.0296	0.0566	0.1609	0.0575	0.0032	0.0259	0.0033	0.0091	0.0032	0.0092
6	190	3.0	3.0	5.2471	1.0986	1.0986	0.1985	0.3432	0.1265	0.0394	0.1178	0.0060	0.0681	0.0251	0.0434
7	200	3.0	3.3	5.2983	1.0986	1.1939	0.2507	0.3432	0.2218	0.0628	0.1178	0.0492	0.0860	0.0556	0.0761
8	220	4.0	3.4	5.3937	1.3863	1.2238	0.3451	0.6309	0.2517	0.1190	0.3980	0.0633	0.2177	0.0860	0.1622
=	—	—	—	$\Sigma Y =$ 40.3894	$\Sigma X_2 =$ 6.0431	$\Sigma X_3 =$ 7.7767	$\Sigma x_1 = 0$	$\Sigma x_2 = 0$	$\Sigma x_3 = 0$	$\Sigma y_i^2 =$ 0.5021	$\Sigma x_2^2 =$ 1.5049	$\Sigma x_3^2 =$ 0.2658	$\Sigma yx_2 =$ 0.8646	$\Sigma yx_3 =$ 0.3594	$\Sigma x_2 x_3 =$ 0.6189

$$\bar{Y} = 5.0486; \quad \bar{X}_2 = 0.7554; \quad \bar{X}_3 = 0.9721$$

(v) The regression results can be presented in the following form:

$$\log_e Q = 4.3900 + 0.4349 \log_e L + 0.3395 \log_e K \qquad R^2 = 0.99$$
$$ (0.1133) \qquad\qquad (0.2697)$$

or, $\hat{Q} = A(L)^{0.4349} (K)^{0.3395}$ where, $A = e^{4.39}$

From the above estimated results, it is observed that the output elasticities (which are constant) of labour and capital are 0.4349 and 0.3395 respectively. In other words, holding the capital input constant, a one per cent increase in the labour input leads on the average to about 0.44 per cent increase in the output. Similarly, holding the labour input constant, a one per cent increase in the capital input leads on the average to about 0.34 per cent increase in the output.

From a statistical view point, the estimated model fits the data quite well. the R^2-value of 0.99 means that about 99 per cent of the variation in the (log of) output is explained by the (log of) labour and capital. However on the basis of estimated standard errors, capital input coefficient does not appear to be statistically significant.

7.5.4 Testing of Returns to Scale

Adding the two output elasticities, we obtain 0.7744, which gives the value of the "returns to scale" parameter.

One may ask: can it be said that the output is, therefore, characterised by decreasing returns to scale statistically?

If there are constant returns to scale, economic theory would suggest that $\beta_1 + \beta_2 = 1$. Hence, to test statistically 'returns to scale' of the production function, a test of hypothesis of 'constant returns to scale' is constructed as:

$$H_0 : \beta_1 + \beta_2 = 1$$
$$H_A : \beta_1 + \beta_2 \neq 1, \text{ and}$$

$$t = \frac{(\hat{\beta}_1 + \hat{\beta}_2) - 1}{\sqrt{\text{Var}(\hat{\beta}_1) + \text{Var}(\hat{\beta}_2) + 2\,\text{Cov}(\hat{\beta}_1, \hat{\beta}_2)}}$$

If the t-value thus computed exceeds the critical t-value at the chosen level of significance, we reject the hypothesis of constant returns to scale; otherwise we may accept.

7.6 CONSTRAINED ESTIMATION

Many a time we are required to estimate the regression parameters of a model under certain conditions or restrictions. For example, suppose we had believed *a priori* that there were constant returns to scale and had, therefore, wished to impose the constraint that $\beta_1 + \beta_2 = 1$ when estimating the parameters of the production function: $Q_i = AL_i^{\beta_1} K_i^{\beta_2} U_i$

In the case of such simple linear restriction, the modifications to our estimating procedure can be made as under:

Production Function: $Q_i = AL_i^{\beta_1} K_i^{\beta_2} U_i$

$$\log_e Q_i = \log_e A + \beta_1 \log_e L_i + \beta_2 \log_e K_i + \log_e U_i$$

Substituting $\quad \beta_2 = 1 - \beta_1$,

$$\log_e Q_i = \log_e A + \beta_1 \log_e L_i + (1 - \beta_1) \log_e K_i + \log_e U_i$$

$$\log_e Q_i - \log_e K_i = \log_e A + \beta_1 (\log_e L_i - \log_e K_i) + \log_e U_i$$

$$\log_e \left(\frac{Q}{K}\right)_i = \log_e A + \beta_1 \log_e \left(\frac{L}{K}\right)_i + \log_e U_i$$

This function can be treated as a simple regression model involving one explanatory variable by putting it in the form:

$$Y_i = A^* + \beta_1 X_i + U_i^*,$$

where; $\qquad Y_i = \log\left(\frac{Q}{K}\right)_i \text{ and, } X_i = \log_e \left(\frac{L}{K}\right)_i$

Therefore least squares estimator of the parameter β_1 of the model: $Y_i = A^* + \beta_i X_i + U_i^*$ shall be given:

$$\hat{\beta}_1 = \frac{\Sigma x_i y_i}{\Sigma x_i^2} = \frac{\Sigma(X_i - \bar{X})(Y_i - \bar{Y})}{\Sigma(X_i - \bar{Y})^2}$$

$$(X_i - \bar{X}) = [(\log L - \log K) - (\overline{\log L} - \overline{\log K})]$$

$$= [(\log L - \overline{\log L}) - (\log K - \overline{\log K})]$$

$$(Y_i - \bar{Y}) = \left[(\log Q - \log K) - (\overline{\log Q} - \overline{\log K})\right] =$$

$$[(\log Q - \overline{\log Q}) - (\log K - \overline{\log K})]$$

Let, $\quad (\log L - \overline{\log L}) = l, \; (\overline{\log K} - \log K) = k$

and, $\quad (\log Q - \log Q) = q,$

$$\therefore \quad \hat{\beta}_1 = \frac{\Sigma(l_i - k_i)(q_i - k_i)}{\Sigma(l_i - k_i)^2} = \frac{\Sigma q_i l_i - \Sigma q_i k_i - \Sigma l_i k_i + \Sigma k_i^2}{\Sigma l_i^2 - 2\Sigma l_i k_i + \Sigma k_i^2}$$

To illustrate a number of the points involved in the above derivation, we consider a hypothetical example of the estimation of a Cobb-Douglas production function with constant returns to scale.

Example 3: Assume that following data (*converted into logarithms*) relates to 28 firms:

$$\Sigma Q_i^2 = 25213.6; \; \Sigma L_i K_i = 5610.0; \; \bar{Q} = 30.0$$

$$\Sigma K_i^2 = 2830.0; \; \Sigma Q_i K_i = 8415.0 \; \bar{K} = 10.0$$

$$\Sigma L_i^2 = 11220.0; \; \Sigma L_i Q_i = 16815.0; \; \bar{L} = 20.0$$

This data can be converted into deviations form as shown under.

$$\Sigma q_i^2 = \Sigma Q_i^2 - n \overline{Q}^2 = 25213.6 - 25200.0 = 13.6$$

$$\Sigma k_i^2 = \Sigma K_i^2 - n \overline{K}^2 = 2830.0 - 2800.0 = 30.0$$

$$\Sigma l_i^2 = \Sigma L_i^2 - n \overline{L}^2 = 11220.0 - 11200.0 = 20.0$$

$$\Sigma k_i l_i = \Sigma K_i L_i - n \overline{KL} = 5610.0 - 5600.0 = 10.0$$

$$\Sigma k_i q_i = \Sigma K_i Q_i - n \overline{KQ} = 8415.0 - 8400.0 = 15.0$$

$$\Sigma l_i q_i = \Sigma L_i Q_i - n \overline{LQ} = 16815.0 - 16800.0 = 15.0$$

Substituting the values in

$$\hat{\beta}_1 = \frac{\Sigma q_i \, li - \Sigma q_i k_i - \Sigma l_i \, k_i + \Sigma k_i^2}{\Sigma l_i^2 - 2\Sigma l_i k_i + \Sigma k_i^2} = \frac{20}{30} = 0.67$$

and, $\hat{\beta}_2 = 1 - \hat{\beta}_1 = (1 - 0.67) = 0.33$

The estimated production function under the imposed restriction of constant returns to scale is:

$$Q_i = e^{13.3} L_i^{0.67} K_i^{0.33}$$

In case the imposed restriction of the constant returns to scale is removed, the estimated results with the same data turn out to be:

$$Q_i = e^{15.0} L_i^{0.60} K_i^{0.30}$$

(Also refer section 8.8 in chapter 8 for 'Generalization' of this problem.)

How do we compare the unrestricted and restricted estimated production functions?

In other words, how do we know that the imposed restriction is valid? This can be tested by applying the F-test in the following way (Refer Tintner Test in section 4.5.3 of chapter 4).

Let, Σe_1^2 = RSS (Residual Sum of Squares) of the unrestricted function

Σe_2^2 = RSS of the restricted function

n = number of observations

k = number of parameters in the unrestricted function

m = number of linear restrictions imposed

(it is one restriction in the present case)

Then, $F = \dfrac{(\Sigma e_2^2 - \Sigma e_1^2)/m}{\Sigma e_1^2/(n-k)}$

follows the F-distribution with m, $(n - k)$ degrees of freedom.

If the computed F-value is statistically not significant, one may accept the hypothesis that the linear restriction is valid. If, on the other hand, the estimated F-value is statistically significant, it means that the restricted and unrestricted functions are different; hence one may reject the hypothesis that the parameters obey the linear restriction.

(**Note:** Above test can be applied even if the number of linear restrictions are more than one.)

7.7 ALTERNATIVE METHODS OF ESTIMATION OF COBB-DOUGLAS PRODUCTION FUNCTION

There are *Five* different methods of estimating the parameters of the Cobb-Douglas Production Function, involving alternative assumptions and econometric problems.

(i) The first is that of estimating the production function itself in log-linear form.

This method requires no further assumptions, such as, with regards to returns to scale, but it leads to some specific econometric estimation problems which are dealt in the other chapters of this book. However, we may point out here the problems that are generally encountered while estimating the C-D function in log-linear form. The usual problems are: simultaneity, multicollinearity and hetroscedasticity.

(ii) The second method is that of estimating the production function through the *intensive form equation* which relates the output per worker to the capital-labour ratio. The production function is reduced to this form by assuming constant returns to scale.

$$\log \left(\frac{Q_i}{K_i} \right) = \beta_0 + \beta_1 \log \left(\frac{L_i}{K_i} \right) + U_i$$

This method reduce the problem of multicollinearity and hetroscedasticity, but it does require the basic assumption of constant returns to scale hence cannot be used to test for increasing or decreasing returns to scale. It also has an endogenous explanatory variable.

(iii) Third method is based on the share of labour income in the total output by assuming once again constant returns to scale, along with the assumptions of perfect competition and profit maximisation.

This method is actually classical approach to estimation of C-D function. Classical conditions of equilibrium require that marginal productivity equals the real wage:

$$\frac{\partial Q_i}{\partial L_i} = \beta_1 \frac{Q_i}{L_i} = \frac{w}{p} \qquad \qquad ...(i)$$

$$\frac{\partial Q_i}{\partial K_i} = \beta_2 \frac{Q_i}{K_i} = \frac{\gamma}{p} \qquad \qquad ...(ii)$$

(w = wages, γ = rate of interest, p = price of product)

With an additional assumption of constant returns to scale;

$$\beta_1 = \frac{wL_i}{pQ_i} = S_L \text{ (share of labour in National Output)}$$

$$\beta_2 = 1 - \beta_1$$

In this way, the shares yield direct estimates of both β_1 and β_2 under classical economists assumptions. With cross-section or time-series data, the shares can be estimated as the geometric means of shares calculated for each production unit or at each time-period.

This method requires no data on capital input but it does depend on the assumption of constant returns to scale, hence cannot be used to test hypothesis about various returns to scale.

(iv) The fourth method is once again based or classical assumption. It utilises the marginal productivity equations (i) and (ii) of the third method.

Equation (i) implies a log-linear relation between output per worker and real-wage:

$$\log \frac{Q_i}{L_i} = \log \frac{w}{p} - \log \beta_1$$

Adding a stochastic disturbance term to above log-linear relation, one would obtain relation from which elasticity β_1 (which is the intercept here) can be estimated.

The third and fourth methods eliminate the simultaneity, multicollinearity and hetroscedasticity problems, but require the assumptions of constant returns to scale, perfect competition and profit maximisation. None could be said to be a better one than the other. Each is appropriate in particular situation, depending upon what can be assumed and what is required to be investigated. The estimates of parameters obtained through each of these two methods will generally be different and there is little evidence to suggest which estimates come closest to true values.

(v) The C-D function is transformed into a simultaneous-equation model for estimating the elasticity coefficients in this method. The model consists of three equations.

$$Q_i = AL_i^{\beta_1} K_i^{\beta_2} e^{u_i}$$

$$\frac{\partial Q_i}{\partial L_i} = \frac{\beta_1 Q_i}{L_i} = \frac{w}{p} \cdot e^{v_i}$$

$$\frac{\partial Q_i}{\partial K_i} = \frac{\beta_2 Q_i}{K_i} = \frac{\gamma}{p} \cdot e^{w_i}$$

In logarithmic terms:

$$\log Q_i = A + \beta_1 \log L_i + \beta_2 \log K_i + U_i$$

$$\log Q_i = -\log \beta_1 + \log L_i + \log\left(\frac{w}{p}\right) + V_i$$

$$\log Q_i = -\log \beta_2 + \log K_i + \log\left(\frac{\gamma}{p}\right) + W_i$$

This is the structural form for a system in which $\log Q_i$, $\log L_i$ and $\log K_i$ are the endogenous variables, and $\log\left(\dfrac{w}{p}\right)$ and $\log\left(\dfrac{\gamma}{p}\right)$ are the exogenous variables on the assumption that there exists perfect competition. Since the system is not identified (Refer chapter 13 on Identification), various restrictions are to be imposed to estimate the Simultaneous Model.

ASSIGNMENTS

1. Show how by appropriate transformations of variables the following nonlinear models relating Y to the explanatory variables X_1 and X_2 and the stochastic disturbances term U can be converted to models that are linear in the parameters:
   1. $Y = AX_1^{\beta_1} X_2^{\beta_2} U$
   2. $Y = \exp. (\beta_0 + \beta_1 X_1 + \beta_2 X_2 + U)$
   3. $Y = (\beta_0 + \beta_1 X_1 + \beta_2 X_2 + U)^{-1}$
   4. $Y = [1 + \exp. (\beta_0 + \beta_1 X_1 + \beta_2 X_2 + U)]^{-1}$
   5. $Y = \exp. (\beta_0 + BX^{-1})$
   6. $\exp. Y = \beta_0 + X\beta_1$

2. Can you convert the following into models that are linear in the parameters?
   1. $Y = \beta_0 + \beta_1 \rho^{x1} + U, \ 0 < \rho < 1$
   2. $Y = \exp. (\beta_0 + \beta_1 X_1 + \beta_2 X_1^2) + U$
   3. $Y = \beta_0 (e^{\beta_1 X_1} + e^{\beta_2 X_2}) + U$

3. Determine whether the following models are linear in the parameters, or in the variables, or in both. Which of these models are linear regression models?
   1. $Y_i = \beta_0 X_i^{\beta_1} + U_i$
   2. In $Y_i = \beta_0 + \beta_1 X_i + U_i$
   3. $Y_i = \beta_0 + \beta^3 X_i + U_i$
   4. $Y_i = \beta_0 + \beta_1 \ln X_i + U_i$
   5. $Y_i = \beta_0 + (0.75 - \beta_0)e^{-\beta_1 X_i} + U_i$

4. Explain why the linear regression model may not be really so restrictive even though many economic relationships are nonlinear. In particular, use an appropriate transformation and then derive the observation matrix for the following model.

$$Y_i = \beta_0 + \beta_1 \left(\frac{1}{1 - X_i}\right) + U_i$$

when, $n = 3$, and $Y_i = 1, 10$ and 12
$X_i = 0, 0.1$ and 0.5 } n denotes number of observations.

5. Some researchers believe that productivity of labour is determined by the level of aggregate demand, which is approximately measured by aggregated output. Denoting aggregate labour by L and aggregate output by X, investigate the equation:

$$Y = \alpha(X)^\beta, \text{ where } Y = \frac{X}{L}$$

Show that this might be expressed as:

$$\log L = (-) \log \alpha + (1 - \beta) \log X,$$

or as: $\log X = [1/(1 - \beta)] \log L + [1/1 - \beta)] \log \alpha.$

6. Which of the following models would you choose for the Engel expenditure curve and why?

(Engel curve, named after the German Statistician Ernest Engel, relates a consumer's expenditure on a commodity to his total income).

1. $Y_i = \beta_0 + \beta_1 (X_i) + U_i$

2. $Y_i = \beta_0 + \beta_1 \left(\dfrac{1}{X_i}\right) + U_i$

3. $\text{In } Y_i = \text{In } \beta_0 + \beta_1 \text{In} X_i + U$

4. $\text{In } Y_i = \text{In } \beta_0 + \beta_1 \left(\dfrac{1}{X_i}\right) + U_i$

5. $Y_i = \beta_0 + \beta_1 \text{ In } X_i + U_i$

[In = Natural log, Y = Consumption Expenditure, and X = Consumer income

7. Consider the model: $Y_i = \beta_0 + \beta_1 X_i + \beta_2 X_i^2 + U_i$. Write the normal equations for the following observations:

Y:	−1	−1	2	4
X:	0	1	2	5

8. From the following data find the Linear and Logarithmic regression of value added per worker on the wage of production worker and capital-labour ratio:

Value added (Rs. per man-hr)	7.12	8.28	6.70	7.16	6.78	9.24
Wage: →	2.96	3.29	3.64	3.37	3.73	3.41
C/L (in Rs.): →	14.99	15.20	20.09	21.89	22.71	17.72

9. Assuming that $C_i = AI_i^\beta U_i$ represents an Engel curve where C_i is expenditure per capita on commodity, I_i is income per capita and U_i is the random error. Fit this curve to the following data and estimate the income elasticity at mean income level.

(Rs. per day)

C_i: →	8	12	15	18	22	23	26
I_i: →	17	27	36	46	57	67	81

10. Suppose to study the behaviour of sales of automobiles over a number of years, following two models are used:

$$Y_t = \beta_0 + \beta_1 t$$
$$Y_t = \beta_0 + \beta_1 t + \beta_2 t^2,$$

where Y_t = sales at time t, and t = time measured in years.

(a) Discuss the properties of these models.

(b) In what situations will be quadratic model be useful?

11. In an application of Cobb-Douglas production function the following results are obtained:

$$\text{In } Y_t = 2.35 + 0.95 \text{ In } X_2 + 0.82 \text{ In } X_3$$
$$(0.3022) \qquad (0.3571)$$
$$R^2 = 0.84 \qquad df = 12$$

Y = Output, X_2 = Labour input, X_3 = Capital input.

Test the hypothesis that the labour and capital elasticities are equal to one, assuming covariance between the estimated labour and capital coefficient is (i) zero, and (ii) it is (−) 0.097.

12. By logarithmic transformation, estimate the parameters of the demand curve: $Q_t = \alpha \, (P_{t-1})^\beta \cdot e^{U_i}$ from the following data:

    Demand this
    week: 12   10   13   11.5   12   13   12   12   12   13
    (Q_t)

    Price of
    last week: 0.54   0.51   0.49   0.49   0.48   0.48   0.48   0.47   0.47   0.44
    (P_{t-1})

    What meaning is attached to the parameters α and β?

13. Following model is used to measure the elasticity of substitution between capital and labour inputs:

$$\log\left(\frac{V}{L}\right) = \log \beta_0 + \beta_1 \log W + U$$

where $\dfrac{V}{L}$ = value added per unit of labour, L = labour input, and W = real wage rate. The coefficient β_1 measures the elasticity of substitution between Labour and Capital. Fit the above equation to the following data and test the hypothesis that the elasticity of substitution is not statistically different from unity.

Industry	$\log\left(\dfrac{V}{L}\right)$	$\log (W)$
I_1	3.6973	2.9617
I_2	3.4795	2.8532
I_3	4.0004	3.1158
I_4	3.6609	3.0371
I_5	3.2321	2.8727
I_6	3.3418	2.9745
I_7	3.4308	2.8287
I_8	3.3158	3.0888
I_9	3.5062	3.0086
I_{10}	3.2352	2.9680
I_{11}	3.8823	3.0909
I_{12}	3.7309	3.0881
I_{13}	3.7716	3.2256
I_{14}	3.6601	3.1025
I_{15}	3.7554	3.1354

14. Consider the following cost curves. For each, determine what conditions economic theory imposes on the coefficients, assuming fixed cost is non-negative; average and marginal cost are both positive; and average and marginal cost initially decrease but eventually increase.

    (i) $C = \beta_1 Q + \beta_2 Q^2 + \beta_3 Q^3$

    (ii) $C = \beta_0 + \beta_1 Q + \beta_2 \sqrt{Q}$

    (iii) $C = \beta_1 Q^{B_2} e^{B_3 Q}$

    (iv) $C = \beta_1 Q^{B_2} e^{B_3 (\log Q)^2}$

    (v) $C = \beta_1 Q^{1/\beta_2} (\beta_2 + \beta_3 Q)^{-1/\beta_2}$

    [C = Total cost, and Q = Total output]

15. The following is the true Cobb-Douglas form of production function:

$$Y_i = \alpha_0 \, L_{1i}^{\alpha_1} \, L_{2i}^{\alpha_2} \, K_i^{\alpha_3}$$

where; Y = output, L_1 = production labour,
L_2 = non-production (administration) labour, and K = capital.

Suppose the regression actually used in empirical investigation was:

$$Y_i = \beta_0 \, L_{1i}^{\beta_1} \, K_i^{\beta_2}$$

Assuming that cross-sectional data was used of empirical investigation;

(i) Will $E(\hat{\beta}_1) = \alpha_1$?

(ii) Will $E(\hat{\beta}_2) = \alpha_3$?

16. Discuss: "The residual sum of squares from the restricted least-squares regression is never less than the corresponding sum of squares from the unrestricted least-squares regression."

17. Suppose in place of true model:

$$Y_i = \alpha X_i U_i \qquad \qquad \text{...(i)}$$

the following model is estimated:

$$Y_i = \beta X_i + V_i \qquad \qquad \text{...(ii)}$$

Would the β estimated from (ii) be an unbiased estimator of α in (i). If no, then does the bias disappear as the sample size increases?

18. Suggest the method of estimating the parameters of the CES production function:

$$Y_i = A \left[\alpha \, K_i^{-\rho} + (1 - \alpha) \, L_i^{-\rho} \right]^{-v/\rho}$$

19. Interpret the following regression model:

$$\log \left(\frac{Y_i}{L_i} \right) = \log A + \beta_2 \log \left(\frac{K_i}{L_i} \right) + U_i$$

where: Y = output, L = labour input and, K = capital input

20. Discuss the choice of the form of econometric equations (e.g., linear in variables, linear in logarithms of variables, linear in unknown parameters) and the choice of variables to be included and variables to be excluded.

8

Multiple Regression and Generalised Estimation Methods

In the last chapter we considered regression model in which the dependent variable was a linear function of one independent or explanatory variable. This was a case of a simple Regression Model. To generalize the analysis, a relationship in which dependent variable is function of any (or, say n-number) number of explanatory variables has to be considered. Such regression models are termed Multiple Variable Regression Models.

A simplest case of multiple regression model involves two explanatory variables.

8.1 MULTIPLE REGRESSION MODEL

Suppose $Y = f(X_2, X_3)$ and the functional relationship is linear; thus the multiple regression model for three variables can be stated in the form:

$$Y_i = \beta_1 + \beta_2 X_{2i} + \beta_3 X_{3i} + U_i \qquad ...(8.1)$$
$$(i = 1, ..., i)$$

Given n-observations on Y, X_2 and X_3 our problem is to estimate β_1, β_2 and β_3. We apply least squares criteria to obtain their estimates: $\hat{\beta}_1, \hat{\beta}_2$ and $\hat{\beta}_3$.

We have defined: $\quad e_i = Y_i - \hat{Y}_i = Y_i - \hat{\beta}_1 - \hat{\beta}_2 X_{2i} - \hat{\beta}_3 X_{3i}$

$$\therefore \qquad \Sigma e_i^2 = \Sigma (Y_i - \hat{\beta}_1 - \hat{\beta}_2 X_{2i} - \hat{\beta}_3 X_{3i})^2 \qquad ...(8.2)$$

To obtain expressions for the least squares estimators, we partially differentiate Σe_i^2 with respect to $\hat{\beta}_1, \hat{\beta}_2$ and $\hat{\beta}_3$ and set these partial derivatives equal to zero.

$$\frac{\partial}{\partial \hat{\beta}_1} \left[\Sigma e_i^2 \right] = -2\Sigma \left(Y_i - \hat{\beta}_1 - \hat{\beta}_2 X_{2i} - \hat{\beta}_3 X_{3i} \right) = 0 \qquad ...(8.3)$$

$$\frac{\partial}{\partial \hat{\beta}_2} \left[\Sigma e_i^2 \right] = -2\Sigma X_{2i} (Y_i - \hat{\beta}_1 - \hat{\beta}_2 X_{2i} - \hat{\beta}_3 X_{3i}) = 0 \qquad ...(8.4)$$

$$\frac{\partial}{\partial\hat{\beta}_3}\left[\Sigma e_i^2\right] = -2\Sigma X_{3i}\left(X_i - \hat{\beta}_1 - \hat{\beta}_2 X_{2i} - \hat{\beta}_3 X_{3i}\right) = 0 \quad ...(8.5)$$

Summing from 1 to n, the multiple regression equation produces three normal equations:

$$\Sigma Y_i = n\hat{\beta}_1 + \hat{\beta}_2\Sigma X_{2i} + \hat{\beta}_3\Sigma X_{3i} \qquad ...(8.6)$$

$$\Sigma Y_{2i}Y_i = \hat{\beta}_1\Sigma X_{2i} + \hat{\beta}_2\Sigma X_{2i}^2 + \hat{\beta}_3\Sigma X_{2i}X_{3i} \qquad ...(8.7)$$

$$\Sigma Y_{3i}Y_i = \hat{\beta}_1\Sigma X_{3i} + \hat{\beta}_2\Sigma X_{2i}X_{3i} + \hat{\beta}_3\Sigma X_{3i}^2 \qquad ...(8.8)$$

From (8.6) we obtain $\hat{\beta}_1$,

$$\hat{\beta}_1 = \bar{Y} - \hat{\beta}_2\bar{X}_2 - \hat{\beta}_3\bar{X}_3 \qquad ...(8.9)$$

Substituting $\hat{\beta}_1$ in (8.7) and (8.8) we get:

$$\Sigma X_{2i}Y_i = (\bar{Y} - \hat{\beta}_2\bar{X}_2 - \hat{\beta}_3\bar{X}_3)\,\Sigma X_{2i} + \hat{\beta}_2\Sigma X_{2i}^2 + \hat{\beta}_3\Sigma_{2i}X_{3i}$$

$$\Sigma X_{3i}Y_i = (\bar{Y} - \hat{\beta}_2\bar{X}_2 - \hat{\beta}_3\bar{X}_3)\,\Sigma X_{3i} + \hat{\beta}_2\Sigma X_{2i}X_{3i} + \hat{\beta}_3\Sigma X_{3i}^2$$

or, $\quad \Sigma X_{2i}Y_i - \bar{Y}\Sigma X_{2i} = \hat{\beta}_2\left(\Sigma X_{2i}^2 - \bar{X}_2\Sigma X_{2i}\right) + \hat{\beta}_3\left(\Sigma X_{2i}X_{3i} - \bar{X}_3\Sigma X_{2i}\right)$

$$\Sigma X_{3i}Y_i - \bar{Y}\Sigma X_{3i} = \hat{\beta}_2\left(\Sigma X_{2i}X_{3i} - \bar{X}_2\Sigma X_{3i}\right) + \hat{\beta}_3\left(\Sigma X_{3i}^2 - \bar{X}_3\Sigma X_{3i}\right)$$

Using the results: $\quad \Sigma X_iY_i - \bar{Y}\Sigma X_i = \Sigma(X_i - \bar{X})(Y_i - \bar{Y}) = \Sigma x_i y_i$

$$\Sigma X_i^2 - \bar{X}\Sigma X_i = \Sigma(X_i - \bar{X})^2 = \Sigma x_i^2;$$

we obtain the normal equations in deviation form:

$$\Sigma x_2 y = \hat{\beta}_2\Sigma x_2^2 + \hat{\beta}_3\Sigma x_2 x_3 \qquad ...(8.10)$$

$$\Sigma x_3 y = \hat{\beta}_2\Sigma x_2 x_3 + \hat{\beta}_3\Sigma x_3^2 \qquad ...(8.11)$$

Solving (8.10) and (8.11) for $\hat{\beta}_2$ and $\hat{\beta}_3$:

$$\hat{\beta}_2 = \frac{\Sigma x_2 y \cdot \Sigma x_3^2 - \Sigma x_2 x_3 \cdot \Sigma x_3 y}{\Sigma x_2^2\,\Sigma x_3^2 - (\Sigma x_2 x_3)^2} \qquad ...(8.12)$$

and, $\quad \hat{\beta}_3 = \dfrac{\Sigma x_3 y \cdot \Sigma x_3^2 - \Sigma x_2 x_3 \cdot \Sigma x_2 y}{\Sigma x_2^2\,\Sigma x_3^2 - (\Sigma x_2 x_3)^2} \qquad ...(8.13)$

· **Note:** For the sake of simplicity, we avoid mentioning 'i' in the subscripts.

8.2 RELATION BETWEEN SIMPLE AND MULTIPLE REGRESSION COEFFICIENTS

The expressions (8.12) and (8.13) can also be written in terms of the simple regression coefficients. We break three-variable-regression model into simple regressions of:

$$Y \text{ on } X_2: \qquad Y_i = \beta_{1\cdot 2} + \beta_{12} X_{2i} + U_{(1\cdot 2)i} \left[\therefore \hat{\beta}_{12} = \frac{\Sigma x_2 y}{\Sigma x_2^2} \right]$$

$$Y \text{ on } X_3: \qquad Y_i = \beta_{1\cdot 3} + \beta_{13} X_{3i} + U_{(1\cdot 3)i} \left[\therefore \hat{\beta}_{13} = \frac{\Sigma x_3 y}{\Sigma x_3^2} \right]$$

$$\text{and, } X_2 \text{ on } X_3: \qquad X_{2i} = \beta_{2\cdot 3} + \beta_{23} X_{3i} + U_{(2\cdot 3)i} \left[\therefore \hat{\beta}_{23} = \frac{\Sigma x_2 x_3}{\Sigma x_3^2} \right]$$

The regression model: $Y_i = \beta_1 + \beta_2 X_{2i} + \beta_3 X_{3i} + U_i$ can also be written as: $\qquad Y_i = \beta_{1\cdot 23} + \beta_{12\cdot 3} X_{2i} + \beta_{13\cdot 2} X_{3i} + U_{(1\cdot 23)i}$

The barrage of subscripts associated with the regression coefficients needs to be explained.

First subscript number refers to the variable to be explained (i.e., Y), while the remaining subscripts refer to the explanatory variables and the full stop is used to separate the explanatory variable being considered from other explanatory variables in the regression model.

In the simple regressions, β_{12} and β_{13} indicate the effect of X_2 and X_3 on Y respectively while β_{23} represents the effect of X_2 on X_3. Since there is only one explanatory variable, no full stop has been used in the subscripts of the coefficients in these cases.

Coefficient $\beta_{12\cdot 3}$ indicates the existence of variable X_3 (by the fact that 3 appears in the subscript after full stop) but represents only the effect of X_2 on Y; similarly coefficient $\beta_{13\cdot 2}$ indicates the existence of X_2 in the model but represents only the effect of X_3 on Y. $\beta_{1\cdot 23}$ is the constant term indicating the existence of X_2 and X_3 in the regression model. Multiple regression coefficient: $\beta_{12\cdot 3}$ and $\beta_{13\cdot 2}$, are usually called partial regression coefficient. Let us relate their estimates with simple regression coefficients: β_{12}, β_{13} and β_{23}.

Divide numerator and denominator of (8.12) and (8.13) by $\Sigma x_2^2 \Sigma x_3^2$:

$$\hat{\beta}_{12\cdot 3} = \hat{\beta}_2 = \frac{\dfrac{\Sigma x_2 y}{\Sigma x_2^2} - \left(\dfrac{\Sigma x_2 x_3}{\Sigma x_2^2} \right)\left(\dfrac{\Sigma x_3 y}{\Sigma x_3^2} \right)}{1 - \left(\dfrac{\Sigma x_2 x_3}{\Sigma x_2^2} \right)\left(\dfrac{\Sigma x_2 x_3}{\Sigma x_3^2} \right)} = \frac{\hat{\beta}_{12} - \hat{\beta}_{32}\hat{\beta}_{13}}{1 - \hat{\beta}_{32}\hat{\beta}_{23}}$$

$$\hat{\beta}_{13.2} = \hat{\beta}_3 = \cfrac{\cfrac{\Sigma x_3 y}{\Sigma x_3^2} - \left(\cfrac{\Sigma x_2 x_3}{\Sigma x_3^2}\right)\left(\cfrac{\Sigma x_2 y}{\Sigma x_2^2}\right)}{1 - \left(\cfrac{\Sigma x_2 x_3}{\Sigma x_2^2}\right)\left(\cfrac{\Sigma x_2 x_3}{\Sigma x_3^2}\right)} = \cfrac{\hat{\beta}_{13} - \hat{\beta}_{23}\hat{\beta}_{13}}{1 - \hat{\beta}_{32}\hat{\beta}_{23}}$$

Considering the terms $\hat{\beta}_{32} \cdot \hat{\beta}_{23}$ of the denominators:

$$\hat{\beta}_{32} \cdot \hat{\beta}_{23} = \frac{(\Sigma x_2 x_3)^2}{\Sigma x_2^2 \Sigma x_3^2} = \frac{(\Sigma x_2 x_3)^2}{n^2 \sigma_{x_2}^2 \sigma_{x_3}^2} = \left(\frac{\Sigma x_2 x_3}{n \sigma_{x_2} \sigma_{x_3}}\right)^2$$

That is $\hat{\beta}_{32} \cdot \hat{\beta}_{23} = r_{23}^2$, which denotes the simple correlation coefficient between x_2 and x_3

$$\therefore \qquad \hat{\beta}_{12\cdot3} = \hat{\beta}_2 = \frac{\hat{\beta}_{12} - \hat{\beta}_{32}\hat{\beta}_{13}}{1 - r_{23}^2} \qquad\qquad ...(8.14)$$

and, $$\qquad \hat{\beta}_{13\cdot2} = \hat{\beta}_3 = \frac{\hat{\beta}_{13} - \hat{\beta}_{23}\hat{\beta}_{12}}{1 - r_{23}^2} \qquad\qquad ...(8.15)$$

(8.14) and (8.15) show the relationship between the estimate of the simple and partial regression coefficients.*

It can be observed in the expression (8.14) that to obtain the estimate of $\beta_{12\cdot3}$, we adjust β_{12} by deducting the compound effect of X_2 on Y_3 and the

---

* Similarly simple and partial correlation coefficients need to be differentiated.

Simple correlation coefficient, r measures the degrees of linear association between two variables. A partial correlation coefficient measures the linear relation or association between any two variables when all other variables connected with those two are kept constant.

For example, for the two explanatory regression model, we can compute three correlation coefficients: r_{12} (correlation between Y and X_2), r_{12} (correlation coefficient between Y and X_2), and r_{13} (correlation between Y and X_3). These coefficients are called simple correlation coefficients, or correlation coefficients of *zero order*.

But here r_{12} does not measure the true degrees of association between Y and X_2 when third variable X_3 is also associated with both of them. In other words generally r_{12} is not likely to reflect the "true" degree of association between Y and X_2 in presence of X_3. As a matter of fact, it is likely to give a "false" impression of the nature of association between Y and X_2. Therefore, what we need is a correlation coefficient that is independent of influence, if any, of X_3 on X_2 and Y. Such a correlation coefficient can be obtained and is known appropriately as the *Partial Correlation Coefficient*. Conceptually, it is similar to the partial regression coefficient. Symbolically, therefore, *against simple correlation coefficient r_{12}, $r_{12\cdot3}$ depicts the partal correlation coefficient* between Y and X_2 holding X_3 constant. The three partial correlations; $r_{12\cdot3}$, $r_{13\cdot2}$ and $r_{23\cdot1}$ are called first-order correlation coefficients.

transmitted effect of X_3 on Y. The so adjusted value is then modified by the fraction of the variance of X_2 which is explained by X_3.

If the variables X_2 and X_3 are not correlated in the given sample, not only would $r_{23}^2 = 0$, but also $\hat{\beta}_{23} = \hat{\beta}_{32} = 0$. In such a case, $\hat{\beta}_{12\cdot3} = \hat{\beta}_{12}$ and $\hat{\beta}_{13\cdot2} = \hat{\beta}_{13}$; i.e., simple regression coefficient are equal to the partial regression coefficients.

8.3 STATISTICAL PROPERTIES OF $\hat{\beta}_1, \hat{\beta}_2$ AND $\hat{\beta}_3$

In order to investigate the statistical properties of the least squares estimates of multiple regression on coefficients in: $Y_i = \beta_1 + \beta_2 X_{2i} + \beta_3 X_{3i} + U_i$, we need some assumptions about the random variable U. These assumptions are the same as in the simple regression model (i.e., with one explanatory variable) developed in the preceding chapter.

Assumption 1: U_i is a random real variable and has a normal distribution.
Assumption 2: The mean value of U_i for each X_i is zero.
$$E(U_i) = 0$$
Assumption 3: The variance of each U_i is the same for all the X_i values;
$$E(U_i^2) = \sigma_u^2 \quad (\sigma_u^2 \text{ is a constant}).$$
Assumption 4: The values of U_j (corresponding to X_j) are independent of U_i (corresponding to X_i);
$$E(U_i U_j) = 0 \text{ for } i \neq j$$
Assumption 5: Every disturbance term U_i is independent of the explanatory variables,
$$E(X_{2i} U_i) = X_{2i} E(U_i) = 0$$
$$E(X_{3i} U_i) = X_{3i} E(U_i) = 0$$

Let us now discuss the statistical properties of the estimators:

(i) *Linearity*

From (8.12) $$\hat{\beta}_2 = \frac{\Sigma x_2 y \cdot \Sigma x_3^2 - \Sigma x_2 x_3 \, \Sigma x_3 y}{\Sigma x_2^2 \, \Sigma x_3^2 - (\Sigma x_2 x_3)^2}$$

Using the results, $\Sigma x_2 y = \Sigma Y_i (X_{2i} - \bar{X}_2) - \bar{Y} \Sigma (X_{2i} - \bar{X}_2)$

$$= \Sigma Y_i (X_{2i} - \bar{X}_2)$$

$$= \Sigma x_2 Y_i$$

and, $$\Sigma x_3 y = \Sigma Y_i (X_{3i} - \bar{X}_3) - \bar{Y} \Sigma (X_{3i} - \bar{X}_3)$$

$$= \Sigma Y_i (X_{3i} - \bar{X}_3)$$

$$= \Sigma x_3 Y_i$$

We obtain, $\hat{\beta}_2 = \dfrac{\Sigma x_2 Y_i \Sigma x_3^2 - \Sigma x_3 \, Y_i \Sigma x_2 x_3}{\Sigma x_2^2 \, \Sigma x_3^2 - (\Sigma x_2 x_3)^2}$ which expresses $\hat{\beta}_2$ as linear

function of Y_i. The same can be proved in case of $\hat{\beta}_3$ and $\hat{\beta}_1$.

(ii) *Unbiasedness*

$$Y_i = \beta_1 + \beta_2 X_{2i} + \beta_3 X_{3i} + U_i$$

and,

$$y_i = \beta_2 x_{2i} + \beta_3 x_{3i} + (U_i - \bar{U})$$

Substituting for y_i in (8.12) we obtain:

$$\hat{\beta}_2 =$$

$$\frac{\Sigma x_{2i} \left[\beta_2 x_{2i} + \beta_3 x_{3i} + (U_i - \bar{U}) \right] \Sigma x_{3i}^2 - \Sigma x_{2i} x_{3i} \Sigma x_{3i} \left[\beta_2 x_{2i} + \beta_3 x_{3i} + (U_i - \bar{U}) \right]}{\Sigma x_{2i}^2 \, \Sigma x_{3i}^2 - (\Sigma x_{2i} x_{3i})^2}$$

$$\Sigma x_{2i} \bar{U} = \bar{U} \Sigma x_{2i} = \bar{U} \Sigma (X_{2i} - \bar{X}_2) = 0; \text{ similarly } \Sigma x_{3i} \bar{U} = 0$$

$$\therefore \quad \hat{\beta}_2 = \frac{\beta_2 \left[\Sigma x_{2i}^2 \, \Sigma x_{3i}^2 - (\Sigma x_{2i} x_{3i})^2 \right] - \beta_3 \left[\Sigma x_{2i}^2 \, \Sigma x_{2i} x_{3i} - \Sigma x_{2i}^2 \, \Sigma x_{2i} x_{3i} \right]}{\Sigma x_{2i}^2 \, \Sigma x_{3i}^2 - (\Sigma x_{2i} x_{3i})^2}$$

$$+ \frac{\Sigma x_{3i}^2 \, \Sigma x_{2i} U_i - \Sigma x_{2i} x_{3i} \, \Sigma x_{3i} U_i}{\Sigma x_{2i}^2 \, \Sigma x_{3i}^2 - (\Sigma x_{2i} x_{3i})^2}$$

or,

$$\hat{\beta}_2 = \beta_2 + \frac{\Sigma x_{3i}^2 \, \Sigma x_{2i} \, U_i - \Sigma x_{2i} x_{3i} \, \Sigma x_{3i} U_i}{\Sigma x_{2i}^2 \, \Sigma x_{3i}^2 - (\Sigma x_{2i} x_{3i})^2} \qquad \ldots (8.16)$$

$$\therefore \quad E(\hat{\beta}_2) = \beta_2 + \frac{\Sigma x_{3i}^2 \, \Sigma x_{2i} \, E(U_i) - \Sigma x_{2i} x_{3i} \Sigma x_{3i} \, E(U_i)}{\Sigma x_{2i}^2 \, \Sigma x_{3i}^2 - (\Sigma x_{2i} x_{3i})^2}$$

or, $E(\hat{\beta}_2) = \beta_2$ since $E(U_i) = 0$.

In other words $\hat{\beta}_2$ is unbiased estimator of β_2. Similarly it can be shown that $\hat{\beta}_1$ and $\hat{\beta}_3$ are the unbiased estimators.

(iii) *Sampling variance*

From (8.16) we obtain:

$$\text{Var } (\hat{\beta}_2) = E[(\hat{\beta}_2 - \beta_2)^2] = E \left[\frac{\Sigma x_{3i}^2 \, \Sigma x_{2i} \, U_i - \Sigma x_{2i} x_{3i} \, \Sigma x_{3i} U_i}{\Sigma x_{2i}^2 \, \Sigma x_{3i}^2 - (\Sigma x_{2i} x_{3i})^2} \right]^2$$

Considering numerator: $(\Sigma x_{3i}^2 \, \Sigma x_{2i} \, U_i - \Sigma x_{2i} x_{3i} \Sigma x_{3i} U_i)^2$

$$= \left[\Sigma x_{3i}^2 \left(x_{21}U_1 \ldots\ldots + x_{22}U_2 + \ldots\ldots + x_{2n}U_n \right) \right.$$

$$\left. - \Sigma x_{2i}x_{3i} \left(x_{31}U_1 + \ldots\ldots + x_{2n}U_n \right) \right]^2$$

$$= (\Sigma x_{3i})^2 \left[\Sigma x_{2i}^2 U_i^2 + \underset{i \neq j}{\Sigma} x_{2i}x_{3j}U_iU_j \right]$$

$$- 2\Sigma x_{3i}^2 \, \Sigma x_{2i}x_{3i} \left[\Sigma x_{2i}x_{3i}U_i^2 + \underset{i \neq j}{\Sigma} x_{2i}x_{3j}U_iU_j \right]$$

$$+ (\Sigma x_{2i}x_{3i})^2 \left[\Sigma x_{3i}^2 U_i^2 + \underset{i \neq j}{\Sigma} x_{2i}x_{3j} \, U_i U_j \right]$$

Making use of the assumptions: $E(U_i^2) = \sigma_n^2$ and $E(U_i U_j) = 0$,

$$\Sigma \left[\Sigma x_{3i}^2 \Sigma x_{2i}U_i - \Sigma x_{2i}x_{3i}\Sigma x_{3i}U_i \right]^2 = \sigma_n^2 \left[(\Sigma x_{3i}^2)^2 \, \Sigma x_{2i}^2 - 2\Sigma x_{2i}^2 \left(\Sigma_{2i}x_{3i} \right)^2 \right.$$

$$\left. + \Sigma x_{3i}^2 \left(\Sigma x_{3i}x_{2i} \right)^2 \right]$$

$$= \sigma_u^2 \, \Sigma x_{3i}^2 \left[\Sigma x_{2i}^2 \, \Sigma x_{3i}^2 - (\Sigma x_{2i}x_{3i})^2 \right]$$

$$\therefore \qquad \text{Var } (\hat{\beta}_1) = \frac{\sigma_u^2 \, \Sigma x_{3i}^2 \, [\Sigma x_{2i}^2 \Sigma x_{3i}^2 - (\Sigma x_{2i}x_{3i})^2]}{[\Sigma x_{2i}^2 \Sigma x_{3i}^2 - (\Sigma x_{2i}x_{3i})^2]^2}$$

or, $\qquad \text{Var } (\hat{\beta}_2) = \dfrac{\sigma_u^2 \, \Sigma x_{3i}^2}{\Sigma x_{2i}^2 \, \Sigma x_{3i}^2 - (\Sigma x_{2i}x_{3i})^2}$ $\qquad\qquad$ ...(8.17)

Similarly, $\quad \text{Var } (\hat{\beta}_3) = \dfrac{\sigma_u^2 \, \Sigma x_{2i}^2}{\Sigma x_{2i}^2 \, \Sigma x_{3i}^2 - (\Sigma x_{2i}x_{3i})^2}$ $\qquad\qquad$ ...(8.18)

These variances can also be expressed in terms of simple correlation coefficients.

$$\text{Var } (\hat{\beta}_2) = \frac{\sigma_u^2}{\Sigma x_{2i}^2 - \dfrac{(\Sigma x_{2i}x_{3i})^2}{\Sigma x_{3i}^2}} = \frac{\sigma_u^2}{\Sigma x_{2i}^2 \left[1 - \dfrac{(\Sigma x_{2i}x_{3i})^2}{\Sigma x_{2i}^2 \, \Sigma x_{3i}^2} \right]}$$

i.e., $\qquad \text{Var } (\hat{\beta}_2) = \dfrac{\sigma_u^2}{\Sigma x_{2i}^2 \, (1 - r_{23}^2)}$ $\qquad\qquad$ ...(8.19)

Similarly, $\quad \text{Var } (\hat{\beta}_3) = \dfrac{\sigma_u^2}{\Sigma x_{3i}^2 \, (1 - r_{23}^2)}$ $\qquad\qquad$ ...(8.20)

σ_u^2 (variance of disturbance terms) is unknown, an unbiased estimator of

σ_u^2 is defined as $\overset{*}{\sigma}{}_u^2 = \dfrac{\Sigma e_i^2}{n-k}$, k being the total number of parameters which are estimated. In the two explanatory variables model

$$k = 3, \text{ and } \overset{*}{\sigma}{}_u^2 = \frac{\Sigma e_i^2}{n-3}.$$

[Refer (6.22) and (8.27) for the derivation of unbiased estimator of σ_u^2]

8.3.1 Tests of Significance

The traditional test of significance of the parameter estimates is the standard error test, which is equivalent to the student's 't' test.

(i) *The standard error test*

$$SE(\hat{\beta}_2) = \sqrt{\mathrm{Var}(\hat{\beta}_2)} = \sqrt{\frac{\overset{*}{\sigma}{}^2 \Sigma x_{3i}^2}{\Sigma x_{2i}^2 \Sigma x_{3i}^2 - (\Sigma x_{2i} x_{3i})^2}}$$

where, $\overset{*}{\sigma}{}^2 = \dfrac{\Sigma e_i^2}{n-3}$.

If $SE(\hat{\beta}_i) > \frac{1}{2}\hat{\beta}_i$, we accept the null hypothesis, that is, we accept that the estimate β_i is not statistically significant.

If $SE(\hat{\beta}_i) < \frac{1}{2}\hat{\beta}_i$, we reject the null hypothesis, that is, we accept that estimate is statistically significant.

The smaller the standard errors, the stronger the evidence that the estimates are statistically reliable.

(ii) *The student's t-test of the null hypothesis*

We compute the *t-ratio* for each $\hat{\beta}_i$:

$$t^* = \frac{\hat{\beta}_i - \beta_i}{SE(\hat{\beta}_i)}, \text{ which follows the } t\text{-}distribution \text{ with}$$

$(n - k)$ degrees of freedom.

In the present case $t^* = \dfrac{\hat{\beta}_2 - \beta_2}{SE(\hat{\beta}_2)}$ with $(n - 3)$ degrees of freedom.

If our null hypothesis is $\beta_2 = 0$, then $t^* = \dfrac{\hat{\beta}_2}{SE(\hat{\beta}_2)}$

If $t^* < t$ (tabulated), we accept the null hypothesis, that is, we accept that $\hat{\beta}_2$ is not significant and hence the regressor does not appear to contribute to the explanation of the variations in Y.

If $t^* > t$ (tabulated), we reject the null hypothesis and we accept the alternative one: $\hat{\beta}_2$ is statistically significant. Thus, greater the value of t^* the stronger the evidence that β_i is statistically significant.

8.3.2 Goodness of Fit (R^2)

By (6.25) we have: $R^2 = 1 - \dfrac{\Sigma e_i^2}{\Sigma y_i^2}$.

In present model of two explanatory variables:

$$\Sigma e_i^2 = \Sigma\,(y_i - \hat{\beta}_2 x_{2i} - \hat{\beta}_3 x_{3i})^2$$

$$= \Sigma e_i\,(y_i - \hat{\beta}_2 x_{2i} - \hat{\beta}_3 x_{3i})$$

$$= \Sigma e_i y_i - \hat{\beta}_2\,\Sigma e_i x_{2i} - \hat{\beta}_3\,\Sigma e_i x_{3i}$$

$$= \Sigma e_i y_i\ \left\{\because \Sigma e_i x_{2i} = \Sigma e_i x_{3i} = 0\right\}$$

$$= \Sigma y_i\,(y_i - \hat{\beta}_2 x_{2i} - \hat{\beta}_3 x_{3i})$$

i.e., $$\Sigma e_i^2 = \Sigma y_i^2 - \hat{\beta}_2 \Sigma x_{2i} y_i - \hat{\beta}_3 \Sigma x_{3i} y_i$$

or $$\underbrace{\Sigma y_i^2}_{} = \underbrace{\hat{\beta}_2 \Sigma x_{2i} y_i + \hat{\beta}_2 \Sigma x_{3i} y_i}_{} + \underbrace{\Sigma e_i^2}_{}$$

Total Sum of   Explained Sum of Squares   Residual Sum
Square (Total   (Explained variations)   of Squares
variation)   (Unexplained variations)

$\therefore$ $$R^2 = \frac{\hat{\beta}_2 \Sigma x_{2i} y_i + \hat{\beta}_3 \Sigma x_{3i} y_i}{\Sigma y_i^2}.$$

$$R^2 = \left(\frac{\text{Sum of Squares Explained by } X_2\ \&\ X_3}{\text{Total Sum of Squares}}\right)$$

8.4 AN APPLICATION

Example 1. Table 8.1 contains observations on the expenditure on clothing (Y), total expenditure (X_2) and the price of clothing (X_3). We fit a linear regression to these observations and test the overall goodness of fit (R^2) as well as the statistical reliability of the estimates; $\hat{\beta}_2$ and $\hat{\beta}_3$. The relevant calculations are shown in the worksheet, Table 8.1.

(i) Substituting in (8.12) and (8.13) to obtain $\hat{\beta}_2$ and $\hat{\beta}_3$

$$\hat{\beta}_2 = \frac{(775.22)(192.20) - (-1019.62)(-125.61)}{(6086.10)(192.20) - (-1019.62)^2} = 0.1608$$

Table 8.1: Worksheet for Model: $Y = \beta_1 + \beta_2 X_2 + \beta_3 X_3 + U$

n	Y Exp. on clothing	X_2 Total expenditure	X_3 Price of clothing	$y_i = (Y_i - \bar{Y})$	$x_2 = (X_2 - \bar{X}_2)$	$x_3 = (X_3 - \bar{X}_3)$	y_i^2	x_2^2	x_3^2	$y_i x_2$	$y_i x_3$	$x_2 x_3$
1	3.5	15	16.0	-4.38	-37.3	8.95	19.18	1391.29	80.10	163.37	-39.20	-333.83
2	4.3	20	13.0	-3.58	-32.3	5.95	12.81	1043.29	35.40	115.63	-21.30	-192.18
3	5.0	30	10.0	-2.88	-22.3	2.95	8.29	497.29	8.70	64.22	-8.49	-65.78
4	6.0	42	7.0	-1.88	-10.3	-0.05	3.53	106.09	0	19.36	0.09	0.51
5	7.0	50	7.0	-0.88	-2.3	-0.05	0.77	5.29	0	2.02	0.04	0.11
6	9.0	54	5.0	1.12	1.7	-2.05	1.25	2.89	4.20	1.90	-2.29	-3.48
7	8.0	65	4.0	0.12	12.7	-3.05	0.01	161.29	9.30	1.52	-0.36	-38.73
8	10.0	72	3.0	2.12	19.7	-4.05	4.49	388.09	16.40	41.76	-8.58	-79.78
9	12.0	85	3.5	4.12	32.7	-3.55	16.97	1069.29	12.60	134.72	-14.62	-116.08
10	14.0	90	2.0	6.12	37.7	-5.05	37.45	1421.29	25.50	230.72	-30.90	-190.38
$n = 10$	$\Sigma Y = 78.8$	$\Sigma X_2 = 523$	$\Sigma X_3 = 70.5$	$\Sigma y_i = 0$	$\Sigma x_{2i} = 0$	$\Sigma x_{3i} = 0$	$\Sigma y_i^2 = 104.75$	$\Sigma x_{2i}^2 = 6086.10$	$\Sigma x_{3i}^2 = 192.20$	$\Sigma y_i x_{2i} = 775.22$	$\Sigma y_i x_{3i} = (-)125.60$	$\Sigma x_{2i} x_{3i} = (-)1019.62$
	$\bar{Y} = 7.88$	$\bar{X}_2 = 52.3$	$\bar{X}_3 = 7.05$									

$$\hat{\beta}_3 = \frac{(-125.61)(6086.10) - (-1019.62)(775.22)}{(6086.10)(192.20) - (-1019.62)^2} = 0.1995$$

Therefore, $\hat{\beta} = \bar{Y} - \hat{\beta}_2 \bar{X}_2 - \hat{\beta}_3 \bar{X}_3$

$$= 7.88 - (0.1608)(52.3) + (0.1995)(7.05) = (-)\ 1.9356$$

(ii) $R^2 = \dfrac{\hat{\beta}_2 \Sigma x_{2i} y_i + \hat{\beta}_3 \Sigma x_{3i} y_i}{\Sigma y_i^2}$

$$= \frac{(0.1608)(775.22) + (0.1995)(-125.61)}{104.75} = 0.9507$$

(iii) For estimation of the standard errors of $\hat{\beta}_2$ and $\hat{\beta}_3$ we need an estimate of σ_u^2.

$$R^2 = 1 - \frac{\Sigma e_i^2}{\Sigma y_i^2} \quad \text{or,} \quad \Sigma e_i^2 = \Sigma y_i^2 (1 - R^2)$$

Substituting the relevant terms Σy_i^2 and R^2 we obtain:

$$\Sigma e_i^2 = 104.75 (1 - 0.9507) = 5.1553$$

Therefore, $\sigma_u^{*2} = \dfrac{5.1553}{10 - 3} = 0.7377$

(iv) The variances of $\hat{\beta}_2$ and $\hat{\beta}_3$ may be obtained by substituting the relevant terms in (8.17) and (8.18).

$$\text{Var}\ (\hat{\beta}_2) = \frac{(0.7377)(192.20)}{(6086.10)(192.20) - (-1019.62)^2} = 0.0011$$

$$\text{Var}\ (\hat{\beta}_3) = \frac{(0.7377)(6086.10)}{(130123.5)} = 0.0345$$

Therefore standard errors of the estimates are:

$$SE\ (\hat{\beta}_2) = \sqrt{0.0011} = 0.0331$$

and, $\qquad SE\ (\hat{\beta}_3) = \sqrt{0.0345} = 0.1857$

(v) The regression results may now be presented in the following form:

$$\hat{Y} = -1.9356 + 0.1608\ X_2 + 0.1995\ X_3 \qquad R^2 = 0.95$$

$$SE\ (\beta_i) \qquad\qquad (0.033) \qquad (0.1858)$$

$$t^* \qquad\qquad\quad (4.8711) \qquad (1.0738)$$

The interpretation of the above estimated regression model is this: if both X_2 and X_3 are fixed at zero value, the average value of expenditure on clothing is negative. But such a mechanical interpretation of the intercept should be taken with a grain of salt. The partial regression coefficient of 0.1608 means that, holding all the other variables constant, an increase in total expenditure of, say, a rupee is accompanied by an increase in the mean expenditure on clothing of about 16 paise. In other words, marginal propensity to spend on clothing is estimated to be about 0.16 or 16 per cent. Similarly, holding all other variables constant, the mean expenditure on clothing increases by about 20 paise with a unit increase in the price of clothing. The R^2 value of 0.9507 shows that the two explanatory variables accounted for 95 per cent of the variations in the expenditure on clothing.

Turning to the statistical significance of the estimated coefficients, we see from the above model that only β_2 coefficient is statistically significant at the 5 per cent level of significance: The ratios of the estimated coefficients to their standard errors (that is, t ratios) are 4.8711 and 1.0738 respectively. Using a two tail t-test at 5 per cent level of significance, we see that the critical t-value for 8 degrees of freedom is 2.365. Only computed t-value for the first coefficient exceeds this critical value. Hence we may reject the null hypothesis; i.e., the true population value of the coefficient (β_2) is zero.

It is also important to note here that we cannot apply the usual t-test to test the hypothesis that $\beta_2 = \beta_3 = 0$ simultaneously because t-test procedure assumes that an independent sample is drawn every time the t-test is applied. If the same sample is used to test hypothesis about β_2 and β_3 simultaneously, it is likely that the estimators $\hat{\beta}_2$ and $\hat{\beta}_3$ are correlated thus violating the assumption underlying the t-test procedure.

A null hypothesis like $\beta_2 = \beta_3 = 0$ simultaneously can be tested only by the Analysis of Variance technique.

8.5 GENERALISED LINEAR REGRESSION MODEL

We have so far discussed the regression models containing one or two explanatory variables. Let us now generalise the model assuming that it contains k–number of explanatory variables. It will be of the form:

$$Y = \beta_0 + \beta_1 X_1 + \beta_2 X_2 \ldots\ldots \beta_k X_k + U$$

There are K parameters to be estimated ($K = k + 1$). System of normal equations will consist of K equations, in which the unknowns are the parameters $\beta_0, \beta_1, \beta_2\ldots, \beta_k$, and the known terms will be the sums of squares and the sums of products of all the variables in the structural equation.

Least squares estimators of the unknown parameters are obtained by minimising the sum of the squared residuals:

$$\Sigma e_i^2 = \Sigma (Y_i - \hat{\beta}_0 - \hat{\beta}_1 X_{1i} - \hat{\beta}_2 X_{2i} - \ldots - \hat{\beta}_k X_{ki})^2$$

with respect to $\hat{\beta}_j [j = 1, 2, \ldots, (k+1)]$

The partial derivations are equated to zero to obtain normal equations:

$$\frac{\partial}{\partial \hat{\beta}_0}\left[\Sigma e_i^2\right] = -2\Sigma\,(Y_i - \hat{\beta}_0 - \hat{\beta}_1 X_{1i} \ldots - \hat{\beta}_k X_{ki}) = 0$$

$$\frac{\partial}{\partial \hat{\beta}_1}\left[\Sigma e_i^2\right] = -2\Sigma X_{1i}\,(Y_i - \hat{\beta}_0 - \hat{\beta}_1 X_{1i} \ldots - \hat{\beta}_k X_{ki}) = 0$$

$$\cdots \quad \cdots \quad \cdots \quad \cdots \quad \cdots \quad \cdots \quad \cdots \quad \cdots \quad \cdots \quad \cdots \quad \cdots$$

$$\cdots \quad \cdots \quad \cdots \quad \cdots \quad \cdots \quad \cdots \quad \cdots \quad \cdots \quad \cdots \quad \cdots \quad \cdots$$

$$\frac{\partial}{\partial \hat{\beta}_k}\left[\Sigma e_i^2\right] = -2\Sigma X_{ki}\,(Y_i - \hat{\beta}_0 - \hat{\beta}_1 X_{1i} \ldots - \hat{\beta}_k X_{ki}) = 0$$

The general form of the above equations (except first one) may be written as:

$$\frac{\partial}{\partial \hat{\beta}_j}[\Sigma e_i^2] = -2\Sigma X_{ji}\,(Y_i - \hat{\beta}_0 - \hat{\beta}_1 X_{1i} \ldots - \hat{\beta}_k X_{ki}) = 0$$

$$(j = 1, 2, \ldots k)$$

Thus, we find that the general model is just a natural extension of the simple regression model. But, as we explain hereunder, the normal equations for a model with any number of explanatory variables may be derived in a mechanical way, without recourse to differentiation.

(I) Regression model with one explanatory variable:

Structural form : $Y_i = \beta_0 + \beta_1 X_{1i} + U$

Basic form : $Y_i = \hat{\beta}_0 + \hat{\beta} X_{1i}$

Normal equations :
$$\begin{cases} \Sigma Y_i = n\hat{\beta}_0 + \hat{\beta}_1 \Sigma X_{1i} \\ \Sigma X_1 Y_i = \hat{\beta}_0 \Sigma X_{1i} + \hat{\beta}_1 \Sigma X_{1i}^2 \end{cases}$$

(II) Regression model with two explanatory variables:

Structural form : $Y_i = \beta_0 + \beta_1 X_{1i} + \beta_2 X_{2i} + U_i$

Basic form : $Y_i = \hat{\beta}_0 + \hat{\beta}_1 X_{1i} + \hat{\beta}_2 X_{2i}$

Normal equations :
$$\begin{cases} \Sigma Y_i = n\hat{\beta}_0 + \hat{\beta}_1 \Sigma X_{1i} + \hat{\beta}_2 \Sigma X_{2i} \\ \Sigma Y_i X_{1i} = \hat{\beta}_0 \Sigma X_{1i} + \hat{\beta}_1 \Sigma X_{1i}^2 + \hat{\beta}_2 \Sigma X_{1i} X_{2i} \\ \Sigma Y_i X_{2i} = \hat{\beta}_0 \Sigma X_{2i} + \hat{\beta}_1 \Sigma X_{1i} X_{2i} + \hat{\beta}_2 \Sigma X_{2i}^2 \end{cases}$$

Comparing the normal equations of the above two models we observe the following:

(i) The first normal equation is derived by summing the basic form over all sample observations.

(ii) The second normal equation is derived by multiplying the basic form by X_1 and summing over all sample observations.

(iii) The third normal equation is derived by multiplying the basic form by X_2 and subsequently summing over the n-sample observations.

The generalisation of this procedure to the k-explanatory variable model is, therefore, very straightforward.

For example the kth equation of the model may be obtained by multiplying the basic form of the k-explanatory variable model by X_k and then summing over the sample observations.

The basic form of this model is   : $Y_i = \hat{\beta}_0 + \hat{\beta}_1 X_{1i} + \hat{\beta}_2 X_{2i} + ... + \hat{\beta}_k X_k$

Multiplying through by X_k : $Y_i X_k = \hat{\beta}_0 X_k + \hat{\beta}_1 X_{1i} X_k + ... + \hat{\beta}_k X_k^2$

Summation over n-sample observations   : $\Sigma Y_i X_{ki} = \hat{\beta}_0 \Sigma X_{ki} + \hat{\beta} \Sigma X_{1i} X_{ki} + ...$

$$+ \hat{\beta}_k \Sigma X_{ki}^2$$

8.5.1   Generalisation of the Formulae of the Variances

(I) In regression model with one explanatory variable:

$$Y_i = \beta_0 + \beta_1 X_{1i} + U_i$$

$$\text{Var } (\hat{\beta}_1) = \frac{\sigma_u^2}{\Sigma x_{1i}^2}$$

(II) In regression model with two explanatory variables:

$$Y_i = \beta_0 + \beta_1 X_{1i} + \beta_2 X_{2i} + U_i$$

$$\text{Var } (\hat{\beta}_1) = \frac{\sigma_u^2 \Sigma x_{2i}^2}{\Sigma x_{1i}^2 \Sigma x_{2i}^2 - (\Sigma x_{1i} x_{2i})^2}$$

$$\text{Var } (\hat{\beta}_2) = \frac{\sigma_u^2 \Sigma x_{1i}^2}{\Sigma x_{1i}^2 \Sigma x_{2i}^2 - (\Sigma x_{1i} x_{2i})^2}$$

These variances can also be put in the form of determinants as follows:
The normal equations of the model with two explanatory variables, *in deviation form*, are:

$$\Sigma x_1 y = \hat{\beta}_1 \Sigma x_1^2 + \hat{\beta}_2 \Sigma x_1 x_2$$

$$\Sigma x_2 y = \hat{\beta}_1 \Sigma x_1 x_2 + \hat{\beta}_2 \Sigma x_2^2$$

Let us define determinant A which is formed by the known terms appearing in the right hand side of the normal equations, i.e.,

$$|A| = \begin{vmatrix} \Sigma x_1^2 & \Sigma x_1 x_2 \\ \Sigma x_1 x_2 & \Sigma x_2^2 \end{vmatrix}$$

Then,

$$\text{Var}(\hat{\beta}_1) = \frac{\sigma_u^2 \begin{vmatrix} \Sigma x_1^2 & \to & \Sigma x_1 x_2 \\ & \downarrow & \\ \Sigma x_1 x_2 & & \Sigma x_2^2 \end{vmatrix}}{\begin{vmatrix} \Sigma x_1^2 & & \Sigma x_1 x_2 \\ \Sigma x_1 x_2 & & \Sigma x_2^2 \end{vmatrix}} = \frac{\sigma_u^2 \Sigma x_2^2}{|A|}$$

$$\text{Var}(\hat{\beta}_2) = \frac{\sigma_u^2 \begin{vmatrix} \Sigma x_1^2 & & \Sigma x_1 x_2 \\ & & \uparrow \\ \Sigma x_1 x_2 & \leftarrow & \Sigma x_2^2 \end{vmatrix}}{\begin{vmatrix} \Sigma x_1^2 & & \Sigma x_1 x_2 \\ \Sigma x_1 x_2 & & \Sigma x_2 \end{vmatrix}} = \frac{\sigma_u^2 \Sigma x_1^2}{|A|}.$$

(III) Regression model with three explanatory variables:

$$Y_i = \beta_0 + \beta_1 X_{1i} + \beta_2 X_{2i} + \beta_3 X_{3i} + U_i$$

The determinant of the known terms appearing in the *RHS* of the normal equations is:

$$\begin{vmatrix} \Sigma x_1^2 & \Sigma x_1 x_2 & \Sigma x_1 x_3 \\ \Sigma x_1 x_2 & \Sigma x_2^2 & \Sigma x_2 x_3 \\ \Sigma x_1 x_3 & \Sigma x_2 x_3 & \Sigma x_3^2 \end{vmatrix} = |B|$$

∴

$$\text{Var}(\hat{\beta}_1) = \frac{\sigma_u^2 \begin{vmatrix} \Sigma x_1^2 & \to \Sigma x_1 x_2 & \to \Sigma x_1 x_3 \\ \downarrow & & \\ \Sigma x_2 x_1 & \Sigma x_2^2 & \Sigma x_2 x_3 \\ \downarrow & & \\ \Sigma x_1 x_3 & \Sigma x_2 x_3 & \Sigma x_3^2 \end{vmatrix}}{|B|}$$

$$= \frac{\sigma_u^2 \begin{vmatrix} \Sigma x_2^2 & \Sigma x_2 x_3 \\ \Sigma x_2 x_3 & \Sigma x_3^2 \end{vmatrix}}{|B|} = \frac{\sigma_u^2 \left\{ \Sigma x_2^2 \Sigma x_3^2 - (\Sigma x_2 x_3)^2 \right\}}{|B|}$$

Following the procedure explained above, we can derive the variances of $\hat{\beta}_2$ and $\hat{\beta}_3$.

Variance of $\hat{\beta}_k$ will be given by the following expression.

$$\text{Var}\ (\hat{\beta}_k) = \frac{\sigma_u^2 \begin{vmatrix} \Sigma x_1^2 & \Sigma x_1 x_2 ...... \Sigma x_1 x_k \\ & \quad\quad\quad\downarrow \\ \Sigma x_1 x_2 & \Sigma x_2^2 ...... \Sigma x_2 x_k \\ \vdots & \vdots \quad\quad\quad\quad \downarrow \\ \Sigma x_1 x_k \leftarrow \Sigma x_2 x_k \leftarrow \Sigma x_k^2 \end{vmatrix}}{\begin{vmatrix} \Sigma x_1^2 & \Sigma x_1 x_2 ...... \Sigma x_1 x_k \\ \Sigma x_1 x_2 & \Sigma x_2^2 \quad ...... \Sigma x_2 x_k \\ \vdots & \vdots \quad\quad \vdots \\ \Sigma x_1 x_k & \Sigma x_2 x_k ...... \Sigma x_k^2 \end{vmatrix}}$$

8.5.2 Generalisation of the Formula for (R^2)

(1) Model with one explanatory variable gives:

$$R^2 = \frac{\hat{\beta}_1 \Sigma x_{1i} y_i}{\Sigma y_i^2}$$

(II) Model with two explanatory variables gives:

$$R^2 = \frac{\hat{\beta}_1 \Sigma x_{1i} y_i + \hat{\beta}_2 \Sigma x_{2i} y_i}{\Sigma y_i^2}$$

By inspection we find that for each additional explanatory variable, R^2 includes an additional term in the numerator, formed by the estimate of the parameter corresponding to the new variable multiplied by the sum of products of the deviations of the new variable and the dependent one.

Thus, R^2 with k explanatory variables will be equal to:

$$R^2 = \frac{\hat{\beta}_1 \Sigma x_{1i} y_i + \hat{\beta}_2 \Sigma x_{2i} y_i + ... + \hat{\beta}_k \Sigma x_{ki} y_i}{\Sigma y_i^2}$$

8.5.3 The Adjusted Coefficient of Determination ($\bar{R}^2$)

It is important to note that R^2 is a nondecreasing function of the number of explanatory variables present in the regression model. As the number of explanatory variables increases, R^2 almost invariably increases and never decreases. In other words, an additional explanatory variable will not decrease R^2. This can be understood in the following way:

$$R^2 = \frac{ESS}{TSS} = 1 - \frac{\Sigma e_i^2}{\Sigma y_i^2} \quad \text{(See 6.25)}$$

Σy_i^2 is independent of the number of variables present in the model because it is simply $\Sigma (Y_i - \bar{Y})^2$. Σe_i^2, however, depends on the number of explanatory variables (including the intercept term) present in the model. Since, in most cases, the coefficient of the additional variables appear with the value different from zero; Σe_i^2 is bound to decrease (at least it will not increase); hence R^2 as defined in 6.25 will increase. In view of this, in comparing two regression models with same dependent variable but different number of explanatory variables, one should be very wary of choosing the model with the highest R^2.

To correct for the above defect, we adjust R^2 by taking into account the *degrees of freedom*, which, as we know, get decreased with inclusion of additional explanatory variable in the model.

$$R^2 = 1 - \frac{\Sigma e_i^2}{\Sigma y_i^2}$$

$$\Sigma e_i^2 = \Sigma y_i^2 (1 - R^2)$$

i.e., unexplained $SS = TSS (1 - R^2)$.

We define $\bar{R}^2$ as the '*Adjusted Coefficient of Determination*' by dividing both sides of above expression by their respective degrees of freedom keeping the above equality true. In case of model with $(k - 1)$ explanatory variables ($\therefore k$ is number of parameters to be estimated).

$$\frac{\text{Unexplained } SS}{n - k} = \frac{\text{Total } SS}{n - 1} (1 - \bar{R}^2)$$

$$\bar{R}^2 = 1 - \left(\frac{n-1}{n-k} \right) \left\{ \frac{\text{Unexplained } SS}{\text{Total } SS} \right\}$$

$$\bar{R}^2 = 1 - \left(\frac{n-1}{n-k} \right) (1 - R^2) \left\{ \because \frac{\Sigma e_i^2}{\Sigma y_i^2} = 1 - R^2 \right\}$$

$$\bar{R}^2 = 1 - \left\{ \frac{\Sigma e_i^2 / (n-k)}{\Sigma y_i^2 / (n-1)} \right\}$$

The following points are important with regard to $\bar{R}^2$.

(i) Value of $\bar{R}^2$ will vary with respect to the number of explanatory variables. In other words, $\bar{R}^2$ can decrease when a new variable is added to a regression model (even though R^2 necessarily increases). However an increase in $\bar{R}^2$ does not necessarily imply that the new variable included is statistically significant. The ultimate decision on inclusion or exclusion of a variable should be based on theoretical considerations, *t*-test of the parameter estimate and the value of $\bar{R}^2$.

(ii) $\bar{R}^2$ is always less than R^2; $\bar{R}^2 = R^2$ only when $R^2 = 1$.

(iii) $\bar{R}^2$ can be < 0 only when $\left(\dfrac{n-1}{n-k}\right)\dfrac{\sum e_i^2}{\sum y_i^2} > 1$. This means that

regression model explains a very small fraction of the total sum of squares. For example, if $n = 10$, $k = 3$, and $R^2 = 0.10$, then $\bar{R}^2 = -0.0125$. In this sense $\bar{R}^2$ is misleading (see relation between R^2 and F under section of chap. 4.4.3).

It is crucial to note also that in comparing two models on the basis of the coefficient of determination, whether adjusted or not, *the dependent variable must be the same*; explanatory variables may take any form. Consider, for example, the following two models:

$$Y_i = \alpha_0 + \alpha_1 X_1 + \alpha_2 X_2 + U_1 \qquad \text{...(i)}$$

$$\log Y_i = \beta_0 + \beta_1 X_1 + \beta_2 X_2 + U_2 \qquad \text{...(ii)}$$

The specification of the model, the error terms, and the computation of R^2 for these two models are entirely different, hence provide no common ground for comparison of R^2s. The reason is as follows: By definition, R^2 measures the proportion of the variation in the dependent variable accounted for by the explanatory variables. In model (ii), R^2 measures the proportion of variation in *log Y* explained by X_1 and X_2, whereas in model (i), it measures the proportion of the variation in Y and two are not the same thing.

There is again another note of warning. At times researchers play the game of maximising $\bar{R}^2$, that is, choosing the model that gives the highest $\bar{R}^2$. But this may be dangerous. In any regression model, our aim is not to obtain high $\bar{R}^2$ *per se* but rather to obtain dependable estimates of the true population regression coefficients and draw inferences about them. If we obtain high $\bar{R}^2$, well and good, but if $\bar{R}^2$ is low, it does not necessarily mean the model is bad. (Refer below section 8.6 for further discussion).

8.5.4 Importance of Different Statistical Tests

There is no general agreement among econometricians as to which of the two statistical criteria is more important: a high R^2 (or $\bar{R}^2$), or low standard error of the parameter estimates.

R^2 is a more important criterion when the model is to be used for forecasting, but when the objective is testing of a null hypothesis based on parameter estimates, then we are interested in unbiased estimates of the parameters. The standard errors acquire a greater importance under such circumstances.

A high R^2 has a clear merit only when combined with significant estimates (low standard errors). We should be very careful in our interpretation and acceptance of the results when high R^2 is not found along with the low standard errors in a particular study. But all the same, standard errors also do not necessarily reflect the true precision of the parameter estimates which is based on the theoretical variance of the distribution of an estimate (remember that theoretical variance, however is unknown). Nevertheless priority should always be given to the fulfilment of the economic *a priori* criteria (i.e., sign and size of the parameter estimate). Only when the economic criteria are satisfied then one should proceed with application of different tests.

Again one may encounter different combinations while dealing with empirical problems. For instance;

(i) R^2 and only some of β's (regression coefficients) may be significant; or
(ii) R^2 may be significant but none of the β's might be significant; or
(iii) all β's may be significant but R^2 may not be significant; or
(iv) neither all β's nor R^2 may be significant.

The first case is very common, particularly when we have a large number of variables in the regression equation. Here the problem, therefore, is to decide which of the non-significant variables to drop. The second case indicates the presence of multicollinearity, while the third case is very rare; rather it may never happen so. The last case is a bit problematic. If R^2 is not significant, one would be inclined to drop the equation. But since some coefficients are significant, we would be tempted to include them and drop the rest. Then the resulting R^2 could turn out to be significant too.

In all cases, the capacity to judge and give the right interpretation is something that *cannot be taught; it can be learnt only by experience.*

8.6 IDENTIFICATION OF EXPLANATORY VARIABLES

The problem of which variables are to be included in the model is a major problem in applied econometrics. Though, as we have mentioned earlier, it is economic theory which ultimately helps to decide upon the variables to be included, it is difficult to estimate the effect of all those variables with any reasonable precision. This is because, at times some included variables turn out to be *superfluous** and *dominant* variables** in the model; while at other times problem of multicollinearity and qualitative nature of the variables present problems of estimation technique. Hence researcher has to consider which variables to include and which to drop to enhance the use of model for which it is estimated.

Some procedures have been developed for systematically adding and deleting variables, but let us not forget that the tests and procedures suggested here under are merely helpful; they are not to be treated as rules of thumb to make final decisions. Any one of the following procedures can be adopted depending on to what use the model is to be put ultimately:

1. Compute all possible regressions and choose the one with maximum $\bar{R}^2$.

2. Follow 'Backward-elimination' procedure and drop the explanatory variables progressively to arrive at final regression with maximum $\bar{R}^2$ and high t-values.

3. Follow 'Forward-selection' procedure and include the explanatory variable systematically to arrive at the final regression with maximum $\bar{R}^2$ and significant coefficients.

4. Follow 'Step-wise regression' procedure to arrive at the final regression with maximum $\bar{R}^2$ and significant coefficients.

In all above four procedures, the inclusion or deletion of the explanatory variable is attempted on the examination of R^2, $\bar{R}^2$, F and, t statistic (s) alongwith partial and simple correlation coefficients.

We have discussed the use of $R^2, \bar{R}^2$, F and t tests to determine the relative importance of different variables in the model. Here we discuss the role of *partial, simple* and *multiple* correlation coefficients in deciding whether to include or drop the explanatory variable in the model.

(i) $r_{yx_1}^2, r_{yx_2}^2$ and $r_{yx_3}^2$ (simple correlation coefficients) respectively measure the proportion of the variance in y that x_1 *alone*, x_2 *alone* and x_3 *alone* explain.

(ii) R^2 measures the proportion of the variance in y that x_1, x_2 and x_3 *together* explain.

---

* A superfluous variable is the one which on addition or deletion in a regression model does not significantly damage the regression coefficients of the other variables. We use or discard the superfluous variable to suit out convenience.

** When a dependent variable is functionally related to an independent variable in fixed proportions, all the variations in the dependent variable are explained by this independent variable; leaving thereby nothing to be explained by other variables—it is called dominant variable.

(iii) $r^2_{yx_1.x_2}$ (partial correlation coefficient) measures the effect of x_1 on y after the impact of the previously included variable x_2 has been eliminated. So that $r^2_{yx_1.x_2x_3}$ measures the effect of x_1 on y after the impact of previously included variables x_2 and x_3 has been eliminated. Partial correlations are, therefore, very important in deciding whether or not to include more explanatory variables.

For example, assume that we are given two explanatory variables x_1 and x_2 and we are asked to choose the one or both. The best procedure would be first to look at $r^2_{yx_1}$ and $r^2_{yx_2}$ (simple correlation coefficients) then include the one that has higher correlation. If x_1 is first chosen, we next look at $r^2_{yx_2.x_1}$ and include x_2 only if this is high. If x_2 is choosen first, we decide about x_1 after looking at $r^2_{yx_1.x_2}$. Sometimes we may first decide to include both variables instead of the two variables separately. In this case both $r^2_{yx_1}$ and $r^2_{yx_2}$ are high and $r^2_{yx_2.x_1}$ and $r^2_{yx_1.x_2}$ may be very low. Then what this suggests is that the separation of the two variables does not help us in explaining the variation in the dependent variable. So we include both variables in the model simultaneously.

Let us now explain the later two procedures in detail.

Forward Selection Procedure: In this procedure we just select the explanatory variable that has the highest simple correlation with dependent variable (Y). Then we look at the partial correlation coefficients of Y with other variables after we have included the one with highest simple correlation. We select the variable which has the highest partial correlation coefficient and include it. This procedure of inclusion of variables with next highest partial correlation is continued as long as the $\bar{R}^2$ increases or as long as F-value associated with the new variable (that is t-value) being included is significant.

Step-wise Regression Procedure: The above procedure has one drawback. A variable which may have been the best single variable at an early stage (because of high simple correlation) may be *superfluous* at a later stage. For example, in the above procedure, say x_3 variable was the one which was first included for being best in terms of highest simple correlation coefficient, it may turn out to be superfluous after the inclusion of variables x_2 and x_4. The step-wise regression method avoids such a situation by checking the F-value after each step-regression. Suppose we start with x_3 in the model. Then we enter x_2 (having highest $r^2_{yx_2.x_3}$) using forward selection method. After x_2 is entered, we look at x_3 and decide whether to retain it (or not) by looking at the F-value (or t^2) for x_3. If it is retained, we include the next variable—say x_4 having next highest $r^2_{yx_4.x_2x_3}$ by forward selection method. After x_4 has been entered, we look again at the F-value for the variables already included, i.e., x_3 and x_4 and delete any of two variables that is superfluous. In this way, at each stage, the forward selection procedure is used to decide which variable to be included and the backward-elimination procedure is used to decide which variable to eliminate.

In all the above procedures, one has to be careful in analysing the effect on $\overline{R}^2$ of deletion or addition of sets of variables. A regression equation with higher $\overline{R}^2$ is not necessarily better than an equation fitted with a lower $\overline{R}^2$. What one should do is exercise some judgement in the initial selection of variables and also examine at each stage whether the coefficients estimated have right signs and whether they make sense. The involves an examination of the signs and magnitudes of the coefficients and thorough analysis of the regression residuals.

8.7 MATRIX APPROACH TO LINEAR REGRESSION MODEL

In section 8.5 we observed that general linear regression model is just an extension of simple regression model. However the derivation of the required results from these (normal) equations will involve algebraic complexities. With the use of matrix algebra, the derivation of the results becomes much easier.

Generalising the two- and three-variable linear regression models, the regression model involving the dependent variable Y and generalised k-explaratory variables $X_1, X_2 ..., X_k$ may be written as

$$Y_1 = \beta_0 + \beta_1 X_1 i + \beta_2 X_2 i + ... + \beta_k X_{ki} + U_i$$
$$(i = 1, 2, 3, ..., n)$$

where β_0 = the intercept, β_1 to β_k = partial slope coefficients, U = stochastic disturbance term and i = ith observation, n being the size of the population. Since subscript i represents the ith observation, we shall have n number of equations with n number of observations on each variable:

$$Y_1 = \beta_0 + \beta_1 X_{11} + \beta_2 X_{21} + \beta_3 X_{31} ...... + \beta_k X_{k1} + U_1$$
$$Y_2 = \beta_0 + \beta_1 X_{12} + \beta_2 X_{22} + \beta_3 X_{32} ...... + \beta_k X_{k2} + U_2$$
$$... \quad ... \quad ... \quad ... \quad ... \quad ... \quad ... \quad ... \quad ...$$
$$... \quad ... \quad ... \quad ... \quad ... \quad ... \quad ... \quad ... \quad ...$$
$$... \quad ... \quad ... \quad ... \quad ... \quad ... \quad ... \quad ... \quad ...$$
$$Y_n = \beta_0 + \beta_1 X_{1n} + \beta_2 X_{2n} + \beta_3 X_{3n} ...... + \beta_k X_{kn} + U_n$$

These equations are put in matrix form:
$$\mathbf{Y} = \mathbf{X}\boldsymbol{\beta} + \mathbf{U} \qquad ...(8.21)$$

where;

$$Y = \begin{bmatrix} Y_1 \\ Y_2 \\ \vdots \\ Y_n \end{bmatrix} \cdot X = \begin{bmatrix} 1 & X_{11} & X_{21} \ldots X_{k1} \\ 1 & X_{12} & X_{22} \ldots X_{k2} \\ \vdots & \vdots & \vdots \\ 1 & X_{1n} & X_{2n} \ldots X_{kn} \end{bmatrix}$$

$$\beta = \begin{bmatrix} \beta_0 \\ \beta_1 \\ \vdots \\ \beta_k \end{bmatrix}, \text{ and } U = \begin{bmatrix} U_1 \\ U_2 \\ \vdots \\ U_n \end{bmatrix}$$

The order of matrix and vectors involved are:

$Y = (n \times 1)$, $X = \{n \times (k + 1)\}$, $\beta = \{(k + 1) \times 1\}$ and $U = (n \times 1)$

To derive the OLS estimators of β, under the usual (classical) assumptions mentioned below, we define two vectors of β and e as;

$$\hat{\beta} = \begin{bmatrix} \hat{\beta}_0 \\ \hat{\beta}_1 \\ \vdots \\ \hat{\beta}_k \end{bmatrix} \text{ and } e = \begin{bmatrix} e_1 \\ e_2 \\ \vdots \\ e_n \end{bmatrix}$$

We can write eq. 8.21 as $\quad Y = X\hat{\beta} + e$

or, $\quad e = Y - X\hat{\beta}$ ...(8.22)

We have to minimise: $\quad \sum_{i-1}^{n} e_i^2 = e_1^2 + e_2^2 + e_3^2 \ldots + e_n^2$

$$\sum_{i=1}^{n} e_i^2 = [e_1 \ e_2 \ \ldots \ldots \ e_n] \begin{bmatrix} e_1 \\ e_2 \\ \vdots \\ e_n \end{bmatrix} = e'e \qquad \text{...(8.23)}$$

$$\sum_{i-1}^{n} e_i^2 = e'e$$

$$= (Y - X\hat{\beta})' (Y - X\hat{\beta})$$

$$= Y'Y - \hat{\beta}'X'Y - Y'X\hat{\beta} + \hat{\beta}'X'X\hat{\beta}$$

Since $\hat{\beta}'X'Y$ is scalar (1×1), it is equal to its transpose;

i.e. $\qquad \hat{\beta}'X'Y = Y'X\hat{\beta}$

$$\therefore \qquad e'e = Y'Y - 2\hat{\beta}'X'Y + \hat{\beta}'X'X\hat{\beta} \quad ...(8.24)$$

Minimising $e'e$ with respect to elements in $\hat{\beta}$,

$$\frac{\partial}{\partial\hat{\beta}}(\Sigma e_i^2) = \frac{\partial}{\partial\hat{\beta}}(e'e) = -2X'Y + 2X'X\hat{\beta}$$

$$\left[\because \frac{\partial}{\partial X}(X'AX) = 2AX \text{ and also to } 2X'A\right]$$

Equating the expression to null vector O, we obtain:

$$-2X'Y + 2X'X\hat{\beta} = O$$

or, $$X'X\hat{\beta} = X'Y$$

i.e., $$\hat{\beta} = (X'X)^{-1}X'Y \qquad ...(8.25)$$

Here $\hat{\beta}$ is the vector of required least squares estimators $\hat{\beta}_0, \hat{\beta}_1, \hat{\beta}_2, ... \hat{\beta}_k$.

Statistical Properties of the Estimators

In order to examine the properties of the parameter estimators (derived in matrix form), we make use of the assumptions which we restate in matrix notations.

Assumption 1. $\quad E(U) = 0$ corresponding to assumption $E(U) = 0$

Assumption 2. We defined $U = \begin{bmatrix} U_1 \\ U_2 \\ \vdots \\ U_n \end{bmatrix}$, $U' = [U_1 \; U_2 \; U_3 ...... U_n]$

$$\therefore \qquad UU' = \begin{bmatrix} U_1^2 & U_1U_2 & U_1U_2... & U_1U_n \\ U_2U_1 & U_2^2 & U_2U_3... & U_2U_n \\ \vdots & \vdots & \vdots \;\; ... & \vdots \\ U_nU_1 & U_nU_2 & U_nU_3... & U_n^2 \end{bmatrix}$$

$$\therefore \qquad E(UU') = \begin{bmatrix} E(U_1^2) & E(U_1U_2) & ... & E(U_1U_n) \\ E(U_2U_1) & E(U_2^2) & ... & E(U_2U_n) \\ \vdots & \vdots & ... & \vdots \\ E(U_nU_1) & E(U_nU_2) & ... & E(U_n^2) \end{bmatrix}$$

$$= \begin{bmatrix} \sigma_u^2 & 0 & \cdots & 0 \\ 0 & \sigma_u^2 & \cdots & 0 \\ \vdots & \vdots & \cdots & \vdots \\ 0 & 0 & \cdots & \sigma_u^2 \end{bmatrix}$$

$$\because \quad E(U_i^2) = \sigma_u^2 \text{ and } E(U_i U_j) = 0 \ (i \neq j)$$

$$\therefore \quad E(UU') = \sigma_u^2 \begin{bmatrix} 1 & 0 & 0 & \cdots & 0 \\ 0 & 1 & 0 & \cdots & 0 \\ \vdots & \vdots & \vdots & \cdots & \vdots \\ 0 & 0 & 0 & \cdots & 1 \end{bmatrix} = \sigma_u^2 I_n$$

Note that $E(UU') = \sigma_u^2 I_n$ is the assumption corresponding to assumptions of variance and covariance of disturbance terms, i.e., $E(U_i^2) = \sigma_u^2$ and $E(U_i U_j) = 0$ for $i \neq j$.

Assumption 3. **X** is a set of fixed numbers.

Assumption 4. The rank of **X** is $(k+1)$ $(< n)$. This assumption is a necessary condition for $(X'X)$ to be non-singular.

Now we proceed to examine the desired properties of the estimators in matrix notations:

(1) *Linearity*

$$\hat{\beta} = (X'X)^{-1} X'Y$$
$$\hat{\beta} = (X'X)^{-1} X'(X\beta + U)$$
$$\hat{\beta} = \beta + (X'X)^{-1} X'U \qquad [\text{since } (X'X)^{-1} X'X = I]$$

The above equation states that $\hat{\beta}$ is the linear functions of β and U.

(2) *Unbiasedness*

$$\begin{aligned} E(\hat{\beta}) &= E\{\beta + (X'X)^{-1} X'U\} \\ &= E(\beta) + E[(X'X)^{-1} X'U] \\ &= \beta + (X'X)^{-1} X'E(U) \\ &= \beta, \text{ since } E(U) = 0 \text{ i.e., least square estimators} \\ &\quad \text{are unbiased.} \end{aligned}$$

(3) *Sampling Variance*

We know, $\quad \text{Var}(\beta') = E\left[(\hat{\beta} - \beta)^2\right]$

$$\text{Var}(\hat{\beta}) = E[(\hat{\beta} - \beta)(\hat{\beta} - \beta)']$$

$$E[(\hat{\beta} - \beta)(\hat{\beta} - \beta)'] =$$

$$\begin{bmatrix} E(\hat{\beta}_1 - \beta_1)^2 & E[(\hat{\beta}_1 - \beta_1)(\hat{\beta}_2 - \beta_2)] & \cdots & E[(\hat{\beta}_1 - \beta_1)(\hat{\beta}_k - \beta_k)] \\ E[(\hat{\beta}_2 - \beta_2)(\hat{\beta}_1 - \beta_1)] & E[(\hat{\beta}_2 - \beta_2)^2] & \cdots & E[(\hat{\beta}_2 - \beta_2)(\hat{\beta}_k - \beta_k)] \\ \vdots & \vdots & \cdots & \vdots \\ E[(\hat{\beta}_k - \beta_k)(\hat{\beta}_1 - \beta_1)] & E[(\hat{\beta}_k - \beta_k)(\hat{\beta}_2 - \beta_2)] & \cdots & E[(\hat{\beta}_k - \beta_k)^2] \end{bmatrix}$$

$$= \begin{bmatrix} \text{Var}(\hat{\beta}_1) & \text{Cov}(\hat{\beta}_1, \hat{\beta}_2) & \cdots\cdots & \text{Cov}(\hat{\beta}_1, \hat{\beta}_k) \\ \text{Cov}(\hat{\beta}_2, \hat{\beta}_1) & \text{Var}(\hat{\beta}_2) & \cdots\cdots & \text{Cov}(\hat{\beta}_2, \hat{\beta}_k) \\ \vdots & \vdots & \cdots\cdots & \vdots \\ \text{Cov}(\hat{\beta}_k, \hat{\beta}_1) & \text{Cov}(\hat{\beta}_k, \hat{\beta}_2) & \cdots\cdots & \text{Var}(\hat{\beta}_k) \end{bmatrix}$$

The above matrix is a symmetric matrix containing variances along its main diagonal and covariances of the estimators everywhere else. This matrix is, therefore, called the *Variance-Covariance matrix* of least squares estimators of the regression slopes. Again,

$$\text{Var}(\hat{\beta}) = E[(\hat{\beta} - \beta)(\hat{\beta} - \beta)']$$

Substituting $(X'X)^{-1} X'U$ for $(\hat{\beta} - \beta)$

$$\text{Var}(\hat{\beta}) = E[\{(X'X)^{-1} X'U\}\{(X'X)^{-1} X'U\}']$$

$$\text{Var}(\hat{\beta}) = E[\{(X'X)^{-1} X' UU' X(X'X)^{-1}]$$

$$= (X'X)^{-1} X' E(UU') X(X'X)^{-1}$$

$$= (X'X)^{-1} X' \sigma_u^2 I_n X (X'X)^{-1}$$

$$= \sigma_u^2 (X'X)^{-1} X'X (X'X)^{-1}$$

$$= \sigma_u^2 (X'X)^{-1}$$

(**Note:** σ_u^2 being a scalar can be moved in front or behind of a matrix while identity matrix I_n can be suppressed).

Thus we obtain,

$$\text{Var}(\hat{\beta}) = \sigma_u^2 (X'X)^{-1} \qquad \qquad ...(8.26)$$

where,
$$(X'X)^{-1} = \begin{bmatrix} n & \Sigma X_{1n} & \cdots\cdots & \Sigma X_{kn} \\ \Sigma X_{1n} & \Sigma X_{1n}^2 & \cdots\cdots & \Sigma X_{1n} X_{kn} \\ \vdots & \vdots & \cdots\cdots & \vdots \\ \vdots & \vdots & \cdots\cdots & \vdots \\ \Sigma X_{kn} & \Sigma X_{1n} X_{kn} & \cdots\cdots & \Sigma X_{kn}^2 \end{bmatrix}^{-1}$$

We can, therefore, obtain the variance of any estimator say $\hat{\beta}_i$ by taking the ith term from the principal diagonal $(X'X)^{-1}$ and then multiplying it by σ_u^2.

Let us take a two explanatory variables model to make use of matrix formulation to derive variances.

In derivation form: $y_i = \hat{\beta}_1 x_1 + \hat{\beta}_2 x_2$

$$\text{Var}\,(\hat{\beta}) = E[(\hat{\beta} - \beta)\,(\hat{\beta} - \beta)']$$

In this model; $(\hat{\beta} - \beta) = \begin{bmatrix} (\hat{\beta}_1 - \beta_1) \\ (\hat{\beta}_2 - \beta_2) \end{bmatrix}$

$$(\hat{\beta} - \beta)' = [(\hat{\beta}_1 - \beta_1)\,(\hat{\beta}_2 - \beta_2)]$$

$$\therefore \quad (\hat{\beta} - \beta)\,(\hat{\beta} - \beta)' = \begin{bmatrix} (\hat{\beta}_1 - \beta_1) \\ (\hat{\beta}_2 - \beta_2) \end{bmatrix} [(\hat{\beta}_1 - \beta_1)\,(\hat{\beta}_2 - \beta_2)]$$

and, $E[(\hat{\beta} - \beta)\,(\hat{\beta} - \beta)] = E\begin{bmatrix} (\hat{\beta}_1 - \beta_1)^2 & (\hat{\beta}_1 - \beta_1)\,(\hat{\beta}_2 - \beta_2) \\ (\hat{\beta}_1 - \beta_1)\,(\hat{\beta}_2 - \beta_2) & (\hat{\beta}_2 - \beta_2)^2 \end{bmatrix}$

$$= \begin{bmatrix} \text{Var}\,(\hat{\beta}_1) & \text{Cov}\,(\hat{\beta}_1, \hat{\beta}_2) \\ \text{Cov}\,(\hat{\beta}_1, \hat{\beta}_2) & \text{Var}\,(\hat{\beta}_2) \end{bmatrix}$$

In case of two explanatory variables, X in the deviation form shall be:

$$X = \begin{bmatrix} x_{11} & x_{21} \\ x_{12} & x_{22} \\ \vdots & \vdots \\ x_{1n} & x_{2n} \end{bmatrix} \text{ and } X' = \begin{bmatrix} x_{11} & x_{12}...x_{1n} \\ x_{21} & x_{22}...x_{2n} \end{bmatrix}$$

$$\therefore \quad \sigma_u^2\,(X'X)^{-1} = \sigma_u^2 \begin{bmatrix} \Sigma x_1^2 & \Sigma x_1 x_2 \\ \Sigma x_1 x_2 & \Sigma x_2^2 \end{bmatrix}^{-1}$$

or, $\qquad \sigma_u^2\,(X'X)^{-1} = \dfrac{\sigma_u^2 \begin{bmatrix} \Sigma x_2^2 & -\Sigma x_1 x_2 \\ -\Sigma x_1 x_2 & \Sigma x_1^2 \end{bmatrix}}{\begin{vmatrix} \Sigma x_1^2 & \Sigma x_1 x_2 \\ \Sigma x_1 x_2 & \Sigma x_2^2 \end{vmatrix}}$

i.e., $$\text{Var}(\hat{\beta}_1) = \frac{\sigma_u^2 \, \Sigma x_2^2}{\Sigma x_1^2 \, \Sigma x_2^2 - (\Sigma x_1 x_2)^2}$$

and $$\text{Var}(\hat{\beta}_2) = \frac{\sigma_u^2 \, \Sigma x_1^2}{\Sigma x_1^2 \, \Sigma x_2^2 - (\Sigma x_1 x_2)^2}$$

Thus the same results have been obtained as in case of (8.17) and (8.18) when no matrix algebra was used. In the present case we can also derive

$$\text{cov}(\hat{\beta}_1, \hat{\beta}_2) = \frac{(-)\, \sigma_u^2 \, \Sigma x_1 x_2}{\Sigma x_1^2 \, \Sigma x_2^2 - (\Sigma x_1 x_2)^2}$$

The only unknown part in variances and covariances of the estimators is σ_u^2.

The derivation of unbiased estimator of σ_u^2, in case of one explanatory variable, is given in (6.22). Similarly, we can obtain the estimator of σ_u^2 in case of two explanatory variables as follows:

$$\begin{aligned}
\Sigma e_i^2 &= \Sigma(Y_i - \hat{Y})^2 \\
&= \Sigma(Y_i - \hat{\beta}_0 - \hat{\beta}_1 X_1 - \hat{\beta}_2 X_2)^2 \\
&= \Sigma(y_i - \hat{\beta}_1 x_1 - \hat{\beta}_2 x_2)^2 \\
&= \Sigma(\beta_1 x_1 + \beta_2 x_2 - \hat{\beta}_1 x_1 - \hat{\beta}_2 x_2 + U_i - \bar{U})^2 \\
&= \Sigma[(U_i - \bar{U}) - x_1(\hat{\beta}_1 - \beta_1) - x_2(\hat{\beta}_2 - \beta_2)]^2 \\
E(\Sigma e_i^2) &= E\Sigma(U_i - \bar{U})^2 + E\Sigma x_1^2 \, (\hat{\beta}_1 - \beta_1)^2 + E\Sigma x_2^2(\hat{\beta}_2 - \beta_2)^2 \\
&\quad + 2E\Sigma x_1 x_2 \, (\hat{\beta}_1 - \beta_1)(\hat{\beta}_2 - \beta_2) - 2E(\hat{\beta}_1 - \beta_1)\Sigma x_1 u_i \\
&\quad - 2E(\hat{\beta}_2 - \beta_2)\, \Sigma x_2 u_i . \\
&= E\Sigma(U_i - \bar{U})^2 + \Sigma x_1^2 \, \text{Var}(\hat{\beta}_1) + \Sigma x_2^2 \, \text{Var}(\hat{\beta}_2) \\
&\quad + 2\Sigma x_1 x_2 \, \text{cov}(\hat{\beta}_1, \hat{\beta}_2) - 2E(\hat{\beta}_1 - \beta_1)\Sigma x_1 u_i \\
&\quad - 2E(\hat{\beta}_2 - \beta_2)\, \Sigma x_2 u_i .
\end{aligned}$$

On substituting for the variances and covariance in second, third and fourth terms of the above expression, we obtain:

$$\Sigma x_1^2 \, \text{Var}(\hat{\beta}_1) + \Sigma x_2^2 \, \text{Var}(\hat{\beta}_2) + 2\Sigma x_1 x_2 \, \text{cov}(\hat{\beta}_1, \hat{\beta}_2)$$

$$= \frac{\sigma_u^2 \, \Sigma x_1^2 \, \Sigma x_2^2 + \sigma_u^2 \, \Sigma x_1^2 \, \Sigma x_2^2 - 2\sigma_u^2(\Sigma x_1 x_2)^2}{\Sigma x_1^2 \, \Sigma x_2^2 - (\Sigma x_1 x_2)^2} = 2\sigma_u^2$$

Again; $\quad E\Sigma(U_i - \bar{U})^2 = E\Sigma U_i^2 - 2E(\Sigma U_i \bar{U}) + nE(U_i^2)$

$$= n\sigma_u^2 - 2\sigma_u^2 + \sigma_u^2 = n\sigma_u^2 - \sigma_u^2$$

and, $\quad -2E(\hat{\beta}_1 - \beta_1)\Sigma x_1 u_i = \dfrac{-2\sigma_u^2[\Sigma x_1^2 \, \Sigma_2^2 - (\Sigma x_1 x_2)^2]}{\Sigma x_1^2 \, \Sigma x_2^2 - (\Sigma x_1 x_2)^2} = -2\sigma_u^2$

Similarly, $\quad -2E(\hat{\beta}_2 - \beta_2)\Sigma x_2 u_i = -2\sigma_u^2$

On substituting for all the terms;

$$E(\Sigma e_i^2) = (n\sigma_u^2 - \sigma_u^2 + 2\sigma_u^2 - 2\sigma_u^2 - 2\sigma_u^2)$$

$$E(\Sigma e_i^2) = n\sigma_u^2 - 3\sigma_u^2$$

or $\qquad\qquad E(\Sigma e_i^2) = (n - 3)\sigma_u^2 \qquad\qquad\qquad …(8.27)$

In other words, an unbiased estimator of σ_u^2 (in case of two explanatory variables model) is $= \left\{\dfrac{\Sigma e_i^2}{n-3}\right\}$. In case of one explanatory variable model, it was $\left\{\dfrac{\Sigma e_i^2}{n-2}\right\}$. Thus, generalising for k-explanatory variables, unbiased estimator for $\sigma_u^2 = \left\{\dfrac{\Sigma e_i^2}{n-k-1}\right\}$. Putting this in matrix notation,

$\because \qquad\qquad \Sigma e_i^2 = e'e, \qquad E(e'e) = (n - k - 1)\sigma_u^2 \qquad …(8.28)$

(4) *Minimum Variance of* $\hat{\beta}$

To show that all the β_i's in the $\hat{\beta}$ vector are Best Estimators, we have also to prove that the variances obtained in (8.26) are the smallest amongst all other possible linear unbiased estimators. We follow the same procedure as followed in case of single explanatory variable model where, we first assumed an alternative linear unbiased estimator and then it was established that its variance is greater than the estimator of the regression model.

Assume that $\hat{\hat{\beta}}$ is *an alternative unbiased and linear estimator of* β.

Suppose that $\hat{\hat{\beta}} = [(X'X)^{-1} X' + B]Y$.

where **B** is $(k \times n)$ matrix of known constants.

$\therefore \qquad\qquad \hat{\hat{\beta}} = [(X'X)^{-1} X' + B] [X\beta + U]$

$$\hat{\hat{\beta}} = (X'X)^{-1} X' (X\beta + U) + B(X\beta + U)$$

$\therefore \qquad E(\hat{\hat{\beta}}) = E[X'X)^{-1} X'(X\beta + U) + B(X\beta + U)]$

$$= E[(X'X)^{-1} X'X\beta + (X'X)^{-1} X'U + BX\beta + BU]$$
$$= \beta + BX\beta \ [\because \ E(U) = 0]$$

Since our assumption regarding an alternative $\hat{\hat{\beta}}$ is that it is to be an unbiased estimator of β, therefore, $E(\hat{\hat{\beta}})$ should be equal to β; on other words $(BX\beta)$ should be a null matrix.

In other words, BX should be $= 0$ if $\hat{\hat{\beta}} = [(X'X)^{-1} X' + B]Y$ is to be an unbiased estimator.

Let us now find variance of this alternative estimator.

$$\text{Var} \ (\hat{\hat{\beta}}) = E[(\hat{\hat{\beta}} - \beta)(\hat{\hat{\beta}} - \beta)']$$
$$= E[\{[(X'X)^{-1} X' + B]Y - \beta\} \{[(X'X)^{-1} X' + B]Y - \beta\}']$$
$$= E[\{[(X'X)^{-1} X' + B] (X\beta + U) - \beta\} \{[(X'X)^{-1} X' + B]$$
$$(X\beta + U) - \beta\}']$$
$$= E[\{(X'X)^{-1} X'X\beta + (X'X)^{-1} X'U + BX\beta + BU - \beta\}$$
$$\{(X'X)^{-1} X' X\beta + (X'X)^{-1} X'U + BX\beta + BU - \beta\}']$$
$$= E[\{(X'X)^{-1} X'U + BU\} \{X'X)^{-1} X'U + BU\}']$$
$$(\because \ BX = 0)$$
$$= E[\{(X'X)^{-1} X'U + BU\} \{U'X (X'X)^{-1} + U'B'\}]$$
$$= E[\{(X'X)^{-1} X' + B\}UU'\{X(X'X)^{-1} + B'\}]$$
$$= [(X'X)^{-1} X' + B] \ E(UU') \ [X(X'X)^{-1} + B']$$
$$= \sigma_u^2 I_n[X'X)^{-1} X' + B] \ [X(X'X)^{-1} + B']$$
$$= \sigma_u^2 [(X'X)^{-1} X'X(X'X)^{-1} + BX(X'X)^{-1} +$$
$$(X X)^{-1} X'B' + BB']$$
$$= \sigma_u^2 [(X'X)^{-1} + BB'] \ (\because \ BX = 0)$$
$$= \sigma_u^2 (X'X)^{-1} + \sigma_u^2 BB'$$

or, in other words, $\text{Var}(\hat{\hat{\beta}})$ is greater than $\text{Var}(\hat{\beta})$ by an expression $\sigma_u^2 \ BB'$ and hence it proves that $\hat{\beta}$ is the best estimator.

Coefficient of Determination (R^2)

From (8.24) we have,

$$\Sigma e_i^2 = e'e = Y'Y - 2\hat{\beta}'X'Y + \hat{\beta}'X'X\hat{\beta}$$

Since $\qquad (X'X)\hat{\beta} = X'Y$

$\therefore \qquad\qquad e'e = Y'Y - 2\hat{\beta}'X'Y + \hat{\beta}'X'Y$

$$e'e = Y'Y - \hat{\beta}'X'Y$$

$$\hat{\beta}'X'Y = Y'Y - e'e \qquad \qquad ...(8.29)$$

We know $\qquad y_i = Y_i - \bar{Y}$

$\therefore \qquad\qquad \Sigma y_i^2 = \Sigma Y_i^2 - \dfrac{1}{n}(\Sigma Y_i)^2$

In matrix notation $\Sigma Y_i^2 = Y'Y$

$$\Sigma y_i^2 = Y'Y - \frac{1}{n}(\Sigma Y_i)^2 \qquad\qquad ...(8.30)$$

Equation (8.30) gives the *total sum of squares* variations in the model.
Explained Sum of Squares

$$ESS = \Sigma y_i^2 - \Sigma e_i^2$$

$$= Y'Y - \frac{1}{n}(\Sigma Y_i)^2 - e'e$$

$$= Y'Y - e'e - \frac{1}{n}(\Sigma Y_i)^2$$

$$= \hat{\beta}'X'Y - \frac{1}{n}(\Sigma Y_i)^2 \quad ...(\text{by } 8.29)$$

Since, $\quad R^2 = \dfrac{\text{Explained Sum of Squares}}{\text{Total Sum of Squares}}$

$\therefore \qquad\qquad R^2 = \dfrac{\hat{\beta}'X'Y - \dfrac{1}{n}(\Sigma Y_i)^2}{Y'Y - \dfrac{1}{n}(\Sigma Y_i)^2} = \dfrac{\hat{\beta}'X'Y - n\bar{Y}^2}{Y'Y - n\bar{Y}^2}$

Summary of the Results

For the general linear regression model involving k-explanatory variables,
following results are obtained with the use of matrix algebra. All the results
are in matrix notations:

(i) Model: $\qquad\qquad\qquad\qquad Y = X\hat{\beta} + U$

(ii) Estimators: $\qquad\qquad\qquad \hat{\beta} = (X'X)^{-1} X'Y$

(iii) Statistical Properties: $\qquad$ (a) Linear (b) Unbiased, and
$\qquad\qquad\qquad\qquad\qquad\qquad$ (c) minimum variance

(iv) Variance-Covariance: $\qquad \text{Var}(\hat{\beta}) = \sigma_u^2 (X'X)^{-1}$

(v) Estimation of $(e'e)$: $\qquad\qquad e'e = Y'Y - \hat{\beta}'X'Y$

(vi) Coeff. of Determination: $\quad R^2 = \dfrac{\hat{\beta}'X'Y - \dfrac{1}{n}(\Sigma Y_i)^2}{Y'Y - \dfrac{1}{n}(\Sigma Y_i)^2}$

In order to help the students to understand the working of matrix algebra in the estimation of the regression coefficients, following examples are given.

Applications Using Matrix Method of Estimation

Example 2: Consider the data given in Table 8.2 to fit the linear function:

$$Y = \alpha + \beta_1 X_1 + \beta_2 X_2 + \beta_3 X_3 + U$$

In the matrix notation: $\hat{\beta} = (X'X)^{-1} X'Y$, where (when we use the data in deviation form),

$$\hat{\beta} = \begin{bmatrix} \hat{\beta}_1 \\ \hat{\beta}_2 \\ \hat{\beta}_3 \end{bmatrix} \quad X = \begin{bmatrix} x_{11} & x_{21} & x_{31} \\ x_{12} & x_{22} & x_{32} \\ \vdots & \vdots & \vdots \\ x_{1n} & x_{2n} & x_{3n} \end{bmatrix},$$

For three explanatory variables;

$$X'X = \begin{bmatrix} \Sigma x_1^2 & \Sigma x_1 x_2 & \Sigma x_1 x_3 \\ \Sigma x_1 x_2 & \Sigma x_2^2 & \Sigma x_2 x_3 \\ \Sigma x_1 x_3 & \Sigma x_2 x_3 & \Sigma x_3^2 \end{bmatrix} \text{ and, } X'Y = \begin{bmatrix} \Sigma x_1 y \\ \Sigma x_2 y \\ \Sigma x_3 y \end{bmatrix}$$

(i) Substituting the relevant quantities from the worksheet Table 8.2 we obtain:

$$X'X = \begin{bmatrix} 270 & 240 & -330 \\ 240 & 630 & -420 \\ -330 & -420 & 750 \end{bmatrix} \text{ and } X'Y = \begin{bmatrix} 319 \\ 492 \\ -625 \end{bmatrix}$$

Note: The calculations may be made easier by taking 30 as common factor from all the elements of matrix $(X'X)$. This will not effect the final results.

$$|X'X| = \begin{bmatrix} 270 & 240 & -330 \\ 240 & 630 & -420 \\ -330 & -420 & 750 \end{bmatrix} = 3852000, \text{ and}$$

$$(X'X)^{-1} = \begin{bmatrix} 0.0085 & -0.0012 & 0.0031 \\ -0.0012 & 0.0027 & 0.0009 \\ 0.0031 & 0.0009 & 0.0032 \end{bmatrix}$$

$$\therefore \quad \hat{\beta} = \begin{bmatrix} \hat{\beta}_1 \\ \hat{\beta}_2 \\ \hat{\beta}_3 \end{bmatrix} = (X'X)^{-1} X'Y =$$

Table 8.2: Worksheet for the Model: $Y = \alpha + \beta_1 X_1 + \beta_2 X_2 + \beta_3 X_3 + U$

n	Y	X_1	X_2	X_3	y_i	x_1	x_2	x_3	y_i^2	x_1x_2	x_2x_3	x_1x_3	x_1^2	x_2^2	x_3^2	x_1y_i	x_2y_i	x_3y_i
1	49	35	53	200	-3	-7	-9	0	9	63	0	0	49	81	0	21	27	0
2	40	35	53	212	-12	-7	-9	12	144	63	-108	-84	49	81	144	84	108	-144
3	41	38	50	211	-11	-4	-12	11	121	48	-132	-44	16	144	121	44	132	-121
4	46	40	64	212	-6	-2	2	12	36	-4	24	-24	4	4	144	12	-12	-72
5	52	40	70	203	0	-2	8	3	0	-16	24	-6	4	64	9	0	0	0
6	59	42	68	194	7	0	6	-6	49	0	-36	0	0	36	36	0	42	-42
7	53	44	59	194	1	2	-3	-6	1	-6	18	-12	4	9	36	2	-3	-06
8	61	46	73	188	9	4	11	-12	81	+44	-132	-48	16	121	144	36	99	-108
9	55	50	59	196	3	8	-3	-4	9	-24	12	-32	64	9	16	24	-9	-12
10	64	50	71	190	12	8	9	-10	144	72	-90	-80	64	81	100	96	108	-120
	520	420	620	2000	0	0	0	0	594	240	-420	-330	270	630	750	319	492	-625
	$\bar{Y}=52$	$\bar{X}_1=42$	$\bar{X}_2=62$	$\bar{X}_3=200$	$\Sigma y_i=$	$\Sigma x_1=$	$\Sigma x_2=$	$\Sigma x_3=$	$\Sigma y_i^2=$	$\Sigma x_1x_2=$	$\Sigma x_2x_3=$	$\Sigma x_1x_3=$	$\Sigma x_1^2=$	$\Sigma x_2^2=$	$\Sigma x_3^2=$	$\Sigma x_1y_i=$	$\Sigma x_2y_i=$	$\Sigma x_3y_i=$

$$\begin{bmatrix} 0.0085 & -0.0012 & 0.0031 \\ -0.0012 & 0.0027 & 0.0009 \\ 0.0031 & 0.0009 & 0.0032 \end{bmatrix} \begin{bmatrix} 319 \\ 492 \\ -625 \end{bmatrix} = \begin{bmatrix} 0.2063 \\ 0.3309 \\ -0.5572 \end{bmatrix} = \begin{bmatrix} \hat{\beta}_1 \\ \hat{\beta}_2 \\ \hat{\beta}_3 \end{bmatrix}$$

and,
$$\begin{aligned} \hat{\alpha} &= \bar{Y} - \hat{\beta}_1\bar{X}_1 - \hat{\beta}_2\bar{X}_2 - \hat{\beta}_3\bar{X}_3 \\ &= 52 - (0.2063)(42) - (0.3309)(62) - (-0.5572)(200) \\ &= 52 - 8.6633 - 20.5139 + 111.4562 = 134.2789 \end{aligned}$$

Important Note: Students may not obtain exactly the similar values of estimators ($\hat{\beta}$'s) as given above. This is because we approximated four figures after decimal (deleting remaining four figures actually obtained).

(ii) The elements in the principal diagonal of $(\mathbf{X'X})^{-1}$ when multiplied σ_u^2 give the variances of the regression parameters, i.e.,

$$\left. \begin{aligned} \text{Var}(\hat{\beta}_1) &= \sigma_u^2(0.0085) \\ \text{Var}(\hat{\beta}_2) &= \sigma_u^2(0.0027) \\ \text{Var}(\hat{\beta}_3) &= \sigma_u^2(0.0032) \end{aligned} \right\} = \hat{\sigma}_u^2 = \frac{\Sigma e_i^2}{n-k} = \frac{17.11}{6} = 2.851$$

$\therefore$ $\text{Var}(\hat{\beta}_1) = 0.0243$ and $SE(\hat{\beta}_1) = 0.1560$

     $\text{Var}(\hat{\beta}_2) = 0.0077$ and $SE(\hat{\beta}_2) = 0.0877$, and

     $\text{Var}(\hat{\beta}_3) = 0.0093$ and $SE(\hat{\beta}_3) = 0.0962$

(iii) $R^2 = \dfrac{\hat{\beta}'\mathbf{X'Y} - \dfrac{1}{n}(\Sigma Y_i)^2}{\mathbf{Y'Y} - \dfrac{1}{n}(\Sigma Y_i)^2} = \dfrac{\hat{\beta}_1\Sigma x_1 y + \hat{\beta}_2\Sigma x_2 y + \hat{\beta}_3\Sigma x_3 y}{\Sigma y_i^2}$

$$= \frac{575.89}{594} = 0.97$$

(iv) The estimated relation may be put in the following form:

$$\hat{Y} = 134.28 + 0.2063X_1 + 0.3309X_2 - 0.5572X_3 \qquad R^2 = 0.97$$

$SE(\beta_i)$ (0.1560)   (0.0877)   (0.0962)

t^* (1.3221)   (3.7719)   (5.7949)

The variables X_1, X_2, and X_3 explain 97 per cent of total variations. Only X_1 is not statistically significant.

Example 3: The following matrix gives the variances and covariances of the three variables:

$$
\begin{array}{cccc}
 & X_1 & X_2 & X_3 \\
X_1 & \begin{bmatrix} 7.59 & 3.12 & 26.99 \\ X_2 \\ X_3 \end{bmatrix}
\end{array}
$$

$$
\begin{array}{c}
X_1 \\ X_2 \\ X_3
\end{array}
\begin{bmatrix}
7.59 & 3.12 & 26.99 \\
- & 29.16 & 30.80 \\
- & - & 133.00
\end{bmatrix}
$$

where, X_1: log food consumption per capita; X_2: log food price; and, X_3: log disposable income per capita.

Fit the function (for $n = 20$): $Y_1 = A Y_2^{\alpha} Y_3^{\beta}$ ($X_i = \log Y_i$)

In the present example, fitting of function of the form:

$$Y_1 = A Y_2^{\alpha} Y_3^{\beta}$$

requires transformation in the following way,

$$\log Y_1 = \log A + \alpha \log Y_2 + \beta \log Y_3$$

But since it is given that

$$\log Y_1 = X_1, \ \log Y_2 = X_2 \text{ and, } \log Y_3 = X_3,$$

hence the above transformation changes to:

$$X_1 = A^* + \alpha X_2 + \beta X_3$$

For estimation of α and β, the relevant matrices are:

$$
\hat{\beta} = \begin{bmatrix} \hat{\alpha} \\ \hat{\beta} \end{bmatrix}
\quad \text{and,} \quad
\mathbf{X} = \begin{bmatrix}
x_{21} & x_{31} \\
x_{22} & x_{33} \\
\vdots & \vdots \\
x_{2n} & x_{3n}
\end{bmatrix}
$$

$$
\therefore \quad \mathbf{X'X} = \begin{bmatrix}
\Sigma x_2^2 & \Sigma x_2 x_3 \\
\Sigma x_3 x_3 & \Sigma x_3^2
\end{bmatrix}
\quad \text{and,} \quad
\mathbf{X'Y} = \begin{bmatrix}
\Sigma x_2 y \\
\Sigma x_3 y
\end{bmatrix}
$$

Substituting the relevant quantities from the given variance-covariance matrix, we obtain:

$$
\mathbf{X'X} = \begin{bmatrix}
29.16 & 30.80 \\
30.80 & 133.00
\end{bmatrix}
\quad \text{and, } \mathbf{X'Y} = \begin{bmatrix}
3.12 \\
26.99
\end{bmatrix}
$$

$$
|\mathbf{X'X}| = \begin{vmatrix}
29.16 & 30.80 \\
30.80 & 133.00
\end{vmatrix} = 2929.64
$$

$$
\therefore \quad (\mathbf{X'X})^{-1} = \frac{1}{2929.64} \begin{bmatrix}
133.00 & -30.80 \\
-30.80 & 29.16
\end{bmatrix} \approx \begin{bmatrix}
0.0454 & -0.0105 \\
-0.0105 & 0.0099
\end{bmatrix}
$$

(i) $\hat{\beta} = (\mathbf{X'X})^{-1} \mathbf{X'Y} = \begin{bmatrix} \hat{\alpha} \\ \hat{\beta} \end{bmatrix}$

$$\begin{bmatrix} 0.0454 & -0.0105 \\ -0.0105 & 0.0099 \end{bmatrix} \begin{bmatrix} 3.12 \\ 26.99 \end{bmatrix} \approx \begin{bmatrix} (-)\,0.1421 \\ 0.2358 \end{bmatrix} = \begin{bmatrix} \hat{\alpha} \\ \hat{\beta} \end{bmatrix}$$

(ii) The element in the principal diagonal of $(\mathbf{X'X})^{-1}$ when multiplied by σ_u^2 give the variances of the $\hat{a}$ and $\hat{\beta}$.

To obtain Σe_i^2, we need R^2.

(iii) $\qquad R^2 = \dfrac{\hat{\alpha}\Sigma x_2 y + \hat{\beta}\Sigma x_3 y}{\Sigma y_i^2} = \dfrac{-(0.1421)\,(3.12) + (0.2358)\,(26.99)}{7.59}$

$\therefore \qquad R^2 = 0.78; \quad \Sigma e_i^2 = (1 - R^2)\,(\Sigma y_i^2) \approx 1.6680$

$\therefore \qquad \hat{\sigma}_u^2 = \dfrac{1.6680}{17} = 0.0981$

$\text{Var}\,(\hat{\alpha}) = (0.0981)\,(0.0454) \approx 0.0045, \quad \therefore \quad (\hat{\alpha})\ SE = 0.0667$

$\text{Var}\,(\hat{\beta}) = (0.0981)\,(0.0099) \approx 0.0009, \quad \therefore \quad (\hat{\beta})\ SE = 0.0312$

(iv) The results may be put in the following form:

$$\hat{Y}_1 = A \qquad Y_2^{(-0.1421)} \quad Y_3^{(0.2358)} \qquad\qquad R^2 = 0.78$$

SE		(0.0667)	(0.0312)
t^*		(−2.13)	(7.55)

The (constant) food price elasticity is negative but income elasticity is positive. Also income elasticity is highly significant. About 78 per cent of the variations in the consumption of food are explained by its price and income of the consumer.

8.8 ESTIMATION UNDER RESTRICTIONS* (GENERALIZATION OF SECTION 7.6)

On many occasions in regression analysis, one may have an exact information relative to a particular parameter from certain extraneous sources. For example, as we have discussed under section 7.6 of the Chapter 7 the

---

* "...... a priori information, particularly restrictions on the values of population parameters, plays an important role in econometrics. On the one hand the econometric investigator often has small samples which he cannot extend or reproduce so that the opportunity for increasing efficiency by increasing the sample size or repeating the experiment is not available. On the other hand, there is a large body of economic theory on which he can draw restrictions to increase to reliability of his inferences". Econometric Theory, A.S. Goldberger, J. Wiley & Sons, New York (1966), pp. 141–142.

estimation of Cobb-Douglas production function with linear restriction of $\beta_1 + \beta_2 = 1$. Such estimation of OLS estimators is called Restricted Least Squares procedures of estimation.

Alternatively, in estimating a demand relation, information may be available from consumer theory on the homogeneity condition, or an estimate of say, the income response coefficient may be available from previous empirical work. We utilise such an extraneous information in our estimation in the following procedure.

Here we develop matrix method to incorporate given information in the least squares method.

The exact linear restrictions on coefficients are to be first expressed in matrix form as under

$$\mathbf{R\beta} = \mathbf{\gamma} \qquad\qquad ...(8.31)$$

where, $\mathbf{R}$ is known restriction matrix of order $J \times k$ (J = number of restrictions to be incorporated), β is a vector of the coefficients to be estimated, γ is a $J \times 1$ known vector.

Assume that we wish to incorporate the given information concerning the parameters in the model: $\mathbf{Y} = \mathbf{X\beta} + \mathbf{U}$ with K number of explanatory variables. The procedure of incorporation of given information (restriction) works in the following way.

(i) *Information that:* $\beta_1 = k$ *(some constant value),* we would set:

$$\gamma = [k], \quad \mathbf{R} = [1 \quad 0 \quad 0 \quad ..... \quad 0]$$

so that $[1 \quad 0 \quad 0...0] \begin{bmatrix} \beta_1 \\ \beta_2 \\ \vdots \\ \beta_k \end{bmatrix} = [k]$

(ii) *Information that:* $\beta_1 + \beta_2 + ... + \beta_k = 1$
We would set:

$$\gamma = [1], \mathbf{R} = [1 \quad 1......1]$$

so that $[1 \quad 1......1] \begin{bmatrix} \beta_1 \\ \beta_2 \\ \vdots \\ \beta_k \end{bmatrix} = [1]$

(iii) *Information that:* $\beta_1 = \beta_2$ and $\beta_1 + 2\beta_4 + \beta_5 = 1$

In this case, $\gamma = \begin{bmatrix} 0 \\ 1 \end{bmatrix}$ and $\mathbf{R} = \begin{bmatrix} 1 & -1 & 0 & 0 & 0 & 0...0 \\ 1 & 0 & 0 & 2 & 1 & 0...0 \end{bmatrix}$

Hence we write:
$$\begin{bmatrix} 1 & -1 & 0 & 0 & 0 & 0...0 \\ 1 & 0 & 0 & 2 & 1 & 0...0 \end{bmatrix} \begin{bmatrix} \beta_1 \\ \beta_2 \\ \vdots \\ \beta_k \end{bmatrix} = \begin{bmatrix} 0 \\ 1 \end{bmatrix}.$$

(iv) *Information that:* $\dfrac{\beta_2}{\beta_1} = k_1$ and, $\dfrac{\beta_1}{\beta_2} = k_2$

Therefore,
$$\gamma = \begin{bmatrix} 0 \\ 0 \end{bmatrix} \qquad R = \begin{bmatrix} -k_1 & 1 & 0 & 0...0 \\ 0 & -k_2 & 1 & 0...0 \end{bmatrix}$$

so that:
$$\begin{bmatrix} -k_1 & 1 & 0 & 0...0 \\ 0 & -k_2 & 1 & 0...0 \end{bmatrix} \begin{bmatrix} \beta_1 \\ \beta_2 \\ \vdots \\ \beta_k \end{bmatrix} = \begin{bmatrix} 0 \\ 0 \end{bmatrix}.$$

(v) *Information that:* $\beta_1 = k$, $\beta_1 + \beta_2 + ... + \beta_k = 1$, and $\beta_2 = \beta_3$.

Here we set,
$$\gamma = \begin{bmatrix} k \\ 1 \\ 0 \end{bmatrix}, \qquad R = \begin{bmatrix} 1 & 0 & 0 & 0 & 0...0 \\ 1 & 1 & 1 & 1 & 1...1 \\ 0 & 1 & -1 & 0 & 0...0 \end{bmatrix}$$

The information on linear combination (restriction) has been expressed in the matrix form (8.31).

Given this information of the form (8.31), the question is how to combine it with the information contained in the sample observations **Y**. Because information on the individual parameter and combinations is specified to be known with certainty, there is no sampling variability from sample to sample. Consequently, the coefficients are not independent and the restrictions on particular coefficients or their combinations reflected in (8.31) above, condition the values that other coefficients may take on. Therefore, if we use the least squares criterion applied to both sample information expressed in equation 8.21 above and the non-sample information described by (8.31), we are faced with the problem of finding the vector β^* that minimises the quadratic form: $(Y - X\beta)' (Y - X\beta)$ subject to restriction

$$R\beta = \gamma, \text{ that is } R\beta - \gamma = 0$$

We, therefore, minimise the Lagrange function of the form:

$$S = (Y - X\beta)' (Y - X\beta) - 2\lambda' (R\beta - \gamma)$$

where λ is a column vector of *Lagrange Multiplier*. The 2 in front of the last term appears to make the manipulations easier later on and does not affect the outcome, since $R\beta - \gamma = 0$ by assumption.

To determine the minimizing value β^* we set the partial derivatives of S with respect to β and λ equal to zero:

$$\frac{\partial S}{\partial \beta} = -2X'Y + 2X'X\beta^* - 2R'\lambda = 0 \qquad ...(8.32)$$

$$\frac{\partial S}{\partial \lambda} = 2(\gamma - R\beta^*) = 0 \qquad ...(8.33)$$

From (8.32) we get:

$$X'X\beta^* = X'Y + R'\lambda$$
$$(X'X)^{-1} (X'X)\beta^* = (X'X)^{-1} (X'Y + R'\lambda)$$
$$\beta^* = \hat{\beta} + (X'X)^{-1} R'\lambda \qquad ...(8.34)$$

where β^* is the restricted least squares estimator, while $\hat{\beta}$ is the unrestricted least squares estimator.

Now only λ is to be removed from (8.34)

$$R\beta^* = R\hat{\beta} + R(X'X)^{-1} R'\lambda \quad \text{[on premultiplying (8.34) by } R]$$

Imposing the given information $R\beta^* = \gamma$ gives:

$$\gamma = R\beta^* = R\hat{\beta} + R(X'X)^{-1} R'\lambda$$

so that,

$$\lambda = [R(X'X)^{-1} R']^{-1} [\gamma - R\hat{\beta}] \qquad ...(8.35)$$

It may now be observed that the restricted estimator β^* differs from the unrestricted estimator β by a linear function of the vector $(\gamma - R\hat{\beta})$.

Mean and Variance of Restricted Least Squares Estimator (β^*): Since β is a random vector, β^* in (8.35) shall also be a random vector. The restricted least squares random vector has mean and variance as given under:

Mean:

$$E(\beta^*) = E\{\hat{\beta} + (X'X)^{-1} R'[R(X'X)^{-1} R']^{-1} [\gamma - R\hat{\beta}]\}$$
$$= E(\hat{\beta}) + (X'X)^{-1} R' [R(X'X)^{-1} [\gamma - R\, E(\hat{\beta})]$$
$$= \beta + (X'X)^{-1} R' [R(X'X)^{-1} R']^{-1} [\gamma - R\beta]$$
$$= \beta + 0 \qquad \because (\gamma - R\beta) = 0$$
$$= \beta$$

Hence it may be said that β^* is an unbiased estimator only if $\gamma - R\beta = 0$; that is only when restrictions are *correct*.

Further,

$$\beta^* = \hat{\beta} + (X'X)^{-1} R'[R(X'X)^{-1} R']^{-1} [\gamma - R\hat{\beta}] \qquad ...(8.36)$$
$$\text{using (8.34) and (8.35)}$$
$$\hat{\beta} = (X'X)^{-1} X'Y = (X'X)^{-1} X' (X\beta + U)$$
$$\hat{\beta} = \beta + (X'X)^{-1} X'U \qquad ...(8.37)$$

Substituting (8.36) in (8.34):

$$\beta^* - \beta = (X'X)^{-1} X'U + (X'X)^{-1} R' [R (X'X)^{-1} R']'$$
$$[\gamma - R(\beta + (X'X)^{-1} X'U)]$$

which may be written as:

$$\beta^* - \beta = M(X'X)^{-1} X'U \qquad \qquad ...(8.38)$$

because, $\qquad \gamma - R\beta = 0$ and,

$$M = I - (X'X)^{-1} R'[R(X'X)^{-1} R']^{-1} R$$

Now we proceed to obtain variance of β^*

$$\text{Var } (\beta^*) = E\{[\beta^* - E(\beta^*)] [\beta^* - E(\beta^*)]'\}$$
$$= E[(\beta^* - \beta) (\beta^* - \beta)'] \qquad \qquad ...(8.38)$$

Substituting (8.37) in (8.38),

$$\text{Var } (\beta^*) = E[M(X'X)^{-1} X'UU'X (X'X)^{-1} M']$$
$$= M(X'X)^{-1} X' E(UU') X(X'X)^{-1} M'$$
$$= \sigma^2 M(X'X)^{-1} M' \qquad \qquad ...(8.39)$$

Again, since

$$M(X'X)^{-1} M' = \{I - (X'X)^{-1} R'[R(X'X)^{-1} R']^{-1} R\} (X'X)^{-1}$$
$$\times \{I - (X'X)^{-1} R' [R(X'X)^{-1} R']^{-1} R\}'$$
$$= (X'X)^{-1} - 2(X'X)^{-1} R'[R(X'X)^{-1} R']^{-1} R(X'X)^{-1}$$
$$+ (X'X)^{-1} R'[R(X'X)^{-1} R']^{-1} R(X'X)^{-1} R'$$
$$\times [R(X'X)^{-1} R']^{-1} R(X'X)^{-1}$$
$$= (X'X)^{-1} - (X'X)^{-1} R'[R(X'X)^{-1} R']^{-1} R(X'X)^{-1}$$
$$= \{I - (X'X)^{-1} R'[R(X'X)^{-1} R']^{-1} R\} (X'X)^{-1}$$
$$= M(X'X)^{-1}$$

Therefore, by (3.39)

$$\text{Var } (\beta^*) = \sigma^2 M(X'X)^{-1} \qquad \qquad ...(8.40)$$
$$= \sigma^2 (X'X)^{-1} - \sigma^2(X'X)^{-1} R[R(X'X)^{-1} R']^{-1}$$
$$R(X'X)^{-1}$$
$$= \text{Var } (\hat{\beta}) - C \quad (C \text{ is a positive definite matrix})$$

That is to say $\text{Var } (\beta^*) - \text{Var } (\hat{\beta}) = (-) C$, consequently we conclude that the variance of the each element of β^* is less than or equal to the variance of the corresponding element of $\hat{\beta}$.

An Illustration: Estimate the coefficients of the relation:

$$Y = \beta_1 + \beta_2 X_2 + \beta_3 X_3 + U;$$

on considering the following three restrictions on the coefficients taking each separately:

(i) $\beta_2 + \beta_3 = 1$ (ii) $\beta_2 = \beta_3$ (iii) $\beta_3 = 0.75$

You are given that the number of observations is 25, which yield following information:

$$X'X = \begin{pmatrix} 20 & 0 \\ 0 & 40 \end{pmatrix} \text{ and, } X'Y = \begin{pmatrix} 15 \\ 25 \end{pmatrix}$$

(i) *Restriction:* $\beta_3 + \beta_2 = 1$. Expressing it in the matrix form of $R\beta = \gamma$, we obtain:

$$R = [1 \; 1], \; \gamma = [1] \text{ so that}$$

$$R\hat{\beta} = \gamma \text{ is expressed as } [1 \; 1] \begin{bmatrix} \hat{\beta}_2 \\ \hat{\beta}_3 \end{bmatrix} = [1]$$

β^* from (8.36) gives:

$$\beta^* = (X'X)^{-1} X'Y + (X'X)^{-1} R'[R(X'X)^{-1} R']^{-1} [\gamma - R\hat{\beta}]$$

Using the given information:

$$(X'X)^{-1} = \frac{1}{800} \begin{bmatrix} 40 & 0 \\ 0 & 20 \end{bmatrix}$$

Unrestricted Estimators:

$$(X'X)^{-1} X'Y = \frac{1}{800} \begin{bmatrix} 40 & 0 \\ 0 & 20 \end{bmatrix} \begin{bmatrix} 15 \\ 25 \end{bmatrix} = \begin{bmatrix} 6/8 \\ 5/8 \end{bmatrix} = \begin{bmatrix} \hat{\beta}_2 \\ \hat{\beta}_3 \end{bmatrix}$$

$$(X'X)^{-1} R' = \frac{1}{800} \begin{bmatrix} 40 & 0 \\ 0 & 20 \end{bmatrix} \begin{bmatrix} 1 \\ 1 \end{bmatrix} = \frac{1}{800} \begin{bmatrix} 40 \\ 20 \end{bmatrix} = \begin{bmatrix} 1/20 \\ 1/40 \end{bmatrix}$$

$$R(X'X)^{-1} R' = [1 \; 1] \frac{1}{800} \begin{bmatrix} 40 & 0 \\ 0 & 20 \end{bmatrix} \begin{bmatrix} 1 \\ 1 \end{bmatrix} = [3/40]$$

$$[R(X'X)^{-1} R']^{-1} = (3/40)^{-1}$$

$$(\gamma - R\hat{\beta}) = (1) - [1 \quad 1] \begin{bmatrix} \hat{\beta}_2 \\ \hat{\beta}_3 \end{bmatrix}$$

$$= (1) - [1 \quad 1] \begin{bmatrix} 6/8 \\ 5/8 \end{bmatrix} = (-3/8)$$

Therefore, $$\beta^* = \begin{bmatrix} 6/8 \\ 5/8 \end{bmatrix} + (40/3) \; [1 - \hat{\beta}_2 - \hat{\beta}_3]$$

$$= \begin{bmatrix} 6/8 \\ 5/8 \end{bmatrix} + \begin{bmatrix} 2/3 \\ 1/3 \end{bmatrix} [-3/8] = \begin{bmatrix} 1/2 \\ 1/2 \end{bmatrix}$$

Thus, we have obtained $\beta^* = \begin{bmatrix} \hat{\beta}_2 \\ \hat{\beta}_3 \end{bmatrix} = \begin{bmatrix} 1/2 \\ 1/2 \end{bmatrix}$ satisfying the restriction

$\hat{\beta}_2 - \hat{\beta}_3 = 1$ (Note that unrestricted least squares estimators are 6/8 and 5/8 respectively).

(ii) *Restriction:* $\hat{\beta}_2 = \hat{\beta}_3$. In this case $\gamma = [0]$ and $R = [1 \quad -1]$

so that, $[1 \quad -1] \begin{bmatrix} \hat{\beta}_2 \\ \hat{\beta}_3 \end{bmatrix} = [0]$

Here we have $(X'X)^{-1} X'Y = \begin{bmatrix} 6/8 \\ 5/8 \end{bmatrix}$

$$(X'X)^{-1} R' = \frac{1}{800} \begin{bmatrix} 40 & 0 \\ 0 & 20 \end{bmatrix} \begin{bmatrix} 1 \\ -1 \end{bmatrix} = \begin{bmatrix} 1/20 \\ -1/40 \end{bmatrix}$$

$$[R(X'X)^{-1} R']^{-1} = [1 \quad -1] \begin{bmatrix} 1/20 \\ -1/40 \end{bmatrix} = [3/40]^{-1} = [40/3].$$

Therefore, $\beta^* = \begin{bmatrix} 6/8 \\ 5/8 \end{bmatrix} + \begin{bmatrix} 1/20 \\ -1/40 \end{bmatrix} [40/3] [-6/8 + 5/8]$

$= \begin{bmatrix} 2/3 \\ 2/3 \end{bmatrix} = \begin{bmatrix} \hat{\beta}_2 \\ \hat{\beta}_3 \end{bmatrix}$ and which satisfies the

required restriction of $\hat{\beta}_2 = \hat{\beta}_3$.

(iii) *Restriction:* $\beta_3 = 0.75$. Here we have; $\gamma = [.75]$ and $R = [0 \quad 1]$

$$(X'X)^{-1} X'Y = \begin{bmatrix} 6/8 \\ 5/8 \end{bmatrix}$$

$$(X'X)^{-1} R' = \frac{1}{800} \begin{bmatrix} 40 & 0 \\ 0 & 20 \end{bmatrix} \begin{bmatrix} 0 \\ 1 \end{bmatrix} = \begin{bmatrix} 0 \\ 1/40 \end{bmatrix}$$

$$[R(X'X)^{-1} R']^{-1} = [0 \quad 1] \begin{bmatrix} 0 \\ 1/40 \end{bmatrix} = [1/40]^{-1} = [40]$$

Therefore, $\beta^* = \begin{bmatrix} 6/8 \\ 5/8 \end{bmatrix} + \begin{bmatrix} 0 \\ 1/40 \end{bmatrix} [4] [1/8]$

$$= \begin{bmatrix} 3/4 \\ 3/4 \end{bmatrix}; \text{ that is the restriction of } \hat{\beta}_3 = 0.75 \text{ get}$$

satisfied (though $\hat{\beta}_2$ also turns out to be 0.75 in the present case)

An Application

Production function of the C–D form is required to be estimated from a cross-section data of 23 firms. You are given the data in deviation form in the following way:

$$\Sigma x_{1i}^2 = 12, \ \Sigma x_{2i}^2 = 12, \ \Sigma x_{1i} x_{2i} = 8$$

$$\Sigma x_1 y_i = 10, \ \Sigma x_2 y = 8 \text{ and } \Sigma y_i^2 = 10$$

[y = log output, x_1 = log labour input and,
x_2 = log capital input: in the production function $Y = AL^\alpha K^\beta$]

   (i) Estimate the production function and R^2
   (ii) Test the hypothesis whether returns to scale are constant.
   (iii) Estimate the production function with a *priori* restriction of Constant Returns to Scale. What is the value of R^2 in this case?

ASSIGNMENTS

1. Use the following data to estimate the parameters in the equation:
   $$Y_i = \beta_1 + \beta_2 X_{2i} + \beta_3 X_{3i} + U_i:$$
   $$\Sigma y_i^2 = 1000, \ \Sigma x_{2i}^2 = 200, \ \Sigma x_{3i}^2 = 100, \ \Sigma x_{2i} y_i = 400,$$
   $$\Sigma x_{3i} y_i = (-)100, \ \Sigma x_{2i} x_{3i} = 0, \ \bar{Y} = 50, \ \bar{X}_2 = 15, \ \bar{X}_3 = 10 \text{ and } n = 28.$$

2. From the following data compute the regression of automobile expenditure on consumer expenditure and other travel expenditure.

Average automobile exp. (Rs.) per year	Other travel exp. (Rs.) per year	Average consumer exp. (Rs.) per year
212	29	2,437
158	46	2,476
180	28	2,132
253	26	2,256
175	29	2,258
429	64	3,566
437	119	4,486
419	81	3,602
318	74	3,446
355	66	3,736

Interpret your results carefully.

3. Many monetary economists argue that the level of deposits is determined by the stock of bills and the liquidity ratio. Discuss the statistical evidence for this hypothesis.

Stock of bills (Lakhs Rs.)	3390	3070	3270	3170	3500	2890
Liquidity ratio (per cent)	35.3	35.1	33.5	32.7	32.1	32.2
Deposits (Lakhs Rs.)	6294	6447	6682	6817	7207	7818

4. From the following sample data, estimate the parameters of the saving function: $S_t = \alpha + \beta Y_{t-1} + \gamma I_t$, where S_t denotes aggregate saving in year t, Y_{t-1} denotes national income in year $(t-1)$ and I_t denotes the average interest rate in year t.

Year	:	1950	1951	1952	1953	1954	1955	1956	1957	1958	1959	1960
Saving	:	20	25	25	30	33	38	35	45	43	50	55
NI	:	100	110	130	140	160	170	170	200	240	250	260
Interest	:	.02	.02	.03	.02	.03	.04	.03	.04	.04	.05	.05

What percentage of the total variation in saving is explained by both income and the interest rate? Compute the marginal propensity to save out of income.

5. In a study of 89 firms, the total cost (C) was assumed to be dependent on rate of output (X_1) and the rate of absenteeism (X_2). The mean values were: $\bar{C} = 5.8$. $\bar{X}_1 = 2.9$ and $\bar{X}_2 = 3.9$. The matrix showing sums of squares and cross products *adjusted* for means is:

$$\begin{array}{c} \\ c \\ x_1 \\ x_2 \end{array} \begin{array}{ccc} c & x_1 & x_2 \\ \left[\begin{array}{ccc} 113.6 & 36.8 & 39.1 \\ & 50.5 & (-)66.2 \\ & & 967.1 \end{array}\right] \end{array}$$

Estimate the relationship (Linear) between C and the other two variables.

6. Estimate the coefficients of the relation:

$Y = \beta_1 + \beta_2 X_2 + \beta_3 X_3 + U$ subject to the restriction $\hat{\beta}_2 = \hat{\beta}_3$. where data from 23 observations in *deviation form* yield:

$$\mathbf{X'X} = \begin{bmatrix} 20 & 0 \\ 0 & 40' \end{bmatrix} \text{ and } \mathbf{X'Y} = \begin{bmatrix} 15 \\ 25 \end{bmatrix}$$

7. From 67 pairs of values of Y on X; the following quantities are calculated:

$$\Sigma y_i^2 = 1.16, \ \Sigma y_i x_{1i} = (-)8, \ \Sigma x_i^2 = 100$$

(a) Find the least squares coefficient $\hat{\beta}_1$ of Y on X_1 and estimate its standard error. It is observed that variations in Y are also affected by another variable X_2. For the same set of data.

$$\Sigma x_{2i}^2 = 100, \ \Sigma x_{2i} x_{1i} = (-)80, \text{ and } \Sigma x_{2i} y_i = 10$$

(b) Find the coefficients of X_1 and X_2 in the least squares relationship of Y on X_1 and X_2 and estimate their standard errors.

(c) Why does the coefficient of X_1 in part (b) differ from that in part (a) and what conclusions do you draw from your calculations in parts (a) and (b)?

8. Suppose the equation of an *indifference curve* between two goods is:
$$X_iY_i = \beta_0 + \beta_1X_i$$
How would you estimate the parameters of this model? Apply this model to the following data and comment:

Consumption of good X:	1	2	3	4	5
Consumption of good Y:	4	3.5	2.8	1.9	0.8

9. Examine whether the following version of the *Phillips Curve* provides a good fit to the data given in the table and interpret your results:

Phillips Curve Model: $Y = \beta_0 + \beta_1X_i + \beta_2X_i^2 + U_i$

where, Y = rate of change of money wages, and
         X = unemployment rate

Years:
1960 1961 1962 1963 1964 1965 1966 1967 1968 1969

Average hourly earnings (in Rs.):
2.19 2.26 2.32 2.39 2.46 2.53 2.61 2.72 2.83 3.01

Unemployment rate (%):
6.1 6.2 7.8 5.8 5.7 5.0 4.0 3.2 3.6 3.3

$$\left[\text{Note: } Y \text{ may be computed as } \frac{Y_t - Y_{t-1}}{Y_{t-1}}. \right]$$

10. From a certain data, you have been given the following matrices, where all the variables are measured in the deviation form:

$$X'X = \begin{bmatrix} 1103111.33 & 16984.00 \\ 16984.00 & 210.00 \end{bmatrix}, \; X'Y = \begin{bmatrix} 955099.33 \\ 14854.00 \end{bmatrix}$$

$$Y'Y = 57420003, \quad n = 15 \quad \bar{Y} = 1942.33$$

(a) Estimate β_2 and β_3.
(b) How would you estimate intercept term β_1?
(c) Estimate the variance of $\hat{\beta}_2$ and $\hat{\beta}_3$ and their covariances.
(d) Obtain R^2 and $\bar{R}^2$.

11. The following table gives data on output and total cost of production of a commodity in the short run:

Output:	1	2	3	4	5	6	7	8	9	10
Total cost (Rs.):	193	226	240	244	257	260	274	297	350	420

Test whether this data fits well to the U-shaped average and marginal cost curves typically encountered in the short run by using the following-model:

$$Y_i = \beta_0 + \beta_1X_i + \beta_2X_i^2 + \beta_3X_i^3 + U_i$$
$$Y = \text{total cost}, \quad X = \text{output}.$$

(a) Express the data in the deviation form and obtain $X'X$, $X'Y$ and $(X'X)^{-1}$.
(b) Estimate β_1, β_2 and β_3.
(c) Estimate β_0. Interpret $\hat{\beta}_1$ in the context of this problem.
(d) Obtain R^2 and $\bar{R}^2$.
(e) If $\beta_2 = \beta_3$, what is the nature of marginal cost function?

12. "In the general linear regression mode: $Y = X\beta + U$, the X-variables are often called the independent variables, the columns of X are assumed to be linearly independent, and the elements of U are assumed to be independently distributed random variables." Explain what is meant by 'independent' in each of those three uses and the role which each concept of independence plays in the theory of estimating the elements of β.

13. Consider $Y = X\beta + U$ with the number of explanatory variables including the constant equal to 2. Show by writing out all matrices in full, that the least squares formulae for the multiple regression model give the same results as a formula for simple regression model without the use of matrix algebra.

14. If $E(Y) = X\beta$, $Var(Y) = \sigma^2 I_n$, $\beta = [\beta_1, \beta_2......,\beta_n]$, and

$$X = \begin{bmatrix} 1 & x_{21} & x_{31} & \cdots & x_{k1} \\ 1 & x_{22} & x_{32} & \cdots & x_{k2} \\ \hline & & & & \\ \hline 1 & x_{2n} & x_{2n} & \cdots & x_{kn} \end{bmatrix} , \text{ show that}$$

$$R^2 = \frac{\hat{\beta}'X'Y - \dfrac{1}{n}\Sigma(Y)^2}{Y'Y - \dfrac{1}{n}(\Sigma Y)^2}$$

15. Following two income determination equations for India for the period 1951–63 (at constant prices) were estimated:

   (a) $\quad Y_t = 11.20 + 0.406 \ I_t + 0.887 \ Y_{t-1} \qquad R^2 = 0.96$
   $\qquad\qquad (11.42) \quad (0.455) \quad\ \ (0.147)$

   (b) $\quad Y_t = 77.27 + 2.997 \ I_t \qquad\qquad\qquad R^2 = 0.84$
   $\qquad\qquad (4.40) \quad\ \ (0.377)$

   Y_t denotes national income in the year t and I_t denotes the investment in the year t.
   Compare the two equations and interpret the given results carefully.

16. In any practical situation the following cases may be encountered at any given level of significance:
   (a) R^2 and all β_i are significant
   (b) All β_i significant but not R^2
   (c) Some β_i significant but not all, nor R^2
   (d) R^2 and some but not all β_i significant
   (e) R^2 but none of the β_i significant
   (f) Neither R^2 nor any β_i significant
   How would you interpret these cases?

17. Consider the following Wage-determination equation:
   $$W_t = 8.582 + 0.364 \ (PF)_t + 0.004(PF)_{t-1} - 2.56 \ U_t$$
   $$\qquad\qquad\ \ (0.08) \qquad\qquad (0.072) \qquad\qquad (0.658)$$
   W = Wages and salaries,
   PF = Prices of final output at factor cost, and
   U = unemployment rate
   (a) Interpret the results.
   (b) Are the coefficients significant statistically?

(c) Compute the elasticity of wages and salaries per employee with respect to the unemployment rate.

(d) What is the rationale for introduction of $(PF)_{t-1}$?

18. Consider the multiple linear regression with two explanatory variables:

$$Y_i = \beta_1 X_1 + \beta_2 X_2 + \beta_3 + U_i$$

Show that if $\hat{v}_i$ are the least-squares residuals in the simple regression of Y_i on X_2 and $\hat{w}_i$ are the least-squares residuals in the simple regression of X_1 on X_2, then the least-squares estimator of β_1 can be obtained as the estimated slope in the simple regression of $\hat{v}_i$ on $\hat{w}_i$.

19. State and explain the Gauss-Markov theorem in matrix notations.

20. Consider the model:

$$y_i = \beta_1 x_1 + \beta_2 x_2 + U_i,$$
$$E(u_i) = 0$$
$$E(u_i u_j) = \begin{cases} \sigma^2 \text{ if } i = j \\ 0 \text{ if } i \neq j \end{cases}$$

where all three variables have mean zero.

If β_1 estimated from the regression y on x_1 with x_2 omitted, show that the resulting estimate is, in general, biased but has a smaller variance than the estimate obtained with x_2 included.

(c) Compute the elasticity of wages and salaries per employee with respect to the unemployment rate.

(d) What is the rationale for introduction of (PE)?

Consider the multiple linear regression with two explanatory variables:

$Y = \beta_0 + \beta_1 X_1 + \beta_2 + U$

Show that if Y_i are the least-square residuals in the simple regression of Y on X, ...

9

Serial Correlation (Autocorrelation) and Heteroscedasticity

We have thus far discussed the procedure of estimation of Classical Linear Regression Model with FIVE basic assumptions which play an important role in sampling distribution of the variables included in the model.

To repeat them, in the model:

$$y_i = \beta_0 + \beta_1 x_{1i} + \beta_2 x_{2i} + \ldots + \beta_k x_{ki} + U_i;$$

(i) the explanatory variables (x_i's) have finite mean and variance and are uncorrelated with the errors in the model (U_i's). No linear relationship exists between two or more of the independent variables (that is, no collinearity), and

(ii) the disturbance terms are independently distributed from a normal population with zero expected value and constant variance.

Importance of above assumptions is discussed in section 6.2.1 of the Chapter 6. Also, correct specification of the model (in terms of its functional form and variables to be included) is important. Chapter 7 and section 8.8 of Chapter 8 discuss these two aspects of the model in details. But in practice, one usually does not have sufficient knowledge to specify accurately both relevant functional form and the variables which should appear in the model.

The purpose of this chapter is to determine those situations in which two assumptions, relating to independence of errors (i.e., no serial correlation) and relating to constant variance of error terms get violated and how estimation procedure can be improved upon if these two assumptions get violated.

9.1 AUTOCORRELATION (SERIAL CORRELATION)

9.1.1 Meaning

The term *autocorrelation* may be defined as 'correlation between members of series of observations ordered in time or space (as in cross-sectional data)':

As per the fourth assumption of ordinary least squares model:

$$\text{Cov } (U_i \ U_j) = E\{[U_i - E(U_i)] \ [U_j - E(U_j)]\}$$
$$= E(U_i U_j) = E(U_i) \ E(U_j)$$
$$= 0 \text{ for } (i \neq j); \ E(U_i) = E(U_i) = 0$$

The above assumption implies that the successive values of disturbance occurring at one point of observation is not related to any other disturbance. This means that when observations are made over time, the effect of disturbance occurring at one period does not carry over into another period.

If the above assumption is not satisfied, that is, if the value of U in any particular period is correlated with its own preceding value(s), we say that the error terms is *autocorrelated* (serially correlated).

Autocorrelation is a special case of correlation. It refers to the relationship between the successive values of the same variable, while correlation refers to the relationship between two or more different variables. Autocorrelation is a common phenomenon in most economic variables. For instance, in a study of relationship between output and inputs of a firm from monthly observations, non-autocorrelation of disturbances implies that unusual happening affecting the production of the firm in a particular month, is strictly temporary in the sense that only the current month's output is affected. One can readily observe autocorrelation in the time-series sample which exhibits a secular trend or long run movement over time. Cyclical fluctuations also impose regularity among successive observations of the variable over time and, therefore, are the cause of autocorrelation.

Autocorrelation also arises due to specification bias arising due to true variables excluded from the regression equation or due to assumption of incorrect functional form of the regression model. Also, at times the regression model is such that one of the explanatory variables is lagged value of the dependent variable itself; such as:

Consumption $(t) = f$ [Income (t), Consumption $(t - 1)$]

If the lagged term is neglected, the resulting error term will reflect a systematic pattern due to influence of lagged consumption on current consumption.

Generally autocorrelation is also called as serial correlation. Some econometricians, however, prefer to distinguish between these two terms. According to G. Tintner, autocorrelation is the lag correlation of a given series with itself but lagged by a number of time units. The term serial correlation is defined by him as, "lag correlation between two different series". Hence, correlation between two time-series such as $U_1, U_2, ..., U_{20}$ and $U_2, U_3, ..., U_{21}$ (where the former is the latter's series lagged by one time period) is autocorrelation; whereas, correlation between time-series such $U_1, U_2, ..., U_{20}$ and, $V_2, V_3, ..., V_{21}$ (where U and V are two different time-series) is called serial correlation. Such a distinction between the two terms may be useful, but we shall treat these terms synonymously in our discussions to follow.

Autocorrelation usually does not arise in cross-section data. Such data refers to a given point of time; hence temporal dependence is ruled out by the very nature of the data itself. For example, in a cross-section sample, data on income and expenditure of different families, the dependence between the expenditure behaviours of two families is completely ruled out.

9.1.2 Matrix Representation of Autocorrelation

Given the assumption of homoscedasticity, i.e., $E(U_i^2) = \sigma_u^2$, the variance-covariance matrix developed in Chapter 8 is represented as:

$$E(UU') = \begin{bmatrix} \sigma_u^2 & E(U_1U_2) & \cdots & E(U_1U_n) \\ E(U_2U_1) & \sigma_u^2 & \cdots & E(U_2U_n) \\ \vdots & \vdots & & \vdots \\ E(U_nU_1) & E(U_nU_2) & \cdots & \sigma_u^2 \end{bmatrix}$$

In case the assumption of non-autocorrelation i.e., $E(U_iU_j) = 0$ for all $i \neq j$; the above variance-covariance matrix reduces to a particularly simple diagonal form, that of a constant σ_u^2 times the identity matrix, i.e.,

$$E(UU') = \sigma_u^2 \begin{bmatrix} 1 & 0 & 0 & \cdots & 0 \\ 0 & 1 & 0 & \cdots & 0 \\ \vdots & & & & \vdots \\ 0 & 0 & 0 & \cdots & 1 \end{bmatrix} = \sigma_u^2 I_n$$

The assumption of no autocorrelation is responsible for the appearance of zeros in the off-diagonal places, whereas the assumption of homoscedasticity establishes the equality of diagonal terms.

Following three examples of variance-covariance matrices help to understand the concept of autocorrelation and homoscedasticity.

$$\begin{bmatrix} 3 & 0 & 0 \\ 0 & 5 & 0 \\ 0 & 0 & 3 \end{bmatrix} \qquad \begin{bmatrix} 1 & 1/2 & 0 \\ 1/2 & 1 & 1/2 \\ 0 & 1/2 & 1 \end{bmatrix} \qquad \begin{bmatrix} 3 & 1/2 & 1/4 \\ 1/2 & 1 & 1/2 \\ 1/4 & 1/2 & 2 \end{bmatrix}$$

| Hetroscedasticity with no autocorrelation | Homoscedasticity with autocorrelation | Hetroscedasticity with autocorrelation |

9.1.3 Detection of Autocorrelation

While dealing with the problem of autocorrelation, we shall use t, $t-1$, $t-2$, ..., $t-n$ as subscripts to disturbance term U so as to show clearly the fact that we are mainly concerned with temporal dependence of the disturbance terms, i.e., their dependence through time. Thus we shall write

U_t for the value of U in period t, U_{t-1} for the value of U in period $(t-1)$ and so on.

There are two method that are commonly used to obtain a rough idea of the existence or absence of autocorrelation in the disturbance terms. Since e's are estimates of the true value of U, if the e's are found to be correlated it will suggest autocorrelation of the true U's. The following methods are based on such logic.

(1) *By plotting scatter diagram of e's:* Since the variables whose correlation we attempt to detect are e_t and e_{t-1}, the observation points to be plotted are: (e_1, e_2), (e_2, e_3), (e_3, e_4), ..., (e_{n-1}, e_n).

The series of the variables are tabulated as follows:

Variable I: e_t			*Varibles II:* e_{t-1}		
e_{t+1}	or	e_2	e_t	or	e_1
e_{t+2}	or	e_3	e_{t+1}	or	e_2
$\vdots$		$\vdots$	$\vdots$		$\vdots$
$e_{t+(n-1)}$	or	e_n	$e_{t+(n-2)}$	or	e_{n-1}
e_{t+n}	or	e_{n+1}	$e_{t+(n-1)}$	or	e_n

Mean of both series is zero: $\bar{e} = 0$.

If on plotting, it is found that most of the points fall in quadrants I and III, as shown in Fig. 9.1, the autocorrelation will be said to be positive. If most of the points fall in quadrants II and IV, the autocorrelation will be said to be negative as shown in Fig. 9.2.

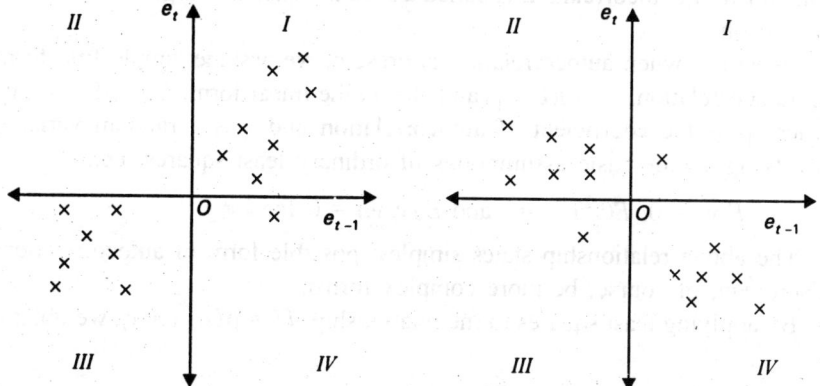

Fig. 9.1: Positive Autocorrelation   **Fig. 9.2:** Negative Autocorrelation

(2) *By plotting e's against time t:* Whether autocorrelation occurs, can be determined by plotting successive e_t's against time t. In general if the successive values of e's rapidly alternate in sign, there is negative autocorrelation. If e's do not change signs frequently, i.e., several positive e's are followed by several positive values of e, or several negative e's are followed by several of its negative values, autocorrelation is positive. This is shown in Figs. 9.3 and 9.4 respectively.

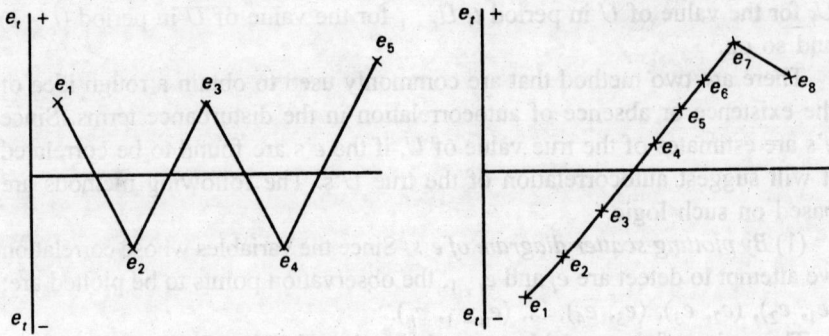

Fig. 9.3: Negative Autocorrelation   **Fig. 9.4:** Positive Autocorrelation

9.1.4   The Coefficient of Autocorrelation

Autocorrelation, as stated earlier, is a kind of lag correlation between successive values of same variables. Thus we treat autocorrelation in the same way as correlation in general. Simple case of linear correlation is termed here as autocorrelation of first order. In other words if the value of U in any particular period depends on its own value in the preceding period alone, we say U's follow a first order autoregressive scheme (or first order Markov scheme): $U_t = f(U_{t-1})$.

If U depends on the values of the two previous periods, then

$$U_t = f(U_{t-1}, U_{t-2})$$

This form of autocorrelation is called a *second order autoregressive* scheme and so on.

Generally when autocorrelation is present, we assume simple first form of autocorrelation: $U_t = f(U_{t-1})$ and also in the linear form: $U_t = \rho U_{t-1} + v_t$, where ρ is the coefficient of autocorrelation and v is a random variable satisfying all the basic assumptions of ordinary least squares, i.e.,

$$E(v) = 0, \; E(v^2) = \sigma_v^2 \; \text{and} \; E(v_i v_j) = 0 \; \text{for} \; i \ne j.$$

The above relationship states simplest possible form of autocorrelation. There can, of course, be more complex forms.

By applying least squares to the relationship: $U_t = \rho U_{t-1} + v_t$, we obtain:

$$\hat{\rho} = \frac{\sum\limits_{t=2}^{n} U_t U_{t-1}}{\sum\limits_{i=2} U_{t-1}^2} \qquad \qquad ...(9.1)$$

Given that for large samples: $\Sigma U_t^2 \approx U_{t-1}^2$, we observe that coefficient of autocorrelation ρ represents a simple correlation coefficient r.

$$\hat{\rho} = \frac{\Sigma U_t U_{t-1}}{\Sigma U_{t-1}^2} = \frac{\Sigma U_t U_{t-1}}{\sqrt{(\Sigma U_{t-1}^2)^2}}$$

$$\hat{\rho} \approx \frac{\Sigma U_t U_{t-1}}{\sqrt{\Sigma U_t^2}\sqrt{\Sigma U^2_{t-1}}} = \gamma_{U_t,\, U_{t-1}} \qquad \ldots(9.2)$$

ρ represents the first order autocorrelation coefficient.

If $\rho = 0$ in $U_t = \rho U_{t-1} + v_t$ then $U_t = v_t$, i.e., U_t is not autocorrelated (on the assumption that v_t is not autocorrelated).

9.1.5 Mean, Variance and Covariance of Disturbance Terms in Autocorrelated Model

To examine the consequences of autocorrelation on ordinary least squares estimators, it is required to study the properties of U if its values are found to be correlated with simple *Markov* process; i.e.,

$$U_t = \rho U_{1-t} + v_t \text{ with } |\rho| < 1$$

and v_t fulfilling all the usual assumptions of a random variable. First, our object is to obtain value of U_t in terms of autocorrelation coefficient ρ and random variable v_t.

The complete form of the first order autoregressive scheme may be described as under:

$$
\begin{aligned}
Ut &= f(U_{t-1}) &&= \rho U_{t-1} + v_t \\
U_{t-1} &= f(U_{t-2}) &&= \rho U_{t-2} + v_{t-1} \\
U_{t-2} &= f(U_{t-3}) &&= \rho U_{t-3} + v_{t-2} \\
&\;\;\vdots &&\;\;\vdots \\
U_{t-r} &= f(U_{t-(r+1)}) &&= \rho U_{t-(r+1)} + v_{t-r}
\end{aligned}
$$

We make use of above relations to perform continuous substitutions in $U_t = \rho U_{t-1} + v_t$ as follows:

Since, $\quad U_t = \rho U_{t-1} + v_t$

$\therefore \qquad U_t = \rho(\rho U_{t-2} + v_{t-1}) + v_t$

$\qquad\qquad U_t = \rho^2 U_{t-2} + (\rho\, v_{t-1} + v_t)$

Again, $\quad U_t = \rho^2(\rho v_{t-2} + \rho v_{t-2}) + (\rho v_{t-1} + v_t)$

$\qquad\qquad U_t = \rho^3 U_{t-2} + (\rho^2 v_{t-2} + \rho v_{t-1} + v_t)$

In this way, if we continue the substitution process for r periods (assuming that r is very large), we shall obtain:

$$U_t = v_t + \rho v_{t-1} + \rho^2_{t-2} + \rho^3 v_{t-3}\ldots \qquad \ldots(9.3)$$

$$[\because \rho^r \to 0, \text{ for } |\rho| < 1]$$

$$\therefore \qquad U_t = \sum_{r=0}^{\infty} \rho^r v_{t-r} \qquad \ldots(9.4)$$

(i) To obtain Mean: $E(U_t) = E\left\{\sum_{r=0}^{\infty} \rho^r v_{t-r}\right\}$

i.e., $\qquad E(U_t) = \Sigma \rho^r E(v_{t-r})$

$\qquad\qquad\qquad = 0;\ [E(v_{t-r}) = 0\ \text{by assumption}]$

$\therefore \qquad\qquad E(U_t) = 0 \qquad\qquad\qquad\qquad ...(9.5)$

In other words we find that mean of autocorrelated U's turns out to be zero.

(ii) To obtain variance: By definition of variance,

$$E(U_t^2) = E\left\{\sum_{r=0}^{\infty} \rho^r \cdot v_{t-r}\right\}^2$$

$$= \sum_{r=0}^{\infty} (\rho^r)^2\, E(v_{t-r})^2$$

$$= \sum_{r=0}^{\infty} \rho^{2r} \text{Var.}\,(v_{t-r})$$

$$= \sum_{r=0}^{\infty} \rho^{2r} \cdot \sigma_v^2$$

$$= \sigma_v^2 \left(1 + \rho^2 + \rho^4 + \rho^6 + ... \infty\right)$$

$$= \sigma_v^2 \left\{\frac{1}{1-\rho^2}\right\} \quad [\because |\rho| < 1]$$

$$\text{Var.}(U_t) = \frac{\sigma_v^2}{1-\rho^2} \qquad\qquad ...(9.6)$$

Thus, variance of autocorrelated U's is $\dfrac{\sigma_v^2}{1-\rho^2}$ which is a constant value (since it does not involve t and all U_t's will have same variance.)

(iii) To obtain covariance: By definition of covariance,

$\qquad$ Cov. $(U_t U_{t-1}) = E\{[(U_t - E(U_t)][U_{t-1} - E(U_{t-i})]\}$

Since; $\qquad U_t = v_t + \rho v_{t-1} + \rho^2_{t-2} \cdots \qquad\qquad$ [from (9.3)]

$\therefore \qquad\quad U_{t-1} = v_{t-1} + \rho v_{t-2} + \rho^2_{t-2} \cdots$

Substituting in: Cov $(U_t U_{t-1})$, we obtain;

$$\text{Cov. } (U_t U_{t-1}) = E[(v_t + \rho v_{t-1} + \rho^2 v_{t-2} + ...)(v_{t-1} + \rho v_{t-2} + \rho^2 v_{t-3} + ...)]$$

$$= E[\{v_t + \rho(v_{t-1} + \rho v_{t-2} + ...)\}(v_{t-1} + \rho v_{t-2} + ...)]$$

$$= E[(v_t)(v_{t-1} + \rho v_{t-2} + ...)] + E[\rho(v_{t-1} + \rho v_{t-2} + ...)^2]$$

$$= 0 + \rho E[(v_{t-1} + \rho v_{t-2} + \rho^2 v_{t-3} ...)^2]$$

$$= \rho E(v_{t-1}^2 + \rho^2 v_{t-2}^2 + ... + \text{cross products})$$

$$= \rho(\sigma_v^2 + \rho^2 \sigma_v^2 + \rho^4 \sigma_v^2 + ...)$$

$$= \rho[\sigma_v^2 (1 + \rho^2 + \rho^4 + ...)]$$

$$= \rho \sigma_v^2 \left(\frac{1}{1-\rho^2}\right) \quad \text{for } |\rho| < 1$$

$$\therefore \quad \text{Cov. } (U_t U_{t-1}) = \rho \left(\frac{\sigma_v^2}{1-\rho^2}\right) = \rho \sigma_u^2 \qquad ...(9.7)$$

Similarly, $\qquad \text{Cov. } (U_t U_{t-2}) = \rho^2 \sigma_u^2$
$$\text{Cov. } (U_t U_{t-3}) = \rho^3 \sigma_u^2$$

and generalising, $\text{Cov. } (U_t U_{t-s}) = \rho^s \sigma_u^2$ (for $s \neq t$)

Summarising on the basis of (i), (ii) and (iii), we find that when U_t's are autocorrelated, then

$$U_t \sim N\left(0, \frac{\sigma_v^2}{1-\rho^2}\right) \quad \text{and, Cov.}(U_t U_{t-1}) \neq 0.$$

9.1.6 Effect of Autocorrelation on OLS Estimators

Ordinary least squares technique is based on the five basic assumptions of which three are with respect to mean, variance and covariance of disturbance terms. Naturally therefore, if these assumptions do not hold good on whatsoever account, the estimators derived by OLS procedure may not be efficient.

In 9.1.5 above, we obtained mean, variance and covariance of disturbance terms when they were assumed to exhibit serial correlation. We are now in a position to examine the effect of autocorrelation on OLS estimators.

Following are the effects on the estimators if OLS method is applied in presence of autocorrelation in the given data.

1. *OLS estimates are unbiased:* In deviation form of simple regression model,

$$\hat{\beta} = \frac{\Sigma x_i y_i}{\Sigma x_i^2}$$

$$\hat{\beta} = \frac{\Sigma x_i (\beta x_i + u_i)}{\Sigma x_i^2} = \beta + \frac{\Sigma x_i u_i}{\Sigma x_i^2}$$

or, $$E(\hat{\beta}) = \beta + \frac{\Sigma x_i E(u_i)}{\Sigma x_i^2}$$

∴ Bias in $\hat{\beta} = E(\hat{\beta}) - \beta = \dfrac{\Sigma x_i E(u_i)}{\Sigma x_i^2} = 0$ (because it has been proved

by (9.5), that expected value of random term U even when autocorrelated, is zero).

2. *The variances of OLS estimators are underestimated:* The variance of estimate $\hat{\beta}$ in simple regression model will be biased downwards (i.e. underestimated) when U's are (positively) autocorrelated, can be shown as follows.

We have established in eq. (6.12) of chpt. 6 that variance of the least squares estimator $\hat{\beta}$ is given by the formula:

$$\text{Var}(\hat{\beta}) = \Sigma k_i^2 E(U_i^2) + 2\Sigma k_i k_j E(U_i U_j),$$

Replacing Σk_i and Σk_i^2,

$$\text{Var}(\hat{\beta}) = \Sigma \left[\frac{x_i}{\Sigma x_i^2}\right]^2 E(U_i^2) + 2\Sigma \left[\frac{x_i x_j}{(\Sigma x_i^2 . \Sigma x_j^2)^2}\right] E(U_i U_j)$$

If $E(U_i U_j) = 0$, the last term disappears, so that;

$$\text{Var}(\hat{\beta}) = \sigma_u^2 \Sigma k_i^2 = \frac{\sigma_u^2}{\Sigma x_i^2} \quad \text{[See eq. (6.12)]}$$

However, it is observed in (9.7) above that $E(U_t U_{t-s}) \neq 0$ but is equal to $\rho^s \sigma_u^2$. In such a case

$$\text{Var}(\hat{\beta}) = \sigma_u^2 \left(\frac{1}{\Sigma x_i^2}\right) + 2\sigma_u^2 \Sigma \left\{\frac{x_i x_j}{(\Sigma x_i^2)^2} \rho^s\right\}$$

Expanding the second term in the above expression, we obtain:

$$\text{Var}(\hat{\beta}) = \frac{\sigma_u^2}{\Sigma x_i^2} + 2\sigma_u^2 \left\{\rho \cdot \frac{\sum\limits_{i}^{n-1} x_i x_{i+1}}{\left(\sum\limits_{i}^{n} x_i^2\right)^2} + \rho^2 \cdot \frac{\sum\limits_{i}^{n-2} x_i x_{i+2}}{\left(\sum\limits_{i}^{n} x_i^2\right)^2} + \ldots\right\}$$

or,
$$\text{Var}(\hat{\beta}) = \frac{\sigma_u^2}{\Sigma x_i^2} \left\{ 1 + 2\rho \cdot \frac{\overset{n-1}{\underset{i}{\Sigma}} x_i x_{i+1}}{\overset{n}{\underset{i}{\Sigma}} x_i^2} + 2\rho^2 \cdot \frac{\overset{n-2}{\underset{i}{\Sigma}} x_i x_{i+2}}{\overset{n}{\underset{i}{\Sigma}} x_i^2} + \ldots \right.$$

$$\left. + 2\rho^{n-1} \cdot \frac{x_1 x_n}{\Sigma x_i^2} \right\}$$

In the absence of autocorrelation, $\text{Var}(\hat{\beta}) = \frac{\sigma_u^2}{\Sigma x_i^2}$, i.e., all the terms of the bracket disappear.

But presently, in case ρ is positive (case of positive autocorrelation) and if x is also positively correlated ($\Sigma x_i x_j \neq 0$), the expression in the bracket is almost certainly greater than unity. This, in turn proves that estimate of variance, in most cases, will have downward bias due to positive autocorrelation. In other words, in case of positive serial correlation, the regression estimates will be unbiased but it does affect their efficiency. This loss of efficiency will be reflected in the estimates of standard errors; that is, though the regression estimators will be unbiased, the standard errors of the regression will be biased downwards. It will then lead to the conclusion that: (i) the parameters estimates are more precise than they actually are, and (ii) there will be tendency to reject the null hypothesis when, infact, it should not be rejected.

3. *The predictions will not be efficient:* If U's are autocorrelated, the predictions based on OLS estimate will be inefficient. This may be perceived diagrammatically as depicted in Figs. 9.5 and 9.6. Both diagrams illustrate the presence of positive autocorrelation in a model with a single explanatory variable (X_t). These two diagrams show clearly how seriously the fitted regression line distorts the true regression line; both in terms of estimation of intercept and slope.

In Fig. 9.5, the first four U_i's (related to first four observations) happen to be positively related and the last two are negatively. In this case the estimated regression slope ($\hat{\beta}$) is lower than the true slope (β) while intercept appears over-estimated.

In Fig. 9.6, the first four disturbance terms appear negatively related while two being positive. The slope has been overestimated and intercept underestimated.

Since both cases are equally likely to occur, the estimates of the slope are likely to turn up correct on an average; that is slope estimates will be unbiased. On the other, as it may be observed very clearly that in both cases the least squares regression line ($\hat{Y}_t = \hat{\alpha} + \hat{\beta} X_t$) fits the observed sample data points more closely than the true regression line. This leads to two

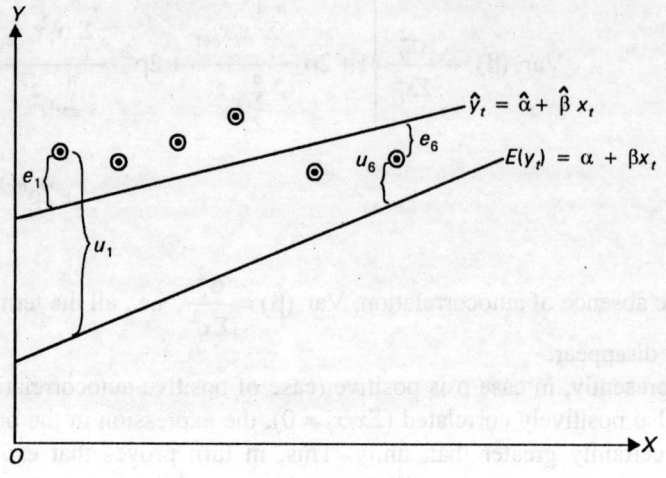

Fig. 9.5

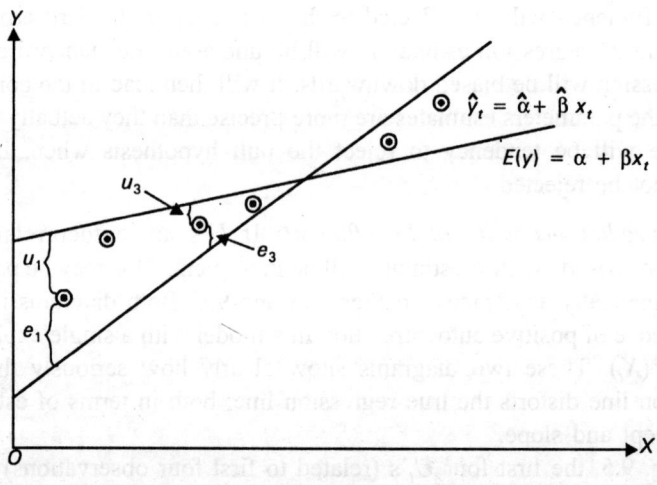

Fig. 9.6

consequences: one, we obtain higher value of an (R^2) reflecting *overly* optimistic picture of the success of fitted regression line: $\hat{Y}_t = \hat{\alpha} + \hat{\beta} X_t$. Secondly, the OLS tend to underestimate the variance of U_t terms which in turn tend to impair the standard errors of α and β estimators. This ultimately leads to wrong statistical results, interpretation and predictions from the fitted regression line.

The above analysis, therefore, makes clear that in presence of autocorrelation, the values as well as the standard errors of the OLS parameter estimates are definitely affected. As such, it is very essential to examine for the existence of autocorrelation before applying OLS procedure. Though a rough idea of the existence of autocorrlelation may be gained by methods explained under 9.1.3, there are more accurate tests for detecting the incidence of autocorrelation. The traditionally applied tests are the *von Neumann ratio test* and the *Durbin-Watson test*.

9.1.7 The von Neumann Ratio Test

The von Neumann ratio is defined as the ratio of the mean square successive difference to the variance of the estimated disturbance values; i.e.,

$$\frac{\delta^2}{s^2} = \frac{\sum\limits_{t=2}^{n}(e_t - e_{t-1})^2/(n-1)}{\sum\limits_{t=2}^{n}(e_t - \bar{e})^2/n}$$

However, in an OLS procedure $\bar{e} = 0$.

For *large n*, von Neumann ratio δ^2/s^2 may be taken as approximately normally distributed with:

$$\text{Mean} = E\left(\frac{\delta^2}{s^2}\right) = \frac{2n}{n-1}, \text{ and}$$

$$\text{Variance} = \text{Var.}\left(\frac{\delta^2}{s^2}\right) = \frac{4n^2(n-2)}{(n+1)(n-1)^3}.$$

The formulae for the mean and variance are only true if the *e*-values are independently distributed and this, in fact, is not true of least squares residuals, even when the true disturbances are independently distributed. A large sample test for positive autocorrelation can be made by *first*, computing the von Neumann ratio. *Secondly*, by using the formulae for the mean and variance of the ratio, obtain from the Normal Distribution table, how many σ units does the estimated ratio lie from the mean value. If it lies more than 3σ units from the mean, one may accept the hypothesis of presence of autocorrelation in the data.

For example: Assume that the ratio with 100 observation is equal to 2.88, with mean = 2.02 and variance = 0.0399.

From the normal distribution table it is observed that $2.02 \pm 3 \, (0.1997)$ = (1.4203, 2.6197) covers about 99.7 per cent of the area under the normal curve. Hence hypothesis of no autocorrelation is rejected.

9.1.8 The Durbin-Watson Test

The test of general kind concerning autocorrelation was developed by J. Durbin and G. Watson in 1951. This test uses what is usually referred to as the *Durbin-Watson d-statistic*, and is based on the sum of the squared differences in successive values of the estimated disturbance terms:

$$d = \frac{\sum_{t=2}^{n} (\hat{U}_t - \hat{U}_{t-1})^2}{\sum_{t=1}^{n} \hat{U}_t^{2}}$$

Somewhat intuitively, we can see that, if we have positive autocorrelation, the successive values of the disturbance terms will tend to close to another; i.e., positive value of the U_t would most likely be followed by another positive value U_{t+1}. This suggests that terms in the numerator of *d-statistic* will be relatively small. We would, therefore, expect positive autocorrelation to result in small value for *d*. Conversely, negative autocorrelation tends to generate large differences between successive values of U_t. The signal for this type of autocorrelation is an unusually large value of *d*.

This test now can be explained in two steps as follows.

Step 1. The null hypothesis; $H_0 : \rho = 0$ is to be tested against alternative hypothesis; $H_1 : \rho \neq 0$

We compute *d-statistic* to test the null hypothesis:

$$d = \frac{\sum_{t=2}^{n} (\hat{U}_t - \hat{U}_{t-1})^2}{\sum_{t=1}^{n} (\hat{U}_t^{2})} \approx \frac{\sum_{t=2}^{n} (e_t - e_{t-1})^2}{\sum_{t=1}^{n} e_t^2}$$

Step 2. We compare the calculated value of *d* with the theoretical value of *d*; with $(n - k)$ degrees of freedom (k being the number of explanatory variables including constant term). The theoretical value of *d* is the value which *d* would assume if null hypothesis were true, i.e., if there is no autocorrelation.

Two values; *upper bound d_n, and lower bound d_L,* have been assigned to theoretical value of d which can be understood as follows:

Suppose that null hypothesis is true. In that case we would also expect the covariance between the estimated residuals $\hat{e}_t$ and $\hat{e}_{t-1}$ to be approximately zero. When this is true, we find that if n is large, d is close to $2(1-\hat{\rho})$.

$$d = \frac{\sum (e_t - e_{t-1})^2}{\sum e_t^2} = \frac{\sum (e_t^2 + e_{t-1}^2 - 2e_t e_{t-1})}{\sum e_t^2}$$

$$d = \frac{\sum_{t=1}^{n} e_t^2 + \sum_{t=2}^{n} e_{t-1}^2 - 2 \sum_{t=2}^{n} e_t e_{t-1}}{\sum_{t=2}^{n} e_t^2}$$

If n is very large, then $\sum_{t=2}^{n} e_t^2 \approx \sum_{t=2}^{n} e_{t-1}^2 \approx \sum_{t=1}^{n} e_t^2$

$$\therefore \qquad d \approx \left\{ \frac{2\Sigma e^2_{t-1}}{\Sigma e^2_{t-1}} - 2\frac{\Sigma e_t e_{t-1}}{\Sigma e^2_{t-1}} \right\}$$

or, $\qquad d \approx 2\left(1 - \frac{\Sigma e_t e_{t-1}}{\Sigma e^2_{t-1}}\right)$

or, $\qquad d \approx 2(1-\hat{\rho}) \left\{ \because \frac{\Sigma e_t e_{t-1}}{\Sigma e^2_{t-1}} = \hat{\rho} \right\}$

From the above relation, therefore,

$\hat{\rho} = 0$ *suggests* $d \approx 2$,

$\hat{\rho} = 1$ *suggests* $d \approx 0$,

$\hat{\rho} = -1$ *suggests* $d \approx 4$.

Thus we obtain two important conclusions:

(i) Values of d lie between 0 and 4, and

(ii) If there is no autocorrelation, $\hat{\rho} = 0$ then $d = 2$.

Whenever, therefore, the calculated value of d turns out to be sufficiently close to 2, we accept null hypothesis, and if it is close to zero or four, we reject the null hypothesis.

However, because the exact value of d is never known, there exist a range of values within which we can neither accept nor reject null hypothesis.

Specifically, for the two-tailed *Durbin-Watson test*, we have set of five regions for the value of d as depicted in Fig. 9.7.

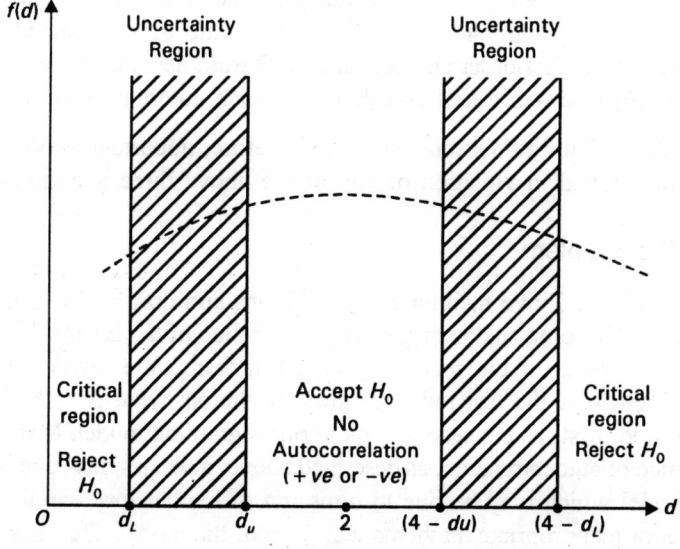

Fig. 9.7

The Fig. 9.7 may be translated in the following words.

(i) If d is less than d_L or greater than $(4 - d_L)$, reject the null hypothesis in favour of the alternative, which implies autocorrelation.

(ii) If, d lies between d_u and $(4 - d_u)$, accept the null hypothesis of no autocorrelation.

(iii) If, however, the value of d lies between d_L and d_u or between $(4 - d_u)$ and $(4 - d_L)$, the Durbin-Watson test is inconclusive. For these values, we cannot, at a specified level of significance, conclude either that we do or do not have autocorrelation among the disturbance terms.

The above test is widely used in econometric applications. A great advantage of this test being that it is based on the estimated residuals. Because of this advantage, it is a common practice to report the Durbin-Watson d-statistic along with other summary statistic (s) such as; as R^2, $\bar{R}^2$ and t-ratios.

Important Assumptions: It is important to note the three basic assumptions underlying the d-statistic:

(i) The regression equation includes an intercept term. If the regression is assumed through the origin, it is then necessary to re-run the regression by including the intercept term to obtain e's.

(ii) The disturbances U_t are generated by the first order auto-regressive scheme.

(iii) The regression equation does not include lagged values of dependent variable as one of the explanatory variables. The test is not applicable in that situation. If applied mistakenly, the value of d in such cases will often be around 2, which is the value of d expected in the absence of first-order autocorrelation. Durbin developed the so-called *h-statistic* to test serial correlation in such autoregressive models.

In using the Durbin-Watson test, it is, therefore, important to note that it can not be applied in violation of any of the above three assumptions.

9.1.9 The Problem

Even with all the above mentioned assumptions and drawbacks of the test, it has, in fact, become customary to report the value of *d-statistic* along with the other estimates of the regression equation from time series data. The problem then is, if the test indicates autocorrelation, what is to be done?

We should, first, take a second look at our regression model. Many times the presence of autocorrelation, as described above, indicates mis-specification of our model which may be due to omission of explanatory variable from the model or inappropriate mathematical form of the model. The appropriate procedure, under such circumstances, is to include the missing variable (s) in the set of explanatory variables or change the initial (linear) form of the model to 'linear in logs' or quadratic form and then re-run the regression to test *d-statistic* once again.

At times autocorrelation may not be due to above reasons. It may be due to the presence of some unexplained systematic influence on the explanatory variables present in the model. It is then a case of true autocorrelation because its root lies in *U*-term itself, and therefore, we have reason to be concerned. What is the appropriate method(s) to remove the autocorrelation in the random variables in such cases? It is described under.

9.1.10 The Methods

Once the autocorrelation is detected, the appropriate corrective procedure is: (i) to obtain an estimate of autocorrelation coefficient ρ, (ii) the original data is transformed (i.e., wiping off the effect of ρ), and (iii) OLS is applied to the transformed data.

First we explain the second step of the above procedure assuming that the value of ρ is known.

Suppose that our model is:

$$Y_t = \alpha + \beta X_t + U_t \qquad \qquad \text{...(9.8)}$$

and,
$$U_t = \rho U_{t-1} + v_t \qquad |\rho| < 1 \qquad \text{...(9.9)}$$

If we take a lagged form of (9.8) and multiply through by ρ, we obtain,

$$\rho Y_{t-1} = \rho \alpha + \rho \beta X_{t-1} + \rho U_{t-1} \qquad \text{...(9.10)}$$

Subtracting (9.10) and (9.8), we have

$$Y_i - \rho Y_{t-1} = (\alpha - \rho \alpha) + \beta (X_t - \rho \beta X_{t-1}) + (U_t - \rho U_{t-1}) \qquad \text{...(9.11)}$$

By rearranging the terms in (9.9),
$$v_t = U_t - \rho U_{t-1}$$
which on substituting in the last term of (9.11) gives;

$$Y_t - \rho Y_{t-1} = (\alpha - \rho \alpha) + \beta (X_t - \rho X_{t-1}) + v_t \qquad \text{...(9.12)}$$

(9.12) may be written as,

$$Y_t^* = a + \beta X_t^* + v_t \qquad \text{...(9.13)}$$

where,
$$Y_t^* = Y_t - \rho Y_{t-1}$$
$$a = \alpha - \rho \alpha = \alpha (1 - \rho)$$

and,
$$X_t^* = X_t - \rho X_{t-1}$$

It may be noted that in transforming (9.8) into (9.13), one observation shall be lost because of lagging and subtracting. We can apply OLS to the transformed relation (9.13) to obtain $\hat{a}$ and $\hat{\beta}$ for our two parameters α and β in (9.8).

$$\hat{\alpha} = \frac{\hat{a}}{1 - \rho}, \text{ and it can be shown that}$$

$$\text{Var} \ (\hat{\alpha}) \ = \ \left(\frac{1}{1-\rho}\right)^2 \cdot \text{Var} \ (\hat{a}),$$

because α is perfectly and linearly related to $\hat{a}$. Again since v_t satisfies all standard assumptions, the variances of $\hat{a}$ and $\hat{\beta}$ would be given by our standard OLS formulae;

$$\text{Var} \ (\hat{\alpha}) \ = \ \frac{\sigma_u^2 \ \sum\limits_{t=2}^{n} X_t^{*2}}{n^* \ \sum\limits_{t=2}^{n} (X_t^* - \bar{X}_t^*)^2},$$

$$\text{Var} \ (\hat{\beta}) \ = \ \frac{\sigma_u^2}{\sum\limits_{t=2}^{n} (X_t^* - \bar{X}_t^*)^2}$$

where $n^* = n - 1$, since one observation is lost in lagging and subtracting to obtain X_t^*.

Estimators obtained from (9.13) are efficient, only if our sample size is large so that loss of one observation becomes negligible.

The above procedure is possible only if value of ρ is known.

We now describe the methods through which the parameters of the autocorrelated models can be estimated.

Method I. A priori information on ρ

Many times an investigator makes some reasonable guess about the value of the autoregressive coefficient by using his knowledge or intuition about the relationship under study.

A usual case is to assume that $\rho = 1$.

The transformed model then becomes:

$$(Y_t - Y_{t-1}) = \beta \ (Y_t - Y_{t-1}) + v_t$$

where $$v_t = U_t - U_{t-1}$$

Note that the constant term gets suppressed in this case. $\hat{\beta}$ is obtained by taking merely the first differences of the variables and obtaining the regression line that passes through the origin.

Suppose that one assumes $\rho = -1$; instead of $\rho = 1$; i.e., case of perfect negative serial correlation.

In such case the transformed model (9.12) becomes:

$$Y_t + Y_{t-1} = 2\alpha + \beta \ (X_t + X_{t-1}) + v_t$$

or,

$$\frac{Y_t + Y_{t-1}}{2} = \alpha + \beta \ \left(\frac{X_t + X_{t-1}}{2}\right) + \frac{v_t}{2}$$

This model is then called two-period moving average regression model because actually we are regressing the value of one moving average $\left(\dfrac{Y_t + Y_{t-1}}{2}\right)$ on another $\left(\dfrac{X_t + X_{t-1}}{2}\right)$.

This model of *first differences* is quite popular in applied research for its simplicity. But the method rests on the assumption that either there is perfect positive or perfect negative autocorrelation in the data.

The question is how to know whether such an assumption is justifiable in any given situation? The answer is in the method that follows.

Method II. Estimation of ρ from the d-statistic

In the section 9.1.8, we obtained $d \approx 2(1-\hat{\rho})$. Suppose that we calculate certain value of *d-statistic* = d^* in case of certain data.

$$\therefore \qquad d^* = 2(1-\hat{\rho}) \text{ so that, } \hat{\rho} = 1 - \frac{1}{2}d^*$$

As already pointed out, $\hat{\rho}$ will not be accurate if the sample size is small. The above relationship is true only for large samples.

Under the restrictive assumption on explanatory variables Professors H. Theil and A.L. Nagar expounded following relation among number of observations, number of explanatory variables and Durbin-Watson statistic for the small samples to obtain value of $\hat{\rho}$:

$$\hat{\rho} = \frac{n^2(1-d/2)+k^2}{n^2-k^2}$$

where n = total number of observations, d = Durbin-Watson statistic, and k = number of coefficients (including intercept) to be estimated. The relation coincides with that of above for large value of n.

Method III. The Cochrane-Orcutt iterative procedure

In this method we remove autocorrelation gradually starting from the simplest form of a first-order scheme.

First we obtain the residuals and apply OLS to them;

$$e_t = \rho e_{t-1} + v_t$$

With the estimated $\hat{\rho}$ from above relation, we transform the original data and then apply OLS to the model:

$$(Y_t - \hat{\rho}Y_{t-1}) = \alpha(1-\hat{\rho}) + \beta(X_t - \hat{\rho}X_{t-1}) + U_t^*$$

We once again apply OLS to the newly obtained residuals e_t^* from the above transformed data:

$$e_t^* = \rho e_{t-1}^* + w_t$$

We use this second estimate $\hat{\rho}$ to transform the original observations and so on we keep proceeding until the value of the estimate of ρ converges. It can be shown that the procedure is convergent. When the data is transformed only by using this second stage estimate of ρ, it is then called a two-stage Cochrane-Orcutt method.

However, one can follow an alternative approach to use at each step of the iteration, the Durbin-Watson d-statistic to residuals for autocorrelation or till the estimates of ρ do not differ substantially from one another.

Method IV. Durbin's two-stage method

Assuming in the first-order autoregressive scheme, Durbin suggests a two-stage procedure for resolving the serial correlation problem.

In Step I, an estimate of ρ is obtained from the equation (9.12) by writing it in the form:

$$Y_t = \alpha(1-\rho) + \rho Y_{t-1} + \beta X_t - \beta \rho X_{t-1} + U_t$$

$$Y_t = \alpha^* + \rho Y_{t-1} + \beta X_t + \gamma X_{t-1} + U_t$$

The equation is now treated as a regression equation with three explanatory variables, X_t, X_{t-1} and Y_{t-1}. This provides estimate of ρ which is used to construct new variables $(Y_t - \hat\rho Y_{t-1})$ and $(X_t - \hat\rho X_{t-1})$. In second step, estimators of α and β are obtained from the regression equation:

$$(Y_t - \hat\rho Y_{t-1}) = \alpha^* + \beta(X_t - \hat\rho X_{t-1}) + U_t^*$$

where $\alpha^* = \alpha (1 - \rho)$.

9.1.11 Applications

Example 1. Consider the model; $Y_t = \alpha + \beta X_t + U_t$. Test for autocorrelation with the following observations on Y and X:

X	1	2	3	4	5	6	7	8	9	10	11	12	13	14	15
Y	2	2	2	1	3	5	6	6	10	10	10	12	15	10	11

Table 9.1 gives the necessary calculations to estimate $\hat\alpha$ and $\hat\beta$ in the model: $Y_t = \alpha + \beta X_t + U_t$.

The estimated model is: $\overline{Y}_t = -0.28 + 0.91 X_t$ $R^2 = 0.85$

$$(0.107)$$

$$\text{Durbin-Watson } statistic \quad d^* = \frac{\Sigma(e_t - e_{t-1})^2}{\Sigma e_t^2} = \frac{60.213}{41.767} = 1.442$$

Values of d_L and d_u on 5% level of significance, with $n = 15$ and one explanatory variable, are:

$$d_L = 1.08 \text{ and } d_u = 1.36$$

Since $d^* = 1.44 > d_u$ (= 1.36), null hypothesis is accepted.

In other words there is no autocorrelation in the given sample of observations on X and Y.

Example 2. Simple Consumption Function is estimated from the hypothetical data on consumption expenditure and disposable income given in Table 9.2. It is given that the estimated function is:

$$\hat{C}_t = 3.29 + 0.906\ Y_t \qquad R^2 = 0.99$$

$$(0.0055)$$

Table 9.1: Calculations of 'Durbin-Watson' statistic

t	Y_t	X_t	X_t^2	X_tY_t	y_t	y_t^2	x_t	x_ty_t	x_t^2	$\hat{Y}_t$	$e_t = (Y_t - \hat{Y}_t)$	e_t^2	e_{t-1}	$e_t - e_{t-1}$	$(e_t - e_{t-1})^2$
1	2	1	1	2	−5	25	−7	35	49	0.63	1.37	1.876	=	=	=
2	2	2	4	4	−5	25	−6	30	36	1.54	0.46	0.211	+1.37	−0.91	0.828
3	2	3	9	6	−5	25	−5	25	25	2.45	−0.45	0.203	+0.46	−0.91	0.828
4	1	4	16	4	−6	36	−4	24	16	3.36	−2.36	5.570	−0.45	−1.91	3.648
5	3	5	25	15	−4	16	−3	12	9	4.27	−1.27	1.612	−2.36	+1.09	1.188
6	5	6	36	30	−2	4	−2	4	4	5.18	−0.18	0.032	−1.27	+1.09	1.188
7	6	7	49	42	−1	1	−1	1	1	6.09	−0.09	0.008	−0.18	+0.09	0.008
8	6	8	64	48	−1	1	0	0	0	7.00	−1.00	1.000	−0.09	−0.91	0.828
9	10	9	81	90	3	9	1	3	1	7.91	2.09	4.368	−1.00	+3.09	9.548
10	10	10	100	100	3	9	2	6	4	8.82	1.18	1.392	+2.09	−0.91	0.828
11	10	11	121	110	3	9	3	9	9	9.73	0.27	0.073	+1.18	−0.91	0.828
12	12	12	144	144	5	25	4	20	16	10.64	1.36	1.850	+0.27	+1.09	1.188
13	15	13	169	195	8	64	5	40	25	11.55	3.45	11.903	+1.36	+2.09	4.369
14	10	14	196	140	3	9	6	18	36	12.46	−2.46	6.052	+3.45	−5.91	34.928
15	11	15	225	165	4	16	7	28	49	13.37	−2.37	5.617	−2.46	+0.09	0.008

$\underline{X} = 8$ $\underline{Y} = 7$ $\Sigma y_t^2 = 274$ $\Sigma x_ty_t = 255$ $\Sigma x_t^2 = 280$ $\Sigma e_t^2 = 41.767$ $\Sigma (e_t - e_{t-1})^2 = 60.213$

The estimated equation explains almost all the variations in consumption; moreover, the variance of $\hat{\beta}$ is also extremely small.

Let us now examine the error terms to see if we find any evidence of autocorrelation.

The required calculations are shown in the worksheet, Table 9.2.

Substituting the relevant values in the formula for *d-statistic*,

$$d = \frac{\Sigma(e_t - e_{t-1})^2}{\Sigma e_t^2} = \frac{142.08}{143.69} = 0.9887$$

At 5% level of significance for $n = 19$, $d_L = 1.18$ and $d_u = 1.40$. Our *d*-statistic falls below the lower bound value, and we, therefore, reject the null hypothesis of no autocorrelation in favour of the alternative hypothesis of (positive) autocorrelated disturbance terms.

Assuming that there exists first order autoregressive form of autocorrelation: $e_t = \rho e_{t-1} + v_t$, we go to estimate the value of ρ:

$$\hat{\rho} = \frac{\Sigma e_t e_{t-1}}{\Sigma e^2_{t-1}} = \frac{69.13}{141.86} = 0.4873$$

With this estimated value of ρ, we obtain:
(i) transformed consumption expenditure:

$$C_t^* = C_t - \hat{\rho}C_{t-1} = C - 0.48C_{t-1}$$

and (ii) transformed disposable income:

$$Y_t^* = Y_t - \hat{\rho}Y_{t-1} = Y_t - 0.48Y_{t-1}$$

The relevant computations to obtain C_t^* and Y_t^* have been shown in Table 9.3.

It is now required to regress C_t^* on Y_t^* to get estimates of parameters in $C_t^* = a + \beta Y_t^* + v_t$ as shown in (9.13).

The relevant summations are found to be as under:

$$\Sigma c_t^* y_t^* = 40755.45, \ \Sigma y_t^{*2} = 44969.84$$

$$\overline{C}^* = 163.74, \ \overline{Y}^* = 178.58 \text{ and } \hat{\rho} = 0.48$$

$$\therefore \qquad \hat{\beta} = \frac{40755.45}{44969.84} = 0.905$$

$$\hat{a} = 163.74 - (0.905)\,178.58 = 2.12$$

$$\hat{\alpha} = \frac{\hat{a}}{1-\hat{\rho}} = \frac{2.12}{1-0.48} = 4.08$$

Thus the regression model in the transformed form is:

$$\hat{C}_t^* = 2.12 + 0.905 \ Y_t^*$$

Table 9.2: Calculations of *d-statistics* for $\hat{C}_t = 3.29 + 0.906\ Y_t$

Year	Consumption expenditure C_t (Rs.)	Disposable Income Y_t (Rs.)	Estimated Consumption $\hat{C} = 3.29 + 0.906\ Y_t$	$(C_t - \hat{C}_t)$ e_t	e_t^2	e_{t-1}	e_{t-1}^2	$e_t - e_{t-1}$	$(e_t - e_{t-1})^2$	$e_t \cdot e_{t-1}$
1951	206.3	226.5	208.6	-2.3	5.29	=	=	=	=	=
1952	216.7	238.6	219.5	-2.8	7.84	-2.3	5.29	-0.5	0.25	6.44
1953	230.0	252.6	232.1	-2.1	4.41	-2.8	7.85	+0.4	0.16	5.88
1954	236.5	257.4	236.5	0	0	-2.1	4.41	+2.1	4.41	0
1955	254.4	275.3	252.7	1.7	2.89	0	0	+1.7	2.89	0
1956	266.7	293.2	268.9	-2.2	4.84	1.7	2.89	-3.9	15.21	-3.74
1957	281.4	308.5	282.8	-1.4	1.96	-2.2	4.84	+0.8	0.64	3.08
1958	290.1	318.8	292.1	-2.0	4.00	-1.4	1.96	-0.6	0.36	2.8
1959	311.2	337.3	308.9	2.3	5.29	-2.0	4.00	+4.3	18.49	-4.6
1960	325.2	350.0	320.4	4.8	23.04	2.3	5.29	+2.5	6.25	11.04
1961	335.2	364.4	333.4	1.8	3.24	4.8	23.04	-3.0	9.00	8.64
1962	355.1	385.5	352.6	2.6	6.25	1.8	3.24	+0.8	0.50	4.68
1963	375.0	404.6	369.6	5.1	26.01	2.7	7.29	+2.4	5.76	13.77
1964	401.2	438.1	400.2	1.0	1.00	5.1	26.01	-4.1	16.81	5.1
1965	432.8	473.2	432.0	0.8	0.64	1.0	1.00	-0.2	0.04	0.8
1966	466.3	511.9	467.1	-0.8	0.64	0.8	0.64	-1.6	2.56	-0.64
1967	492.1	546.3	498.2	-6.1	37.21	-0.8	0.64	-5.3	28.09	4.88
1968	536.2	591.0	538.7	-2.5	6.25	-6.1	37.21	+3.6	12.96	15.25
1969	579.6	634.2	577.9	1.7	2.89	-2.5	6.25	+4.2	17.64	-4.25
					$\Sigma e_t^2 =$ 143.69		$\Sigma e_{t-1}^2 =$ 141.86		$\Sigma (e_t - e_{t-1})^2 =$ 142.08	$\Sigma e_t e_{t-1} =$ 67.58

Table 9.3: Calculations of transformed variables C_t^* and Y_t^*

Year	C_t	$0.48\,C_t$	$0.48\,C_{t-1}$	$C_t^* = C_t - 0.48\,C_{t-1}$	Y_t	$0.48\,Y_t$	$0.48\,Y_{t-1}$	$Y_t^* = Y_t - 0.48\,Y_{t-1}$
1951	206.3	99.02	104.01	102.29	226.6	108..76	114.38	112.22
1952	216.7	104.01	110.40	106.30	238.3	114.38	121.24	117.06
1953	230.0	110.40	113.52	116.48	252.6	121.24	123.55	129.05
1954	236.5	113.52	122.11	114.39	257.4	123.55	132.14	125.26
1955	254.4	122.11	128.01	126.39	275.3	132.14	140.73	134.57
1956	266.7	128.01	135.07	131.63	293.2	140.73	148.08	145.12
1957	281.4	135.07	139.24	142.16	308.5	148.08	153.02	155.48
1958	290.1	139.24	149.237	140.73	318.8	153.02	161.90	156.90
1959	311.2	149.37	156.09	155.11	337.3	161.90	168.00	169.30
1960	325.2	156.09	160.89	164.31	350.0	168.00	174.72	175.28
1961	335.2	160.89	170.44	164.76	364.4	174.72	185.04	179.36
1962	355.1	170.44	180.00	175.10	385.5	185.04	194.20	191.30
1963	375.0	180.00	192.57	182.43	404.6	194.20	210.28	194.32
1964	401.2	192.57	207.74	193.46	438.1	210.28	227.13	210.97
1965	432.8	207.74	223.82	208.98	473.2	227.13	245.71	224.49
1966	466.3	223.82	236.20	230.10	511.9	245.71	262.22	249.68
1967	492.1	236.20	257.37	234.73	546.3	262.22	283.68	262.62
1968	536.2	257.37	273.88	262.32	591.0	213.68	304.41	286.59
1969	570.6	273.88	=	=	634.2	304.41	=	=

$$\bar{C}_t^* = 163.74 \qquad\qquad \bar{Y}_t^* = 178.58$$

which may now be stated in terms of original variables as

$$\hat{C}_t^* = 4.08 + 0.905 \, Y_t \qquad\qquad n = 18$$
$$(0.0092) \qquad\qquad R^2 = 0.998$$

The value of *d-statistic* for the transformed variables is not indicative of serial correlation in the disturbance terms.

9.2   HETROSCEDASTICITY

9.2.1   Meaning

The third assumption about the disturbance terms is that their probability distribution remains same over all observations of X; i.e., the variance of each U_i is the same for all the values of the explanatory variable.

Symbolically:

$$\text{Var } (U_i) = E\{[U_i - E(U_i)]\}^2 = E(U_i^2) = \sigma_u{}^2; \text{ a constant value.}$$

This feature of homogeneity of variance (or constant variance) is known as homoscedasticity. It may be the case, however, that all of the disturbance terms do not have the same variance. This condition of non-constant variance or non-homogeneity of variance is known as hetroscedasticity. Thus we say that U's are hetroscedastic when

$$\text{Var } (U_i) \neq \sigma_u{}^2 \text{ (a constant value) but } = \sigma^2{}_{ui} \text{ (a value that varies).}$$

9.2.2   Graphical Representation

The assumption of homoscedasticity states that the variation of each U_i around its zero mean does not depend on the value of explanatory variable. The variance of each U_i remains the same irrespective of small or large values of X; the explanatory variable. Mathematically, $\sigma_u{}^2$ is not a function of X; i.e., $\sigma_u{}^2 \neq f(X_i)$.

If the variance of U were the same at every point or for all values of X, definite restriction would be placed on the scatter of Y against X; and when plotted in three dimensions, we should observe something approximating the pattern of Fig. 9.8. In contrast, consider Fig. 9.9, which shows that the conditional variance of Y_i (which in fact is U_i) increases as X increases. When seen in two dimensions, there should be no evident tendency for the scatter of Y and X to widen or narrow appreciably anywhere along the range of X as shown in Fig. 6.3 of Chapter 6.

If σ_u^2 is not constant but its values depend on the values of X; it means that $\sigma^2 ui = f(X_i)$. Such dependence is depicted diagrammatically in panels of Fig. 9.10. Three cases of hetroscedasticity are shown by increasing or decreasing dispersion of the observations from the regression line.

In panel (a), σ_u^2 seems to increase with X. In panel (b) the error variance appears greatest in X's middle range, tapering off toward the extremes. Finally, in panel (c), the variance of the error term is greatest for low values of X, declining and levelling off rapidly as X increases.

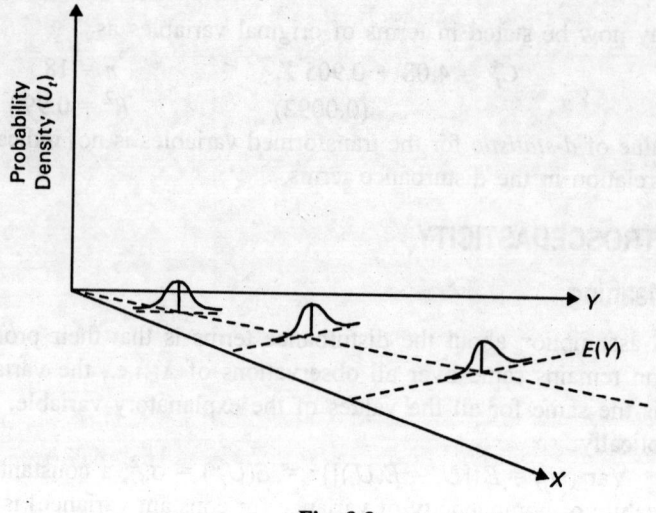

Fig. 9.8

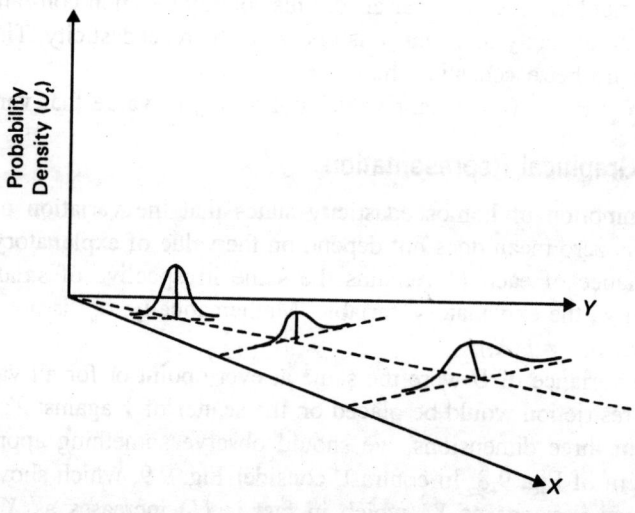

Fig. 9.9

The pattern of hetroscedasticity would depend on the signs and values of the coefficients of the relationship $\sigma_{u_i}^2 = f(X_i)$; but U_i's are not observable. As such in applied research we make convenient assumptions that hetroscedasticity is of the forms,

(i) $\sigma_{u_i}^2 = k^2(X_i^2)$, (ii) $\sigma_{u_i}^2 = k(X_i)$, and (iii) $\sigma_{u_i}^2 = \dfrac{k}{X_i^2}$

where K is a constant, the value of which we try to estimate from the given data.

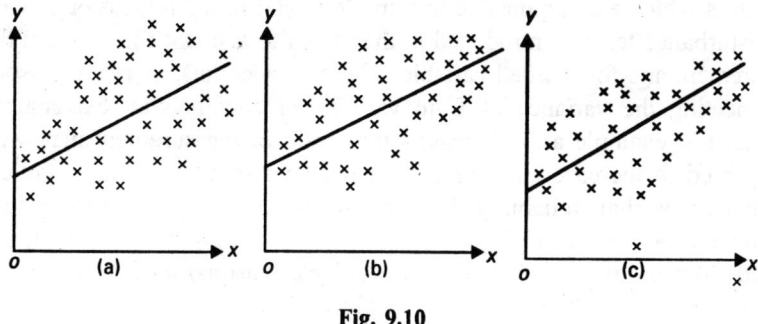

Fig. 9.10

The above three cases of known variances is based on different degree of prior knowledge of the sample and error variances. This may occur very occasionally but it is important to undertake such assumptions here just to illustrate how to correct for hetroscedasticity. This is explained under section 9.2.7.

9.2.3 Matrix Notation of Hetroscedasticity

The variance-covariance matrix developed in Chapter 7, is represented as:

$$E(\mathbf{UU'}) = \begin{bmatrix} E(U_i^2) & E(U_1U_2) & ... & E(U_1U_n) \\ E(U_1U_2) & E(U_2^2) & ... & E(U_2U_n) \\ \vdots & \vdots & & \vdots \\ E(U_1U_n) & E(U_2U_n) & ... & E(U_n^2) \end{bmatrix}$$

Presently if $E(U_i^2) \neq \sigma_u^2$ (a constant value), then $E(UU')$ is $\neq I_n\sigma_u^2$ {given that $E(U_iU_j) = 0$}. It shall be equal to:

$$E(\mathbf{UU'}) = \begin{bmatrix} \lambda_1 & 0 & 0...0 \\ 0 & \lambda_2 & 0...0 \\ \vdots & \vdots & \\ 0 & 0 & 0...\lambda_n \end{bmatrix}, \text{ where } \lambda_i = E(U_i^2).$$

In other words, variance-covariance matrix in the present case is a diagonal matrix with unequal elements in the diagonal. Refer different examples of hetroscedasticity with autocorrelation in section 9.1.2. above and section 9.3 which deals with more generalized case with the use of GLS estimation.

9.2.4 Violation of Assumption of Homoscedasticity

In actuality the assumption of constant variance of the disturbance terms may be expected not to hold. This can be understood if we take into account the factors which are responsible to bring term (U) in the regression model. The disturbance term is introduced in the model to account for errors in the measurement and for omitted variables. On both accounts, there are reasons for expecting the variance of U to vary systematically with explanatory variable. For example as Y increases, the errors of measurement may well be expected to increase also; because it becomes more difficult to collect data and check their reliability. In this case variance of U_i would increase with increasing values of X. On the other hand, the variables which are omitted from the model (for some unavoidable reasons) tend to change in the same direction with explanatory variable; thereby causing an increase of the variation of the observations from the estimated regression line. Thus it may be said that on *priori* grounds there are reasons to believe that the assumption of homoscedasticity may often be violated in practice.

We present two examples in support of this argument.

(i) *Consumption function:* Suppose we are to study the consumption expenditure from a given cross-section sample of family budgets:

$$C_1 = \alpha + \beta Y_i + U_i$$

where C_i = Consumption expenditure of ith household and Y_i = disposable income of ith household.

Here, the assumption of homoscedasticity is not very plausible on *a priori* grounds since we would expect variance in consumption to rise with level of income. At low levels of income the average level of consumption is low, and the variation below this level is less possible; consumption cannot fall too far below because this might mean starvation. On the other hand, it cannot rise too far above because money income does not permit it. Such constraints may not be found at higher income levels. Thus consumption patterns are more regular at lower income levels than at higher levels. This implies that at high incomes the U_i's will be high, while at low incomes the U_i's will be small. The assumption of constant variance of U's therefore, does not hold when estimating the consumption function from a cross-section of family budgets.

(ii) *Production function:* Suppose we are required to estimate the production function. $X = f(K, L)$ of the sugar industry from a cross-section random sample of firms of the industry. Disturbance terms in the production function would stand for many factors; like entrepreneurship, technological differences, selling and purchasing procedures, differences in organisations, etc., other than inputs labour (L) and capital (K) considered in the production function. The factors mentioned above, which are not considered explicitly in the production function show considerable variance in large firms than in the small ones. This leads to breakdown of our assumption on homogeneity of variances of the disturbance terms.

It should be noted that the problem of hetroscedasticity is likely to be more common in cross-sectional data than in time-series data. In cross-sectional data, one deals with members of population at a given point of time, such as individual consumers or their families, firms, industries. These members may be of different sizes, such as small, medium or large firms or low, medium, or high income. In time-series data, on the other hand, the variables tend to be of similar orders of magnitude because one generally collects data for the same entity over a period of time.

Since, the assumption of homoscedasticity in ordinary least squares procedure is one of the critical requirements for consistency and best, linear, unbiasedness of the parameter, it is important to examine the consequences of violation of this assumption on ordinary least squares estimates.

9.2.5 Consequences

What happens when we use ordinary least squares procedure to a model with hetroscedastic disturbance terms?

Following shall be the consequences:

(i) The OLS estimators will have no bias:

$$\hat{\beta} = \frac{\Sigma x_i y_i}{\Sigma x_i^2} = \beta + \frac{\Sigma x_i u_i}{\Sigma x_i^2}$$

$$\therefore \quad E(\hat{\beta}) = \beta + E\left\{\frac{\Sigma x_i u_i}{\Sigma x_i^2}\right\} = \beta$$

Similarly, $\quad \hat{\alpha} = \bar{Y} - \hat{\beta}\bar{X} = (\alpha + \beta\bar{X} + \bar{U}) - \hat{\beta}\bar{X}$

$$\therefore \quad E(\hat{\alpha}) = \alpha + \beta\bar{X} + E(\bar{U}) - E(\hat{\beta})X = \alpha$$

That is, the least squares estimators are unbiased even under the condition of hetroscedasticity. It is because we do not make use of assumption of homoscedasticity here. The variances of the error terms play no role in the proof that least squares estimates are unbiased.

(ii) Variance of OLS coefficients will be incorrect.

By (6.12), it was shown: $\mathrm{Var}(\hat{\beta}) = \sigma^2 \Sigma k_i^2 = \dfrac{\sigma^2}{\Sigma x_i^2}$, but under the hetroscedasticity assumption we shall have:

$$\mathrm{Var}(\hat{\beta}) = \Sigma k_i^2 E(U_i^2) = \Sigma k_i^2 \sigma_{ui}^2 \neq \sigma^2 \Sigma k_i^2$$

σ_{ui}^2 is no more a finite constant figure, but rather it tends to change with an increasing range of value of X and hence cannot be taken out of the summation (notation). If the variations σ_{ui}^2, $i = 1, 2, \ldots$ were known, then we could substitute these values into $\Sigma k_i \sigma_{ui}^2$ and compute the correct value of the sampling variance of $\hat{\beta}$. The problem is that the values of the U are not known and have to be estimated from the sample data, using the residuals as proxies of the unobservable errors. In this case we have to estimate n variables from n observations, that is, one for each variance; (a situation in which estimation is obviously impossible) because we cannot estimate a variance from one observation.

(iii) OLS estimators shall be inefficient; in other words the OLS estimators do not have the smallest variance in a class of unbiased estimators and, therefore, they are not efficient both in small and in large samples.

Under the hetroscedastic assumption, therefore,

$$\text{Var}\,(\hat{\beta}) = \Sigma k_i^2\, E(U_i^2)$$

$$= \Sigma \left(\frac{x_i}{\Sigma x_i^2}\right)^2 E(U_i^2)$$

$$= \frac{\Sigma x_i^2\, \sigma_{ni}^2}{(\Sigma x_i^2)^2} \qquad\qquad \text{...(i)}$$

(i) is different from the variance of β under homoscedastic assumption. In other words, under hetroscedastic assumption although β is unbiased, but it is inefficient. Its variance is larger than necessary. Under homoscedastic assumption variance of β is given by usual formula, namely:

$$\text{Var}\,(\hat{\beta}) = \frac{\sigma^2}{\Sigma x_i^2} \qquad\qquad \text{...(ii)}$$

To see the consequences of using (ii) instead of (i), let us assume that:
$$\sigma_{ui}^2 = k_i \sigma^2,$$

where k_i are same nonstochastic constant weights. This assumption merely states that the hetroscedastic variances are proportional to k_i; σ^2 being factor of proportionality.

Substituting this value of σ_{ui}^2 in (i), we obtain:

$$\text{Var}\,(\hat{\beta}) = \frac{\sigma^2 \Sigma k_i x_i^2}{(\Sigma x_i^2)^2} = \frac{\sigma^2 \Sigma k_i x_i^2}{(\Sigma x_i^2)(\Sigma x_i^2)}$$

$$= \left(\frac{\sigma^2}{\Sigma x_i^2}\right)\left(\frac{\Sigma k_i x_i^2}{\Sigma x_i^2}\right)$$

$$= \left(\begin{array}{c}\text{Var}\,(\hat{\beta})\ \text{under homos-}\\ \text{cedastic assumption}\end{array}\right)\left(\frac{\Sigma k_i x_i^2}{\Sigma x_i^2}\right) \qquad \text{...(iii)}$$

That is to say that if x_i^2 and k_i are positively correlated, and if second term of (iii) is greater than 1, the Var $(\hat{\beta})$ under hetroscedasticity will be greater than its variance under homoscedasticity. As a result, true standard error of $\hat{\beta}$ shall be underestimated. As such the t-value associated with it, will be overestimated which might lead to the conclusion that in a specific case at hand $\hat{\beta}$ is statistically significant (which in fact may not be true).

The consequence of (iii) above is that the confidence limits and the tests of significance will not be applicable. That is, if we proceed with our model under false belief of homogeneity of variances, our inferences and predictions about the population coefficients would be incorrect.

9.2.6 Tests for Hetroscedasticity

We have observed that the consequences of hetroscedasticity are fairly serious on OLS estimates. As such it is desirable to examine whether or not the regression model is in fact homoscedastic. Various tests have been suggested for establishing hetroscedasticity. We describe two of them.

Tests I. The Spearman Rank Correlation Test

This is a most simple and approximate test for detecting the hetroscedasticity. This test is performed in the following way.

First regress Y on X (explanatory variable) to obtain the residuals (e) which are estimates of the disturbance terms (U). Next arrange e's (ignoring signs) and the values of X in ascending or descending order to compute *Rank Correlation Coefficient* between X and e (remember, simple correlation coefficient will always be zero; since $\Sigma ex = 0$ in OLS).

A high coefficient suggests the presence of hetroscedasticity. One can compute the rank correlation coefficient between e_i's and each one of explanatory variables in case there are more than one explanatory variable in the model.

Test II. The Goldfeld-Quandt Test

This test is based on two basic assumptions: (1) that, the number of observations is (at least) twice the number of explanatory variables in the model, (2) U_i's are non-autocorrelated and normally distributed.

This test involves estimating two least squares regression lines, one using data thought to be associated with low variance errors and the other using data thought to be associated with high variance errors. If the variances associated with each regression line are approximately equal, the homoscedasticity assumption can not be rejected.

The G-Q test can be carried out in the following steps:

First Step: Order the observations according to the magnitude of explanatory variable (X_i).

Second Step: Omit a certain number of central observations (say c) from the analysis. The remaining observations, i.e., ($n - c$) observations are, then, divided into two equal parts. Each part, therefore, now consists of $\left(\dfrac{n-c}{2}\right)$ number of observations. One part includes the small values of X while the other the large values of X. (c must be small enough to ensure that enough degrees of freedom are available to allow for proper estimation of each of the seperate regressions).

Third Step: Fit separate regression by OLS procedure to each part and obtain the sum of squared residuals from each of them.

Fourth Step: Let Σe_1^2 denote the sum of squared residuals from the sample of low values of X and Σe_2^2 from the sample of large values of X.

Then calculate $F = \dfrac{\Sigma e_2^2}{\Sigma e_1^2}$; which will have the F-distribution with $\left\{\dfrac{n-c}{2} - k\right\}$ degrees of freedom for both numerator and denominator of the ratio. (n = total number of observations, c = number of central observations omitted, and k = number of parameters to be estimated including constant term).

If U's are homoscedastic, the two variances, i.e. Σe_1^2 and Σe_2^2 should turn out to be equal and therefore, F will tend to 1. Otherwise it will tend to be large indicating hetroscedasticity.

Fifth Step: Test the hypothesis of homoscedasticity in the following way:

$$H_0 : U_i\text{'s are homoscedastic}$$
$$H_1 : U_i\text{'s are hetroscedastic}$$

If the calculated value of F^* from fourth step is greater than theoretical or tabulated F, rejected H_0 (i.e., we reject the U's are homoscedastic). If F^* is less than F, accept H_0.

The power of test depends on the value of c. It has been found from some experiments by Goldfeld and Quandt that for samples larger than $n = 30$, the optimum number of central observations to be omitted from the test is approximately a quarter of observations; for example $c = 8$ for $n = 30$ and $c = 15$ for $n = 60$.

However, the choice of the number of middle observations to eliminate from the test is somewhat arbitrary. If no middle observations are eliminated, the test is still correct.

Test III. The Park Test

There are at least two limitations in G-Q test discussed above. One, that it does not help us to obtain the pattern or form of hetroscedasticity in the observed data and, secondly, it does not test the presence of hetroscedasticity statistically directly.

Park-Glejser tests remove these limitations and also possess advantage of being easy to use. Prof. R.E. Park suggested a specific functional form between the σ_{ui}^2 and the explanatory variable to detect hetroscedasticity.

$$\sigma_{ui}^2 = f(X_i) = \sigma^2 X_i^\beta e^{vi}$$

$$\ln \sigma_{ui}^2 = \ln \sigma^2 + \beta \ln X_i + v_i$$

Since σ_{ui}^2 is not observable, he suggested e_i^2 as a proxy. Therefore;

$$\ln e_i^2 = \ln \sigma^2 + \beta \ln X_i + v_i$$

$$= \alpha + \beta \ln X_i + v_i$$

According to him, if β in the above regression turns out to be statistically significant, it would suggest that hetroscedasticity is present in the data.

This test is two-stage procedure.

Stage I: Run the OLS regression disregarding the hetroscedasticity. Obtain e_i from this regression.

Stage II: Run the log-linear regression between e_i^2's and X_i's and examine whether β is significant.

Test IV. The Glejser Test

Glejser test is similar to Part test. The only difference being that Glejser suggests as many as seven functional forms instead of only one (i.e., log-linear) as suggested by Park.

Glejser used the following functional forms to detect hetroscedasticity:

$$|e_i| = \beta X_i + v_i, \qquad\qquad |e_i| = \beta \sqrt{X_i} + v_i$$

$$|e_i| = \frac{\beta}{X_i} + v_i, \qquad\qquad |e_i| = \frac{\beta}{\sqrt{X_i}} + v_i$$

$$|e_i| = \alpha + \beta X_i + v_i, \qquad |e_i| = \sqrt{\alpha + \beta X_i} + v_i$$

$$(v_i \text{ is the error term}).$$

If β in above regressions turns out to be significant, it would suggest presence of hetroscedasticity in the data.

It should be clear that the above four tests merely specify whether or not the disturbance terms are hetroscedastic but not the manner in which they are hetroscedastic. In other words by using these tests we only come to know whether or not $E(U_i^2) = \sigma_u^2$, a constant value.

In case $E(U_i^2) \neq \sigma_u^2$, then it means $E(U_i^2) = \sigma_{ui}^2 = f(X_i)$. But the above tests are not able to specify the nature or particular form of this relationship. Nevertheless in order to decide as to what approximate transformation of data is needed (to remove heteroscedasticity), we must know the exact form of the above relationship.

9.2.7 Different Hetroscedastic Structures

Assume that our original model is: $Y_i = \alpha + \beta X_i + U_i$ where U_i satisfied all the assumptions except that U_i is hetroscedastic, i.e.,

$$U_i \sim N(0, \sigma_{ui}^2), \text{ and}$$
$$E(U_i^2) = \sigma_{ui}^2 = f(X_i).$$

Our problem is, what is the exact nature of $f(X_i)$?

As has been explained already, empirically it is not possible to obtain the exact form of this relationship. We can only assume possible types of hetroscedastic structures.

Case (a): Suppose the hetroscedasticity is of the form:

$$E(U_i^2) = \sigma_{ui}^2 = k^2 X_i^2,$$

where k is some finite constant to be estimated from the model.

Given that
$$\sigma_{ui}^2 = k^2 X_i^2; \qquad k^2 = \frac{\sigma_{ui}^2}{X_i^2}$$

or,
$$k = \frac{\sigma_{ui}}{X_i}.$$

In other words, the required transformation should be

$$\frac{Y_i}{X_i} = \frac{\alpha}{X_i} + \frac{\beta X_i}{X_i} + \frac{U_i}{X_i}$$

or,
$$\frac{Y_i}{X_i} = \frac{\alpha}{X_i} + \beta + \frac{U_i}{X_i}$$

Let us now examine whether the disturbance terms in the transformed form are homoscedastic. For this we have to obtain variance of $\left(\dfrac{U_i}{X_i}\right)$.

$$\text{Var}\left(\frac{U_i}{X_i}\right) = E\left(\frac{U_i}{X_i}\right)^2 = \frac{1}{X_i^2} E(U_i^2) = \frac{\sigma_{ui}^2}{X_i^2}$$

Since we have assumed $\sigma_{ui}^2 = k^2 X_i^2$

$$\therefore \quad \text{Var}\left(\frac{U_i}{X_i}\right) = \frac{\sigma_{ui}^2}{X_i^2} = \frac{k^2 X_i^2}{X_i^2} = k^2 \text{ (a constant), which proves that}$$

new random term in the model has a finite constant variance ($= k^2$). We can, therefore, apply to OLS the transformed version of the model:

$$\frac{Y_i}{X_i} = \frac{\alpha}{X_i} + \beta + \frac{U_i}{X_i}$$

Note that in this transformation the position of the coefficients has changed; the parameter of the variable $\dfrac{1}{X_i}$ in the transformed model is the constant intercept of the original model, while the constant term of the transformed model is the parameter of the explanatory variable X in the original model. Therefore, to get back to the original model, we shall have to multiply the estimated regression by X_i.

Case (b): Suppose hetroscedasticity is of the form:

$$E(U_i^2) = \sigma_{ui}^2 = k^2 X_i.$$

Given that, $E(U_i^2) = \sigma_{ui}^2 = k^2 X_i,$

$\therefore$ $$k^2 = \frac{\sigma_{ui}^2}{X_i}; \quad k = \frac{\sigma_{ui}}{\sqrt{X_i}};$$

which means that the required transformation should be;

$$\frac{Y_i}{\sqrt{X_i}} = \frac{\alpha}{\sqrt{X_i}} + \frac{\beta X_i}{\sqrt{X_i}} + \frac{U_i}{\sqrt{X_i}}$$

$$\frac{Y_i}{\sqrt{X_i}} = \frac{\alpha}{\sqrt{X_i}} + \beta\sqrt{X_i} + \frac{U_i}{\sqrt{X_i}}$$

The disturbance term in the transformed version is homoscedastic.

$$E\left(\frac{U_i}{\sqrt{X_i}}\right)^2 = \frac{1}{X_i} E(U_i^2) = \frac{1}{X_i}(\sigma_{ui}^2) = \frac{k^2 X_i}{X_i} = k^2$$

In other words, we can apply OLS to transformed model:

$$\frac{Y_i}{\sqrt{X_i}} = \frac{\alpha}{\sqrt{X_i}} + \beta\sqrt{X_i} + \frac{U_i}{\sqrt{X_i}}.$$

There is no intercept term in the transformed model. Therefore, one will have to use the 'regression through the origin' model to estimate α and β. In this case, therefore, to get back to the original model, we shall have to multiply estimated regression by $\sqrt{X_i}$.

Case (c): Suppose hetroscedasticity is of the form:

$$E(U_i^2) = \sigma_{ui}^2 = k^2 [E(Y_i)]^2$$

In this case it is assumed that the variance of the disturbance terms is proportional to the squared mean of dependent variable.

$$\sigma_{ui}^2 = k^2 [E(Y_i)]^2 = k^2 [(\alpha + \beta X_i)^2]$$

$\therefore$ $$k^2 = \frac{\sigma_{ui}^2}{(\alpha + \beta X_i)^2}; \quad k = \frac{\sigma_{ui}}{\alpha + \beta X_i}$$

The required transformation should be:

$$\frac{Y_i}{\alpha + \beta X_i} = \frac{\alpha}{\alpha + \beta X_i} + \frac{\beta X_i}{\alpha + \beta X_i} + \frac{U_i}{\alpha + \beta X_i} \qquad \text{...(i)}$$

The new random term is homoscedastic because;

$$E\left\{\frac{U_i}{\alpha + \beta X_i}\right\}^2 = \left(\frac{1}{\alpha + \beta X_i}\right)^2 E(U_i^2)$$

$$= \left(\frac{1}{\alpha + \beta X_i}\right)^2 k^2(\alpha + \beta X_i)^2 = k^2$$

The transformed model described in (i) above is however, not operational in this case. It is because values of x and β are not known. But since we can obtain the regression: $\hat{Y}_i = \hat{\alpha} + \hat{\beta} X_i$, the transformation can be made through the following two steps:

First we run the usual OLS regression disregarding the hetroscedasticity problem in the data and obtain $\hat{Y}_i$. Using the estimated $\hat{Y}_i$, we transform our model as follows:

$$\frac{Y_i}{\hat{Y}_i} = \alpha\left(\frac{1}{\hat{Y}_i}\right) + \beta\left(\frac{X_i}{\hat{Y}_i}\right) + \frac{U_i}{\hat{Y}_i} \qquad \text{...(ii)}$$

In the second step, we run the regression (ii) to obtain α and β.

From the above analysis it may therefore be generalised that if the hetroscedasticity is of the form: $E(U_i^2) = \sigma_{ui}^2 = k^2 f(X_i)$, *the transformed version of the model may be obtained by dividing throughout the original model by* $\sqrt{f(X_i)}$.

It should, be clear that in order to adopt the necessary corrective measure (which is through transformation of the original data in such a way as to obtain a form in which the transformed disturbance terms possess constant variance), we must have information on the form of hetroscedasticity. Also, since our transformed data no more possesses hetroscedasticity, it can be shown that the estimates of the transformed model are more efficient (i.e., they possess a smaller variance) than the estimates obtained from the application of OLS to the original data.

Let us assume that test reveals the original data possesses hetroscedasticity; and that hetroscedasticity of the form: $\sigma_{ui}^2 = k^2 X_i^2$ is being assumed.

Our original model, therefore, is: $Y_i = \alpha + \beta X_i + U_i$ with $E(U_i^2) = k^2 X_i^2$. Applying OLS to the above hetroscedastic model,

$$\hat{\beta} = \beta + \frac{\Sigma x_i U_i}{\Sigma x_i^2}$$

$$\text{Var}\,(\hat{\beta}) = E\,(\hat{\beta}-\beta)^2 \;=\; E\left[\beta + \frac{\Sigma x_i U_i}{\Sigma x_i^2} - \beta\right]^2$$

$$= E\left[\frac{\Sigma x_i U_i}{\Sigma x_i^2}\right]^2$$

$$= E\left[\frac{\Sigma x_i^2 U_i^2 + 2\Sigma x_i x_j U_i U_j}{(\Sigma x_i^2)^2}\right] = \left[\frac{\Sigma x_i^2 E(U_i^2)}{(\Sigma x_i^2)^2}\right]$$

$$= k^2 \cdot \frac{\Sigma x_i^2 X_i^2}{(\Sigma x_i^2)^2} \qquad \left(\because E(U_i^2) = k^2 X_i^2\right)$$

$$\therefore \quad \text{Var}\,(\hat{\beta}) = \frac{k^2[n^2(\Sigma X_i^4) - 2n\,(\Sigma X_i^3)\,(\Sigma X_i) + (\Sigma x_i^2)\,(\Sigma X_i)^2]}{[n\Sigma X_i^2 - (\Sigma X_i)^2]^2} \qquad \ldots(i)$$

On transforming the original model, we obtain:

$$\frac{Y_i}{X_i} = \beta + \frac{\alpha}{X_i} + \frac{U_i}{X_i} = \frac{\alpha}{X_i} + \beta + V_i$$

The transformed disturbance terms: $\dfrac{U_i}{X_i}$ possess constant variance k^2.

On applying OLS to above transformed model we obtain:

$$\hat{\beta} = \overline{\left(\frac{Y_i}{X_i}\right)} - \hat{\alpha}\,\overline{\left(\frac{1}{X_i}\right)}$$

($\hat{\beta}$ is the OLS estimator of the transformed model)

$$\text{Var}\,(\hat{\beta}) = \left[\sigma_v^2\,\frac{\Sigma(1/X_i)^2}{n\Sigma\{(1/X_i) - (\overline{1/X_i})\}^2}\right]$$

$$\text{Var}(\hat{\beta}) = k^2 \cdot \frac{\Sigma(1/X_i)^2}{n\Sigma\{(1/X_i) - (\overline{1/X_i})\}^2} \;=\; \frac{k^2\Sigma(1/X_i^2)}{n\Sigma(1/X_i^2) - [(\Sigma 1/X_i)]^2} \qquad \ldots(ii)$$

$$\left[\because \text{Var}\,(\hat{\beta})\ \text{in}\ OLS = \sigma_u^2\left(\frac{\Sigma X_i^2}{n\Sigma x_i^2}\right)\right]$$

On dividing variances of the estimators of two models, i.e., (ii) by (i), it is clear that

$$\frac{\text{Var.}(\hat{\hat{\beta}})}{\text{Var.}(\hat{\beta})} < 1$$

in other words, the OLS estimator is unbiased but less efficient (i.e., has higher variance) than the transformed least-squares estimator. This shows that the application of simple least squares to the original data with hetroscedasticity will provide less efficient estimator. The OLS estimator would have been comparatively more efficient had the original data departed less from the assumption of homoscedasticity.

For instance, had our original model been:

$$Y_i = \alpha + \beta X_i + U_i \text{ with } E(U_i) = k^2 \ (X_i),$$

the ratio of Var.$(\hat{\beta})$ to Var.$(\hat{\hat{\beta}})$ would have been larger than that of in the earlier case of hetroscedasticity $\left[\text{of } (U_i^2) = k^2 \left(X_i^2\right)\right]$.

9.2.8 Applications

Example 3: Consider the following data on monthly expenditures for clothing and on incomes of 10 families.

Assuming that the variance of the disturbance term is proportional to the square of expenditure on clothing, obtain the appropriate transformation so as to make the resulting disturbance term homoscedastic. Compare the regression equation of the so transformed data with that of the original data.

Expenditure on clothing (in Rs.)

| 20 | 25 | 30 | 40 | 45 | 50 | 55 | 60 | 65 |

Income (in Rs.)

| 1500 | 2000 | 3000 | 3500 | 4500 | 4500 | 5500 | 6000 | 5500 |

The relationship between expenditure on clothing and income is hypothesized to be:

$$Y_i = \alpha + \beta X_i + U_i$$

where Y = expenditure on clothing, X = income, U = random disturbance, and the subscript i refers to the ith family.

(i) First assume that there is no hetroscedasticity in the data. Thus the explanatory variable X_i is considered to be nonstochastic, and the disturbance term U_i is assumed to be a normally distributed, non-autoregressive random variable with zero mean and constant variance = σ^2.

The OLS estimators of the regression coefficient are:

$$\hat{\beta} = \frac{\Sigma x_i y_i}{\Sigma x_i^2} = \frac{206250}{22525000} = 0.009156$$

Table 9.4: Calculation of Transformed Variables

Expenditure (Y)	Income (X)	$\left[\left(\dfrac{Y_i}{X_i}\right) \times 1000\right]$	$\left[\left(\dfrac{1}{X_i}\right) \times 10000\right]$	$\left[\left(\dfrac{Y_i}{X_i^2}\right) \times 1000\right]$	$\left[\left(\dfrac{1}{X_i^2}\right) \times 10000\right]$
20	1500	13.333	6.666	0.0088	0.0044
25	2000	12.500	5.000	0.0063	0.0025
30	3000	10.000	3.333	0.0033	0.0011
35	3500	10.000	2.857	0.0028	Nearly zero
40	4500	8.888	2.222	0.0019	,,
45	4500	10.000	2.222	0.0022	,,
50	5500	9.090	1.818	0.0016	,,
55	5500	10.000	1.818	0.0018	,,
60	6000	10.000	1.666	0.0017	,,
65	5500	10.909	1.818	0.0021	,,

$$\hat\alpha = \bar Y - \hat\beta \bar X = 4.50094$$

$$R^2 = \frac{\hat\beta \Sigma x_i y_i}{\Sigma y_i^2} = 0.9156$$

(ii) Now if we assume that the pattern of hetrosedasticity is:

$$\sigma u_i^2 = k^2 X_i^2$$

So that the appropriate transformation of the original model is:

$$\frac{Y_i}{X_i} = \alpha\left(\frac{1}{X_i}\right) + \beta + \frac{U_i}{X_i}$$

The transformed variables (Y_i/X_i and $1/X_i$) are shown in the third and fourth columns of Table 9.4.

Applying OLS procedure to the new variables, we obtain:

$$\frac{Y_i}{X_i} = \hat\alpha\left(\frac{1}{X_i}\right) + \hat\beta = 3.5898 \left(\frac{1}{X_i}\right) + 0.00013$$

To get back to the original model, multiply this estimated regression by X_i. The *new expenditure function,* therefore, is:

$$Y_i^* = 3.5898 + 0.00013 X_i \qquad\qquad R^2 = 0.786$$

As compared to the previous function (with homoscedastic assumption) is:

$$Y_i = 4.5009 + 0.00915 X_i \qquad\qquad R^2 = 0.915$$

Note that the R^2 of the transformed model is lower than R^2 in the original model. Can you say why?

Note: One can use the following direct formula to obtain estimators of α and β for the transformed model. Columns 5 and 6 of Table 9.4 have been obtained for this purpose.

$$\hat\beta = \frac{(\Sigma 1/X_i^2)(\Sigma Y_i/X_i) - (\Sigma 1/X_i)(\Sigma Y_i/X_i^2)}{n(\Sigma 1/X_i^2) - [\Sigma(1/X_i)]^2} \text{, and}$$

$$\hat\alpha = \left[\frac{\Sigma(Y_i/X_i^2)}{\Sigma(1/X_i^2)}\right] - \left[\frac{\Sigma(1/X_i)}{\Sigma(1/X_i^2)}\right](\hat\beta)$$

9.3   GENERALIZED LEAST SQUARES ESTIMATION (GLS)

The classical regression model is based on rather restrictive assumptions concerning the behaviour of regression residuals.

While specifying the classical model in Chapters 6 and 8, we made two assumptions; one, that elements of residual vector were uncorrelated $E(U_i U_j) = 0$, $i \neq j$, and two, that they have an identical variances

$E(U_i^2) = \sigma^2$, for all i. This made $E(U\,U') = \sigma_u^2\,I_n$ possible. Failure to satisfy either of the assumptions shall not produce covariance matrix of such an 'identity-scalar' type of matrix. In that case residuals are said to *nonspherical*.

We examined nonsphericalness in the form of autocorrelation and heteroscedasticity in the sections 9.1 and 9.2 of the present chapter. The 'identity-scalar' covariance matrix no more holds good under such circumstances. Although we have dealt these problems in details, the object of present section is to generalize the classical linear model to apply to cases where autocorrelation and heteroscedasticity simultaneously coexist in the sample data.

We begin with matrix generalization form of multiple regression model:

$$Y = X\beta + U,$$

where $\mathbf{Y}$, $\mathbf{X}$, β and $\mathbf{U}$ denote as described by section 8.6.

Assume the error structure with heteroscedasticity and first-order serial correlation in this model so that

$$E(\mathbf{UU'}) = \phi \ (= \sigma^2 \ \Psi), \text{ where}$$

$$\phi = \sigma^2\psi = \begin{bmatrix} \sigma_1^2 & \sigma_{12} & \cdots & \sigma_{1n} \\ \sigma_{21} & \sigma_2^2 & \cdots & \sigma_{2n} \\ \cdots & \cdots & \cdots & \cdots \\ \cdots & \cdots & \cdots & \cdots \\ \sigma_{n1} & \sigma_{n2} & \cdots & \sigma_n^2 \end{bmatrix}$$

(σ_{ii} denotes the variances of U_i and σ_{ij} the covariance of U_i and U_j)

We now pose the question of how best to estimate the unknown parameters of the vector β by accounting for the information provided by the knowledge in the form of matrix ϕ. (remember that no other classical assumption gets violated).

We have already explained in the earlier sections of chapter that though OLS estimator remains unbiased in such circumstances, it nevertheless loses the sampling precision quality. This is specifically because variance-covariance matrix is no longer identity-scalar matrix. What is, therefore, required is to transform the original data so that the covariance matrix of transformed residuals equals $\sigma^2 I_n$. Once this is done, it will then be easier to obtain generalized estimators.

A theorem of matrix algebra, which states that there exists a non-singular $(n \times n)$ matrix $\mathbf{P}$ such that

$$\mathbf{P\psi P'} = \mathbf{I}_n$$

helps to do the job of desired transformation.

$$\mathbf{P\psi P'} = \mathbf{I} \text{ also implies that}$$

$$\psi = \mathbf{P}^{-1}\,(\mathbf{P'})^{-1} = (\mathbf{P'P})^{-1}$$

i.e., $$\mathbf{P'P} = \psi^{-1}$$

Returning to the classical linear model and premultiplying it with matrix $\mathbf{P}$:

$$\mathbf{Y} = \mathbf{X}\beta + \mathbf{U}$$
$$\mathbf{PY} = \mathbf{PX}\beta + \mathbf{PU}$$
$$\mathbf{Y_*} = \mathbf{X_*}\beta + \mathbf{U_*} \qquad \qquad ...(9.14)$$

where;
$$\mathbf{Y_*} = \mathbf{PY}$$
$$\mathbf{X_*} = \mathbf{PX}$$
$$\mathbf{U_*} = \mathbf{PU}$$

The residual property of zero mean and zero covariance is restored by transforming the model in the way as described in (9.14). Let us examine it:

$$E\left(\mathbf{U_*}\,\mathbf{U_*}'\right) = E(\mathbf{PU}\;\mathbf{U}\;\mathbf{P}')$$
$$= \mathbf{P}E\left(\mathbf{U}\;\mathbf{U}'\right)\mathbf{P}'$$
$$= \sigma^2\mathbf{P}\psi\mathbf{P}'$$
$$= \sigma^2\mathbf{I}_n \qquad \qquad \textit{(using the above stated theorem)}$$

Since (9.14) obeys all the classical assumptions now, application of OLS procedure yields BLU parameters estimates.

Applying OLS to (9.14), the generalized least squares (GLS) estimator shall be given by:

$$\hat{\mathbf{b}} = (\mathbf{X_*'X_*})^{-1}\mathbf{X_*'}\,\mathbf{Y_*}$$

On substituting for $\mathbf{X_*}$ and $\mathbf{Y_*}$

$$\hat{\mathbf{b}} = [(\mathbf{PX})'\mathbf{PX}]^{-1}\,(\mathbf{PX})'\mathbf{PY}$$
$$\hat{\mathbf{b}} = (\mathbf{X'P'PX})^{-1}\,\mathbf{X'P'PY}$$
$$\hat{\mathbf{b}} = (\mathbf{X'}\Psi^{-1}\mathbf{X})^{-1}\,\mathbf{X'}\psi^{-1}\mathbf{Y} \qquad \qquad ...(9.15)$$

ψ^{-1} is a known $(n \times n)$ matrix.

Testing Gauss-Markov Least Squares Theorem in Generalized Case:

(i) Unbiasedness: $E(\hat{\mathbf{b}}) = E(\mathbf{X'}\psi^{-1}\mathbf{X})^{-1}\,\mathbf{X'}\Psi^{-1}\mathbf{Y}]$
$$= E(\mathbf{X'}\Psi^{-1}\mathbf{X})^{-1}\,\mathbf{X'}\Psi^{-1}\,(\mathbf{X}\beta + \mathbf{U})]$$
$$= \beta + E[(\mathbf{X'}\psi^{-1}\mathbf{X})^{-1}\,\mathbf{X'}\Psi^{-1}\mathbf{U}] \qquad ...(9.16)$$
$$= \beta$$

$\hat{\mathbf{b}}$ GLS is an unbiased estimators

(ii) Variance: $E[(\hat{\mathbf{b}} - \beta)\,(\hat{\mathbf{b}} - \beta)']$
$$= E(\mathbf{X'}\Psi^{-1}\mathbf{X})^{-1}\,\mathbf{X'}\psi^{-1}\,\mathbf{U}\mathbf{U}'\psi^{-1}\mathbf{X}(\mathbf{X'}\psi^{-1}\mathbf{X})^{-1}]$$
$$\qquad \qquad ...(bv\ 9.16)$$

$$= (X'\psi^{-1}X)^{-1}X'\psi^{-1} \; E(UU')\psi^{-1}X(X'\psi^{-1}X)^{-1}$$
$$= \sigma^2(X'\psi^{-1}X)^{-1} \qquad\qquad \ldots(9.17)$$

(iii) Theorem: *Aitken's generalized Gauss Markov least squares theorem* states that in the generalised least squares regression model, the GLS estimator (**b**) is given by:

$$\hat{b} = (X'\psi^{-1}X)^{-1}X'\psi^{-1}Y, \text{ and}$$

whose variance covariance matrix is:

$$\Sigma_{\hat{b}\hat{b}} = \sigma^2(X'\Psi^{-1}X)^{-1}$$

It is worth noting here that the GLS results (9.15) and (9.17) immediately coincide with those of OLS when ψ is an identity matrix.

It can also be proved that OLS estimator would have lost the minimum variance property, had we applied OLS procedure in the presence of heteroscedastic and autocorrelated residuals.

Variance of $\hat{\beta}$ in case of OLS is defined:

$$\text{Var } (\hat{\beta}) = E[(\hat{\beta} - \beta) \, (\hat{\beta} - \beta)']$$
$$= E\{X'X)^{-1} \; X'UU'X(X'X)^{-1}]$$
$$E(UU') \neq \sigma^2 I_n \text{ in the present case, but}$$
$$= \sigma^2\psi.$$

Therefore, $\quad$ Var $(\beta) = \sigma^2(X'X)^{-1}X'\psi X(X'X)^{-1}$ while by (9.17)

we have $\quad$ Var $(\hat{b}) = \sigma^2(X'\psi^{-1}X)^{-1}$

Therefore,

$$\text{Var } (\hat{\beta}) - \text{Var}\,(\hat{b}) = \sigma^2(X'X)^{-1}X'\psi X(X'X)^{-1} - \sigma^2 \; (X'\psi^{-1}X)^{-1}$$
$$= \sigma^2(X'X)^{-1}X\psi X(X'X)^{-1}$$
$$\quad - \sigma^2(X'\psi^{-1}X)^{-1}X'\psi^{-1}\psi\psi^{-1}X(X'\psi^{-1}X)^{-1}$$
$$= \sigma^2[(X'X)^{-1}X' - X'(\psi^{-1}X)^{-1}\,X'\psi^{-1}]$$
$$\quad \times \psi \; [X'X)^{-1}X' - (X'\psi^{-1}X)^{-1}X'\psi^{-1}]'$$
$$= \sigma^2(A\psi^{-1}A')$$

where $\qquad\qquad A = (X'X)^{-1}X' - (X'\psi^{-1}X)^{-1}X'\psi^{-1}.$

Since ψ is a positive definite matrix, $A\psi A'$ is a non-negative definite. The variance-covariance of $\hat{\beta}$, therefore, exceeds that of the GLS estimator by the positive definite matrix $A\psi A'$.

9.3.1 Estimation of ψ and σ^2

In order to apply GLS estimation procedure, we need two things: *first*, knowledge of ψ matrix and *second*, estimate of σ^2 to perform various statistical tests on the estimated coefficients.

(A) *Knowledge of ψ matrix:* In applied econometric work, ψ matrix is seldom known or observable, and when ψ is unknown the GLS estimator **b** is no longer a feasible alternative to the least squares estimator $\beta = (X'X)^{-1} X'Y$. The use of GLS estimation requires construction of an appropriate or estimation of such a matrix.

Let us consider few special cases of matrix ψ.

(1) If $\phi = \sigma^2 \psi = \sigma^2 I$; the generalized model reduces to the classical model.

(2) If $\phi = \sigma^2 \psi =$
$$\begin{bmatrix} \sigma_1^2 & 0 & \cdots & 0 \\ 0 & \sigma_2^2 & \cdots & 0 \\ \vdots & \vdots & & \vdots \\ 0 & 0 & \cdots & \sigma_n^2 \end{bmatrix}$$ where

σ_i^2 is the variance of the ith stochastic disturbance term; $i = 1, 2, \ldots n$, the inverse ψ used in GLS estimator is then (omitting σ^2, which cancels in (9.15)),

$$\psi^{-1} = \begin{bmatrix} \dfrac{1}{\sigma_1^2} & 0 & \cdots & 0 \\ 0 & \dfrac{1}{\sigma_2^2} & \cdots & 0 \\ \cdots & \cdots & \cdots & \cdots \\ \cdots & \cdots & \cdots & \cdots \\ 0 & \cdots & \cdots & \dfrac{1}{\sigma_n^2} \end{bmatrix}$$

That is to say the Aitken's GLS estimator is the same as the BLU estimator developed for the heteroscedastic model.

(3) Finally, if $\phi = \sigma^2 \psi$

$$= \sigma^2 \begin{bmatrix} 1 & \rho & \rho^2 & \cdots & \rho^{n-1} \\ \rho & 1 & \rho & \cdots & \rho^{n-2} \\ \cdots & \cdots & \cdots & \cdots & \cdots \\ \cdots & \cdots & \cdots & \cdots & \cdots \\ \rho^{n-1} & \rho^{n-2} & \rho^{n-3} & \cdots & 1 \end{bmatrix}$$

That is if the disturbance follows a first-order autoregressive scheme, we obtain;

$$\psi^{-1} = \frac{1}{1-\rho^2} \begin{bmatrix} 1 & (-)\rho & 0 & \dots & 0 \\ (-)\rho & (1+\rho^2) & (-)\rho & \dots & 0 \\ \dots & \dots & \dots & \dots & \dots \\ \dots & \dots & \dots & \dots & \dots \\ 0 & 0 & 0 & \dots & (-)\rho \end{bmatrix}$$

In this case GLS estimator is the same as the BLU estimator derived for the regression model with autogressive disturbances.

In the three cases discussed above, a simple structure of the ψ matrix has been assumed so that it is possible to apply GLS procedure and obtain a generalized estimator.

The model is called '*Generalized*' not only because it is applicable in these three special cases but (as we shall observe below) it can be applied under special residual structures.

Above three cases may not exist in certain situations. In that case we find consistent estimator of ψ first so that (9.15) yields:

$$\hat{b} = (X'\hat{\psi}^{-1}X)^{-1} X'\hat{\psi}^{-1} Y \qquad \dots(9.18)$$

(9.18) estimator is called an *estimated generalized least squares* estimator or a feasible generalized least squares estimator.

Since ψ matrix involves only two unknown parameters, σ^2 and ρ, these may be readily estimated on the basis of the pattern of the residuals from the classical regression which can be suggestive as to the nature of the nonsphericalness of the disturbances.

(B) *Estimator of σ^2:* An unbiased estimator of σ^2 is obtainable by an argument parallel to that used in the classical case.

In classical linear model, an unbiased estimator of σ^2 is given by:

$$\hat{\sigma}^2 = \left(\frac{e'e}{n-k}\right) = \frac{(Y-X\beta)'(Y-X\beta)}{n-k}$$

In GLS, $\qquad \hat{\sigma}^2_g = \left(\frac{e'_* e_*}{n-k}\right)$

$$\hat{\sigma}^2_g = \frac{(Y_* - X_* b)'(Y_* - X_* b)}{n-k}$$

$$\hat{\sigma}^2_g = \frac{1}{n-k}(Pe)'(Pe)$$

$$\hat{\sigma}_g^2 = \frac{1}{n-k} [e' \ \psi^{-1} e] \qquad \qquad ...(9.19)$$

$$\left[\because \ P'P = \psi^{-1} \right]$$

GLS has various applications in the estimation of regression coefficients under various situations. We have examined its application in the spherical and nonspherical situations in the residuals of the model. One of the most important applications of GLS occurs in the estimation of *Seemingly unrelated equations*.

The seemingly unrelated type of equations are often observed while modeling the business or economic phenomenon. As the term suggests, such type of equations though appear unrelated outwardly, they are infact inter-related and hence require a more sophisticated estimation technique.

ASSIGNMENTS

1. Consider the model:
$$Y_t = \alpha + \beta X_t + U_t$$
$$U_t = \rho U_{t-1} + v_t$$

   Show that our usual formula for the variance of $\hat{\beta}$, namely; $Var\ (\beta) = \frac{\sigma_u^2}{\Sigma x_i^2}$ no longer holds.

2. Consider the model:
$$I_t = \alpha_0 + \alpha_1 X_t + \alpha_2 Y_t + U_t$$
$$U_t = \rho_1 U_{t-1} + \rho_2 U_{t-2} + v_t,$$

   where I = investment, X_i = change in income, and Y_t = interest rate.
   Assume that v_t is independent of all the regressors, is not autocorrelated, has a mean of zero, and a constant variance. Outline a procedure for obtaining estimates of α_0, α_1 and α_2 that accounts for the autocorrelation when values ρ_1 and ρ_2 are assumed $\hat{\rho}_1$ and $\hat{\rho}_2$ respectively.

3. Suppose we have the following model and initial conditions:
$$Y_t = 20 + X_t + U_t$$
$$U_t = U_{t-2} + v_t,\ U_{t-1} = 5,\ U_0 = 6 \text{ and } v_t = 0$$

   for all observations.
   Assume that X_t takes the values from 1 to 20.
   (a) generate an artificial sample of 20 observations.
   (b) use this generated sample to estimate $\hat{\alpha}$ and $\hat{\beta}$ by OLS and compute *d*-statistic to test for first order autocorrelation, and
   (c) estimate ρ and apply OLS to the transformed data.

4. Generate a sample of ten Y values from the model:

$$Y_t = 3.0 + 0.5X_t + U_t$$

where, $U_t = 0.9\ U_{t-1} + v_t$. Assume $U_0 = 10$ and that X_t takes the values from 1 to 20; $v_t = 0$.

5. Given a sample of 50 observations and four explanatory varables, what can you say about the existence of autocorrelation if following values of d-statistic(s) are obtained.

    (i) $d = 1.05$, (ii) $d = 3.97$, (iii) $d = 2.50$, and (iv) $d = 1.40$

6. The data of the following table are the OLS residuals of a consumption function:

   $\hat{C}_t = -3.02 + 0.93Y_t$. Show that d-statistic = 1.42. Can you test for existence of autocorrelation?

Years $\rightarrow$	1954	1955	1956	1957	1958	1959	1960	1961	1962	1963	1964	1965
e_t $\rightarrow$	0.6	1.9	−1.8	−2.7	−2.9	1.4	3.3	0.3	0.8	2.3	−1.4	−1.1

7. Based on the Durbin-Watson d-statistic, how would you distinguish 'pure' autocorrelation from specification bias?

8. Give reasons for the following:

    (i) If negative autocorrelation exists, null hypothesis H_0: $\rho = 0$ would be rejected on the average using the usual OLS estimates and a t-test.

    (ii) The upper limit of D–W statistic is 4 when perfect negative autocorrelation exists. Its lower limit is zero.

    (iii) $\rho = \dfrac{1}{2}(2 - d)$; ρ is estimate of first order autoregressive coefficient and d is d-statistic.

9. Examine whether the following statements are true or false.

    (i) Least squares technique when applied to time-series data usually yields biased estimates because many economic time-series are autocorrelated.

    (ii) The D-W test for serial correlation is not applicable if the residuals are hetroscedastic.

    (iii) The D-W test is not applicable in distributed lag models.

    (iv) If one applies OLS to estimate the parameters of a regression equation with autocorrelated errors, one will obtain unbiased estimators but one is likely to obtain a serious underestimate of their sampling errors.

    (v) Hetroscedasticity is due to mis-specification of explanatory variables in the model and not due to mis-specification of the distribution of U.

10. Summarise and compare critically the tests and corrective procedure associated with hetroscedasticity.

11. Given that: $Y_i = \alpha + \beta\ X_i + U_i$ with $E(U_i^2) = k^2X_i^2$; prove that OLS estimates of α and β possess greater variance than OLS estimates of the transformed version of the original model.

12. Consider the model: $Y_i + \alpha + U_i$ where $U_i \sim N(0, \sigma^2X_i)$, $E(U_i\ U_j) = 0$, $i \neq j$ and X_i is non-stochastic. Find best linear ubiased estimator of α and its variance.

13. What is the problem of hetroscedasticity of disturbances? How does it arise? Discuss with illustrations.

14. Discuss the most likely pattern of hetroscedasticity in the following cases:

    (i) A food expenditure function is to be estimated from a cross-section sample of family expenditures:

    $E_i = \alpha_0 + \beta_1 Y_i + \beta_2 S_i + U_i$

    E = Food expenditure, Y = Income, S = Size of family.

    (ii) A short-run production function of a firm is to be estimated.

    $X_t = \alpha + \beta L_t + U_t$

    X = Output and L = Labour input

    (iii) A long-run cost function is to be estimated from a cross-section sample of firms:

    $C_i = \alpha + \beta X_i + U_i$

    C_i = total cost and X_i = total output of ith firm.

15. When are disturbance terms in the Classical model said to be Non-spherical? Describe such an economic behaviour that can cause Non-sphericalness in the disturbances. Discuss on appropriate model when the distrubances are Non-spherical in nature.

10

Miscellaneous Problems in Regression Analysis

In the earlier Chapter our purpose was to examine the impact of violation of two important assumptions of residual terms on OLS technique of estimation of general linear regression model. Presently, our goal is to study how mis-specification, lagged values of explanatory variables and inter-relationship among the regressors or explanatory variables create problems in applied econometrics.

Of the above three problems, last one is one of the five assumptions of classical linear regression model. It is that there has to be no exact linear relations among the observed values of explanatory variables. Violation of this assumption breaks down the least squares estimation procedure.

10.1 MULTICOLLINEARITY: MEANING AND PROBLEM

The term multicollinearity is used to denote the presence of linear relationship among explanatory variables of the regression model.

When the explanatory variables are perfectly correlated we speak of perfect multicollinearity and use the word multicollinearity* to mean that there is high degree of collinearity between the explanatory variables. When the explanatory variables are perfectly correlated, the method of least squares breaks down. On the other hand, the variables are said to be *orthogonal* if they are uncorrelated. It is then a case of absence of multicollinearity. In practice neither of these extreme cases is often met. In most cases there is some degree of intercorrelation among the explanatory variables due to interdependence of many economic variables over time.

Before discussing problem of multicollinearity, following three points should be understood clearly.

1. Multicollinearity is essentially a sample phenomenon.

When we assume a theoretical or population regression model, we believe that all explanatory variables included in the model have independent

---

* The term 'Multicollinearity' was first introduced by R. Frisch in his book, 'Statistical Confluence Analysis by Means of Complete Regression System' in 1934.

influence on the dependent variable Y. But it may happen that in any given sample that is used to test our population regression model some or all explanatory variables are so highly correlated that we can not isolate their individual influence on Y. In other words our sample does not stand the basic assumption of independency among the explanatory variables included.

2. Secondly, multicollinearity is a question of degree and not of kind.

That is to say, it is not a matter of concern whether the correlation among the explanatory variables is negative or positive; what matters is the existence of correlation (and its extent or degree) among the explanatory variables.

3. Thirdly, it is to be noted that multicollinearity is the problem that arises with the presence of linear relationship among the explanatory variables. It rules out the non-linear relationships among them.

For example, consider the following regression model:

$$Y_i = \alpha + \beta_1 X_i + \beta_2 X_i^2 + \beta_3 X_i^3 + U_i,$$

where; Y = Total cost and X = Output.

The variables X_i^2 (output squared) and X_i^3 (output cube) are obviously functionally related to X_i (output), but the relationship is nonlinear. Therefore, in such a model the assumption of no multicollinearity is not violated. As a matter of fact to depict the U-shaped cost curves of economic theory, the model has to be in this form.

Problem of multicollinearity may arise for various reasons.

Firstly, it is due to an inherent characteristic of many economic variables to move together over time. Economic magnitudes are influenced by the same factors. Therefore, once such influencing factors become operative, all the variables tend to change in the one direction. For example: income, saving, investment, consumption, prices and employment tend to rise in the periods of boom and decrease in the periods of depression. In time series data, therefore, growth and trend factors are the main causes of multicollinearity.

Secondly, multicollinearity arises due to use of lagged values of certain explanatory variables in the regression model. To estimate the consumption function, for example, past income may also be included as a separate explanatory variable along with the present income; and it is very natural to observe the correlation between the past and present incomes. Hence the problem of multicollinearity is generally observed in distributed lag models.

Thus, considering the very basic nature of the data, multicollinearity is expected to appear in most economic relationships. We are, therefore, not concerned whether or not multicollinearity exists, but to what extent it exists in the sample study. Although, as reasoned above, multicollinearity is usually a serious problem in time series data, it is quite frequent in cross-section data also.

Presence of multicollinearity affects the least squares estimators and renders them inefficient. The problem of multicollinearity must therefore, be regarded as a 'black mark' that reduces the confidence in conventional tests of significance of least squares estimators.

10.1.1 Consequences of Multicollinearity

If there exists a perfect correlation between the two explanatory variables (it is then a case of perfect multicollinearity), then:

(i) least squares estimators are indeterminate, and
(ii) the variances and covariances of the estimators become infinitely large.

It may be proved as follows:

(i) Suppose $X_1 = a(X_2)$ (a is an arbitrary constant) and it is required to estimate the parameters of the equation:

$$Y = \alpha + \beta_1 X_1 + \beta_2 X_2 + U$$

Under these circumstances, all the variations in Y come ultimately from X_1, X_2 and U. When we collect sample data on Y, X_1 and X_2 and try to run multiple regression, we find that all sample points lie in a single plane, perpendicular to the plane of X_1 and X_2.

The OLS formulae for the estimation of $\hat{\beta}_1$ and $\hat{\beta}_2$ are:

$$\hat{\beta}_1 = \frac{\Sigma x_1 y \Sigma x_2^2 - \Sigma x_2 y \, \Sigma x_1 x_2}{\Sigma x_1^2 \, \Sigma x_2^2 - (\Sigma x_1 x_2)^2} \quad \text{and}$$

$$\hat{\beta}_2 = \frac{\Sigma x_2 y \Sigma x_1^2 - \Sigma x_1 y \Sigma x_1 x_2}{\Sigma x_1^2 \Sigma x_2^2 - (\Sigma x_1 x_2)^2}$$

Substituting aX_2 for X_1,

$$\hat{\beta}_1 = \frac{a \Sigma x_2 y \Sigma x_2^2 - a \Sigma x_2 y \Sigma x_2^2}{a^2 \Sigma x_2^2 \Sigma x_2^2 - a^2 (\Sigma x_2^2)^2} = \frac{0}{0}$$

and,

$$\hat{\beta}_2 = \frac{a \Sigma x_2 y \Sigma x_2^2 - a \Sigma x_2 y \Sigma x_2^2}{a^2 \Sigma x_2^2 \, \Sigma x_2^2 - a^2 (\Sigma x_2^2)^2} = \frac{0}{0}$$

Thus the parameters are indeterminate.

In the matrix notation, in two explanatory variables case,

$$X'X = \begin{bmatrix} \Sigma x_1^2 & \Sigma x_1 x_2 \\ \Sigma x_1 x_2 & \Sigma x_2^2 \end{bmatrix}$$

To obtain $\hat{\beta}$ vector, we need inversion $(\mathbf{X'X})$. Since $|\mathbf{X'X}|$ is zero it is impossible to form $(\mathbf{X'X})^{-1}$.

Substituting αX_2 for X_1 in $|\mathbf{X'X}|$, we obtain:

$$|\mathbf{X'X}| = \begin{vmatrix} a^2 \Sigma x_2^2 & a\Sigma x_2^2 \\ a\Sigma x_2^2 & \Sigma x_2^2 \end{vmatrix} = (\Sigma x_2^2)^2 \begin{vmatrix} a^2 & a \\ a & 1 \end{vmatrix} = 0$$

(ii) The formulae for the variances of $\hat{\beta}_1$ and $\hat{\beta}_2$ are:

$$\text{Var } (\hat{\beta}_1) = \frac{\sigma_u^2 \Sigma x_2^2}{\Sigma x_1^2 \Sigma x_2^2 - (\Sigma x_1 x_2)^2} \quad \text{and}$$

$$\text{Var } (\hat{\beta}_2) = \frac{\sigma_u^2 \Sigma x_1^2}{\Sigma x_1^2 \Sigma x_2^2 - (\Sigma x_1 x_2)^2}$$

Substituting aX_2 for X_1, we obtain:

$$\text{Var } (\hat{\beta}_1) = \frac{\sigma_u^2 \Sigma x_2^2}{a^2 \Sigma x_2^2 \Sigma x_2^2 - a^2 (\Sigma x_2^2)^2} = \frac{\sigma_u^2 \Sigma x_2^2}{0} = \infty$$

$$\text{Var } (\hat{\beta}_2) = \frac{a^2 \sigma_u^2 \Sigma x_1^2}{a^2 \Sigma x_2^2 \Sigma x_2^2 - a^2 (\Sigma x_2^2)^2} = \frac{a^2 \sigma_u^2 \Sigma x_1^2}{0} = \infty$$

Unless σ_u^2 is also zero, the variances of β's become infinite. The same can be observed in the matrix notation.

The above case is that of perfect multicollinearity, and it is observed that it is not possible to estimate the separate influence of X_1 and X_2. In fact, estimating method breakdowns. But such an extreme case is not very frequent in practical applications. Most data exhibit only some multicollinearity. We study such cases.

In the section 8.2, formulae of regression coefficients and their variances in terms of simple correlation coefficients is as follows.

In the model: $Y = \alpha + \beta_1 X_1 + \beta_2 X_2 + U;$

$$\hat{\beta}_1 = \frac{\hat{\beta}_{11} - \hat{\beta}_{21}\hat{\beta}_{12}}{(1 - r_{12}^2)}, \text{ and Var } (\hat{\beta}_1) = \frac{\sigma_u^2}{\Sigma x_1^2 (1 - r_{12}^2)}$$

$$\hat{\beta}_2 = \frac{\hat{\beta}_{11} - \hat{\beta}_{12}\hat{\beta}_{11}}{(1 - r_{12}^2)}, \text{ and Var } (\hat{\beta}_2) = \frac{\sigma_u^2}{\Sigma x_2^2 (1 - r_{12}^2)}$$

$$\text{Cov } (\hat{\beta}_1, \hat{\beta}_2) = \frac{-\sigma_u^2 r_{12}}{\sqrt{\Sigma x_1^2} \sqrt{\Sigma x_2^2} (1 - r_{12}^2)};$$

where r_{12} is the coefficient of correlation between X_1 and X_2.

Clearly, therefore, as r_{12} tends to $+1$ or -1, $\hat{\beta}_1$, $\hat{\beta}_2$, Var $(\hat{\beta}_1)$ and Var $(\hat{\beta}_2)$ tend to infinity.

The above result also implies that higher the value r_{12}^2 (i.e., high degree of multicollinearity), the larger the variances and the covariances of $\hat{\beta}_1$ and $\hat{\beta}_2$. Nevertheless we can always obtain a determinate solution for the least squares estimators so long as there is no such a *one to one* relation between explanatory variables.

It is, therefore, concluded that a high degree of multicollinearity renders the regression coefficients highly imprecise; imprecise in the sense that multicollinearity gives rise to very large variances. But appearance of large variances should not be regarded as an *acid-test* of multicollinearity. Large variances of the regression coefficients may exist even if there is no multicollinearity at all, but because the explanatory variables have a small dispersion or because σ_u^2 itself is large (see Section 6.6). Thus if we want to put the whole blame on multicollinearity, we should be able to explain it by measuring its degree. Here also, it is easier to measure the degree of multicollinearity in case of two explanatory variables, but when there are more than two explanatory variables, measurement of degree of multicollinearity becomes more complicated. Not only this, but even though the correlation between the independent variables is nearly unity, the variation in the independent variable, i.e., Σx_1^2 or Σx_2^2 may offset the term $(1 - r_{12}^2)$ and make the theoretical (calculated) variances very small.

To summarize, therefore, if multicollinearity is severe (but not perfect), then following consequences ensue:

1. Although OLS estimators may be obtainable, their standard errors tend to be large as the degree of correlation between the variables increase.
2. Because of large standard errors the probability of accepting a false hypothesis (i.e., type error II) increases.
3. The OLS estimates and their standard errors become very sensitive to slightest change in the sample data.
4. If multicollinearity is high, one may obtain a high R^2 but none of or very few estimated regression coefficients are statistically significant. (Refer Section 8.5.4 of Chapter 8)

10.1.2 Tests For Detecting Multicollinearity

(A) *Test based on Frisch's Confluence Analysis*: A recognisable set of symptoms for the existence of multicollinearity on which one can rely are:

(a) Coefficient of determination (R^2)
(b) Partial correlation coefficients ($r_{x_i x_j}$'s), and
(c) Standard errors of the regression parameters.

None of these symptoms by itself is a satisfactory indicator of multi-collinearity, because:

(i) large standard errors may arise for various reasons and not only because of the presence of linear relationships among explanatory variables.

(ii) a high $r_{x_i x_j}$ is only a sufficient but not a necessary condition (i.e., adequate criterion) for the existence of multicollinearity; and

(iii) R^2 may be high and yet the estimates may not be significant and imprecise.

However, a combination of all these criteria should help the detection of multicollinearity; as has been suggested in the Frisch's Test. In this test, it is required to estimate all possible regressions between two variables which are present in a relationship, taking each variable successively as the dependent variable and considering all possible regressions of each variable on all others which are gradually introduced into the analysis.

For example, if the regression model is assumed to be: $Y = f(X_1, X_2, X_3)$, then according to this test, it is required to consider following relations for the different regressions:

$$X_1 = f(X_2); \qquad X_2 = f(X_1); \qquad X_3 = f(X_1)$$
$$X_1 = f(X_3); \qquad X_2 = f(X_3); \qquad X_3 = f(X_2)$$
$$X_1 = f(X_2, X_3); \qquad X_2 = f(X_1, X_3); \qquad X_3 = f(X_1, X_2)$$

As may be observed, this test therefore involves many regressions and computations so that comparison of the results become more complicated.

This test is also used in another form generally known as *Stepwise regression.*

In deciding on the 'best' set of explanatory variables for a regression model, the method of stepwise regression is often followed. In this method one proceeds either by introducing the X variables one at a time (stepwise forward regression) or by including all possible X variables in one multiple regression model and rejecting them one at a time (stepwise backward regression). The decision to add or drop a variable is usually made on the basis of the contribution of that variable to the Error Sum of Squares as judged by the F-test.

(B) *Test based on Simple and Partial Correlations:* More often high simple correlation coefficient between the values of two regressors along with high (R^2) are considered as the indication of presence of collinearity among the variables. A commonly used rule is that if the correlation coefficient between the two regressors is greater than 0.8 or 0.9 (and also this value is greater than R^2), then multicollinearity is a serious problem.

In fact, high simple correlations are first sufficient but not necessary conditions for the existence of multicollinearity because it can exist even though the simple correlation are comparatively low.

Another test of existence of multicollinearity is when (R^2) for equation is high but partial r^2's are low. For instance in case of three regressors, $R^2_{y \cdot x_1 x_2 x_3}$ can be very high but $r^2_{y x_1 \cdot x_2 x_3}$, $r^2_{y x_2 \cdot x_1 x_3}$ and $r^2_{y x_3 \cdot x_2 x_3}$ could all be low. This will happen if x_1, x_2 and x_3 are highly intercorrelated. Though this criterion is often used to decide whether collinearity is serious or not, but at times reverse is also observed. Sometimes it is seen that even if multicollinearity is serious, partial r^2's are not low (with high R^2).

Finally, a rule of thumb in judging when multicollinearity is harmful, is suggested by econometrician L.R. Klein.

According to him, "Intercorrelation of variables is not necessary a problem unless it is high relative to the overall degree of multiple correlation". In other words, in case of three explanatory variables by Klein's rule, multicollinearity would be regarded as a problem only if $R^2_{y \cdot x_1 x_2 x_3}$ is less than R^2_i ($R^2_i = R^2_{x_1 \cdot x_2 x_3}, R^2_{x_2 \cdot x_1 x_3}$ and $R^2_{x_3 \cdot x_2 x_3}$). Here 'intercorrelations' is interpreted as multiple correlation of each explanatory variable with the other explanatory variables.

All the above criteria are simple guides to detecting whether or not multicollinearity is present or whether it is severe. What criterion to apply in particular situation depends largely on the nature of problem and one's own judgement.

(C) *The Farrar-Glauber Test:* Since the problem of multicollinearity is likely to be detected through Multiple, Partial and Simple Correlation Coefficients among the explanatory variables, Farrar and Glauber suggested testing of all the three intercorrelations by formulation of three hypothesis and testing them by three different statistic(s).

(i) Testing overall orthogonality among the explanatory variables included in the model through χ^2 (Chi-Square) test.

This is attempted by testing the statistical significance of the value of $|X'X|$ through the χ^2 statistic.

The elements of $X'X$ are the standardised values of explanatory variables rather than their original values; that is, they have mean of zero and standard deviation of unity.

The standardised form of $|X'X|$ is obtained in the following manner.

Consider model of three explanatory variables. $|X'X|$ in deviation form shall be:

$$|X'X| = \begin{vmatrix} \Sigma x_1^2 & \Sigma x_1 x_2 & \Sigma x_1 x_3 \\ \Sigma x_2 x_1 & \Sigma x_2^2 & \Sigma x_2 x_3 \\ \Sigma x_3 x_1 & \Sigma x_3 x_2 & \Sigma x_3^2 \end{vmatrix}$$

On dividing each element of $\Sigma x_i x_j$ by $\sqrt{\Sigma x_i^2} \sqrt{\Sigma x_j^2}$, $|X'X|$ gets transformed into its standardised format.

$$\begin{vmatrix} \dfrac{\Sigma x_i^2}{\sqrt{\Sigma(x_1^2)^2}} & \dfrac{\Sigma x_1 x_2}{\sqrt{\Sigma x_1^2}\sqrt{\Sigma x_2^2}} & \dfrac{\Sigma x_1 x_3}{\sqrt{\Sigma x_1^2}\sqrt{\Sigma x_3^2}} \\[3mm] \dfrac{\Sigma x_2 x_1}{\sqrt{\Sigma x_2^2}\sqrt{\Sigma x_1^2}} & \dfrac{\Sigma x_2^2}{\sqrt{\Sigma(x_2^2)^2}} & \dfrac{\Sigma x_2 x_3}{\sqrt{\Sigma x_2^2}\sqrt{\Sigma x_3^2}} \\[3mm] \dfrac{\Sigma x_3 x_1}{\sqrt{\Sigma x_3^2}\sqrt{\Sigma x_1^2}} & \dfrac{\Sigma x_3 x_2}{\sqrt{\Sigma x_3^2}\sqrt{\Sigma x_2^2}} & \dfrac{\Sigma x_3^2}{\sqrt{(\Sigma x_3^2)^2}} \end{vmatrix}$$

Each element of $|X'X|$ in the above form now depicts partial correlation coefficients, that is,

$$\begin{array}{c} |X'X| \\ \text{(in standardised form)} \end{array} = \begin{vmatrix} r_{11} & r_{12} & r_{13} \\ r_{21} & r_{22} & r_{23} \\ r_{31} & r_{32} & r_{33} \end{vmatrix} = \begin{vmatrix} 1 & r_{12} & r_{13} \\ r_{21} & 1 & r_{23} \\ r_{31} & r_{32} & 1 \end{vmatrix}$$

In the above case, the value of determinant $|X'X|$ falls in the interval of $[0,1]$. If the determinant $(X'X) = 0$ then one or more exact linear dependence exist among the column of X. If det. $(X'X) = 1$, then the columns of X are orthogonal.

Given these facts, Glauber and Farrar (1967)* suggested χ^2 (Chi-square) test in the following manner:

H_0 : X's are orthogonal

H_1: X's are not orthogonal

value of χ^2 (Chi-square) $= (-)\left[(n-1) - \dfrac{1}{6}(2k + 5) \right] \log_e |X'X|$. The empirical value of χ^2 is then tested with $[1/2\ k\ (k-1)]$ degrees of freedom.

(ii) Testing Multiple Correlation Coefficients through *F*-test.

This is attempted by formulating all possible regressions when each explanatory variable in turn is regressed on the remaining explanatory variables.

In case of three explanatory variables model:

$R_{1.23}^2, R_{2.13}^2$ and $R_{3.21}^2$ are estimated and then tested for their significance through *F*-test.

Orthogonality is inversely proportional to the R^2's values. Zero-value of R^2's will depict perfectly orthogonal explanatory variables, while significant value of multiple correlation coeff. depicts existence of multicollinearity.

---

* Farrar, D.E., and Glauber, R.R. (1967); 'Multicollinearity in Regression Analysis: The Problem Revisited'. The Review of Economics and Statistics, 49: 22–107.

For testing hypothesis, the procedure is as follows:

$$F^* = \frac{R^2_{x_i \cdot x_1 x_2 \ldots x_k}/(k-1)}{(1 - R^2_{x_i \cdot x_1 x_2 \ldots x_k})/(n-k)}$$

In case of three explanatory variables, three F-ratios shall be:

$$F_1^* = \frac{R^2_{x_1 \cdot x_2 x_3}/(k-1)}{(1 - R^2_{x_1 \cdot x_2 x_3})/(n-k)} ;$$

$$F_2^* = \frac{R^2_{x_2 \cdot x_1 x_3}/(k-1)}{(1 - R^2_{x_2 \cdot x_1 x_3})/(n-k)}$$

and

$$F_3^* = \frac{R^2_{x_3 \cdot x_1 x_2}/(k-1)}{(1 - R^2_{x_3 \cdot x_1 x_2})/(n-k)}$$

In case $\mathbf{F}^* > \mathbf{F}$ (tabulated value) on $[(k-1), (n-k)]$ degrees of freedom, it will be inferred that the explanatory variable involved in that R^2 is most affected by multicollinearity.

(iii) Testing Partial Correlation Coefficient Through t-test

In this case all the possible partial correlation coefficients are tested by describing the Null-hypothesis in the following way:

$$H_0 : r^2_{x_i x_j \cdot x_1 x_2 x_3 \ldots x_k} = 0$$

$$H_A : r^2_{x_i x_j \cdot x_1 x_2 x_3 \ldots x_k} \neq 0.$$

In three variable models:

$$r^2_{x_1 x_2 \cdot x_3} = \frac{(r_{12} - r_{13} r_{23})^2}{(1 - r_{23}^2)(1 - r_{13}^2)}$$

$$r^2_{x_1 x_3 \cdot x_2} = \frac{(r_{13} - r_{12} r_{23}^2)}{(1 - r_{23}^2)(1 - r_{12}^2)}, \text{ and}$$

$$r^2_{x_2 x_3 \cdot x_1} = \frac{(r_{23} - r_{12} r_{13})^2}{(1 - r_{13}^2)(1 - r_{12}^2)}$$

t^*-ratio is computed by:
$$t^* = \frac{(r^2_{x_i x_j \cdot x_1 x_2 \ldots x_k})\sqrt{(n-k)}}{\sqrt{(1 - r^2_{x_i x_j \cdot x_1 x_2 x_3 \ldots x_k})}}$$

If $t^* > t$ (tabulated), H_0 is rejected.

If $t^* < t$ (tabulated), H_0 is accepted, i.e., we accept that X_i and X_j are not the cause of multicollinearity (since $r_{x_i x_j}$ is not significant).

10.1.4 Corrective Measures

As has been mentioned above, it is rather more difficult to deal with models indicating the existence of multicollinearity than detecting the problem of multicollinearity. Different procedures have been suggested by econometicians depending on the severity of the problem, availability of other sources of data and the importance of variables which are found to be multicollinear in the model.

Some econometricians suggest that minor degree of multicollinearity can be tolerated although one should be a bit careful while interpreting the model under such conditions.

Others suggest the factors which show multicollinearity but are not so important in the model and such factors should be excluded from the model. Nevertheless by doing so, the desired character of the model may then get affected.

However, following corrective procedures are suggested if the problem of multicollinearity is found to be serious.

1. *Increase the Size of the Sample:* It is suggested that multicolinearity may be avoided or reduced if the size of the sample is increased. With the increase in the size of the sample, the covariances among the parameters get reduced. It is because these covariances are inversely related to the sample size. But we should remember that this will be true when intercorrelation happens to exist only in the sample but not in the population of the variables. If the variables are collinear in the population, the procedure of increasing the size of the sample will not help to reduce the multicollinearity.

2. *Introduce an Additional Equation in the Model:* The problem of multicollinearity may be overcome by expressing explicitly the relationship between multicollinear variables. Such relation in a form of an equation may then be added to original model. The addition of new equation transforms our single equation (original) model to simultaneous equation model. The reduced form method (which is usually applied for estimating simultaneous equation models) can then applied to avoid multicollinearity.

3. *Use extraneous Information:* Extraneous information is the information obtained from any other source outside the sample which is being used for the estimation. Extraneous information may be available from economic theory or from some empirical studies already conducted in the field in which we are interested. Three methods, through which extraneous information is utilised in order to deal with the problem of multicollinearity, are explained as follows:

(A) *Method of Using Prior Information:* Suppose that the correct specification of the model is: $Y = \alpha + \beta_1 X_1 + \beta_2 X_2 + U$; and also X_1 and X_2 are found to be collinear. If it is possible to gather information on the exact value of

β_1, or β_2 from extraneous source, we then make use of such information in estimating the influence of the remaining variable of the model in the following way.

Suppose, $\beta_2{}^*$ is known *a priori*, then

$$(Y - \beta_2{}^*X_2) = \alpha + \beta_1 X_1 + U$$

Applying OLS method; $\hat{\beta}_1 = \dfrac{\Sigma x_1(y - \beta_2{}^* x_2)}{\Sigma x_1^2} = \dfrac{\Sigma x_1 y - \beta_2^* \Sigma x_1 x_2}{\Sigma x_1^2}$

i.e., $\hat{\beta}_1$ is the OLS estimator of the slope of the regression of $(y - \beta_2^* x_2)$ on x_1.

Thus the estimating procedure described is equivalent to correcting dependent variable for the influence of those explanatory variables with known coefficients (from extraneous source of information) and regressing this residual on the remaining explanatory variables.

(B) *Method of Transformation of Variables:* This method is used when the relationship between certain parameters is known a *priori*. For instance, suppose that we want to estimate the production function expressed in the form: $Q = AL^\alpha K^\beta e^u$; where, $Q =$ quantity (of particular commodity) produced, $L =$ labour input and $K =$ the input of capital. It is required to estimate α and β. On logarithmic transformation, the function becomes:

$$Q^* = A^* + \alpha L^* + \beta K^* + U;$$

The asteriks indicate *logs* of the variables.

Suppose, it is observed that K and L move together so closely that it is difficult to separate the effect of changing quantities of labour inputs on output from the effect of variation in the use of capital. Again, let us also assume that on the basis of information from some other source, we have a solid evidence that the present industry is characterised by constant returns to scale. This implies that $\alpha + \beta = 1$. We can, therefore, on the basis of this information, substitute $\beta = (1 - \alpha)$ in the transformed function:

$$Q^* = A^* + \alpha L^* + (1 - \alpha)K^* + U$$

And thus we do away with one of the collinear explanatory variable. Estimation of such models have been dealt under sections 7.6 and 8.8. To conclude, therefore, a *priori* information (in a form of relationship or value of parameter) help us to tackle the multicollinearity by removing one of the variables creating trouble.

(C) *Method of Pooling Cross-section and Time-Series Data:* This method is, in fact, a special case of restricted least squares method; because in this method, at first, one of the parameters of the (original) function is estimated and then, this estimated parameter is used as a restriction on (original) function to estimate the remaining parameter (s).

Let us illustrate the procedure by taking a problem of estimation of a simple demand function of the form:

$$D_t = \alpha + \beta_1 p_t + \beta_2 Y_t + U_t$$

where D = demand for particular commodity, p = price of commodity, and Y = consumer's income.

Suppose further that time-series data is provided for the estimation of above demand function. But since in the time-series sample, price and income are generally found to be collinear; price and income effects (β_1 and β_2) cannot be separated. On the other it is not possible to obtain price effect (β_1) from the cross-section sample (because price structure is the same for all the consumers at a particular point of time). Under such conditions, it is suggested to use pooling technique which avoids to a certain extent the problems associated with both types of sample data.

Pooling technique can be outlined as follows:

In the first stage, cross-section sample is used to obtain an estimate of the income coefficient β_2^*. Next the influence of changes in income (Y) on D_t is eliminated by subtracting $\beta_2^* \, Y$ from the demand (D_t). This way a new variable: say Z is obtained:

$$Z_t = D_t - \beta_2^* Y_t$$

In the second stage, the new variable of first stage (Z) is regressed on price variable using time series sample to estimate price coefficient ($\hat{\beta}_1$):

$$Z_t = \alpha + \beta_1 p_1 + U_t.$$

On combining the results, the relationship becomes

$$\hat{D}_t = \alpha + \hat{\beta}_1 p_t + \beta_2 * Y_t$$

where $\hat{\beta}_1$ is derived from the time series data and β_2* is obtained by using the cross-section data. By following the pooling technique we have skirted the multicollinearity between income and price.

The methods described above are no sure methods to get rid of the problem of multicollinearity. These are just rules of thumb, which of these will work in practice will depend on the nature of the data under investigation and severity of the multicollinearity problem. One has to use one's judgement is any particular problem.

10.1.5 Multicollinearity and Prediction

The final stage of any econometric research is concerned with the evaluation of the forecasting validity of the model or function estimated. However, the purpose of estimation is not always the prediction of value of the dependent variable in a future period for policy decisions. Many times, the purpose of estimation may be to examine or verify the theory. In other words, many times a researcher is interested in the individual coefficient of the variable and not the overall effect of the variables. The problem of multicollinearity will severely affect the results in such circumstances. The researcher will have to be careful in case existence of multicollinearity has been established. On the other hand, if the purpose of estimation is only to forecast the values of dependent variable, the problem of multicollinearity can be ignored—but only on the assumption that the same pattern of collinearity continues in the period of prediction as observed in the sample period. But in case the correlation between the explanatory variables is expected to change in the period of forecast, then accurate forecasting requires dealing with the problem of multicollinearity.

10.1.6 Multicollinearity and Identification

The problem of multicollinearity, like under-identification, creates estimating difficulties for the structural parameters. Thus incidence of multicollinearity possesses a close affinity with problem of identification. Since till now the student has not been introduced to the problem of identification (which arises when we deal with the estimation of simultaneous-equation model), we shall examine this affinity in Chapter 13 under section 13.4.

10.2 SPECIFICATION BIAS

10.2.1 Meaning

The most important step of any econometric research is the correct specification of the model. The specification of a model consists of formulation of the regression equation and of assumptions concerning the variables and the disturbance term. Obviously, the specification of the model, therefore, presupposes knowledge of economic theory as well as familiarity with the problem being studied. Specification involves three things:

(i) determination of dependent and explanatory variables which will be included in the model. (See section 8.6 of Chapter 8)
(ii) determination of *a priori* theoretical expectations about the magnitude and sign of the parameters of the function, and
(iii) determination of the mathematical form of the model (e.g., linear, non linear, simultaneous or single equation model).

A *specification error* occurs whenever the assumption relating to any of the above three specifications is incorrect. The reasons for incorrect specification of economic models are:

(a) the limitation of (our) knowledge of the variables which are operative in any economic phenomenon,
(b) non-availability of the required data, or
(c) imperfection of the economic theory itself which forms the basis for the specification of the model.

The most common specification errors are those resulting from:

(a) *omission* of some of the variable(s) from the function.
(b) *inclusion* of some of the variable(s) in the function,
(c) *omission of some equation* (s) from the model, and
(d) *incorrect mathematical form* of the function.

Our main concern here will be to determine the consequences of three types of errors of specification for the least squares estimators of the regression parameters and their standard errors.

10.2.2   Case of Omission of Explanatory Variable

The use of ordinary least squares when some variables are left out may introduce bias into the estimates. Bias that originates in this way is called *specification bias*. For instance, the true function explaining variation in y is given as: $y = \beta_1 x_1 + \beta_2 x_2 + u$. However, either due to ignorance of the true relation or because of non-availability of data on x_2, following regression equation is estimated: $y = \beta_1^* x_1 + U$. It can be shown that β_1^* is different from β_1.

On applying OLS to $y = \beta_1^* x_1 + u$, we obtain, $\beta_1^* = \dfrac{\Sigma x_1 y}{\Sigma x_1^2}$. On the other hand, the normal equations of the true function: $y = \beta_1 x_1 + \beta_2 x_2 + U$ are:

$$\Sigma x_1 y = \beta_1 \Sigma x_1^2 + \beta_2 \Sigma x_1 x_2$$

$$\Sigma x_2 y = \beta_1 \Sigma x_1 x_2 + \beta_2 \Sigma x_2^2$$

Dividing the first equation Σx_1^2, we obtain

$$\frac{\Sigma x_1 y}{\Sigma x_1^2} = \beta_1 + \beta_2 \left(\frac{\Sigma x_1 x_2}{\Sigma x_1^2} \right)$$

Since
$$\beta_1^* = \frac{\Sigma x_1 y}{\Sigma x_1^2}, \quad \therefore \ \beta_1^* = \beta_1 + \beta_2 \left(\frac{\Sigma x_1 x_2}{\Sigma x_1^2} \right)$$

As such $\beta_1^* = \beta_1$ only if $\left(\dfrac{\Sigma x_1 x_2}{\Sigma x_1^2} \right) = 0$, i.e., if $\Sigma x_1 x_2 = 0$.

In other words, when x_1 and x_2 are orthogonal, which in fact will be rarely observed in case of economic relations (because most economic magnitudes are interdependent).

$$\therefore \ \text{Specification error} = (\beta_1^* - \beta_1) = \beta_2 \left(\frac{\Sigma x_1 x_2}{\Sigma x_1^2} \right)$$

It is, hence, proved that β_1^* from incorrect specification (through OLS procedure) is a biased estimate of the parameter β_1. The bias, which is equal to $\left\{\beta_2\left(\dfrac{\Sigma x_1 x_2}{\Sigma x_1^2}\right)\right\}$, depends on two terms; namely, the regression coefficient of the omitted variable in the true relation (β_2), and the covariance of the omitted variable with the included variable $\left(\dfrac{\Sigma x_1 x_2}{\Sigma x_1^2}\right)$.

The foregoing analysis suggests that if the omitted explanatory variable is uncorrelated with the included explanatory variable, its omission may not lead to serious consequences for least square estimation.

The above analysis may easily be now extended to functions with three explanatory variables.

Assume a true relation: $y = \beta_1 x_1 + \beta_2 x_2 + \beta_2 x_3 + u$. Suppose x_2 and x_3 are omitted from the true relation; thus, $y = \beta_1^* x_1 + u$;

so that
$$\beta_1^* = \frac{\Sigma x_1 y}{\Sigma x_1^2}$$

The specification error in this case will be:

$$(\beta_1^* - \beta_1) = \beta_2\left(\frac{\Sigma x_1 x_2}{\Sigma x_1^2}\right) + \beta_3\left(\frac{\Sigma x_1 x_3}{\Sigma x_1^2}\right)$$

or,
$$(\beta_1^* - \beta_1) = \beta_2(\alpha_1) + \beta_3(\alpha_2),$$

where α_1 is the coefficient of the regression of x_2 on x_1, and
α_2 is the coefficient of the regression of x_3 and x_1.

Let us now examine the variances of the estimators.

For $y = \beta_1^* x_1 + U$, $\text{Var}(\beta_1^*) = \dfrac{\sigma u^2}{\Sigma x_1^2} = \dfrac{\Sigma e_i^2/(n-2)}{\Sigma x_1^2}$

$$\text{Var}(\beta_1^*) = \frac{\Sigma(y - \beta_1^* x_1)^2}{(n-2)\Sigma x_1^2}$$

Substituting for y from the true function: $y = \beta_1 x_1 + \beta_2 x_2 + u$

$$\text{Var}(\beta_1^*) = \frac{\Sigma(\beta_1 x_1 + \beta_2 x_2 - \beta_1^* x_1)^2}{(n-2)\,\Sigma x_1^2}$$

$$= \frac{\Sigma\left[-(\beta_1^* - \beta_1)x_1 + \beta_2 x_2\right]^2}{(n-2)\,\Sigma x_1^2}$$

$$= \text{Var}(\beta_1^*) + \frac{\Sigma \beta_2^2 \Sigma x_2^2}{(n-2) \Sigma x_1^2}$$

This implies that estimator of (β_1^*) is positively biased.

Therefore, the usual tests of significance concerning β_1 shall be invalid in the present circumstances. Also, the estimator of the constant intercept of the incorrectly specified function turns out to be a biased one.

$$E(\beta_0^*) = E(\bar{Y} - \beta_1 \bar{X}_1)$$

$$= E(\beta_0 + \beta_1 \bar{X}_1 + \beta_2 \bar{X}_2 - \beta_1 \bar{X}_1)$$

$$= \beta_0 + \beta_1 \bar{X}_1 + \beta_2 \bar{X}_2 - \beta_1 \bar{X}_1$$

$$= \beta_0 + \beta_2 \bar{X}_2, \text{ which means } \beta_0^* \text{ is biased unless}$$

$$\bar{X}_2 = 0$$

The above discussion can now be summarised as follows:

(i) If the omitted or left out explanatory variable(s) is correlated with the included explanatory variable, the OLS estimator of β_1 will be biased and inconsistent.

(ii) If the omitted variable(s) is *not* correlated with the included variable; the estimator of constant term will still be biased and inconsistent, but estimator of β_1 will be unbiased.

(iii) The variance of β_1 will contain an upward bias. Therefore, the test on significance of the estimator would not lead to correct conclusions.

10.2.3 Case of Inclusion of an Irrelevant Explanatory Variable

Another type of specification error occurs when the set of relevant explanatory variables is enlarged by inclusion of one or more irrelevant variables. This is just an inverse case of the one discussed above.

Suppose a true regression is: $y_t = \beta_1 x_1 + u_t$, instead a regression equation estimated is: $y_t = \beta_1 x_1 + \beta_2 x_2 + u_t$. The specification error involved (in the wrong regression equation) occurs because $\beta_2 = 0$ is ignored in the equation actually estimated.

Suppose that this is not considered, and as a result β_1 and β_2 are estimated in the usual manner. What will be the consequences? Will (β_1) remain unbiased?

The answer to this question fortunately, is *yes* in the present case; but only under the condition that none of the basic assumptions concerning the disturbance term is violated.

Least squares estimate of $\hat{\beta}_1$ in $y_t = \beta_1 x_1 + \beta_2 x_2 + u_t$ is given by:

$$\hat{\beta}_1 = \frac{\Sigma x_2^2 \, \Sigma x_1 y - \Sigma x_2 x_1 \Sigma x_2 y}{\Sigma x_1^2 \, \Sigma x_2^2 - (\Sigma x_1 x_2)^2}$$

Substituting y from the true relation: $y_t = \beta_1 x_1 + u_t$,

$$\hat{\beta}_1 = \beta_1 + \frac{\Sigma x_2^2 \Sigma x_1 u - \Sigma x_1 x_2 \Sigma x_2 u}{\Sigma x_1^2 \, \Sigma x_2^2 - (\Sigma x_1 x_2)^2}$$

Therefore, $E(\hat{\beta}_1) = \beta_1$

Again, $E(\hat{\beta}_2) = E\left[\dfrac{\Sigma x_1^2 \, \Sigma x_2 y - \Sigma x_1 x_2 \Sigma x_1 y}{\Sigma x_1^2 \, \Sigma x_2^2 - (\Sigma x_1 x_2)^2}\right]$

or, $E(\hat{\beta}_2) = E\left[\dfrac{\Sigma x_1^2 \, \beta_1 \Sigma x_1 x_2 - \Sigma x_1 x_2 \cdot \beta_1 \cdot \Sigma x_1^2}{\Sigma x_1^2 \Sigma x_2^2 - (\Sigma x_1 x_2)^2}\right]$

(By substituting for y from the true relation)

i.e., $E(\hat{\beta}_2) = 0$

Turning to variances of the estimates:

$$\text{Var}(\hat{\beta}_1) = \frac{\sigma_u^2 \Sigma x_2^2}{\Sigma x_1^2 \, \Sigma x_2^3 - (\Sigma x_1 x_2)^3} = \frac{\sigma_u^2}{\Sigma x_1^2 (1 - r_{12}^2)}$$

But, in fact, the variance of β_1 from the true regression equation is

$$\text{Var}(\hat{\beta}_1^{\,*}) = \frac{\sigma u^2}{\Sigma x_1^2}$$

The ratio of the two variances:

$$\frac{\text{Var}(\hat{\beta}_1)}{\text{Var}(\hat{\beta}_1^*)} = \frac{1}{(1 - r_{12}^2)}; \text{ Since } 0 \le r_{12}^2 \le 1,$$

$$\therefore \quad \frac{\text{Var}(\hat{\beta}_1)}{\text{Var}(\hat{\beta}_1^*)} \ge 1.$$

If $r_{12} = 0$, then Var $(\hat{\beta}_1) = $ Var $\hat{\beta}_1^*$.

But since the square of correlation coefficient is always a positive fraction and non-zero quantity, the variance of $\hat{\beta}_1$ will be usually larger than the variance of $\hat{\beta}_1^*$. The implication of this result therefore is that $\hat{\beta}_1$ is generally a non-efficient estimator.

To conclude, therefore, if the specification error consists of including some irrelevant explanatory variable(s) in the model, the least squares estimators of the parameters are unbiased but not efficient. The larger variance reduces the precision of the estimates. In consequence, therefore, confidence intervals become wider; a variables appearing to be statistically not significant might, in fact, be having a systematic effect on the dependent variable.

10.2.4 Specification Bias: Incorrect Functional Form

Suppose that the 'true' or correct marginal cost model is as follows:

$$MC_i = \alpha + \beta_1(\text{output})_i + \beta_2(\text{output})_i^2 + U_i$$

but instead the following model is used for estimation:

$$MC_i = \alpha_0 + \alpha_1(\text{output})_i + V_i$$

The marginal cost curve corresponding to the true model is depicted in Fig. 10.1 along with the incorrect linear marginal cost curve. Between points P and Q, the linear marginal cost curve will consistently overestimate the true marginal cost, whereas beyond these points, it will consistently underestimate the true marginal cost. This is going to happen because the disturbance term V_i is, in fact, equal to $[(\text{output})^2 + U_i]$ and hence the (specification) bias in the estimator of α_1. (For detailed discussion on different functional forms, their choice and tests are presented in Chapter 7.)

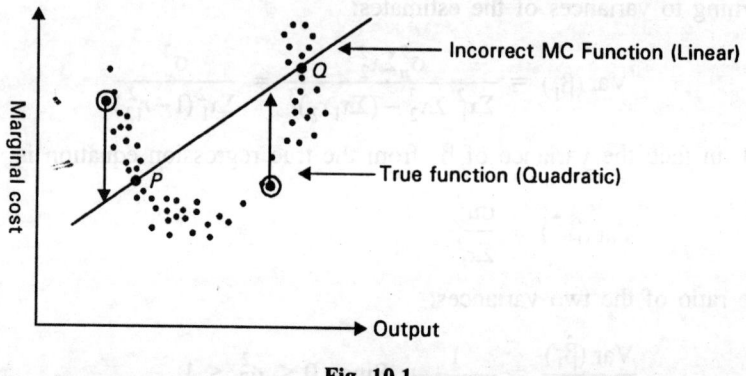

Fig. 10.1

10.2.5 Matrix Notation in Understanding Specification Error

Using the matrix notation for the general case of linear regression model; suppose, as usual, that the true model with k-explanatory variable is: $Y = X\beta + U$. X is a data matrix as explained in Section 8.6 of Chapter 8.

Assume now that mistakenly instead of using X, we employ a data matrix $\bar{X}$ of different order $n \times (k + 1)$.

Note that number of rows of X and $\bar{X}$ are same, they only differ column-wise. Nevertheless these matrices will have certain columns in common; that is, we assume that at least some of correct variables are included in the model. But X and $\bar{X}$ may differ in the omission of some relevant variables from $\bar{X}$ or in the inclusion of some irrelevant variables.

The least squares estimator, using $\bar{X}$, shall be:

$$\beta^* = (\bar{X}'\,\bar{X})^{-1}\,\bar{X}'\,Y$$

Substituting for $Y = X\beta + U$, which is the true relation, we obtain,

$$\beta^* = (\bar{X}'\,\bar{X})^{-1}\,\bar{X}'\,(X\beta + U)$$

$$\beta^* = (\bar{X}'\,\bar{X})^{-1}\,\bar{X}'X\beta + (\bar{X}'\,\bar{X})^{-1}\bar{X}'U$$

Hence, $$E\,(\beta^*) = (\bar{X}'\,\bar{X})^{-1}\,\bar{X}'X\beta = B\beta$$

where $$B = (\bar{X}'\,\bar{X})^{-1}\,\bar{X}'X$$

$E(\beta^*) = \beta$ only if $(\bar{X}'\,\bar{X})^{-1}\,\bar{X}'X$ is an Identity Matrix. This leads to the presence of specification error in the ordinary least squares estimates of the population parameters of the model: $Y = X\beta + U$.

10.3 LAGGED VARIABLES AND DISTRIBUTED LAG MODELS

10.3.1 Meaning

While considering the standard linear regression model, we did not pay any attention to the timing of the effect of explanatory variables(s) on the dependent variable. The standard linear regression implies that change in one of the explanatory variables causes a change in the dependent variable during the same time period and during that period alone. But in economics, such specification is rarely found. In economic phenomenon, generally, a cause often produces its effect only after a lapse of time; this lapse of time (between cause and its effect) is called a *lag*. Therefore, realistic formulations of economic relations often require the insertion of lagged values of the explanatory (or insertion of lagged dependent) variables.

Few examples from economics are given under:

Consumption function: $C_t = f(Y_t)$; generally it is assumed that current level of consumption (C_t) depends on the current level of income (Y_t). But there is no reason, however, why current consumption should depend solely on present income. One may very well postulate that the current level of consumption depends not only on current income, but also on past levels of income and past levels of consumption (due to psychological, technical and institutional factors); i.e.,

$$C_t = f(Y_t,\ Y_{t-1},\ Y_{t-2}\ \cdots\ C_{t-1},\ C_{t-2}\ldots)$$

Investment function: Investment expenditure (I_t) of a firm depends on the present as well as the past sales and other many factors: i.e.,

$$I_t = f(X_t,\ X_{t-1},\ X_{t-2}\ldots)$$

Demand function: Demand for durable good (D) depends not only on its price (p) but on present and past levels of income (Y) which, in fact, determine the amount saved for acquiring that durable good; i.e.,

$$D = f(Y_t, Y_{t-1}, Y_{t-2} \cdots p_t)$$

The demand for non-durable depends, among other factors, on past levels of consumption (Q) of that commodity; i.e.,

$$D = f(Y_t, p_t, Q_{t-1})$$

Hence we observe that lags are involved nearly in all economic relationships. Yet our micro economic theory does not specify them; it is mostly static.

The lags involved in the economic phenomenon are rarely mentioned, yet these lags are of great importance for decision making. It is crucial for the planners to know how fast will be consumers (or producers) react to changes of various policy decisions undertaken. For example, how fast will the consumers react to the imposition of a tax or rise in interest rate? How fast will the producers react to certain incentives provided for increasing the investment expenditures? Many such questions underline the importance of lagged values of the explanatory variables in the formulation of econometric models to understand the real nature of the problem.

Such a casual relation, in which a change in the dependent variable can be explained by the lagged values of the explanatory variables, is called *disturbed lag model*. For example.

$$C_t = \alpha + \beta_0 Y_t + \beta_1 Y_{t-1} + \beta_2 Y_{t-2} \cdots \beta_k Y_{t-k} + U_t$$

is a distributed lag model of consumption function. This means that the value of the consumption expenditure (C_t) at any given time depends on past values of the disposable income (Y_t).

The *general form* of a distributed lag model (with only lagged exogenous variables) is written as,

$$Y_t = \alpha + \beta_0 X_t + \beta_1 X_{t-1} + \beta_2 X_{t-2} + \ldots + \beta_s X_{t-s} + \cdots + U_t$$

$$Y_t = \alpha + \sum_{s=0}^{\infty} \beta_s X_{t-s} + U_t$$

The number of lags, s, may be either finite or infinite. But generally it is assumed to be finite.

In the above relation, the coefficient β_0 is known as the *short run multiplier* because it gives the change in mean value of Y following a unit change in X in the same time period t.

$\beta_1, \beta_2, \ldots \beta_s$ are called *delay*, or *interim multipliers* because they measure the impact on mean Y of a unit change in X in various previous time periods.

Also,

$$\sum_{i=0}^{s} \beta_i = \beta_0 + \beta_1 + \beta_2 + \cdots + \beta_s = \beta$$

is called the long run distributed-lag multiplier provided the sum β exists.

It should be noted that *Distributed lag model* is not to be confused with *Autoregressive model*. If the regression model includes the lagged values of explanatory variables, it is called a distributed lag model. Whereas, if the model includes one or more lagged values of dependent variables among its explanatory variables, it is called an Autoregressive model.

For example, $Y_i = \alpha + \beta_0 X_t + \beta X_{t-1} + U_t$ represent a Distributed lag model, whereas $Y_i = \alpha + \beta X_t + \gamma Y_{t-1} + W_t$ is an example of an Autoregressive model.

10.3.2 The Reasons for Lag

The above examples of distributed lag models point out the nature of lagged phenomenon, they do not fully explain why lags occur. There are several reasons why there might be a lag in the system, specially a lapse of time between a change in an explanatory variable and a change in the dependent variable. Of these, the major are:

1. *Technical reasons:* Production requires time, therefore, supply of particular commodity, depending on its production process, depends on lagged variables; such as lagged prices of inputs. The time must elapse between application of inputs and obtaining output. Again, suppose the price of capital relative to labour declines making substitution of capital for labour attractive for the producers. But addition of capital to the production process takes time. Moreover, if the drop in price of labour is expected to be temporary, firms may not rush to substitute capital for labour—specially if they expect that after the temporary drop the price of capital may increase beyond its previous level. Also durable goods last more than one period. The durability of capital goods implies that current output depends, in part, on the past investment decisions.

2. *Institutional reasons:* It takes time to respond to external events. For example, contractual obligations may prevent the firms to switch over from one source of labour or raw material to another (though the switching over may be very beneficial). Secondly, certain rules also lead to lagged responses. For instance, those who have placed funds in long-term savings accounts for fixed duration of 3 years or 7 years are essentially 'locked in' even though money market conditions may be such that higher yields are available elsewhere.

3. *Psychological reasons:* Behaviour is often based on inertia and habit. It is due to force of habit that people do not change their consumption habits immediately following a price decrease or income increase. Probably because process of such change involves immediate disutility. The change in consumption habit is therefore a slow process depending on whether the change in come is permanent or transitory.

10.3.3 Average or Mean Lag

A summary statistic known as Mean or Average lag is computed in order to compare the lag structure of different lag models. The mean lag is defined as a lag weighted average of time.

For the model: $y_t = \alpha + \beta_0 X_t + \beta_1 X_{t-1} + \cdots + U_t$;

$$\text{Mean lag} = \frac{\sum\limits_{i=0}^{s} i \cdot \beta_i}{\sum\limits_{i=0}^{s} \beta_i} \text{ (Finite case); Mean lag} = \frac{\sum\limits_{i=0}^{\infty} i \cdot \beta_i}{\sum\limits_{i=0}^{\infty} \beta_i} \text{ (Infinite case)}$$

For the model: $y_t = \alpha + \beta X_t + \beta\lambda X_{t-1} + \beta\lambda^2 X_{t-2} \cdots\cdots U_t$;

or; $y_t = \alpha + \beta \sum\limits_{i=0}^{\infty} \lambda^i X_{t-i} + U_t$; $\quad 0 < \lambda < 1$

The size of mean lag is

$$= \frac{0.\beta\lambda^0 + 1.\beta\lambda^1 + 2.\beta\lambda^2 + 3\beta\lambda^3 + \cdots\cdots}{\beta\lambda^0 + \beta\lambda^1 + \beta\lambda^2 + \cdots\cdots}$$

$$= \frac{\beta\left[0 + \lambda + 2\lambda^2 + 3\lambda^3 + \cdots\right]}{\beta\left[1 + \lambda + \lambda^2 + \cdots\right]}$$

$$= \frac{\lambda + (1-\lambda)^2}{\lambda + (1-\lambda)} = \frac{1}{1-\lambda}$$

For the distributed lag model, when lags occur in the dependent as well as in independent variables together, the average lag is defined in a different way.

Suppose the distributed lag model is in the following deviation form:

$$y_t = \alpha_0 x_t + \alpha_1 x_{t-1} + \alpha_2 x_{t-2} + \cdots + \alpha_m x_{t-m} + \beta_1 y_{t-1} + \beta_2 y_{t-2} + \cdots + u_t$$

The mean lag is, then, defined as,

$$\text{Mean lag} = \left[\frac{\sum\limits_{i=0}^{m} i \cdot \alpha_i}{\sum\limits_{i=0}^{m} \alpha_i} + \frac{\sum\limits_{i=1}^{n} i \cdot \beta_i}{1 - \sum\limits_{i=1}^{n} \beta_i} \right]$$

Mean lag, for the model: $y_t = \alpha_0 x_t + \alpha_1 x_{t-1} + \beta y_{t-1} + u_t$ is given by:

$$\text{Mean lag} = \left(\frac{\alpha_1}{\alpha_0 + \alpha_1} + \frac{\beta}{1-\beta} \right)$$

10.3.4 Estimation of Distributed-Lag Models

Can the distributed lag model be estimated through ordinary least square procedure under the usual specifications about disturbance term?

The answer, unfortunately, is *no*. It is because *two* problems are almost certain to arise which make the least squares estimates biased and inefficient.

Firstly: if the number of lags is large and the sample size is small it may not be possible to estimate the parameters. With every additional lagged value of the variable, one observation is lost which in turn leads to fall in the degrees of freedom.

This may be understood through the following observations table:

Observations on Y: $Y_1\ Y_2\ Y_3$......Y_n
Observations on X: $X_0\ X_1\ X_2$......X_{n-1}

which are to used for the model: $Y_t = f(X_{t-1})$. Though n observations on X and Y are available to us, yet we are able to use only $(n-1)$ observations. We are unable to use Y_1 observation since we do not have an observed value of X_0, and likewise we cannot make use of X_n since we do not know Y_{n+1}. Thus one period lag model reduces the size of sample by one.

Secondly, problem of multicollinearity is encountered in such type of models since there is every possibility to find a strong correlation between the successive values of same variables. With strong collinearity the values of the estimates will turn out to be imprecise and their variances will be very large.

Thus, the two basic problems associated with distributed lag models are:

(i) observations are lost due to lags, and
(ii) there are too many parameters to estimate reliably.

Various methods have been suggested to deal with these problems. The basic aim of these methods therefore is—"to reduce the number of lagged variables in the model".

The important methods, in the form of models, generally used for estimating Distributed lag Models, are described below.

10.3.5 The Koyck Approach to Distributed-Lag Model

In order to reduce the number of lags in the given distributed lag model, the present model makes an assumption that the impact of explanatory variables (on the dependent variable) in the most distant past is less than what is in more recent periods. More specifically, the *Koyck lag formulation* assumes that the weights (impacts) are declining continuously, following a pattern of a geometric progression.

Assume that original model is:

$$Y_t = \alpha_0 + \beta_0\ X_t + \beta_1\ X_{t-1} + \beta_2 X_{t-2} + \ldots + U_t$$

where $U_i \sim N(0, \sigma_u^2)$

$$E(U_i U_j) = 0 \; (i \neq j)$$

$$E(U_i X_j) = 0 \; (j = 1, 2,..., k)$$

As stated above, the Koyck lag scheme hypothesises that more recent values of X exert greater influence on Y than remoter values of X. The influence declines in the form of a geometric progression as follows:

$$\beta_1 = \lambda \beta_0$$

$$\beta_2 = \lambda^2 \beta_0$$

$$\beta_2 = \lambda^3 \beta_0 \text{ and, so on.}$$

So that,

$$\beta_i = \lambda^i \cdot \beta_0 \quad \text{where } 0 < \lambda < 1$$

λ is known as the rate of decline, or decay, of the distributed lag and $(1 - \lambda)$ is known as the speed of adjustment.

By assuming non-negative values λ, Koyck rules out the β's from changing sign, and by assuming $\lambda < 1$, lesser weight is assigned to the distant β's than the current one.

Substituting the values of β's in the original model, we obtain

$$Y_t = \alpha_0 + \beta_0 X_t + (\lambda \beta_0) X_{t-1} + (\lambda^2 \beta_0) X_{t-2} + ... + U_t$$

Lagging by one period and multiplying through by λ, we get,

$$\lambda Y_{t-1} = \lambda \alpha_0 + (\lambda \beta_0) X_{t-1} + (\lambda^2 \beta_0) X_{t-2} + (\lambda^3 \beta_0) X_{t-3} + ... + \lambda U_{t-1}$$

or,

$$Y_t - \lambda Y_{t-1} = \alpha_0 (1 - \lambda) + \beta_0 X_t + (U_t - \lambda U_{t-1})$$

or,

$$Y_t = \alpha_0^* + \beta_0 X_t + \lambda Y_{t-1} + V_t$$

where,

$$V_t = U_t - \lambda U_{t-1} \quad \text{and,} \quad \alpha_0^* = \alpha_0 (1 - \lambda)$$

The above procedure of transformation is known as Koyck transformation. It may now be observed that the original model has been tremendously simplified. The effects of all the lagged values of X's on the current value of Y are captured in a single term; the value of Y itself is lagged by one period only. We need only to estimate the value of λ instead of coefficients for each of the lagged values of explanatory variables. In other words, if the Koyck hypothesis concerning the lag scheme and assumptions concerning V_t are accepted, ordinary least squares can be applied to obtain estimates of α_0^*, β_0 and λ. From these estimates, the estimates of original parameters: α_0, β_0, β_1, β_2... can then be easily obtained through the following two relations:

$$\hat{\alpha}_0 = \frac{\hat{\alpha}_0^*}{1 - \hat{\lambda}} \quad \text{and} \quad \hat{\beta}_i = (\hat{\lambda}_i) \hat{\beta}_0$$

The present estimation method would also require the loss of only one observation.

However, following features of the Koyck transformation may be taken note of:

1. In the original model, the disturbance term was U_t, whereas in the transformed model it is $V_t (= U_t - \lambda U_{t-1})$. Hence the statistical properties of V_t depend on what is assumed about the statistical properties of U_t.
2. Our original model was a distributed lag model but the transformed model is autoregressive model because Y_{t-1} appears as one of the explanatory variables. Koyck transformation, therefore, also helps to convert distributed lag model into an autoregressive model.
3. Presence of lagged dependent variable in the transformed model poses some statistical problems. These are discussed under.

(i) In the new formulation the error term $V_t (= U_t - \lambda U_{t-1})$ is found to be autocorrelated despite the fact that the disturbance term of the original model is non autocorrelated. It can be seen as under

$$E(V_t V_{t-1}) = E[U_t - \lambda U_{t-1}) (U_{t-1} - \lambda U_{t-2})]$$
$$= E[U_t U_{t-1} - U_t \lambda U_{t-2} - \lambda U^2_{t-1} + \lambda^2 U_{t-1} U_{t-2}]$$
$$= -\lambda E(U^2_{t-1})$$
$$= -\lambda \sigma^2_u \neq 0 \qquad [\because 0 < \lambda < 1]$$

(ii) The lagged variable Y_{t-1} is also not independent of the error term V_t; i.e., $E(V_t Y_{t-1}) \neq 0$. This is because Y_t directly depends on V_t; similarly Y_{t-1} on V_{t-1}. But since V_t and V_{t-1} are not independent, Y_{t-1} will obviously be related to V_t.

Due to above two problems, the Koyck transformation of the distributed lag model will give rise to biased and inconsistent estimates. In addition to these estimation problems, the Koyck hypothesis is quite a restrictive one in the sense that it assumes the impact of past periods decline successively in a specific way. This may not always be the case.

Following could be the cases:

(a) There may be a declining lag scheme. That is, in the distributed lag model: $Y_t = \alpha_0 + \beta_0 X_t + \beta_1 X_{t-1} + \beta_2 X_{t-2} + ... + U_t$, the impact of more recent values of X have greater influence than the past.
Mathematically, $\beta_0 > \beta_1 > \beta_2 > \beta_3$ ... and so on.
(b) There may be a rectangular lag scheme. That is, each past value of X has the same influence on Y.
Mathematically, $\beta_0 = \beta_1 = \beta_2 = \beta_3$ ... and so on.
(c) There may be an inverted 'V' lag scheme. That is, at first the impact increases but decreases subsequently.
Mathematically, $\beta_0 < \beta_1 < \beta_2 > \beta_3 > \beta_4$ and so on.

10.3.6   The Almon Approach to Distributed-Lag Models

The Almon lag model possesses two advantages over the Koyck procedure.

First, it does not violate any of the ordinary least squares basic assumptions concerning the disturbance term.

Second, it is far more flexible than Koyck method in terms of the form of lag scheme.

It is because, this method does not hypothesise any form of lag scheme before hand. But, on the other hand, this method does not like the Koyck formulation, reduce the number of observations that are lost due to presence of lagged variables. Nevertheless Almon method does reduce the number of parameters to be estimated in the original model.

This model, as stated above, does not assume any rigid relationship among β_i's. It assumes that any pattern of lag scheme among β_i's can be described by polynomial.* This idea is based on a theorem in mathematics known as *Weierstrass's theorem*, which states that under general conditions a curve may be approximated by a polynomial whose degree is one more than the number of turning points in the curve. Supposing that β's in a given distributed lag model are expected to decrease first, then the increase and again decrease is as illustrated in Fig. 10.2.

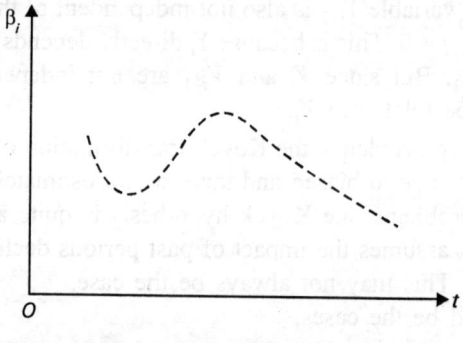

Fig. 10.2

Applying the rule to Fig. 10.2 the degree of polynomial would be three. In Fig. 10.3, number of possible lag patterns along with degree of the corresponding polynomial have been depicted.

Assuming that β_i's show a lag pattern as depicted in Fig. 10.2 in our original distributed lag model, the polynomial, as per Almon's technique, would be: $\beta_i = a_0 + a_1 i + a_2 i^2 + a_3 i^3$, where a_0, a_1, a_2 and a_3 are the parameters to be estimated.

---

*Degree of polynomial refers the highest power to which the variable is raised. Thus, $y = a_0 + b_1 x + b_2 x^2$ is a second degree polynomial, while $Y = a_0 + b_1 x_1 + b_2 x^2 + b_3 x^3$ is a polynomial of the third degree.

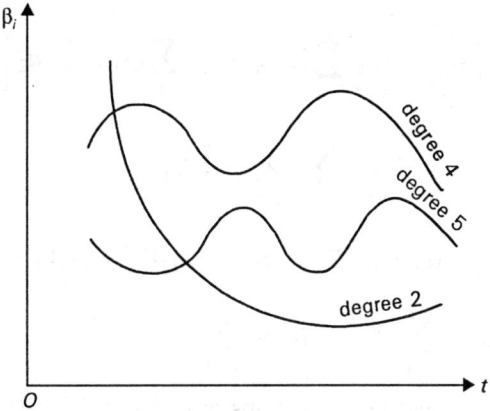

Fig. 10.3

Note that, if our original model to be estimated is:

$Y = \alpha_0 + \beta_0 X_t + \beta_1 X_{t-1} + \beta_2 X_{t-2} + \ldots + U_t$; then by using the relationship: $\beta_i = a_0 + a_1 i + a_2 i^2 + a_2 i^3$, we are in a position to obtain all β's by setting i equal to the values of the subscript of the particular coefficient.

$$\beta_0 = a_0$$
$$\beta_1 = a_0 + a_1 + a_2 + a_3$$
$$\beta_2 = a_0 + 2a_1 + 4a_2 + 8a_3$$
$$\beta_3 = a_0 + 3a_1 + 9a_2 + 27a_3$$
$$\vdots$$
$$\beta_k = a_0 + ka_1 + k^2 a_2 + k^3 a_3$$

Naturally therefore, what is needed to be estimated is only the four parameters of the polynomial function: $\beta_i = a_0 + a_1 i + a_2 i^2 + a_3 i^3$. Obtaining the values of a_0, a_1, a_2, a_3, we are able to estimate all the parameters of the original distributed lag model. Also, we are at liberty to change the polynomial function to any other degree of polynomial as per our assumptions relating to lag scheme. This, in other words, demonstrates the flexibility of the Almon technique.

The working of this technique is explained as follows:

Let our original distributed lag model required to be estimated be:

$$Y_t = \alpha_0 + \beta_0 X_t + \beta_1 X_{t-1} + \beta_2 X_{t-2} + \ldots + U_t$$

Suppose that economic theory suggests that a third degree polynomial is appropriate to describe the form of lag. So we take:

$$\beta_i = a_0 + a_1 i + a_2 i^2 + a_3 i^3$$

Substituting value of β's in the original model,

$$Y_t = \alpha_0 + (a_0) X_t + (a_0 + a_1 + a_2 + a_3) X_{t-1}$$
$$+ (a_0 + 2a_1 + 4a_2 + 8a_3) X_{t-2} + \ldots + U_i$$

or,
$$Y_t = \alpha_0 + a_0 \sum_{i=0}^{k} X_{t-i} + a_1 \left(\sum_{i=1}^{k} iX_{t-i} \right) + a_2 \left(\sum_{i=1}^{k} i^2 X_{t-i} \right)$$

$$+ a_3 \left(\sum_{i=1}^{k} i^3 X_{t-i} \right) + U_t$$

or
$$Y_t = \alpha_0 + a_0 W_0 + a_1 W_1 + a_2 W_2 + a_3 W_3 + U_t$$

where,
$$W_0 = \sum_{i=0}^{k} X_{t-i} , \; W_1 = \sum_{i=1}^{k} iX_{t-i}, \; \ldots\ldots$$

This, then, is the final form (or transformed form) of Almon lag model.

We can now apply OLS method to estimate $\hat\alpha_0, a_0, a_1, a_2,$ and a_3 to obtain β's in the original form.

Note that U_t remains in its original form.

Almon model is possible only if we know: (i) the length of the lag in the original model (i.e., value of k), and (ii) the general pattern of the β's so that order of polynomial can be determined.

In practice neither k nor the pattern of β's may be known. Different procedures, however, are recommended for obtaining both.

Before proceeding to a numerical example, the advantages of the Almon transformation may be re-emphasised:

(i) Almon method provides a flexible method of incorporating variety of leg structures; whereas the Koyck technique is quite rigid in that it assumes that the β's decline geometrically.

(ii) Unlike Koyck technique, in the Almon method, one has not to worry about presence of the lagged dependent variable as an explanatory variable in the transformed form of the model and the problems it creates for estimation.

(iii) If the sufficiently low-degree of polynomial is assumed, the number of coefficients to be estimated (i.e., a's) will be considerably smaller than the original number of coefficients (i.e., β's).

10.3.7 Applications

To illustrate the procedures for estimating Koyck and Almon lag models, we take up a hypothetical problem on estimation of consumption function from the following data.

Year	1965	1966	1967	1968	1969	1970	1971	1972	1973	1974
Consumption Expenditure	32	33	35	37	40	43	47	49	54	58
Disposable Income	34	36	38	40	44	47	51	55	59	63

We assume that consumption expenditure depends on disposable income with distributed lag:

$$C_t = \alpha_0 + \beta_0 Y_t + \beta_1 Y_{t-1} + \beta_2 Y_{t-2} + \ldots + U_t$$

I. *Estimation of Consumption Function through Koyck Approach.*

To estimate the Koyck transformed model:

$$C_t = \alpha_0^* + \beta_0 Y_t + \lambda C_{t-1} + V_t$$

where
$$\alpha_0^* = \alpha_0 (1 - \lambda);$$

we assume that V_t follows all the basic assumptions of the OLS disturbance term. The observations for this model shall be:

C_t	33	35	37	40	43	47	49	54	58
C_{t-1}	32	33	35	37	40	43	47	49	54
Y_t	36	38	40	44	47	51	55	59	63

(Note that only one observation of the year 1965 has been lost)

Using the above data, the transformed model is estimated. The results are:

$$\hat{C}_t = 0.3550 + 0.8160\ Y_t + 0.1092\ C_{t-1} \qquad R^2 = 0.91$$

i.e., $\qquad \alpha^* = 0.3550$ and $\lambda = 0.1092$

$$\alpha_0 = \frac{\alpha^*}{1 - \lambda} = \frac{0.3550}{1 - 0.1092} = 0.3985$$

$\beta_0 = 0.8160,$
$\beta_1 = \lambda^1 \beta_0 = (0.1092)(0.8160) = 0.0891;$
$\beta_2 = \lambda^2 \beta_0 = (0.1092)^2 (0.8160) = 0.0097;$
$\beta_3 = \lambda^3 \beta_0 = (0.1092)^3 (0.8160) = 0.0011;$ and so on.

Substituting value of β's in the original model, we obtain the original distributed log model as under:

$$\hat{C}_t = 0.3985 + 0.8160\ Y_t + 0.0891\ Y_{t-1} + 0.0097\ Y_{t-2} + 0.0011\ Y_{t-3} + \ldots$$

It may be observed that the impact of the distant Y's is successively decreasing. It should be remembered that we have estimated the Koyck lag model assuming that U follows OLS assumptions; which in fact is not true. We have estimated the function only to illustrate the procedure of estimating and comparing it with Almon model.

II. *Estimation of Consumption Function through Almon Approach*

We shall have to assume two things here: (i) lag scheme, and (ii) the length of lag in consumption function.

Suppose that lag takes the form of second-degree polynomial and that consumption depends on disposable income in the current year and in the four preceding years.

Specification of consumption function is, then,

$$C_t = \alpha_0 + \beta_0 Y_t + \beta_1 Y_{t-1} + \beta_2 Y_{t-2} + \beta_3 Y_{t-3} + \beta_4 Y_{t-4} + U_t$$

where, $\beta_t = a_0 + a_1 i + a_2 i^2$

The transformed model, then, becomes:

$$C_t = \alpha_0 + a_0 Y_t + (a_0 + a_1 + a_2) Y_{t-1} + (a_0 + 2a_1 + 4a_2) Y_{t-2}$$
$$+ (a_0 + 3a_1 + 9a_2) Y_{t-3} + (a_0 + 4a_1 + 16a_2) Y_{t-4} + U_t$$
$$C_t = \alpha_0 + a_0 (Y_t + Y_{t-1} + Y_{t-2} + Y_{t-3} + Y_{t-4})$$
$$+ a_1 (Y_{t-1} + 2Y_{t-2} + 3Y_{t-3} + 3Y_{t-4})$$
$$+ a_2 (Y_{t-1} + 4Y_{t-2} + 9Y_{t-3} + 16Y_{t-4}) + U_t$$

$$C_t = \alpha_0 + a_0 \left(\sum_{i=0}^{4} Y_{t-i} \right) + a_1 \left(\sum_{i=1}^{4} i . Y_{t-i} \right) + a_2 \left(\sum_{i=1}^{4} i^2 . Y_{t-i} \right) + U_t$$

$$C_t = \alpha_0 + a_0 W_0 + a_1 W_1 + a_2 W_2 + U_t$$

The given data on consumption and disposable income will have to be reshaped in the following way.

$$C_{1969} = \alpha_0 + a_0 (Y_{1969} + Y_{1968} + Y_{1967} + Y_{1966} + Y_{1965})$$
$$+ a_1 (Y_{1968} + 2Y_{1967} + 3Y_{1966} + 4Y_{1965}) + a_2 (......)$$
$$C_{1970} = \alpha_0 + a_0 (Y_{1970} + Y_{1969} + Y_{1968} + Y_{1967} + Y_{1966})$$
$$+ a_1 (Y_{1969} + 2Y_{1968} + 3Y_{1967} + 4Y_{1966}) + a_2 (......)$$
$$\vdots$$
$$C_{1974} = \alpha_0 + a_0 (Y_{1974} + Y_{1973} + Y_{1972} + Y_{1971} + Y_{1970})$$
$$+ a_1 (Y_{1973} + 2Y_{1972} + 3Y_{1971} + 4Y_{1970}) + a_2 (......)$$

As a result of having four period lag in the original consumption function, we have lost four observations on consumption and income; they are relating to years 1965, 1966, 1967 and 1968. We shall obtain only six observations on consumption and transformed Y in the form of W_0, W_1 and W_2.

The new generated data has thus been computed as;

Year	C	Y	W_0	W_1	W_2
1965	32	34	—	—	—
1966	33	36	—	—	—
1967	35	38	—	—	—
1968	37	40	—	—	—
1969	40	44	192	360	1060
1970	43	47	205	382	1122
1971	47	51	220	407	1191
1972	49	55	237	437	1275
1973	54	59	256	474	1386
1974	58	63	275	510	1490

Using the above data, we use standard ordinary least squares procedure to estimate the equation:

$$C_t = \alpha_0 + a_0 W_0 + a_1 W_1 + a_2 W_2 + U_t$$

The estimate results are:

$$\hat{C}_t = -0.4853 + 0.0764 W_0 + 0.0944 W_1 - 0.0073 W_3$$

Since our assumption relating to β_i's is as follows:

$$\beta_i = a_0 + a_1 i + a_2 i^2$$

$$\therefore \quad \hat{\beta}_0 = \hat{a}_0 = .0764$$

$$\hat{\beta}_1 = \hat{a}_0 + \hat{a}_1 + \hat{a}_2 = 0.0764 + .0944 - .0073 = 0.1635$$

$$\hat{\beta}_2 = \hat{a}_0 + 2\hat{a}_1 + 4\hat{a}_2 = 0.0764 + 2(.0944) - 4(.0073) = 0.2360$$

$$\hat{\beta}_3 = \hat{a}_0 + 3\hat{a}_1 + 9\hat{a}_2 = 0.0764 + 3(.0944) - 9(.0073) = 0.2939$$

$$\hat{\beta}_4 = \hat{a}_0 + 4\hat{a}_1 + 16\hat{a}_2 = 0.0764 + 4(.0944) - 16(.0073) = 0.3372$$

Substituting all the β's in the original consumption function, the estimated (Almon lag model) consumption function becomes:

$$\hat{C}_t = -0.4853 + 0.0764\, Y_t + 0.1635\, Y_{t-1} + 0.2360\, Y_{t-2}$$
$$+ 0.2939\, Y_{t-3} + 0.3372\, Y_{t-4} \qquad R^2 = 0.92$$

We have not computed the variances of the coefficients. But such additional information is provided by most computer programmes with Almon lag schemes.

10.3.8 Lagged Endogenous Variables (Partial Adjustment and Adaptive Expectation Models)

So far we have discussed the lagged models which include lagged values of exogenous or explanatory variables only. But we also observed that the application of a Koyck lag scheme to the lagged values of explanatory variables (X_t) produced a final model with lagged value of dependent variable (Y_t) and as such it is also called *Autoregressive model*. There are such other Autoregressive models. The two such models are: Nerlove's Partial Adjustment model and Cagan's Adaptive Expectations model.

These models are based on a bit more realistic behavioural hypothesis of economic units in the form of lag models. These models are, therefore, frequently quoted and used in applied econometrics in the area of Agricultural Economics.

(I) *Partial Adjustment Model*

Under this model, a desired or optimal value of dependent variable (Y_t^*) is related with the value of explanatory variable in a particular time period (X_t); i.e., $Y_t^* = \alpha + \beta_1 X_t$; where Y_t^* depicts optimal value of Y.

For instance, in case of consumption function: $C_t^* = \alpha + \beta_1 Y_t$; Y_t = consumer's disposable income, and C_t^* = optimal or desired level of consumption expenditure adjusting to increased disposable income. The once for all (immediate) changes in the income of the consumer that has been produced, say Y_t, may be large one with which it may not be possible for him to adjust immediately to new situation. As such, the change in the income which happens in one stroke exerts its lag effects on consumption expenditure of the consumer. These lags arise chiefly because of technological and institutional rigidities which have been described under 10.3.2 above.

In the consumption model: $C_t^* = \alpha + \beta_1 Y_t + U_t$, C_t^* is not observable, hence it must be replaced so as to estimate the model.

For this purpose certain specific hypothesis concerning the consumer's behaviour is made, which is described as follows in mathematical relation:

$$C_t - C_{t-1} = \delta_t (C_t^* - C_{t-1}) + U_t \quad 0 < \delta \leq 1$$

This, in other words, means that the 'Adjustment' to the 'Desired level' of consumption (C_t^*) from his initial position of consumption (C_{t-1}) is only gradual due to factors mentioned above. In the above hypothesis

$C_t - C_{t-1}$ = Actual change in the consumption expenditure,

$C_t^* - C_{t-1}$ = Desired change in the consumption expenditure, and

δ = Adjustment coefficient.

Another example of such adjustment may be given from the theory of investment in fixed capital. The capital stock is determined by the level of output. Due to gestation period involved in all the investment projects, the actual change in the capital stock in any period is only a fraction of the desired change.

If $\delta = 1$, it means that the actual stock of capital is equal to the desired stock; that is, actual stock adjusts to the desired stock instantaneously (in the same time period).

If $\delta = 0$, it means that nothing changes since actual stock at time t is the same as that observed in the previous time period. Typically, δ is expected to lie between these two extremes. In other words the adjustment of capital stock to the desired level is gradual due to technological, financial or administrative constraints.

Substituting the original consumption function:

$$C_t^* = \alpha_0 + \beta_1 Y_t + U_t \text{ into the behavioural hypothesis:}$$

$$C_t - C_{t-1} = \delta (C_t^* - C_{t-1}) + U_t, \text{ we obtain:}$$

$$C_t - C_{t-1} = \delta [\alpha_0 + \beta_1 Y_t - C_{t-1}] + U_t$$

$$C_t = (\delta\alpha_0) + (\delta\beta_1) Y_t + (1 - \delta) C_{t-1} + U_t$$

$$C_t = \alpha^* + \beta_1^* Y_t + \beta_2^* C_{t-1} + U_t$$

where, $\alpha^* = \alpha_0\delta$, $\beta_1^* = \delta\beta_1$ and $\beta_2^* = (1 - \delta)$.

It may be observed here that the final form of the consumption function is similar to autoregressive Koyck scheme (which is: $C_t = \alpha_0^* + \beta_0 Y_t + \lambda C_{t-1} + V_t$). The only differences are:

(i) that the disturbance term in the partial adjustment model does not involve any autoregressive scheme, and

(ii) that the coefficient $(1 - \delta)$ of the lagged consumption C_{t-1} in the present case possesses a certain economic meaning. In contrast, λ in the Koyck model is merely an arbitrary assumed coefficient having no economic interpretation.

The above behavioural adjustment hypothesis has been used by Houthokker and Taylor to explain the demand for non-durables in their well-quoted book, 'Consumer demand in the United States, 1929-1970, Analysis and Projections.' They argue that the quantity demanded in any one period depends upon the demand of the same commodity in the previous period. This is due to a habit formation process which is a basic to human behaviour. Thus according to them, the demand for non-durables may be described as:

$$q_t = \alpha_0 + \beta_1 x_t + \beta_2 q_{t-1} + \beta_3 p_t + U_t$$

q_t = demand for a particular non-durable commodity
q_{t-1} = lagged demand
x_t = income of the consumer
p_t = price of commodity under study.

The only weak point in the Partial Adjustment Model seems to be that it sometimes may not be true to hypothesis: that optimum or desired level of consumption (C_t^*) depends on the current and only on the current level of income (Y_t), because Y_t may itself be changing from period to period. One might therefore, think in terms of permanent or the expected level of income rather than current level of income. It is this idea which has been incorporated in the Adaptive Expectations Model explained below.

(II) *Adaptive Expectations Model*

This model is based on the behavioural hypothesis which states that the present level of consumption (C_t) depends not on the present level of income but on the expected or permanent level of income (Y_t^*), i.e.,

$$C_t = \alpha + \beta Y_t^* + U_t$$

Here again the above equation is nonoperational since Y_t^* is unobservable. It is, therefore, supplemented with another assumption; as to know how the expectations are formed on the *Adaptive* Principle.

Expectations are seldom fully realised, there is usually a gap between what is actually achieved and what was expected. On the basis of this discrepancy we go on reformulating or modifying our expectations.

The Adaptive Principle can therefore be mathematically stated as:

$$Y_t^* - Y_{t-1}^* = \lambda (Y_t - Y_{t-1}^*)$$
$$0 < \lambda \leq 1 \ (\lambda \text{ is expectation coefficient})$$

In other words, the change (or modification) in the expectations ($Y_t^* - Y_{t-1}^*$) depends on a fraction (λ) of the difference between the actually achieved and the past expectations ($Y_t - Y_{t-1}^*$).

We have original model as: $C_t = \alpha + \beta Y_t^* + U_t$,
with adaptive expectations hypothesis: $Y_t^* - Y_{t-1}^* = \lambda (Y_t - Y_{t-1}^*)$

$$\text{or,} \quad Y_t^* = -\frac{\alpha}{\beta} + \frac{1}{\beta} C_t - \frac{1}{\beta} U$$

$$\text{and,} \quad Y_{t-1}^* = -\frac{\alpha}{\beta} + \frac{1}{\beta} C_{t-1} - \frac{1}{\beta} U_{t-1}$$

Substituting these values in the adaptive hypothesis, we obtain:

$$\left(-\frac{\alpha}{\beta}+\frac{1}{\beta}C_t-\frac{1}{\beta}U_t\right)-\left(-\frac{\alpha}{\beta}+\frac{1}{\beta}C_{t-1}-\frac{1}{\beta}U_{t-1}\right)$$

$$=\lambda\left[Y_t-\left\{-\frac{\alpha}{\beta}+\frac{1}{\beta}C_{t-1}-\frac{1}{\beta}U_{t-1}\right\}\right]$$

i.e., $\qquad C_t = (\lambda\alpha) + (\lambda\beta)\,Y_t + (1-\lambda)\,C_{t-1} + [U_t - (1-\lambda)\,U_{t-1}]$.

which is the final equation of a Simple Adaptive Expectations Model.

On comparing with the final equations of the Koyck's model and Adaptive Expectation model, we observe that same variables appear on the right hand side of the equations; hence all the three models are identical. The reason for equivalence of the three models is due to the fact that the underlying assumption regarding the lag-pattern (which being the declining geometric pattern of lag coefficients) is similar in all the three models. But it should, nevertheless, be remembered that although similar in appearance, the Adaptive Expectation and Partial Adjustment models are conceptually very much different. The former is based on uncertainty (about the future course of prices and interest rates), whereas the latter is due to technical and institutional rigidities, inertia and cost of the change. These two models are theoretically much sounder than the Koyck model.

10.3.9 Compound Geometric Lag Model

We have discussed partial adjustment and adaptive expectation models above. Operational form of both the models is the same; that is, the declining geometric pattern of lag coefficients.

As a matter of interest, both these models can be combined into one compound geometric lag model. This combined form can be visualized as the modification of the simple regression model:

$$Y_t = \alpha + \beta X_t + U_t.$$

In the adaptive expectation model X_t is replaced by its 'expected' value X_t^*; and in the partial adjustment model, Y_t is replaced by its 'desired' value Y_t^*. Combining two specifications, we write:

$$Y_t^* = \alpha + \beta X_t^* + U_t \qquad\qquad ...(10.1)$$

This means that the mean of desired value of Y is a linear function of the expected level of X.

Examples of such combinations expressed in the form (10.1) may be many:

(i) A firm anticipates some change in the demand for its product. So the firm desires to increase the capital stock equal to K_t^* provided the expected sales are S_t^*. The model in this case becomes:

$$K_t^* = \alpha + \beta S_t^* + U_t \qquad\qquad ...(10.2)$$

(ii) Farmers desire to go for the area sown equal to A_t^* provided the price (expected) is P_t^*, that is

$$A_t^* = \alpha + \beta P_t^* + U_t \qquad \text{...(10.3)}$$

Thus in the model (10.1), we have to see how the X_t^* and Y_t^* are transformed into operational variables. Both partial adjustment and expectation mechanism or hypothesis work under such model;

Adaptive Expectation Hypothesis: $X_t^* - X_{t-1}^* = \lambda(X_t - X_{t-1}^*)$ ...(A)

Partial Adjustment Hypothesis: $Y_t - Y_{t-1} = \delta(Y_t^* - Y_{t-1})$ ...(B)

λ = reaction of expectations, and δ = speed of adjustment

To begin, omit residual term (for the sake of convenience) in (10.1)

$$Y_t^* = \alpha + \beta X_t^*$$

$$Y_{t-1}^* = \alpha + \beta X_{t-1}^* \qquad \text{...(10.4)}$$

$$Y_t^* - Y_{t-1}^* = \beta(X_t^* - X_{t-1}^*)$$

$$Y_t^* - Y_{t-1}^* = \lambda\beta(X_t - X_{t-1}^*) \qquad \text{(using Hyp. A)}$$

$$Y_t^* - Y_{t-1}^* = \lambda\beta X_t - \lambda\beta X_{t-1}^* \qquad \text{...(10.5)}$$

Also $\beta X_{t-1}^* = Y_{t-1}^* - \alpha$ from (10.4)

Substituting (10.4) in (10.5);

$$Y_t^* - Y_{t-1}^* = \lambda\beta X_t - \lambda(Y_{t-1}^* - \alpha)$$

$$Y_t^* - (1-\lambda)Y_{t-1}^* = \lambda\alpha + \lambda\beta X_t \qquad \text{...(10.6)}$$

Hypothesis (B) can also be stated as follows:

$$Y_t^* = \frac{1}{\delta}[Y_t - (1-\delta)Y_{t-1}] \qquad \text{...(10.7)}$$

So that $Y_{t-1}^* = \frac{1}{\delta}[Y_{t-1} - (1-\delta)Y_{t-2}]$

Multiplying throughout by $(1 - \lambda)$,

$$(1 - \lambda)Y^*_{t-1} = \left(\frac{1-\lambda}{\delta}\right)[Y_{t-1} - (1-\delta)Y_{t-2}] \qquad \text{...(10.8)}$$

Using (10.7) and (10.8) in (10.6),

$$\frac{1}{\delta}[Y_t - (1-\delta)Y_{t-1}] - \left(\frac{1-\lambda}{\delta}\right)[Y_{t-1} - (1-\delta)Y_{t-2}] = \lambda\alpha + \lambda\beta X_t$$

$$\left(\frac{1}{\delta}\right)Y_t + \left(\frac{\delta - 2 + \lambda}{\delta}\right)Y_{t-1} + \left\{\frac{(1-\lambda)(1-\delta)}{\delta}\right\}Y_{t-2} = \lambda\alpha + \lambda\beta X_t$$

or, $Y_t = \delta\lambda\alpha + \delta\lambda\beta X_t + (2 - \lambda - \delta) Y_{t-1} - (1-\lambda)(1-\delta) Y_{t-2}$ ...(10.9)

(10.9) possesses all variables in operational form; we may write it as:

$$Y_t = b_0 + b_1 X_t + b_2 Y_{t-1} + b_3 Y_{t-2}$$

where, $\hat{b}_0 = \delta\lambda\alpha$ ...(i)

$$\hat{b}_1 = \delta\lambda\beta \qquad\qquad\text{...(ii)}$$

$$\hat{b}_2 = (2 - \lambda - \delta) \qquad\qquad\text{...(iii)}$$

$$\hat{b}_3 = (-)(1-\lambda)(1-\delta) \qquad\qquad\text{...(iv)}$$

Four estimated values $(\hat{b}_0, \hat{b}_1, \hat{b}_2, \hat{b}_3)$ of coefficient, which we obtain by regressing Y_t on Y_{t-1}, Y_{t-2} and X_t in (10.9), give rise to four equations with four unknown parameters α, β, λ and δ.

Solving these equations, we obtain:

$$\hat{\alpha} = \frac{\hat{b}_0}{1 - \hat{b}_2 - \hat{b}_3}$$

$$\hat{\beta} = \frac{\hat{b}_1}{1 - \hat{b}_2 - \hat{b}_3}$$

$$\hat{\delta} = \frac{2 - \hat{b}_2 \pm \sqrt{\hat{b}_2^2 - 4\hat{b}_3}}{2}$$

$$\hat{\lambda} = 2 - \hat{b}_2 - \hat{\delta}$$

It may be observed that though we can determine α and β unambiguously, δ and λ are not determined unquitely.

Procedure for Obtaining δ and λ: Suppose that (10.9) describes capital stock requirements (Y_t) which depends on sales (X_t), past acquired capital (Y_{t-1}) and (Y_{t-2}). The speed of adjustment coefficient (δ) and reaction of expectation coefficient (λ) can then be obtained by introducing other variables in this multiple regression; say L_t, the amount of labour hired. The initial model (10.1) then changes to

$$Y_t^* = \alpha + \beta_1 X_t^* + \beta_2 L_t + U_t$$

This model in the form of (10.9) changes to:

$$Y_t = \delta\lambda\alpha + \delta\lambda\beta_1 X_t + (2 - \lambda - \delta) Y_{t-1} - (1-\lambda)(1-\delta) Y_{t-2}$$
$$+ \delta\beta_2 L_t - \delta(1-\lambda)\beta_2 L_{t-1} \qquad\qquad\text{...(10.10)}$$

which may be written in the following form:

$$Y_t = b_0 + b_1 X_t + b_2 Y_{t-1} - b_3 Y_{t-2} + b_4 L_t - b_5 L_{t-1} \qquad\qquad\text{...(10.11)}$$

On regressing Y_t on X_t, Y_{t-1}, Y_{t-2}, L_t and L_{t-2} in (10.10), we shall obtain two more coefficients of L_t and L_{t-1}. Though from these two coefficients, we can determine unique value of λ, it nevertheless give rise to two values of δ; one from the coefficient of Y_{t-1} and another from the coefficient of Y_{t-2}. Corresponding to each value of δ we get one set of estimates of α, β_1 and β_2. Therefore, δ is said to be 'over identified' in (10.10). This is also obvious from the fact that (10.10) involves *six* coefficients (b_0, b_1, b_2, b_3, b_4 and b_5) but only *five* parameters (α, β_1, β_2, λ and δ).

Coefficients of (10.11) describe:

$$\left.\begin{array}{l} \hat{b}_0 = \delta\lambda\alpha \\[4pt] \hat{b}_1 = \delta\lambda\beta_1 \\[4pt] \hat{b}_2 = (2-\lambda-\delta) \\[4pt] \hat{b}_3 = (-)(1-\lambda)(1-\delta) \\[4pt] \hat{b}_4 = \delta\beta_2 \\[4pt] \hat{b}_5 = (-)\delta(1-\lambda)\beta_2 \end{array}\right\} \quad \therefore\ = 1+\frac{\hat{b}_5}{\hat{b}_4}.$$

(i) The estimate of δ from the coefficient of Y_{t-1} is

$$\delta = (2-b_2-\lambda) = 1-\hat{b}_2-\frac{\hat{b}_5}{\hat{b}_4}$$

(ii) The estimate of δ from the coefficient of Y_{t-2} is

$$\delta = 1+\frac{\hat{b}_3}{1-\lambda} = 1-\frac{\hat{b}_3\hat{b}_4}{\hat{b}_5}$$

The two estimates of δ should be equal. Hence we develop a restriction that:

$$1-b_2-\frac{b_5}{b_4} = 1-\frac{b_3b_4}{b_5}$$

that is, $-b_3b_4^2 + b_2b_4b_5 + b_5^2 = 0$ ...(10.12)

This restriction is non-linear restriction. To obtain the unique estimates of b_0, b_1, b_2, b_3, b_4 and b_5, we shall have to minimise

$$\Sigma(Y_t - b_0 - b_1X_t - b_2Y_{t-1} - b_2Y_{t-2} - b_4L_t - b_5L_{t-1})^2$$

subject to non-linear restriction (10.12). This procedure is called non-linear least squares method of estimation which is beyond the scope of the present text.

ASSIGNMENTS

1. In matrix notation: $\hat{\beta} = (X'X)^{-1}X'Y$ and, Var-Cov $(\hat{\beta}) = \sigma^2(X'X)^{-1}$

   (a) What happen to $\hat{\beta}$ when there is perfect collinearity among X's?

   (b) How would you know if perfect collinearity exists?

   (c) What happens to Var-Cov $(\hat{\beta})$ matrix if there is perfect multicollinearity, and if collinearity is high but not perfect.

2. "Due to the existence of multicollinearity in the data, the OLS estimates of the regression coefficients and their standard errors become very sensitive." Examine this statement by assuming the following hypothetical data on Y, X_1 and X_2 in the first instance, and then interchanging the third and fourth values of X_2 only.

Y	X_1	X_2
1	2	4
2	0	2
3	4	12
4	6	0
5	8	16

Y	X_1	X_2
1	2	4
2	0	2
3	4	0
4	6	12
5	8	16

3. How would you find out from the given zero-order (simple) correlation matrix whether:

   (i) there is perfect collinearity,

   (ii) there is less than perfect collinearity, and

   (iii) there is no multicollinearity in the data.

4. Examine whether the model: $Y_t = \alpha + \beta_1 X_{1i} + \beta_2 X_{2i} + U_i$ can be fitted to the following hypothetical data:

Y	X_1	X_2
-10	1	1
-8	2	3
-6	3	5
-4	4	7
-2	5	9
0	6	11
2	7	13
4	8	15
6	9	17
8	10	19

   How would you modify the model in case it is not possible to estimate the above given model?

5. Suppose in the regression model:
   $$Y_t = \alpha + \beta_1 X_{1i} + \beta_2 X_{2i} + U_i,$$
   γ_{12} which depicts coefficient of correlation between X_1 and X_2 is zero. Would you suggest to run the following regressions:
   $$Y_t = \alpha_0 + \alpha_1 X_{1i} + U_1 \text{ and,}$$
   $$Y_t = \gamma_0 + \gamma_2 X_{2i} + U_{2i}?$$

Also examine whether:

(i) $\hat{\alpha}_1 = \hat{\beta}_1$ and $\hat{\gamma}_2 = \hat{\beta}_2$?

(ii) $\hat{\alpha} = \hat{\alpha}_0$ and $\hat{\alpha} = \hat{\gamma}_0$?

6 It is required to estimate the short-run average and marginal cost curves of a commodity from a given data. The model suggested is of the form:

$$Y_i = \alpha + \beta_1 X_i + \beta_2 X_i^2 + \beta_3 X_i^3 + U_i$$

where, Y = total cost, and X = output

The zero-order (simple) correlation matrix from the data obtained is as follows:

$$
\begin{array}{cccc}
 & X_i & X_i^2 & X_i^3 \\
X_i & \begin{bmatrix} 1.0 & 0.97 & 0.93 \\ - & 1.0 & 0.99 \\ - & - & 1.0 \end{bmatrix} \\
X_i^2 \\
X_i^3
\end{array}
$$

(i) Would you say that since the zero-order correlations are very high, there must be serious multicollinearity?

(ii) Would you drop variables X_i^2 and X_i^3 from the model?

(iii) What will happen to the value of the coefficient of X_i (i.e., β_1) if you drop X_i^2 and X_i^3?

7 Discuss the problem of pooling cross-section and time-series data on household per capita total consumption expenditure and per capita expenditure on a given commodity in estimating expenditure elasticity of demand for that commodity. Can you give a set of sufficient conditions under which such data can be validly pooled?

8 If in a production function, we include two inputs, land and labour but fail to include an important input—capital; show how this mis-specification will affect the coefficient of land and labour. Are the estimates of these inputs likely to be biased?

9 Based on the Durbin-Watson d-statistic, how would you distinguish 'pure' autocorrelation from specification bias?

10 Define specification bias.

Will the least squares method yield an unbiased estimate of β_1 when $Y_i = \alpha + \beta_1 X_{1i} + \beta_2 X_{2i} + U_i$ is the correct model but the investigator assumes the model: $Y_i = \alpha + \beta_1 X_{1i} + v_i$; X_1 and X_2 being nostochastic, U and v being disturbances? Explain whether estimate of α be unbiased?

11 The true demand function of a commodity is represented as:

$$Q = \beta_0 + \beta_1 P + + \beta_2 Y + U;$$

where Q = quantity demanded, P = price of commodity, and Y = personal disposable income.

Suppose Y is mistakenly omitted from the above model.

(a) Derive an expression for the specification bias imported in $\hat{\beta}_1$.

(b) Under what conditions will $\hat{\beta}_1$ be upwardly or downwardly biased?

(c) What is the most plausible type of bias in $\hat{\beta}_1$ on *a priori* economic criteria?

12 Define Mean lag and Median lag. Show that for Koyck model the mean lag is $[\lambda/(1 - \lambda)]$ and median lag is $-\left(\dfrac{\log 2}{\log \lambda}\right)$; where λ is the rate of decline of the lagged coefficients.

Evaluate the median lag for λ = 0.2, 0.4 and 0.8.

13 Consider the Koyck model:

$$Y_t = \alpha (1 - \lambda) + \beta_0 X_t + \lambda Y_{t-1} + (U_t - \lambda U_{t-1})$$

Suppose in the original model U_t follows the first order autoregressive scheme: $U_t - \rho u_{t-1} = v_t$, where ρ is the coefficient of autocorrelation and v_t satisfies all the classical OLS assumptions.

(a) If $\rho = \lambda$, can the Koyck model be estimated by OLS?

(b) Will the estimates thus obtained be unbiased and consistent?

(c) How reasonable is it to assume that $\rho = \lambda$?

14   Show under what conditions Koyck's distributed lag model can provide a solution to the problem of multicollinearity.

15   Discuss the economic rationale for using the distributed lag model associated with Koyck. Why is the OLS procedure unsatisfactory for such models? Indicate methods for estimating such models.

16   Consider the model: $Y_t = \alpha + b_0 X_t + ... + b_6 X_{t-6} + U_t$.

Suppose that we employ the Almon technique with a polynomial of degree 4 to estimate the parameter of this model. Suppose also that our results are

$$\hat{a}_0 = 1, \ \hat{a}_1 = 3, \ \hat{a}_2 = 5, \ \hat{a}_3 = 4 \ \text{and} \ \hat{a}_4 = -10$$

Write up the estimated model.

17   Consider the following distributed-lag model:

$$Y_t = \alpha + \beta_0 X_{t-1} + \beta_2 X_{t-2} + \beta_3 X_{t-3} + \beta_4 X_{t-4} + U$$

Assume that β_i can be adequately expressed by the second degree polynomial as follows:

$$\beta_i = a_0 + a_1 i + a_2 i^2$$

How would you estimate the β's if we want to impose the restriction that $\beta_0 = \beta_4 = 0$?

18   Bring out the 'duality' between 'Partial Adjustment' and 'Adaptive Expectations' models. Discuss their utility in applied econometric research.

19   Examine whether the following statements are true, false or uncertain. Give reasons in each case.

(a) The omission of a variable from a regression equation biases the estimates of the coefficients of the included variables.

(b) Multicollinearity among the independent variables in a regression equation implies that the OLS estimates of the coefficients are not BLU.

(c) The omission of income variable in a demand function results in an underestimate of the price elasticity in absolute terms.

(d) If a variable X is uncorrelated with Z, the addition of Z to a regression in which X is used as an independent variable will not change either the coefficient of X or the standard error of the coefficient.

(e) An estimation of the demand function for a commodity gave its price elasticity of demand = −0.4. This finding should be interpreted to mean that the price elasticity of supply is at least + 0.4.

(f) The omission of an explanatory variable will not lead to serious consequences for OLS estimation if it is uncorrelated with the included explanatory variable.

(g) The inclusion of an irrelevant explanatory variable(s) in the regression equation reduces the precision of the estimates of the true explanatory variable(s).

(h) The model: $Y = \alpha_0 + \beta_1 X_1 + \beta_2 X_1^2 + U$ involves the problem of perfect multicollinearity.

(i) If regression in the form $Y = \alpha_0 + \beta_1 X_1 + U$ is run instead of true regression of the form given in (h), the slope coefficient shall be biased upwards.

(j) The mean lag of an estimated Equation:

$$Y_t = 0.10 + .25 \, X_t + 0.35 \, X_{t-1} + 0.15 \, X_{t-2} + 0.05 \, X_{t-3} + U_t \text{ is } 1.78.$$

11

Adhoc Procedures in Regression Analysis (Instrumental and Dummy Variables)

One of the five basic assumptions in Classical Linear Regression model requires that the explanatory variables are measured without errors and that they be nonstochastic in nature. This, in a way, makes the explanatory variables uncorrelated with the disturbance terms*. If such an assumption is withdrawn, that is, if a regressor is correlated with disturbance, then least squares estimation gives a misleading estimate of the influence of variations in the regressor on the variations in the regressand (Independent Variable). This may be explained by taking simple two variables model with both variables measured in deviation form:

$$\hat{\beta} = \frac{\Sigma x_i y_i}{\Sigma x_i^2} \quad ; \quad \text{where} \quad y_i = \beta x_i + u_i$$

or,
$$\hat{\beta} = \frac{\Sigma x_i (\beta x_i + u_i)}{\Sigma x_i^2} = \frac{\beta \Sigma x_i^2 + \Sigma x_i u_i}{\Sigma x_i^2}$$

$$\hat{\beta} = \beta + \frac{\Sigma x_i u_i}{\Sigma x_i^2} \qquad \qquad ...(11.1)$$

It was hence proved that $\hat{\beta}$ is an unbiased estimator of β only when observations on X variable were assumed to be fixed in repeated samples (nonstochastic). This makes the $\Sigma x_i u_i$ term vanish and the desired result is achieved.

But, as it is generally observed, such an ideal situation is not met in practice. All economic data are subject to some errors of measurement for a variety of reasons:

(a) Most of the aggregate (published) series are obtained from samples which are *blown up* to cover the aggregate macro-variables. Errors in

---

* If on the other, dependent variable (regressand) is not error free in measurements, disturbance term takes care of it in the classical linear regression model.

sampling and, therefore, the errors in extrapolation of the samples are certain to occur.

(b) Many times the variable required by economic theory is different in the content than what is available, but still it is used due to non-availability of the variable (required by economic theory). For instance, for estimation of consumption function at macro-level data on GNP is used in place of disposable income. Use of GNP is bound to have an error of measurement in the explanatory variable.

(c) Many times current values of variables are deflated through price indices in order to express the relationship in the particular time period. If the index of prices is not appropriate or not without errors, the deflating procedure is bound to have errors.

(d) Sometimes the indices of wages, prices, income, etc., are used as explanatory variables for the regression model. These indices may not be without errors.

For such other reasons it seems that the presumption of no errors in the variables in regressors should be questioned in all econometric applications. The challenge to this presumption becomes more strong and meaningful if it could be proved that the coefficients of the regression model are greatly affected if such an assumption is withdrawn.

11.1 ERRORS IN VARIABLES

Consequences of violation of the above assumption are explained by considering three cases systematically.

Case 1: *When Y is measured with Error*

Consider a classical simple linear regression model:

$$Y_i^* = \alpha + \beta X_i + U_i \qquad \qquad ...(11.2)$$

where,
$Y_i^* = $ true but unobservable value of the dependent variable

$Y_i = $ observable value of the dependent variable

$Y_i = Y_i^* + V_i$; where V_i denote errors of measurement in Y_i^*. Therefore, instead of estimating (11.2), we estimate:

$$Y_i = (\alpha + \beta X_i + U_i) + V_i$$
$$= \alpha + \beta X_i + (U_i + V_i)$$
$$= \alpha + \beta X_i + \varepsilon_i \qquad \qquad ...(11.3)$$

where $\varepsilon_i = U_i + V_i$ is a composite error term, containing the population disturbance term and the measurement error term.

For simplicity assume that:

$E(U_i) = E(V_i) = 0$, $Cov(X_i, V_i) = 0$ [that is to say that errors of measurement in Y_i^* are uncorrelated with X_i], $Cov(X_i, U_i) = 0$, and $Cov(U_i, V_i) = 0$; which means that the equation error and the measurement error are not correlated. Also that ε_i is homosedastic with known constant variance.

With these assumptions, it can be proved that β estimated from (11.3) will be an unbiased estimator of true β.

From (11.3), $\qquad \hat{\beta} = \dfrac{\Sigma x_i y_i}{\Sigma x_i^2} = \dfrac{\Sigma x_i (\beta x_i + \varepsilon_i)}{\Sigma x_i^2}$

$$E(\hat{\beta}) = E\left\{\beta + \frac{\Sigma x_i \varepsilon_i}{\Sigma x_i^1}\right\} \qquad \text{[since } Cov(X_i, \varepsilon_i) = 0\text{]},$$

$E(\hat{\beta}) = \beta$; that is, the errors of measurement in the dependent variable Y do not destroy the characteristic of unbiasedness of the OLS estimators.

What about the variance of $\hat{\beta}$ estimated from (11.6)? Applying the usual formula, we obtain:

$$\text{Var}(\hat{\beta}) = \frac{\sigma_\varepsilon^2}{\Sigma x_i^2} = \frac{\sigma_u^2 + \sigma_v^2}{\Sigma x_i^2} \qquad \qquad ...(11.4)$$

Had there been no errors of measurement in Y,

$$\text{Var}(\hat{\beta}) \text{ would have been } = \frac{\sigma_u^2}{\Sigma x_i^2}$$

which obviously is smaller than the variance obtained in (11.4).

It may, therefore, be concluded that although the errors of measurement in the dependent variable give unbiased estimates of the parameters, the estimated variances are larger than in the case when there are no such errors of measurement.

Case 2: *When X is measured with Error*

Instead of (11.2), assume the simple linear regression model as:

$$Y_i = \alpha + \beta X_i^* + U_i \qquad \qquad ...(11.5)$$

where $\qquad Y_i =$ true and observable value of the dependent variable

$\qquad X_i^* =$ true but unobservable value of the explanatory variable

$\qquad X_i =$ observable value of the explanatory variable

$\qquad X_i = X_i^* + W_i$; that is W_i denote errors of measurement in X_i^*. Therefore, instead of estimating (11.5), we estimate:

$$Y_i = \alpha + \beta(X_i + W_i) + U_i$$
$$= \alpha + \beta X_i + (U_i + \beta W_i)$$
$$= \alpha + \beta X_i + U_i^* \qquad \qquad ...(11.6)$$

where $U_i^* = U_i - \beta W_i$; a compound of equation and measurement errors.

In this case, even if it is assumed that U_i^* has zero mean, it is nonautocorrelated, and is uncorrelated with population disturbance term U_i, it is not possible to assume that the composite error term U_i^* is independent of the explanatory variable X_i.

$$\text{Cov }(X_i, U_i^*) = E(X_i - E(X_i)][U_i^* - E(U_i^*)]$$
$$\text{(assuming the } E(U_i^*) = 0)$$

$$\text{Cov }(X_i, U_i^*) = E(U_i - \beta W_i)(W_i)$$
$$= E(-\beta W_i^2)$$
$$= -\beta \sigma_w^2 \neq 0,$$

because neither β can be zero (there will be then no relation between the variables) nor σ_w^2 can be zero (because it is a square). Thus, the observed explanatory variable and error term in (11.6) are correlated. This, then is the violation of an important assumption of classical linear regression model. The OLS estimators, therefore, will not only be biased (even asymptotically) but also inconsistent. This may be proved as follows:

On applying OLS to (11.5):

$$\hat{\beta} = \frac{\Sigma x_i^* y_i}{\Sigma x_i^{*2}} = \frac{\Sigma[(X_i^* - \bar{X}^*)(Y_i - \bar{Y})]}{\Sigma(X_i^* - \bar{X}^*)^2}$$

$$\hat{\beta} = \frac{\Sigma[\{(X_i - \bar{X}) - (W_i - \bar{W})\}(Y_i - \bar{Y})]}{\Sigma[(X_i - \bar{X}) - (W_i - \bar{W})]^2}$$

$$\hat{\beta} = \frac{\Sigma[\{(X_i - \bar{X})(Y_i - \bar{Y}) - (W_i - \bar{W})(Y - \bar{Y})]}{\Sigma(X_i - \bar{X})^2 - 2\Sigma(X_i - \bar{X})(W_i - \bar{W}) + \Sigma(W_i - \bar{W})^2}$$

The last term of the numerator and the middle term of the denominator vanish as $n \to \infty$.

$$\therefore \quad \text{plim} \cdot (\hat{\beta}) = \frac{\Sigma(X_i - \bar{X})(Y_i - \bar{Y})}{\Sigma(X_i - \bar{X})^2 + n\sigma_w^2}$$

$$\text{or,} \quad \text{plim} \cdot (\hat{\beta}) = \frac{\{\Sigma(X_i - \bar{X})(Y_i - \bar{Y})\} \div \Sigma(X_i - \bar{X})^2}{1 + [n\sigma_w \div \Sigma(X_i - \bar{X})^2]}$$

$$\text{plim} \cdot (\hat{\beta}) = \frac{\beta}{1 + \left\{\dfrac{n\sigma_w^2}{n}\right\} \div \left\{\dfrac{\Sigma(X_i - \bar{X})^2}{n}\right\}}$$

$$\text{plim} \cdot (\hat{\beta}) = \left[\frac{1}{1 + \dfrac{\sigma_w^2}{\sigma_x^2}}\right] \neq \beta$$

(σ_w^2 = variance of the measurement error in X^* and σ_x^2 = variance of X values), hence $\hat{\beta}$ is biased.

Again, the condition of consistency is also violated since the ratio $\left(\sigma_w^2/\sigma_x^2\right)$ shall always be greater than zero (being the ratio of two squares) even if the size of sample is increased, plim $\cdot (\hat{\beta}) < \beta$;

$\therefore$ $(\hat{\beta})$ is asymptotically biased and hence inconsistent. For instance, if σ_w^2 is 10 per cent of σ_x^2, $\hat{\beta}$ is likely to be underestimated by about 10 per cent no matter how large a sample size is available.

The effect of measurement of errors can also be shown diagrammatically. Suppose our observations correspond to just two values of X. If the measurement of errors are in Y, the effect will merely be to increase the dispersion of Y values around their expected value at each value of X as shown in Fig. 11.1 and 11.2; and there is no consequential bias. If however, the measurement errors are in X, the result will be a horizontal dispersion of X values around each value of X^* as shown in Fig. 11.3.

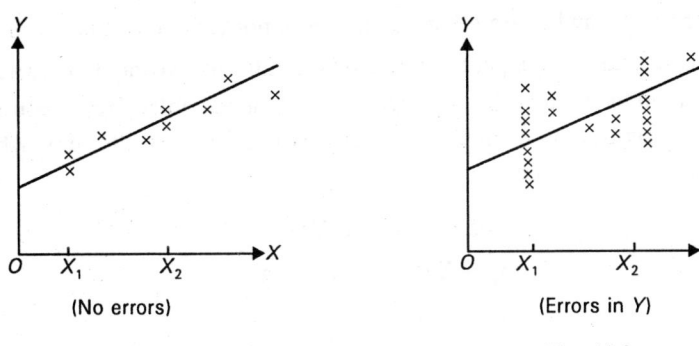

(No errors)   (Errors in Y)

Fig. 11.1   **Fig. 11.2**

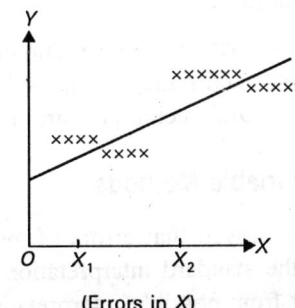

(Errors in X)

Fig. 11.3

Case 3: *When X and Y both are measured with Errors.*

Though under this case no new conclusions compared to above two cases are derived, the present case is important from the point of view of understanding it in some other details.

Considering the same two variable case that:

$$Y_i^* = \alpha + \beta X_i^* + U_i \qquad \qquad ...(11.7)$$

where,
$$Y_i = Y_i^* + V_i \ ; \quad V_i \sim N(0, \sigma_w^2)$$
$$X_i = X_i^* + W_i; \quad W_i \sim N(0, \sigma_w^2)$$

W_i, V_i are uncorrelated with each other and that each error involves no serial correlation. Finally, in the present case: $y_i^* = \beta x_i^*$ (since there are no other types of errors).

Consider the ordinary least-squares estimator $\hat{\beta}$ from (11.7).

$$\hat{\beta} = \frac{\Sigma x_i^* y_i^*}{\Sigma x_i^{*2}} = \frac{\Sigma(x_i - w_i)(y_i - v_i)}{\Sigma(x_i - w_i)^2} = \frac{\Sigma(x_i - w_i)(\beta x_i - v_i)}{\Sigma(x_i - w_i)^2}$$

$$\hat{\beta} = \frac{\beta \Sigma x_1^2 - \beta \Sigma x_i w_i - \Sigma x_i v_i - \Sigma w_i v_i}{\Sigma x_i^2 + \Sigma w_i^2 - 2\Sigma x_i w_i}$$

Since x_i, w_i and v_i are all stochastic, it is not easy to evaluate the bias of $\hat{\beta}$. It is because the expected value of the ratio of two random variables is not equal to the ratio of the expected value of the variables. Hence consistency of $\hat{\beta}$ is obtained by evaluating the expression for $\hat{\beta}$ in the limit when the sample size gets large.

$$\text{plim} \cdot \hat{\beta} = \text{plim} \cdot \frac{\beta \Sigma x_i^2}{\Sigma x_i^2 + \Sigma w_i^2} = \frac{\beta \cdot \text{Var}(x)}{\text{Var}(x) + \sigma_w^2}$$

$$= \frac{\beta}{1 + \sigma_w^2 \Big/ \text{Var}(x)}$$

This, therefore, suggests that in case measurement error are present in both the variables (regressor and regressand), the true regression parameter shall be under estimated if OLS techniques are used.

11.1.1 Instrumental-Variable Methods

The above discussion has proved that errors of measurement pose a great threat to the validity of the standard interpretation of the estimators.

How are we to protect from possible interpretation of OLS results if we become aware of the existence of errors in measurement?

In fact econometricians do not have much to offer in the way of useful solution; while on the other, Maximum Likelihood procedure can not be used in such a situation. Hence, some 'grouping' procedures of estimation have been suggested to solve the measurement error problem. All these grouping methods can be regarded as "Instrumental-Variable" methods*.

The method of instrumental variable involves the search for a new variable (say it is Z) which is both highly correlated with the independent variable (X) and at the same time uncorrelated with the error term in the equation; as well as the errors of measurement in explanatory variable(s).

The reason we can not use OLS to derive unbiased estimator of β for the equation (11.6) is that $(u_i - \beta w_i)$ is correlated with (X_i). In case a new variable (here called instrumental variable) Z is a variable uncorrelated with residual $(u_i - \beta w_i)$ but correlated with (X), the instrumental variable estimator of β is obtained by solving two 'Normal Equations' put in deviation form:

$$\Sigma y_i = \hat{\beta} \Sigma x_i + \Sigma u_i \qquad \text{...(i)}$$
$$\Sigma z_i y_i = \hat{\beta} \Sigma x_i z_i + \hat{\beta} z_i u_i \qquad \text{...(ii)}$$

(second equation has now completely changed)

$$\underset{\text{(I.V estimator)}}{\hat{\beta}^*} = \frac{\Sigma z_i y_i}{\Sigma x_i z_i} \qquad \text{(solving eq. (ii))}$$

$$\text{plim} \cdot \hat{\beta}^* = \frac{\Sigma(\beta x_i + u_i - \beta w_i) z_i}{\Sigma x_i z_i}$$

$$= \beta + \text{plim} \cdot \frac{(1/n) \Sigma(u_i - \beta w_i) z_i}{(1/n) \Sigma x_i z_i}$$

$$= \beta \text{ [because (Z_i) is uncorrelated with $(u_i - \beta w_i)$,}$$
$$\text{provided plim} \cdot (1/n) \Sigma x_i z_i = \text{Cov} \cdot (xz) \neq 0]$$

Any random variable can be considered as an instrumental variable only if:

(i) the correlation between (Z) and (U), (V) and (W) in the equation approach zero as the sample size gets larger, and
(ii) the correlation between (Z) and (X) is non zero as the sample size gets large.

The three main grouping methods of instrumental variables suggested by

---

* This technique is an important estimation technique when one is dealing with models consisting of system of simultaneous equations. Refer section 14.7 of Chapter 14 on Simultaneous Eq. Methods.

Wald, Bartlett and Durbin are presented here.

1. *Wald's Two Group Method*

This method may be outlined as follows:

(i) The observations of explanatory variable X are ordered in ascending magnitude and then divided into two equal subgroups. If the total number of observations is odd, the central observations are omitted. Assuming that the subscripts actually indicate the order of magnitude, our ordered array shall be:

$$X_1, X_2, X_3, ..., X_m, X_{m+1}, X_{m+2}, ..., X_n$$

and the corresponding Y values,

$$Y_1, Y_2, Y_3, ..., Y_m, Y_{m+1}, Y_{m+2}, ..., Y_n$$

(ii) Compute the means for the below group of observations (below median) and for the above group of observations (above median).

$$\bar{X}_1 = \frac{1}{m}\sum_{i}^{m} X_i, \quad \bar{X}_2 = \frac{1}{m}\sum_{m+1}^{n} X_i$$

$$\bar{Y}_1 = \frac{1}{m}\sum_{i}^{m} Y_i \quad \bar{Y}_2 = \frac{1}{m}\sum_{m+1}^{n} Y_i$$

(iii) Obtain estimate of the slope parameter by the following formula:

$$\text{Estimate of } \beta = \beta^* = \frac{\bar{Y}_2 - \bar{Y}_1}{\bar{X}_2 - \bar{X}_1}$$

The assumption underlying this method is, to obtain the slope of regression line which passes through the means of the two subgroups. This may be understood by Fig. 11.4.

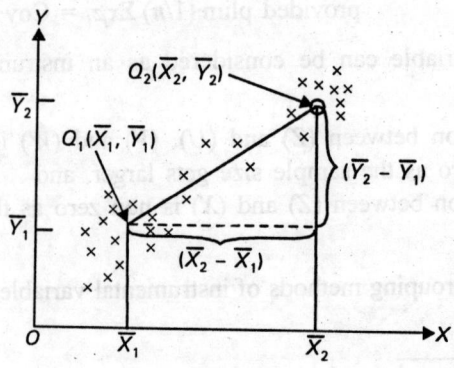

Fig. 11.4

Q_1 and Q_2 depict the means of sub-groups and slope of the line joining Q_1 and Q_2 points is given by*

$$\beta^* = \frac{\overline{Y}_2 - \overline{Y}_1}{\overline{X}_2 - \overline{X}_1}$$

The constant intercept is obtained in the usual way:

$$\alpha^* = \overline{Y} - \beta^* \overline{X}$$

α^* and β^* are consistent but are not best. In other words, the estimates, obtained through this procedure, are no doubt asymptotically unbiased but they do not possess the minimum variance property.

2. Barlett's Three-Group Method

The underlying idea in this method is the same as that of two group method: that is, fitting a straight line to the data passing through the means of sub-groups as shown in Fig. 11.5. The only difference is that, in the present method, the total observations are divided into three sub-groups instead of two sub-groups. This method can be outlined as follows:

(i) Observations are arranged in ascending order and divided into three equal groups (or approximately equal);

(ii) The means for the lowest and the highest group are computed. The middle one is ignored; and

(iii) The estimate of the slope parameter, then, is obtained by the formula,

$$\beta^* = \frac{\overline{Y}_3 - \overline{Y}_1}{\overline{X}_3 - \overline{X}_1}$$

Figure 11.5 shows that it merely amounts to drawing a straight line through two points $Q_1(\overline{X}_1, \overline{Y}_1)$ and $Q_3(\overline{X}_3, \overline{Y}_3)$.

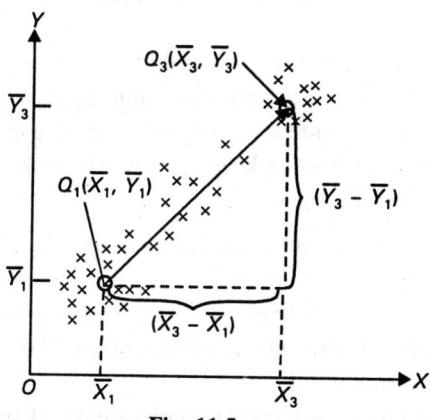

Fig. 11.5

---

* This amounts to using the instrumental variable as: $Z_i = 1$ if $X_i >$ median value; $Z_i = -1$ if $X_i < -$ median value and then using the estimator $\hat{\beta}^* = \Sigma Y_i Z_i / \Sigma X_i Z_i$.

This method gives unbiased and consistent estimate of the slope coefficient. This estimate of slope coefficient is more efficient (i.e., it possesses smaller variance) than the Two Group method suggested by A. Wald.

3. Durbin's Method

Use of above grouping methods become cumbersome and tedious when more than one explanatory variables are involved in regression equation. Method suggested by Durbin does not possess such drawback.

In Durbin's method ranks of (X_i) operate as instrumental variables.

Matrix $\mathbf{Z}$ in general classical linear regression model is defined after $(\mathbf{X})$ values are put in ascending order, that is,

$$\mathbf{Z'} = \begin{bmatrix} 1 & 1 & 1 & \text{......} & 1 \\ 1 & 2 & 3 & \text{......} & n \end{bmatrix}$$

where the second row indicates the rank values of the X's in the

$$\hat{\beta}^* = (\mathbf{Z'X})^{-1} \mathbf{Z'Y}$$

In two variable case (in deviational form):

$$\hat{\beta}^* = \frac{\Sigma i \cdot y_i}{\Sigma i \cdot x_i}, \text{ and}$$

intercept: $\qquad\qquad \hat{\alpha}^* = \dfrac{\overline{Y}\Sigma i \cdot X_i - \overline{X}\Sigma i \cdot Y_i}{\Sigma i \cdot X_i}$

If the errors are large, the ranks will be correlated with the errors and then Durbin's procedure will give poor instrumental variable estimator. In this case Durbin suggests arranging the (X) values according to magnitude forming them into groups, and taking the instrument $Z_i = i$ for all X's in the i-th group.

With the above three instrumental variable estimators, there is a reduction in the bias but an increase in variance as compared to OLS estimators; yet the methods appear to provide a simple solution to a difficult problem.

Every researcher must always keep in view the following while dealing with problem of measurement errors:

 (i) that, OLS estimation technique is only *a special case* of instrumental variables;

 (ii) that, instrumental variable estimation guarantees consistent estimation, but it does not guarantee unbiased estimation. The loss of unbiasedness is not to be taken lightly;

 (iii) that, one instrument is needed to replace each of the regressors which are infected with measurement errors; and

 (iv) that, the parameter estimates obtained by instrumental methods are sensitive to the specific choice of instruments made.

11.2 DUMMY (EXPLANATORY) VARIABLES

Up to now we have dealt exclusively with variables which we can measure in quantitative terms. But at times certain variables which we believe are important, are of qualitative character. The presence of such variables cannot be measured but can only be noted whether the given characteristic is present or not. For example, suppose that we want to explain the consumption behaviour of different households. In addition to the levels of disposable income, we may believe that the household's level of consumption spending depends on number of other characteristics: the presence or absence of children, whether or not the householder owns his own house, its religion, literacy of the head of household, and so on.

To such characteristics which cannot be measured, we assign a value of 1 to the presence and 0 to the absence of the attribute in question. In this way an attribute is transformed into a type of variable which is restricted to two (Binary) values only. Such a variable, therefore, is called a *dummy variable*. Alternative terms used are *indicator variables, categorical variables, qualitative variables,* and *dichotomous variables.*

Dummy variables are commonly used in econometric research for qualitative factors such as profession, religion, sex, region, literacy and for such other attributes.

In order to explain working of regression analysis with dummy variables, let us take an example of simple regression model in which the explanatory variable is represented by a dummy variable.

Assume that in a factory, the salary offered to a person depends on his literacy. We may describe this situation by a regression with salary as the dependent variable and literacy as the explanatory variable, i.e.,

$$Y_i = \alpha + \beta D_i + U_i, \qquad \qquad ...(11.8)$$

where, Y_i = salary of the ith worker, and

D_i = is the dummy variable

such that if the person has passed high school then we assign X_i value equal to one and if the qualification of the person is below high school, then we assign D_i value equal to 0. The model, then, is formally depicted as follows:

$$Y_i = \alpha + \beta D_i + U_i$$

$D_i = 1$, if the worker has passed high school

$D_i = 0$, otherwise

Assuming that the disturbance term U_i satisfies all the basic assumptions of the ordinary least squares, we obtain from (11.8)

If, $D_i = 0$, then $E(Y_i) = \alpha$

If, $D_i = 1$, then $E(Y_i) = \alpha + \beta$

That is, the intercept constant (α) measures mean salary of the person who has qualification below high school, while the slope coefficient (β) measures the difference between mean salary of a person who is high school and a person who is below high school in literacy. A test of a hypothesis: $\beta = 0$ is then equivalent to the test that there is no difference between the mean salary of the persons qualified differently (below or high school).

The preceding illustration can easily be modified if more than two qualitative values are to be represented through explanatory variables. For example, assume that in the above example three different levels of literacy are to be accounted for the fact that the salary of each of the literate category may not be identical. Two dummy variables can be introduced to account for this. (This is a general procedure to be followed while using dummy variables. If (N) number of qualitative values are to be differentiated, ($N - 1$) dummy variables will suffice).

Consider the model with two dummy variables:

$$Y_i = \alpha + \beta_i D_{1i} + \beta_2 D_{2i} + U_i$$

In the present case: $D_{1i} = \begin{cases} 1, \text{ if person has passed only high school;} \\ 0 - \text{otherwise.} \end{cases}$

$$D_{2i} = \begin{cases} 1, \text{ if person is graduate or above} \\ 0 - \text{otherwise.} \end{cases}$$

In the above model, three levels of literacy are represented by following combination of values taken by the dummy variables:

	Level of Literacy	D_1	D_2
1.	Below High School	0	0
2.	High School	1	0
3.	Graduation and above	0	1

By taking expected values for each of these cases, the regression results may be interpreted as follows:

$$E(Y_i) = \begin{cases} \alpha \text{ when } D_{1i} = 0, D_{2i} = 0 \\ \alpha + \beta_1 \text{ when } D_{1i} = 1, D_{2i} = 0 \\ \alpha + \beta_2 \text{ when } D_{1i} = 0, D_{2i} = 1 \end{cases}$$

The regression intercept (α) represents the expected salary of a person who is literate below high school level.

The first slope coefficient (β_1) represents the difference in the salary associated with a change in the literacy levels from below high school to high school.

The second slope coefficient (β_2) represents the average increased salary associated with change in literacy levels from below high school to graduation and above.

Significance of t-test on β_1 coefficient would mean that there is significant difference between the salaries of a person who is below high school level and the one who is high school level literate. Similarly, t-test on β_2 coefficient would provide difference between salaries of below high school and graduate persons.

In the above two illustrations, no explanatory variable of quantitative nature is used.

Models that contain explanatory variables that are described exclusively through dummy variables, are called *Analysis of Variance* (AOV) Regression Models.

AOV models of above two types are common in sociology, psychology, education, and market research. Such models are rare in economics. In most economic research, regression model contains admixture of quantitative and qualitative variables. Such models are called *Analysis of Covariance* (ACOV) *Models*.

For example, suppose that it is required to explain the consumption behaviour of different households not only on the basis of disposable income (Y), but also considering children, owning of house, and age of head of the household. If we were to obtain all this information from a sample of households, we could then estimate the regression equation using dummy variables in the following procedure:

$$C_i = \beta_0 + \beta_1 Y_i + \beta_2 D_{1i} + \beta_3 D_{2i} + \beta_4 D_{3i} + U_i$$

where, C_i = consumption expenditure of ith household.

$$D_1 \begin{cases} = 1, \text{ if the household has children} \\ = 0, \text{ if no children} \end{cases}$$

$$D_2 \begin{cases} = 1, \text{ if the household owns its own house} \\ = 0, \text{ otherwise} \end{cases}$$

$$D_3 \begin{cases} = 1, \text{ if the head of the household is over 50 yrs of age} \\ = 0, \text{ if 50 or below} \end{cases}$$

U_i = the Disturbance term

The consumption function of a household, whose head of the family is below 50 years of age, has no children and also does not own his house will correspond to the function:

$$C_i = \beta_0 + \beta_1 Y_i + U_i$$

The range of application of dummy variables in applied econometric research is virtually unlimited. We discuss only three important cases of dummy variables through ACOV models.

Case 1: Dummy Variables for Measuring the Shift of a Function.

A shift of a function implies that the constant intercept changes in a different period while the other coefficients remain unchanged. Such type of shifts can be examined by introducing a dummy variable in the function formulated for the study.

For example, we wish to study the aggregate consumption function for the period 1910–1950. During this period there were two wars, partition of the country and also a deep depression. Hence conditions could not be assumed to be normal during this whole period of 40 years. During war times, moral suasion and actual controls restrict the availability of consumer goods so that, for any given level of disposable income we might expect lower level of consumption than in normal times. The consumption function might have, for such reasons, shown a shift downwards.

Suppose we hypothesise that slope (marginal propensity to consume) coefficient of the consumption function in the two periods remain unchanged, but they are assumed to change in respect of intercept (subsistence level) as shown in Fig. 11.6.

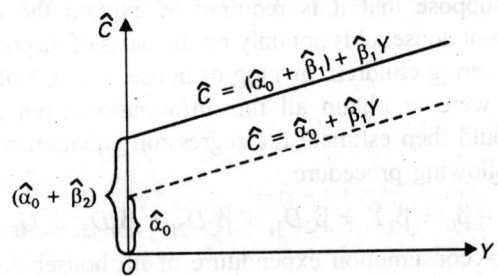

Fig. 11.6

The consumption functions of both the periods in terms of a single regression equation may be expressed as follows:

$$C_t = \alpha_0 + \beta_1 Y_t + \beta_2 D_t + U_t \qquad \qquad ...(11.9)$$

$$D_t \begin{cases} = 1 \text{ for normal years} \\ = 0 \text{ for war years} \end{cases}$$

$$(t = 1, 2, ..., n)$$

Therefore, for normal years the function would be:

$$\hat{C}_t = \hat{\alpha}_0 + \hat{\beta}_1 Y_t + \hat{\beta}_2$$

$$\hat{C}_t = (\hat{\alpha}_0 + \hat{\beta}_2) + \hat{\beta}_1 Y_t \qquad \qquad ...(11.9 \text{ A})$$

for war years;
$$\hat{C}_t = \hat{\alpha}_0 + \hat{\beta}_1 Y_t \qquad \qquad ...(11.9 \text{ B})$$

The type of data we shall use to estimate the function:

$$C_t = \alpha_0 + \beta_1 Y_t + \beta_2 D_t + U_t$$

will be in a form as given in Table 11.2.

Table 11.2

t	C_t	Y_t	D_t
1	C_1	Y_1	0
2	C_2	Y_2	0
⋮	⋮	⋮	⋮
5	C_5	Y_5	0
6	C_6	Y_6	1
Normal 7	C_7	Y_7	1
years 8	C_8	Y_8	1
9	C_9	Y_9	1
10	C_{10}	Y_{10}	1
11	C_{11}	Y_{11}	0
⋮	⋮	⋮	⋮
n	C_n	Y_n	0

With Y_t and D_t as two explanatory variables, we apply OLS procedure to obtain estimates of Y_t and D_t in the regression equation:

$$\hat{C}_t = \hat{\alpha}_0 + \hat{\beta}_1 Y_t + \hat{\beta}_2 D_t$$

Assume that estimation equation is as under:

$$\hat{C}_t = 19.5 + 0.85 Y_t + 10\, D_t$$

Also assume that t-ratio corresponding to (D_t) variable is of sufficient size to suggest that parameter β_2 in the estimated regression equation is not zero. We would then conclude that the estimated function during two periods would be:

$$\hat{C}_t = 29.5 + 0.85\ Y_t\ ; \qquad \text{...for Normal years,}$$
$$\hat{C}_t = 19.5 + 0.85\ Y_t\ ; \qquad \text{...for War years.}$$

The above functions suggest that war had a significantly negative impact on consumption expenditure.

Case 2: Dummy Variables for Measuring the Change in Parameters (Slopes)

As against the above analysis, we might have hypothesised that war time conditions reduced the marginal propensity to consume (that is, slope coefficient), but not the constant term in the consumption function. In this case, the consumption functions of both the periods would then be represented by the following equation:

$$C_t = \alpha_0 + \beta_1 Y_t + \beta_2 (Y_t D_t) + U_t \qquad \text{...(11.10)}$$

$$D_t \begin{cases} = 1 \text{ in normal years, and} \\ = 0 \text{ in war years} \end{cases}$$

Since here we assume that there is a shift in the slope coefficient, the dummy variable has been clipped with the disposable income to form a new explanatory variable of the function.

The two functions, would then be:

$$C_t = \alpha_0 + (\beta_1 + \beta_2)Y_t + U_t \quad \text{...for Normal years,}$$
$$C_t = \alpha_0 + \beta_1 Y_t + U_t \quad \text{...for War years}$$

We could use data such as those given in Table 11.2 to estimate equation:

$$C_t = \alpha_0 + \beta_1 Y_t + \beta_2(Y_t D_t) + U_t$$

The resulting functions would be similar to the curves depicted in Fig. 11.7.

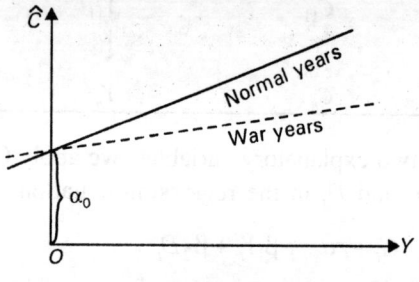

Fig. 11.7

Case 3: The third and final possibility of distinguishing between war time and peace time functions is to let both intercept (representing subsistence level) and the slope (representing MPC) coefficient of the consumption change. The regression equation then would be:

$$C_t = \alpha_0 + \beta_1 Y_t + \beta_2 D_t + \beta_3 Y_t D_t + U_t \quad \text{...(11.11)}$$
$$D_t = 1 \text{ in war years, and}$$
$$= 0 \text{ in normal years.}$$

Then the estimated functions would be:

$$C_t = (\alpha_0 + \beta_2) + (\beta_1 + \beta_3)Y_t + U_t \text{...in war years,}$$
$$C_t = \alpha_0 + \beta_1 Y_t + U_t \quad \text{...in normal years.}$$

These functions may be depicted as in Fig. 11.8.

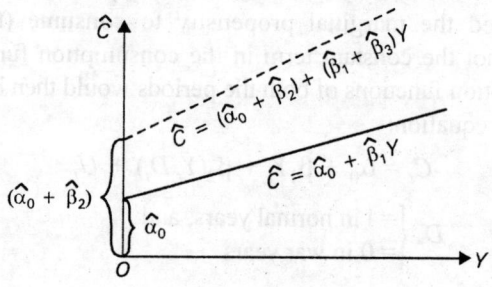

Fig. 11.8

11.2.1 Features of Dummy Variable

Following features of the dummy-variable models should be apparent from the models considered above.

1. One dummy variable suffices to distinguish two categories. To distinguish the two categories, normal year and year of war, we introduced only one dummy variable D_t. For, if $D_t = 1$ always denotes normal year, when $D_t = 0$ we know that it is a war year since there are only two possible outcomes in the given data. Now suppose we introduce two dummies for these two categories in the model (11.9) as:

$$C_t = \alpha_0 + \beta_1 Y_t + \beta_2 D_{1t} + \beta_3 D_{2t} + U_t \qquad ...(11.12)$$

where C_t and Y_t are as defined before

$$D_{1t} = 1 \quad \text{for normal year}$$
$$= 0 \quad \text{otherwise}$$
$$D_{2t} = 1 \quad \text{for war year}$$
$$= 0 \quad \text{otherwise,}$$

then model (11.12) cannot be estimated because of multicollinearity between D_1 and D_2. This could be easily seen from the data matrix which will now look like as described under:

			C_t	Y_t	D_1	D_2
Normal year	:	(NY)	C_1	Y_1	1	0
War year	:	(WY)	C_2	Y_2	0	1
		WY	C_3	Y_3	0	1
		WY	C_4	Y_4	0	1
		NY	C_5	Y_5	1	0
		NY	C_6	Y_6	1	0
		WY	C_7	Y_7	0	1
		NY	C_8	Y_8	1	0
		⋮	⋮	⋮	⋮	⋮

It can be seen readily from above data matrix that $D_1 = 1 - D_2$ or, $D_2 = 1 - D_1$; that is, D_1 and D_2 are perfectly collinear. The estimation through OLS procedure is not possible in case of perfect multicollinearity. To do away with the problem of multicollinearity, it is required to assign the dummies in the procedure we did in model (11.9). There was no column labeled D_2 in Table 11.2 thereby avoiding the problem of multicollinearity.

The general rule, therefore, is:

If a qualitative variable has n categories, introduce only $n - 1$ dummy variables.

If the above rule is not followed, the estimation is not possible and the problem is said to be trapped into the *Dummy Variable Trap*.

2. The assignment of values 0 and 1 to two categories, war year and normal year is arbitrary in the sense that one could assign $D = 1$ for war year and

$D = 0$ for normal year in model (11.11). But in this situation, the two regression equations obtained from model (11.9) will be

$$\hat{C}_t = \hat{\alpha}_0 + \hat{\beta}_1 Y_t \qquad \text{...for normal years}$$

$$\hat{C}_t = (\hat{\alpha}_0 + \hat{\beta}_2) + \hat{\beta}_1 Y_t \qquad \text{...for war years}$$

Now as compared with (11.9.A) and (11.9.B), in the preceding models, $\hat{\beta}_2$ tells by how much the mean subsistence level of consumption in war time differs from the mean subsistence level of consumption in normal time. In the present model, $\hat{\beta}_2$ is expected to be negative whereas before it was expected to be positive (see Fig. 11.6). As such, it is essential to know how the 1 and 0 values are assigned before one interprets the results of the models which use dummy variables.

3. The category which is assigned the value 0 is often referred to as the *base* or *control* category in these models. In model (11.9) the war year is the base category. Which one is to be taken as a base category is a matter of choice; sometimes dictated by *a priori* considerations.

4. The coefficient β_2 attached to the dummy variable is called the *differential intercept coefficient* because it tells by how much the value of the intercept term of the category that receives the value of 1 differs from the intercept coefficient of the *base category*.

11.2.2 Dummy Variables in Seasonal Analysis

In general, any economic time-series based on monthly or quarterly data exhibits four basic components—*trend*, representing long-term movements; *cycle*, representing sinusoidal movements; *seasonal*, representing cyclical movements within a period of a year; and *irregular*, representing residual movements.

Various methods are available to isolate these components. The series can be then adjusted after these components are isolated and estimated. Isolation of trend component was discussed in the seventh chapter under section 7.4.

The use of dummy variables help to isolate the seasonal component from the time-series. The process of removing the seasonal component from a time-series is known as *deseasonalisation*, or *seasonal adjustment*. The time-series obtained after deseasonalisation is then called the *deseasonalised* time-series or *seasonally-adjusted* time-series. Many economic time-series in our country are usually published in the seasonally adjusted form.

To illustrate how the dummy variables can be used to capture the seasonal effects in the economic time-series, consider the following regression equations:

$$Y_t = \alpha_1 + \beta X_t + U_t \quad \text{(First quarter)}$$
$$Y_t = \alpha_2 + \beta X_t + U_t \quad \text{(Second quarter)}$$
$$Y_t = \alpha_3 + \beta X_t + U_t \quad \text{(third quarter)} \quad \Bigg\} \quad ...(11.13)$$
$$Y_t = \alpha_4 + \beta X_t + U_t \quad \text{(fourth quarter)}$$

The seasonal effects are presumed to shift the intercept of the regression function (the slope coefficient does not change).

The above model (11.13) can be described through a single equation by the help of dummy variables depicting the various quarters:

$$Y_t = \alpha + \beta X_t + \gamma_1 D_1 + \gamma_2 D_2 + \gamma_3 D_3 + U_t \quad ...(11.14)$$

where:
$$D_1 = 1, \quad \text{if it is a second quarter,}$$
$$= 0 \quad \text{otherwise;}$$
$$D_2 = 1, \quad \text{if it is third quarter,}$$
$$= 0 \quad \text{otherwise;}$$
$$D_3 = 1, \quad \text{if it is fourth quarter,}$$
$$= 0 \quad \text{otherwise.}$$

Note that since it has been assumed that the variable "season" has *four* quarters of a year, only three (not four) dummy variables have been used in the model. Thus if there is a seasonal pattern in various quarters, the estimated differential intercepts will reveal it as depicted under:

$$Y_t = \alpha + \beta X_t \qquad \text{First quarter equation}$$
$$Y_t = (\alpha + \gamma_2) + \beta X_t \qquad \text{Second quarter equation}$$
$$Y_t = (\alpha + \gamma_3) + \beta X_t \qquad \text{Third quarter equation}$$
$$Y_t = (\alpha + \gamma_4) + \beta X_t \qquad \text{Fourth quarter equation}$$

(First quarter of the year is treated as the Base Quarter)

The significance of the intercepts will reflect the presence of seasonal pattern. It is possible that only some of these differential intercepts are statistically significant so that only some quarters may reflect the seasonal effect.

An alternative way of introducing the dummy for seasonal variations is:
$$Y_t = \alpha + \beta X_t + \gamma_1 D_1 X_t + \gamma_2 D_2 X_t + \gamma_3 D_3 X_t + U_t \qquad ...(11.15)$$

where,
$$D_1 = 1 \quad \text{if it is a second quarter}$$
$$= 0 \quad \text{otherwise;}$$
$$D_2 = 1 \quad \text{if it is a third quarter}$$
$$= 0 \quad \text{otherwise;}$$
$$D_3 = 1 \quad \text{if it is a fourth quarter}$$
$$= 0 \quad \text{otherwise.}$$

The seasonal effects will now be revealed by the slope of the regression equation:

$$Y_t = \alpha + (\beta + \gamma_1)X_i \qquad \text{Second quarter}$$
$$Y_t = \alpha + (\beta + \gamma_2)X_t \qquad \text{Third quarter}$$
$$Y_t = \alpha + (\beta + \gamma_3)X_t \qquad \text{Fourth quarter}$$

First quarter is the base quarter: $Y_t = \alpha + \beta X_t$. The relevance of the seasonal effects can now be examined by testing the hypothesis that γ_1, γ_2 and γ_3 are jointly zero.

A final possibility, we could let the intercept and the slope (both) be affected by the seasonal factors as depicted by Fig. 11.8.

The dummy variables also play an important role in describing *Temporal Effects* (where different classes refer to different time periods), *Spatial Effects* (where classes refer to different areas or spaces) and *Industrial Effects* (where different types refer to particular industries).

11.3 MODELS WITH QUALITATIVE DEPENDENT VARIABLES (PROBIT, LOGIT AND TOBIT PROBABILITY MODELS)

When one or more of the explanatory variables in a regression model are qualitative (reflecting dichotomous choices) in nature, we can represent them as dummy variables and proceed as described in foregoing chapter under 11.2. However, economist many a times deal with the problems in which the dependent variables is assumed to be dichotomous in character. For instance, questions about whether to produce or consume, rather than how much to produce and consume, are also of great importance. At micro-level in the study of consumer durable goods, an econometrician can study the factors determining whether a family will buy a scooter in a certain period. Many such situations which include '*buy-no buy*' decision, '*yes-no*' response, and various choices between two alternatives are analysed through the models with Qualitative Dependent Variables.

Following three situations can arise in case of qualitative dependent variables:

(a) Dependent variable is of Dichotomous or Binary nature; that is when Y (the dep. variable) takes the value one or zero according to which one of the events (or results) occurs. For instance, if $Y_i = 1$ (or zero) if the i-th family buys a house (or not); if the i-th person is married (or not) and so on.

(b) Dependent variable is of polytomous nature; that is when more than two possible events (or results) occur. For instance, educational achievements of a person may be (i) Below high school, (ii) High school, (iii) Graduation and (iv) Postgraduation.

(c) Dependent variable is of limited (or truncated) nature; that is when qualitative dependent variable is subject to some limit or can be observed over a limited range. For example, non-zero values of dependent variables are available only for some of the observations.

In the present section, estimation procedures of the first case are presented.

Models in which individuals or families are faced with a choice between two alternatives fall in the first category of *Binary Choice Models*. Assuming that we have information about the choices of the individuals they make, the problem is whether it is possible to estimate regression equation which will predict the choices of individuals not in the original data. For instance, it may be required to build a model which will allow us to make predictions about how disposable income is a primary determinant of purchasing a scooter. No doubt, as has been assumed, it is reasonable to expect a direct relationship between income and going for scooter purchase; but our information is not sufficient enough to predict how each and every family or the individual will purchase the scooter with perfect accuracy.

Purpose of qualitative dependent variable models is to determine the probability that an individual with a given set of variables (or attributes) will make one choice (purchase scooter) rather than the alternative (not purchase scooter). More generally, in these models our object is to find a relationship between a set of attributes (explanatory or some other variables) describing an individual and the probability that the individual will make a given choice. Such relationships may be described in several possible model specifications. The most simplest form is to assume that the probability of an individual making a given choice (any of the two) is a *linear* function of the given set of variables; it is then called Linear Probability Model.

Linear Probability Model: Suppose 'to buy or not to buy' decision of family with a given level of disposable income is described by the model

$$Y_i = \alpha + \beta X_i + U_i \qquad \qquad ...(11.16)$$

X_i is the disposable income of the i-th family and Y_i is binary variable such that:

$$Y_i = \begin{cases} 1, \text{ if } i\text{-th family opts for a scooter} \\ 0, \text{ otherwise} \end{cases}$$

X_i = Nonstochastic and independent of U_i

The mean value of dependent variable is given by:

$$E(Y_i) = E(\alpha + \beta X_i + U_i) = \alpha + \beta X_i \qquad ...(11.17)$$

Since Y_i is either 1 or 0, we describe the probability of Y by letting:

$$P_i = \text{Prob.} \quad (\text{when } Y_i = 1)$$

$$1 - P_i = \text{Prob.} \quad (\text{when } Y_i = 0)$$

Therefore, $\qquad E(Y_i) = P_i(1) + (1 - P_i)(0) = P_i$

Hence the Linear Probability Model (11.17) should be interpreted as describing the probability (P_i) that a household shall opt for a scooter given the information about its disposable income.

The slope of the model $\left(\dfrac{dY_i}{dX_i} = \dfrac{dP_i}{dX_i} = \beta \right)$ *does not* measure the effect on the probability (P_i) due to a unit change in the income of the household.

An example of linear probability model may be cited from Goldberger's text on Econometric Theory (page 249) as: $\hat{Y} = (-)\,0.008 + 0.0022X$; where X = disposable income in hundred rupees, and $Y = 1$ for purchases and 0 for non purchases (for car), the function has been estimated by classical least squares.

As per this model, the estimate of probability that an individual with Rs. 10,000 disposable income will buy a new car in a year is $= (-)\,0.008 + 0.0022(100) = 0.212$.

However, there are few basic weaknesses in this model which are analysed below.

Let us examine the probability distribution of disturbance term U_i in the Linear Probability Model:

Equation (11.16) gives
$$U_i = Y_i - \alpha - \beta X_i$$
$$U_i = 1 - \alpha - \beta X_i\,; \quad \text{if} \quad Y_i = 1$$
$$U_i = -\alpha - \beta X_i\,; \quad \text{if} \quad Y_i = 0$$

It then follows that U_i can also assume only two discrete values. The only assumption that remains to be checked is the homoscedastic character of the residuals.

$$E(U_i) = (1 - \alpha - \beta X_i)\,(P_i) + (-\alpha - \beta X_i)\,(1 - P_i) \qquad \text{...(11.18)}$$

$$E(U_i^2) = (1 - \alpha - \beta X_i)^2\,(P_i) + (-\alpha - \beta X_i)^2\,(1 - P_i) \qquad \text{...(11.19)}$$

Substituting assumption of zero mean in (11.18) gives:

$$0 = (1 - \alpha - \beta X_i)\,(P_i) - (-\alpha - \beta X_i)\,(1 - P_i)$$

Solving for P_i, we obtain

$$P_i = \alpha + \beta X_i,\ 1 - P_i = 1 - \alpha - \beta X_i \qquad \text{...(11.20)}$$

Substituting (11.20) in (11.19), we get:

$$E(U_i^2) = (1 - \alpha - \beta X_i)^2\,(\alpha + \beta X_i) + (-\alpha - \beta X_i)^2\,(1 - \alpha - \beta X_i)$$
$$= (1 - \alpha - \beta X_i)\,(\alpha + \beta X_i)$$
$$= P_i(1 - P_i) \neq 0.$$

This means that U_i is not homoscedastic; rather its variance depends on $E(Y_i)$, because $P_i(1 - P_i) = E(Y_i)\,[1 - E(Y_i)]$.

Observations for which P_i is close to zero or close to 1 will have relatively low variance, while observations with P_i closer to half will have higher variances.

In case OLS rule is applied to (11.16), the presence of heteroscedasticity shall result in a loss of efficiency but will not affect biasedness and consistency of the estimate.

Because of the special nature of the dependent variable, the application of OLS procedure to the linear probability model poses three problems.

(i) The classical assumption of homoscedasticity is untenable. An obvious way out is to apply GLS procedure by assuming heteroscedastic pattern of the residuals.

(ii) The second problem concerns the non-normal distribution of residuals. This violation does not allow us to apply tests of significance to the estimated parameters.

(iii) The third problem concerns the prediction of linear probability model. When we attempt to use this model for prediction, a serious weakness of the model becomes apparent.

Since $E(Y_i)$ is interpreted as a probability, its range is confined to the interval from 0 to 1. However, as the predicted value of Y is point on a straight line, its range is from $-\infty$ to $+\infty$ (unless the line is perfectly horizontal). As such even if the true linear probability model is correct, it is certainly possible that for a given income (X), the value of Y may be outside the (0, 1) interval. Such a possibility as shown in Fig. 11.9 may occur when X takes some value beyond 4.

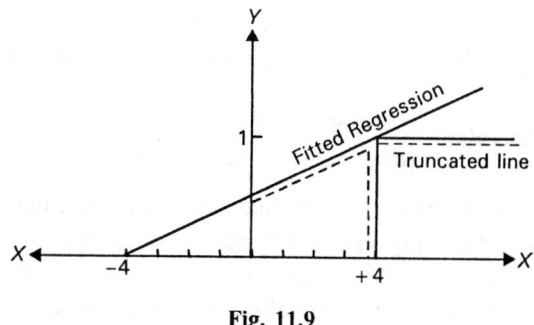

Fig. 11.9

Of the above three limitations of linear probability model, it is the last one that led to search for alternative model specifications and distributional assumptions with an object that all predictions must lie within the appropriate interval. An obvious solution to the problem is to transform the original model in such a way that predictions will lie in the (0, 1) interval for all values of X.

As such, our transformation must achieve following two objectives:

(i) that all the values of explanatory variable(s) (or all the attributes of X) must give rise to probability which range in value from zero to one only; and

(ii) that such transformation must take care of maintaining the monotonic property between (X) and dependent variable (Y); in other words increases (or decreases) in (X) are associated with increases (or decreases) in (Y) for all values of (X).

The function which fulfills these two requirements is Cumulative Probability Function (CPF).

CPF incorporates the above requirements by transforming the LPM (Linear Probability Model) into two different types of Cumulative Functions; (i) Cumulative Normal Probability Functions (leading to Probit Probability Model) and (ii) Cumulative Logistic Probability Function (leading to Logit Probability Model).

Probit (Probability) Model

Equation (11.17) gives; $\quad E(Y_i) = \alpha + \beta X_i$

which is equivalent to; $\qquad P_i = \alpha + \beta X_i$

To understand Probit Model, let us assume that there exists some unobservable (theoretical) index variable (I_i) which is linear function of explanatory variable (X_i) in the linear probability model. The monotonic relationship between (I_i) and probability (P_i) of an event occurring is established by saying that larger the value of (I_i), the greater the probability of occurrence of event. In other words, if Y = scooter ownership and X = income, an individual (or family) with index as high as I_i^* would own a scooter only if his income (X) is so high that $I_i \geq I_i^*$.

With above modifications, the linear probability model is stated as follows:

$$\text{An individual} \begin{cases} \text{owns a scooter if index } I_i \geq I_i^* \\ \text{does not own scooter if index } I_i < I_i^* \end{cases}$$

This also means that each individual makes a choice between ownership of scooter and not owning a scooter as per the value of index (I_i) to threshold level, say, I_i^*. Value I_i^* is determined by many independent factors.

Since I_i is assumed to be normally distributed, therefore:

$$P_i = F(I_i) = \int_{-\infty}^{I_i} \frac{1}{\sqrt{2\pi}} \cdot e^{-s^2/2} \cdot ds \qquad \ldots(11.21)$$

where; $\quad s \sim N(0, 1)$

P_i depicts the probability of the individual opting for scooter. Since this probability is measured by the area under the Standard Normal Curve from $-\infty$ to I_i, the event will be more likely to occur the larger the value of index I_i.

The graphical representation of Cumulative Probability Distribution Function is given in Fig. 11.10.

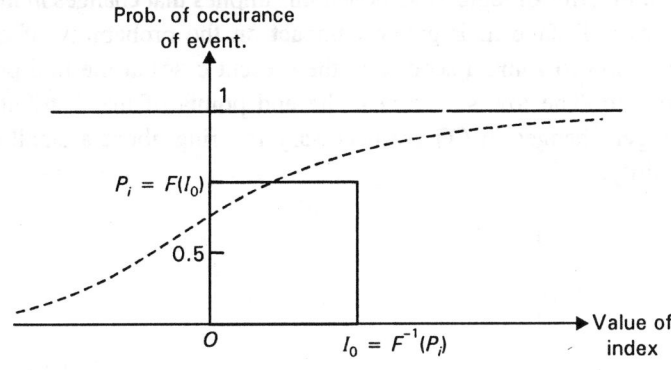

Fig. 11.10

Our object is to obtain estimate of unobservable index I_i, for this inverse of the cumulative distribution function expressed by (11.21).

Since,
$$P_i = F(I_i)$$
$$I_i = F^{-1}(P_i) = (\alpha + \beta X_i) \qquad \text{...(11.22)}$$

Model expressed through (11.22) is called *Probit Model*.

The probability resulting from Probit model may be interpreted as an estimate of the conditional probability that an individual will opt for scooter, given that the individual's income is X_i. This is equivalent to the probability that standard normal variate will be less than or equal to $(\alpha + \beta X_i)$.

It can be observed that Probit model appears more appealing and also plugs the limitations of the linear probability model. But all the same, this model, for being based on Cumulative Probability Function which is nonlinear function, the estimation of Probit model involves non-linear estimation procedure through Maximum Likelihood method. In practical applications, therefore, Logit model is preferred and is often used as substitute for the Probit model.

Logit (Logistic) Probability Model

In this model, the probabilities are transformed into logarithmic formulation through the function as shown below:

$$P_i = f(I_i) = F(\alpha + \beta X_i) = \frac{1}{1 + e^{-I_i}} = \frac{1}{1 + e^{-(\alpha + \beta X_i)}} \qquad \text{...(11.23)}$$

In (11.23), (P_i) is constrained to the $(0, 1)$ interval. It increases monotonically with the stimulus $(\alpha + \beta X_i)$ and equals 0.5 when $\alpha + \beta X_i = 0$. It has a shape similar to that of cumulative normal probability (Probit) function as could be seen from Fig. 11.11; the only difference is that the

Logistic model is slightly less slopped above probability level of 0.5. In other words, the slope of the cumulative logistic distribution is greatest at $P = 0.5$. In terms of regression model, this implies that changes in independent variables will have their greatest impact on the probability of choosing a given option (owning a scooter in the present case) at the mid point of the distribution. The low slopes near the end points of the distribution imply that larger changes in (X) are necessary to bring about a small change in probability.

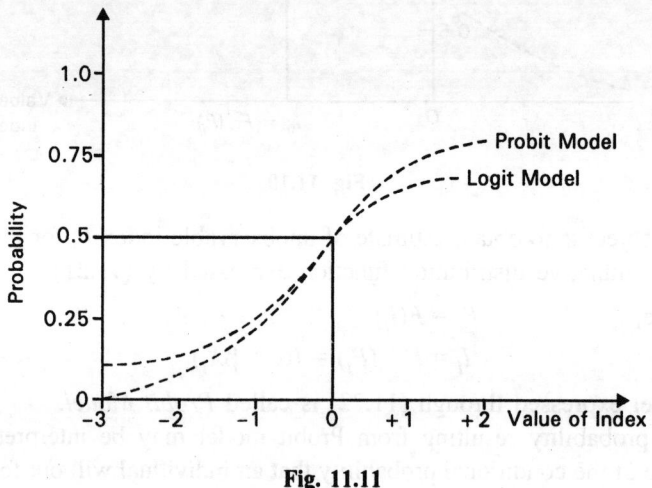

Fig. 11.11

Interpretation of our example through Logit model would be that an increase in income will raise the probability of opting a scooter 'only slightly' for those who are low income earning individuals (or families); this means that low income individuals are unlikely to alter their choice under any conditions. On the other, high income individuals generally opt for owing a scooter even before they experience rise in their incomes. As for the individuals who fall within middle income ranges, they are indifferent to making a choice either way ($P = 0.5$) and any change in their incomes is likely to have a substantial impact on the probability of choice for owing a scooter.

For estimation purpose, the logit model is to be specified as described in (11.23), i.e;

$$P_i = F(\alpha + \beta X_i) = \frac{1}{1 + \exp[-(\alpha + \beta X_i)]}$$

P_i is the probability that i-th household will opt for a scooter, given its disposable income X_i and e is the base of natural logarithm.

(11.23) can be rewritten as:

$$P_i[1 + \exp\{-(\alpha + \beta X_i)\}] = 1$$

$$\alpha + \beta X_i = \log_e\left(\frac{P_i}{1 - P_i}\right) \qquad ...(11.24)$$

(11.24) is then operational specification of the logit model.

The ratio $\left(\dfrac{P_i}{1 - P_i}\right)$ is called the odd-ratio (*or ratio of option*) and hence

$\log\left(\dfrac{P_i}{1 - P_i}\right)$ is called log-odds (*or logit*) which acts as dependent variable.

Specification (11.24) has a unique feature since it ensures that no matter what values are taken by the explanatory variable, the predicted value of the probability will fall within a (0, 1) interval.

The logit model in the form (11.24) suffers from one serious drawback.

If P_i happens to equal either 0 or 1, the ratio $\left(\dfrac{P_i}{1 - P_i}\right)$ will equal 0 or infinity and the logarithm of the ratio will be undefined.

The application of OLS estimation to (11.24) is then clearly not possible. The model is, therefore, estimated by considering group of households (of identical income) as a unit (rather than individual household). The data are converted to relative frequencies by determining the proportion who buy the scooter at a particular level of income.

That is; $$\hat{P}_i = \frac{r_i}{n_i};$$

r_i = number of households having income Rs. X_i

n_i = number of times scooter is opted by the households with income of Rs. X_i

Using $\hat{P}_i$ in place of P_i (11.24) can now be specified as:

$$\log_e\left(\frac{r_i}{n_i - r_i}\right) = \alpha^* + \beta^* X_i + U_i \qquad ...(11.25)$$

(11.25) is the operational form of the logit model to be estimated by OLS procedure.

For small samples the estimated parameters are found to be biased, but as the number of observation of (*X*) increases the results improve. Also, estimated parameters are consistent only when sample in each group gets larger. Such a requirement may be difficult to observe in practical situations.

ASSIGNMENTS

1. What are the assumptions of instrumental variable method of estimation. Discuss the properties of the estimators obtained through this method.
2. Differentiate between AOV model and ACOV model. How would you write a AOV model incorporating income of a college teacher as the dependent variable against the teacher being male or female representing an explanatory variable? How would you write this model if "years of teaching experience" is also introduced as an explanatory variable of the income of the teacher.
3. Is it essential that dummy variable must be given values only 0 and 1? Can it take any two arbitrary values other than these two values? Give an example of such a case.
4. Describe how the dummy variables can be used to take into account the seasonal effects.
   If you have monthly data over a number of years, how many dummy variables will you introduce to test whether all the 12 months of the year exhibit seasonal pattern.
5. Describe how would you make a model involving dependent dummy variable. What are the main problems that are faced in estimating such models?
   To what extent these problems get solved through the use of Logit and Probit Models.
6. Explain briefly why measurement error in the explanatory variables leads to inconsistent and biased parameter estimates while measurement error in the dependent variables does not.
7. Discuss the models that are used to consider the qualitative characteristic of the regrassand. Obtain the operational specification of these models.

Simultaneous-Equation Models

12.1 THE NATURE OF SIMULTANEOUS-EQUATION MODEL

We were thus far concerned exclusively with the problems and estimation of single equation regression models. In such models, dependent variable is expressed as a linear function of one or more explanatory variable(s). In such models, the cause-and-effect relationship between dependent and independent variables is unidirectional. That is, the explanatory variables are the cause and the dependent variable is the effect. But there are situations where such a one-way causation in the function is not meaningful. This occurs if Y (dependent) variable is not only function of X (explanatory) variable but also X is function of Y. There is, therefore, a two-way flow of influence between Y and (some of) the X which in turn makes the distinction between dependent and independent variables a little doubtful. Under such circumstances, we need to consider more than one regression equation; one for each interdependent variable to understand the multi-flow of influence among the variables. This is precisely what is done in the simultaneous-equation models.

A system describing the joint dependence of variables is called a system of simultaneous-equations or *Simultaneous-equation model*. The number of equations in such models is equal to the number of jointly dependent or endogenous variables involved in the phenomenon under analysis. Also unlike the single-equation models, in simultaneous-equation models it is not possible (possible only under specific assumptions) to estimate a single equation of the model without taking into account information provided by other equations of the system. If one applies OLS to estimate the parameters of each equation disregarding other equations of the model, the estimates so obtained are not only biased but also inconsistent; that is, as the sample size increases indefinitely, the estimators do not converge to their true (parameter) values.

The bias arising from application of such procedure of estimation which treats each equation of the simultaneous-equation model as though it were a single-equation model is known as *Simultaneity bias* or *Simultaneous-equation bias*.

To illustrate the source of such bias, let us consider the following examples:

Demand Function: Demand for any particular commodity depends on its own price (P), on other prices (P_0), and on income (I); so that;

$$Q_d = \alpha_0 + \alpha_1 P + \alpha_2 P_0 + \alpha_3 I + U_1 \qquad ...(12.1)$$

Can OLS be applied to obtain estimates of α_1, α_2 and α_3?

Recall that one of the crucial assumptions of the OLS procedure is that the explanatory variables are either nonstochastic, or if stochastic, are distributed independently of the stochastic disturbances. This assumption does not hold true in the present case. Since the price of the commodity is also affected by the quantity demanded of that commodity, the above single-equation model cannot be treated as a complete model. In other words there is two-way causation of the following type:

$$Q_d = f(P), \text{ and also}$$
$$P = f(Q_d).$$

That is, there needs to be at least one more equation (to describe relation between P and Q_d) to estimate the given demand function.

Assume that the required relation is described as under:

$$P = f(Q_d) = \beta_0 + \beta_1 Q_d + \beta_2 W + U_2 \qquad ...(12.2)$$

(W depicts the weather conditions).

To obtain estimates of α_1, α_2 and α_3 of the demand function through OLS procedure, it is to be shown that explanatory variables P_0 and I in (12.1) are distributed independently of U_1 and the explanatory variable Q_d and W in (12.2) are distributed independently of U_2.

Combining (12.1) and (12.2):

$$P = \beta_0 + \beta_1(\alpha_0 + \alpha_1 P + \alpha_2 P_0 + \alpha_3 I + U_1) + \beta_2 W + U_2.$$

It is clear that P is not independent of U_1 in the above relation; i.e., $E(PU_1) \neq 0$. The estimates of α_1, α_2 and α_3 will, therefore, turn out to be biased if OLS is applied to (12.1).

Money-supply function: The main determinant of the supply of money is real level of income: $M = f(Y)$; i.e.,

$$M = \alpha_0 + \alpha_1 Y + U$$

But since the level of income, in turn, is influenced by the supply of money itself and also by the investment decisions of the entrepreneurs, the above equation cannot be treated as a single-equation model. In other words, Y is not truly exogenous as it is thought to be. There ought to be another relation to explain the variations in Y due to certain other factors. Suppose:

$$Y = \beta_0 + \beta_1 M + \beta_2 I + ... + V.$$

Combining the two equations now:

$$Y = \beta_0 + \beta_1(\alpha_0 + \alpha_1 Y + U) + \beta_2 I + ... + V$$

Obviously $Y = f(U)$, i.e., $E(YU) \neq 0$. Thus in money-supply function: $M = \alpha_0 + \alpha_1 Y + U$, the explanatory variable (Y) is not independent of disturbance term. OLS cannot be applied.

Both the above examples show that the simultaneity-bias originates from the violation of one of the OLS assumptions, which states that explanatory variable(s) and disturbance term should be independent of each other.

12.2 PROBLEMS OF SIMULTANEOUS-EQUATION MODELS

Simultaneous-equations models create three distinct problems. These are:

1. *Mathematical completeness of the model:* Any model is said to be (mathematically) complete only when it possesses as many independent equations as endogenous variables. In other words if we happen to know values of disturbance terms, exogenous variables and structural parameters, then all the endogenous variables are uniquely determined.

2. *Identification of each equation of the model:* Many times it so happens that a given set of values of disturbance terms and exogenous variables yield the same values of different endogenous variables included in the model. It is because the equations are *observationally indistinguishable.*

What is needed is that parameters of each equation in the system should be uniquely determined. Hence certain tests are required to examine the identification of each equation before its estimation.

3. *Statistical estimation of each equation of the model:* Since application of OLS yields biased and inconsistent estimates, different statistical techniques are to be developed to estimate the structural parameters.

The last two problems form the subject matter of the next two chapters.

Presently our concern is to examine the consequences that follow when OLS procedure is applied to estimate the simultaneous-equation model.

12.3 INCONSISTENCY AND SIMULTANEITY BIAS OF OLS ESTIMATORS

It is shown above that the two-way causation in a relationship leads to violation of the important assumption of linear regression model.

Let us examine it more formally.

We assume a simple simultaneous-equation model:

$$Y = \alpha_0 + \alpha_1 X + U$$
$$X = \beta_0 + \beta_1 Y + \beta_2 Z + V;$$

Assumptions being: $\quad E(U) = 0 \qquad\qquad E(V) = 0$

$$E(U^2) = \sigma_u^2 \qquad\qquad E(V^2) = \sigma_v^2$$
$$E(U_i U_j) = 0 \qquad\qquad E(V_i V_j) = 0, \quad \text{and} \quad E(UV) = 0$$

The model is mathematically complete in the sense that it contains two equations in two *endogenous* variables; X and Y.

Z is an *exogenous* variable.

Substituting Y in the equation of X,

$$X = \beta_0 + \beta_1(\alpha_0 + \alpha_1 X + U) + \beta_2 Z + V$$

$$X = \frac{\beta_0 + \alpha_0\beta_1}{1 - \alpha_1\beta_1} + \left(\frac{\beta_2}{1 - \alpha_1\beta_1}\right)Z + \left(\frac{\beta_1 U + V}{1 - \alpha_1\beta_1}\right)$$

It can now be proved that the covariance of X and U is not zero.

$$\text{Cov}(X,U) = E[\{X - E(X)\}\{U - E(U)\}]$$

$$= E[\{X - E(X)\}U]$$

$$= E\left[\left\{\frac{\beta_0 + \alpha_0\beta_1}{1 - \alpha_1\beta_1} + \left(\frac{\beta_2}{1 - \alpha_1\beta_1}\right)Z + \left(\frac{\beta_1 U + V}{1 - \alpha_1\beta_1}\right)\right.\right.$$

$$\left.\left. - \left(\frac{\beta_0 + \alpha_0\beta_1}{1 - \alpha_1\beta_1}\right) - \left(\frac{\beta_2}{1 - \alpha_1\beta_1}\right)Z\right\}U\right]$$

$$= E\left[\left\{\frac{U}{1 - \alpha_1\beta_1}(\beta_0 + \alpha_0\beta_1 + \beta_2 Z + \beta_1 U + V - \beta_0 - \beta_1\alpha_0 - \beta_2 Z)\right\}\right]$$

$$= E\left[\left\{\frac{U}{1 - \alpha_1\beta_1}(\beta_1 U + V)\right\}\right]$$

$$= \frac{1}{1 - \alpha_1\beta_1} E(\beta_1 U^2 + UV); \text{ that is}$$

$$= \frac{\beta_1}{1 - \alpha_1\beta_1} E(U^2) = \frac{\beta_1\sigma_u^2}{1 - \alpha_1\beta_1} \neq 0 \qquad \text{...(i)}$$

That is, covariance between X and U is not zero. As a consequence, if OLS is applied to each equation of the model separately the coefficients will turn out to be biased and inconsistent.

Let us examine this.

One of the normal equations (in deviation form) of a single equation model: $\qquad Y = \alpha_0 + \alpha_1 X + U$ is given by

$$\Sigma xy = \alpha_1 \Sigma x^2 + \Sigma xu$$

i.e.,

$$\frac{\Sigma xy}{\Sigma x^2} = \alpha_1 + \frac{\Sigma xu}{\Sigma x^2}$$

Setting

$$\hat{\alpha}_1 = \frac{\Sigma xy}{\Sigma x^2}; \quad \hat{\alpha}_1 = \alpha_1 + E\left(\frac{\Sigma xu}{\Sigma x^2}\right) \qquad \text{...(ii)}$$

On taking the expected values:

$$E(\hat{\alpha}_1) = \alpha_1 + E\left(\frac{\sum xu}{\sum x^2}\right)$$

In case $E(xu) \neq 0$; $E(\hat{\alpha}_1) \neq \alpha_1$, that is $\hat{\alpha}_1$ will be biased by the amount equivalent to $\dfrac{\sum xu}{\sum x^2}$.

Turning to consistency property, an estimator is said to be consistent if its probability limit (or *plim.* for short) is equal to its population value. Therefore, to show that $\hat{\alpha}$, the estimator of α is consistent, it is required to be shown that its plim. is equal to α;

i.e., $\quad$ plim $(\hat{\alpha}) = \alpha$

$$\text{plim } (\hat{\alpha}_1) = \text{plim } (\alpha_1) + \text{plim } \left(\frac{\sum xu}{\sum x^2}\right)$$

$$= \text{plim } (\alpha_1) + \frac{\text{plim} \cdot \left(\sum xu / N\right)}{\text{plim} \cdot \left(\sum x^2 / N\right)}$$

$$= \alpha_1 + \frac{\text{plim} \cdot \left(\sum xu / N\right)}{\text{plim} \cdot \left(\sum x^2 / N\right)} \qquad \text{...(iii)}$$

The quantities in the brackets of the second term of (iii) describe sample covariance between X and U and the sample variance of X, respectively. In other words, the probability limit of $\hat{\alpha}$ is given by true α_1 *plus* the ratio of the plim. of the sample variance of X. As the sample size N increases, the sample covariance between X and U would approximate to the true population covariance given by (i). Similarly, as $N \to \infty$, the sample variance of X will approximate its population variance, say, α_x^2. Therefore, equation (iii) may now be written as (using (i));

$$\text{plim } (\hat{\alpha}_1) = \alpha_1 + \frac{\beta_1 \sigma_u^2 / (1 - \alpha_1 \beta_1)}{\sigma_x^2}$$

$$= \alpha_1 + \frac{\beta_1}{1 - \alpha_1 \beta_1} \left(\frac{\sigma_u^2}{\sigma_x^2}\right) \qquad \text{...(iv)}$$

Since σ_u^2 and σ_x^2 are both positive, it is obvious from (iv) that plim $(\hat{\alpha}_1)$ will be greater or less than α_1. In other words, $\hat{\alpha}_1$ is a biased estimator, and the bias will not disappear even when $N \to \infty$. In general, however, the direction of the bias will depend on the structure of the particular model and the values of the regression coefficients.

12.4 STRUCTURAL, REDUCED-FORM AND RECURSIVE MODELS

One needs to acquaint himself with some important definitions and notations frequently used in the estimation of simultaneous-equation models.

(A) *Endogenous and Exogenous Variables:* The nature of such variables has been already described in the first chapter. Presently we shall redefine them in the context of simultaneous-equations models.

The variables entering any simultaneous-equations models are of two types: endogenous and Predetermined (or Exogenous).

Endogenous variables are regarded as stochastic and their values are determined within the model. Predetermined variables are treated as nonstochastic and their values are given.

In the conventional notation endogenous and exogenous variables are denoted by Y's and X's respectively; while structural parameters or coefficients are depicted by β's and γ's.

Predetermined variables are again divided into two categories: exogenous (current and lagged) and lagged endogenous. For instance; X_t and X_{t-1} depict the current and lagged exogenous variables respectively; and Y_{t-1} depicts a lagged endogenous variable. X_t, X_{t-1} and Y_{t-1} are thus regarded as predetermined variables whose values are not determined by the model in the current time period.

Every variable entering the simultaneous equations model should be clearly specified before the estimation of the model.

(B) *Structural Models:* A structural model describes the complete structure of the relationships among the economic variables.

Structural equations of the model may be expressed in terms of endogenous variables, exogenous variables and disturbances.

Structural parameters express the *direct effect* of each explanatory variable on the dependent variable. Variables not appearing in any function explicitly may have an indirect effect on the dependent variable of the function. Such effect is known as *indirect effect* and is taken into account by the simultaneous solution of the system.

For instance, a change in consumption affects the investment indirectly and is not considered in the consumption function. The effect of consumption on investment cannot be measured directly by any structural parameter, but is measured indirectly by considering the system as a whole.

Structural Model	*Structural Model in Standard Notations*
$C_t = \alpha_0 + \alpha_1 Y_t + U_1$	$y_1 = \beta_{13} y_3 + u_1$
$Y_t = \beta_0 + \beta_1 Y_t + \beta_2 Y_{t-1} + U_2$	$y_2 = \beta_{23} y_3 + \gamma_{21} x_1 + u_2$
$Y_t = C_t + I_t + G_t$	$y_3 = y_1 + y_2 + x_2$

(C) *Reduced-form Models:* Reduced form models express endogenous variable as a function of exogenous variables.

The reduced form of any model can be obtained or described in two ways:

Let us consider a simple demand-supply model for this purpose

$$Q^d = \beta_0 + \beta_1 P + \beta_2 Y + U$$
$$Q^s = \alpha_0 + \alpha_1 P + V$$
$$Q^d = Q^s$$

The first method merely expresses the endogenous variables directly as a function of the exogenous variables

$$Q = \pi_{11} + \pi_{12} Y + e_{11}$$
$$P = \pi_{21} + \pi_{22} Y + e_{22}$$

The second method of obtaining the reduced form of a model is to solve the structural system of endogenous variables in terms of the exogenous variables, structural parameters and the disturbances.

The reduced form, by this procedure, would be:

$$Q = \frac{\alpha_1 \beta_0 - \alpha_0 \beta_1}{\alpha_1 - \beta_1} + \left(\frac{\beta_2 \alpha_1}{\alpha_1 - \beta_1} \right) Y + \frac{\alpha_1 U - \beta_1 V}{\alpha_1 - \beta_1}$$

$$P = \frac{\beta_0 - \alpha_0}{\alpha_1 - \beta_1} + \left(\frac{\beta_2}{\alpha_1 - \beta_1} \right) Y + \frac{U - V}{\alpha_1 - \beta_1}.$$

On comparing the above two methods, the following relationships between π's and the structural parameters must hold good, i.e.,

$$\pi_{11} = \frac{\alpha_1 \beta_0 - \alpha_0 \beta_1}{\alpha_1 - \beta_1}, \quad \pi_{12} = \frac{\beta_2 \alpha_1}{\alpha_1 - \beta_1}, \quad e_{11} = \frac{\alpha_1 U - \beta_1 V}{\alpha_1 - \beta_1}$$

$$\pi_{21} = \frac{\beta_0 - \alpha_0}{\alpha_1 - \beta_1}, \quad \pi_{22} = \frac{\beta_2}{\alpha_1 - \beta_1}, \quad e_{22} = \frac{U - V}{\alpha_1 - \beta_1}$$

As it may be observed π's bear a definite relationship with the structural parameters. The reduced form parameters measure the total effect (direct and indirect) of a change in the exogenous variables on the endogenous variable. For instance in the above model, π_{12} measures the total effect of unit change in the disposable income on the quantity. The effect is β_2 (which is direct effect) times the $\dfrac{\alpha_1}{\alpha_1 - \beta_1}$ (which is indirect effect).

(D) *Recursive Models:* It has been shown above that because of the interdependence between the disturbance term and the endogenous variables, the OLS technique is not appropriate for estimation of an equation in a simultaneous-equations model. However, in a special type of simultaneous-equations model called Recursive, *Triangular*, or *Casual* model, the use of OLS procedure of estimation is appropriate.

Consider the following three-equation system to understand the nature of such models:

$$Y_1 = \alpha_{10} + \beta_{11}X_1 + \beta_{12}X_2 + U_1$$
$$Y_2 = \alpha_{20} + \alpha_{21}Y_1 + \beta_{21}X_1 + \beta_{22}X_2 + U_2$$
$$Y_3 = \alpha_{30} + \alpha_{31}Y_1 + \alpha_{32}Y_2 + \beta_{31}X_1 + \beta_{32}X_2 + U_3$$

In the above illustration, as usual, the X's and Y's are the exogenous and endogenous variables respectively. The disturbance terms follow the following assumption:

$$E(U_1, U_2) = E(U_1, U_3) = E(U_2, U_3) = 0$$

The above assumption is the most crucial assumption that defines the recursive model. If this does not hold good, the above system is no longer recursive and recursive OLS is also no longer valid.

The first equation of the above system contains only the exogeneous variables on the right hand side. Since by assumption, the exogenous variables are independent of U_1, first equation satisfies the critical assumption of the OLS procedure. Hence OLS can be applied straightforwardly to this equation.

Consider the second equation. It contains the endogenous variable Y_1 as one of the explanatory variables along with the non-stochastic X's. OLS can be applied to this equation only if it can be shown that Y_1 and U_2 are independent of each other. This is true, because U_1 which affects Y_1 is by assumption uncorrelated with U_2, i.e., $E(U_1 U_2) = 0$. Y_1 in fact acts as a predetermined variable insofar as Y_2 is concerned. Hence OLS can be applied to this equation also.

Similar argument can be stretched to the third equation because Y_1 and Y_2 are independent of U_2.

In this way, in the recursive system OLS can be applied to each equation separately.

The unidirectional flow in the recursive system is illustrated in the Fig. 12.1 through an arrow diagram.

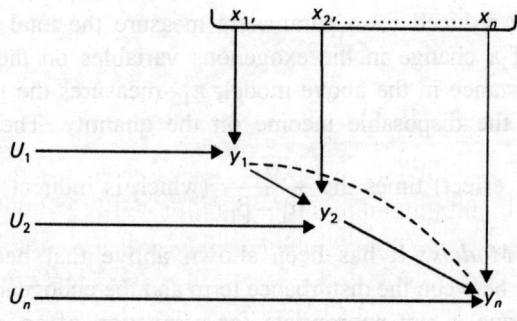

Fig. 12.1

All the predetermined variables and U_1 determine Y_1.

Then Y_1, all the predetermined variables, and U_2 determine Y_2.

Then Y_1, Y_2, all the predetermined variables, and U_3 determine Y_3.

Let us build a hypothetical recursive model for an agricultural commodity, say *wheat*.

The production of wheat $= Y_1$ may be assumed to depend on exogenous factors: $X_2 = $ climatic conditions, and $X_3 = $ last season's price. The retail price $= Y_2$ may be assumed to be the function of production level $= Y_1$ and exogenous factor $X_4 = $ disposable income. Finally the price obtained by the producer $= Y_3$ can be expressed in terms of the retail price Y_2 and exogenous · factor $X_5 = $ the cost of marketing the product.

The relevant equations of the model may be described as under:

$$Y_1 = \alpha_1 + \alpha_2 X_2 + \alpha_3 X_3 + U_1$$
$$Y_2 = \alpha_4 + \beta_1 Y_1 + \alpha_5 X_4 + U_2$$
$$Y_3 = \alpha_6 + \beta_2 Y_2 + \alpha_7 X_5 + U_3$$

In the first equation, there are only exogenous variables and are assumed to be independent of U_1. In the second equation, the casual relation between Y_1 and Y_2 is in one direction. Also Y_1 is independent of U_2 and can be treated just like exogenous variable. Similarly since Y_2 is independent of U_3, OLS can be applied to the third equation.

$$\text{Thus we have} \quad \begin{cases} Y_1 - \alpha_1 - \alpha_2 X_2 - \alpha_3 X_3 = U_1 \\ -\beta_1 Y_1 + Y_2 - \alpha_4 - \alpha_5 X_4 = U_2 \\ -\beta_2 Y_2 + Y_3 - \alpha_6 - \alpha_7 X_5 = U_3 \end{cases}$$

$$\underbrace{\begin{bmatrix} 1 & 0 & 0 \\ -\beta_1 & 1 & 0 \\ 0 & -\beta_2 & 1 \end{bmatrix}}_{\substack{\text{Coefficient matrix} \\ \text{of endogenous variables}}} \begin{bmatrix} Y_1 \\ Y_2 \\ Y_3 \end{bmatrix} + \underbrace{\begin{bmatrix} -\alpha_1 & -\alpha_2 & -\alpha_3 & 0 & 0 \\ -\alpha_4 & 0 & 0 & -\alpha_5 & 0 \\ -\alpha_6 & 0 & 0 & 0 & -\alpha_7 \end{bmatrix}}_{\substack{\text{Coefficient matrix of} \\ \text{exogenous variables}}} \begin{bmatrix} 1 \\ X_2 \\ X_3 \\ X_4 \\ X_5 \end{bmatrix} = \begin{bmatrix} U_1 \\ U_2 \\ U_3 \end{bmatrix}$$

The coefficient matrix of endogenous variables is thus a triangular one, hence recursive models are also called as *Triangular models*.

Assuming $\text{Cov}(U_{it}, U_{jt}) = 0$; $i \neq j$, for both $i, j = 1, 2, 3$; OLS can be applied to the estimate α's and β's.

12.5 SIMULTANEOUS-EQUATION METHODS

We have discussed the nature of simultaneous-equations models and the problems encountered in the estimation of the parameters of such models in the above sections. It follows then, that different estimation methods (other than single-equation estimation methods) are necessary for estimation of consistent parameters of these models.

There are several methods of estimation, with varying statistical properties, that have been designed. These methods may be divided into two categories; namely *single-equation methods* (also known as limited information methods) and *system methods* (also known as full information methods).

There are three single-equation methods:

(i) The Indirect Least Squares (ILS)
(ii) The Method of Instrumental Variables (IV)
(iii) Two Stage Least Squares (2 SLS)

The system methods are:

(i) Limited Information Maximum Likelihood (LIML)
(ii) Three Stage Least Squares (3 SLS)
(iii) Full Information Maximum Likelihood (FIML)

In the single-equation methods, each equation of simultaneous-equations model is estimated individually disregarding the restrictions on the other equations in the model. The alternative name *limited information methods* stems from this fact.

In the system methods, all the equations of the model are considered together and estimated simultaneously taking into account all restrictions placed on the equations; hence the name *full information methods*. Ideally, the system methods should be used for estimation. It is because these methods obtain the parameters while considering all the equations of the model simultaneously; which is the very idea on which these models are built. In practice, however, the system methods are not commonly used for their complex nature, enormous computational work and sensitiveness to specification errors.

In view of the introductory nature of the present text, we shall discuss only the limited information methods of estimation.

ASSIGNMENTS

1. Distinguish between Single-Equation and Simultaneous-Equations models.
   Can we use OLS technique for estimating equations belonging to a system of simultaneous relation? Why?
2. Define Simultaneous-Equation model. What are the main issues that face us while building any simultaneous-equation model?
   Construct a simultaneous-equation model describing the market mechanism of an agricultural commodity.
3. Discuss the nature of the following models:
   (i) Structural Models, (ii) Reduced-form Models, (iii) Recursive Models and its various forms. Give example of each model.
4. What is Simultaneity Bias? How does it differ from other bias?
   Derive an expression for simultaneity-bias considering the following models:

(i)
$$Q_d = \alpha_0 + \alpha_1 P + U_1$$
$$Q_s = \beta_0 + \beta_1 P + U_2$$
$$Q_d = Q_s$$

(ii)
$$C_t = \beta_0 + \beta_1 Y_t + U_t$$
$$Y_t = C_t + I_t (= S_t)$$

5. Consider the following model:

$$C_t = \alpha_0 + \alpha_1 Y_t + U_1$$
$$I_t = \beta_0 + \beta_1 Y_t + \beta_2 Y_{t-1} + U_2$$
$$Y_t = C_t + I_t + G_t$$

(i) What is the economic meaning of the structural and of the reduced-form parameters.

(ii) Define the reduced-form parameters in terms of the structural parameters.

(iii) Obtain the total effect of a change in the exogenous variables on the endogenous variable in any of the equations of the model.

13

The Identification Problem

Problem of identification refers to model formulation. It does not concern the estimation of the model.

The estimation of the model depends upon the empirical data and the form of the model. If the model is not in the proper statistical form, it may turn out that the parameters may not be uniquely estimated even though adequate and relevant data are available. In the language of econometrics, we say that model is not *Identified*. A model is said to be identified only when it is in unique statistical form to enable us to obtain unique estimates of its parameters from the sample data.

13.1 PROBLEM OF IDENTIFICATION

To understand the meaning of identification problem, let us take an example of a simple static econometric model of market for a single commodity;

$$Q_d = \beta_0 + \beta_1 P + U \qquad ...(13.1)$$
$$Q_s = \alpha_0 + \alpha_1 P + V \qquad ...(13.2)$$

With market clearing condition: $Q_d = Q_s$ \qquad ...(13.3)

Q_d and Q_s are the quantities demanded and supplied while P depicts the price of that commodity.

Suppose the sample data consists of two time-series showing the equilibrium price and quantity exchanged during each period of time. If we use these data for estimation, we would actually measure coefficient of a function of the form: $Q = f(P)$. But a question now arises; how do we know which equation (demand or supply) has been approximated by the observed data?—or in other words, with which equation are we to identify the estimated equation?

This is an example of the problem of identification and is usually faced in the construction of all econometric models involving more than single equation. Obviously therefore we need to evolve some tests or conditions which enable us to verify that the estimated coefficients belong to the supply or the demand equation. Such conditions are called "*Conditions of Identification*" and shall be developed in a subsequent section.

In some instances scatter diagram of the sample observations helps us to determine what the data show. Suppose we plot our observed time-series sample data on a diagram. The scatter of points may reveal one of the patterns shown in the Figs. 13.1, 13.2 and 13.3 which lead us to conclusions which may not be necessarily true.

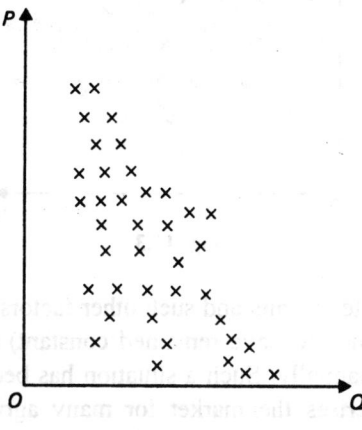

Fig. 13.1

If the scatter of data is in the form of Fig. 13.1, we conclude that the sample data identifies the demand function; while if it turns out in the form of Fig. 13.2, it identifies the supply function. It identifies neither function in case scatter of data is as depicted in Fig. 13.3.

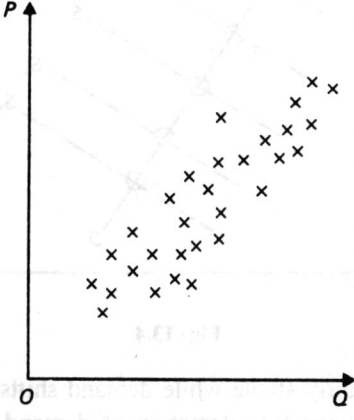

Fig. 13.2

The above assertions may be taken to be true only under certain assumed conditions described under:

(a) The scatter of points in Fig. 13.1 depict observations under the condition that the demand curve has remained unchanged over the sample period

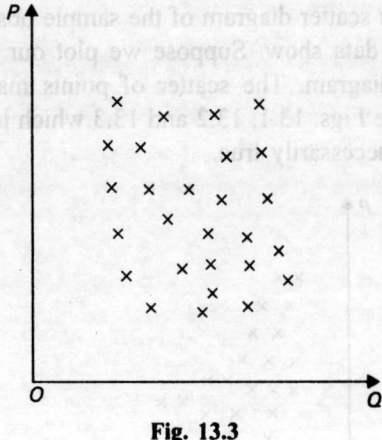

Fig. 13.3

(i.e., income, tastes, habits and such other factors which affect demand have been assumed to have remained constant) and the supply curve has shifted substantially. Such a situation has been represented in Fig. 13.4. It characterises the market for many agricultural commodities where supply is mainly influenced by weather conditions while their demand does not shift much over time.

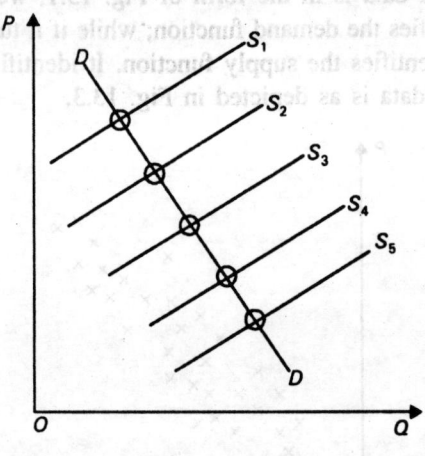

Fig. 13.4

(b) If the supply is fairly stable while demand shifts within a wide range, then the observations by interaction of demand and supply trace the supply function as shown in Fig. 13.5.

(c) Finally, if demand and supply both shift appreciably, their interaction gives observations scattered all over depicting neither supply nor demand function as shown in Fig. 13.6.

The above diagrammatic analysis can be explained in econometric terminology also.

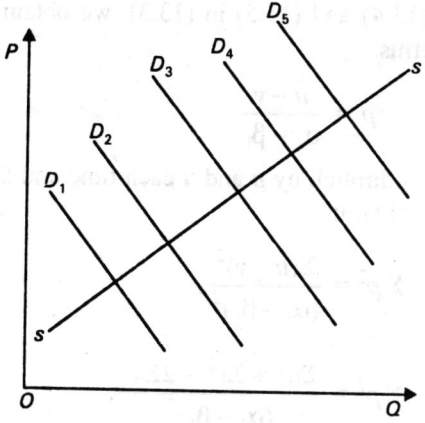

Fig. 13.5

We rewrite our model in *deviation* form:

$$q_d = \beta_1 p + u \qquad \qquad ...(13.4)$$
$$q_s = \alpha_1 p + v \qquad \qquad ...(13.5)$$

On applying OLS to estimate the demand curve, we obtain,

$$\hat{\beta}_1 = \frac{\Sigma pq}{\Sigma p^2}$$

$$\hat{\beta}_1 = \frac{\Sigma p(\beta_1 p + u)}{\Sigma p^2} = \frac{\beta_1 \Sigma p^2 + \Sigma pu}{\Sigma p^2}$$

i.e.
$$\hat{\beta}_1 = \beta_1 + \frac{\Sigma pu}{\Sigma p^2} \qquad \qquad ...(13.6)$$

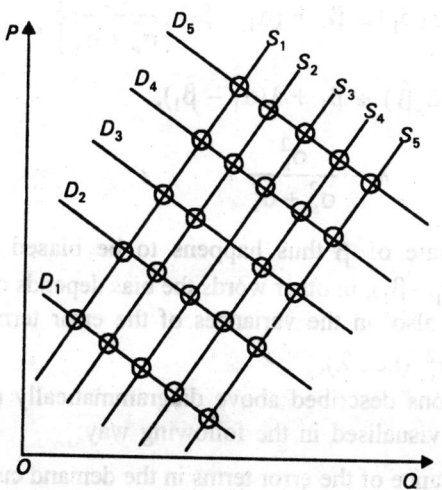

Fig. 13.6

On substituting (13.4) and (13.5) in (13.3), we obtain equilibrium price in terms of error terms.

$$p = \frac{u - v}{\alpha_1 - \beta_1} \qquad \qquad ...(13.7)$$

Multiplying (13.7) through by p and u each time and then summing over all observations we obtain:

$$\Sigma p^2 = \frac{\Sigma(u - v)^2}{(\alpha_1 - \beta_1)^2},$$

$$\Sigma p^2 = \frac{\Sigma u^2 + \Sigma v^2 - 2\Sigma uv}{(\alpha_1 - \beta_1)^2}, \qquad \qquad ...(13.8)$$

and $$\Sigma pu = \frac{\Sigma u^2 - \Sigma uv}{\alpha_1 - \beta_1} \qquad \qquad ...(13.9)$$

Substituting (13.8) and (13.9) in (13.6), we go to obtain an expression for bias of OLS estimate:

$$\hat{\beta}_1 = \beta_1 + (\alpha_1 - \beta_1) \frac{\Sigma u^2 - \Sigma uv}{\Sigma u^2 + \Sigma v^2 - 2\Sigma uv}$$

Taking expected values:

$$E(\hat{\beta}_1) \approx \beta_1 + (\alpha_1 - \beta_1) \frac{n\sigma_u^2 - n \cdot Cov(u, v)}{n \cdot \sigma_u^2 + n \cdot \sigma_v^2 - 2n Cov(u, v)}$$

On the assumption that u and v are generated independently; i.e., $Cov(u, v) = 0$

$$E(\hat{\beta}_1) \approx \beta_1 + (\alpha_1 - \beta_1) \left\{ \frac{\sigma_u^2}{\sigma_u^2 + \sigma_v^2} \right\} \qquad \qquad ...(13.10)$$

or, $$E(\hat{\beta}) \approx \beta_1 + \lambda(\alpha_1 - \beta_1),$$

where, $$\lambda = \frac{\sigma_u^2}{\sigma_u^2 + \sigma_v^2}$$

The OLS estimate of $\hat{\beta}$ thus happens to be biased by the quantity equivalent to $\lambda \cdot (\alpha_1 - \beta_1)$; in other words the bias depends on the parameters of the model, and also on the variances of the error terms in the model, namely, σ_u^2 and σ_v^2 (i.e., λ).

Now the situations described above diagrammatically (Figs. 13.4, 13.5 and 13.6) may be visualised in the following way:

(a) When the variance of the error terms in the demand curve is very small relative to the variance of errors in the supply curve, then λ will be close to zero and the estimated regression equation will be very close representation of the demand curve. The observed data on price-quantity pairs in such situation represent interaction of shifting supply curve (because of existence of errors terms in it) on a stable demand curve, as depicted in Fig. 13.4.

(b) When only demand curve has non-zero errors while errors in the supply curve have zero variance; λ will be close to unity and all observed price-quantity pairs represent movements along a stable supply curve as represented in Fig. 13.5.

Thus we are faced with the same question once again: Is the estimated equation closer to the demand curve or to the supply curve?

The answer, as we observe in the above analysis, depends on the magnitude of λ; or on the relative variances of the error terms. We are in a problematic situation because the equations, in the model actually involve two *'observationally equivalent'* relationships so that the parameters for one relationship can well be the estimators of the other relationship. Under such a situation the technique of estimation definitely fails, because the problem before using the technique of estimation is to know or to identify the relationship *which we think we are estimating.*

The foregoing discussion has made at least one point clear; that we trace the supply function if it is fairly stable while demand shows enough variability; while in case of identification of demand function, the supply function must be changing over the period of the sample.

Let us examine the above conclusion in a bit more formal way.

The reduced-form model from (13.1) through (13.3) may be written as:

$$P = \frac{\alpha_0 - \beta_0}{\beta_1 - \alpha_1} + \frac{V - U}{\beta_1 - \alpha_1} \qquad \qquad ...(13.11)$$

$$Q = \frac{\alpha_0\beta_1 - \alpha_1\beta_0}{\beta_1 - \alpha_1} + \frac{\beta_1 V - \alpha_1 U}{\beta_1 - \alpha_1} \qquad \qquad ...(13.12)$$

(13.11) and (13.12) contain no (endogenous or exogenous) variables, therefore;

$$E(P) = \frac{\alpha_0 - \beta_0}{\beta_1 - \alpha_1} = (\bar{P}), \text{ i.e., } a \text{ constant price.}$$

and, $$E(Q) = \frac{\alpha_0\beta_1 - \alpha_1\beta_0}{\beta_1 - \alpha_1} = (\bar{Q}), \text{ i.e., } a \text{ constant quantity.}$$

That is to say that the parameters of the two reduced-form equations can be estimated simply as $\bar{P}$ and $\bar{Q}$. We are in no way able to estimate the structural parameters.

Let us make a small change in our model by introducing one more variable in it. Suppose that demand besides depending on price, depends on income (Y) as well; i.e.,

$$Q_d = \beta_0 + \beta_1 P + \beta_2 Y + U \qquad \text{...(13.13)}$$

$$Q_s = \alpha_0 + \alpha_1 P + V \qquad \text{...(13.14)}$$

The reduced-form equations shall now be:

$$\left[\begin{array}{l} P = \dfrac{\beta_0 - \alpha_0}{\alpha_1 - \beta_1} + \left(\dfrac{\beta_2}{\alpha_1 - \beta_1} \right) Y + \dfrac{U - V}{\alpha_1 - \beta_1} \\[3mm] Q = \dfrac{\alpha_1 \beta_0 - \alpha_0 \beta_1}{\alpha_1 - \beta_1} + \left(\dfrac{\beta_2 \alpha_1}{\alpha_1 - \beta_1} \right) Y + \dfrac{\alpha_1 U - \beta_1 V}{\alpha_1 - \beta_1} \end{array} \right.$$

or

$$\begin{cases} P = \pi_{11} + \pi_{12} Y + e_{11} & \text{...(13.15)} \\ Q = \pi_{21} + \pi_{22} Y + e_{21} & \text{...(13.16)} \end{cases}$$

The constant terms and coefficients of (13.15) and (13.16) are obtained by OLS; so that $\hat{\pi}_{12}$ and $\hat{\pi}_{22}$ are known. The price coefficient of the supply equation, α_1 can now be obtained by:

$$\hat{\alpha}_1 = \frac{\hat{\pi}_{22}}{\hat{\pi}_{12}}$$

Again,

$$\hat{\pi}_{21} = \frac{\alpha_1 \beta_0 - \alpha_0 \beta_1}{\alpha_1 - \beta_1} = \frac{\alpha_1 \beta_0 - \alpha_1 \alpha_0 + \alpha_0 \alpha_1 - \alpha_0 \beta_1}{\alpha_1 - \beta_1}$$

$$= \alpha_1 \left(\frac{\beta_0 - \alpha_0}{\alpha_1 - \beta_1} \right) + \alpha_0 \left(\frac{\alpha_1 - \beta_1}{\alpha_1 - \beta_1} \right)$$

i.e.,

$$\hat{\pi}_{21} = \hat{\alpha}_1 (\hat{\pi}_{11}) + \alpha_0$$

On substituting the estimated values of $\hat{\pi}_{21}$, $\hat{\pi}_{11}$ and $\hat{\alpha}_1$, we obtain estimate of α_0 also. Thus supply equation gets identified. Nevertheless we are still not in a position to obtain any of the coefficients of demand equation. It still remains *underidentified*.

Notice an interesting fact in the above analysis:

Inclusion of new variable in the demand curve enables us to identify the supply function. Why?

It is because the introduction of the income variable in the demand function provides some additional information about the variability of the function as described through the Fig. 13.5. The above analysis has validated the argument described in this figure; that is, the interaction of stable supply curve (no change is made in supply curve) with the shift in the demand curve (on account of changes in income) traces or identifies the supply curve.

Let us proceed further and make another change in the original model. Let us now assume that demand depends not only on price and income but also on some other price of a complement or substitute (P').

$$Q_d = \beta_0 + \beta_1 P + \beta_2 Y + \beta_2 P' + U \qquad ...(13.17)$$

$$Q_s = \alpha_0 + \alpha_1 P + V \qquad ...(13.18)$$

The two equations depicting the reduced-form of this model shall be:

$$P = \pi_{11} + \pi_{12} Y + \pi_{13} P' + e_{11} \qquad ...(13.19)$$

$$Q = \pi_{21} + \pi_{22} Y + \pi_{23} P' + e_{21} \qquad ...(13.20)$$

That is:

$$P = \frac{\beta_0 - \alpha_0}{\alpha_1 - \beta_1} + \left(\frac{\beta_2}{\alpha_1 - \beta_1}\right) Y + \left(\frac{\beta_3}{\alpha_1 - \beta_1}\right) P' + \left(\frac{U - V}{\alpha_1 - \beta_1}\right) \qquad ...(13.21)$$

$$Q = \frac{\alpha_1 \beta_0 - \alpha_0 \beta_1}{\alpha_1 - \beta_1} + \left(\frac{\alpha_1 \beta_2}{\alpha_1 - \beta_1}\right) Y + \left(\frac{\alpha_1 \beta_2}{\alpha_1 - \beta_1}\right) P' + \left(\frac{\alpha_1 U - \beta_1 V}{\alpha_1 - \beta_1}\right) \qquad ...(13.22)$$

Surprisingly, we obtain two estimates of α_1 from (13.19) and (13.20):

$$\hat{\alpha}_1 = \frac{\hat{\pi}_{22}}{\hat{\pi}_{12}} \quad \text{and also,} \quad \hat{\alpha}_1 = \frac{\hat{\pi}_{23}}{\hat{\pi}_{13}}$$

Will these two estimates coincide?

There is no reason to suppose so; nor is there any reason to prefer one estimate to the other. That is to say, supply equation in the present situation gets *over-identified;* yet the demand equation remains unestimated or *under-identified.*

Suppose now we introduce a new variable in the supply curve and redefine the model as:

$$Q_d = \beta_0 + \beta_1 P_t + \beta_2 Y_t + U_t \qquad ...(13.23)$$

$$Q_s = \alpha_0 + \alpha_1 P_t + \alpha_2 P_{t-1} + V_t \qquad ...(13.24)$$

The demand function is similar to (13.13) while supply function describes that the quantity supplied depends on its current and previous period's price. P_{t-1} is a new variable and is a predetermined variable.

The reduced-form of the model shall be:

$$P_t = \pi_{11} + \pi_{12} Y_t + \pi_{13} P_{t-1} + e_{11} \qquad ...(13.25)$$

$$Q_t = \pi_{21} + \pi_{23} Y_t + \pi_{23} P_{t-1} + e_{21} \qquad ...(13.26)$$

Solving (13.23) and (13.24), we obtain:

$$\pi_{11} = \frac{\alpha_0 - \beta_0}{\beta_1 - \alpha_1}, \quad \pi_{12} = \frac{-\beta_2}{\beta_1 - \alpha_1}, \quad \pi_{13} = \frac{\alpha_2}{\beta_1 - \alpha_1}, \quad e_{11} = \frac{V_t - U_t}{\beta_1 - \alpha_1}.$$

$$\pi_{21} = \frac{\beta_1\alpha_0 - \beta_0\alpha_1}{\beta_1 - \alpha_1}, \quad \pi_{22} = \frac{-\beta_2\alpha_1}{\beta_1 - \alpha_1}, \quad \pi_{23} = \frac{\beta_1\alpha_2}{\beta_1 - \alpha_1}, \quad e_{21} = \frac{\beta_1 V_t - \alpha_1 U_t}{\beta_1 - \alpha_1}$$

We have thus *six* reduced-form coefficients: $\pi_{11}, \pi_{12}, \pi_{13}, \pi_{21}, \pi_{22}$ and π_{23} to estimate *six* structural coefficients: $\alpha_0, \alpha_1, \alpha_2, \beta_0, \beta_1$ and β_2. That is, we have six equations in six unknowns. Mathematically, therefore, it should be possible to obtain unique values of six unknowns.

$$\frac{\hat{\pi}_{22}}{\hat{\pi}_{12}} = \hat{\alpha}_1 \; ; \; \frac{\hat{\pi}_{23}}{\hat{\pi}_{13}} = \hat{\beta}_1 .$$

On substituting these values further, the other four structural coefficients can be obtained.

Inclusion of extra variable in the supply function has enabled us to identify the parameters of both the demand and supply equations. Hence the model gets identified.

The above three manipulations in the original model have further analysed the problem of identification; it is observed that the equation may get identified (or *overidentified*) by inclusion (or exclusion) of the exogenous (or endogenous) variable(s) in the model.

Following are the important *conclusions* from the foregoing analysis:
1. Identification of a system (or model) means identification of each equation of the system.
2. Identification of any equation is established if we can prove that its structural form is unique.
   There are two formal rules with which we can establish the identification of an equation. These are developed in 13.2.
3. It is possible to identify an equation by including (or excluding) some exogenous (or endogenous) variables in the equation. Such a procedure of identification is known as *identification through restriction*. This is discussed in 13.3.

There can be two situations of identification:
(a) Equation may be said to be underidentified,
(b) Equation may be said to be identified, under this situation, equation is exactly identified or, equation is overidentified.

The problem of identification should not be confused with bias or statistical inference.

Identification is purely a *non-statistical concept* and comes logically prior to estimation or statistical inference.

13.2 THE GENERAL ECONOMETRIC MODEL: STRUCTURAL AND REDUCED FORM

In the previous section the simultaneous equation system and problems relating to its identification were discussed through simple illustrations. The main object was to understand the concepts underlying the simultaneous equation models. To understand various estimating and identification problems in case of models involving more than two or three equations, we have to develop a vocabulary, notation and statistical model for the general case of a system of simultaneous linear economic equations.

The general econometric model containing G number of endogenous variables: $y_{1t}, y_{2t}, ..., y_{Gt}$ and, K number of predetermined variables: $x_{1t}, x_{2t}, ..., x_{Kt}$ can be described as:

$$\beta_{11}y_{1t} + \beta_{12}y_{2t} + ... + \beta_{1G}y_{Gt} + \gamma_{11}x_{1t} + \gamma_{12}x_{2t} + ... \gamma_{1K}x_{Kt} = U_{1t}$$
$$\beta_{21}y_{1t} + \beta_{22}y_{2t} + ... + \beta_{2G}y_{Gt} + \gamma_{21}x_{1t} + \gamma_{22}x_{2t} + ... \gamma_{2K}x_{Kt} = U_{2t}$$
$$\vdots \qquad\qquad\qquad\qquad\qquad\qquad\qquad\qquad\qquad \vdots$$
$$\beta_{G1}y_{1t} + \beta_{G2}y_{2t} + ... + \beta_{GG}y_{Gt} + \gamma_{G1}x_{1t} + \gamma_{G2}x_{2t} + ... \gamma_{GK}x_{Kt} = U_{Gt}$$

The whole system of equations may be written in matrix notations as (13.2.1):

$$\mathbf{B}\mathbf{Y}_t + \mathbf{\Gamma}\mathbf{X}_t = U_t \qquad\qquad ...(13.2.1)$$
$$(t = 1, 2, .., n)$$

where

$$\mathbf{Y}_t = \begin{bmatrix} Y_{1t} \\ Y_{2t} \\ \vdots \\ y_{Gt} \end{bmatrix}_{(G \times 1)}, \quad \mathbf{X}_t = \begin{bmatrix} X_{1t} \\ X_{2t} \\ \vdots \\ X_{Kt} \end{bmatrix}_{(K \times 1)}, \quad U_t = \begin{bmatrix} U_{1t} \\ U_{2t} \\ \vdots \\ U_{Gt} \end{bmatrix}_{(G \times 1)}$$

$$\mathbf{B} = \begin{bmatrix} \beta_{11} & \beta_{12} \cdots \beta_{1G} \\ \beta_{21} & \beta_{22} \cdots \beta_{2G} \\ \vdots & \\ \beta_{G1} & \beta_{G2} \cdots \beta_{GG} \end{bmatrix}_{(G \times G)}, \quad \mathbf{\Gamma} = \begin{bmatrix} \gamma_{11} & \gamma_{12} \cdots \gamma_{1K} \\ \gamma_{21} & \gamma_{22} \cdots \gamma_{2K} \\ \vdots & \\ \gamma_{G1} & \gamma_{G2} \cdots \gamma_{GK} \end{bmatrix}_{(G \times K)}$$

Thus $\mathbf{Y}_t$ and $\mathbf{X}_t$ are, respectively, vectors of G number of endogenous and K number of predetermined variables and, U_t is the vector of G stochastic disturbance terms; one for each of the G equations of the system. The coefficient matrices to be estimated are $\mathbf{B}$ and $\mathbf{\Gamma}$, representing respectively, coefficient of endogenous and predetermined variables. $\mathbf{B}$ is square matrix and is assumed to be non-singular: while $\mathbf{\Gamma}$ is generally not square.

The subscript t refers to the observation number, indexing the n-observation.

Note that (13.2.1) which describes the *Structural form* of the general econometric model refers to only a single joint observation.

To write the system in terms of all the observations, let us consider any one equation of the system; say first structural equation. It is:

$$\beta_{11}y_{1t} + \beta_{12}y_{2t} + \dots + \beta_{1G}y_{Gt} + \gamma_{11}x_{1t}$$
$$+ \gamma_{12}x_{2t} + \dots + \gamma_{1K}x_{Ki} = U_{1t}$$

Similarly mth equation of the system may be written as: $\left.\right\}$ ...(13.2.2)

$$\beta_{m1}y_{mt} + \beta_{m2}y_{mt} + \dots \beta_{mG}y_{Gt} + \gamma_{m1}x_{1t}$$
$$+ \gamma_{m2}x_{2t} + \dots + \gamma_{mK}x_{Kt} = U_{mt}$$

The n-observations on each of the G endogenous variables of the first equation can be summarised by the following *data matrix*:

$$\mathbf{Y}_{1t} = \begin{bmatrix} y_{11} & y_{21} & y_{G1} \\ y_{12} & y_{22} & y_{G2} \\ \vdots & \vdots & \vdots \\ y_{1n} & y_{2n} & y_{Gn} \end{bmatrix}_{(n \times G)} \qquad ...(13.2.3)$$

Similarly, the n observations on each of the K predetermined variables of the equation can be summarised by the following data matrix:

$$\mathbf{X}_{1t} = \begin{bmatrix} x_{11} & x_{21} & \cdots & x_{K1} \\ x_{12} & x_{22} & \cdots & x_{K2} \\ \vdots & \vdots & & \vdots \\ x_{1n} & x_{2n} & & x_{Kn} \end{bmatrix}_{(n \times K)} \qquad ...(13.2.4)$$

The first structural equation of (13.2.1) in terms of all the observations may, therefore, be described as:

$$\mathbf{Y}_{1t}\,\mathbf{B}_1 + \mathbf{X}_{1t}\,\Gamma_1 = \mathbf{U}_{1t} \qquad ...(13.2.5)$$

where

$$\mathbf{B}_1 = \begin{bmatrix} \beta_{11} \\ \beta_{12} \\ \vdots \\ \beta_{1G} \end{bmatrix}_{(G \times 1)}, \quad \Gamma_1 = \begin{bmatrix} \gamma_{11} \\ \gamma_{12} \\ \vdots \\ \gamma_{1K} \end{bmatrix}_{(K \times 1)}, \quad \text{and} \quad \mathbf{U}_{1t} = \begin{bmatrix} U_{11} \\ U_{12} \\ \vdots \\ U_{1n} \end{bmatrix}_{(n \times 1)}$$

With respect to the stochastic disturbances, it is assumed that each disturbance satisfies the assumptions of the classical normal linear regression model, i.e., that

$$U_{gt} \sim N(0, \sigma_{gg}), \qquad g = 1, 2, \dots, G$$
$$E(U_{gt}\,U_{gs}) = 0, \qquad t, s = 1, 2, \dots, n$$
$$t \neq s$$

However the possibility of disturbances being correlated across the structural equations may not be ruled out, i.e., that

$$E(U_{gt}\,U_{ht}) = \sigma_{gh} \qquad (g, h = 1, 2, \dots, G)$$

The above assumptions can be put in matrix notation:

$$\mathbf{U}_t \sim N(\mathbf{0}, \Sigma),$$

$$E(\mathbf{U}_t \ \mathbf{U}_s') = \mathbf{0} \qquad \text{where,}$$

$$\Sigma = \begin{bmatrix} \sigma_{11} & \sigma_{12} \cdots \sigma_{1G} \\ \sigma_{21} & \sigma_{22} \cdots \sigma_{2G} \\ \vdots & \\ \sigma_{G1} & \sigma_{G2} \cdots \sigma_{GG} \end{bmatrix}_{(G \times G)} \qquad ...(13.2.6)$$

Σ is a symmetric positive definite matrix of variances and covariances of the structural disturbances.

Returning to general model of (13.2.1), since it is assumed that **B** is a non-singular matrix, it is possible to solve for the vector of endogenous variables $\mathbf{Y}_t$ by transposing **B** matrix in the following way:

$$\mathbf{B}\,\mathbf{Y}_t + \Gamma\,\mathbf{X}_t = \mathbf{U}_t$$

$$\mathbf{Y}_t = -\mathbf{B}^{-1}\,\Gamma\,\mathbf{X}_t + \mathbf{B}^{-1}\,\mathbf{U}_t \qquad ...(13.2.7)$$

$$\underset{(G \times 1)}{\mathbf{Y}_t} = \underset{(G \times K)}{\pi}\ \underset{(K \times 1)}{\mathbf{X}_t} + \underset{(G \times 1)}{\mathbf{V}_t} \qquad ...(13.2.8)$$

Here, $$\underset{(G \times K)}{\pi} = -\underset{(G \times G)}{\mathbf{B}^{-1}}\ \underset{(G \times K)}{\Gamma} \qquad ...(13.2.9)$$

and $$\underset{(G \times 1)}{\mathbf{V}_t} = \underset{(G \times G)}{\mathbf{B}^{-1}}\ \underset{(G \times 1)}{\mathbf{U}_t} \qquad ...(13.2.10)$$

(13.2.7) can also be written as:

$$\mathbf{Y}_t' = (-\mathbf{B}^{-1}\,\Gamma\,\mathbf{X}_t)' + (\mathbf{B}^{-1}\,\mathbf{U}_t)'$$

$$\mathbf{Y}_t' = \mathbf{X}_t'[-\Gamma'(\mathbf{B}')^{-1}) + \mathbf{U}_t'(\mathbf{B}')^{-1}$$

$$\mathbf{Y}_t' = \mathbf{X}_t'\ \pi' + \mathbf{V}_t' \qquad ...(13.2.11)$$

In (13.2.11) $$\pi' = -\Gamma'(\mathbf{B}')^{-1} \qquad ...(13.2.12)$$

and, $$\mathbf{V}_t' = \mathbf{U}_t'\,(\mathbf{B}')^{-1} \qquad ...(13.2.13)$$

Equations (13.2.8) and (13.2.11) describe the *reduced form* of the structural form expressed by (13.2.1).

The distinctive feature of the reduced form is that in each of its equations only one endogenous variable appears. This contrast with the structural form is made explicit if we write out (13.2.8) algebraically, analogously to general econometric model described, in equation-form:

First eqn: $$y_{1t} = \pi_{11}x_{1t} + \pi_{12}x_{2t} + ... + \pi_{1k}x_{kt} + V_{1i}$$

$$y_{2t} = \pi_{21}x_{1t} + \pi_{22}x_{2t} + ... + \pi_{2k}x_{kt} + V_{2t}$$

$$\vdots \qquad\qquad\qquad\qquad\qquad \vdots$$

mth eqn: $$y_{mt} = \pi_{m1}x_{1t} + \pi_{m2}x_{2t} + ... + \pi_{mk}x_{kt} + V_{mt}$$

$$\vdots \qquad\qquad\qquad\qquad\qquad \vdots$$

Gth eqn: $$y_{Gt} = \pi_{G1}x_{1t} + \pi_{G2}x_{2t} + ... + \pi_{Gk}x_{kt} + V_{Gt}$$

$$...(13.2.14)$$

so that:

$$\pi = -\mathbf{B}^{-1}\mathbf{\Gamma} = \begin{bmatrix} \pi_{11} & \pi_{12} \cdots \pi_{1k} \\ \pi_{21} & \pi_{22} \cdots \pi_{2k} \\ \vdots \\ \pi_{m1} & \pi_{m2} \cdots \pi_{mk} \\ \vdots \\ \pi_{G1} & \pi_{G2} \cdots \pi_{Gk} \end{bmatrix}_{(G \times k)} \qquad \ldots(13.2.15)$$

$$\mathbf{V}_t = \mathbf{B}^{-1}\mathbf{U}_t = \begin{bmatrix} V_{1t} \\ V_{2t} \\ \vdots \\ \vdots \\ V_{Gt} \end{bmatrix}_{(G \times 1)} = \begin{bmatrix} V_{11} & V_{12} \cdots V_{1n} \\ V_{21} & V_{22} \cdots V_{2n} \\ \vdots \\ V_{m1} & V_{m2} \cdots V_{mn} \\ \vdots \\ V_{G1} & V_{G2} \cdots V_{GN} \end{bmatrix}_{(G \times n)} \qquad \ldots(13.2.16)$$

To account for all the n observations in the equation of (13.2.14), let us consider the first equation of it only and describe in matrix notation:

First equation of the reduced form:

$$\begin{pmatrix} y_{11} \\ y_{12} \\ \vdots \\ y_{1n} \end{pmatrix} = \begin{pmatrix} x_{11} & x_{21} \cdots x_{k1} \\ x_{12} & x_{22} \cdots x_{k2} \\ \vdots \\ x_{1n} & x_{2n} \cdots x_{kn} \end{pmatrix} \begin{pmatrix} \pi_{11} \\ \pi_{12} \\ \vdots \\ \pi_{1k} \end{pmatrix} + \begin{pmatrix} V_{11} \\ V_{12} \\ \vdots \\ V_{1n} \end{pmatrix}$$

That is:
$$\begin{array}{cccc} \mathbf{Y}_1 & = & \mathbf{X}_t & \mathbf{\pi}_1 & + & \mathbf{V}_1 \\ (n \times 1) & & (n \times k)\,(k \times 1) & & (n \times 1) \end{array} \qquad \ldots(13.2.17)$$

mth equation of the reduced form:

$$\begin{array}{cccc} \mathbf{Y}_m & = & \mathbf{X}_t & \mathbf{\pi}_m & + & \mathbf{V}_m \\ (n \times 1) & & (n \times k)\,(k \times 1) & & (n \times 1) \end{array}$$

where
$$\mathbf{Y}_m = \begin{pmatrix} y_{m1} \\ y_{m2} \\ \vdots \\ y_{mn} \end{pmatrix}, \quad \mathbf{\pi}_m = \begin{pmatrix} \pi_{m1} \\ \pi_{m2} \\ \vdots \\ \pi_{mk} \end{pmatrix}, \quad V_m = \begin{pmatrix} V_{m1} \\ V_{m2} \\ \vdots \\ V_{mn} \end{pmatrix}, \quad \text{and}$$

$\mathbf{X}_t$ is similar as defined in (13.2.17).

In (13.2.17),

$\mathbf{Y}_1$ or $\mathbf{Y}_m$ is the col. vector of n observations on the first of mth endogenous variable.

X,   is the $n \times k$ matrix of n observations on all the predetermined variables.

π_1 or π_m is the col. vector of coefficients of first or mth reduced form equation, i.e., the first or mth row vector of π defined by (13.2.15).

$\mathbf{V}_1$ or $\mathbf{V}_m$ is the col. vector of disturbances in the first (or mth) reduced form equation, i.e., first or mth row vector of $\mathbf{V}_t$ defined by (13.2.16).

As it shall be observed, it is much easier to obtain reduced form of the system involving any number of equations through matrix algebra. It becomes computationally difficult to derive reduced form directly (without using matrices) when number of equations increase in the simultaneous equations model. One may adopt any of the two procedures (13.2.8) or (13.2.11) to obtain the reduced form, depending on his requirements.

Both the procedures lead to same result. This can be demonstrated by taking illustration of simple Keynesian model:

$$\left.\begin{array}{l} C_t = \alpha + \beta Y_t + V_t \\ Y_t = C_t + I_t \end{array}\right\} \begin{array}{l} c = \beta y + U \\ y = c + i \end{array}$$

$$\left.\begin{array}{l} C_t - \alpha - \beta Y = V \\ -C + Y - I = 0 \end{array}\right\} \begin{array}{l} -c + \beta y = U \\ y - c - i = 0 \end{array}$$

$$\underset{\mathbf{B}}{\begin{bmatrix} 1 & -\beta \\ -1 & 1 \end{bmatrix}} \underset{\mathbf{Y}_t}{\begin{bmatrix} C \\ Y \end{bmatrix}} + \underset{\Gamma}{\begin{bmatrix} -\alpha & 0 \\ 0 & -1 \end{bmatrix}} \underset{\mathbf{X}_t}{\begin{bmatrix} 1 \\ I \end{bmatrix}} = \underset{\mathbf{U}_t}{\begin{bmatrix} V \\ 0 \end{bmatrix}}$$

Deviation-form:

$$\begin{bmatrix} 1 & -\beta \\ -1 & 1 \end{bmatrix} \begin{bmatrix} c \\ y \end{bmatrix} + \begin{bmatrix} 0 \\ -1 \end{bmatrix} [i] = \begin{bmatrix} U \\ 0 \end{bmatrix}$$

or,

$$\begin{bmatrix} -1 & \beta \\ 1 & -1 \end{bmatrix} \begin{bmatrix} c \\ y \end{bmatrix} + \begin{bmatrix} 0 \\ 1 \end{bmatrix} [i] + \begin{bmatrix} U \\ 0 \end{bmatrix} = \begin{bmatrix} 0 \\ 0 \end{bmatrix}$$

The reduced form expressed in (13.2.8) can now be acquired by obtaining π of (13.2.9) and $\mathbf{V}_t$ of (13.2.10)

$$\pi = -\mathbf{B}^{-1}\Gamma = \begin{bmatrix} \pi_{11} & \pi_{12} \\ \pi_{21} & \pi_{22} \end{bmatrix}$$

$$= -\begin{pmatrix} 1 & -\beta \\ -1 & 1 \end{pmatrix}^{-1} \begin{pmatrix} -\alpha & 0 \\ 0 & -1 \end{pmatrix}$$

$$= -\left(\frac{1}{1-\beta}\right)\begin{pmatrix} 1 & \beta \\ 1 & 1 \end{pmatrix}\begin{pmatrix} -\alpha & 0 \\ 0 & -1 \end{pmatrix}$$

$$= -\left(\frac{1}{1-\beta}\right)\begin{pmatrix} -\alpha & -\beta \\ -\alpha & -1 \end{pmatrix}$$

$$\mathbf{V}_t = \mathbf{B}^{-1}\mathbf{U} = -\begin{pmatrix} 1 & -\beta \\ -1 & 1 \end{pmatrix}^{-1}\begin{pmatrix} V \\ 0 \end{pmatrix}$$

$$= \left(\frac{1}{1-\beta}\right)\begin{pmatrix} 1 & \beta \\ 1 & 1 \end{pmatrix}\begin{pmatrix} V \\ 0 \end{pmatrix}$$

$$= \left(\frac{1}{1-\beta}\right)\begin{pmatrix} V \\ V \end{pmatrix}$$

Placing the relevant matrices in the form of (13.2.8), we obtain:

$$\begin{pmatrix} C \\ Y \end{pmatrix} = -\left(\frac{1}{1-\beta}\right)\begin{pmatrix} -\alpha & -\beta \\ -\alpha & -1 \end{pmatrix}\begin{pmatrix} 1 \\ I \end{pmatrix} + \left(\frac{1}{1-\beta}\right)\begin{pmatrix} V \\ V \end{pmatrix}$$

which reduces to two reduced-form equations:

$$\left. \begin{aligned} C &= \frac{\alpha}{1-\beta} + \left(\frac{\beta}{1-\beta}\right)I + \frac{V}{1-\beta} \\ Y &= \frac{\alpha}{1-\beta} + \left(\frac{1}{1-\beta}\right)I + \frac{V}{1-\beta} \end{aligned} \right\} \quad ...(13.2.18)$$

If one starts with the deviation-form of the model, then

$$\pi = -\mathbf{B}^{-1}\Gamma = -\begin{pmatrix} 1 & -\beta \\ -1 & 1 \end{pmatrix}^{-1}\begin{pmatrix} 0 \\ -1 \end{pmatrix} = -\left(\frac{1}{1-\beta}\right)\begin{pmatrix} -\beta \\ -1 \end{pmatrix}$$

and $$\mathbf{V}_t = \mathbf{B}^{-1}\mathbf{U} = \left(\frac{1}{1-\beta}\right)\begin{pmatrix} u \\ u \end{pmatrix}$$

So that the reduced form shall be:

$$\begin{pmatrix} c \\ y \end{pmatrix} = -\left(\frac{1}{1-\beta}\right)\begin{pmatrix} -\beta \\ -1 \end{pmatrix}(i) + \left(\frac{1}{1-\beta}\right)\begin{pmatrix} u \\ u \end{pmatrix}$$

which gives rise to two reduced-form equations that do not contain constant term:

$$c = \left(\frac{\beta}{1-\beta}\right)i + \frac{u}{1-\beta}$$

$$y = \left(\frac{1}{1-\beta}\right)i + \frac{u}{1-\beta}$$

...(13.2.19)

(13.2.18) is similar to (13.2.19).

To obtain reduced-form of the given model expressed by (13.2.11), the frame of the model shall have to be changed accordingly:

$$-C_t + \beta Y_i + \alpha + V_t = 0$$

$$C_t - Y_t + I_t = 0$$

$$(C \quad Y)\begin{pmatrix} -1 & 1 \\ \beta & -1 \end{pmatrix} + (1 \quad I)\begin{pmatrix} \alpha & 0 \\ 0 & 1 \end{pmatrix} + (V \quad 0) = (0 \quad 0)$$

$$\quad\quad \mathbf{Y_t'} \quad\quad \mathbf{B'} \quad\quad\quad \mathbf{X_t'} \quad \mathbf{\Gamma'} \quad\quad \mathbf{U_t'} \quad\quad\quad \mathbf{O'}$$

In the present case;

$$\pi' = -\Gamma(\mathbf{B'})^{-1} = -\begin{pmatrix} \alpha & 0 \\ 0 & 1 \end{pmatrix}\begin{pmatrix} -1 & 1 \\ \beta & -1 \end{pmatrix}^{-1}$$

$$= -\begin{pmatrix} \alpha & 0 \\ 0 & 1 \end{pmatrix}\left\{\left(\frac{1}{1-\beta}\right)\begin{pmatrix} 1 & \beta \\ 1 & 1 \end{pmatrix}\right\}$$

$$= \begin{bmatrix} \alpha/1-\beta & \alpha/1-\beta \\ \beta/1-\beta & 1/1-\beta \end{bmatrix}$$

$$\mathbf{V_t'} = \mathbf{U_t'}(\mathbf{B'})^{-1} = (V \quad 0)\begin{pmatrix} -1 & 1 \\ \beta & -1 \end{pmatrix}^{-1}$$

$$= (V \quad 0)\left\{\left(\frac{1}{1-\beta}\right)\begin{pmatrix} 1 & \beta \\ 1 & 1 \end{pmatrix}\right\}$$

$$= (V/1-\beta \quad V/1-\beta)$$

Placing the relevant matrices in the form of (13.2.11), we obtain:

$$(C \quad Y) = (1 \quad I)\begin{pmatrix} \alpha/1-\beta & \alpha/1-\beta \\ \beta/1-\beta & 1/1-\beta \end{pmatrix} + (V/1-\beta \quad V/1-\beta)$$

...(13.2.20)

(13.2.20) is similar to (13.2.18).

In case one assumes deviation form in the above formulation, then

$$\pi' = -\Gamma'(\mathbf{B}')^{-1} = -(0 \quad 1) \begin{pmatrix} -1 & 1 \\ \beta & -1 \end{pmatrix}^{-1}$$

$$= -(0 \quad 1) \begin{pmatrix} -1/1-\beta & -1/1-\beta \\ -\beta/1-\beta & -1/1-\beta \end{pmatrix}$$

$$= \left[\dfrac{\beta}{1-\beta} \quad \dfrac{1}{1-\beta} \right]$$

and $$\mathbf{V}_t' = \mathbf{U}_t'(\mathbf{B}')^{-1} = (U \quad 0) \begin{pmatrix} 1/1-\beta & \beta/1-\beta \\ 1/1-\beta & 1/1-\beta \end{pmatrix}$$

$$= [U/1-\beta \quad U/1-\beta]$$

The reduced-form can then be expressed as:

$$(c \quad y) = (i) \left(\dfrac{\beta}{1-\beta} \quad \dfrac{1}{1-\beta} \right) + \left(\dfrac{U}{1-\beta} \quad \dfrac{U}{1-\beta} \right) \qquad \text{...(13.2.21)}$$

(13.2.21) is similar to (13.2.19).

13.3 CONDITIONS FOR IDENTIFICATION (RANK AND ORDER CONDITIONS)

In section 13.1, it was observed that identification of a simultaneous equations model can be established only by examining its reduced form.

Certain rules for examining the identification have been developed to cut-short the above procedure. The rules are known as **Rank** and **Order** conditions of identification, and are applied directly to the structural form of the model.

The relationships among the reduced form parameters and structural form parameters are summarised by (13.2.9):

$$\pi = -\mathbf{B}^{-1}\Gamma$$

Basically, the problem of identification is that of using *a priori* information[1] contained in the specification to determine estimates of $\mathbf{B}$ and Γ from estimates of the reduced form parameters contained by π. π, therefore, represents the available *a posteriori* information.[2] In case absence of certain

---

[1] In general, *a priori* information includes all knowledge of the system prior to parameter estimation. This information, therefore, includes information as to which variables are included, which one are endogenous, which one are exogenous, the form of the model, and specific information about the values of variances and covariances.

[2] *A priori* information precedes the estimation, *a posteriori* information follows estimation. The information that provides knowledge about the estimation of reduced form equations is *a posteriori* information. Thus the information in (13.2.9) is *a posteriori* information.

endogenous and predetermined variables from a certain equation of the model is specified, *a priori* information takes the form of zeros in **B** and **Γ** coefficient matrices, representing, respectively, endogenous and predetermined variables omitted from those equations.

Let us now consider the identification of the first structural equation[3] of model described by (13.2.1). This equation, when it contains all the endogenous and predetermined variables (contained by the model) may be written as:

$$(\beta_{11}.\beta_{12}...\beta_{1G}) \begin{pmatrix} y_{1t} \\ y_{2t} \\ \vdots \\ y_{Gt} \end{pmatrix} + (\gamma_{11} \ \gamma_{12}...\gamma_{1K}) \begin{pmatrix} x_{1t} \\ x_{2t} \\ \vdots \\ x_{Kt} \end{pmatrix} = U_{1t} \qquad ...(13.3.1)$$

That is;

$$\mathbf{B}_1\mathbf{Y}_t + \mathbf{\Gamma}_1\mathbf{X}_t = \mathbf{U}_1 \qquad ...(13.2.2)[4]$$

Assume that this equation does not contain all the endogenous and predetermined variables; but of the G endogenous variables and K predetermined variables, only G^* and K^* enter this first equation. (13.3.1) will now take the form:

$$(\beta_{11} \ \beta_{12}...\beta_{1G^*} \ 0 \ 0...0) \begin{pmatrix} y_{1t} \\ y_{2t} \\ \vdots \\ y_{Gt} \end{pmatrix} + (\gamma_{11} \ \gamma_{12}...\gamma_{1K^*} \ 0 \ 0...0) \begin{pmatrix} x_{1t} \\ x_{2t} \\ \vdots \\ x_{Kt} \end{pmatrix} = U_{1t} \ ...(13.3.3)$$

Note that zeros have been put at the end of each of the two row vectors of parameters. This has been done by changing the order of the variables, that is variables have been renumbered so that the excluded variables are listed after the variables which are present in the equation. Accordingly, therefore, G^{**} $(= G - G^*)$ endogenous variables which are *omitted* from the equation are placed last in the column vector $(y_{1t} \ y_{2t}...y_{Gt})'$ so that the first column of the $\mathbf{B}_1$ matrix ends in G^{**} zeros as shown in (13.3.3).

Similarly, of the K predetermined variables, it is assumed that only the first K^* enter the equation. The remaining predetermined variables are placed last in the vector $(x_{1t} \ x_{2t}...x_{Kt})'$ so that the first column of $\mathbf{\Gamma}_1$ matrix ends in K^{**} $(= K - K^*)$ zeros, as shown in (13.3.3). Such a procedure has been adopted merely to simplify our mathematical manipulations that

---

[3] There will be no loss of generality in doing so, because equations can be renumbered in whatsoever procedure one wants.

[4] (13.3.2) and (13.2.5) describe the same first structural equation of the model, but they differ in notational form. The former one has not been described in terms of observations.

follow.

(13.3.3) can be rewritten as:

$$(\beta_{11}y_{1t} + \beta_{12}y_{2t} + ...\beta_{1G*}y_{G*t}) +$$
$$(\gamma_{11}x_{1t} + \gamma_{12}x_{2t} + ... + y_{1K*}x_{K*t}) = U_1 \qquad ...(13.3.4)$$

To express the relation between reduced form and structural form coefficients of (13.3.4), let us recall (13.2.9):

$$\pi = -\mathbf{B}^{-1}\Gamma$$

which can be written, by premultiplying **B** matrix as

$$\mathbf{B}\pi = -\Gamma \qquad ...(13.3.5)$$

Note that only first row of **B** and Γ in (13.2.9) correspond to the (13.3.1).

Considering the zero values in (13.3.3), the π matrix can be partitioned so that the first structural equation may be expressed in the form of (13.2.9) as:

$$\begin{bmatrix} \beta_{11} \beta_{12}...\beta_{1G*} & | & 0...0 \end{bmatrix} \begin{bmatrix} \pi_1^{*\cdot*} & \vdots & \pi_3^{*\cdot**} \\ \cdots & \cdots & \cdots \\ \pi_2^{**\cdot*} & \vdots & \pi_4^{**\cdot**} \end{bmatrix}_{(G \times K)} =$$

$$-\begin{bmatrix} \gamma_{11} \gamma_{12}...\gamma_{1K*} & | & 0...0 \end{bmatrix} \qquad ...(13.3.6)$$

In (13.3.6) π_1, π_2, π_3 and π_4 are submatrices of π corresponding to the variables included in and excluded from the first equation. The order of these submatrices is as under:

$\pi_1^{*,*}$	is of order	$G^* \times K^*$	That is, first star(s) refers to
$\pi_2^{**,*}$	is of order	$G^{**} \times K^*$	endogenous variable(s) and the
$\pi_3^{*,**}$	is of order	$G^* \times K^{**}$	second stars(s) refers to
$\pi_4^{**,**}$	is of order	$G^{**} \times K^{**}$	predetermined variable(s)

Performing the matrix multiplications, two sets of equations are obtained:

$$(\beta_{11} \beta_{12}...\beta_{1G*}) \cdot \pi_1^{*,*} = -(\gamma_{11} \gamma_{12}...\gamma_{1K*}) \qquad ...(13.3.7)$$

$$(\beta_{11} \beta_{12}...\beta_{1G*}) \cdot \pi_2^{*,**} = (0 \ 0.0...0) \qquad ...(13.3.8)$$

(13.3.7) involves K^* number of equations.

(13.3.8) involves K^{**} number of equations.

The problem of identification in the present case is that of solving these equations (total $K^* + K^{**} = K$) described by (13.3.7) and (13.3.8) simultaneously for β's and γ's, given the estimates of π.

Since (13.3.7) involves both β's and γ's, solution of above equations is possible by solving (13.3.8) for β's first and then inserting these estimates in (13.3.7) to acquire the γ's. The problem, thus, reduces to that of solving (13.3.8) for β's.

The system in (13.3.8) is a homogenous system of K^{**} linear equations in G^* unknowns. If the rank of coefficient matrix $\pi_2^{*,**}$ in (13.3.8) is exactly G^*, then, the only solution would the trivial *solution* where $\beta_{11} = \beta_{12} = ... = \beta_{1G^*} = 0$ (Since we have null matrix on the right side of equality). But this can never be the case, as it is assumed that there is at least one endogenous variable included in the first equation. Hence the system shall have a nontrivial solution if an only if the coefficient matrix $\pi_3^{*,**}$ satisfies the rank condition of:

$$\rho(\pi_3^{*,**}) = G^* - 1 \qquad ...(13.3.9)$$

$$(\rho = \text{stands for rank})$$

(13.3.9) is known as the *rank condition* of identification. It is necessary and sufficient for identification of the equation, and if it holds, there exist solution for $\beta_{11}, \beta_{12}, ..., \beta_{1G^*}$.

Condition described by (13.3.9) states:

An equation containing G^* endogenous variables is identified if and only if it is possible to construct at least one non-zero determinant of order $G^* - 1$ (that is rank = $G^* - 1$) from the reduced form coefficients of the predetermined variables *excluded* from that particular equation.

But again, since $\pi_3^{*,**}$ in (13.3.8) is a $G^* \times K^{**}$ matrix, for rank condition (13.3.9) to be satisfied it is necessary that

$$K^{**} \geq G^* - 1 \qquad ...(13.3.10)$$

That is, the number of columns in $\pi_3^{*,**}$ must be at least as great as number of its rows less one, in order that non-zero determinant of order $(G^* - 1)$ could be framed from it.

(13.3.10) is known as order condition of identification, which is necessary but not sufficient for identification. Since this condition involves merely counting zeros in the relevant columns of **B** and **Γ** matrices (to know K^{**}), it is easy to check. This condition is, therefore, checked first.

(13.3.9) and (13.3.10) state the conditions for identification applicable to the reduced form of the given model. Traditionally, identification has been approached via reduced form, because basically the term identification is used to denote the possibility of deducing the values of the parameters of the structural relations from the knowledge of the reduced form parameters. However, as the reader must have realised by now, the *reduced form approach* is conceptually confusing and computationally difficult (because this approach would require the derivation of the reduced form first and then examination of the rank of the matrix from some of the reduced form coefficient). It would be convenient if the two conditions are so changed as to make them applicable directly to the structural form of the model.

13.4 CONDITIONS OF IDENTIFICATION FOR STRUCTURAL FORM

Conditions in (13.3.9) and (13.3.10) can also be restated in the forms so as to apply them directly to structural form of the system.

Order Condition

This condition states:

For an equation to be identified, the total number of variables (endogenous and predetermined) excluded from it but included in other equations must be at *least* as great as the number of endogenous variables in the system *less one*.[5]

The condition may be described in notation form:

$$G^{**} + K^{**} \geq G - 1 \qquad \qquad ...(13.4.1)$$

Rank Condition

This condition states:

For an equation to be identified, the rank of the matrix of the parameters of all the excluded variables (endogenous and predetermined) from that equation, but contained in other equations of the model, is equal to number of endogenous variables *less one*.

The above condition[6] may be described in notation form:

$$\rho[\beta^{**} : \Gamma^{**}] = G - 1 \qquad \qquad ...(13.4.2)$$

The theory of identification[7] developed in the form of Rank and Order Conditions enables us to set up the following general rule for determing the identification status of an equation in a given simultaneous equations model:

(i) An equation is *over identified* if:

$$\rho(B^{**} \; \Gamma^{**}) = G - 1, \text{ and } K^{**} + G^{**} > G - 1$$

---

[5] This condition can be obtained from (13.3.10) as follows:

$$K^{**} \geq G^{*} - 1,$$

on adding G^{**} to both sides of the inequality;

$$K^{**} + G^{**} \geq G^{**} + G^{*} - 1,$$

that is: $\qquad K^{**} + G^{**} \geq G - 1$

[6] The proof of equivalence of (13.4.2) and (13.3.9) involves use of a bit difficult matrix algebra. It has, therefore, been avoided here.

[7] It should be remembered that this theory of identification is applicable to models which are linear in variables and parameters. Many realistic models, however, may be non-linear in variables. Identification theory of such models is difficult and has been partially developed.

(ii) An equation is *just identified* if:
$$\rho(\mathbf{B}^{**}\ \Gamma^{**}) = G - 1, \text{ and } K^{**} + G^{**} = G - 1$$

(iii) An equation is *under identified* if:
$$K^{**} + G^{**} < G - 1$$

(iv) An equation is *unidentified* if:
$$\rho(\mathbf{B}^{**}\ \Gamma^{**}) < G - 1, \text{ and } K^{**} + G^{**} \geq G - 1$$

The *basic condition* for a structural equation to be identified is the rank condition which is both necessary as well as sufficient condition.

The application of the theory of identification developed above may be explained through the following two illustrations.

Example 1: Discuss the identification of the following model, assuming Y's as endogenous and X's as predetermined variables.

$$Y_1 = \alpha_{10} + \alpha_{12}Y_2 + \alpha_{13}Y_3 + \beta_{11}X_1 + U_1$$
$$Y_2 = \alpha_{20} + \alpha_{23}Y_3 + \beta_{21}X_1 + \beta_{22}X_2 + U_2$$
$$Y_3 = \alpha_{30} + \alpha_{31}Y_1 + \beta_{31}X_1 + \beta_{32}X_2 + U_3$$
$$Y_4 = \alpha_{40} + \alpha_{41}Y_1 + \alpha_{42}Y_2 + \beta_{43}X_3 + U_4$$

To check Order Condition:

(i) First Equation: $Y_1 = \alpha_{10} + \alpha_{12}Y_2 + \alpha_{13}Y_3 + \beta_{11}X_1 + U_1$

$$
\left.
\begin{array}{rcl}
G^* &=& 3 \\
G^{**} &=& 1 \\
K^* &=& 1 \\
K^{**} &=& 2 \\
G &=& 4
\end{array}
\right\}
\begin{array}{l}
G^{**} + K^{**} = 1 + 2 = 3 \\
G - 1 = 4 - 1 = 3
\end{array}
$$

That is; order condition is satisfied.

(ii) Second Equation: $Y_2 = \alpha_{20} + \alpha_{23}Y_3 + \beta_{21}X_1 + \beta_{22}X_2 + U_2$

$$
\left.
\begin{array}{rcl}
G^* &=& 2 \\
G^{**} &=& 2 \\
K^* &=& 2 \\
K^{**} &=& 1 \\
G &=& 4
\end{array}
\right\}
\begin{array}{l}
G^{**} + K^{**} = 2 + 1 = 3 \\
G - 1 = 4 - 1 = 3
\end{array}
$$

That is; order condition is satisfied.

(iii) Third Equation: $Y_3 = \alpha_{30} + \alpha_{31}Y_1 + \beta_{31}X_1 + \beta_{32}X_2 + U_3$

$$
\left.\begin{array}{l}
G^* \ \ = 2 \\
G^{**} = 2 \\
K^* \ \ = 2 \\
K^{**} = 1 \\
G \ \ \ = 4
\end{array}\right\} \text{Order condition is satisfied.}
$$

(iv) Fourth Equation: $Y_4 = \alpha_{40} + \alpha_{41}Y_1 + \alpha_{42}Y_2 + \beta_{43}X_3 + U_4$

$$
\left.\begin{array}{l}
G^* \ \ = 3 \\
G^{**} = 1 \\
K^* \ \ = 1 \\
K^{**} = 2 \\
G \ \ \ = 4
\end{array}\right\} \begin{array}{l} G^{**} + K^{**} = 1 + 2 = 3 \\[6pt] G - 1 = 4 - 1 = 3 \end{array}
$$

That is; order condition is satisfied.

To check Rank Condition:

The model has to be put in the following form to facilitate the formulation of the required matrix.[8]

$$-\alpha_{10} + Y_1 - \alpha_{12}Y_2 - \alpha_{13}Y_3 + 0Y_4 - \beta_{11}X_1 + 0X_2 + 0X_3 = U_1$$

$$-\alpha_{20} + 0Y_1 + Y_2 - \alpha_{23}Y_3 + 0Y_4 - \beta_{21}X_1 - \beta_{22}X_2 + 0X_3 = U_2$$

$$-\alpha_{30} - \alpha_{31}Y_1 + 0Y_2 + Y_3 + 0Y_4 - \beta_{31}X_1 - \beta_{32}X_2 + 0X_3 = U_3$$

$$-\alpha_{40} - \alpha_{41}Y_1 + \alpha_{42}Y_2 + 0Y_3 + Y_4 + 0X_1 + 0X_2 - \beta_{43}X_3 = U_4$$

To frame the $\mathbf{B^{**}\Gamma^{**}}$ matrix from the above model, following tabular form is to be made:

Eq. No.	Constant term	Coefficients of						
		Y_1	Y_2	Y_3	Y_4	X_1	X_2	X_3
1.	$-\alpha_{10}$	1	$-\alpha_{12}$	$-\alpha_{13}$	0	$-\beta_{11}$	0	0
2.	$-\alpha_{20}$	0	1	$-\alpha_{23}$	0	$-\beta_{21}$	$-\beta_{22}$	0
3.	$-\alpha_{30}$	$-\alpha_{31}$	0	1	0	$-\beta_{31}$	$-\beta_{32}$	0
4.	$-\alpha_{40}$	$-\alpha_{41}$	$-\alpha_{42}$	0	1	0	0	$-\beta_{43}$

(i) *First Equation:* It excludes Y_4, X_2 and X_3 variables. This is represented by zeros in the first row of the above table. We are required to examine

---

[8] The dropping of constant terms from all the equations will not change the result of rank and order conditions.

the rank of the matrix formed by the coefficients of the variables excluded from this equation. Let this matrix be denoted by **A**, so that

$$[\mathbf{B}^{**} \vdots \Gamma^{**}] = \mathbf{A} = \begin{bmatrix} 0 & -\beta_{22} & 0 \\ 0 & -\beta_{32} & 0 \\ 1 & 0 & -\beta_{43} \end{bmatrix}$$

But since $|\mathbf{A}| = 0$, $\rho(\mathbf{A}) < (G - 1) = 3$
Rank condition for this equation, is not satisfied.

(ii) *Second Equation:* It exclude Y_1, Y_4 and X_3 variables

$$[B^{**} \vdots \Gamma^{**}] = \mathbf{A} = \begin{bmatrix} 1 & 0 & 0 \\ -\alpha_{31} & 0 & 0 \\ -\alpha_{41} & 1 & -\beta_{43} \end{bmatrix}$$

Since $|\mathbf{A}| = 0$, $\rho(\mathbf{A}) < 3$
Rank condition for second equation is not satisfied.

(iii) *Third Equation:* It excludes Y_2, Y_4 and X_3 variables

$$[\mathbf{B}^{**} \vdots \Gamma^{**}] = \mathbf{A} = \begin{bmatrix} -\alpha_{12} & 0 & 0 \\ 1 & 0 & 0 \\ -\alpha_{42} & 1 & -\beta_{43} \end{bmatrix}$$

Since $|\mathbf{A}| = 0$, $\rho(\mathbf{A}) < 3$

Rank condition is not satisfied.

(iv) *Fourth Equation:* It excludes Y_3, X_1 and X_2 variables

$$[\mathbf{B}^{**} \vdots \Gamma^{**}] = \mathbf{A} = \begin{bmatrix} -\alpha_{13} & -\beta_{11} & 0 \\ -\alpha_{23} & -\beta_{21} & -\beta_{22} \\ 1 & -\beta_{31} & -\beta_{32} \end{bmatrix}$$

hence, $|\mathbf{A}| \neq 0$, $\rho(\mathbf{A}) = 3$.
The fourth equation satisfies rank condition.
The above results may now be summarised as:

Eq. No.	Order condition	Rank condition	Result
1.	Satisfied	Not satisfied	*Unidentified*
2.	Satisfied	Not satisfied	*Unidentified*
3.	Satisfied	Not satisfied	*Unidentified*
4.	Satisfied	Satisfied	*Just identified*

Since any system is said to be identified only if each of the equations of the structural form is identified, the present model is found to be unidentified.

Example 2: Examine the identification of the following Keynesian model of income determination:

$$C_t = \alpha_0 + \alpha_1 Y_t + \alpha_2 T_t + U$$
$$I_t = \beta_0 + \beta_1 Y_{t-1} \qquad + V$$
$$T_t = \gamma_0 + \gamma Y_t \qquad + W$$
$$Y_t = C_t + I_t + G_t$$

Endogenous variables are: C_t, I_t, T_t and Y_t.

In the present model, identification status has to be examined only of three[9] structural functions: consumption, investment and taxation functions.

Order Condition

(i) Consumption Function:

$$\left. \begin{array}{l} G^{**} + K^{**} = 3 \\ G - 1 \qquad\quad = 3 \end{array} \right\} \text{ hence order condition is satisfied.}$$

(ii) Investment Function:

$$\left. \begin{array}{l} G^{**} + K^{**} = 4 \\ G - 1 \qquad\quad = 3 \end{array} \right\} \text{ hence order condition is satisfied.}$$

(iii) Taxation Function:

$$\left. \begin{array}{l} G^{**} + K^{**} = 4 \\ G - 1 \qquad\quad = 3 \end{array} \right\} \text{ hence order condition is satisfied.}$$

Rank Condition

	C_t	Y_t	T_t	I_t	Y_{t-1}	G
			Structural Coefficients			
Consumption:	-1	α_1	α_2	0	0	0
Investment:	0	0	0	-1	β_1	0
Taxation:	0	γ_1	-1	0	0	0

(i) Consumption Function:

$$[B^{**} \vdots \Gamma^{**}] = A = \begin{bmatrix} -1 & \beta_1 & 0 \\ 0 & 0 & 0 \end{bmatrix}$$

$\rho(A) \neq 3$, hence rank condition is not satisfied.

---

[9] Problems of identification arise only for those equations which contain coefficients and, which could be estimated statistically from the given simple data. Identification problems do not arise for definitional equations, identities or statement of equilibrium conditions. Such relations do not require measurement as well.

(ii) Investment Function:

    Rank condition remains unsatisfied.

(iii) Taxation Function:

    Rank condition is not satisfied.

Tabulating the result as attempted in case of first example, it is found that given model remains *unidentified.*

The preceding analysis of identifiability conditions remain confined to the specification of the structural equations. Identification is examined on the basis of *a priori* zero restrictions. As the reader must have observed, the rank and order conditions establish the identifiability of the model only through the examination of *a priori* restrictions on its structural form matrices. **B** and **Γ**. If there were no *a priori* restrictions, all the equations would look alike statistically and the situation would indeed be hopeless. Each equation would then be a linear combination of all *G*-endogenous and all *K*-predetermined variables and no equation in the model would be identifiable.

It may, therefore, be said that econometrician, in order to achieve identification of the model must impose *a priori* zero restrictions on the coefficient matrices **B** and **Γ**. This is the most common way of achieving the identification of the model.

Nevertheless, identification can also be achieved by non-zero restrictions on the coefficient matrices **B** and **Γ** e.g., by specifying relations between the coefficients via various linear homogenous restrictions. Such restrictions are called *linear restrictions* on the coefficients. These restrictions are discussed under the Section 13.5.

These are two other approaches to identification also. Of these two approaches, one approach is through imposition of restrictions on **Σ** matrix; the matrix of variance and covariances of the disturbances described in (13.2.6). The other approach is mixture of all types restrictions described above. Here restrictions of equalities or inequalities are imposed on **B**, **Γ** and **Σ** simultaneously. An example of such an approach is that of a *recursive system* in which certain zero restrictions are imposed on both **B** and **Σ**.

13.5 IDENTIFICATION THROUGH (ADDED) RESTRICTIONS

Three forms of restrictions other than zero restrictions described above, shall be discussed in the present section.

I. Linear Homogenous Restrictions

The connection between structural and reduced form coefficients is given by (13.2.9) as

$$\pi = -\mathbf{B}^{-1}\mathbf{\Gamma}$$

This connection can also be expressed as:

$$\mathbf{B}\pi + \mathbf{\Gamma} = 0 \qquad\qquad ...(13.5.1)$$

Let two matrices $\mathbf{W}$ and $\mathbf{A}$, and one vector α_1 be defined as under:

(i) $\mathbf{A}$ matrix is the matrix of all coefficients (endogenous and predetermined) of the structural form and, defined as follows:

$$\underset{[G\times(G+K)]}{\mathbf{A}} = \left[\begin{array}{c|c} \underset{(G\times G)}{B} & \underset{(G\times K)}{\Gamma} \end{array}\right] = \left[\begin{array}{ccc|ccc} \beta_{11} & \cdots & \beta_{1G} & \gamma_{11} & \cdots & \gamma_{K1} \\ \beta_{21} & \cdots & \beta_{2G} & \gamma_{21} & \cdots & \gamma_{K2} \\ \vdots & & & \vdots & & \\ \beta_{G1} & \cdots & \beta_{GG} & \gamma_{G1} & \cdots & \gamma_{GK} \end{array}\right]$$

(ii) α_1 vector is the first row of $\mathbf{A}$

$$\underset{[1\times(G+K)]}{\alpha_1} = \left[\begin{array}{ccc|ccc} \beta_{11} & \cdots & \beta_{1G} & \gamma_{11} & \cdots & \gamma_{K1} \end{array}\right]$$

(iii) $\mathbf{W}$ is partitioned coefficient matrix of elements of π and identity matrix of order K

$$\mathbf{W} = \left[\begin{array}{c} \pi_{(G\times K)} \\ \cdots\cdots\cdots \\ \mathbf{I}_K \end{array}\right] \text{ and } \rho[\mathbf{W}] = K$$

Premultiplying $\mathbf{A}$ to $\mathbf{W}$;

$$\mathbf{A}\,\mathbf{W} = [\mathbf{B} \quad \Gamma]\left[\begin{array}{c} \pi \\ \mathbf{I}_K \end{array}\right] = \mathbf{B}\,\pi + \Gamma = \mathbf{0}$$

Therefore, $\qquad \mathbf{A}\,\mathbf{W} = \mathbf{0}$ \qquad\qquad ...(13.5.2)

In particular situations also;

$$\underset{[1\times(G+K)]}{\alpha_1} \quad \underset{[(G+K)\times K]}{\mathbf{W}} = \underset{(1\times K)}{\mathbf{O}} \qquad\qquad ...(13.5.3)$$

Since the rank of $\mathbf{W}$ is K, (13.5.3) constitutes a set of K independent equations in $(G + K)$ unknowns (which are the elements of α_1 vector), α_1 cannot be determined from this equation alone (note that there is null matrix on the right hand side). To put this point another way, no unknown can be determined unless certain *a priori* restrictions are assumed. *A priori* restrictions may be of '*zero restrictions*' form or they may be linear homogenous restrictions involving two or more of the elements of vector α_1.

These restrictions may be expressed in the form:

$$\alpha_1 \phi = 0 \qquad\qquad ...(13.5.4)$$

where, ϕ has $(G + K)$ rows and a column for each restriction.

The *a priori* restrictions (13.5.4) and the *a posteriori* restrictions (13.5.3) for each equation can be combined in the single system of homogenous equation as under:

$$[\alpha_1]\, [\mathbf{W}\, \phi] = 0 \qquad\qquad ...(13.5.5)$$

Since α_1 has $(G + K)$ elements, identification of this equation requires that rank of $[\mathbf{W} \quad \phi]$ should be $(G + K - 1)$. In other words a non-trivial solution of (13.5.5) exists if and only if the matrix $[\mathbf{W} \quad \phi]$ satisfies the following rank condition,

$$\rho\,[\mathbf{W} \quad \phi] = (G + K - 1) \qquad \qquad ...(13.5.6)$$

(13.5.6) is the **rank condition** of identification.

The rank condition stated in (13.5.6) is not a convenient one to apply since it requires the construction of the π matrix ($\mathbf{W}$ involves π and $\mathbf{I}_K$). A condition that is equivalent to [(13.5.6)] is the general rank condition of identification which involves matrix $\mathbf{A}$ in the following way[10];

$$\rho[\mathbf{A}\ \phi] = G - 1 \qquad \qquad ...(13.5.7)$$

This rank condition is a necessary and sufficient condition for identification. From (13.5.7) and the fact that multiplying a matrix by another cannot increase its rank, it follows that a necessary condition of identification is·

$$\rho(\phi) \geq G - 1 \qquad \qquad ...(13.5.8)$$

This is the **order condition** of identification.

It is called an 'order' condition even though it involves the rank of a matrix; and it is necessary but not sufficient for identification. This condition along with rank condition defines over identified, just identified and under identified status of the equation under examination.

(i) Equation is over identified; if

$$\rho(\mathbf{A}\ \phi) = G - 1, \text{ and } \rho(\phi) > G - 1$$

(ii) Equation is just identified; if

$$\rho(\mathbf{A}\ \phi) = G - 1, \text{ and } \rho(\phi) = G - 1$$

(iii) Equation is under identified; if $\rho(\phi) < G - 1$

(iv) Equation is unidentified; if

$$\rho(\mathbf{A}\ \phi) < G - 1, \text{ and } \rho(\phi) \geq G - 1$$

To illustrate the application of conditions derived above, let the following two-equations model be assumed:

$$\beta_{11}y_1 + \beta_{12}y_2 + \gamma_{11}x_1 + \gamma_{12}x_2 = u_1$$
$$\beta_{21}y_1 + \beta_{22}y_2 + \gamma_{21}x_1 + \gamma_{22}x_2 = u_2$$

Both the above equations, as they stand, are unidentifiable since all the variables (y's and x's) are contained by both the equations, that is no *a priori* restriction have yet been imposed.

---

[10]Note carefully that $[\mathbf{W}\ \phi]$ is a matrix consisting of two indicated sub-matrices; while $\mathbf{A}\ \phi$ is the product of two matrices of which order is $[(G + K) \times (K + R) - R$ is no. of col. in $\phi]$. Hence $\rho(\mathbf{W}\ \phi)$ shall be $(G + K - 1)$ if and only if $\rho(\mathbf{A}\ \phi) = G - 1$.

Assume the following cases of *a priori* restrictions:

Case (a): $\gamma_{12} = 0$, and $\gamma_{21} = 0$

(b): $\gamma_{12} = 0$, and $\gamma_{22} = 0$

(c): $\gamma_{11} = 0$, $\gamma_{12} = 0$, and $\gamma_{22} = 0$

(d): $\gamma_{11} = 0$, and $\gamma_{12} = 0$

(e): $\gamma_{11} = 0$, $\gamma_{12} = 0$, $\gamma_{22} = 0$, and $\beta_{21} = -\gamma_{21}$.

Two matrices $\mathbf{A}$ and ϕ shall have to be constructed for each case. $\mathbf{A}$ matrix is the matrix of coefficients of all the variables. ϕ matrix has: rows $= G + K$, with **unit** coefficient for each zero-restriction but **zero** otherwise, columns $=$ number of restrictions.

$$\mathbf{A} = \begin{bmatrix} \beta_{11} & \beta_{12} & \gamma_{11} & \gamma_{12} \\ \beta_{21} & \beta_{12} & \gamma_{21} & \gamma_{22} \end{bmatrix}$$

Case (a):

Considering first equation $\phi = \begin{bmatrix} 0 \\ 0 \\ 0 \\ 1 \end{bmatrix}$, $\mathbf{A}\,\phi = \begin{bmatrix} \gamma_{12} \\ \gamma_{22} \end{bmatrix}$

On using the restrictions; $\gamma_{12} = 0$,

$$\mathbf{A}\phi = \begin{bmatrix} 0 \\ \gamma_{22} \end{bmatrix}, \text{ and } \rho(\mathbf{A}\phi) = 1 = G - 1$$

Rank condition for the first equation gets satisfied. Again, since $\rho(\phi) = 1$, which is $= G - 1$, the first equation is just identified, provided of course if $\gamma_{22} \neq 0$.

Considering second equation: $\phi = \begin{bmatrix} 0 \\ 0 \\ 1 \\ 0 \end{bmatrix}$

$$\mathbf{A}\phi = \begin{bmatrix} \gamma_{11} \\ \gamma_{21} \end{bmatrix} = \begin{bmatrix} \gamma_{11} \\ 0 \end{bmatrix} \text{ on considering } \gamma_{21} = 0.$$

Therefore, $\rho(\mathbf{A}\phi) = 1 = G - 1$

Also, $\rho(\phi) = 1 = G - 1$

Second equation is, therefore, just identified, provided $\gamma_{11} \neq 0$.

Since both the equations are identified, the system stands to be just identified.

Case (b):

Considering restriction on first equation: $\phi = \begin{bmatrix} 0 \\ 0 \\ 0 \\ 1 \end{bmatrix}$

$$\mathbf{A}\phi = \begin{bmatrix} \gamma_{12} \\ \gamma_{22} \end{bmatrix}, \text{ using restrictions } \gamma_{12} = \gamma_{22} = 0$$

$$\mathbf{A}\phi = \begin{bmatrix} 0 \\ 0 \end{bmatrix}, \ \rho(\mathbf{A}\phi) = 0.$$

The first equation is not identified, nor is the second. Hence, the model is not identifiable with restrictions given under case (b).

Case (c):

Considering the restrictions on first equation: $\phi = \begin{bmatrix} 0 \\ 0 \\ 1 \\ 1 \end{bmatrix}$

$$\mathbf{A}\phi = \begin{bmatrix} \gamma_{11} & \gamma_{12} \\ \gamma_{21} & \gamma_{22} \end{bmatrix} = \begin{pmatrix} 0 & 0 \\ \gamma_{21} & 0 \end{pmatrix} \text{ (on considering the restrictions)}$$

$$\left.\begin{array}{l} \rho(\mathbf{A}\phi) = 1 = G - 1 \\ \rho(\phi) = 1 = G - 1 \end{array}\right\} \text{ Equation is identified.}$$

But the second equation remains unidentified.

Case (d):

Considering the restrictions on first equation: $\phi = \begin{bmatrix} 0 & 0 \\ 0 & 0 \\ 1 & 0 \\ 0 & 1 \end{bmatrix}$

(For two restrictions)

$$\mathbf{A}\phi = \begin{bmatrix} 0 & 0 \\ \gamma_{21} & \gamma_{22} \end{bmatrix} \text{ using the restrictions.}$$

$$\left.\begin{array}{l} \rho(\mathbf{A}\phi) = 1 = G - 1 \\ \rho(\phi) = 1 = G - 1 \end{array}\right\} \text{ Equation is identified.}$$

Here also, second equation is not identified. The model, therefore, remains unidentified in case (d).

Case (e):

Restrictions on the first equation ($\gamma_{11} = 0$, $\gamma_{12} = 0$) are the same as in Case (d). These make the first equation identifiable.

Considering the second equation: $\gamma_{22} = 0$ and $\beta_{21} + \gamma_{21} = 0$;

$$\phi = \begin{bmatrix} 1 & 0 \\ 0 & 0 \\ 1 & 0 \\ 0 & 1 \end{bmatrix}$$

$$A\phi = \begin{bmatrix} \beta_{11} + \gamma_{11} & \beta_{21} + \gamma_{21} \\ \gamma_{12} & \gamma_{22} \end{bmatrix} = \begin{bmatrix} \beta_{11} & 0 \\ 0 & 0 \end{bmatrix}$$

$$\rho(A\phi) = 1 = G - 1.$$

Hence the second equation now gets identified (which was not under Case (d) and the model is identified.

II. Restrictions on Variances and Covariances

Thus far, while developing the theory of identification conditions, no reference was made to the matrix of variances and covariances of the simultaneous equations model described by (13.2.6). That is, our explicit assumption of serial independence among the disturbances across the structural equations remained undisturbed while establishing the identification status of the model.

Recall (13.2.6):

$$\Sigma = \begin{bmatrix} \sigma_{11} & \sigma_{12} & \cdots & \sigma_{1G} \\ \sigma_{21} & \sigma_{22} & \cdots & \sigma_{2G} \\ \vdots & & & \\ \sigma_{G1} & \sigma_{G2} & \cdots & \sigma_{GG} \end{bmatrix}_{(G \times G)}$$

Σ is $(G \times G)$ matrix, the terms in the principal diagonal indicate the variances (assumed constant) of the disturbances in the G structural equations and, the off-diagonal terms indicating the covariances between pairs of disturbances. If specific restriction can be placed on some of the elements of this matrix, they would constitute an additional source of the identifying power.

For instance, zero restrictions could be assumed on variances and covariances: e.g., $\sigma_{11} = \sigma_{22} = 0$; $\sigma_{12} = \sigma_{23} = 0$.

Second procedure could be the assumptions relating to relative sizes of variances or covariances; e.g., $\sigma_{11} > \sigma_{22}$; $\sigma_{23} > \sigma_{34}$. In general, the source of such restrictions is the knowledge of the conditions of the particular phenomenon described by the model. However, since the disturbances are defined by so many unknown and complex forces, the assumptions concerning their variances and covariances would usually be highly arbitrary.

For the sake of conceptual understanding, consider a simple demand-supply model to understand how the identification status of the model changes with the imposition of restrictions on the covariances of disturbances.

$$Q_s = \alpha_0 + \alpha_1 P + V$$
$$Q_d = \beta_0 + \beta_1 P + \beta_2 Y + U$$
$$Q_s = Q_d$$

Supply equation of this model is identifiable, demand equation is not.

The reduced form of the model:

$$Q = \pi_{11} + \pi_{12} Y + e_1$$
$$P = \pi_{21} + \pi_{22} Y + e_2,$$

where,

$$e_1 = \frac{\alpha_1 U - \beta_1 V}{\alpha_1 - \beta_1}$$

and

$$e_2 = \frac{U - V}{\alpha_1 - \beta_1},$$

so that,

$$\left. \begin{array}{l} U = e_1 - \beta_1 e_2 \\ V = e_1 - \alpha_1 e_2 \end{array} \right\} \qquad \qquad ...(13.5.9)[11]$$

Let us now add a restriction by specifying that the disturbances in the two equations (i.e., U and V) are mutually independent; i.e., that $E(UV) = 0$.

The restriction implies that:

$$E[(e_1 - \beta_1 e_2)(e_1 - \alpha_1 e_2)] = 0$$

$$E[(e_1^2 - \beta e_1 e_2 - \alpha_1 e_1 e_2 + \alpha_1 \beta_1 e_2^2)] = 0$$

$$\sigma_{11} - \beta_1 \sigma_{12} - \alpha_1 \sigma_{12} + \sigma_1 \beta_1 \sigma_{22} = 0 \qquad \qquad ...(13.5.10)$$

(σ's are element of Σ matrix)

Since supply equation is identified, α_1 is estimated directly from the reduced form coefficients:

$$\alpha_1 = \pi_{12}/\pi_{22}, \text{ substituting this in (13.5.10),}$$

---

[11]Equalities of e_1 and e_2 involve same denominator, therefore:
$$(\alpha_1 U - \beta_1 V) / e_1 = (U - V)/e_2$$
$$U(e_1 - \alpha e_2) = V(e_1 - \beta_1 e_2); \text{ hence the result.}$$

$$\beta_1 = \frac{\pi_{12}\sigma_{12} - \pi_{22}\sigma_{11}}{\pi_{12}\sigma_{22} - \pi_{22}\sigma_{12}}$$

$$\beta_1 = -\left(\frac{\pi_{22}\sigma_{11}}{\pi_{12}\sigma_{22}}\right) \qquad (\because \sigma_{12} = \sigma_{23} = 0)$$

$$\beta_2 = \pi_{12} - \beta_1\pi_{22}$$

In this way, it is observed that β_1 and β_2 coefficients of demand function are uniquely obtained due to added restriction imposed on the covariances of the structural disturbances. In other words, previously under-identified demand equation becomes identified with added restriction on covariances.

III. Restrictions on Coefficients and Covariances

In certain simultaneous equations models, the endogenous variables and the structural equations can be arranged in such an order that **B** matrix of the coefficients of endogenous variables is a *triangular* matrix and Σ, the matrix of variances and covariances of stochastic disturbance terms is a *diagonal* matrix. Such simultaneous equation system is called *Recursive system*.

The two sets of restrictions that characterise the system recursive are described under:

$$\mathbf{B} = \begin{bmatrix} \beta_{11} & \beta_{12} & \beta_{13} & \cdots & \beta_{1G} \\ 0 & \beta_{22} & \beta_{23} & \cdots & \beta_{2G} \\ 0 & 0 & \beta_{33} & \cdots & \beta_{3G} \\ \vdots & & & \ddots & \\ 0 & 0 & 0 & \cdots & \beta_{GG} \end{bmatrix} \qquad ...(13.5.11)$$

$$\Sigma = \begin{bmatrix} \sigma^2 & 0 & 0 & \cdots & 0 \\ 0 & \sigma^2 & 0 & \cdots & 0 \\ 0 & 0 & \sigma^2 & \cdots & 0 \\ \vdots & & & \ddots & \\ 0 & 0 & & & \sigma^2 \end{bmatrix} \qquad ...(13.5.12)$$

(13.5.11) requires that the structural equations can be expressed so that no equation includes those endogenous variables included in higher numbered equation. Each endogenous variable can, therefore, be explained in terms of lower numbered endogenous variable(s), disturbance term and predetermined variable(s).

(13.5.12) requires that all the covariances between stochastic disturbance terms in any two different equation vanish. This set of restrictions, along with the first set (13.5.11), makes each structural equation stand alone without its disturbance term 'contaminating' the other structural equation. As such both sets of restrictions are essential for the simultaneous equations system to be recursive.

The recursive models are always *exactly identified*. That is, with the zero restrictions in **B** and Σ matrices, it is always possible to infer the non-zero structural coefficients from the reduced-form coefficients.

13.6 IDENTIFICATION AND MULTICOLLINEARITY

There is a close affinity between identification and multicollinearity.

1. Multicollinearity is a special case of underidentification. When variables happen to be multicollinear, they are practically the same from the statistical point of view. Two multicollinear variables cannot be treated as two distinct variables in the model; hence one of them is often dropped to do away with the problem of multicollinearity. Similarly if identification of any relationships is established on the basis of zero or exclusion restrictions, it can be viewed as the case of multicollinearity where we drop some of the variables which happen to be collinear.

2. Both problems create estimation difficulties; therefore absence of multicollinearity and identification are the prerequisites for the estimation of a model. Strong collinearity of the explanatory variables does not allow us to obtain the structural coefficients; while in case of underidentification we have observationally equivalent relations in the model which make it impossible to identify the coefficients of any particular relationship.

3. Both type of problems arise because of many relationships between the variables in the model under study. We are, thus, not able to assess statistically the influence of each variable on the dependent variable.

The above points show the close relation between the problems of multicollinearity and identification.

ASSIGNMENTS

1. In a model of the money market, the demand for money (M_d) depends linearly on national income (Y), the interest rate (γ), and population (N); the supply of money (M_s) depends linearly on national income and lagged interest rate (γ_{t-1}); and, in equilibrium, money demand equals money supply. Y and N are treated exogenous, while γ and stock of money (M) are treated as endogenous. All equations contain constant terms (intercepts).
   State the structural equations and express them as a matrix equation. Also obtain the reduced-form equations in matrix form.

2. In a certain political-economic model, the proportion of votes cast for the particular party (D) depends linearly on unemployment rate (U) and union membership (M); unemployment rate depends linearly on the government deficit ($G-T$) and war (W, a dummy variable, equal to 1 if war, 0 if no war); and the government deficit depends linearly on unemployment and war.

   D, U and $G-T$ are treated as endogenous. All equations contain constant terms. Obtain the structural form and the reduced-form of the model.

3. In a certain inflation-unemployment model, rate of inflation (I) depends on the growth of the money supply (M), the interest rate (γ), past wage increases (W_{t-1}), and the government deficit (d). Unemployment rate (U) depends on inflation (I), the rate of interest (γ), current wages (W_t), and the union membership (n). Treat only I and U as endogenous and find the structural form and reduced-form of this model.

4. A macroeconomic model is of the form:

$$C = \alpha_1 + \alpha_2 Y + \alpha_3 W + U_1$$
$$I = \beta_1 + \beta_2 Y + \beta_3 Y_{t-1} + \beta_4 \gamma + U_2$$
$$Y = C + I + G$$

   where C, I and Y are endogenous;

   Y_{t-1} W, γ and G are predetermined;

   U_1 and U_2 are stochastic.

   (W = Wealth and γ = Interest rate).

   Determine the reduced-form of the model.

5. Bring out the essential character of the problem of identification with the help of a simple demand and supply model for a single commodity.

6. Explain the rank and order conditions of identifiability. Can you construct an econometric model in which the order condition is satisfied but rank condition is not?

7. Are the structural equations of the following model identified?

$$Y_1 = \beta_{10} + \beta_{12} Y_2 + \alpha_{11} X_1 + U_1$$
$$Y_2 = \beta_{20} + \beta_{21} Y_1 + \alpha_{22} X_2 + U_2$$

   What happens to identification if it is assumed that $\alpha_{11} = 0$?

8. Obtain the estimates of the structural parameters if the estimated reduced-form equations of the model described in exercise 13.7 are as follows:

$$Y_1 = 3.5 + 3X_1 + 8.5X_2$$
$$Y_2 = 2.5 + 6X_1 + 10.5X_2.$$

9. Obtain the reduced-form of the model:

$$Y_1 = \beta_{10} + \beta_{12} Y_2 + \alpha_{11} X_1 + U_1$$
$$Y_2 = \beta_{20} + \beta_{21} Y_1 + U_2$$

   Is it identified?

   Assume that the estimated reduced-form equations of this model are as follows:

$$Y_1 = 3.5 + 7X_1$$
$$Y_2 = 2.5 + 15X_1$$

   Which structural coefficients can you estimate from the reduced-form equations? How would your answer change if it is assumed that (i) $\beta_{10} = 0$ and (ii) $\beta_{12} = 0$.

10. Given the structural equations:

$$[y_1 \ y_2 \ y_3] \begin{bmatrix} -1 & \alpha_{21} & 0 \\ 0 & -1 & 0 \\ \alpha_{31} & \alpha_{32} & -1 \end{bmatrix} +$$

$$[x_1 \ x_2 \ x_3 \ x_4] \begin{bmatrix} \beta_{11} & 0 & \beta_{13} \\ \beta_{21} & \beta_{22} & 0 \\ \beta_{31} & 0 & 0 \\ \beta_{41} & \beta_{42} & \beta_{43} \end{bmatrix} = [u_1 \ u_2 \ u_3]$$

Determine the identification status of the model.

11. Structural equations of a certain model are:

$$S = f_1(p, M, T); \ p = f_2(S, p_{-1}, I); \ M = f_3(p, T)$$

where
S = shipment of steel (Endogenous)
p = price of steel (Endogenous)
M = Imports of steel (Endogenous).

Following are predetermined variables:

T = time variable, I = inventory, and lagged price (p_{t-1}).

Show that model is not identified.

Can you respecify the model to make it identified?

12. A structural model of a firm using a Cobb-Douglas production function takes the form:

$$y = a_1 + \alpha_1 l + \beta_1 k$$
$$w = a_2 + \alpha_2 l + \beta_2 k$$
$$\gamma = a_3 + \alpha_3 l + \beta_3 k$$

where,
y = logarithm of the total production
l = logarithm of the labour input
k = logarithm of the capital input
w = logarithm of the money wage
g = logarithm of the interest rate.

Assuming that w and γ are exogenous, obtain the reduced-form and show that each equation is exactly identified.

Indicate how the structural parameters can be estimated from the reduced-form equations.

13. Discuss the identification problem in the context of a structural-equation system. Do you think it is an estimation problem arising out of estimation of the structural parameters or does it arise prior to estimation in the very specification of the system?

14. Obtain the reduced form of the following model:

$$y_1 = -2y_2 + 7x_1 + 4x_2 + x_3 - 8x_4 + e_1$$
$$y_2 = 2y_1 + y_3 - x_1 + 7x_3 - 9x_5 + e_2$$
$$y_3 = 2y_1 - 7x_2 + 7x_3 + 14x_4 + e_3$$

Also investigate the identifiability of each equation.

15. Show that there is a close affinity between the concept of multicollinearity and the idea of identification.

16. Test the identifiability of the structural equations of the following models:

(i) $C = \alpha + \beta x + u_1$

$$i = \gamma + \delta y + u_2$$
$$t = y - x$$
$$y = C + i + g;$$

y, C, i and x are endogenous.

(ii) $\alpha_1 y_{1t} + \alpha_2 y_{2t} + \alpha_3 z_{1t} + \alpha_4 z_{2t} = u_{1t}$
$$\beta_2 y_{1t} + \beta_2 y_{2t} + \beta_3 y_{3t} + \beta_4 y_{2t-1} + \beta_6 z_{2t} = u_{2t}$$
$$\gamma_1 \gamma_{1t} + \gamma_2 y_{3t} + \gamma_3 z_{2t} = u_{3t}$$

y's are endogenous and z's are exogenous.

(iii) $b_{11} y_1 + b_{13} y_3 + b_{14} y4 + c_{41} z_1 = e_1$
$$b_{22} y_2 + b_{23} y_3 + b_{24} y_4 + c_{21} z_1 = e_2$$
$$b_{31} y_1 + b_{33} y_3 + c_{32} z_2 = e_3$$
$$b_{42} y_2 + b_{44} y_4 + c_{43} z_3 + c_{44} z_4 = e_4$$

y's are endogenous and z's are exogenous.

(iv) $y_{1t} = \alpha_{12} x_{2t} + u_{1t}$
$$y_{2t} = \beta_{21} y_{1t} + \alpha_{21} x_{1t} + u_{2t}$$
$$x_{3t} = \beta_{31} y_{1t} + \alpha_{32} x_{2t} + u_{3t}$$

y's are endogenous and x's are exogenous.

(v) $Q^d = \alpha_0 + \alpha_1 P + \alpha_2 Y + U$
$$Q^s = \beta_0 + \beta_1 P_{t-1} + \beta_2 W + V$$
$$Q^d = Q^s;$$

W is weather index.

(vi) $y_{1t} = -2y_{2t} + 7x_{1t} + 4x_{2t} + x_{3t} - 8x_{4t} + u_{1t}$
$$y_{2t} = 2y_{1t} + y_{3t} - x_{1t} + 7x_{3t} - 9x_{5t} + u_{2t}$$
$$y_{3t} = 2y_{1t} - 7x_{2t} + 7x_{3t} + 14x_{4t} + u_{3t}$$

(vii) $y_{1t} + \beta_{12} y_{2t} + \gamma_{11} x_{1t} = u_{1t}$
$$\beta_{21} y_{1t} + y_{2t} + \beta_{22} x_{2t} = u_{2t}$$

(viii) $y_{1t} + \beta_{12} y_{2t} + U_{1t}$
$$\beta_{21} y_{1t} + y_{2t} + \gamma_{21} x_{1t} = U_{2t}$$

y's are jointly dependent and x's are predetermined variables.

17. Determine the identifiability of each equation of the following *five* equations model with *five* endogenous (Y) and *four* exogenous (X) variables.

Eq. No.	Y_1	Y_2	Y_3	Y_4	Y_5	X_1	X_2	X_3	X_4
1.	1	α_{12}	0	α_{14}	0	β_{11}	0	0	β_{14}
2.	0	1	α_{23}	α_{24}	0	0	β_{22}	β_{23}	0
3.	α_{31}	0	1	α_{34}	α_{35}	0	0	β_{33}	β_{34}
4.	0	α_{42}	0	1	0	β_{41}	0	β_{42}	0
5.	α_{51}	0	0	α_{54}	1	0	β_{42}	β_{53}	0

14

Estimation of Simultaneous-Equation Models

Assuming that the given simultaneous-equation model is identified, there are several methods to estimate it. These methods have been referred in the chapter 12. Unlike estimation of single-equation models, the problem of estimation of simultaneous-equation models is rather complex and difficult too. Since the system methods are beyond the scope of the present introductory text, our discussion on estimation problem will be simple and often heuristic; dealing with single-equation methods of estimation.

14.1 INDIRECT LEAST SQUARES (ILS)

This method is designed to estimate one equation at a time with limited reference to the rest of the system. The method is named indirect least squares since it estimates the parameters indirectly by estimating the reduced-form equations, in which endogenous variables are expressed only as a function of the exogenous variables and of the error terms. Naturally therefore, this technique of estimation is appropriate only when we are required to estimate an exactly identified structural equation belonging to system of simultaneous equations with no restrictions on the variance-covariance matrix of the disturbances.

To illustrate the working with this method, let us take an exactly identified simple demand-supply model.

$$D_t = \alpha_0 + \alpha_1 P_t + \alpha_2 Y_t + U_1$$
$$S_t = \beta_0 + \beta_1 P_t + \beta_2 W_t + U_2$$
$$D_t = S_t$$

where $D_t = S_t$ = quantity demanded and supplied, P = price of the commodity in question, Y = income, and W = weather index. The above model is mathematically complete, i.e., there are three endogenous variables (D, S, P) and three equations in the model. It can also be observed that the model is exactly identified.

The first step to apply ILS is to obtain the reduced-form of the model,

$$D_t = \frac{\alpha_0\beta_1 - \alpha_1\beta_0}{\beta_1 - \alpha_1} + \left(\frac{\alpha_2\beta_1}{\beta_1 - \alpha_1}\right)Y_t - \left(\frac{\alpha_1\beta_2}{\beta_1 - \alpha_1}\right)W_t + \frac{\beta_1 U_1 - U_2\alpha_1}{\beta_1 - \alpha_1}$$

$$P_t = \frac{\alpha_0 - \beta_0}{\beta_1 - \alpha_1} + \left(\frac{\alpha_2}{\beta_1 - \alpha_1}\right)Y_t - \left(\frac{\beta_2}{\beta_1 - \alpha_1}\right)W_t - \frac{U_1 - U_2}{\beta_1 - \alpha_1}$$

or
$$D_t = \pi_{10} + \pi_{11}\,Y_t + \pi_{12}\,W_t + V_1$$
$$P_t = \pi_{20} + \pi_{21}\,Y_t + \pi_{22}\,W_t + V_2$$

where π's and V's depict the coefficients and disturbances of the reduced-form model. Since the reduced-form disturbances satisfy all the assumptions of the classical linear regression model (because equations do not contain endogenous variables) the application of the OLS method to each reduced-form equation leads to unbiased estimates of π's. Hence using sample data on $D(= S)$, P, Y and W, we obtain estimates of π's. We are, however, not interested in π's. We are interested in the original structural parameters of the model. Since the estimated π's are functions of these parameters, we estimate them indirectly from the π's through the following simple manipulations.

(a) Calculation of α_0:

$$\frac{\hat{\pi}_{10}}{\hat{\pi}_{20}} = \frac{\alpha_0\beta_1 - \alpha_1\beta_0}{\alpha_n - \beta_0}; \quad \text{and} \quad \frac{\hat{\pi}_{12}}{\hat{\pi}_{22}} = \alpha_1$$

Hence,
$$\hat{\pi}_{20}\left(\frac{\hat{\pi}_{10}}{\hat{\pi}_{20}} - \frac{\hat{\pi}_{12}}{\hat{\pi}_{22}}\right) = \frac{\alpha_0 - \beta_0}{\beta_1 - \alpha_1}\left(\frac{\alpha_0\beta_1 - \alpha_0\alpha_1}{\alpha_0 - \beta_0}\right) = \alpha_0$$

To obtain α_0, we, therefore, substitute the relevant estimated π's in

$$\left[\hat{\pi}_{20}\left(\frac{\hat{\pi}_{10}}{\hat{\pi}_{20}} - \frac{\hat{\pi}_{12}}{\hat{\pi}_{22}}\right)\right] = \text{estimated value of } \alpha_0$$

(b) Calculation of β_0:

$$\frac{\hat{\pi}_{10}}{\hat{\pi}_{20}} = \frac{\alpha_0\beta_1 - \alpha_1\beta_0}{\alpha_0 - \beta_0}, \quad \text{and} \quad \frac{\hat{\pi}_{11}}{\hat{\pi}_{21}} = \beta_1$$

Hence,
$$\hat{\pi}_{30}\left(\frac{\hat{\pi}_{10}}{\hat{\pi}_{20}} - \frac{\hat{\pi}_{11}}{\hat{\pi}_{21}}\right) = \frac{\alpha_0 - \beta_0}{\beta_1 - \alpha_1}\left(\frac{\beta_0\beta_1 - \beta_0\alpha_1}{\alpha_0 - \beta_0}\right) = \beta_0$$

Therefore, to obtain β_0, we substitute $\hat{\pi}$'s in $\left[\hat{\pi}_{20}\left(\frac{\hat{\pi}_{10}}{\hat{\pi}_{20}} - \frac{\hat{\pi}_{11}}{\hat{\pi}_{21}}\right)\right]$

(c) Calculation of α_2:

$$\frac{\hat{\pi}_{11}}{\hat{\pi}_{21}} = \frac{\alpha_2\beta_1}{\alpha_2}; \frac{\hat{\pi}_{12}}{\hat{\pi}_{22}} = \alpha_1$$

$$\therefore \qquad \hat{\pi}_{21}\left(\frac{\hat{\pi}_{11}}{\hat{\pi}_{21}} - \frac{\hat{\pi}_{12}}{\hat{\pi}_{22}}\right) = \frac{\alpha_2}{\beta_1 - \alpha_1}\left(\frac{\alpha_2\beta_1 - \alpha_2\alpha_1}{\alpha_2}\right) = \alpha_2$$

Therefore, to obtain α_2, we substitute π's in $\left[\hat{\pi}_{21}\left(\dfrac{\hat{\pi}_{11}}{\hat{\pi}_{21}} - \dfrac{\hat{\pi}_{12}}{\hat{\pi}_{22}}\right)\right]$

(d) Calculation of β_2:

$$\frac{\hat{\pi}_{12}}{\hat{\pi}_{22}} = \alpha_1, \frac{\hat{\pi}_{11}}{\hat{\pi}_{21}} = \frac{\alpha_2\beta_1}{\alpha_2}$$

$$\therefore \qquad \hat{\pi}_{22}\left(\frac{\hat{\pi}_{12}}{\hat{\pi}_{22}} - \frac{\hat{\pi}_{11}}{\hat{\pi}_{21}}\right) = \frac{-\beta_2}{\beta_1 - \alpha_1}\left(\frac{\alpha_2\alpha_1 - \alpha_2\beta_1}{\alpha_2}\right) = \beta_2$$

Relevant π's are to be substituted in $\left[\hat{\pi}_{22}\left(\dfrac{\hat{\pi}_{12}}{\hat{\pi}_{22}} - \dfrac{\hat{\pi}_{11}}{\hat{\pi}_{21}}\right)\right]$ to obtain β_2.

(e) Calculation of α_1 and β_1:

$$\alpha_1 = \frac{\hat{\pi}_{12}}{\hat{\pi}_{22}} \quad \text{and} \quad \beta_1 = \frac{\hat{\pi}_{11}}{\hat{\pi}_{21}}$$

It should be noted here that the relation between the structural coefficients and the π's will give rise to unique values of α's and β's only when the simultaneous-equation model is exactly identified. In case the system is overidentified, the multiple estimates of a structural parameter(s) will be obtained by ILS.

The two assumptions underlying the ILS procedure, therefore, are following:

1. The structural equations must be exactly identified.
2. The disturbance term of the reduced-form equation must satisfy all the stochastic assumptions of OLS. This is essential because this method is merely application of OLS to the reduced form equations. If these assumptions are not fulfilled, the bias in π's will be transmitted to the estimates of the structural parameters.

It may, therefore, be said that ILS method is based on all the assumptions of OLS along with an additional assumption that the model be exactly identified.

Are the estimates obtained through ILS unbiased and consistent? ILS method yields biased (yet asymptotically unbiased) but consistent estimates of the structural parameters. In other words bias in the ILS estimates depends inversely on the sample size. As the sample size approaches infinity, the bias approaches zero and the distribution collapses on the true value of the structural parameter.

Had we applied OLS to each equation of the model directly, the estimates would have been biased (which is simultaneity bias). Also these estimates would not have been consistent because they are not even asymptotically unbiased. As such the choice between the two estimates (OLS and ILS) crucially depends on the sample size. In a given practical situation when we are not able to increase the sample size we have to settle for the better of the two estimates.

To illustrate the application of the ILS, we take an example of demand-supply model.

$$D_t = \alpha_0 + \alpha_1 P_t + \alpha_2 Y_t + U_1$$
$$S_t = \beta_0 + \beta_1 P_t + \beta_2 W_t + U_2$$
$$D_t = S_t$$

The data relevant for the estimation of the structural parameters of the above model are given in the first four columns (D_t, P_t, Y_t and W_t) of Table 14.1.

We apply ordinary least squares to the first of the reduced-form equations:

$$D_t = \pi_{10} + \pi_{11} Y + \pi_{12} W + V_1$$

By substituting the calculated values in the relevant formulae from the Table 14.1, we obtain:

$$\hat{\pi}_{10} = (-)12.40, \hat{\pi}_{11} = 1.573, \hat{\pi}_{12} = 0.266, R^2 = 0.92$$

We next apply ordinary least squares to the second of the reduced-form equations:

$$P_t = \pi_{20} + \pi_{21} Y + \pi_{22} W + V_2$$

and obtain the estimates

$$\pi_{20} = (-)25.52, \hat{\pi}_{21} = 6.422, \hat{\pi}_{22} = (-)0.159, \text{ and } R^2 = 0.84$$

We substitute these estimates into the different relations explained above to obtain the estimates of the structural parameters.

(a) $\hat{\alpha}_0 = \hat{\pi}_{20} \left(\dfrac{\hat{\pi}_{10}}{\hat{\pi}_{20}} - \dfrac{\hat{\pi}_{12}}{\hat{\pi}_{22}} \right) = -25.52 \left(\dfrac{-12.40}{-25.52} - \dfrac{0.266}{-0.159} \right) = -55.13$

(b) $\hat{\alpha}_1 = \dfrac{\hat{\pi}_{12}}{\hat{\pi}_{22}} = \dfrac{0.266}{-0.159} = -1.675$

(c) $\hat{\alpha}_2 = \hat{\pi}_{21} \left(\dfrac{\pi_{11}}{\hat{\pi}_{21}} - \dfrac{\hat{\pi}_{12}}{\hat{\pi}_{21}} \right) = 6.442 \left(\dfrac{1.573}{6.442} - \dfrac{0.266}{-0.159} \right) = 12.360$

Table 14.1: Worksheet for the estimation of demand-supply model by OLS, ILS and 2SLS

$D_t = S_t$	P_t	Y_t	W_t	$d_t = s_t$	p_t	y_t	w_t	d_t^2	p_t^2	y_t^2	w_t^2	$d_t y_t$	$d p_t$	$d_t w_t$	$p y_t$	$p_t w_t$	$w_t y_t$
11	20	8.1	42	-3.1	-4.4	-0.8	-4.7	9.61	19.36	0.64	22.09	2.48	13.64	14.57	3.52	20.68	3.76
16	18	8.4	58	1.9	-6.4	-0.5	11.3	3.61	40.96	0.25	127.69	-0.95	-12.16	21.47	3.20	-72.32	-5.65
11	22	8.5	35	-3.1	-2.4	-0.4	-11.7	9.61	5.76	0.16	136.89	1.24	7.44	36.27	0.96	28.08	4.68
14	21	8.5	46	-0.1	-3.4	-0.4	-0.7	0.01	11.56	0.16	0.49	0.04	0.34	0.07	1.36	2.38	0.28
13	27	8.8	41	-1.1	2.6	-0.1	-5.7	1.21	6.76	0.01	32.49	0.11	-2.86	6.27	-0.26	-14.82	0.57
17	26	9.0	56	2.9	1.6	0.1	9.3	8.41	2.56	0.01	86.49	0.29	4.64	26.97	0.16	14.88	0.93
14	25	8.9	48	-0.1	0.6	0	1.3	0.01	0.36	0	1.69	0	-0.06	-0.13	0	0.78	0
15	27	9.4	50	0.9	2.6	0.5	3.3	0.81	6.76	0.25	10.89	0.45	2.34	2.97	1.30	8.58	1.65
12	30	9.5	39	-2.1	5.6	0.6	-7.7	4.41	31.36	0.36	59.29	-1.26	-11.76	16.17	3.36	-43.12	-4.62
18	28	9.9	52	3.9	3.6	1.0	5.3	15.21	12.96	1.0	28.09	3.90	14.04	20.67	3.60	19.08	5.30
141	244	89	467					52.90	138.40	2.84	506.10	6.30	15.60	145.30	17.20	(-)35.82	6.9

$\underline{D}_t = 14.1$ $\bar{P} = 24.4$ $\underline{Y} = 8.9$ $\underline{W}_t = 46.7$

$\Sigma d_t^2 =$ $\Sigma p_t^2 =$ $\Sigma y_t^2 =$ $\Sigma w_t^2 =$ $\Sigma d_t y_t =$ $\Sigma d p_t =$ $\Sigma d_t w_t =$ $\Sigma p y_t =$ $\Sigma p_t w_t =$ $\Sigma w_t y_t =$

(d) $\hat{\beta}_0 = \hat{\pi}_{20}\left(\dfrac{\hat{\pi}_{10}}{\hat{\pi}_{20}} - \dfrac{\hat{\pi}_{11}}{\hat{\pi}_{21}}\right) = -25.52\left(\dfrac{-12.40}{-25.52} - \dfrac{1.573}{6.442}\right) = -6.168$

(e) $\hat{\beta}_1 = \dfrac{\hat{\pi}_{11}}{\hat{\pi}_{21}} = \dfrac{1.573}{6.442} = 0.244.$

(f) $\hat{\beta}_2 = \hat{\pi}_{22}\left(\dfrac{\hat{\pi}_{12}}{\hat{\pi}_{22}} - \dfrac{\hat{\pi}_{11}}{\hat{\pi}_{21}}\right) = -0.159\left(\dfrac{0.266}{-0.159} - \dfrac{1.573}{6.422}\right) = 0.304$

(*Note:* All figures have been rounded up to three places after decimal)

Thus the estimated model may now be written as follows:

$$\hat{D}_t = -55.13 - 1.675\,P_t + 12.360\,Y_t$$

$$\hat{S}_t = -6.168 + 0.244\,P_t + 0.304\,W_t$$

For the sake of comparison we have computed the estimates of $\hat{\alpha}$'s and $\hat{\beta}$'s by inappropriately applying OLS to the original structural model. The results are:

$$D_t = -25.09 - 0.659\,P_t + 6.209Y_t, \qquad R^2 = 0.54$$
$$\qquad\qquad (0.317) \qquad (2.212)$$

$$S_t = -4.57 + 0.191\,P_t + 0.301\,W_t, \qquad R^2 = 0.88$$
$$\qquad\quad (0.273) \quad (0.143)$$

The OLS estimates are not consistent. The results also show how OLS procedure can distort the true picture of structure of the model when it is applied in inappropriate conditions.

14.2   TWO STAGE LEAST SQUARES (2SLS)

This method also being a single-equation method seeks to remove the defect of existence of the correlation between the disturbance term and the independent variable(s) so that when we apply OLS technique to each structural equation separately, the simultaneity bias gets eliminated. Theoretically therefore, 2SLS may be considered as an extension of ILS method. In ILS interdependence between explanatory variable and disturbance term is bypassed by applying OLS to reduced-form equation; here we purge the explanatory variable(s) which is correlated with the error term with its (their) own estimated value. This is done in two stages which we explain by taking the same demand-supply model considered in 14.1.

$$D_t = \alpha_0 + \alpha_1 P_t + \alpha_2 Y_t + U_1$$
$$S_t = \beta_0 + \beta_1 P_t + \beta_2 W_t + U_2$$
$$D_t = S_t$$

The reduced-form equations are:

$$D_t = \pi_{10} + \pi_{11} Y_t + \pi_{12} W_t + V_1$$

$$P_t = \pi_{20} + \pi_{21} Y_t + \pi_{22} W_t + V_2$$

where π's and V's are defined as before in 14.1. π's are estimated by applying OLS to these reduced-form equations. *This is the first stage of estimation.*

Having estimated the π's, we obtain values of $\hat{P}_t$ for different values of Y_t and w_t. We now replace Pt in the structural model by $\hat{P}_t$ obtained in the first stage as follows:

$$D_t = \alpha_0 + \alpha_1 \hat{P}_t + \alpha_2 Y_t + U_1$$

$$S_t = \beta_0 + \beta_1 \hat{P}_t + \beta_2 W_t + U_2$$

This is now a transformed model.

Since $\hat{P}_t$ is based on the estimates from the reduced-form equations, it acts as an instrumental variable for the original data on P_t.

All the structural parameters are estimated by applying OLS to these transformed equations. *This is second stage of estimation.*

Since in 2SLS, the endogenous variable(s) is purged by its own estimated value by taking into consideration all the exogenous variables, this method assumes complete knowledge of exogenous variables in the model. If the specification of these variables is not correct, the estimates of the structural parameters will not possess the desired properties. 2SLS estimates are thus sensitive to specification errors. They are also asymptotically unbiased and consistent; i.e., their distribution collapses on the true parameter (value) as sample size tends to infinity. As such this method requires rather large number of observations, specially if the model includes many exogenous variables, which will be used in the first stage to estimate $\hat{P}_t$ (endogenous) variable.

As already stated, ILS fails when our model is overidentified. It is in this situation that 2SLS technique has an advantage over ILS. 2SLS provides a single estimate of the parameter which is overidentified.

However, when model is exactly identified the ILS and 2SLS procedures give identical estimates.

Two stage least squares procedure is, therefore, used extensively in practice for the following points over the indirect least squares procedure of estimation:

(i) Unlike ILS, which provides multiple estimates of the parameters when applied to over-identified equations, 2SLS provides only one estimate per parameter.

(ii) Although 2SLS has been specially designed to handle over-identified equations, this method can also be applied to exactly identified equations. ILS and 2SLS give identical results in such situation.

(iii) In the application ILS, there is no simple method of estimation of standard errors of the structural coefficients from the standard errors of the reduced-form coefficients. But this can be done easily in case of 2SLS estimates because the structural coefficients are directly estimated from the second stage (OLS) regressions. However, the estimated standard errors in the second-stage regression need to be modified.

Let us now consider the estimation of the same demand-supply model by 2SLS with the same data used in ILS procedure.

That is, our model is:

$$D_t = \alpha_0 + \alpha_1 P_t + \alpha_2 Y_t + U_1$$

$$S_t = \beta_0 + \beta_1 P_t + \beta_2 W_t + U_2$$

$$D_t = S_t$$

and the relevant data on the variables is given in the *first four columns* of Table 14.1.

We first obtain the reduced-form equations of the endogenous variables (already obtained under 14.1):

$$\hat{D}_t = -12.40 + 1.573 Y_t + 0.266 W_t \qquad \text{...(i)}$$

$$\hat{P}_t = -25.52 + 6.442 Y_t - 0.159 W_t \qquad \text{...(ii)}$$

This is *first stage* of estimation.

We next substitute the calculated value of price $(\hat{P}_t)$ for the original $\hat{P}_t$ variable and perform the regressions

$$D_t^* = \alpha_0^* + \alpha_1^* \hat{P}_t + \alpha_2^* Y_t + U^* \qquad \text{...(iii)}$$

$$S_t^* = \beta_0^* + \beta_1^* \hat{P}_t + \alpha_2^* W_t + U^{**} \qquad \text{...(iv)}$$

The new data on $\hat{P}_t$ is calculated with the help of second reduced-form equation as shown in the Table 14.2.

Using the new series on $\hat{P}_t$ along with the exogenous variables W_t and Y_t, as shown in Table 14.3 on page 401, we estimate α^*'s and β^*s of (iii) and (iv) equations by applying OLS.

This then is the *second stage of estimation*.

The final results are as follows:

$$\hat{D}_t = -51.09 - 1.654 \hat{P}_t + 12.821 Y_t \qquad\qquad R^2 = 0.93$$
$$(0.1922) \ (1.1965)$$

$$\hat{S}_t = -5.841 + 0.236 \hat{P}_t + 0.304 W_t \qquad\qquad R^2 = 0.90$$
$$(0.083) \ \ (0.039)$$

Table 14.2: Calculation of $\hat{P}_t$

n	$(6,4416)Y_t$	$(-0.1586)W_t$	$\hat{P}_t = -25.52 + 6.4416\,Y_t$ $-0.1586\ W_t$
1.	52.17	−6.66	19.99
2.	54.11	−9.20	19.39
3.	54.75	−5.55	23.68
4.	54.75	−7.29	21.94
5.	56.68	−6.50	24.66
6.	57.97	−8.88	23.57
7.	57.33	−7.61	24.20
8.	60.55	−7.93	27.10
9.	61.19	−6.81	28.86
10.	63.17	−8.25	29.40

The results obtained through ILS were as follows:

$$\hat{D}_t = -55.13 - 1.675P_t + 12.360\ Y_t$$

$$\hat{S}_t = -6.17 + 0.244P_t + 0.304\ W_t$$

That shows that if the model is exactly identified the results obtained through ILS and 2SLS are identical (except for constant coefficients).

We have, thus far, explained the methodology underlying the ILS and 2SLS procedures through simple illustrations. The purpose was to acquaint the students with underlying principles in methodology of these two procedures of estimation. It should now be easy to follow and understand the derivation of ILS and 2SLS estimators for the general econometric model.

14.3 THEORETICAL DERIVATION OF ILS ESTIMATORS

Let us recall the first equation of general econometric model containing G endogenous variables and K predetermined variables:

$$\beta_{11}y_{1t} + \beta_{12}y_{2t} +... + \beta_{1G}y_{Gt} + \gamma_{11}x_{1t} + \gamma_{12}x_{2t} +... \gamma_{1K}x_{Kt} = U_t$$

Let us suppose further that β_{11} is equal to unity, and that the *included* endogenous variables are: $y_{1t}, y_{2t},..., y_{G*t}$ and *included* predetermined variables are: $x_{1t}, x_{2t},..., x_{K*t}$.

Then first equation can be written as:

$$y_{1t} = -\beta_{12}y_{2t} - \beta_{13}y_{3t} -...- \beta_{1G*}y_{G*t} - \gamma_{11}x_1t - \gamma_{12}x_{2t} -... - \gamma_{1K*}x_{K*t} + U_t$$
$$...(14.3.1)$$

where $t = 1, 2,..., n$ observations.

The (14.3.1) form of equation is called '**normalized**' form of the first equation which in matrix notation can be expressed as:

$$y_1 = Y_1\beta_1 + X_1\Gamma_1 + U_1 \qquad ...(14.3.2)$$

where, $\mathbf{y}_1$ is the first column of $\mathbf{Y}_{1t}$ described in (13.2.3). $\mathbf{X}_1$ is as described in (13.2.4), while element of $\mathbf{B}_1$ and $\mathbf{\Gamma}_1$ acquire *minus* sign as expressed under:

$$\mathbf{y}_1 = \begin{bmatrix} y_{11} \\ y_{12} \\ \vdots \\ y_{1n} \end{bmatrix}_{(n \times 1)}, \qquad \mathbf{Y}_1 = \begin{bmatrix} y_{21} & y_{31} \cdots y_{G^{*}1} \\ y_{22} & y_{32} \cdots y_{G^{*}2} \\ \vdots \\ y_{2n} & y_{3n} \cdots {}_{G^{*}n} \end{bmatrix}_{(n \times (G^{*}-1))},$$

$$\mathbf{\beta}_1 = \begin{bmatrix} -\beta_{12} \\ -\beta_{13} \\ \vdots \\ -\beta_{1G^{*}} \end{bmatrix}_{(G^{*}-1) \times 1} \qquad \mathbf{\Gamma}_1 = \begin{bmatrix} -\gamma_{11} \\ -\gamma_{12} \\ \vdots \\ -\gamma_{1K^{*}} \end{bmatrix}_{(K^{*} \times 1)}, \qquad \text{and}$$

$$\mathbf{X}_1 = \begin{bmatrix} x_{11} & x_{21} \cdots x_{K^{*}1} \\ x_{12} & x_{22} \cdots x_{K^{*}2} \\ \vdots & \vdots \\ x_{1n} & x_{2n} \cdots x_{K^{*}n} \end{bmatrix}_{(n \times K^{*})}$$

The data on all variables of the system, summarised by $\mathbf{Y}_{1t}$ and $\mathbf{X}_{1t}$ matrices in (13.2.3) and (13.2.4) can be divided into data on the variables indicated by (14.3.2).

The matrix of data on the endogenous variables $\mathbf{Y}_{1t}$ can be partitioned into:

$$\underset{(n \times G)}{Y_{1t}} = \left[\underset{(n \times 1)}{\mathbf{Y}_1} \mid \underset{(n \times (G^{*}-1))}{\mathbf{Y}_1} \mid \underset{(n \times G^{**})}{\mathbf{Y}_2} \right] \qquad ...(14.3.3)$$

Here, $\mathbf{y}_1$ is the column vector of data on dependent endogenous variables (the one on which first equation has been normalised), $\mathbf{Y}_1$ is matrix data on $G^{*}-1$ explanatory endogenous variables and $\mathbf{Y}_2$ is the matrix of data on G^{**} excluded endogenous variables.

Similarly as (14.3.3), the matrix data on the predetermined variable $\mathbf{X}$ can be partitioned into:

$$X_1 t = \left[\underset{(n \times K^{*})}{\mathbf{X}_1} \mid \underset{(n \times K^{**})}{\mathbf{X}_2} \right] \qquad ...(14.3.4)$$

where $\mathbf{X}_2$ is the matrix of data on the K^{**} excluded predetermined variables and $\mathbf{X}_1$ is the matrix of data on K^{*} included predetermined variables.

(14.3.2) can also be written as:

$$-\mathbf{y}_1 + \mathbf{Y}_1 \mathbf{B}_1 + \mathbf{X}_1 \mathbf{\Gamma}_1 = \mathbf{U}_1 \qquad ...(14.3.5)$$

Using (14.3.3) and (14.3.4), (14.3.5) can be expressed into partitioned matrix notation,

$$[y_1 \mid Y_1 \mid Y_2] \begin{bmatrix} -1 & \mid & - \\ \hline \Gamma_1 & \mid & - \\ \hline 0 & \mid & - \end{bmatrix} + [X_1 \mid X_2] \begin{bmatrix} \gamma_1 & \mid & - \\ \hline 0 & \mid & - \end{bmatrix} = [-U_1 \mid -] \qquad ...(14.3.6)$$

The reduced form of first equation, as expressed by (13.2.17), may also be put in partitioned matrix form:

$$\begin{bmatrix} y_1 & \bigg| & Y_1 & \bigg| & Y_2 \\ {}_{(n\times 1)} & & {}_{n\times G^*-1} & & {}_{n\times G^{**}} \end{bmatrix}_{(n\times G)}$$

$$= \begin{bmatrix} X_1 & \bigg| & X_2 \\ {}_{n\times K^*} & & {}_{n\times K^{**}} \end{bmatrix} \begin{bmatrix} \pi_1^* & \bigg| & \pi_1^{**} & \bigg| & \pi_3 \\ {}_{(K^*\times 1)} & & {}_{(K^*\times G^*-1)} & & {}_{(K^*\times G^{**})} \\ \hline \pi_2^* & \bigg| & \pi_2^{**} & \bigg| & \pi_4 \\ {}_{(K^{**}\times 1)} & & {}_{(K^{**}\times G^*-1)} & & {}_{(K^{**}\times G^{**})} \end{bmatrix}_{(K\times G)}$$

$$+ \begin{bmatrix} U_0 & \bigg| & U_1 & \bigg| & U_2 \\ {}_{(n\times 1)} & & {}_{(n\times G^*-1)} & & {}_{(n\times G^{**})} \end{bmatrix}_{(n\times G)} \qquad ...(14.3.7)$$

Here the stochastic disturbance terms have been partitioned in the same way as Y_{1t}, corresponding to the dependent, explanatory and excluded endogenous variables.

The matrix of reduced form coefficient π has been partitioned in (14.3.7) into six submatrices in order to carry out the matrix multiplication. If the first equation (which is required to be estimated) is just identified, then

$$K^{**} = G - 1, \text{ and hence } \pi_2^{**} \text{ is a } \textit{square matrix.}$$

Recollect the relation between the structural form and reduced form parameters as expressed by (13.2.9):

$$\pi = -B^{-1}\Gamma$$

or, $$\pi'B' = -\Gamma'$$

For the first equation, which involves only first column of B and Γ, the above relation, using partitioned π matrix, shall be:

$$\bullet \begin{bmatrix} \pi_1^* & \pi_1^{**} & \pi_3 \\ \pi_2^* & \pi_2^{**} & \pi_4 \end{bmatrix}_{K\times G} \begin{bmatrix} -I \\ \beta_1 \\ 0 \end{bmatrix}_{G\times 1} = -\begin{bmatrix} \Gamma_1 \\ 0 \end{bmatrix}_{K\times 1} \qquad ...(14.3.8)$$

Writing out the resulting two sets of equations, where elements of π are replaced by the estimators $\hat{\pi}$ and the structural coefficients of the first equation are replaced by their estimators; $\hat{\beta}_1$ and $\hat{\Gamma}_1$:

$$-\hat{\pi}_1^* + \hat{\pi}_1^{**}\,\hat{\beta}_1 = \hat{\Gamma}_1 \qquad \text{(involves } K^* \text{ no. of equations)} \quad ...(14.3.9)$$

$$-\hat{\pi}_2^* + \hat{\pi}_2^{**}\,\hat{\beta}_1 = 0 \qquad \text{(involves } K^{**} \text{ no. of equations)} \quad ...(14.3.10)$$

As already noted, if the first equation is just identified, then π_2^{**} is a square matrix. Assuming it is nonsingular also, $\hat{\beta}_1$ can be solved from (14.3.10):

$$\hat{\beta}_1 = \left[\hat{\pi}_2^{**}\right]^{-1}\hat{\pi}_2^* \qquad\qquad ...(14.3.11)$$

Substituting (14.3.11) in (14.3.9)

$$-\hat{\pi}_1^* + \hat{\pi}_1^{**}\left[(\hat{\pi}_2^{**})^{-1}\hat{\pi}_2^*\right] = \hat{\Gamma}_1$$

$$\hat{\Gamma}_1 = \hat{\pi}_1^* - \hat{\pi}_1^{**}\left[(\hat{\pi}_2^{**})^{-1}\,\hat{\pi}_2^*\right] \qquad\qquad ...(14.3.12)$$

(14.3.11) and (14.3.12) give the ILS estimators which may be expressed in terms of endogenous and predetermined variables simultaneously as under:

$$\left[\frac{\hat{\beta}_1}{\hat{\Gamma}_1}\right] = \left[\frac{(\hat{\pi}_2^{**})^{-1}\,\hat{\pi}_2^*}{\hat{\pi}_1^* - \hat{\pi}_1^{**}\,(\hat{\pi}_2^{**})^{-1}\,\hat{\pi}_2^*}\right] \qquad\qquad ...(14.3.13)$$

ILS estimators use the least squares estimators of reduced form coefficients *plus* the identifying restrictions to obtain estimates of the structural parameters of exactly identified equation of the simultaneous system.

The procedure for estimating the full model will mean, therefore, obtaining the OLS estimates of all the reduced form coefficients of the given model. Let us consider the full general simultaneous equation model expressed in (13.2.1)

$$\mathbf{B Y}_t + \mathbf{\Gamma Y}_t = \mathbf{U}_t$$

Of which the reduced form given by (13.2.8) is:

$$\mathbf{Y}_t = \mathbf{\pi X}_t + \mathbf{V}_t$$

In order to obtain π, (13.2.8) must be changed in the form of basic linear regression model:

$$\mathbf{Y}_t = \mathbf{X}_i\mathbf{\beta} + \mathbf{U}_t$$

(13.2.8) may, therefore, be put as expressed in (13.2.11)

$$\mathbf{Y}_t' = \mathbf{X}_t'\,\mathbf{\pi}' + \mathbf{V}_t'$$

The classical least squares estimator of π of (13.2.11) is given by

$$(\hat{\pi})' = [(\mathbf{X}_t')'(\mathbf{X}_t')]^{-1}\,(\mathbf{X}')'\mathbf{Y}_t$$

$$(\hat{\pi})' = [X_t X_t']^{-1} \quad X_t \quad Y_t' \qquad ...(14.3.14)^1$$
$$(K \times G) \quad (K \times k) \quad (K \times K) \quad (1 \times G)$$

(14.3.14) describes set of all least squares estimators of the entire reduced form system; and each column of $\hat{\pi}$ summarises all the parameters in one of the reduced form equations.

Method of obtaining ILS estimates, using matrix notations can now be understood by the following illustration.

Illustration: Estimate the consumption function of the following simple Keynesian model: $\quad C = \alpha + \beta Y + U$

$$Y = C + I,$$

Given:

$$
\begin{bmatrix} X'X & X'Y \\ & Y'Y \end{bmatrix} =
\begin{array}{c} I \\ C \\ Y \end{array}
\begin{bmatrix} & I & C & Y \\ 5710 & 11698 & 17408 \\ & 35887 & 47585 \\ & & 64993 \end{bmatrix}
$$

Since the given model is just identified, we can apply ILS to obtain structural coefficients α and β of the consumption function. For that we must acquire two data matrices X_t and Y_t described by (13.2.4) and (13.2.3).

Also note that data is given in the form of matrices of *moments about mean* (deviation form), therefore, the model has to be changed accordingly:

$$\left.\begin{array}{c} c = \beta y + V \\ y = c + i \end{array}\right\} \qquad ...(14.3.15)$$

Its reduced form shall be described

$$\left.\begin{array}{c} c = \pi_{11}.i + V_i \\ y = \pi_{21}.i + V_2 \end{array}\right\} \qquad ...(14.3.16)$$

Here,

$$Y = \begin{bmatrix} c \\ y \end{bmatrix}, \quad X = [i], \quad \pi = \begin{bmatrix} \pi_{11} \\ \pi_{21} \end{bmatrix}$$

$$Y' = [c \quad y], \quad X' = [i], \quad \pi' = [\pi_{11} \quad \pi_{21}]$$

$$\hat{\pi}' = (XX')^{-1} XY' \qquad \text{(By 14.3.14))}$$

$$X'X = [i^2], \quad X'Y = (i)[c \quad y] = [ci \quad yi]$$

$$\hat{\pi}' = (i^2)^{-1} [ci \quad yi]$$

$$\hat{\pi}' = (5710)^{-1} [11698 \quad 17408] = [2.048 \quad 3.048]$$

$$\hat{\pi}' = [\beta/1 - \beta \quad 1/1 - \beta] \quad \text{(By (13.2.19))}$$

---

[1] If the general structural model is of the form: $Y_t B + X_t \Gamma = U_t$, then the reduced form shall be: $Y_t = X_t \pi + V_t$ so that the $\hat{\pi}$ shall be expressed as: $\hat{\pi} (X'X)^{-1} X'Y_t$

Therefore,

$$\hat{\pi}' = [\beta/1 - \beta \quad 1/1 - \beta] = [2.048 \quad 3.048]$$

$$\hat{\beta}_{ILS} = \frac{2.048}{3.048} = 0.672.$$

14.4   THEORETICAL DERIVATION OF 2SLS ESTIMATORS

As already explained under 14.2, 2SLS avoids the correlation between explanatory endogenous variable(s) and the stochastic disturbance terms by using the estimated reduced form to replace explanatory endogenous variables by their estimated values.

Thus, in the first normalised equation given by (14.3.2)

$$y_1 = Y_1\beta_1 + X_1\Gamma_1 + U_1,$$

Y_1 is replaced by $\hat{Y}_1$, which is the estimated values of each of the explanatory variables at each observation using the reduced form.

How to obtain $\hat{Y}_1$?

The reduced form of (14.3.2) is described by (14.3.7)

$$\left[y_1 \mid \boxed{Y_1} \mid Y_2 \right] = [X_1 \mid X_2] \begin{bmatrix} \hat{\pi}_1^* & \boxed{\hat{\pi}_1^{**}} & \hat{\pi}_3 \\ \hat{\pi}_2^* & \boxed{\hat{\pi}_2^{**}} & \hat{\pi}_4 \end{bmatrix}$$

$$+ \left[U_0 \mid \boxed{U_1} \mid U_2 \right]$$

Solving for the variables of interest, the explanatory endogenous variables in the equation to be estimated:

$$Y_1 = X_1\hat{\pi}_1^{**} + X_2\hat{\pi}_2^{**} + U_1 = \hat{Y}_1 + \hat{U}_1$$

That is;

$$\hat{Y}_1^* = X_1\hat{\pi}_1^{**} + X_2\hat{\pi}_2^{**} \qquad \qquad ...(14.4.1)$$

Furthermore, since in the reduced form model of the form:

$$Y_1 = X\pi_1 + V_1 \quad \text{and,} \quad \hat{\pi}_1 = (X'X)^{-1} X' Y_1,$$

therefore,

$$\hat{Y}_1 = X(X'X)^{-1} X'Y_1 \qquad \qquad ...(14.4.2)$$

$\hat{Y}_1$ can also be expressed as the actual Y_1 less the relevant reduced form residuals:

$$\hat{Y}_1 = Y_1 - \hat{U}_1 \qquad \qquad ...(14.4.3)$$

We have, thus, expressed $\hat{Y}_1$ in *three* equivalent ways: (14.4.1), (14.4.2) and (14.4.3).

2SLS, in order to purge statistical dependence of explanatory endogenous variables on the stochastic terms, replace the explanatory endogenous variables by values estimated from the reduced form. Hence,

$$y_1 = Y_1\beta_1 + X_1\Gamma_1 + U_1$$

becomes;
$$y_1 = (\hat{Y}_1 + \hat{U}_1)\beta_1 + X_1\Gamma_1 + U_1$$

$$y_1 = \hat{Y}_1\beta_1 + X_1\Gamma_1 + (\hat{U}_1\beta_1 + U_1)$$

$$y_1 = \hat{Y}_1\beta_1 + X_1\Gamma_1 + V_1 \qquad\qquad ...(14.4.4)$$

where;
$$V_1 = (\hat{U}_1\beta_1 + U_1)$$

The second stage of 2SLS procedure involves application of OLS to (14.4.4) to obtain estimators of β_1 and Γ_1 from it.

$$y_1 = \hat{Y}_1\beta_1 + X_1\Gamma_1 + V_1$$

$$y_1 = \begin{bmatrix} \hat{Y}_1 & | & X_1 \end{bmatrix} \begin{bmatrix} \beta_1 \\ \hline \Gamma_1 \end{bmatrix} + V_1$$

$$y_1 = Z_1\delta_1 + V_1 \qquad\qquad ...(14.4.5)$$

where;
$$Z_1 = [\hat{Y}_1 \mid X_1] \text{ and } \delta_1 = \begin{bmatrix} \beta_1 \\ \hline \Gamma_1 \end{bmatrix}$$

The OLS estimators of (14.4.5) yield:

$$\hat{\delta}_1 = (\hat{Z}_1 Z_1)^{-1} Z_1' y_1 \qquad\qquad ...(14.4.6)$$

Here,
$$\hat{\delta}_1 = \begin{bmatrix} \beta_1 \\ \hline \hat{\Gamma}_1 \end{bmatrix}, \ \hat{Z}_1' = \begin{bmatrix} \hat{Y}_1' \\ \hline \hat{X}_1' \end{bmatrix}, \text{ so that}$$

$$(Z_1'Z_1)-1 = \begin{bmatrix} \hat{Y}_1'\hat{Y}_1 & | & \hat{Y}_1'X_1 \\ \hline X_1'\hat{Y}_1 & | & X_1'X_1 \end{bmatrix}^{-1} \qquad\qquad ...(14.4.7)$$

Using (14.4.7) in (14.4.6),

$$\hat{\delta}_1 = \begin{bmatrix} \hat{\beta}_1 \\ \hline \hat{\Gamma}_1 \end{bmatrix}_{2SLS} = \begin{bmatrix} \hat{Y}_1' \ \hat{Y}_1 & | & \hat{Y}_1' \ X_1 \\ \hline X_1' \ \hat{Y}_1 & | & X_1' \ X_1 \end{bmatrix}^{-1} \begin{bmatrix} \hat{Y}_1' \\ \hline X_1' \end{bmatrix} y_1 \qquad\qquad ...(14.4.8)$$

Using $\hat{\mathbf{Y}}_1 = \mathbf{Y}_1 - \hat{\mathbf{U}}_1; \hat{\mathbf{Y}}_1' = \mathbf{Y}_1' - \hat{\mathbf{U}}_1'$, the upper left submatrix of (14.4.8) becomes $(\mathbf{Y}_1' \mathbf{Y}_1 - \hat{\mathbf{U}}_1' \, \hat{\mathbf{U}}_1)$ as explained below:

$$\hat{\mathbf{Y}}_1' \hat{\mathbf{Y}}_1 = (\mathbf{Y}_1' - \hat{\mathbf{U}}_1')(\mathbf{Y}_1 - \hat{\mathbf{U}}_1) = \hat{\mathbf{Y}}_1' \, \mathbf{Y}_1 - \hat{\mathbf{U}}_1' \, \hat{\mathbf{U}}_1$$

$$\left[\because \hat{\mathbf{U}}_1 \mathbf{Y}_1 = \mathbf{Y}_1' \hat{\mathbf{U}}_1 = (\hat{\mathbf{Y}}_1 + \hat{\mathbf{U}}_1)' \, \mathbf{U}_1 = \hat{\mathbf{U}}_1' \hat{\mathbf{U}}_1; \hat{\mathbf{Y}}' \, \hat{\mathbf{U}}_1 = 0 \right]$$

Thus the 2SLS estimators described in (14.4.8) become:

$$\left(\begin{matrix} \hat{\beta}_1 \\ \hline \hat{\Gamma}_1 \end{matrix} \right)_{2SLS} = \left[\begin{array}{c|c} \mathbf{Y}_1' \, \mathbf{Y}_1 - \hat{\mathbf{U}}_1' \, \hat{\mathbf{U}}_1 & \mathbf{Y}_1' \mathbf{X}_1 \\ \hline \mathbf{X}_1' \mathbf{Y}_1 & \mathbf{X}_1' \, \mathbf{X}_1 \end{array} \right]^{-1} \left[\begin{matrix} \mathbf{Y}_1' - \hat{\mathbf{U}}_1' \\ \hline \mathbf{X}_1' \end{matrix} \right] \mathbf{y}_1 \quad ...(14.4.9)$$

[because $\hat{\mathbf{Y}}_1' \, \mathbf{X}_1 = (\mathbf{Y}_1 - \hat{\mathbf{U}}_1)' \, \mathbf{X}_1 = \mathbf{Y}_1' \mathbf{X}_1 = \mathbf{X}_1' \, \mathbf{Y}_1; \mathbf{X}_1' \, \hat{\mathbf{U}}_1 = \hat{\mathbf{U}}_1' = \hat{\mathbf{U}}_1' \mathbf{X}_1 = 0$]

A comparative View of Estimators: Finally let us not forget that ILS and 2SLS estimators are consistent estimators, but they are not unbiased. OLS estimators in a system of simultaneous equations model are neither unbiased nor consistent.

ILS estimates are defined only for just identified equations, while 2SLS are defined for both over and just identified equations. Also, 2SLS reduce to the ILS estimators in the just identified case; the exposition of this follows in the next section of present chapter.

ILS are the OLS estimates of the reduced-form coefficients, and 2SLS involve application of OLS procedure in two stages in order to purge the statistical dependence of explanatory endogenous variables on the stochastic terms.

The main difference between OLS and 2SLS is the fact that in 2SLS the reduced form residuals $\hat{\mathbf{U}}_1$ are netted out from $\mathbf{Y}_1$ to derive $\hat{\mathbf{Y}}_1 (\mathbf{Y}_1 = \hat{\mathbf{Y}}_1 + \hat{\mathbf{U}}_1)$.

$\hat{\mathbf{U}}_1$ is zero if the reduced form is estimated exactly; hence $\mathbf{Y}_1 = \hat{\mathbf{Y}}_1$. As such OLS and 2SLS estimates are identical.

Also, under such circumstances, R^2 for each of relevant reduced form equations (those of $\mathbf{Y}_1$) is **unity**. Against this, if the values of R^2 for the relevant reduced form equations are close to **zero**, then it would mean that the data on the explanatory endogenous variables are merely replaced by disturbance terms. 2SLS are meaningless in such a situation.

It may, therefore, be concluded that the method of 2SLS works poorly in the following two situations:

(i) if R^2 values in the first stage are 'too small' or close to zero; and
(ii) if R^2 values in the first stage are 'too large' or close to unity.

It is only in case of 'intermediate' values that the 2SLS estimators make sense.

14.5 AN APPLICATIVE FORMULATION OF ILS AND 2SLS ESTIMATORS

To make the ILS and 2SLS estimators [derived under 14.3.13 and 14.4.8] operational to the given data directly, certain changes are necessary.

Reverting back to our general simultaneous equations model described by (13.2.1):

$$\mathbf{B}\mathbf{Y}_t + \mathbf{\Gamma}\mathbf{X}_t = U_t; \qquad (t = 1, 2, ..., n)$$

where

$$\mathbf{Y}_t = \begin{bmatrix} y_{1t} \\ y_{2t} \\ \vdots \\ y_{Gt} \end{bmatrix}, \qquad \mathbf{X}_t = \begin{bmatrix} X_{1t} \\ X_{2t} \\ \vdots \\ X_{Kt} \end{bmatrix}$$

are respectively $(G \times 1)$ vector of observations on the endogenous variables at time t and $(K \times 1)$ vector t^ε of observations on the exogenous variables at time t.

Let us now define **Y** and **X** as:

$$\mathbf{Y} = \begin{bmatrix} y_{11} & y_{12} \cdots y_{1G} \\ y_{21} & y_{22} \cdots y_{2G} \\ \vdots & \\ y_{n1} & y_{n2} \cdots y_{nG} \end{bmatrix} = \begin{bmatrix} -\mathbf{y}_1' - \\ -\mathbf{y}_2' - \\ \vdots \\ -\mathbf{y}_n' - \end{bmatrix}_{n \times G}$$

$$\mathbf{X} = \begin{bmatrix} x_{11} & x_{12} \cdots x_{1K} \\ x_{21} & x_{22} \cdots x_{2K} \\ \vdots & \vdots \\ x_{n1} & x_{n2} \cdots x_{nK} \end{bmatrix} = \begin{bmatrix} -\mathbf{x}_1' - \\ -\mathbf{x}_2' - \\ \vdots \\ -\mathbf{x}_n' - \end{bmatrix}_{n \times K}$$

so that here **Y** is the $(n \times G)$ matrix of the sample observations on G endogenous variables and **X** is the $(n \times K)$ matrix of sample observations on exogenous variables.

$$\mathbf{B}\mathbf{Y}_t + \mathbf{\Gamma} X_t = \mathbf{U}_t$$

can, therefore, be rewritten as:

$$\mathbf{Y}\mathbf{B}' + \mathbf{X}\mathbf{\Gamma}' = \mathbf{U} \qquad \qquad ...(14.5.1)$$

Here **U** is the $(n \times G)$ matrix of all the sample disturbances so that:

$$\mathbf{U} = \begin{bmatrix} U_{11} & U_{12} \cdots U_{1G} \\ U_{21} & U_{22} \cdots U_{2G} \\ \vdots & \\ U_{n1} & U_{n2} \cdots U_{nG} \end{bmatrix}$$

The reduced form of (14.5.1) shall be given by

$$Y = X\pi' + V \qquad \qquad ...(14.5.2)$$

where;

$$\left. \begin{array}{c} \pi' = -\Gamma'(B')^{-1} \\ V = U(B')^{-1} \end{array} \right\} \qquad ...(14.5.3)$$

(14.5.3) is simplify the transpose of the matrices previously defined in (13.2.9) and (13.2.10).

The estimation of reduced form coefficients (π) is now accomplished by applying OLS to (14.5.2), giving:

$$(\hat{\pi})' = (X'X)^{-1} X'Y \qquad \qquad ...(14.5.4)$$

We are interested in estimating first equation of the model described by (14.3.2) of chapter 14:

$$y_1 = Y_1\beta_1 + X_1\Gamma_1 + U_1$$

This can be rewritten as:

$$[\, y_1 \;\; Y_1 \;\; X_1 \,] \begin{bmatrix} I \\ -\beta \\ -\Gamma_1 \end{bmatrix} = U \qquad \qquad ...(14.5.5)$$

Relation between structural and reduced form equations given by (14.5.3) can also be stated as:

$$\pi'B' = -\Gamma' \qquad \qquad ...(14.5.6)$$

Describing (14.5.5) in terms of (14.5.6), we state:

$$\pi' \begin{bmatrix} I \\ -\beta_1 \\ 0 \end{bmatrix} = \begin{bmatrix} \Gamma_1 \\ 0 \end{bmatrix}$$

Substituting the estimated values of π, β and Γ_1 in the above relation:

$$(X'X)^{-1} X'Y \begin{bmatrix} I \\ -\hat{\beta}_1 \\ 0 \end{bmatrix} = \begin{bmatrix} \Gamma_1 \\ 0 \end{bmatrix}$$

which in case of our equation be:

$$(X'X)^{-1} X' [y_1 \;\; Y_1 \;\; Y_2] \begin{bmatrix} I \\ -\hat{\beta} \\ 0 \end{bmatrix} = \begin{bmatrix} \Gamma_1 \\ 0 \end{bmatrix} \qquad ...(14.5.7)$$

(14.5.7) can be rewritten as:

$$(\mathbf{X}'\mathbf{X})^{-1}\mathbf{X}'\mathbf{y}_1 - (\mathbf{X}'\mathbf{X})^{-1}\mathbf{X}'\hat{\boldsymbol{\beta}}_1\mathbf{Y}_1 = \begin{bmatrix} \hat{\boldsymbol{\Gamma}}_1 \\ 0 \end{bmatrix}$$

Premultiplying both sides by $(\mathbf{X}'\mathbf{X})$, and partitioning $\mathbf{X}$ as $[\mathbf{X}_1 \quad \mathbf{X}_2]$ and finally rearranging gives the pair of equations:

$$\left.\begin{aligned} (\mathbf{X}_1'\mathbf{Y}_1)\hat{\boldsymbol{\beta}}_1 + (\mathbf{X}_1'\mathbf{X}_1)\hat{\boldsymbol{\Gamma}}_1 = \mathbf{X}_1'\mathbf{y}_1 \\ (\mathbf{X}_2'\mathbf{Y}_1)\hat{\boldsymbol{\beta}}_1 + (\mathbf{X}_2'\mathbf{X}_1)\hat{\boldsymbol{\Gamma}}_1 = \mathbf{X}_2'\mathbf{y}_1 \end{aligned}\right\} \qquad ...(14.5.8)$$

(14.5.8) can be described in matrix notations:

$$\begin{bmatrix} \mathbf{X}_2'\mathbf{Y}_1 & \mathbf{X}_2'\mathbf{X}_1 \\ \mathbf{X}_1'\mathbf{Y}_1 & \mathbf{X}_1'\mathbf{X}_1 \end{bmatrix}\begin{bmatrix} \hat{\boldsymbol{\beta}}_1 \\ \hat{\boldsymbol{\Gamma}}_1 \end{bmatrix} = \begin{bmatrix} \mathbf{X}_2'\mathbf{y}_1 \\ \mathbf{X}_1'\mathbf{y}_1 \end{bmatrix}$$

$$\begin{bmatrix} \hat{\boldsymbol{\beta}}_1 \\ \hat{\boldsymbol{\Gamma}}_1 \end{bmatrix}_{ILS} = \begin{bmatrix} \mathbf{X}_2'\mathbf{Y}_1 & \mathbf{X}_2'\mathbf{X}_1 \\ \mathbf{X}_1'\mathbf{Y}_1 & \mathbf{X}_1'\mathbf{X}_1 \end{bmatrix}^{-1}\begin{bmatrix} \mathbf{X}_2'\mathbf{y}_1 \\ \mathbf{X}_1'\mathbf{y}_1 \end{bmatrix} \qquad ...(14.5.9)$$

(14.5.9) is the *operational formula* for obtaining ILS estimates of $\hat{\boldsymbol{\beta}}_1$ and $\hat{\boldsymbol{\Gamma}}_1$. Note that it is equivalent to (14.3.13) obtained above.

Derivation of 2 SLS Estimators: These estimators are obtained in (14.4.8).

To repeat:
$$\begin{bmatrix} \hat{\boldsymbol{\beta}}_1 \\ \hat{\boldsymbol{\Gamma}}_1 \end{bmatrix}_{2SLS} = \begin{bmatrix} \hat{\mathbf{Y}}_1'\hat{\mathbf{Y}}_1 & \hat{\mathbf{Y}}_1'\mathbf{X}_1 \\ \mathbf{X}_1'\hat{\mathbf{Y}}_1 & \mathbf{X}_1'\mathbf{X}_1 \end{bmatrix}^{-1}\begin{bmatrix} \hat{\mathbf{Y}}_1'\mathbf{y}_1 \\ \mathbf{X}_1'\mathbf{y}_1 \end{bmatrix}$$

To make the above expression directly operational to the given data, $\hat{\mathbf{Y}}_1$ is to be replaced as per following manipulations.

Matrix $\mathbf{Y}_1$ can be expressed as; $\mathbf{Y}_1 = \hat{\mathbf{Y}}_1 + \hat{\mathbf{U}}_1$

$$\hat{\mathbf{Y}}_1 = \mathbf{Y}_1 - \hat{\mathbf{U}}_1$$

$$\hat{\mathbf{Y}}_1'\hat{\mathbf{Y}}_1 = \hat{\mathbf{Y}}_1'(\mathbf{Y}_1 - \hat{\mathbf{U}}_1)$$

$$\hat{\mathbf{Y}}_1'\hat{\mathbf{Y}}_1 = \hat{\mathbf{Y}}_1'\mathbf{Y}_1 - \hat{\mathbf{Y}}_1'\hat{\mathbf{U}}_1$$

$$\hat{\mathbf{Y}}_1'\hat{\mathbf{Y}}_1 = \hat{\mathbf{Y}}_1'\mathbf{Y}_1 \qquad [\because \hat{\mathbf{Y}}_1'\hat{\mathbf{U}}_1 = 0]$$

Therefore,
$$\hat{\mathbf{Y}}_1'\hat{\mathbf{Y}}_1 = [\mathbf{Y}_1'\mathbf{X}(\mathbf{X}'\mathbf{X})^{-1}\mathbf{X}']\mathbf{Y}_1 \qquad ...(14.5.10)$$
(By using 14.4.2)

Once again:
$$\hat{\mathbf{Y}}_1 = \mathbf{Y}_1 - \hat{\mathbf{U}}_1$$

i.e.,
$$\hat{\mathbf{Y}}_1' = (\mathbf{Y}_1 - \hat{\mathbf{U}}_1)'$$

$$\hat{Y}_1' \, X_1 = (Y_1 - \hat{U}_1)' X_1$$

$$\hat{Y}_1' \, X_1 = \hat{Y}_1' X_1 - \hat{U}_1' X_1$$

$$\hat{Y}_1' \, X_1 = Y_1' \, X_1 \qquad [\because \hat{U}_1' X_1 = 0]$$

Therefore, $\qquad \hat{Y}_1 \, X_1 = Y_1' \, X_1$ $\qquad\qquad\qquad\qquad$ ...(14.5.11)

substituting (14.5.10) and (14.5.11) in (14.4.8);

$$\begin{bmatrix} \hat{\beta}_1 \\ \hat{\Gamma}_1 \end{bmatrix}_{2SLS} = \begin{bmatrix} [Y_1' X (X'X)^{-1} X'] Y_1 & \vline & Y_1' \, X_1 \\ \hline X_1' \, Y_1 & \vline & X_1' \, X_1 \end{bmatrix}^{-1} \begin{bmatrix} Y_1' X (X'X)^{-1} X' y_1 \\ X_1' y_1 \end{bmatrix} \quad ...(14.5.12)$$

(14.5.12) is the required operational formula for 2SLS estimators.

Illustration: Given the data on the two matrices:

$$X'X = \begin{bmatrix} 10 & 0 & 0 \\ 0 & 5 & 0 \\ 0 & 0 & 10 \end{bmatrix} \qquad X'Y = \begin{bmatrix} 10 & 20 \\ 20 & 10 \\ 30 & 20 \end{bmatrix}$$

Obtain:
   (i) Reduced form estimates
   (ii) ILS estimates and,
   (iii) 2 SLS estimates of the structural parameters of the following model:

$$y_{1t} = \beta_{12} y_{2t} + \gamma_{11} x_{1t} + \gamma_{12} x_{2t} + U_{1t}$$

$$y_{2t} = \beta_{21} y_{1t} + \gamma_{23} x_{3t} + U_{2t}$$

Reduced Form Estimates: We have already explained the procedure of obtaining such estimates by taking illustration on simple Keynesian model. The reduced form of this model was obtained by using the manipulations derived in (13.2.9) and (13.2.12); that is, by using:

$$\pi = -B^{-1} \, \Gamma,$$

$$\pi' = -\Gamma' \, (B')^{-1}$$

The identical results were obtained in (13.2.19) and (13.2.21).

In the present example, since we are given the data on $X'X$ and $X'Y$ matrices, the reduced form estimates can be accomplished by using OLS rule directly as given by (14.5.4) above; i.e.;

$$(\hat{\pi})' = (X'X)^{-1} X'Y.$$

Substituting the matrix data:

$$(\hat{\pi})' = \begin{bmatrix} 10 & 0 & 0 \\ 0 & 5 & 0 \\ 0 & 0 & 10 \end{bmatrix}^{-1} \begin{bmatrix} 10 & 20 \\ 20 & 10 \\ 30 & 20 \end{bmatrix}$$

$$= \begin{bmatrix} 1/10 & 0 & 0 \\ 0 & \frac{1}{5} & 0 \\ 0 & 0 & 1/10 \end{bmatrix}^{-1} \begin{bmatrix} 10 & 20 \\ 20 & 10 \\ 30 & 20 \end{bmatrix} = \begin{bmatrix} 1 & 2 \\ 4 & 2 \\ 3 & 2 \end{bmatrix}$$

which on transforming into equations gives:

$$\left. \begin{array}{l} y_{1t} = x_{1t} + 4x_{2t} + 3x_{3t} + V_{1t} \\ y_{2t} = 2x_{1t} + 2x_{2t} + 2x_{3t} + V_{2t} \end{array} \right\} \qquad ...(14.5.11)$$

Can we obtain $\hat{\pi}$ using: $\hat{\pi} = -\mathbf{B}^{-1}\mathbf{\Gamma}$ in the present example?

Remember, the expression $\hat{\pi} = -\mathbf{B}^{-1}\mathbf{\Gamma}$ was derived from the structural equations specified as: $\mathbf{BY}_t + \mathbf{\Gamma X}_t = \mathbf{U}$, whereas the equations of this model have been specified with just a single endogenous variable on the left hand side of each equation.

ILS and 2SLS Estimates: These estimates are obtained by taking each equation of the model independently. We therefore, calculate ILS and 2SLS estimates taking each of the two equations of the given model separately.

ILS Estimates of First-equation

First equation of the model is:

$$y_{1t} = \beta_{12}y_{2t} + \gamma_{11}x_{1t} + \gamma_{12}x_{2t} + U_{1t}$$

ILS estimators are given by (14.5.9):

$$\begin{bmatrix} \hat{\beta}_1 \\ \hline \hat{\Gamma}_1 \end{bmatrix} = \begin{bmatrix} \hat{\beta}_{12} \\ \hat{\gamma}_{11} \\ \hat{\gamma}_{12} \end{bmatrix} = \begin{bmatrix} \mathbf{X}_2'\mathbf{Y}_1 & \mathbf{X}_2'\mathbf{X}_1 \\ \hline \mathbf{X}_1'\mathbf{Y}_1 & \mathbf{X}_1'\mathbf{X}_1 \end{bmatrix}^{-1} \begin{bmatrix} \mathbf{X}_2'y_1 \\ \mathbf{X}_1'y_1 \end{bmatrix}$$

To obtain these estimates, therefore, we need the data on the matrices involved in (14.5.9). These are to be derived from the given $\mathbf{X'X}$ and $\mathbf{X'Y}$ matrices.

Let us recall the definitions of various matrices on the basis of which ILS estimators in (14.5.9) were obtained:

$$\mathbf{Y}_{1t} = [\mathbf{y}_1 \; \vdots \; \mathbf{Y}_1] \text{ in which for the first equation:}$$

$$\mathbf{y}_1 = \begin{bmatrix} y_{11} \\ y_{12} \\ \vdots \\ y_{1n} \end{bmatrix} \text{ and,} \qquad \mathbf{Y}_1 = \begin{bmatrix} y_{21} \\ y_{22} \\ \vdots \\ y_{2n} \end{bmatrix}$$
$$\text{(included endo.)}$$

$$\mathbf{X}_1 = \begin{bmatrix} x_{11} & x_{21} \\ x_{12} & x_{22} \\ \vdots & \vdots \\ x_{1n} & x_{2n} \end{bmatrix} \text{ and,} \qquad \mathbf{X}_2 = \begin{bmatrix} x_{31} \\ x_{32} \\ \vdots \\ x_{3n} \end{bmatrix}$$
$$\text{(included exog.)} \qquad\qquad \text{(excluded exog.)}$$

Also, $\qquad\qquad \mathbf{X}_{1t} = [\mathbf{X}_1 \vdots \mathbf{X}_2]$

$$\mathbf{X}_{1t}' = \begin{bmatrix} \mathbf{X}_1' \\ \mathbf{X}_2' \end{bmatrix}$$

Note: Remember that $\mathbf{y}_1$ in our case is the column vector of data on dependent endogenous variable for which the first equation has been normalized. Thus, the lower subscript should not be confused while dealing with second equation of the model. In second equation $y_2' = [y_{21} \; y_{22} \cdots y_{2n}]'$

Therefore,

$$\mathbf{X}'\mathbf{X} = \begin{bmatrix} \mathbf{X}_1' \\ \hline \mathbf{X}_2' \end{bmatrix} [\mathbf{X}_1 \vdots \mathbf{X}_2] = \begin{bmatrix} \mathbf{X}_1'\mathbf{X}_1 & \mathbf{X}_1'\mathbf{X}_2 \\ \hline \mathbf{X}_2'\mathbf{X}_1 & \mathbf{X}_2'\mathbf{X}_2 \end{bmatrix} = \begin{bmatrix} 10 & 0 & 0 \\ 0 & 5 & 0 \\ 0 & 0 & 10 \end{bmatrix}$$

$$\mathbf{X}'\mathbf{Y} = \begin{bmatrix} \mathbf{X}_1' \\ \hline \mathbf{X}_2' \end{bmatrix} [\mathbf{y}_1 \vdots \mathbf{Y}_1] = \begin{bmatrix} \mathbf{X}_1\mathbf{y}_1 & \mathbf{X}_1'\mathbf{Y}_1 \\ \hline \mathbf{X}_2'\mathbf{y}_1 & \mathbf{X}_2'\mathbf{Y}_1 \end{bmatrix} = \begin{bmatrix} 10 & 20 \\ 20 & 10 \\ 30 & 20 \end{bmatrix}$$

From the above analysis of $\mathbf{X}'\mathbf{X}$ and $\mathbf{X}'\mathbf{Y}$, we get all the relevant matrices required to obtain ILS and 2SLS estimates of the first equation. They are as follows:

1. $\mathbf{X}_1'\mathbf{Y}_1 = \begin{bmatrix} 20 \\ 10 \end{bmatrix}$

6. $\mathbf{X}_1'\mathbf{y}_1 = \begin{bmatrix} 10 \\ 20 \end{bmatrix}$

2. $\mathbf{Y}_1'\mathbf{X}_1 = [20 \quad 10]$

7. $\mathbf{X}_2'\mathbf{y}_1 = [30]$

3. $\mathbf{X}_2'\mathbf{Y}_1 = [20]$

8. $\mathbf{X}'\mathbf{y}_1 = \begin{bmatrix} 10 \\ 20 \\ 30 \end{bmatrix}$

4. $\mathbf{X}'\mathbf{Y}_1 = \begin{bmatrix} 20 \\ 10 \\ 20 \end{bmatrix}$

9. $\mathbf{X}_1'\mathbf{X}_1 = \begin{bmatrix} 10 & 0 \\ 0 & 5 \end{bmatrix}$

5. $\mathbf{Y}_1'\mathbf{X} = [20 \quad 10 \quad 20]$

10. $\mathbf{X}_2'\mathbf{X}_1 = [0 \quad 0]$

Substituting the relevant matrices in (14.5.9)

$$\begin{bmatrix} \hat{\beta}_{12} \\ \hat{\gamma}_{11} \\ \hat{\gamma}_{12} \end{bmatrix} = \begin{bmatrix} 20 & 0 & 0 \\ 20 & 10 & 0 \\ 10 & 0 & 5 \end{bmatrix}^{-1} \begin{bmatrix} 30 \\ 10 \\ 20 \end{bmatrix}$$

$$= \begin{bmatrix} 1/20 & 0 & 0 \\ -1/10 & 1/10 & 0 \\ -1/10 & 0 & 1/5 \end{bmatrix} \begin{bmatrix} 30 \\ 10 \\ 20 \end{bmatrix} = \begin{bmatrix} 3/2 \\ -2 \\ 1 \end{bmatrix}$$

That is, ILS estimates of the structural parameters of the first equation are: $\hat{\beta}_{12} = 3/2$, $\hat{\gamma}_{11} = -2$ and, $\hat{\gamma}_{12} = 1$

2SLS Estimates of the First Equation

2SLS estimators of the first equation are given by:

$$\begin{bmatrix} \hat{\beta} \\ \hat{\Gamma} \end{bmatrix}_{2SLS} = \begin{bmatrix} \hat{\beta}_{12} \\ \hat{\gamma}_{11} \\ \hat{\gamma}_{12} \end{bmatrix}$$

$$= \begin{bmatrix} Y_1'X(X'X)^{-1}X'Y_1 & Y_1'X_1 \\ X_1'Y_1 & X_1'X_1 \end{bmatrix} = \begin{bmatrix} Y_1'X(X'X)^{-1}X'y_1 \\ X_1'y_1 \end{bmatrix}$$

We need to specify two additional matrices required to be substituted in (14.5.12). They are to be obtained from the above 10 matrices.

(11) $$Y_1'X(X'X)^{-1}X'Y_1 = \begin{bmatrix} 20 & 10 & 20 \end{bmatrix} \begin{bmatrix} 10 & 0 & 0 \\ 0 & 5 & 0 \\ 0 & 0 & 10 \end{bmatrix}^{-1} \begin{bmatrix} 20 \\ 10 \\ 20 \end{bmatrix}$$

$$= \begin{bmatrix} 20 & 10 & 20 \end{bmatrix} \begin{bmatrix} 1/10 & 0 & 0 \\ 0 & 1/5 & 0 \\ 0 & 0 & 1/10 \end{bmatrix} \begin{bmatrix} 20 \\ 10 \\ 20 \end{bmatrix}$$

$$= \begin{bmatrix} 2 & 2 & 2 \end{bmatrix} \begin{bmatrix} 20 \\ 10 \\ 20 \end{bmatrix}$$

$$= [100]$$

(12) $\quad Y_1'X(X'X)^{-1}X'y_1 = [2 \quad 2 \quad 2] \begin{bmatrix} 10 \\ 20 \\ 30 \end{bmatrix}$

$$= [120]$$

Substituting the matrices obtained in the relevant places of (14.5.12):

$$\begin{bmatrix} \hat{\beta}_{12} \\ \hat{\gamma}_{11} \\ \hat{\gamma}_{12} \end{bmatrix} = \begin{bmatrix} 100 & 20 & 10 \\ 20 & 10 & 0 \\ 10 & 0 & 5 \end{bmatrix}^{-1} \begin{bmatrix} 120 \\ 10 \\ 20 \end{bmatrix}$$

$$= \begin{bmatrix} 1/40 & -1/20 & -1/20 \\ -1/20 & 1/5 & 1/10 \\ -1/20 & 1/10 & 3/10 \end{bmatrix} \begin{bmatrix} 120 \\ 10 \\ 20 \end{bmatrix} = \begin{bmatrix} 3/2 \\ -2 \\ 1 \end{bmatrix}$$

That is, the 2SLS estimates of the structural parameters of the first equation are:

$$\hat{\beta}_{13} = 3/2, \quad \hat{\gamma}_{11} = -2 \quad \text{and} \quad \hat{\gamma}_{12} = 1$$

Since the first equation of the given model is *just identified,* the ILS and 2SLS estimates are identical. This is an illustration of a general result that 2SLS and ILS estimates, where the later exist, are identical. (This is also proved theoretically under 14.6 below).

ILS Estimates of the Second Equation

Our second equation is: $y_{2t} = \beta_{21}y_{1t} + \gamma_{23}x_{3t} + u_{2t}$
so that:

$$y_1 = \begin{bmatrix} y_{21} \\ y_{22} \\ \vdots \\ y_{2n} \end{bmatrix}, \qquad \underset{\text{(included endo.)}}{Y_1} = \begin{bmatrix} y_{11} \\ y_{12} \\ \vdots \\ y_{1n} \end{bmatrix}$$

$$\underset{\text{(included exo.)}}{X_1} = \begin{bmatrix} x_{21} \\ x_{32} \\ \vdots \\ x_{3n} \end{bmatrix}, \qquad \underset{\text{(excluded exo.)}}{X_2} = \begin{bmatrix} x_{11} & x_{21} \\ x_{12} & x_{22} \\ \vdots & \vdots \\ x_{1n} & x_{2n} \end{bmatrix}$$

[Note the change in y_1 in the present case. Refer earlier note for this.]

$$X'X = \begin{bmatrix} X_1' \\ X_2' \end{bmatrix} [X_1 \vdots X_2] = \begin{bmatrix} X_1'X_1 & X_1'X_2 \\ X_2'X_1 & X_2'X_2 \end{bmatrix} = \begin{bmatrix} 10 & 0 & 0 \\ 0 & 5 & 0 \\ 0 & 0 & 10 \end{bmatrix}$$

$$X'Y = \begin{bmatrix} X_1' \\ \hline X_2' \end{bmatrix} [y_1 \vdots Y_1] = \begin{bmatrix} X_1'y_1 & X_1'Y_1 \\ \hline X_2'y_1 & X_2'Y_1 \end{bmatrix} = \begin{bmatrix} 10 & 20 \\ 20 & 10 \\ 30 & 20 \end{bmatrix}$$

The above partitioned analysis of $X'X$ and $X'Y$ matrices in case of second equation gives us the following relevant matrices:

1. $X_1'Y_1 = [20]$

6. $X_1'y_1 = [10]$

2. $Y_1'X_1 = [20]$

7. $X_2'y_1 = \begin{bmatrix} 20 \\ 30 \end{bmatrix}$

3. $X_2'Y_1 = \begin{bmatrix} 10 \\ 20 \end{bmatrix}$

8. $X'y_1 = \begin{bmatrix} 10 \\ 20 \\ 30 \end{bmatrix}$

4. $X'Y_1 = \begin{bmatrix} 20 \\ 10 \\ 20 \end{bmatrix}$

9. $X_1'X_1 = [10]$

5. $Y_1'X = [20 \quad 10 \quad 20]$

10. $X_2'X_1 = \begin{bmatrix} 0 \\ 0 \end{bmatrix}$

Substituting these matrices in (14.5.9):

$$\begin{bmatrix} \hat{\beta}_{21} \\ \hat{\gamma}_{23} \end{bmatrix} = \begin{bmatrix} 10 & 0 \\ 20 & 0 \\ \hline 20 & 10 \end{bmatrix}^{-1} \begin{bmatrix} 20 \\ 30 \\ \hline 10 \end{bmatrix}$$

This is an impossible expression. Why?

Since the second equation of the model is *over-identified*, we are not in a position to obtain ILS estimates of the structural parameters of this equation.

2SLS Estimates of the Second-Equation

To acquire 2SLS estimates, we need two additional matrices to substitute in (14.5.12). But on the other, with the changes in the definition of matrices y_1, Y_1, X_1 and X_2 for the second equation, $X'Y_1$ and $X'y$ also change in the following way:

$$X'Y_1 = \begin{bmatrix} 10 \\ 20 \\ 30 \end{bmatrix} \quad \text{and} \quad X'y = \begin{bmatrix} 20 \\ 10 \\ 20 \end{bmatrix}$$

Using these, we obtain following two additional matrices:

$$(11) \quad \mathbf{Y_1'X(X'X)^{-1}X'Y_1} = [10 \quad 20 \quad 30] \begin{bmatrix} 10 & 0 & 0 \\ 0 & 5 & 0 \\ 0 & 0 & 10 \end{bmatrix}^{-1} \begin{bmatrix} 10 \\ 20 \\ 30 \end{bmatrix}$$

$$= [10 \quad 20 \quad 30] \begin{bmatrix} 1/10 & 0 & 0 \\ 0 & 1/5 & 0 \\ 0 & 0 & 1/10 \end{bmatrix} \begin{bmatrix} 10 \\ 20 \\ 30 \end{bmatrix}$$

$$= [1 \quad 4 \quad 3] \begin{bmatrix} 10 \\ 20 \\ 30 \end{bmatrix}$$

$$= [180]$$

$$(12) \quad \mathbf{Y_1'X(X'X)^{-1}X'y_1} = [1 \quad 4 \quad 3] \begin{bmatrix} 20 \\ 10 \\ 20 \end{bmatrix}$$

$$= [120]$$

Substituting the relevant matrices in (14.5.12)

$$\begin{bmatrix} \hat{\beta}_{21} \\ \hat{\gamma}_{23} \end{bmatrix}_{2SLS} = \begin{bmatrix} 180 & | & 20 \\ 20 & | & 10 \end{bmatrix}^{-1} \begin{bmatrix} 120 \\ 10 \end{bmatrix}$$

$$\begin{bmatrix} \hat{\beta}_{21} \\ \hat{\gamma}_{23} \end{bmatrix} = \begin{bmatrix} 5/7 \\ -3/7 \end{bmatrix}$$

That is, the 2SLS estimates of the structural parameters of the second equation are:

$$\hat{\beta}_{21} = 5/7 \quad \text{and} \quad \hat{\gamma}_{23} = -3/7$$

The 2SLS estimates of the given structure are, therefore, to be described as under.

$$y_{1t} = 3/2 y_{2t} - 2x_{1t} + x_{2t} + U_{1t}$$
$$y_{2t} = 5/7 \, y_{1t} - 3/7 \, x_{3t} + U_{2t}$$

14.6 EQUIVALENCE BETWEEN ISL AND 2SLS

It has been stated previously that 2SLS estimators generally reduce in ILS estimators in the just identified case. It is to be proved theoretically.

Consider the first normalized equation expressed in (14.3.2)

$$y_1 = Y_1\beta_1 + x_1\Gamma_1 + U_1$$

Using (14.4.1) to replace Y_1 by $\hat{Y}_1$ for the first stage of 2SLS estimation:

$$y_1 = (x_1\hat{\pi}_1^{**} + x_2\hat{\pi}_2^{**})\beta_1 + x_1\Gamma_1 + U_1$$

$$y_1 = x_1\left[\hat{\pi}_1^{**}\beta_1 + \Gamma_1\right] + x_2\hat{\pi}_2^{**}\beta_1 + V_1 \qquad ..(14.6.1)$$

(14.4.10) may again be put in the partitioned matrix form so as to be expressed in (14.4.5) for the application of OLS for the second stage of estimation:

$$y_1 = \begin{bmatrix} x_1 & | & x_2 \end{bmatrix} \begin{bmatrix} \hat{\pi}_1^{**}\beta_1 + \Gamma_1 \\ \hline \hat{\pi}_2^{**}\beta_1 \end{bmatrix} + V_1$$

$$= [X]\begin{bmatrix} \hat{\pi}_1^{**}\beta_1 + \hat{\Gamma}_1 \\ \hline \hat{\pi}_2^{**}\hat{\beta}_1 \end{bmatrix} + V_1 \qquad ...(14.6.2)$$

Second stage of estimation requires application of OLS to (14.6.2), which yields:

$$\begin{bmatrix} \hat{\pi}_1^{**}\beta_1 + \Gamma_1 \\ \hline \hat{\pi}_2^{**}\beta_1 \end{bmatrix} = [X'X]^{-1}X'y_1$$

But, $$(X'X)^{-1}X'y_1 = \begin{bmatrix} \hat{\pi}_1^* \\ \hat{\pi}_2^* \end{bmatrix}$$

i.e., $(X'X)^{-1}X'y_1$ is simply the first column of the estimated matrix of reduced form coefficients

Hence: $$\begin{bmatrix} \hat{\pi}_1^{**}\hat{\beta}_1 + \hat{\Gamma}_1 \\ \hline \hat{\pi}_2^{**}\hat{\beta}_1 \end{bmatrix} = \begin{bmatrix} \hat{\pi}_1^* \\ \hat{\pi}_2^* \end{bmatrix} \qquad ...(14.6.3)$$

If the given equation (14.3.2) is just identified, then $\hat{\pi}_2^{**}$ will be square, and, assuming it is non-singular, solving for $\hat{\beta}_1$ and $\hat{\Gamma}_1$ (14.6.3) yields:

$$\hat{\beta}_1 = (\hat{\pi}_2^{**})^{-1}\hat{\pi}_2^* \qquad ...(14.6.4)$$

$$\hat{\Gamma}_1 = \hat{\pi}_1^* - \hat{\pi}_1^{**}(\hat{\pi}_2^{**})^{-1}\hat{\pi}_2^* \qquad ...(14.6.5)$$

(14.6.4) and (14.6.5) are precisely the ILS estimators expressed in (14.3.13).

A simple illustration without making use of matrix algebra provides the equivalence between the two procedures in the just identified case.

Let us consider simple model:

$$C = \alpha + \beta Y + U$$

$$Y = C + I.$$

Reduced-form: $C = \pi_{11} + \pi_{12}I + V_1$ ...(14.6.6)

$$Y = \pi_{21} + \pi_{22}I + V_2 \quad ...(14.6.7)$$

$$\pi_{12} = \left(\frac{\beta}{1-\beta}\right), \text{ and } \pi_{22} = \left(\frac{1}{1-\beta}\right) \text{ from (13.2.19)}$$

OLS on (14.6.6) yields: $\hat{\pi}_{12} = \dfrac{\Sigma ci}{\Sigma i^2}$

OLS on (14.6.7) yields : $\hat{\pi}_{22} = \dfrac{\Sigma yi}{\Sigma i^2}$;

hence, $\beta_{ILS} = \dfrac{\hat{\pi}_{12}}{\hat{\pi}_{22}} = \dfrac{\Sigma ci}{\Sigma yi}$ ...(14.6.8)

2SLS estimators are obtained as the least squares estimators of

$$C = \alpha + \beta \hat{Y} + U;$$

where $\hat{Y}$ is the estimated value of Y from the reduced form (14.6.7).

In the first stage: $\hat{\pi}_{22} = \dfrac{\Sigma yi}{\Sigma i^2}$, and

$$\hat{\pi}_{21} = \bar{Y} - \hat{\pi}_{22}\bar{I}$$

That is, $\bar{Y} = \hat{\pi}_{21} + \hat{\pi}_{22}\bar{I}$

$\hat{Y} = \bar{Y} - \hat{\pi}_{22}\bar{I} + \hat{\pi}_{22}I$ (By substituting in 14.6.7)

$$\hat{Y} - \bar{Y} = \hat{\pi}_{22}(I - \bar{I}) = \hat{\pi}_{22}(i)$$

So that $\hat{y} = \hat{\pi}_{22}i$ implying that:

$$\Sigma c\hat{y} = \hat{\pi}_{22}\Sigma ci$$

$$\Sigma \hat{y}^2 = \hat{\pi}_{22}^2\Sigma i^2$$

In the second stage: On applying OLS to $C = \alpha + \beta \hat{Y} + U$

$$\hat{\beta}_{2SLS} = \frac{\Sigma c\hat{y}}{\Sigma \hat{y}^2} = \frac{\hat{\pi}_{22}\Sigma ci}{\hat{\pi}_{22}^2\Sigma i^2} = \frac{\Sigma ci}{\Sigma yi} \quad ...(14.6.9)$$

which proves $\hat{\beta}_{ILS} \equiv \hat{\beta}_{2SLS}$. (refer first equation of illustration of P. 392 in this case)

Table 14.3: Worksheet for the second stage estimation in 2SLS

$D_t = S_t$	$\hat{P}_t$	Y_t	W_t	$d_t = s_t$	$\hat{p}_t$	y_t	w_t	$d_t^2\big|_{s_t^2}$	$\hat{p}_t^2$	y_t^2	w_t^2	$d_t y_t\big|_{s_t y_t}$	$d_t \hat{p}_t\big|_{s_t \hat{p}_t}$	$d_t w_t\big|_{s_t w_t}$	$\hat{p}_t y_t$	$\hat{p}_t w_t$	$w_t y_t$
11	19.99	8.1	42	−3.1	−4.35	−0.8	−4.7	9.61	18.92	0.64	22.09	2.48	13.48	14.57	3.48	20.44	3.76
16	19.39	8.4	58	1.9	−4.95	−0.5	11.3	3.61	24.50	0.25	127.69	−0.95	−9.40	21.47	2.47	−55.94	−5.65
11	23.68	8.5	35	−3.1	−0.66	−0.4	−11.7	9.61	0.43	0.16	136.89	1.24	2.04	36.27	0.26	7.72	4.64
14	21.94	8.5	46	−0.1	−2.40	−0.4	−0.7	0.01	5.76	0.16	0.49	0.04	0.24	0.07	0.96	−1.68	0.28
13	24.66	8.8	41	−1.1	0.32	−0.1	−5.7	1.21	0.10	0.01	32.49	0.11	−0.35	6.27	−0.03	1.82	0.57
17	23.57	9.0	56	2.9	−0.77	0.1	9.3	8.41	0.59	0.01	86.49	0.29	−2.23	26.97	−0.08	−7.16	0.93
14	24.20	8.9	48	−0.1	−0.14	0	1.3	0.01	0.02	0	1.69	0	0.01	−0.13	0	−0.18	0
15	27.10	9.4	50	0.9	2.76	0.5	3.3	0.81	7.62	0.25	10.89	0.45	2.48	2.97	1.38	9.11	1.65
12	28.86	9.5	39	−2.1	4.51	0.6	−7.7	4.41	20.34	0.36	59.29	−1.26	9.47	16.17	2.71	34.73	−4.62
18	29.40	9.9	52	3.9	5.06	1.0	5.3	15.21	25.60	1.0	28.09	3.90	19.73	20.67	5.06	26.82	5.30
141	243.42	8.9	467					52.90	110.06	2.84	506.10	6.30	15.19	145.30	16.59	(−)35.35	6.90
$\sum D_t =$	$\sum \hat{P}_t =$	$\sum Y_t =$	$\sum W_t =$					$\sum d_t^2 =$	$\sum \hat{p}_t^2 =$	$\sum y_t^2 =$	$\sum w_t^2 =$	$\sum d_t y_t =$	$\sum d_t \hat{p}_t =$	$\sum d_t w_t =$	$\sum \hat{p}_t y_t =$	$\sum \hat{p}_t w_t =$	$\sum w_t y_t =$

14.7 THE METHOD OF INSTRUMENTAL VARIABLES (IV)

This method has been explained while dealing with the estimation of a model when data on the relevant variables contain errors. To repeat, the basic idea behind this method is to do away the dependence of U on explanatory variable(s) by introducing an appropriate exogenous variable(s) as an instrument(s).

In section 12.3 we observed that in estimating a single equation out of simultaneous-equation model simultaneity bias creeps in because of correlation between error term and the independent variable(s). If these independent variables can be somehow purged of the disturbance term, the OLS procedure should provide reasonable estimates of the structural parameters. This is what the method of instrumental variables does [Refer section (11.1.1)]. This method involves the transformation of structural equations so that OLS procedure can be applied to each equation separately. Such transformation consists of multiplying the structural equation through by an appropriate instrument variable(s). By carrying out such manipulation we seek to eliminate the defect of the dependence of the explanatory variable(s) in the disturbance term(s) in each equation.

The present method is, therefore, based on all the usual assumptions of least squares method and on the additional assumption of the existence of the appropriate instrumental variable.

The estimates of the structural parameters obtained through this method are biased (yet asymptotically unbiased) but consistent. That is, the estimates are more reliable if our sample size is large enough.

Method of instrumental variables has been thoroughly explained earlier. In the present context we illustrate this method by assuming the possibility of simultaneous-equation bias when the demand for steel is estimated by OLS procedure from the data given in the *first two columns* of Table 14.4.

First we estimate the demand for steel $Y_t = \alpha_0 + \alpha_1 (GNP)_t + U_t$ by applying OLS. Next we estimate the demand for steel by the instrumental variables method, using say housing construction (Z) as an instrument (given in the fourth column of Table 14.4).

OLS procedure gives the following results

$$Y_t = -220.57 + 1.345X_t \qquad R^2 = 0.58$$
$$(0.320)$$

Assuming that the above results are not free from simultaneity bias, we re-estimate the equation by method of instrumental variables. Housing construction may well be expected, on theoretical grounds, to be an exogenous variable highly correlated with $GNP(X)$. Thus we use housing construction (Z) as an instrumental variable for replacing (X) in the structural equation. The system of transformed (Normal) equations will be:

$$\Sigma Y = n\alpha_0{}^* + \alpha_1{}^*\Sigma X$$
$$\Sigma ZY = \alpha_0{}^*\Sigma Z + \alpha_1{}^*\Sigma XZ$$

On substituting the relevant values from the worksheet of Table 14.4, we obtain the solution of these equations. The results are:

$$Y_t = -297.94 + 1.515 X_t \qquad\qquad R^2 = 0.32$$
$$(0.898)$$

In the above hypothetical example, we considered only one of structural equations (demand for steel) from the full simultaneous equations model to explain the working of *Instrumental Variable* procedure of estimation. In fact, researcher, in order to purge the statistical dependence between disturbance terms and the endogenous and exogenous explanatory variables, may have to use any number of such instrumental variables for the model; may be more than one for a single structural equation. The basic assumption underlying use of such variables, as stated above, is that every instrumental variable must be least correlated with the exogenous and endogenous variables already appearing in the structural equation so that OLS procedure could be applied to each single equation in a system of equations.

Let us now generalise the method by using matrix algebra.

Recall once again the first structural equation which was expressed as (14.4.5):

$$y_1 = Z_1 \delta_1 + U_1 \qquad\qquad ...(14.4.5)$$

$$y_1 = (Y_1 \mid X_1)\left[\dfrac{\beta_1}{\Gamma_1}\right] + U_1 \qquad\qquad ...(14.7.1)$$

In (14.4.5), Z_1 depicts the data on all included endogenous and exogenous explanatory variables, and δ_1 summarises all the coefficients in the first equation to be estimated; that is:

$$Z_1 = [Y_1 \mid X_1] \text{ and } \delta_1 = \left[\dfrac{\beta_1}{\Gamma_1}\right]$$

To make the matrix Z_1 a square,[2] (14.4.5) is multiplied throughout by Z_1' yielding:

$$Z_1' y_1 = Z_1' Z_1 \delta_1 + Z_1' U_1 \qquad\qquad ...(14.7.2)$$

---

[2] OLS procedure is based only on such type of manipulation.

Solution of $\hat{\beta}$ from the equation: $Y = X\hat{\beta} + \hat{U}$ is attempted by making X matrix, which is premultiplied to $\hat{\beta}$, a square one (Remember X is $n \times k$). This is done by premultiplying the equation $Y = X\hat{\beta} + \hat{U}$ by X' throughout: $X'Y = X'X\hat{\beta} + X'\hat{U}$

The matrix multiplying $\hat{\beta}$ is $(X'X)$, which is now square $(k \times k)$.

On dropping last term $\left[X'\hat{U}\right]$ from the equation, $\hat{\beta}$ yields the least squares estimator:
$\hat{\beta} = (X'X)^{-1} X'Y$.

Table 14.4: Worksheet for estimation of demand for steel by OLS and IV (Instrumental variable)

n	Y_t (Steel sales)	X_t (GNP)	Instrumental Variable Z_t	y_t	x_t	z_t	y_t^2	x_t^2	z_t^2	$x_t y_t$	$z_t y_t$	$x_t z_t$
1.	385	444	20	−5	−10	−4	25	100	16	+50	+20	+40
2.	392	446	22	+2	−8	−2	4	64	4	−16	−4	+16
3.	398	445	19	+8	−9	−5	64	81	25	−72	−40	+45
4.	396	450	25	+6	−4	+1	36	16	1	−24	+6	−4
5.	368	454	23	−22	0	−1	484	0	1	0	+22	0
6.	365	453	20	−25	−1	−4	625	1	16	+25	+100	+4
7.	364	455	24	−26	+1	0	676	1	0	−26	0	0
8.	376	448	17	−14	−6	−7	196	36	49	+84	+98	+42
9.	372	438	18	−18	−16	−6	324	256	36	+288	+108	+96
10.	371	440	20	−19	−14	−4	361	196	16	+266	+76	+56
11.	387	451	24	−3	−3	0	9	9	0	+9	0	0
12.	407	462	28	+17	+8	+4	289	64	16	+136	+68	+32
13.	406	469	33	+16	+15	+9	256	225	81	+240	+144	+135
14.	432	480	35	+42	+26	+11	1764	676	121	+1092	+462	+286
15.	431	475	32	+41	+21	+8	1681	441	64	+861	+328	+168
Σ→	5850	6810	360				6794	2166	446	2913	1388	916

Dropping the last term from (14.7.2), and solving the resulting *normal equations* yields the OLS estimator:

$$(\hat{\delta}_1)_{OLS} = (\mathbf{Z}_1'\mathbf{Z}_1)^{-1}\mathbf{Z}_1'\mathbf{y}_1 \qquad \ldots(14.7.3)$$

The dropping of the last term $(\mathbf{X}'\hat{\mathbf{U}})$ in the single equation model: $\mathbf{Y} = \mathbf{X}\hat{\boldsymbol{\beta}} + \mathbf{U}$ was justified because the explanatory variables were assumed to be exogenous and hence uncorrelated with the stochastic disturbance terms. In the simultaneous equations model, however, dropping the last term $(\mathbf{Z}_1'\mathbf{U})$ cannot be so justified; because in the present case $\mathbf{Z}_1$ involves explanatory variables of both nature: endogenous and exogenous and, explanatory endogenous variables in $\mathbf{Z}_1$ are not statistically independent of $\mathbf{U}_1$. They are correlated with the $\mathbf{U}_1$'s even in the probability limit.

In order to by-pass such a problem in simultaneous system of equations, a set of such variables are brought into the equation to enable us to drop the last term from (14.7.2) and thereby solve for $(\hat{\delta}_1)$.

Suppose, that there exists such a set of $(G^* - 1 + K^*)$ number of variables (the same number as in $\mathbf{Z}_1$) that are independent of $\mathbf{U}_1$, but at the same time, correlated with $\mathbf{Z}_1$. Such variables are called *instrumental variables.*

Assume that the data on set of these variables is summarised by matrix $\mathbf{W}_1$ of order $[n \times (G^* - 1 + K^*)]$

Premultiplying (14.4.5) by $\mathbf{W}_1'$ yields:

$$\mathbf{W}_1'\mathbf{y}_1 = \mathbf{W}_1'\mathbf{Z}_1\,\delta_1 + \mathbf{W}_1'\,\mathbf{U}_1 \qquad \ldots(14.7.4)$$

Dropping last term $\mathbf{W}_1'\,\mathbf{U}_1$, since now it is assumed that the variables $\mathbf{W}_1$ are uncorrelated with $\mathbf{U}_1$, (14.7.4) can be solved for δ_1;

$$(\hat{\delta}_1)_{IV} = (\mathbf{W}_1'\mathbf{Z}_1)^{-1}\,\mathbf{W}_1'\,\mathbf{y}_1 \qquad \ldots(14.7.5)$$

(14.7.5) gives instrumental variable estimator.

This estimator is extremely useful, since it represents a whole class of estimators (OLS, ILS, and 2SLS estimators) and, is applicable in an overidentified case also.

The three single-equation methods of estimation discussed in 14.1 through 14.7 do not take into account the correlation between disturbances of different structural equations. They are based on the assumption that the disturbance terms in different equations of the model are independently distributed. Along with such a restrictive assumption these methods also rely upon the basic assumptions of the classical linear regression model, consequently they lead to estimates that are consistent but, in *general*, not asymptotically efficient. This deficiency has been overcome by estimating all equations of the system simultaneously in the system methods. LIML is not a system method, but this method as in case of system methods, also allows for contemporaneous dependence of disturbances terms of the various equations.

Therefore the estimates obtained through LIML, 3SLS and FIML methods are not only asymptotically unbiased and consistent but are asymptotically efficient also. However, these methods are extremely sensitive to sample size and specification errors. In addition to sensitivity to sample size and specification errors. In addition to sensitivity to mis-specification errors, these methods, particularly FIML, are computationally more complicated and more costly.

..........*FIML perfoms admirably under favourable conditions, but it losses ground when complications such as high interdependence of the jointly determined variables or structural mis-specification arise. The steadiest method appears to be 2SLS.**

14.8 IDENTIFICATION AND CHOICE OF ESTIMATION METHOD

There are several methods for estimating a simultaneous equation model. As a practical matter, however, one may be required to decide which of the method is more appropriate. There is no clear cut test to suggest the appropriateness of a method in a particular situation; yet the choice amongst the different methods is greatly facilitated by knowing the extent of identification of a model in question.

If the relationship is underidentified, no econometric technique can be useful to estimate is parameters. However an underidentified system may contain some identified structural equations which can be estimated by some procedure.

If all the relationships of a model are exactly identified (i.e., whole model is exactly identified), all the structural coefficients can then be estimated uniquely by any of the techniques of estimation described above. All techniques yield identical estimates, yet 2SLS is the mostly preferred procedure for its simplicity under such circumstances.

If some or all the equations of a system are overidentified the whole system is said to be overidentified. All techniques except ILS can then be applied to estimate the structural coefficients. It is only in this situation that we are faced with the problem of making choice amongst the various techniques available with us. This problem has been widely discussed in econometric literature and yet there is no conclusive evidence. However, the choice of technique, as has been argued by many econometricians, should depend to a considerable extent on the purpose for which the model is to be estimated. As we discussed earlier, the following may be the various purposes:

* R. Summers, "A Capital Intensive Approach to the Small Sample Properties of Various Simultaneous Equation Estimators," Econometrica, Vol 33, 1965, p.32.

(a) The model may be used for testing economic theory.
(b) The model may be used for evaluating the different policy measures.
(c) The model may be used for forecasting purposes.

The statistical properties of the estimates expected under each of the above three purposes are different; hence the choice of technique has to be based on the basis of the statistical properties possessed by the estimates of the various techniques vis-a-vis the properties expected. On the other hand, we expect different statistical properties depending on the size of the sample. For instance, we are mainly concerned with unbiasedness and minimum variance of the estimators while we deal with small samples. On the other asymptotic properties (i.e., consistency and efficiency) are important when we deal with large samples.

Nearly all the methods of estimation shed light only on the asymptotic properties of the estimates. In practice one has to work with finite samples and it is therefore important to study the small sample properties of estimates obtained from these methods. But unfortunately it is not possible to study small-sample properties by direct application of analytical methods to actual observations. The study of small-sample properties of simultaneous-equation estimators has been made through the sampling experiments known as *Monte Carlo Experiments*. These are based on simulated data. The reasons for this being that actual observations usually involve different problems; such as multicollinearity, autocorrelation, errors of measurement, specification errors and such other problems. It is, therefore, not possible to study and establish the theoretical properties of the estimates of various techniques which by assumption exclude all the problems. But simulated data helps the econometrician to conduct research on the properties of the estimators and establish their statistical properties when the sample size is small.

The ranking of different techniques on the basis of the small-sample properties of the estimates as per *Monte Carlo Studies* is summarised in Table 14.5.

Table 14.5: Ranking of different techniques on the basis of small-samples properties of the estimates of the structural parameters with the correct specification of the simultaneous-equation model.

Ranking of the technique on the basis of:

Bias	Variance	Root Mean Square Error*
1. FIML ≡ LIML	1. OLS	1. FIML
2. 2SLS	2. FIML	2. 2SLS
3. OLS	3. 2SLS	3. LIML
	4. LIML	4. OLS

* It is the square root of the mean square error
≡ denotes that the methods yields identical results

The major conclusion from Table 14.5 is that OLS yields the estimates with the greatest bias. Also since OLS estimates possess the lowest variance, there is always a danger of incorrectly accepting the (OLS) coefficients as significant. Thus, it may be said that OLS seems to be the least appropriate method for estimation of structural parameters of a simultaneous-equation model.

There is no problem in making the choice amongst the various estimation techniques on the criterion of consistency. All the estimation methods except OLS yield consistent estimates. On the basis of asymptotic efficiency, the ranking of different techniques (with the assumption that the given data is free from multicollinearity, measurement and specification errors) can be described as follows:

(a) 2SLS and LIML estimates possess same degree of efficiency since these techniques use same amount of information provided in the model. These techniques are more efficient than instrumental variables method.

(b) 3SLS and FIML methods use more information than 2SLS, LIML and IV methods; hence these two techniques could be said to be the best on the basis of criterion of efficiency. However these methods are also more sensitive to specification and measurement errors. Since we are never sure about the non-existence of such errors; 3SLS and FIML techniques are less attractive with the researchers.

Summarising, therefore, we may say that the problem of choice of econometric technique is by no means simple. It depends on many factors; such as the purpose for which we need to estimate the model, the identification condition of the model, the availability of the data (i.e., size of the sample) and the computational complexity of the technique.

ASSIGNMENTS

1. Prove that the ILS estimators of the parameters of an equation in a system of simultaneous linear stochastic equations are identical with the 2SLS estimators if the equation is just identified.

2. Consider the following demand-supply model for pork:

   Demand: $q = \alpha_0 + \alpha_1 p + \alpha_2 y + \alpha_3 w + u$
   Supply: $q = \beta_0 + \beta_1 p + \beta_2 z + v$

   where p = retail price, q = consumption, y = disposable consumer income, z = an estimate of production based wholly on exogenous variables, and w = measure of income distribution: p and q are dependent variables and all the other variables are predetermined.

   What method would you employ to estimate the supply function? Outline the steps.

3. Given the two-equation Keynesian model

$$C_t = \alpha_0 + \alpha Y_t + U_t$$
$$Y_t = C_t + I_t;$$

C_t and Y_t are endogenous variables, I_t is exogenous. Derive the 2SLS estimator of 'α' and stating the necessary conditions, prove that it is 'consistent'. Also find out the variance of the estimator of α.

4. Suggest the simplest but consistent method of estimation for each equation of the following model. Outline the suggested methods and defend your suggestion in each case.

National Income : $\quad Y = \alpha_0 + \alpha_1 I + \alpha_2 Y_{-1} + U_1$

Net Capital Formation : $I = \beta_0 + \beta_1 Y + \beta_2 Q + U_2$

Personal Consumption: $C = \gamma_0 + \gamma_1 Y + \gamma_2 C_{-1} + \gamma_3 P + U_3$

Profits: $\qquad\qquad Q = \delta_0 + \delta_1 Q_{-1} + \delta_2 R + U_4$

The consumer price-index P and index of industrial productivity R are exogenous variables.

5. Given: $\mathbf{X'X} = \begin{bmatrix} 1 & 0 & 0 \\ 0 & 20 & 0 \\ 0 & 0 & 10 \end{bmatrix} \qquad \mathbf{X'Y} = \begin{bmatrix} 5 & 10 \\ 40 & 20 \\ 20 & 30 \end{bmatrix}$

Estimate the model:

$$y_{1t} = \beta_{12} y_{2t} + \gamma_{11} x_{1t} + U_{1t}$$
$$y_{2t} = \beta_{21} y_{1t} + \gamma_{22} x_{2t} + \gamma_{22} x_{3t} + U_{2t}$$

6. Consider the model (in deviation form)
$$y_1 = b_1 y_2 + u$$
$$y_2 = c_1 y_1 + c_2 x_1 + v$$
Estimate the first equation by OLS, ILS and 2SLS and compare the results. Use the following observations (which are in deviation form). Which method would you suggest for second equation?

y_1	y_2	x_1
−4	2	−2
0	3	1
3	2	0
1	−7	3

7. Given the following data in deviation-form:

y_1	y_2	x_1	x_2
−4	2	−2	−1
0	3	−1	+ 2
3	2	0	− 1
1	7	3	0

Estimate the first equation of the following model by 2SLS. Why is this method more appropriate than ILS in this case?
$$y_1 = b_1 y_2 + u_1$$
$$y_2 = c_1 y_1 + c_2 x_1 + c_3 x_2 + u_2$$

8. Consider the following model (in deviation-form):
$$y_1 = \beta_{12} y_2 + \alpha_{11} x_1 + u_1$$
$$y_2 = \beta_{21} y_1 + \alpha_{22} x_2 + \alpha_{23} x_3 + u_2 \ (y\text{'s are endogenous})$$

Use the following information to obtain 2SLS estimates of the coefficients of the first structural equation of the above model.

(a) The OLS estimates of the reduced-form coefficients are

$$\begin{bmatrix} 5 & 10 & 2 \\ 10 & 10 & 5 \end{bmatrix}$$

(b) The variance of the errors of the coefficients in the first reduced-form equation are 1, 0.5 and 0.1.

(c) The corresponding covariances are estimated to be all zero.

(d) The estimated variance of the disturbance term of the first reduced-form equation is 2.

9. The following simultaneous equation system was used for Indian meat market.

Demand: $\qquad y_1 = \alpha_1 y_2 + \beta_1 x_1 + u_1$

Supply: $\qquad y_2 = \alpha_2 y_1 + \beta_2 x_2 + \beta_3 x_3 + u_2$

where, y_1 = per capita meat consumption, y_2 = deflated price index of meat. Both are endogenous variables.

x_1 = per capita disposable income, x_2 = index of cost of processing meat and x_3 = index of cost of agricultural production.

Estimate the structural coefficients of the supply function if the matrix of sum of products of observed values is as follows:

	y_1	y_2	x_1	x_2	x_3
y_1	100	200	30	20	40
y_2		900	0	50	160
x_1			100	0	0
x_2				50	0
x_3					40

$$\cdots = \begin{bmatrix} \mathbf{Y'Y} & \mathbf{Y'X} \\ \mathbf{X'Y} & \mathbf{X'X} \end{bmatrix}$$

10. The following is first equation in a three-equation model which contains three other exogenous variables x_2, x_3 and x_4:

$$y_1 = \alpha_{12} y_2 + \alpha_{13} y_3 + \beta_{11} x_1 + u_1$$

Observations give the following matrices:

$$\mathbf{Y'Y} = \begin{bmatrix} 20 & 15 & -5 \\ 15 & 60 & -45 \\ -5 & -45 & 70 \end{bmatrix} \quad \mathbf{Y'X} = \begin{bmatrix} 2 & 2 & 4 & 5 \\ 0 & 4 & 12 & -5 \\ 0 & -2 & -12 & 10 \end{bmatrix}$$

$$\mathbf{X'X} = \begin{bmatrix} 1 & 0 & 0 & 0 \\ 0 & 2 & 0 & 0 \\ 0 & 0 & 4 & 0 \\ 0 & 0 & 0 & 5 \end{bmatrix}, \quad N = 30$$

Obtain 2SLS estimates of the parameters of the equation and estimate their standard errors. (Hint: In the complete model, therefore, $G = 3$ and $K = 4$)

15

How to Investigate
Goodness of the Model

There has been phenomenal growth in the application of econometric techniques in the day to day affairs of decision makers. Also with the dramatic rise in availability of computers and software facilities, not only these techniques have grown sophisticated but the gap between theoretical and applied econometrics is being felt by the users.

Econometric techniques with remarkable development, are no more regarded reserved for econometricians. Though overtly related to economics, econometric models are also designed by sociologists, political scientists, corporate planners and managers to understand and analyze the various problems of their fields. Every econometric model has a purpose behind it, it could be designed for forecasting purposes or it may be built for purely descriptive purposes and hypothesis testing. An analytical mind of a decision maker is no longer happy with a 'best fit model' with desirable distributional properties; rather a model which provides solution for the problem at hand is more likable and usable. It is therefore essential that when a model has been constructed its overall validation be investigated before it is put into use by the designer. Again the real life situations are so complicated and unique that rarely a text on econometrics can be regarded a comprehensive one in all respects. Every text attempts to explain the complex techniques through simplified illustrative examples (under the given set of assumptions) which might never occur in practical situations. A sound theoretical knowledge may prove to be less than enough while dealing into practical problems. One learns only by intuition, experience and larger exposure.

Model validation of single equation model presents less serious problems than a multi-equation model. In case of single equation there exists a set of statistical tests through which the model can be evaluated and directly used to produce a forecast. Though the same consideration apply to simultaneous equation model but the evaluation criteria is more complicated and may not be straight forward task. In such models each individual equation may be a very good statistical fit but a model as a whole may be far from achieving the purpose. The converse may also be true and the individual equation of a model may prove to be a poor statistical fit yet the model as a whole may do a good predictive job. This happens because the variables of multi-equation model interact with each other across the equation of the model and through different points of time.

In the above background and perspective, the present chapter has been developed to provide a very broad outline for evaluating the goodness of Single Equation Econometric model.

The overall performance model is assessed through four major dimensions on which every econometric model is constructed.

(a) Theoretical robustness of the model

(b) Statistical significance of complete model and individual coefficients;

(c) Predictive performance of the model; and

(d) Purpose and sensitivity of the model.

Theoretical robustness: Theoretical robustness of the model refers to validation about the specification of the process by which unobserved stochastic disturbances are assumed to have been generated and also specification about the relationship connecting these disturbances with the dependant and non-stochastic explanatory variables of the model.* In the Classical Regression model, disturbances are assumed to be generated by a random selection from a normal distribution** with zero mean and constant variance. Assumed statistical process of the disturbances enables us to establish distributional properties of estimators $(\hat{\beta}_i s)$ and derive summary statistics $(t, F$ and $R^2)$ to asses their usefulness. Finally, since true disturbances are unobservable, we require sample residuals $(e_i's)$ to follow all the properties as those assumed for the disturbances $(U_i's)$. The derivation all the estimators and summary statistics are possible only by hypothesizing such correspondence between population and sample related residuals.

Assume two explanatory variables model with explicit linear relation:

Population regression line : $Y_i = \beta_o + \beta_1 X_{1i} + \beta_2 X_{2i} + U_i$ ... (i)

Sample regression line : $Y_i = \hat{\beta}_o + \hat{\beta}_1 X_{1i} + \hat{\beta}_2 X_{2i} + e_i$ ...(ii)

The sample residuals : $e_i = Y_i - \hat{\beta}_o - \hat{\beta}_1 X_{1i} + \hat{\beta}_2 X_{2i}$ ...(iii)

As per the equation of sample residuals the different values of $(\hat{\beta}_i s)$ would generate different sets of values of $e_i's$ even though the values of $x_i's$ are same (fixed in repeated samples); but ideal estimators $(\hat{\beta}_i s)$ would be those which generate set of $e_i's$ which justify same characteristics as those assumed for populations residuals. In other words, values of estimators are such that the

---

* As has been already discussed in the text, specification of the model means a detailed description of (i) all explonatory (or lagged) variables to be included in the models, (ii) functional form required to be used for the model, and (iii) Stochastic proporties of the disturbance terms.

** As mentioned earlier in the text, we need not make the assumption of normality for disturbances except for confidence interval statements and test of significance. Normality assumption is also required to show OLS- estimators are identical to the ML-estimators.

residuals (e_i's) generated by sample observations posses the same distributional properties as those of population residuals (U_i's). To make this happen for the above two variable model, the assumptions are expressed in the form of two constraints on residuals; that is, zero mean and randomness of disturbances. They are $\Sigma e_i = 0$ and $\Sigma x_1 e_i = \Sigma x_2 e_i = 0$ on the residual equation (iii). Satisfactions of two conditions give rise to three normal equations* for deriving the unique values of ideal estimators from the sample observations.

$$\Sigma Y_i = n\hat{\beta}_o + \hat{\beta}_1 \Sigma X_{1i} + \hat{\beta}_2 \Sigma X_{2i}$$

$$\Sigma X_{1i} Y_i = \hat{\beta}_o \Sigma X_{1i} + \hat{\beta}_1 \Sigma X_{1i}^2 + \hat{\beta}_2 \Sigma X_{1i} X_{2i}$$

$$\Sigma X_{2i} Y_i = \hat{\beta}_o \Sigma X_{2i} + \hat{\beta}_1 \Sigma X_{1i} X_{2i} + \hat{\beta}_2 \Sigma X_{2i}^2$$

From the above discussion it should be clear that optimal estimators are those which produce well behaved sample residuals possessing similar properties which are assumed for unknown disturbances. The theoretical robustness or validation of the model therefore means undertaking the analysis of residuals obtained after application of classical linear regression.

The analysis of residuals may reveal:

(i) that relationship is not linear as assumed;

(ii) the residuals formulate systematic pattern and hence they are not randomly obtained as assumed;

(iii) that variance is not constant neither are residuals normally distributed; and

(iv) the residuals are correlated instead of being independent as assumed.

Any of the above irregularity shall formulate a regular pattern in the residuals which signifies that residuals generated are non-random. This, then, indicates that there is something systematically going on in the data which our model has failed to take into account (discussed below). Certain desirable modifications** are therefore required to be carried in order to make the model purposeful and meaningful.

Statistical significance of complete model: Significance of the model can be investigated on two basis; one by examining its overall statistical

---

*However minimization of Σe_i^2 will not generate normal equations if the model does not contains a constant term. In other words if our model does not include constant term, we cannot simultaneously minimize the residuals sum of square (Σe_i^2) and satisfy the required properties of the residuals. Hence it is always advisable to include constant terms in every linear econometric model. Its inclusion guarantees to produce set of residuals (Σe_i^2) to posses same properties as of the non-observable disturbance terms via satisfaction of the conditions. But remember, constant term get suppressed while dealing with deviation-form of the linear model.

**In absence of well-behaved disturbances, different statistical tests get seriously distorted. This calls for revised procedures to derive optimum estimators to regain validity of the model.

soundness, and the other by studying extent of impact of each explanatory variable introduced in the model. Overall significance is examined through four summary statistics; $R^2, \bar{R}^2, F$ and *SEE*. The individual strength of the coefficient is looked into by standard errors (*t*-statistics) and interval estimation statements. All these statistics are explained in details at the relevant places of the present text. The purpose here is to dispel certain misconception about these statistics while making inferences.

The overall goodness of every model depends upon the extent of movement in the dependent variable (*Y*) that is explained by the explanatory variables introduced in the model. If larger (smaller) proportion of the total variation are explained then it indicates that model possesses greater (lesser) predictive power in the format it has been designed.

As explained in the text, total variations in the (*Y*) are decomposed into two parts; Explained (Regression) sum of squares (*RSS*) and unexplained (Error) sum of squares (*ESS*). The four statistics $R^2, \bar{R}^2, F$ and *SEE* study goodness of the model in four different procedures; first three are concerned with the investigation of total explained variations; the last one examines the unexplained part of the total variations described by the residual terms.

(i) R^2–(R–square) : Recall that $R^2 = \dfrac{\text{Variations explained by the model}}{\text{Total variations in } (Y)}$

$$= 1 - \dfrac{\text{Residual Variations}}{\text{Variations in } (Y)}$$

$$= 1 - \dfrac{\Sigma e_i^2}{\Sigma y_i^2}$$

(ii) $\bar{R}^2$ – (R– bar square): Assume that a sample of *n*-number of observations is used to estimate coefficients of *k*-number of explanatory variables. To compute $(\bar{R})^2$, variations in numerator and denominator are converted into variances*. This is done by dividing the variations by respective degrees of freedom**; that is

---

*Variance equals variation divided by degrees of freedom.

**Of the *n*-number of residuals, residuals generated by the equation (iii) only three residuals must assume such specific values so that three conditions that we impose on the residuals must get satisfied. These conditions are $\Sigma e_i = 0$, $\Sigma x_1 e_i = 0$ and $\Sigma x_2 e_i = 0$. The remaining number of residuals, $(n-3)$ can assume any value depending on different values of estimators $(\hat{\beta}_i s)$. In statistical terminology, the impositions of three restrictions on residuals line (iii) above is expressed by saying that there are only $(n-3)$ degrees of freedom in the *n*-number of different values which residuals can take.

$$\bar{R}^2 = 1 - \frac{\text{Var.}(e_i)}{\text{Var.}(y_i)} = 1 - \frac{\Sigma e_i / (n-k)}{\Sigma y_i^2 / (n-1)};\ \text{on simplification this provides the}$$

basic relationship between R^2 and $\bar{R}^2$:

$$\bar{R}^2 = 1 - \left\{ (1 - R^2) \left(\frac{n-1}{n-k} \right) \right\}$$

(iii) Analysis of variance (F-statistic): In the k-explanatory variable model;

$$Y_i = \beta_0 + \beta_1 x_1 + \beta_2 x_2 + \ldots + \beta_k x_k + U_i \qquad (i = 1 \ldots n)$$

the total variations in Y around its mean value are decomposed into explained and unexplained variations. The analysis of these variations is summarized in terms of analysis of variance (ANOVA) by converting these variations into variances to compute F-statistic.

$$F = \frac{\text{Explained Variance}}{\text{Unexplained Variance}} = \frac{Rss / k}{Ess / (n - k - 1)};\ \text{which simplifies to}$$

$$F = \left(\frac{R^2}{1 - R^2} \right) \left(\frac{n - k - 1}{k} \right)$$

This F-ratio follow F-distribution with k-degrees of freedom of numerator (because there are k-no. of explanatory variables to explain variations in Y), while the denominator has $(n-k-1)$ number of degrees of freedom because we use n-observations to estimate $(k+1)$ number of coefficients of the above linear relation.

F-distribution helps us to test the hypothesis, $Ho : \beta_1 = \beta_2 = \ldots = \beta_k = 0$ that is, none of the explanatory variables influence Y; in other words the above relationship is useless.

Notice that for the above linear relationship, null hypothesis does not include intercept term ($\beta_0 = 0$); that is to say we do not test whether this equation passes through origin. The test merely tells us whether or not variations around the mean value Y are explained by all X's jointly. In a way it supports or rejects the significance of R^2 statistic. But rejection of null hypothesis leaves us with more important question; which of the explanatory variables are useful in explaining variations in Y?

t-test helps us to examine the significance of individual coefficients.

(iv) Standard errors : There are two types of standard errors; one is related to regression coefficients, the other to the complete regression model. The former is called standard error of the coefficient while the latter is Standard Error of the Estimate (*SEE*). Both errors are computed by obtaining square root of the estimated variances; square root of estimated variance of the statistical distribution of $(\hat{\beta}_i s)$ is called standard error of the regression coefficient and square root of estimated variance of disturbance terms $(U_i's)$ is called (*SEE*).

In statistical concepts, positive square root of variance is called standard deviation. But in above two cases we compute root of estimated variances rather than true variances; it is, therefore, called standard error to distinguish it from standard deviation. The true variance of disturbance terms is not known (though it is assumed to be constant over each of the fixed values of exploratory variables). An unbiased estimator $(\hat{\sigma}_u^2)$ of true variance (σ_u^2) is computed through OLS residual terms. On the other, variance of the statistical distribution of regression coefficients $(\hat{\beta}_i s)$ is also directly dependent on the true variance of disturbances.

For instance, in one exploratory variable case;

$$\text{true variance } (\hat{\beta}_i) = \frac{\sigma_u^2}{\Sigma x_i^2}; \hat{\sigma}_u^2 = \frac{\Sigma e_i^2}{n-2}; \text{ hence}$$

$$\text{estimated variance: } \hat{V}ar. (\hat{\beta}) = \frac{\Sigma e_i^2 / n - 2}{\Sigma x_i^2} = \frac{\Sigma e_i^2}{\Sigma x_i^2 (n-2)}$$

The basic difference between standard deviation and standard error should always be kept in mind;

$$\text{std. dev. } (\hat{\beta}_i) = \sqrt{\frac{\sigma_u^2}{\Sigma x_i^2}}; \text{ std. error } (\hat{\beta}_i) = \sqrt{\frac{\hat{\sigma}_u^2}{\Sigma x_i^2}} = \sqrt{\frac{\Sigma e_i^2}{\Sigma x_i^2 (n-2)}}$$

Standard error of the coefficient is, in fact, estimate of standard deviation of the coefficient and not the standard deviation itself. In case, estimate of variance of regression coefficient is biased (because of mis-specification of the model or what so ever reason), the computed standard error from it shall not reflect the real precision of the coefficient(s). The true precision of the coefficient ultimately depends upon the theoretical standard deviation of the regression coefficient.

(v) SEE (Criteria for forecast performance of the model): Standard error of the estimate, which is square root of estimated residual variance, is reported by different terms in the computer outputs as per its use and procedure of computation.

(a) Since *SEE* measures dispersion of the residual terms associated with regression model, it is called Standard Error of Regression (*SER*).

(b) At times *SEE* is reported only in terms of *ESS* ($\hat{\sigma}^2$) from which *SEE* is obtained on dividing it by degrees of freedom and then getting its square root.

(c) Since *SEE* is computed through square root of square of residuals divided by degrees of freedom, it is reported as Mean-Square Error or simply (*MSE*).

(d) Finally a model with smaller residual variance also has smaller variance of the error of prediction; hence *SEE* is also called Standard Error of Forecast. In fact, the predictive power of the model (exploratory power of the model) is given by *SEE*. The predictive power decreases when increase in residual is more than the number of degrees of freedom; on the other decrease in *SEE* is indicative of gain in predictive power of the model.

Since there is no useful test for evaluating the magnitude of the standard error, we must rely on qualitative (value) judgment about how low *SEE* is justifiable in the given circumstances. Generally econometrician study; how much percentage is *SEE* of the mean value of dependent variable? Lower this percentage, better the exploratory power of the model. A percentage of *SEE* closer to 10-15 percent is always preferred.

Statistical significance of individual coefficients (standardised regression coefficients): In order to test which of the exploratory variables introduced in the model are statistically significant, tools of hypothesis test are applied. On the assumption that disturbance terms are generated by a normal distribution, every regression coefficient is first standardized before putting it to hypothesis test on *t*-distribution. As in the case of standardization of any value of sample or population, estimated coefficient is also standardized in the similar manner. *t*-ratio is, infact, a standardized form of coefficient:

$$t = \frac{\hat{\beta}_i - \beta_i}{SE(\hat{\beta}_i)}; \text{ where } \hat{\beta}_i = \text{estimated coefficient}; \beta_i = \text{actual or hypothesised}$$

mean value of the coefficient and $SE(\hat{\beta}_i)$ = Std. Error of ($\hat{\beta}_i$) (recall that *SE* is estimated value of the true std. deviation).

We are always interested in question of the form: "Does (*Y*) really depend on explanatory variable (*X*)?" Other way of saying this is; if $\hat{\beta}_i \neq 0$, then (*Y*) does not depend on (*X*) and hence $\hat{\beta}_i = 0$

Generally computer outputs are based on above the hypothesis H_0 : $\beta_i = 0$, H_A: $\beta_i \neq 0$; in case (H_0) cannot be rejected, the standardized coefficients in the format of *t*-ratio is given by : $t = \hat{\beta}_i / SE(\hat{\beta}_i)$.

Remember that *t*-ratio follows *t*-statistical distribution on the satisfaction of two test-rules; one that null hypothesis is true and two that true disturbances (U_i's) are normally distributed. In case alternative hypothesis is changed from $\beta_i \neq 0$ to $\beta_i > 0$ or $\beta_i < 0$, two tail-test changes to right tail or left tail tests.

When *t*-ratio is less than the tabulated *t*-value, the null hypothesis cannot be rejected, meaning thereby that explanatory variable does not cause any movement in the dependant variable. In case one desires to make the rejection of null hypothesis more difficult, he prefers to choose lower significance level. This test also can be extended to any specific parametric mean value and not necessarily as is generally reported in the computer outputs (based on the hypothesis as described above).

Another use of *t*-ratio (standardised coefficient) is made in computing confidence interval statements of individual coefficient. Hypothesis testing and interval estimation are two close knit procedures of describing a similar statistical concept. Following hypothetical illustration makes this point clear.

Suppose an estimated relationship with one explanatory variable for a sample of 8 observations is described as $\hat{Y} = 1.50 + 0.15 \, (X)$ with standard error of the slope coefficient = 0.032. The 95% confidence interval (with 6 degrees of freedom) for the estimated slope parameters would be :

$$\beta = \hat{\beta} \pm (t_c) \text{ (standard error of } \hat{\beta})$$

$$= 0.15 \pm (2.447) \, (0.032) = 0.15 \pm 0.078$$

That is; $\quad\quad\quad P \, (0.072 < \beta < 0.0228) = 0.95$

Since zero value lies outside the estimated confidential interval, it also allows us to reject null hypothesis of $\hat{\beta} = 0$ at 5% level of significance. This fact also gets verified by testing calculated *t*-ratio (= 4.6) directly on 5% level of significance. The null hypothesis of $\beta_i = 0$ is not validated.

Analysis of residual : The validity of various statistical tests that are applied to evaluate statistical significance of the model depends upon the assumptions of disturbance terms which we introduce in the population regression function. Nevertheless, since existence of such error terms is entirely theoretical, the residuals generated by OLS procedure are taken to be similar to these errors. On the other hand, residuals also satisfy certain conditions so as to generate optimum estimators. Residuals are, therefore, dependent on the values of independent variables also. The theoretical errors do not depend on the values of independent variables but residuals do (disturbance terms are introduced entirely for different reasons). Hence, the residuals reflect properties of true errors as well as those of independent variables. Only under the condition of elimination of influence of independent variables that the residuals would ever be regarded exact replica of true error terms. But such a situation is never observed in applied econometrics. Residuals of every model are generally contaminated due to incorrect specification of the model; as such residuals are rarely reflective of true error terms. Analysis of residuals helps us to know (the presence of) influence of mis-specification of the OLS residuals.

Whenever residuals show any non-random pattern, it indicates that there are certain peculiarities going on in the data which require reformulation in the specification of the model. May be the functional form chosen is a wrong one;

or, certain important variables might have been omitted; or, it may be that underlying assumption of the disturbance terms are not valid. Any of these irregularities may tilt away the original data from linear fitted curve and produce systematic pattern in the values of the residuals.

This can be understood through simple diagrams showing how a linear fit mis-represents the actual data of parabolic nature.

Assume that original data points when plotted give rise to the curve as shown in Fig. (a) or, as in Fig. (b). In both cases a linear fit can not be regarded as a good fit. In figure (a), the residuals are first negative, then become positive and finally they turn negative. Reverse to this happens in figure (b); residuals are first positive turn negative and finally become positive. Possibly, parabolic or exponential functions could have been a better fit.

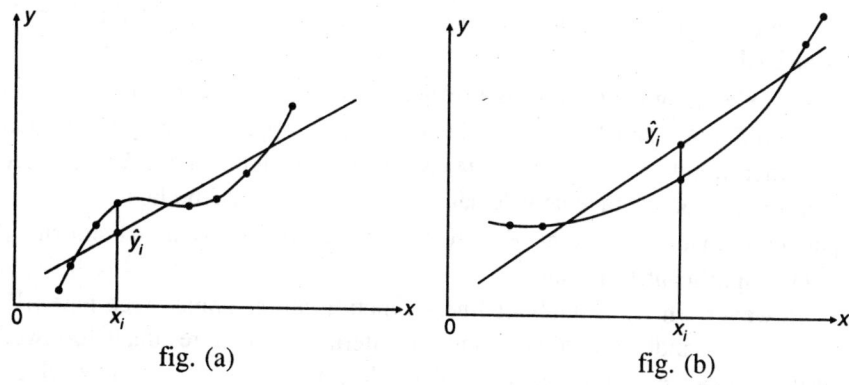

fig. (a)   fig. (b)

Following illustrations would prove to be useful to understand how analysis of residuals helps to detect the possible defects and suggests improved specification of the model.

Illustration: 1. Consider the following data on cellular phones, the popularity of which has been phenomenal ever since their introduction in the market. Which trend curve would be most appropriate for extrapolation?

Year	No. of cellular subscribers
1982	3510
1983	34520
1984	80180
1985	143300
1986	288420
1987	507930
1988	877850
1989	1471200
2000	2342080

Number of socio-economic factors could be said to have been responsible for such a phenomenal growth in the demand for cellular phones. Dynamic changes in the economic activity are representative of all the factors. Changes in economic activities are assumed to be the function of time. On the other, looking to given time-series data on cellular, it is observed that it is steadily moving in one direction. The given series is therefore said to contain a trend component. The influence of this component can be extracted by introducing time as an explicit explanatory variable in the model. The only problem which one faces is; how to determine appropriate nature or type of trend curve? It could be linear or non-linear. The analysis of residuals along with other summary statistics, help us to resolve such problem.

In case of above example, we begin by fitting linear trend and then examine the computed residuals to see whether any non-random pattern is visible amongst the residuals.

The regression results as reported by the computer are presented in parts I, II and III.

On examining the overall significance of the linear function (I (A) & (B)) through R^2, $\bar{R}^2$ and F statistics, this trend curve appears to be good fit. On the other, trend coefficient (=2.604) is also highly significant*. Accordingly therefore, on an average new demand for approximately 2.60 lakh of cellular phones is made every year. R^2 and $\bar{R}^2$ are highly significant as shown by highly significant F statistic.

However when residuals of linear function are examined (see part III), there is clear indication of non-random pattern of positive residuals followed by large negative values. Again, negative values are followed by positive values. Thus a pattern of positive values followed by negative and negative values followed by positive appear amongst the OLS residuals. (see page 422)

A quadratic model would be better. The regression results of quadratic function are presented in parts II (A) and II (B) of Page 422.

Last column of the part (III); table of residual output presents the residual values when quadratic trend curve is tried. It may be very well seen that not

---

* Computer outputs generally provide information on p-value of each explanatory variable and of F-distribution. p-value is used to test significance of the individual coefficients and (R^2) without looking at the t or F distribution tables. In case of estimated coefficients, the entries in the column headed by p-values are 'probability values' for two-tailed test of the hypothesis; H_o: $\hat{\beta} = 0$ against H_A: $\hat{\beta} \neq 0$. p-value is that probability value which provides that level of test on which the observed t-value would fall in the critical (rejection) region. In other words p-value is that level of test that would just barely allow us to reject H_o. Therefore, when p-value is greater than significance level hypothesised by us, $\hat{\beta}_i$ is not significant variable (H_o cannot be rejected) while, when p-value is less than hypothesised significane level, ($\hat{\beta}_i$) is a significant explanatory variable (H_o is rejected). In illustration 1, p-value of coefficient is 0.001. To test it on 1% level, it is observed that 0.001< 0.005, hence we are unable to accept null hypothesis. We say that exp. variable is a significant variable. Also, observed p-value, in case of F-statistic rejects null hypothesis of all the coeff. jointly becoming zero. However, remember that F-distribution has no importance in one variable model. Recall that $F(1, n-2) = t(1, n-2)$ for same level of significance.

only the values of residual terms have decreased to a larger extent, but the pattern has also vanished. Simultaneously, the values of R^2 and $\bar{R}^2$ have increased with significant F-value. Both the trend-coefficients (t) and (t^2) earlier are also significant. Above all, *SEE* has declined from 3.87 lakh subscribers to merely 1.18 lakh. This decrease, in terms of *SEE* as percentage of dependant variable mean, is from 60.6 to 18.5. Thus, all statistics justify quadratic trend a better one with increased explanatory power.

Illustration II : Following data describe the consumption expenditure and disposable income of randomly chosen 12 families with their heads of the house-hold being either male or female. We are required to study whether the expenditure gets affected by the difference in the gender of the head of house-hold.

Head of Household	Income (Rs.)	Consumption Expd. (Rs.)
Male	45100	37070
Male	28070	22700
Female	26080	24260
Male	35000	30420
Female	18860	17360
Male	41270	33520
Male	32940	26960
Female	21440	19360
Male	44700	35680
Female	24400	22360
Female	33620	28640
Male	46000	39720

There are two procedures to examine whether or not gender of the head of household could be the potential explanatory variable in determining the consumption expenditure of the family; one, by directly introducing dummy variable for the gender of the head of the household and two, through the analysis of residual terms when the gender has not been introduced in the model.

Let us therefore, first try model without incorporating gender of the head of the family. The computer results obtained are presented in the Part I (A) and (B) of page 424. The result of consumption function fitted with disposable income as the only explanatory variable appears quite a nice fit. R^2-value is significant and is as high as 98%; the income coefficients is 0.75 which also highly significant. Nevertheless the residual values obtained through this function (see Part III of page 424) clearly indicate presence of non-random pattern. The residual values move from positive to negative values alternatively. This indication puts us in a doubtful situation that gender could be potential explanatory variable. Dummy variable technique is therefore tried by introducing dummy for the gender in the model.

If the head of the household is male; $D = 1$; $D = 0$, otherwise; the results obtained are described in Part II (A) and (B) of page 424. The hypothesis to be

Illustration : I

I (A). Regression Analysis (Linear): Cellular = –6.632 + 2.604(*t*)
(Lakh units)

	Coefficients	SE	*t*-ratio	*p*-value*
Intercept	–6.632	2.812	–2.358	0.050
Time (t)	2.604	0.499	5.211	0.001

$R^2 = 0.795$; $\overline{R}^2$ – bar square = 0.766;   *SEE* = 3.871

I (B). Analysis of variance (Linear):

Source	df	SS	MS	F	*p*-value*
RSS	1	4.068(E+12)	4.068(E+12)	27.156	0.0012
ESS	7	1.048(E+12)	1.498(E+12)	—	—
Total	8	5.177(E+12)	—	—	—

II (A). Regression Analysis (Quadratic function):
Cellular = 3.628–2.992(t) + 0.599(*t*²) (Lakh units)

	Coefficients	SE	*t*-ratio	*p*-value*
Intercept	3.628	1.505	2.409	0.052
Time (*t*)	(–)2.992	0.691	(–)4.328	0.005
Time *t*²	0.559	0.067	8.299	0.000

$R^2 = 0.984$; $\overline{R}^2$ – bar square = 0.978;   *SEE* = 1.183

II (B). Analysis of variance (Quadratic):

Source	df	SS	MS	F	*p*-value*
RSS	2	5.03(E+12)	2.51(E+12)	179.67	0.000
ESS	6	84042754341	14097125723	—	—
Total	8	5.11(E+12)	—	—	—

(III). Residual Output:

Year	Actual no. of cellular subscribers (Y)	Estimated ($\hat{Y}$) in Linear function	Residuals (Linear function)	Estimated ($\hat{Y}$) in Quadratic function	Residuals (Quadratic Function)
1982	0.035 Lakh	(–)4.028	4.063	1.195	(–)0.160
1983	0.345 Lakh	(–)1.423	1.768	(–)0.118	0.463
1984	0.802 Lakh	1.179	(–)0.377	(–)0.313	1.115
1985	1.433 Lakh	3.783	(–)2.350	(–)0.612	0.821
1986	2.884 Lakh	6.387	(–)3.503	2.656	0.228
1987	5.079 Lakh	8.992	(–)3.913	5.820	(–)0.741
1988	8.788 Lakh	11.595	(–)2.807	10.103	(–)1.215
1989	14.712 Lakh	14.199	0.513	15.505	(–)0.793
1990	23.421 Lakh	16.803	6.613	22.027	1.394

tested here would be whether standardised gender coefficient is different from zero; that is,

$$H_o : \beta_2 = 0; H_A : \beta_2 \neq 0;$$

(β_2 depicts the standardised coefficient of gender of head of the family, it will be two-tailed test because gender may affect the expenditure upward or downward)

p-value for gender standardized coefficient is 0.103, it is greater than 0.10 (for testing on 5% level of significance on two-tails), hence it is difficult to reject null hypothesis. It may therefore be concluded that gender of the head of the family does not show whatsoever impact on the consumption expenditure of the family. Also if one looks up to the residual values of this model when dummy is used as explanatory variable (see Part III), the earlier pattern still persist though with less intensity. This is also reflected in the values of the income coefficient which have not changed significantly in the two models. This, then calls for searching some other irregularity in the specification of the model; it may be that some important variable requires to be introduced to model so as to generate randomness in the residuals.

Purpose and sensitivity of the model: Finally, every model's validation depends largely on its sensitivity and purpose for which it has been designed.

A different criteria of evaluation needs to be applied depending on the purpose of the model. Some models are built primarly for hypothesis testing or, to measure some elasticity. In such a situation testing to reasonable statistical significance of the individual coefficient(s) is more desirable than symmary statistic(s). On the other, if model has been built for forecasting, it should have as small a standard error (*ESS*) as possible.

Sensitivity of the model also plays an important role in deciding the goodness of the model. By sensitivity what is meant is that changes in the following (if and whenever encountered) do not affect the inferences derived from the model very drastically.

(a) initial period for which the model is built;

(b) estimated coefficients, and

(c) time path of the explanatory variables.

Having discussed so much on various statistical tests and criteria, the need for some personal element based on judgement and experience still can not be ruled out in the process of taking a final decision on the good performance of the model. "Rules are helpful but they cannot make decisions for the applied econometricians".[1]

For Prof. Chow, specification of a good model is an art and this art is difficult to learn unless one has solid command of the tools of economic

---

1. Rao P. & Miller, R.L.; **Applied Econometrics**, Prentice Hall of India Pvt. Ltd., New Delhi (1972), p. 52.

Illustration: II

I (A). Regression Analysis (without consideration of gender of head of household): $C = 3327.2 + 0.75(Y)$

	Coefficients	SE	t ratio	p-value*
Intercept	3327.198	1220.26	2.726	0.021
Income (Rs.)	0.750	0.035	21.122	0.000

$R^2 = 0.978$; $\bar{R}^2$ – bar square = 0.975;   SEE = 1125.52

I (B). Analysis of variance:

Source	df	SS	MS	F	p-value*
RSS	1	565151988.7	565151988.7	446.129	0.000
ESS	10	12667902.99	1266790.299	—	—
Total	11	577819891.7	—	—	—

II (A). Regression Analysis (with inclusion of Dummy for gender of household): $C = 2036.42 + 0.818(Y) - 1664.8(D)$

	Coefficients	SE	t-ratio	p-value*
Intercept	2036.43	1310.29	1.554	0.154
Income (Rs.)	0.818	0.049	16.564	0.000
Dummy (for gender)	(–)1664.18	916.87	(–)1.815	0.103

$R^2 = 0.983$; $\bar{R}^2$ – bar square = 0.980;   SEE = 1015.07

II (B). Analysis of variance:

Source	df	SS	MS	F	p-value*
ƘSS	2	568546507.6	284273253.8	275.89	0.000
ESS	9	9273384.041	1030376.005	—	—
Total	11	577819891.7	—	—	—

(III). Residual Output:

Actual Consumption (C)	Estimated (Ĉ) without Dummy	Residuals	Estimated (Ĉ) with Dummy	Residuals
37070	37154	(–)84	37278	(–)208
22700	24381	(–)1681	23342	(–)642
24260	22888	1372	23378	882
30420	29578	842	29013	1407
17360	17473	(–)113	17470	(–)110
33520	34281	(–)761	34144	(–)624
26960	28033	(–)1073	27327	(–)367
19360	19408	(–)48	19581	(–)221
35680	36854	(–)1174	36951	(–)1271
22360	21628	732	22003	357
28640	28543	97	29548	(–)908
39720	37829	1891	38015	1705

analysis and sound judgement to select the essential variables of the model.[2] Similar views are held by Johnston for whom the art of formulation of a good econometric model can only be learnt through the vary basic principle of *"Learning by Doing"*.

"Doing or Practicing" has to be undertaken with the help of talented supervisors and colleagues, and by study of best practice examples.[3]

Every search for a good model is to be based on procedure of–*'screen out the bad models rather than generate good model'*.

"Once a model is specified, however, there are statistical criteria to judge whether the model is bad. Since many models can explain the same data about equally well, a given set of data can be used to screen out bad models but not to generate good model, whatever statistical tests are used".[4]

2. Gregory C. Chow, **Econometrics**, McGraw Hill International Book Co. (1985), p. 1
3. J. Johnston; **Econometric Methods**, McGraw Hill International Book Co. (1985.2/E) P. 498 & 510.
4. Gregory C. Chow; Ibid, p. 313

Appendix on Chapter Seven

Estimation of Non-linear Growth Models (Logarithmic and Exponential Functions)

As already emphasized, we rarely come across linear relations among economic variables to describe any economic phenomena. This, however does not hold us back is using OLS procedure of estimations of any non-linear relation of economic theory.

We have explained in the text, that how a model which is linear in parameters can be easily handled with OLS procedure of estimation even if the variables enter non-linearly. Estimation in such relations is attempted by appropriate transformations of the variables. Through such transformations, a relation which is non-linear in the original variables is reduced into one which is linear in the transformed variables. Nevertheless, the statistical soundness of the estimates and justification for application of least squares under such circumstances depend largely on the extent of satisfaction or deviation of the assumptions of disturbance term in the transformed relation for those made in original classical linear regression model.

The two important non-linear relations that are generally required to be estimated in economics are logarithmic and exponential relations. The underlined interactions of the different variables involved in many economic phenomenon are approximated through these functions.

The present appendix provides an additional insight of these two functions to derive exact inference when estimated.

Let us recall two básic properties of these two functions:

(*a*) Exponential function is inverse of logarithmic function and vice-versa.

$Y = f(x) = a^x$ is an exponential function because the variable x is exponent of a fixed number $-a$. In case, constant e (= 2.718...) takes place of this constant $-a$; then: $Y = f(x) = e^x$.

Negative values of constant base are ruled out in this function. Any root value of negative number is imaginary number and unexplainable.

Inverse of above function is to be expressed as $x = f(Y)$; which can also be expressed in logarithmic function; that is:

$$Y = f(x) = a^x; \qquad x = f(Y) = \log_a Y.$$
$$\text{But if; } Y = f(x) = e^x; \quad \text{then,} \quad x = f(Y) = \log_e Y \text{ (natural log.)}$$

An illustration would make this more understandable.

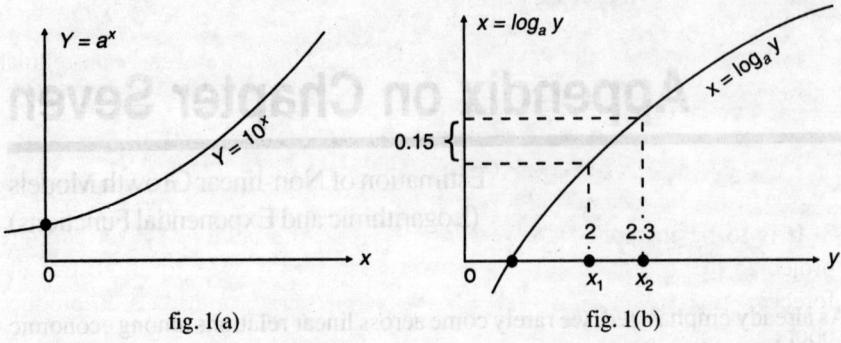

fig. 1(a)   fig. 1(b)

Value of a has been taken to be ten to make the calculations easier and transfer of the exponential-function to common logarithmic.

Since two functions are inverse of each other, the figures 1(a) and 1(b) when superimposed on each other (*i.e.*; Y-axis of 2(a) is put over Y-axis of 1(b) and X-axis of 1(a) on that of 1(b)) the curves coincide.

(*b*) Through log-function relative changes in the original variable can be approximated to the absolute changes in logarithms; that is:

Relative change in the variable (x) »   Absolute changes in log . value
(say from x_1 to x_2)   of those values of variable (x)

(This theorem operates only in cases of small changes in any variable –x).

For instance, relative change in variable x from 2 to 2.3 (see fig. 1(b)) = 0.3/2 = 0.15 or 15%. On the other hand absolute difference in the two log values (natural log) is :

$$\log_e (2.3) - \log_e (2.0) = 0.1496 \text{ which is approx.} = 0.15$$

Both the two characteristics of log-exponential functions explained under 1(a) and 1(b) above are useful in studying the economic models; where in we are required to evaluate proportional changes in the dependent variable when absolute changes are made in the explanatory variables or, also to study proportional changes in dependent variable versus proportional changes in explanatory variables.

Empirical Application of Log and Exponential Functions

I. Estimation of Growth Models: Changes in univariate data over the period of time can be studied through two types of functions with two different underlying assumptions.

(*a*) Linear Trend Function; where changes are assumed to happen at '*a-constant absolute amount*' per unit of time;

(*b*) Growth (or decay) Trend Function; where changes are assumed to happen at '*a-constant proportional rate*' per unit of time; or changes are assumed to take place at '*a-constant proportional rate*' **continuously.**

Linear trend procedure is relatively naïve, because this procedure implies increase (or decrease) in the variable under study take place at a constant amount every time during the whole period.

In the first illustration of *Chapter 15*, estimated linear trend curve on cellular subscribers is:

$$\text{No. of Subscribers (in Lakh nos.)} = -6.60 + 2.60. \ (t),$$

$$R^2 = 0.79, \quad \bar{R}^2 = 0.77$$

It is to be inferred from above model that the cellular subscribers are projected to grow by 2.60 lakhs every year during 1982 to 2000. But the forecasts generated by such a constant change model are likely to produce poor estimates of the actual values.

Logarithmic models (semi-log) assume that changes in the variable take place at a constant annual rate rather than at a constant annual amount. In other words, in the above illustration, on using logarithmic (exponential) model the subscribers would be assumed to change over the time by 'a constant proportional amount' rather than by 'a constant absolute amount' as implied by a linear trend model. Second characteristic of log model is used in growth models; which describes proportional change in subscribers due to absolute unitary change in the time variable.

Recall that amount of rupees (P_0) deposited for t-number of years on $r\%$ interest rate to be compounded annually would turn into: Rs. $P_t = P_0(1 + r)^t$. Changing this to our subscriber illustration;

$$\{\text{No. of subscribers in } t\text{-year}\} = \text{(current no. of subscribers)}$$
$$= (1 + \text{growth rate})^t;$$

$$\text{or;} \qquad C_t = C_0 (1 + g)^t \qquad \qquad \dots(i)$$

Eq. (*i*) above describes that subscribers after time period of t-years are equal to current period subscribers compounded at a constant g-growth rate every year. In case the assumption of 'yearly compounding'; is changed to 'instantaneous or continuous compounding' the equation (*i*) turns into exponential format:

$$P_t = P_0 \, e^{rt} \quad \text{or,} \quad C_t = C_0 \, e^{gt} \qquad \qquad \dots(ii)$$

On transforming equations (*i*) and (*ii*) to logarithmic form, we obtain semi-log type of models*

$$\text{Log } C_t = \log C_0 + [\log (1 + g)] \ .t \qquad \dots(iii) \text{ from } (i)$$

[which is of the form: $\log C_t = a + b.t$, where $b = \log (1 + g)$]

and, $\qquad\qquad\qquad \text{Log}_e \, C_t = \text{Log}_e \, C_0 + g.t. \qquad \dots(iv) \text{ from } (ii)$

---

*We have not taken account of disturbance term (U) while transforming the equation (*i*) & (*ii*) to (*iii*) & (*iv*). In both cases underlying error term would enter as a multiplicative term to get transformed log-form equations.

In equations (*iii*) and (*iv*), '*g*' depicts proportionate growth rate but with different underlying assumptions. Through (*iv*), its estimate is obtained directly while from (*iii*) estimate of growth rate is derived from the estimated value of (*b*) which is [log (1 + *g*)]. Because of different underlying assumptions, values of two growth rates will of course be different; nonetheless it can be proved that both growth relations (*iii*) & (*iv*) are identical and would therefore lead to approximately similar forecast results.

Using common log for both (*iii*) & (*iv*) equations;

$$\log_{10} C_t = \log_{10} C_o + [\log_{10} (1 + g_2)] \cdot t \qquad \ldots(v)$$
$$\log_{10} C_t = \log_{10} C_o + [g_1 \cdot \log_{10} (e)] \cdot t \qquad \ldots(vi)$$

[**Note:** just to make two growth rates differentiated, subscripts are used on (*g*)].

In case (*v*) & (*vi*) are identical then;

$$\log_{10} (1 + g_2) = g_1 \log_{10} (e);$$

$$g_1 = \frac{\log_{10} (1 + g_2)}{\log_{10} (e)} = \frac{[\log_e (1 + g_2) \cdot \log_{10} (e)]}{\log_{10} (e)} *$$

Therefore; $\qquad g_1 = \log_e (1 + g_2)$

In other words, continuous compounding with 'g_1' growth rate would provide same results as discrete compounding with the rate of growth of 'g_2'.

Let us take an example to prove the above logic.

Assume that a given data on sales of a product during last decade (1990-2000) generates following results of constant annual rate of growth model:

$$\text{Log}_{10} S_t = 1.90 + 0.155 \ (t); \quad R^2 = 96.3$$
$$(36.30) \qquad (20.50)$$

(figures in brackets depict t-ratios)

In order to revert back to original format:

$$S_t = (\text{antilog } 1.90) \times (\text{antilog } 0.155)^t$$
$$S_t = (79.43) \times (1.429)^t \qquad \ldots(A)$$

Hence estimated annual growth rate is 1.429 – 1= 0.429 or 42.9%.

The inference derived from this result shall be that sales of the product during the period (1990-2000) grow at a constant annual rate of 42.9 percent.

To see whether similar equation is generated through the continuous compounding procedure, model of the exponential format: $S_t = S_o \cdot e^{gt}$ is to be estimated using same data.

---

* Let $\qquad\qquad\qquad \log_e (1 + g) = m$; then $e^m = (1 + g)$
On taking common log.; $\quad m \log_{10} (e) = \log_{10} (1 + g)$
Substituting for *m*; $\qquad \log_e (1 + g) \cdot \log_{10} (e) = \log_{10} (1 + g)$

The estimated results are:

$$\text{Log}_e\, S_t = \; 4.37 \; + \; 0.356\ (t); \quad R^2 = 96.3$$
$$(36.30) \qquad (20.50)$$

Notice that t- statistics for intercepts and slope coefficients are identical to those obtained for constant annual rate of growth model. R^2- value is also similar.

In the present situation, the estimate of growth rate is directly obtained as 35.60%.

Reverting back to original format:

$$S_t = S_o . e^{gt} = S_o.\ (e^g)^t$$
$$S_t = (\text{exponential } 4.37) \times \ (\text{exponential } 0.356)^t$$
$$S_t = (79.43) \times \ (e^{\,0.356})^t$$
$$S_t = (79.43) \times (1.429)^t \qquad\qquad \ldots(B)$$

Equation (B) is identical to the estimated equation (A).

Note that growth rate in annual compounding is 42.9% while in case of continuous compounding it is 35.60%; nevertheless the two estimated equations prove that both being identical; the two shall lead to identical forecast values.

Appendix on Chapter Eleventh

Estimation of Linear, Logit and Probit Models

We have explained in the text that application of linear regression model when dependent variable is of dichotomous nature is more complex. The problem in such models is to determine the probability that an individual with a given 'set of stimulus' will make a choice (of say purchasing a car) rather than opt for alternative (of not purchasing a car). Set of stimulus which trigger a new car purchase could include such variables as income, wealth, petrol price, depression in car prices, age of present car owned by the individual and so forth.

Beginning from most elementary model specification, we assumed a linear probability model in which probability of an individual making a given choice is a linear function of set of stimulus (x) experienced by the individual. However it is found that at least three major difficulties are associated with linear probability model; they are (i) that this model may predict probabilities of choices outside the $(0,1)$ range; (ii) that the slope coefficient is constant, meaning thereby that a unitary increase in (x) stimulus value leads to constant (and similar) change in the probability value at all levels of stimulus and for all individuals experiencing that level of stimulus. Also the slope of the line largely depends on how the stimulus data (based on given sample) are bunched differently on the extremes (0 & 1 defining making a choice or not making the choice); and finally (iii) error distribution in the linear probability model is neither normal nor are error-variances homoscedastic.

The above limitations of linear model advise against the use of this model; and also point to the need for alternative model specification. Since the most serious limitation arises from the fact that the predictions may lie outside the $(0,1)$ range, alternative model is required which translates all the values of stimulus set (x) to a probability which ranges in values from 0 to 1. Simultaneously the alternative model must also be monotonically increasing function of stimulus levels. The cumulative probability functions fulfill these two basic requirements because we know that the range of such functions is from 0 to unity *(see chapter 2 of this text)*

Of the various cumulative probability functions available, two of them serve our purpose. They are; cumulative standard normal distribution and the other is cumulative logistic probability function. On transformation of stimulus (x)

values to cumulative function; the cumulative normal probability function leads to 'Probit Model' while 'Logit Model' is formulated using logistic cumulative function. Though both models are more appealing than the linear probability model; Probit model involves non-linear estimations and hence its use is rather limited. On the other, logistic cumulative function which is generally preferred transforms the probability values directly into logit model.

The slope of the cumulative normal distribution is similar to that of cumulative logistic function. Both are S- shaped curves with lower and upper asymptotes at 0 & 1, and both are monotonically increasing functions of dependent variable. Again, both possess point of inflexion at half of the saturation level, that is half of the level of upper asymptote.

The general equation of logistic curve is given as:

$$Y = f(x) = \frac{k}{1 + be^{-ax}}; \quad a, b \text{ and } k \text{ are parameters; if } a = b = k = 1, \text{ then;}$$

$$Y = \frac{1}{1 + e^{-x}}; \quad e^{-x} = \frac{1-Y}{Y}; \quad \log_e\left[\left(\frac{Y}{1-Y}\right)\right] = x.$$

By assigning unitary values to these three parameters, point of inflexion of the curve is at $x = 0$. The curve rises with increasing rate below 0 values of (x), while it rises slowly with decreasing rate above zero values of (x), and then slowly getting tapper off to level of $Y = 1$. The curve is quite similar in form to one when bell shaped normally distributed curve is cumulated. Similarity between cumulative normal (Probit Model) and cumulative logistic (Logit Model) functions is shown under section **(11.3)** of this text.

In the logit model, the probability in favor of event is modeled by the cumulative logistic function which relates the stimulus (S_i) with probability of occurrence (P_i) of the event directly;

$$P_i = f(s_i) = \frac{1}{1 + e^{-s_i}}$$

In order to make the model operational for estimation purpose, it is simplified as shown under:

$$P_i = \frac{1}{1 + e^{-s_i}}, \quad e^{s_i} = \frac{P_i}{1 - P_i}, \quad \text{and} \quad s_i = \log_e\left[\left(\frac{P_i}{1 - P_i}\right)\right]$$

Thus it may be observed that with the help of logistic function, probability and stimulus are made to depend on each other directly *via* semi-log relation. P_i is also constrained by $(0,1)$ interval with greatest impact felt at the centre (when $P_i = 0.5$) which tappers off at the extremes. *(see fig. (11.11) in the text)*

Two basic problems still remain to be addressed;

(*i*) since raw observations of zero and one on probability will make the logit ratio blow up; how the observed data is to be recorded, and

(*ii*) how to express set of stimulus exactly linearly dependent on logit ratio.

Since individual observations on probability do not make the logit ratio operationable, the correct estimation procedure becomes possible through grouped data. This methodology involves two major steps which need to understood.

Step 1: Assume that out of total n-number of persons in the first sub-sample (or a group), r-number of persons show the choice in favor of the event so that probabilities are defined as:

$P_1 = r_1/n_1$ (*i.e*; proportion of favorable events occurring in n-number of observations)

$P_2 = r_2/n_2, \ldots, P_i = r_i/n_i \ (i = 1, 2, \ldots, j)$

The observed logits ($\log_e P_i/1 - P_i$) can be computed to make up j-number of observations on the dependent variable.

Step 2: For each sub-sample, we observe $(k \times 1)$ column vector of (X_i) stimulus (explanatory) variables. The (b) vector $(k \times 1)$ of their coefficients is unknown and is required to be estimated.

For example in the question of whether or not to purchase a new car in a given year, the vector (X_i) would include data on k-number of variables such as income, price of petrol, diesel and new car, size of family, age of present car etc. Since total stimulus is to be represented by some linear combination of variables, the i-th level of stimulus shall be expressed in matrix notation*:

$$s_i = X_i' \beta, \text{ and}$$

$$\left[\log_e \left(\frac{P_i}{1 - P_i} \right) \right] = X_i' \beta + U_i$$

Because of presence of problem of hetroscedasticity among the error terms, GLS regression technique is used to estimate (β) vector.

However if the computation of sample sub proportions is not possible, and that we have single observation on probability of zero and one for each $(X_i' \beta,)$; the model reduces to estimation of linear probability regression of (P) on $(X_i' \beta,)$ about which we have discussed in details.**

---

*Since β and X_i are col. vectors of equal order $(k \times 1)$, any of the two, X_i vectors may be put in the transposition form to make multiplication possible, and produce row vector for each sub-group of the j-number of total sub-groups in the population. Hence $s_i = X_i' \beta = \beta' X_i$

**In single variable case; $P_i = \dfrac{1}{1 + e^{-s_i}} = \dfrac{1}{1 + e^{-(\alpha + \beta X_i)}}$; or, $\log_e \left(\dfrac{P_i}{1 - P_i} \right) = \alpha + \beta X_i + U_i$

The Logit model can also be stated in double log model: $P_i = \dfrac{1}{1 + e^{-s_i}}$, that is;

if $s_i = (\alpha + \beta \log X_i)$ then

$P_i = \dfrac{1}{1 + e^{-(\alpha + \beta \log X_i)}}$, or, $\log_e \left(\dfrac{P_i}{1 - P_i} \right) = \alpha + \beta \log X_i + U_i$

Fortunately technique of maximum likelihood estimation help to derive consistent parameters of logit model. Maximum likelihood procedure of estimation of (β) does not necessitates that data be grouped and as such we may use individual observation within the sample to have distinct probability associated with it*.

Interpretation of coefficients:

Interpretation of the individual estimated parameters in qualitative models require extreme care keeping two points in mind;

(*i*) That dependent variable is a dichotomous variable. In such models, therefore it describes conditional probability of occurrence of favourable event with range (0,1) interval; and

(*ii*) Due to transformation of original specification of the models, the dependent variable also gets changed. In logit model, the probability as a dependent variable is transformed to logarithm of the odd ratio while in probit model original probability is inverse of Z-normal variate.

Following illustrations would prove useful in regards to data manipulations, estimation procedure and interpretation of two types of qualitative models.

I. Linear probability models: In linear specifications, each estimated slope coefficient of the model describes the absolute change which would take place in the (conditional) probability of event occurrence for a given unit change in the corresponding explanatory or stimulant variable. (others remaining unchanged)

Assume that the decision to purchase a new house and the decision not to purchase a new house as two options for a household. We can estimate the probability of purchasing a house by a family using linear probability model with cross-sectional data on two variables of yearly family income (in lakh Rs.) and market price of house (in lakh Rs.) in the city in which 250 families are living. The purpose of model is to know whether or not these two variables are important in predicting the probability of house-purchase by a family.

The specification of linear model is : $P_i = \beta_1 + \beta_2$ (income of household)$_i$ + β_3 (price of house)$_i$

Where P_i is dummy variable and describes;

$$P = 1 \text{ if the family opts for house purchase}$$
$$= 0, \text{ otherwise}$$

---

* A very simplified version of max. likelihood technique is given in the International (second) edition of *R*. Pindyek & Rubinfeld's text on 'Econometric Models & Economic Forecasts' (Chapter 10)

Let us assume that estimated results of the model are as below:

$$\hat{P} = -0.82 + 0.328 \ Y - 0.095 \ P; \quad R^2 = 0.35$$
$$(\text{s.e}) \quad (0.22) \ (0.15) \quad (0.45)$$

The goodness of fit (R^2) in classical linear regression model describes the extent of fitness of the linear specification to the given data, and therefore (R^2) close to one indicates a perfect fit. But while working with dichotomous dependent variable, $R^2 = 1$ would indicate that all the predicted probabilities are either equal to zero or one. This is most unlikely to happen. The most likely predicted values of the probability from the estimated model would lie between zero and one but not exactly zero and one. As such, if we are to use (R^2) as a measure of goodness of fit in qualitative models, its upper bound value is going to be substantially less than one. For instance, from the value of $R^2 = 0.35$ (in case of above illustration) one may infer that two variables explain merely a small portion (35%) of the total variations in the dependent variable. But such an inference would be in correct. The significant slope coefficients quite clearly indicate that choice to go for house-purchase largely depends on income and price variables. The negative coefficient of price implies, *ceteris paribus*, an increase in the price by rupees one lakh will decrease the probability of house-purchase by 0.095; in other words the chances of a family to go for new house purchase would rise by about 0.09 (or 9%) if price falls by one lakh rupees. This result is quite expected given other things do not change. Also, income coefficient reveals as usually expected; *i.e.*, rise with yearly income of the household generally raises chances of house purchases. In the present case the probability rises by about 32 percent on one lakh rupees rise in the income of the household.

As has been already pointed out, it is certainly possible that the estimated linear probability model may give rise to probability values outside the (0,1) interval for certain values of price and income variables. In such cases one may censor the predicted probabilities within the zero and one range by assuming probability equal to zero when estimated predicted probability turns out to be negative and one if the predicted probability is estimated to be more than one. However, such solution may not be very satisfactory; but linear probability model suffers from such limitations due to violation of basic OLS assumptions.

II. Logit models: Since left hand side of the equation of such models is the logarithm of the odds of the choices, the estimated coefficients do not indicate absolute increase or decrease in the probability of event occurrence given one unit increase in the corresponding stimulant variable. Rather coefficient value in the logit model reflects the effect of change on [$\log_e (P/1 - P)$] and simultaneously this ratio is not actual or true probability. The interpretation here, would be that one unit change in the stimulant variable will lead to relative change (equivalent to 'coeff.value' of that stimulant variable) in the log of odd ratio.

It is already made clear that it is difficult to define odd ratio if individual observations on choices are recorded. This problem, however, can be by-passed by use of group data. Such procedure is explained below.

Let us assume that it is required to study the behaviour of a households in regards to purchase of a new house (or any durable product) on the basis of information about their income and size of family.

Hypothetically, let income levels be divided into three stratas; *low*, *middle* and *high* income levels. Size of family is categorized on the basis of number of children the family has; with no child, with two or less than two children, and above two children.

Since individual is to be replaced by a group of individuals, in the grouping procedure it is required to ensure that every group has all those attributes which we would have wanted in every individual while dealing with individual observation procedure. Grouping procedure is therefore based on grouping of individuals who are identical in attributes. Suppose in the i-th group of n-number of individuals of identical attributes, r_i- represent the number of individuals who responded by purchasing a new house (occurrence of an event). It, then seems reasonable to assume the probability of occurrence of event of the group as probability of an individual. In other words;

$$\hat{P_i} = \frac{r_i}{n_i}$$ (here ($\hat{P}$) is the *estimated probability* because it is not true

probability of every individual)

For our example, where it is required to study 'choice making' of the households on the basis of income and size of family, following nine sub-groups are to be sampled to obtain estimated probabilities of occurrence of event (purchase of a new house) for all possible combinations for given six attributes :

$\hat{P_1}\left(=\dfrac{r_1}{n_1}\right) =$ Proportion of households with low income and no child but having purchased a new house.

$\hat{P_2}\left(=\dfrac{r_2}{n_2}\right) =$ Proportion of households with low income and 2 or less than two children but purchased a new house.

$\hat{P_3}\left(=\dfrac{r_3}{n_3}\right) =$ Proportion of households with low income and more than two children but purchased a new house.

$\hat{P_4}\left(=\dfrac{r_4}{n_4}\right) =$ Proportion of households with middle income and no child and purchased house.

$\hat{P_5}\left(=\dfrac{r_5}{n_5}\right) =$ Proportion of households with middle income and 2 or less than two children and purchased house.

$\hat{P_6}\left(=\dfrac{r_6}{n_6}\right) =$ Proportion of households with middle income and more than two children and purchased house.

$$\hat{P}_7 \left(= \frac{r_7}{n_7} \right) = \text{Proportion of households with high income and no child and purchased house.}$$

$$\hat{P}_8 \left(= \frac{r_8}{n_8} \right) = \text{Proportion of households with high income and 2 or less than two children and purchased house.}$$

$$\hat{P}_9 \left(= \frac{r_9}{n_9} \right) = \text{Proportion of households with high income and more than two children and purchased house.}$$

Each of the above nine groups represent one observation on probability of house-purchase; therefore in this way we have as many as nine observations of dependent variable.

Dummy variables are used to specify the full logit model in the following way:

$$\log_e \left(\frac{\hat{P}_i}{1 - \hat{P}_i} \right) = \alpha_0 + \beta_1 D_{1i} + \beta_2 D_{2i} + \beta_3 D_{3i} + \beta_4 D_{4i} + U_i; \, (i = 1 \text{ to } 9).$$

Where dummies are defined as:

Level of income

Low Income	Base group (i.e., omitted group)
Middle Income	$D_1 = 1$, when household falls in middle income group
	$= 0$, otherwise.
High Income	$D_2 = 1$, when household falls in high income group
	$= 0$, otherwise.

No. of children

No Child	Base group (*i.e.*, omitted group)
Two or Less than Two Children	$D_3 = 0$, when household has two or less than two children
	$= 0$, otherwise.
More than Two Children	$D_4 = 1$, when household has more than two children
	$= 0$, otherwise.

Interpretation of slope coefficients shall be made as given below:

$\hat{\alpha}_0 \Rightarrow$ Describes the predicted odds in favour of house purchase by low income group of households having no child.

$\hat{\alpha}_0 + \hat{\beta}_3 \Rightarrow$ Predicted odds in favour of low income group with ≤ 2 children

$\hat{\alpha}_0 + \hat{\beta}_4 \Rightarrow$ Predicted odds in favour of low income group with > 2 children

$\hat{\alpha}_0 + \hat{\beta}_1 \Rightarrow$ Predicted odds in favour of middle income group with no children

$\hat{\beta}_1 + \hat{\beta}_3 \Rightarrow$ Predicted odds in favour of middle income group with $\leq$ two children

$\hat{\beta}_1 + \hat{\beta}_4 \Rightarrow$ Predicted odds in favour of middle income group with > 2 children

$\hat{\alpha}_0 + \hat{\beta}_2 \Rightarrow$ Predicted odds in favour of high income group with no children

$\hat{\alpha}_0 + \hat{\beta}_2 + \hat{\beta}_3 \Rightarrow$ Predicted odds in favour of high income group with $\leq$ two children

$\hat{\alpha}_0 + \hat{\beta}_2 + \hat{\beta}_4 \Rightarrow$ Predicted odds in favour of high income group with > 2 children

Two important matters need attention here;

(*i*)   *Regarding number of observation within each sub-group:* There should be reasonable number of observations within each sub-group sampled so that the estimated probability ($\hat{P}$) provides good estimate of true individual probability (*P*).

(*ii*) *Regarding efficiency of OLS procedure:* OLS method would provide accurate parameter estimates of logit model only when basic assumptions are not violated. Unfortunately this is not true when grouped data are used. Error variances are not constant but are hetroscedastic when grouped data (on dependent and independent variables) are used. The estimator from grouped data is always less efficient than estimator from ungrouped observations. The loss of efficiency is minimized by minimizing the 'within – group' variation and maximizing the 'between-group' variation. This is done through use of weighted least square method on which GLS procedure of estimation is based.

In logit model, assuming that each of individual observations in a group is independent, the estimated dependent variable $\left[\log_e \left(\dfrac{\hat{P}_i}{1 - \hat{P}_i}\right)\right] =$

$\left[\log_e \left(\dfrac{n_i}{n_i - r_i}\right)\right]$ will be approximately normally distributed (in large samples)

with zero mean but variance $= \left[\dfrac{n_i}{r_i\,(n_i - r_i)}\right]$. Hence to obtain efficient slope

coefficients in the logit model, it is required to transform hetroscedastic error terms to homoscedastic error terms by obtaining weighted least squares where

each observation is multiplied by the weight $= \dfrac{1}{\sqrt{\text{variance}}}$. This is exactly

what is attempted in GLS procedure.

Again, when ratio (r_i / n_i) approaches either zero or one, the variance tends to become very large which then leads to inaccurate estimates parameters. Hence while sampling sub-groups, care should be taken to see that number of observations in each group are large enough with sufficient number of repeatations.

Tobit models: In economic surveys of middle or lower income households, it is generally observed that expenditure on certain household items is limited in value and fall within certain ranges. These households do not spend any amount on few items: such as luxury or durable items. On the other, a wide variability in the amounts spent is observed among the households who make expenditure on such items.

J. Tobin (in 1957) on observing such characteristics among the households introduced model of limited dependent variables which has been designated the Tobit Model. The point of his deperature was that we should be concerned not only with whether or not an event occurred but also with the extent of its occurrence. In other words, according to Tobin, our concern needs to be with both; with the price for a house if it was bought as well as with whether or not it was bought.

Linear probability model was found to be empirically inappropriate to deal with such a dual situation simultaneously. However, few econometrians experimented with *'twin linear probability model'* as an extention of linear probability model; first linear probability model is fitted to one and zero dependent variable, while the other on restricting the sample to those with dependent variable equal to one only. As such in the twin probability approach, the first model estimates the probability that regressand (i.e., dependent variable) is greater than zero. The second model estimates the expected value of regressand given that value of regressand is greater than zero. Tobin combines both the results in his model which becomes extention of Probit model.

Tobit model, in matrix notation may be stated as under:

(a) $Y = X' \beta + U$; when regressors in equation are greater than zero value;

(b) $Y = 0$; when regressors in equation are zero or negative value.

Tobin assumes that limiting value of dependent variable is not zero but some minimum value; say (α), then two parts of model are combined in following procedure:

$$Y = [X' \ \alpha] \begin{bmatrix} \beta \\ 1 \end{bmatrix}$$

Maximum likelihood method of estimation was used by Tobin to estimate the model.

Selected Bibliography

Bridge, J.T., *Applied Econometrics*, North-Holland Publishing Co., Amsterdam, 1971.

Chow, Gregory C., *Econometric Methods*, McGraw Hill Inc. Book Company, New York—(Second Printing 1985).

Cramer, J.S., *Empirical Econometrics*, North-Holland Publishing Co., Amsterdam, 1969.

Desai, Meghnad, *Applied Econometrics*, McGraw Hill Book Co., New York, 1976.

Dhrymes, Phoebus J., *Mathematics for Econometrics*, Springer-Verlag, New York 1978.

Dhrymes, Phoebus J., *Introductory Econometrics*, 1978.

Goldberger, A.S., *Econometric Theory*, John Wiley & Sons, Inc., New York, Third Printing, 1966.

Goldberger, A.S., *Introductory Econometrics*, Harvard University Press, 1998.

Gujarati, Damodar N., *Essentials of Econometrics*, Tata McGraw Hill Book Co., New York, Second Edition, 1999.

Gujarati, Damodar N., *Basic Econometrics*, McGraw Hill Book Co., New York, Fourth Edition, 2004.

Hu, Teh-Wei., *Econometrics—An Introductory Analysis*, University Park Press, Baltimore, 1973.

Johnson, J., *Econometric Methods*, McGraw Hill Book Co. New York, Third Printing, Third Edition, 1985.

Kelejian, H.A., and Oates, W.E., *Introduction to Econometrics, Principles and Applications*, Harper and Row Publishers, Inc., New York, Second Ed., 1981.

Klein, Lawrence, R., *An Introduction to Econometrics*, Prentice-Hall, Inc., Engle Wood Cliffs, N.J., 1962.

Klein, Lawrence, R., *A Text of Econometrics*, Prentice-Hall, Inc., Englewood Cliffs, N.J., Second Edition, 1974.

Kmenta, Jan, *Elements of Econometrics*, The Macmillan Co., New York, Second Edition, 1986.

Koutsoyiannis, A., *Theory of Econometrics*, Harper and Row Publishers, Inc., New York, 1973.

Murphy, James L., *Introductory Econometrics*, Richard D. Irwin. Inc., Homewood, Ill., 1973.

Maddala, G.S., *Introduction to Econometrics*, McGraw Hill Book Co., Third Printing, 1986.

Malinvaud, E., *Statistical Methods of Econometrics*, North-Holland Publishing Co., Amsterdam, Second Edition, 1976.

Pindyck, R.S. and Rubinfeld, D.L., *Econometric Model and Econometric Forecasts*, McGraw Hill Book Co., Fourth Edition, 1990.

Rama Mohan Rao, T.V.S., *Econometric Analysis of Managerial Decision*, Oxford & IBH Co., 1978.

Theil, Henry, *Principles of Econometrics*, John Wiley & Sons, Inc., New York, 1971.

Tintner Gerhard, *Econometrics*, John Wiley & Sons, Inc., New York, 1965.

Walters, A.A., *An Introduction to Econometrics*, Macmillan & Co., Ltd., London, 1968.

Wonnacott, R.J., Wonnacott, T.H., *Econometrics*, John Wiley & Sons, New York, Second Edition, 1979.

STATISTICAL TABLES

TABLE I: Areas Under the Standardized Normal Distribution

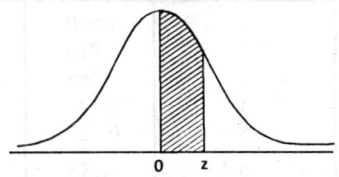

z	.00	.01	.02	.03	.04	.05	.06	.07	.08	.09
0.0	.0000	.0040	.0080	.0120	.0160	.0199	.0239	.0279	.0319	.0359
0.1	.0398	.0438	.0478	.0517	.0557	.0596	.0636	.0675	.0714	.0753
0.2	.0793	.0832	.0871	.0910	.0948	.0987	.1026	.1064	.1103	.1141
0.3	.1179	.1217	.1255	.1293	.1331	.1368	.1406	.1440	.1480	.1517
0.4	.1554	.1591	.1628	.1664	.1700	.1736	.1772	.1808	.1844	.1879
0.5	.1915	.1950	.1985	.2019	.2054	.2088	.2123	.2157	.2190	.2224
0.6	.2257	.2291	.2324	.2357	.2389	.2422	.2454	.2586	.2517	.2549
0.7	.2580	.2611	.2642	.2673	.2703	.2734	.2764	.2794	.2823	.2852
0.8	.2881	.2910	.2939	.2967	.2995	.3023	.3051	.3078	.3106	.3133
0.9	.3159	.3186	.3212	.3238	.3264	.3289	.3315	.3340	.3365	.3389
1.0	.3413	.3438	.3461	.3485	.3508	.3531	.3554	.3577	.3599	.3621
1.1	.3643	.3665	.3686	.3708	.3729	.3749	.3770	.3790	.3810	.3830
1.2	.3849	.3869	.3888	.3907	.3725	.3944	.3962	.3980	.3997	.4015
1.3	.4032	.4049	.4066	.4082	.4099	.4115	.4131	.4147	.4162	.4177
1.4	.4192	.4207	.4222	.4236	.4251	.4265	.4279	.4292	.4306	.4319
1.5	.4332	.4345	.4357	.4370	.4382	.4394	.4406	.4418	.4429	.4441
1.6	.4452	.4463	.4474	.4484	.4495	.4605	.4515	.4525	.4535	.4545
1.7	.4554	.4564	.4573	.4582	.4591	.4599	.4608	.4616	.3625	.4633
1.8	.4641	.4649	.4656	.4664	.4671	.4678	.4686	.4693	.4699	.4706
1.9	.4713	.4719	.4726	.4732	.4738	.4744	.4750	.4756	.4761	.4767
2.0	.4772	4778	.4783	.4788	.4793	.4798	.4803	.4808	.4812	.4817
2.1	.4821	.4826	.4830	.4834	.4838	.4842	.4846	.4850	.4854	.4857
2.2	.4861	.4864	.4868	.4871	.4875	.4878	.4881	.4884	.4887	.4890
2.3	.4893	.4896	.4898	.4901	.4904	.4906	.4909	.4911	.4913	.4916
2.4	.4918	.4920	.4922	.4925	.4927	.4929	.4931	.4932	.4934	.4936
2.5	.4938	.4940	.4941	.4943	.4945	.4946	.4948	.4949	.4951	.4952
2.6	.4953	.4955	.4956	.4957	.4959	.4697	.4961	.4962	.4963	.4951
2.7	.4965	.4966	.4967	.4968	.4969	.4970	.4971	.4972	.4973	.4974
2.8	.4974	.4975	.4976	.4977	.4977	.4978	.4979	.4979	.4980	.4781
2.9	.4981	.4982	.4982	.4983	.4984	.4984	.4985	.4985	.4986	.4986
3.0	.4987	.4987	.4987	.4988	.4988	.4989	.4989	.4989	.4990	.4990

TABLE II: Percentage values of *t*-Distribution
(see example below)

df.	Probability				
	0.25	*0.05*	*0.025*	*0.01*	*0.005*
1	1.000	6.314	12.706	31.821	63.657
2	0.816	2.920	4.303	6.965	9.925
3	0.765	2.353	3.182	4.541	5.841
4	0.741	2.132	2.776	3.747	4.604
5	0.727	2.015	2.571	3.365	4.032
6	0.718	1.943	2.447	3.143	3.707
7	0.711	1.895	2.365	3.00	3.499
8	0.706	1.860	2.306	2.90	3.355
9	0.703	1.833	2.262	2.821	3.250
10	0.700	1.812	2.228	2.764	3.169
11	0.697	1.796	2.201	2.718	3.106
12	0.695	1.782	2.179	2.681	3.055
13	0.694	1.771	2.160	2.650	3.012
14	0.692	1.761	2.145	2.624	2.977
15	0.691	1.753	2.131	2.602	2.947
16	0.690	1.746	2.120	2.583	2.921
17	0.690	1.740	2.110	2.567	2.90
18	0.689	1.734	2.101	2.552	2.878
19	0.688	1.729	2.093	2.539	2.861
20	0.688	1.725	2.086	2.528	2.845
21	0.686	1.721	2.080	2.518	2.831
22	0.686	1.717	2.074	2.508	2.819
23	0.685	1.714	2.069	0.500	2.807
24	0.685	1.711	2.064	2.492	2.80
25	0.684	1.708	2.060	2.485	2.787
26	0.684	1.706	2.056	2.480	2.779
27	0.684	1.703	2.052	2.473	2.771
28	0.683	1.701	2.048	2.476	2.763
29	0.683	1.699	2.045	2.462	2.756
30	0.683	1.697	2.042	2.457	2.750
Normal Distribution	0.674	1.645	1.960	2.326	2.576

Example :

(i)

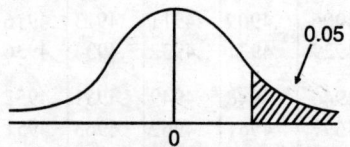

(ii)

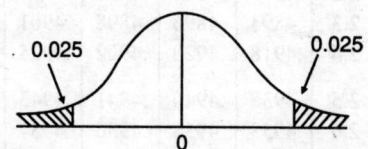

Value of *t*-corresponding to an area of 0.05 (or 5%) in one tail of distrubution, it is = 1.645 ($n = \infty$)

Value of *t*-corresponding to 0.05 in both combined tails (0.025 + .025); it is = 1.960 ($n = \infty$)

TABLE III: Significance Points of the *F*-Distribution

5 per cent points

v_1 / v_2	1	2	3	4	5	6	8	12	24	∞
					Numerator					
1	161.4	199.5	215.7	224.6	230.2	234.0	238.9	243.9	249.0	254.3
2	18.51	19.00	19.16	19.25	19.30	19.33	19.37	19.41	19.45	19.50
3	10.13	9.55	9.28	9.12	9.01	8.94	8.84	8.74	8.64	8.53
4	7.71	6.94	6.59	6.39	6.26	6.16	6.04	5.91	5.77	5.63
5	6.61	5.79	5.41	5.19	5.05	4.95	4.82	4.68	4.53	4.36
6	5.99	5.14	4.76	4.53	4.39	4.28	4.15	4.00	3.84	3.67
7	5.59	4.74	4.35	4.12	3.97	3.87	3.73	3.57	3.41	3.23
8	5.32	4.46	4.07	3.84	3.69	3.58	3.44	3.28	3.12	2.93
9	5.12	4.26	3.86	3.63	3.48	3.37	3.23	3.07	2.90	2.71
10	4.96	4.10	3.71	3.48	3.33	3.22	3.07	2.91	2.74	2.54
11	4.84	3.93	3.59	3.36	3.20	3.09	2.95	2.79	2.61	2.40
12	4.75	3.88	3.49	3.26	3.11	3.00	2.85	2.69	2.50	2.30
13	4.67	3.80	3.41	3.18	3.02	2.92	2.77	2.60	2.42	2.21
14	4.60	3.74	3.34	3.11	2.96	2.85	2.70	2.53	2.35	2.13
15	4.54	3.68	3.29	3.06	2.90	2.79	2.64	2.48	2.29	2.07
16	4.49	3.63	3.24	3.01	2.85	2.74	2.59	2.42	2.24	2.01
17	4.45	3.59	3.20	2.96	2.81	2.70	2.55	2.38	2.19	1.96
18	4.41	3.55	3.16	2.93	2.77	2.66	2.51	2.34	2.15	1.92
19	4.38	3.52	3.13	2.90	2.74	2.63	2.48	2.31	2.11	1.88
20	4.35	3.49	3.10	2.87	2.71	2.60	2.45	2.28	2.08	1.84
21	4.32	3.47	3.07	2.84	2.68	2.57	2.42	2.25	2.05	1.81
22	4.30	3.44	3.05	2.82	2.66	2.55	2.40	2.23	2.03	1.78
23	4.28	3.42	3.03	2.80	2.64	2.53	2.38	2.20	2.00	1.76
24	4.26	4.40	3.01	2.78	2.62	2.51	2.36	2.18	1.98	1.73
25	4.24	3.38	2.99	2.76	2.60	2.49	2.34	2.16	1.96	1.71
26	4.22	3.37	2.98	2.74	2.59	2.47	2.32	2.15	1.95	1.69
27	4.21	3.35	2.96	2.73	2.57	2.46	2.30	2.13	1.93	1.67
28	4.20	3.34	2.95	2.71	2.56	2.44	2.29	2.12	1.91	1.65
29	4.18	3.33	2.93	2.70	2.54	2.43	2.28	2.10	1.90	1.64
30	4.17	3.32	2.92	2.69	2.53	2.42	2.27	2.09	1.89	1.62
40	4.08	3.23	2.84	2.61	2.45	2.34	2.18	2.00	1.79	1.51
60	4.00	3.15	2.76	2.52	2.37	2.25	2.10	1.92	1.70	1.39
120	3.92	3.07	2.68	2.45	2.29	2.17	2.02	1.83	1.61	1.25
∞	3.84	2.99	2.60	2.37	2.21	2.09	1.94	1.75	1.52	1.00

TABLE IV: Significance Points of χ^2-Distribution

Degrees of freedom	0.10	0.05	0.01	Pr / df	0.10	0.05	0.01
1	2.706	3.841	6.635	40	51.805	55.758	63.691
2	4.605	5.991	9.210	50	63.167	67.505	76.154
3	6.251	7.815	11.341	60	74.397	79.082	88.379
4	7.779	9.488	13.277	70	85.527	90.531	100.425
5	9.236	11.070	15.086	80	96.578	101.879	112.329
6	10.645	12.592	16.812	90	107.565	113.145	124.116
7	12.017	14.067	18.475	100	118.498	124.342	135.807
8	13.362	15.507	20.090				
9	14.684	16.919	21.666				
10	15.987	18.307	24.209				
11	17.275	19.675	24.725				
12	18.589	27.026	26.217				
13	19.812	22.362	27.688				
14	21.064	23.685	29.141				
15	22.307	24.996	30.578				
16	23.542	26.296	32.000				
17	24.769	27.587	33.409				
18	25.989	28.869	34.805				
19	27.204	30.144	36.191				
20	28.412	31.410	37.566				
21	29.615	32.671	38.932				
22	30.813	33.924	40.289				
23	32.007	35.172	41.638				
24	33.196	36.415	42.980				
25	34.382	37.652	40.314				
26	35.563	38.885	45.642				
27	36.741	40.311	46.963				
28	37.916	41.337	48.278				
29	39.037	42.557	49.588				
30	40.256	43.773	50.892				

Note: For degrees of freedom greater than 100, the quantity $\sqrt{2\chi^2} - \sqrt{2k-1}$ may be used as a normal variate with unit variance. k = degree of freedom.

TABLE V: The Durbin-Watson *d*-Statistic
Significance Points of d_L and d_v 5%

n	$k' = 1$ d_L	d_v	$k' = 2$ d_L	d_v	$k' = 3$ d_L	d_v	$k' = 4$ d_L	d_v	$k' = 5$ d_L	d_v
15	1.09	1.36	0.95	1.54	0.82	1.75	0.69	1.97	0.56	2.21
16	1.10	1.37	0.98	1.54	0.86	1.73	0.74	1.93	0.62	2.25
17	1.13	1.38	1.02	1.54	0.90	1.71	0.78	1.90	0.67	2.10
18	1.16	1.39	1.05	1.53	0.93	1.69	0.82	1.87	0.71	2.06
19	1.18	1.40	1.08	1.53	0.97	1.68	0.88	1.85	0.75	2.02
20	1.20	1.41	1.10	1.54	1.00	1.68	0.90	1.83	0.79	1.99
21	1.22	1.42	1.13	1.54	1.03	1.67	0.93	1.81	0.83	1.96
22	1.24	1.43	1.15	1.54	1.05	1.66	0.96	1.80	0.86	1.94
23	1.26	1.44	1.17	1.54	1.08	1.66	0.99	1.79	0.90	1.92
24	1.27	1.45	1.19	1.55	1.10	1.66	1.01	1.78	0.93	1.90
25	1.29	1.45	1.21	1.55	1.12	1.66	1.04	1.77	0.95	1.89
26	1.30	1.46	1.22	1.55	1.14	1.65	1.60	1.76	0.98	1.88
27	1.32	1.47	1.24	1.56	1.16	1.65	1.08	1.76	1.01	1.86
28	1.33	1.48	1.26	1.56	1.18	1.65	1.10	1.75	1.03	1.85
29	1.34	1.48	1.27	1.56	1.20	1.65	1.12	1.74	1.05	1.84
30	1.35	1.49	1.28	1.57	1.21	1.65	1.14	1.74	1.07	1.83
31	1.36	1.50	1.30	1.57	1.23	1.65	1.16	1.74	1.09	1.83
32	1.37	1.50	1.31	1.57	1.24	1.65	1.18	1.73	1.11	1.82
33	1.38	1.51	1.32	1.58	1.26	1.65	1.19	1.73	1.13	1.81
34	1.39	1.51	1.33	1.58	1.27	1.65	1.21	1.73	1.15	1.81
35	1.40	1.52	1.34	1.58	1.28	1.65	1.22	1.73	1.16	1.80
36	1.41	1.52	1.35	1.59	1.29	1.65	1.24	1.73	1.18	1.80
37	1.42	1.53	1.36	1.59	1.31	1.66	1.25	1.72	1.19	1.80
38	1.43	1.54	1.37	1.59	1.32	1.66	1.26	1.72	1.21	1.79
39	1.43	1.54	1.38	1.60	1.33	1.66	1.27	1.72	1.22	1.79
40	1.44	1.54	1.39	1.60	1.34	1.66	1.29	1.72	1.23	1.79
45	1.41	1.57	1.43	1.62	1.38	1.67	1.34	1.72	1.29	1.78
50	1.50	1.59	1.46	1.63	1.42	1.67	1.38	1.72	1.34	1.77
55	1.53	1.60	1.49	1.64	1.45	1.68	1.41	1.72	1.38	1.77
60	1.55	1.62	1.51	1.65	1.48	1.69	1.44	1.73	1.41	1.77
65	1.57	1.63	1.54	1.66	1.50	1.70	1.47	1.73	1.44	1.77
70	1.58	1.64	1.55	1.67	1.52	1.70	1.49	1.74	1.46	1.77
75	1.45	1.50	1.42	1.53	1.39	1.56	1.37	1.59	1.34	1.62
80	1.61	1.66	1.59	1.69	1.56	1.72	1.53	1.74	1.51	1.77
85	1.48	1.53	1.46	1.55	1.43	1.58	1.41	1.60	1.39	1.64
90	1.63	1.68	1.61	1.70	1.59	1.73	1.57	1.75	1.54	1.78
95	1.64	1.69	1.62	1.71	1.60	1.73	1.58	1.75	1.56	1.78
100	1.65	1.69	1.63	1.72	1.61	1.74	1.59	1.76	1.57	1.78

Note: k' = Number of explanatory variables excluding the constant term.

n = Number of observations.

TABLE VI: The Durbin-Watson d-Statistic
Significance Points of d_L and d_v 1%

n	$k' = 1$ d_L	d_v	$k' = 2$ d_L	d_v	$k' = 3$ d_L	d_v	$k' = 4$ d_L	d_v	$k' = 5$ d_L	d_v
15	0.81	1.07	0.70	1.25	0.59	1.46	0.49	1.70	0.39	1.96
16	0.84	1.09	0.74	1.25	0.63	1.44	0.53	1.66	0.44	1.90
17	0.87	1.10	0.77	1.25	0.67	1.43	0.57	1.63	0.48	1.85
18	0.90	1.12	0.80	1.26	0.71	1.42	0.61	1.60	0.52	1.80
19	0.93	1.13	0.83	1.26	0.74	1.41	0.65	1.58	0.56	1.77
20	0.95	1.15	0.86	1.27	0.77	1.41	0.68	1.57	0.60	1.74
21	0.97	1.16	0.89	1.27	0.80	1.41	0.72	1.55	0.63	1.71
22	1.00	1.17	0.91	1.28	0.83	1.40	0.75	1.54	0.66	1.69
23	1.02	1.19	0.94	1.29	0.86	1.40	0.77	1.53	0.70	1.67
24	1.04	1.20	0.96	1.30	0.88	1.41	0.80	1.53	0.72	1.66
25	1.05	1.21	0.98	1.30	0.90	1.41	0.83	1.52	0.75	1.65
26	1.07	1.22	1.00	1.31	0.93	1.41	0.85	1.52	0.78	1.64
27	1.09	1.23	1.02	1.32	0.95	1.41	0.88	1.51	0.81	1.63
28	1.10	1.24	1.04	1.32	0.97	1.41	0.90	1.51	0.83	1.62
29	1.12	1.25	1.05	1.33	0.99	1.42	0.92	1.51	0.85	1.61
30	1.13	1.26	1.07	1.34	1.01	1.42	0.94	1.51	0.88	1.61
31	1.15	1.27	1.08	1.34	1.02	1.42	0.96	1.51	0.90	1.60
32	1.16	1.28	1.10	1.35	1.04	1.43	0.98	1.51	0.92	1.60
33	1.17	1.29	1.11	1.36	1.05	1.43	1.00	1.51	0.94	1.59
34	1.18	1.30	1.13	1.36	1.07	1.43	1.01	1.51	0.95	1.59
35	1.19	1.31	1.14	1.37	1.08	1.44	1.03	1.51	0.97	1.59
36	1.21	1.32	1.15	1.38	1.10	1.44	1.04	1.51	0.99	1.59
37	1.22	1.32	1.16	1.38	1.11	1.45	1.06	1.51	1.00	1.59
38	1.23	1.33	1.18	1.39	1.12	1.45	1.07	1.52	1.02	1.58
39	1.24	1.34	1.19	1.39	1.14	1.45	1.09	1.52	1.03	1.58
40	1.25	1.34	1.20	1.40	1.15	1.46	1.10	1.52	1.05	1.58
45	1.29	1.38	1.24	1.42	1.20	1.48	1.16	1.53	1.11	1.58
50	1.32	1.40	1.28	1.45	1.24	1.49	1.20	1.54	1.16	1.59
55	1.36	1.43	1.32	1.47	1.28	1.51	1.25	1.55	1.21	1.59
60	1.38	1.45	1.35	1.48	1.32	1.52	1.28	1.56	1.25	1.60
65	1.41	1.47	1.38	1.50	1.35	1.53	1.31	1.57	1.28	1.61
70	1.43	1.49	1.40	1.52	1.37	1.55	1.34	1.58	1.31	1.61
75	1.45	1.50	1.42	1.53	1.39	1.56	1.37	1.59	1.34	1.62
80	1.47	1.52	1.44	1.54	1.42	1.57	1.39	1.60	1.36	1.62
85	1.48	1.53	1.46	1.55	1.43	1.58	1.41	1.60	1.39	1.63
90	1.50	1.54	1.47	1.56	1.45	1.59	1.43	1.61	1.41	1.64
95	1.51	1.55	1.49	1.57	1.47	1.60	1.45	1.62	1.42	1.64
100	1.52	1.56	1.50	1.58	1.48	1.60	1.46	1.63	1.44	1.65

Note: k' = Number of explanatory variables excluding the constant term.

n = Number of observations.

Index